INFORMATION SECURITY

INFORMATION SECURITY
Principles and Practice

Second Edition

Mark Stamp

San Jose State University
San Jose, CA

A JOHN WILEY & SONS, INC., PUBLICATION

Library of Congress Cataloging-in-Publication Data:

Stamp, Mark.
    Information security: principles and practice / Mark Stamp. — 2nd ed.
        p. cm.
    Includes bibliographical references and index.
    ISBN 978-0-470-62639-9 (hardback)
    1. Computer security. I. Title.
    QA76.9.A25S69 2011
    005.8—dc22   2010045221

Printed in the United States of America.

10 9 8 7 6 5 4 3 2 1

To Miles, Austin, and Melody, with love.

Contents

Preface

Please sir or madam won't you read my book?
It took me years to write, won't you take a look?
— *Lennon and McCartney*

I hate black boxes. One of my goals in writing this book was to illuminate some of those black boxes that are so popular in information security books today. On the other hand, I don't want to bore you to death with trivial details (if that's what you want, go read some RFCs). As a result, I often ignore details that I deem irrelevant to the topic at hand. You can judge whether I've struck the proper balance between these two competing goals.

I've strived to keep the presentation moving along so as to cover a broad selection of topics. My goal is to cover each item in just enough detail so that you can appreciate the basic security issue at hand, while not getting bogged down in details. I've also attempted to regularly emphasize and reiterate the main points so that crucial information doesn't slip by below the radar screen.

Another goal of mine was to present the topic in a reasonably lively and interesting way. If any computing subject should be exciting and fun, it's information security. Security is happening now and it's in the news—it's clearly alive and kicking.

I've also tried to inject a little humor into the material. They say that humor is derived from pain, so judging by the quality of my jokes, I'd say that I've led a charmed life. In any case, most of the really bad jokes are in footnotes so they shouldn't be too distracting.

Some security textbooks offer a large dollop of dry useless theory. Reading one of those books is about as exciting as reading a calculus textbook. Other books offer a seemingly random collection of apparently unrelated facts, giving the impression that security is not really a coherent subject at all. Then there are books that present the topic as a collection of high-level managerial platitudes. Finally, some texts focus on the human factors in security. While all of these approaches have their place, I believe that, first and foremost, a security engineer must have a solid understanding of the inherent strengths and weaknesses of the underlying technology.

Information security is a huge topic, and unlike more established fields, it's not clear what material should be included in a book like this, or how best to organize it. I've chosen to organize this book around the following four major themes:

- Cryptography
- Access Control
- Protocols
- Software

In my usage, these themes are fairly elastic. For example, under the heading of access control I've included the traditional topics of authentication and authorization, along with such nontraditional topics as firewalls and CAPTCHAs. The software theme is particularly flexible, and includes such diverse topics as secure software development, malware, software reverse engineering, and operating systems.

Although this book is focused on practical issues, I've tried to cover enough of the fundamental principles so that you will be prepared for further study in the field. In addition, I've strived to minimize the background requirements as much as possible. In particular, the mathematical formalism has been kept to a bare minimum (the Appendix contains a review of all necessary math topics). Despite this self-imposed limitation, I believe this book contains more substantive cryptography than most security books out there. The required computer science background is also minimal—an introductory computer organization course (or comparable experience) is more than sufficient. Some programming experience is assumed and a rudimentary knowledge of assembly language would be helpful in a couple of sections, but it's not mandatory. Networking basics arise in a few sections. The Appendix contains a brief overview of networking that provides more than sufficient background material.

If you are an information technology professional who's trying to learn more about security, I would suggest that you read the entire book. However, if you want to avoid the material that's most likely to slow you down and is not critical to the overall flow of the book, you can safely skip Section 4.5, all of Chapter 6 (although Section 6.6 is highly recommended), and Section 8.4.

If you are teaching a security class, you need to realize that this book has more material than can be covered in a one-semester course. The schedule that I generally follow in my undergraduate security class appears in Table 1. This schedule allows ample time to cover a few of the optional topics.

If the syllabus in Table 1 is too busy, you could cut Section 8.9 of Chapter 8 and some of the topics in Chapters 12 and 13. Of course, many other variations on the syllabus are possible.

Chapter	Hours	Comments
1. Introduction	1	All
2. Classic Cryptography	3	All
3. Symmetric Key Crypto	4	Omit Section 3.3.5
4. Public Key Crypto	4	Omit Section 4.5
5. Hash Functions++	3	Omit 5.6
		Omit attack details in 5.7
		Omit Section 5.9.1
6. Advanced Cryptanalysis	0	Omit entire chapter
7. Authentication	4	All
8. Authorization	2	Omit 8.4.1 and 8.4.2
		Omit 8.10
9. Authentication Protocols	4	Omit 9.4
10. Real-World Protocols	4	Omit either WEP or GSM
11. Software Flaws and Malware	4	All
12. Insecurity in Software	4	Omit 12.3
13. OS and Security	3	All, time permitting
Total	40	

Table 1: Suggested Syllabus

Security is not a spectator sport—doing a large number of homework problems is essential to learning the material in this book. Many topics are fleshed out in the problems and additional topics are often introduced. The bottom line is that the more problems you solve, the more you'll learn.

A security course based on this book is an ideal venue for individual or group projects. Chapter 6 is a good source for crypto projects, while the annotated bibliography provides a starting point to search for additional project topics. In addition, many homework problems lend themselves well to class discussions or in-class assignments (see, for example, Problem 19 in Chapter 10 or Problem 33 in Chapter 11).

The textbook website is at

http://www.cs.sjsu.edu/~stamp/infosec/

where you'll find PowerPoint slides, all of the files mentioned in the homework problems, errata, and so on. If I were teaching this class for the first time, I would particularly appreciate the PowerPoint slides, which have been thoroughly "battle tested" and improved over several iterations. In addition, a solutions manual is available to instructors (sorry, students) from the publisher.

It is also worth noting how the Appendices fit in. Appendix A-1, Network Security Basics, is relevant to Sections 8.9 and 8.10 of Chapter 8 and also for all of Part III. Even if students have a solid foundation in networking, it's probably worthwhile to review this material, since networking terminology is not always consistent and the focus here is on security.

The Math Essentials of Appendix A-2 are assumed in various places throughout the text. Elementary modular arithmetic (Appendix A-2.2) arises in a few sections of Chapter 3 and Chapter 5, while some of the relatively advanced concepts are required in Chapter 4 and Section 9.5 of Chapter 9. I've found that the vast majority of my students need to brush up on modular arithmetic basics. It only takes about 20 to 30 minutes of class time to cover the material on modular arithmetic and that will be time well spent prior to diving into public key cryptography. Trust me.

Permutations, which are briefly discussed in Appendix A-2.3, are most prominent in Chapter 3, while elementary discrete probability (Appendix A-2.4) appears in several places. The elementary linear algebra in Appendix A-2.5 is only required in Section 6.5.

Just as any large and complex piece of software must have bugs, this book inevitably has errors. I would like to hear about any errors—large or small— that you find. I will maintain a reasonably up-to-date errata on the textbook website. Also, don't hesitate to provide any suggestions you might have for future editions of this book.

What's New for the Second Edition?

> *Cats right themselves; books don't.*
> — *John Aycock*

One major change for this second edition is that the number and quality of the homework problems have both greatly increased. In addition to the new-and-improved homework problems, new topics have been added, some new background material has been included, virtually all of the existing material has been updated and clarified, and all known errors have been corrected. Examples of new topics include a practical RSA timing attack, a discussion of botnets, and coverage of security certification. Examples of added background material include a section on the Enigma cipher and coverage of the classic "orange book" view of security.

Information security is a rapidly evolving field and there have been some significant changes since the first edition of this book was published in 2005. Nevertheless, the basic structure of the book remains intact. I believe the organization and list of topics has held up well over the past five years. Consequently, the changes to the content for this second edition are more evolutionary than revolutionary.

Mark Stamp
San Jose State University

About The Author

I've got nearly 20 years of experience in information security, including extensive work in industry and government. My work experience includes more than seven years at the National Security Agency followed by two years at a Silicon Valley startup company. While I can't say too much about my work at NSA, I can tell you that my job title was Cryptologic Mathematician. In industry I helped design and develop a digital rights management security product. This real-world work was sandwiched between academic jobs. While in academia, my research interests have included a wide variety of security topics.

When I returned to academia in 2002, it seemed to me that none of the available security textbooks had much connection with the real world. I felt that I could write an information security book that would fill this gap, while also containing information that would be useful to working IT professionals. Based on the feedback I've received, the first edition was apparently a success.

I believe that this second edition will prove even more valuable in its dual role as a textbook and as a resource for working professionals, but then I'm biased. I can say that many of my former students who are now at leading Silicon Valley technology companies tell me that the information they learned in my courses has been useful to them. And I certainly wish that a book like this had been available when I worked in industry, since my colleagues and I would have benefitted from it.

I do have a life outside of information security.[1] My family includes my wife, Melody, and two wonderful sons, Austin (whose initials are AES), and Miles (whose initials are not DES, thanks to Melody). We enjoy the outdoors, with regular local trips involving such activities as bicycling, hiking, camping, and fishing. I also spend way too much time working on my fixer-upper house in the Santa Cruz mountains.

---

[1] Well, sort of. . .

Acknowledgments

My work in information security began when I was in graduate school. I want to thank my thesis advisor, Clyde F. Martin, for introducing me to this fascinating subject.

In my seven years at NSA, I learned more about security than I could have learned in a lifetime anywhere else. From my time in industry, I want to thank Joe Pasqua and Paul Clarke for giving me the chance to work on a fascinating and challenging project.

The following San Jose State University students helped greatly with the first edition: Fiona Wong, Martina Simova, Deepali Holankar, Xufen Gao, Subha Rajagopalan, Neerja Bhatnager, Amit Mathur, Ali Hushyar, Smita Thaker, Puneet Mishra, Jianning Yang, Konstantin Skachkov, Jian Dai, Thomas Nikl, Ikai Lan, Thu Nguyen, Samuel Reed, Yue Wang, David Stillion, Edward Yin, and Randy Fort.

Richard Low, a colleague here at SJSU, provided helpful feedback on an early version of the manuscript. David Blockus (God rest his soul) deserves special mention for providing detailed comments on each chapter at a particularly critical juncture in the writing of the first edition.

For this second edition, many of my SJSU masters students "volunteered" to serve as proofreaders. The following students all contributed their time and energy to correct errors in the manuscript: Naidele Manjunath, Mausami Mungale, Deepti Kundu, Jianrui (Louis) Zhang, Abhishek Shah, Sushant Priyadarshi, Mahim Patel, Lin Huang, Eilbroun Benjamin, Neha Samant, Rashmi Muralidhar, Kenny Zhang, Jyotsna Krishnaswamy, Ronak Shah, Gauri Gokhale, Arnold Suvatne, Ashish Sharma, Ankit Patel, Annie Hii, Namrata Buddhadev, Sujandharan Venkatachalam, and Sathya Anandan. In addition, Piyush Upadhyay found several errors in the first edition.

Many other people made helpful comments and suggestions. Here, I would like to specifically thank Bob Harris (Penn State University) for the visual crypto example and exercise, and a very special thanks goes to John Trono (Saint Michael's College) for his many detailed comments and questions.

Undoubtedly, errors remain. Of course, all remaining flaws are my responsibility alone.

Chapter 1

Introduction

> *"Begin at the beginning,"* the King said, very gravely,
> *"and go on till you come to the end: then stop."*
> — Lewis Carroll, *Alice in Wonderland*

1.1   The Cast of Characters

Following tradition, Alice and Bob, who are pictured in Figure 1.1, are the good guys. Occasionally we'll require additional good guys, such as Charlie and Dave.

Figure 1.1: Alice and Bob.

Trudy, pictured in Figure 1.2, is a generic bad "guy" who is trying to attack the system in some way. Some authors employ a team of bad guys where the name implies the particular nefarious activity. In this usage, Trudy is an "intruder" and Eve is an "eavesdropper" and so on. To simplify things, we'll use Trudy as our all-purpose bad guy.[1]

---

[1]You might be wondering why a picture of Tweedledee and Tweedledum is used to represent Trudy. After all, Trudy is typically a female name, so why two bad guys instead of one bad girl? One possible reason is that, occasionally, we need two bad guys, so it's convenient to have both Tweedledee and Tweedledum available. Another plausible

Figure 1.2: Trudy.

Alice, Bob, Trudy, and the rest of the gang need not be humans. For example, one of many possible scenarios would have Alice as a laptop, Bob a server, and Trudy a human.

1.2   Alice's Online Bank

Suppose that Alice starts an online banking business, appropriately named Alice's Online Bank,[2] or AOB. What are Alice's information security concerns? If Bob is Alice's customer, what are his information security concerns? Are Bob's concerns the same as Alice's? If we look at AOB from Trudy's perspective, what security vulnerabilities might we see?

First, let's consider the traditional triumvirate of confidentiality, integrity, and availability, or CIA,[3] in the context of Alice's Bank. Then we'll point out some of the many other possible security concerns.

1.2.1   Confidentiality, Integrity, and Availability

Confidentiality deals with preventing unauthorized reading of information. AOB probably wouldn't care much about the confidentiality of the information it deals with, except for the fact that its customers certainly do. For example, Bob doesn't want Trudy to know how much he has in his savings account. Alice's Bank would also face legal problems if it failed to protect the confidentiality of such information.

Integrity deals with preventing, or at least detecting, unauthorized "writing" (i.e., changes to data). Alice's Bank must protect the integrity of account information to prevent Trudy from, say, increasing the balance in her account or changing the balance in Bob's account. Note that confidentiality and integrity are not the same thing. For example, even if Trudy cannot read the data, she might be able to modify this unreadable data, which, if undetected,

explanation is that you never know who might be acting as "Trudy." While these would be good reasons for choosing the Tweedle brothers, the reality is that your easily amused author finds the picture, well, amusing.

[2]Not to be confused with "Alice's Restaurant" [135].

[3]No, not *that* CIA...

would destroy its integrity. In this case, Trudy might not know what changes she had made to the data (since she can't read it), but she might not care—sometimes just causing trouble is good enough.

Denial of service, or DoS, attacks are a relatively recent concern. Such attacks try to reduce access to information. As a result of the rise in DoS attacks, data *availability* has become a fundamental issue in information security. Availability is an issue for both Alice's Bank and Bob—if AOB's website is unavailable, then Alice can't make money from customer transactions and Bob can't get his business done. Bob might then take his business elsewhere. If Trudy has a grudge against Alice, or if she just wants to be malicious, she might attempt a denial of service attack on Alice's Online Bank.

1.2.2 Beyond CIA

Confidentiality, integrity, and availability are only the beginning of the information security story. Beginning at the beginning, consider the situation when customer Bob logs on to his computer. How does Bob's computer determine that "Bob" is really Bob and not Trudy? And when Bob logs into his account at Alice's Online Bank, how does AOB know that "Bob" is really Bob, and not Trudy? Although these two *authentication* problems appear to be similar on the surface, under the covers they are actually completely different.

Authentication on a standalone computer typically requires that Bob's password be verified. To do so securely, some clever techniques from the field of *cryptography* are required. On the other hand, authentication over a network is open to many kinds of attacks that are not usually relevant on a standalone computer. Potentially, the messages sent over a network can be viewed by Trudy. To make matters worse, Trudy might be able to intercept messages, alter messages, and insert messages of her own making. If so, Trudy can simply replay Bob's old messages in an effort to, say, convince AOB that she is really Bob. Since information security people are professional paranoids,[4] we always assume the worst. In any case, authentication over a network requires careful attention to *protocol*, that is, the composition and ordering of the exchanged messages. Cryptography also has an important role to play in security protocols.

Once Bob has been authenticated by Alice's Bank, then Alice must enforce restrictions on Bob's actions. For example, Bob can't look at Charlie's account balance or install new accounting software on the AOB system. However, Sam, the AOB system administrator, can install new accounting software. Enforcing such restrictions goes by the name of *authorization*. Note that authorization places restrictions on the actions of authenticated users.

---

[4]Rumor has it that the security people at Yahoo proudly carry the title of "Paranoids."

Since authentication and authorization both deal with issues of access to resources, we'll lump them together under the clever title of *access control*.

All of the information security mechanisms discussed so far are implemented in *software*. And, if you think about it, other than the hardware, what isn't software in a modern computing system? Today, software systems tend to be large, complex, and rife with bugs. A software bug is not just an annoyance, it is a potential security issue, since it may cause the system to misbehave. Of course, Trudy loves misbehavior.

What software flaws are security issues, and how are they exploited? How can AOB be sure that its software is behaving correctly? How can AOB's software developers reduce (or, ideally, eliminate) security flaws in their software? We'll examine these software development related questions (and much more) in Chapter 11.

Although bugs can (and do) give rise to security flaws, these problems are created unintentionally by well-meaning developers. On the other hand, some software is written with the intent of doing evil. Examples of such malicious software, or *malware*, includes the all-too-familiar computer viruses and worms that plague the Internet today. How do these nasty beasts do what they do, and what can Alice's Online Bank do to limit their damage? What can Trudy do to increase the nastiness of such pests? We'll also consider these and related questions in Chapter 11.

Of course, Bob has many software concerns, too. For example, when Bob enters his password on his computer, how does he know that his password has not been captured and sent to Trudy? If Bob conducts a transaction at `www.alicesonlinebank.com`, how does he know that the transaction he sees on his screen is the same transaction that actually goes to the bank? That is, how can Bob be confident that his software is behaving as it should, instead of as Trudy would like it to behave? We'll consider these questions as well.

When discussing software and security, we'll need to consider operating system, or OS, topics. Operating systems are themselves large and complex pieces of software and OSs are responsible for enforcing much of the security in any system. So, some basic knowledge of OSs is necessary to fully appreciate the challenges of information security. We'll also briefly consider the concept of a trusted operating system, that is, an operating system that we can actually have reasonable confidence is doing the right thing.

1.3   About This Book

Lampson [180] believes that real-world security boils down to the following.

- Specification/policy — What is the system supposed to do?

- Implementation/mechanism — How does it do it?

- Correctness/assurance — Does it really work?

Your humble author would humbly[5] add a fourth category:

- Human nature — Can the system survive "clever" users?

The focus of this book is primarily on the implementation/mechanism front. Your fearless author believes this is appropriate, nay essential, for an introductory course, since the strengths, weaknesses, and inherent limitations of the mechanisms directly affect all other aspects of security. In other words, without a reasonable understanding of the mechanisms, it is not possible to have an informed discussion of other security issues.

The material in this book is divided into four major parts. The first part deals with cryptography, while the next part covers access control. Part III is on protocols, while the final part deals with the vast and relatively ill-defined topic of software. Hopefully, the previous discussion of Alice's Online Bank[6] has convinced you that these major topics are all relevant to real-world information security.

In the remainder of this chapter, we'll give a quick preview of each of these four major topics. Then the chapter concludes with a summary followed by some lovely homework problems.

1.3.1 Cryptography

Cryptography or "secret codes" are a fundamental information security tool. Cryptography has many uses, including providing confidentiality and integrity, among other vital information security functions. We'll discuss cryptography in detail, since this is essential background for any sensible discussion of information security.

We'll begin our coverage of cryptography with a look at a handful of classic cipher systems. In addition to their obvious historic and entertainment value, these classic ciphers illustrate the fundamental principles that are employed in modern digital cipher systems, but in a more user-friendly format.

With this background, we'll be prepared to study modern cryptography. Symmetric key cryptography and public key cryptography both play major roles in information security, and we'll spend an entire chapter on each. We'll then turn our attention to hash functions, which are another fundamental security tool. Hash functions are used in many different contexts in information security, some of which are surprising and not always intuitive.

Then we'll briefly consider a few special topics that are related to cryptography. For example, we'll discuss information hiding, where the goal is for Alice and Bob to communicate without Trudy even knowing that any

---

[5]This sentence is brought to you by the Department of Redundancy Department.
[6]You did read that, right?

information has been passed. This is closely related to the concept of digital watermarking, which we also cover briefly.

The final chapter on cryptography deals with cryptanalysis, that is, the methods used to break cipher systems. Although this is relatively technical and specialized information, understanding these attack methods makes clear many of the design principles behind modern cryptographic systems.

1.3.2   Access Control

As mentioned above, access control deals with authentication and authorization. In the area of authentication, we'll consider the many issues related to passwords. Passwords are the most often used form of authentication today, but this is primarily because passwords are cheap, and definitely not because they are the most secure option.[7]

We'll consider how to securely store passwords. Then we'll delve into the issues surrounding secure password selection. Although it is possible to select reasonably strong passwords that are relatively easy to remember, it's surprisingly difficult to enforce such policies on clever users. In any case, weak passwords present a major security vulnerability in most systems.

The alternatives to passwords include biometrics and smartcards. We'll consider some of the security benefits of these alternate forms of authentication. In particular, we'll discuss the details of several biometric authentication methods.

Authorization deals with restrictions placed on authenticated users. Once Alice's Bank is convinced that Bob is really Bob, it must enforce restrictions on Bob's actions. The two classic methods for enforcing such restrictions are so-called access control lists[8] and capabilities. We'll look at the plusses and minuses of each of these methods.

Authorization leads naturally to a few relatively specialized topics. We'll discuss multilevel security (and the related topic of compartments). For example, the United States government and military has TOP SECRET and SECRET information—some users can see both types of information, while other users can only see the SECRET information, and some can't view either. If both types of information are stored on a single system, how can we enforce such restrictions? This is a thorny authorization issue that has potential implications beyond classified military systems.

Multilevel security leads naturally into the rarified air of security modeling. The idea behind such modeling is to lay out the essential security requirements of a system. Ideally, by verifying a few simple properties we

---

[7]If someone asks you why some weak security measure is used when better options are available, the correct answer is invariably "money."

[8]Access control list, or ACL, is one of many overloaded terms that arise in the field of information security.

would know that a given system satisfies a particular security model. If so, the system would automatically inherit all of the security properties that are known to hold for such a model. We'll only present two of the simplest security models, both of which arise in the context of multilevel security.

Multilevel security also provides an opportunity to discuss covert channels and inference control. Covert channels are unintended channels of communication. Such channels are common in the real world and create potential security problems. Inference control, on the other hand, refers to attempts to limit the sensitive information that can unintentionally leak out of a database due to legitimate user queries. Both covert channels and inference control are difficult problems to deal with effectively in real-world systems.

Since firewalls act as a form of access control for the network, we stretch the usual definition of access control to include firewalls. Regardless of the type of access control employed, attacks are bound to occur. An intrusion detection system (IDS) is designed to detect attacks in progress. So we include a brief discussion of IDS techniques after our discussion of firewalls.

1.3.3   Protocols

We'll then cover security protocols. First, we consider the general problem of authentication over a network. Many examples will be provided, each of which illustrates a particular security pitfall. For example, replay is a critical problem, and so we must consider effective ways to prevent such attacks.

Cryptography will prove essential in authentication protocols. We'll give example of protocols that use symmetric cryptography, as well as examples that rely on public key cryptography. Hash functions also have an important role to play in security protocols.

Our study of simple authentication protocols will illustrate some of the subtleties that can arise in the field of security protocols. A seemingly insignificant change to a protocol can completely change its security. We'll also highlight several specific techniques that are commonly used in real-world security protocols.

Then we'll move on to study several real-world security protocols. First, we look at the so-called Secure Shell, or SSH, which is a relatively simple example. Next, we consider the Secure Socket Layer, or SSL, which is used extensively to secure e-commerce on the Internet today. SSL is an elegant and efficient protocol.

We'll also discuss IPSec, which is another Internet security protocol. Conceptually, SSL and IPSec share many similarities, but the implementations differ greatly. In contrast to SSL, IPSec is complex and it's often said to be over-engineered. Apparently due to its complexity, some fairly significant security issues are present in IPSec—despite a lengthy and open development process. The contrast between SSL and IPSec illustrates some of the inherent challenges and tradeoffs that arise when developing security protocols.

Another real-world protocol that we'll consider is Kerberos, which is an authentication system based on symmetric cryptography. Kerberos follows a much different approach than either SSL or IPSec.

We'll also discuss two wireless security protocols, WEP and GSM. Both of these protocols have many security flaws, including problems with the underlying cryptography and issues with the protocols themselves, which make them interesting case studies.

1.3.4 Software

In the final part of the book, we'll take a look at some aspects of security and software. This is a huge topic, and in three chapters we barely do more than scratch the surface. For starters, we'll discuss security flaws and malware, which were mentioned above.

We'll also consider software reverse engineering, which illustrates how a dedicated attacker can deconstruct software, even without access to the source code. We then apply our newfound hacker's knowledge to the problem of digital rights management, which provides a good example of the limits of security in software, particularly when that software executes in a hostile environment.

Our final software-related topic is operating systems (OSs). The OS is the arbiter of many security operations, so it's important to understand how the OS enforces security. We also consider the requirements of a so-called trusted OS, where "trusted" means that we can have confidence that the OS is performing properly, even when under attack. With this background in hand, we consider a recent attempt by Microsoft to develop a trusted OS for the PC platform.

1.4   The People Problem

Users are surprisingly adept at damaging the best laid security plans. For example, suppose that Bob wants to purchase an item from `amazon.com`. Bob can use his Web browser to securely contact Amazon using the SSL protocol (discussed in Part III), which relies on various cryptographic techniques (see Part I). Access control issues arise in such a transaction (Part II), and all of these security mechanisms are enforced in software (Part IV). So far, so good. However, we'll see in Chapter 10 that a practical attack on this transaction that will cause Bob's Web browser to issue a warning. If Bob heeds the warning, no attack will occur. Unfortunately, if Bob is a typical user, he will ignore the warning, which has the effect of negating this sophisticated security scheme. That is, the security can be broken due to user error, despite the fact that the cryptography, protocols, access control, and software all performed flawlessly.

To take just one more example, consider passwords. Users want to choose easy to remember passwords, but this also makes it easier for Trudy to guess passwords—as discussed in Chapter 7. A possible solution is to assign strong passwords to users. However, this is generally a bad idea since it is likely to result in passwords being written down and posted in prominent locations, likely making the system less secure than if users were allowed to choose their own (weaker) passwords.

As mentioned above, the primary focus of this book is on understanding security mechanisms—the nuts and bolts of security. Yet in several places throughout the book, various "people problems" arise. It would be possible to write an entire volume on this single topic, but the bottom line is that, from a security perspective, the best solution is to remove the humans from the equation as much as possible. In fact, we will see some specific examples of this as well.

For more information on the role that humans play in information security, a good source is Ross Anderson's book [14]. Anderson's book is filled with case studies of security failures, many of which have at least one of their roots somewhere in human nature.

1.5   Principles and Practice

This book is not a theory book. While theory certainly has its place, in your opinionated author's opinion, many aspects of information security are not yet ripe for a meaningful theoretical treatment.[9] Of course, some topics are inherently more theoretical than others. But even the more theoretical security topics can be understood without getting deeply into the theory. For example, cryptography can be (and often is) taught from a highly mathematical perspective. However, with rare exception, a little elementary math is all that is needed to understand important cryptographic principles.

Your practical author has consciously tried to keep the focus on practical issues, but at a deep enough level to give the reader some understanding of—and appreciation for—the underlying concepts. The goal is to get into some depth without overwhelming the reader with trivial details. Admittedly, this is a delicate balancing act and, no doubt, many will disagree that a proper balance has been struck here or there. In any case, the book touches on a large number of security issues related to a wide variety of fundamental principles,

---

[9]To take but one example, consider the infamous buffer overflow attack, which is certainly the most serious software security flaw of all time (see Section 11.2.1 of Chapter 11). What is the grand theory behind this particular exploit? There isn't any—it's simply due to a quirk in the way that memory is laid out in modern processors.

and this breadth necessarily comes at the expense of some rigor and detail. For those who yearn for a more theoretical treatment of the subject, Bishop's book [34] is the obvious choice.

1.6   Problems

The problem is not that there are problems. The problem is
expecting otherwise and thinking that having problems is a problem.
— Theodore I. Rubin

1. Among the fundamental challenges in information security are confidentiality, integrity, and availability, or CIA.

   a. Define each of these terms: confidentiality, integrity, availability.

   b. Give a concrete example where confidentiality is more important than integrity.

   c. Give a concrete example where integrity is more important than confidentiality.

   d. Give a concrete example where availability is the overriding concern.

2. From a bank's perspective, which is usually more important, the integrity of its customer's data or the confidentiality of the data? From the perspective of the bank's customers, which is more important?

3. Instead of an online bank, suppose that Alice provides an online chess playing service known as Alice's Online Chess (AOC). Players, who pay a monthly fee, log into AOC where they are matched with another player of comparable ability.

   a. Where (and why) is confidentiality important for AOC and its customers?

   b. Why is integrity necessary?

   c. Why is availability an important concern?

4. Instead of an online bank, suppose that Alice provides an online chess playing service known as Alice's Online Chess (AOC). Players, who pay a monthly fee, log into AOC where they are matched with another player of comparable ability.

   a. Where should cryptography be used in AOC?

   b. Where should access control used?

    c. Where would security protocols be used?

    d. Is software security a concern for AOC? Why or why not?

5. Some authors distinguish between secrecy, privacy, and confidentiality. In this usage, secrecy is equivalent to our use of the term confidentiality, whereas privacy is secrecy applied to personal data, and confidentiality (in this misguided sense) refers to an obligation not to divulge certain information.

    a. Discuss a real-world situation where privacy is an important security issue.

    b. Discuss a real-world situation where confidentiality (in this incorrect sense) is a critical security issue.

6. RFID tags are extremely small devices capable of broadcasting a number over the air that can be read by a nearby sensor. RFID tags are used for tracking inventory, and they have many other potential uses. For example, RFID tags are used in passports and it has been suggested that they should be put into paper money to prevent counterfeiting. In the future, a person might be surrounded by a cloud of RFID numbers that would provide a great deal of information about the person.

    a. Discuss some privacy concerns related to the widespread use of RFID tags.

    b. Discuss security issues, other than privacy, that might arise due to the widespread use of RFID tags.

7. Cryptography is sometimes said to be brittle, in the sense that it can be very strong, but when it breaks, it (generally) completely shatters. In contrast, some security features can "bend" without breaking completely—security may be lost as a result of the bending, but some useful level of security remains.

    a. Other than cryptography, give an example where security is brittle.

    b. Provide an example where security is not brittle, that is, the security can bend without completely breaking.

8. Read Diffie and Hellman's classic paper [90].

    a. Briefly summarize the paper.

    b. Diffie and Hellman give a system for distributing keys over an insecure channel (see Section 3 of the paper). How does this system work?

    c. Diffie and Hellman also conjecture that a "one way compiler" might be used to construct a public key cryptosystem. Do you believe this is a plausible approach? Why or why not?

9. The most famous World War II cipher machine was the German Enigma (see also Problem 10).

    a. Draw a diagram illustrating the inner workings of the Enigma.

    b. The Enigma was broken by the Allies and intelligence gained from Enigma intercepts was invaluable. Discuss a significant World War II event where broken Enigma messages played a major role.

10. The German Enigma is the most famous World War II cipher machine (see also Problem 9). The cipher was broken by the Allies and intelligence gained from Enigma messages proved invaluable. At first, the Allies were very careful when using the information gained from broken Enigma messages—sometimes the Allies did not use information that could have given them an advantage. Later in the war, however, the Allies (in particular, the Americans) were much less careful, and they tended to use virtually all information obtained from broken Enigma messages.

    a. The Allies were cautious about using information gained from broken Enigma messages for fear that the Germans would realize the cipher was broken. Discuss two different approaches that the Germans might have taken if they had realized that the Enigma was broken.

    b. At some point in the war, it should have become obvious to the Germans that the Enigma was broken, yet the Enigma was used until the end of the war. Why did the Nazis continue to use the Enigma?

11. When you want to authenticate yourself to your computer, most likely you type in your username and password. The username is considered public knowledge, so it is the password that authenticates you. Your password is something you know.

    a. It is also possible to authenticate based on something you are, that is, a physical characteristic. Such a characteristic is known as a biometric. Give an example of biometric-based authentication.

    b. It is also possible to authenticate based on something you have, that is, something in your possession. Give an example of authentication based on something you have.

c. Two-factor authentication requires that two of the three authentication methods (something you know, something you have, something you are) be used. Give an example from everyday life where two-factor authentication is used. Which two of the three are used?

12. CAPTCHAs [319] are often used in an attempt to restrict access to humans (as opposed to automated processes).

    a. Give a real-world example where you were required to solve a CAPTCHA to gain access to some resource. What do you have to do to solve the CAPTCHA?

    b. Discuss various technical methods that might be used to break the CAPTCHA you described in part a.

    c. Outline a non-technical method that might be used to attack the CAPTCHA from part a.

    d. How effective is the CAPTCHA in part a? How user-friendly is the CAPTCHA?

    e. Why do you hate CAPTCHAs?

13. Suppose that a particular security protocol is well designed and secure. However, there is a fairly common situation where insufficient information is available to complete the security protocol. In such cases, the protocol fails and, ideally, a transaction between the participants, say, Alice and Bob, should not be allowed to occur. However, in the real world, protocol designers must decide how to handle cases where protocols fail. As a practical matter, both security and convenience must be considered. Comment on the relative merits of each of the following solutions to protocol failure. Be sure to consider both the relative security and user-friendliness of each.

    a. When the protocol fails, a brief warning is given to Alice and Bob, but the transaction continues as if the protocol had succeeded, without any intervention required from either Alice or Bob.

    b. When the protocol fails, a warning is given to Alice and she decides (by clicking a checkbox) whether the transaction should continue or not.

    c. When the protocol fails, a notification is given to Alice and Bob and the transaction terminates.

    d. When the protocol fails, the transaction terminates with no explanation given to Alice or Bob.

14. Automatic teller machines (ATMs) are an interesting case study in security. Anderson [14] claims that when ATMs were first developed, most

attention was paid to high-tech attacks. However, most real-world attacks on ATMs have been decidedly low tech.

    a. Examples of high-tech attacks on ATMs would be breaking the encryption or authentication protocol. If possible, find a real-world case where a high-tech attack on an ATM has actually occurred and provide the details.

    b. Shoulder surfing is an example of a low-tech attack. In this scenario, Trudy stands behind Alice in line and watches the numbers Alice presses when entering her PIN. Then Trudy bonks Alice in the head and takes her ATM card. Give another example of a low-tech attack on an ATM that has actually occurred.

15. Large and complex software systems invariably have a large number of bugs.

    a. For honest users, such as Alice and Bob, buggy software is certainly annoying but why is it a security issue?

    b. Why does Trudy love buggy software?

    c. In general terms, how might Trudy use bugs in software to break the security of a system?

16. Malware is software that is intentionally malicious, in the sense that it is designed to do damage or break the security of a system. Malware comes in many familiar varieties, including viruses, worms, and Trojans.

    a. Has your computer ever been infected with malware? If so, what did the malware do and how did you get rid of the problem? If not, why have you been so lucky?

    b. In the past, most malware was designed to annoy users. Today, it is often claimed that most malware is written for profit. How could malware possibly be profitable?

17. In the movie *Office Space* [223], software developers attempt to modify company software so that for each financial transaction, any leftover fraction of a cent goes to the developers, instead of going to the company. The idea is that for any particular transaction, nobody will notice the missing fraction of a cent, but over time the developers will accumulate a large sum of money. This type of attack is sometimes known as a salami attack.

    a. Find a real-world example of a salami attack.

    b. In the movie, the salami attack fails. Why?

18. Some commercial software is closed source, meaning that the source code is not available to users. On the other hand, some software is open source, meaning that the source code is available to users.

    a. Give an example of software that you use (or have used) that is closed source.

    b. Give an example of software that you use (or have used) that is open source.

    c. For open source software, what can Trudy do to search for security flaws in the software?

    d. For closed source software, what can Trudy do to search for security flaws in the software?

    e. For open source software, what can Alice do to make the software more secure?

    f. For closed source software, what can Alice do to make the software more secure?

    g. Which is inherently more secure, open source software or closed source software? Why?

19. It's sometimes said that complexity is the enemy of security.

    a. Give an example of commercial software to which this statement applies, that is, find an example of software that is large and complex and has had significant security problems.

    b. Find an example of a security protocol to which this statement applies.

20. Suppose that this textbook was sold online (as a PDF) by your money-grubbing author for, say, $5. Then the author would make more money off of each copy sold than he currently does[10] and people who purchase the book would save a lot of money.

    a. What are the security issues related to the sale of an online book?

    b. How could you make the selling of an online book more secure, from the copyright holder's perspective?

    c. How secure is your approach in part b? What are some possible attacks on your proposed system?

21. The PowerPoint slides at [255] describe a security class project where students successfully hacked the Boston subway system.

---

[10]Believe it or not.

a. Summarize each of the various attacks. What was the crucial vulnerability that enabled each attack to succeed?

b. The students planned to give a presentation at the self-proclaimed "hacker's convention," Defcon 16 [80], where they would have presented the PowerPoint slides now available at [255]. At the request of the Boston transit authority, a judge issued a temporary restraining order (since lifted) that prevented the students from talking about their work. Do you think this was justified, based on the material in the slides?

c. What are war dialing and war driving? What is war carting?

d. Comment on the production quality of the "melodramatic video about the warcart" (a link to the video can be found at [16]).

Part I

Crypto

Chapter 2

Crypto Basics

The solution is by no means so difficult as you might
be led to imagine from the first hasty inspection of the characters.
These characters, as any one might readily guess,
form a cipher—that is to say, they convey a meaning...
— Edgar Allan Poe, *The Gold Bug*

2.1   Introduction

In this chapter we'll discuss some of the basic elements of cryptography. This discussion will lay the foundation for the remaining crypto chapters which, in turn, underpin much of the material throughout the book. We'll avoid mathematical rigor as much as possible. Nevertheless, there is enough detail here so that you will not only understand the "what" but you will also have some appreciation for the "why."

After this introductory chapter, the remaining crypto chapters focus on:

- Symmetric key cryptography

- Public key cryptography

- Hash functions

- Advanced cryptanalysis

A handful of special topics are also covered.

2.2   How to Speak Crypto

The basic terminology of crypto includes the following.

- *Cryptology* — the art and science of making and breaking "secret codes."

- *Cryptography* — the making of "secret codes."

- *Cryptanalysis* — the breaking of "secret codes."

- *Crypto* — a synonym for any or all of the above (and more), where the precise meaning should be clear from context.

A *cipher* or *cryptosystem* is used to *encrypt* data. The original unencrypted data is known as *plaintext*, and the result of encryption is *ciphertext*. We *decrypt* the ciphertext to recover the original plaintext. A *key* is used to configure a cryptosystem for encryption and decryption.

In a *symmetric* cipher, the same key is used to encrypt and to decrypt, as illustrated by the black box cryptosystem in Figure 2.1.[1] There is also a concept of *public key* cryptography where the encryption and decryption keys are different. Since different keys are used, it's possible to make the encryption key public—thus the name public key.[2] In public key crypto, the encryption key is, appropriately, known as the *public key*, whereas the decryption key, which must remain secret, is the *private key*. In symmetric key crypto, the key is known as a *symmetric key*. We'll avoid the ambiguous term secret key.

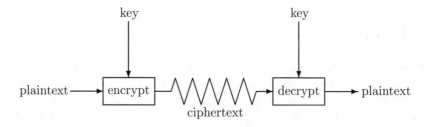

Figure 2.1: Crypto as a Black Box

For an ideal cipher, it is infeasible to recover the plaintext from the ciphertext without the key. That is, even if the attacker, Trudy, has complete knowledge of the algorithms used and lots of other information (to be made more precise later), she can't recover the plaintext without the key. That's the goal, although reality sometimes differs.

---

[1]This is the only black box you'll find in this book!

[2]Public key crypto is also known as asymmetric crypto, in reference to the fact that the encryption and decryption keys are different.

A fundamental tenet of cryptography is that the inner workings of a crypto-system are completely known to the attacker, Trudy, and the only secret is a key. This is known as *Kerckhoffs' Principle*, which, believe it or not, was named after a guy named Kerckhoffs. In the year 1883, Kerckhoffs, a Dutch linguist and cryptographer, laid out six principles of cipher design and use [164]. The principle that now bears his name states that a cipher "must not be required to be secret, and it must be able to fall into the hands of the enemy without inconvenience" [165], that is, the design of the cipher is not secret.

What is the point of Kerckhoffs' Principle? After all, it must certainly be more difficult for Trudy to attack a cryptosystem if she doesn't know how the cipher works. So, why would we want to make Trudy's life easier? There are (at least) a couple of problems with relying on a secret design for your security. For one, the details of "secret" cryptosystems seldom, if ever, remain secret for long. Reverse engineering can be used to recover algorithms from software, and even algorithms embedded in tamper-resistant hardware are sometimes subject to reverse engineering attacks and exposure. And, even more worrisome is the fact that secret crypto-algorithms have a long history of failing to be secure once the algorithms have been exposed to public scrutiny—see [29] for a relatively recent example where Microsoft violated Kerckhoffs' Principle.

Cryptographers will not deem a crypto-algorithm worthy of use until it has withstood extensive public analysis by many cryptographers over an extended period of time. The bottom line is that any cryptosystem that does not satisfy Kerckhoffs' Principle is suspect. In other words, ciphers are presumed guilty until "proven" innocent.

Kerckhoffs' Principle is often extended to cover various aspects of security well beyond cryptography. In other contexts, this basic principle is usually taken to mean that the security design itself is open to public scrutiny. The belief is that "more eyeballs" are more likely to expose more security flaws and therefore ultimately result in a system that is more secure. Although Kerckhoffs' Principle (in both its narrow crypto form and in a broader context) seems to be universally accepted in principle, there are many real-world temptations to violate this fundamental tenet, almost invariably with disastrous consequences. Throughout this book we'll see several examples of security failures that were directly caused by a failure to heed the venerable Mr. Kerckhoffs.

In the next section, we look briefly at a few classic cryptosystems. Although the history of crypto is a fascinating topic [159], the purpose of this material is to provide an elementary introduction to some of the crucial concepts that arise in modern cryptography. In other words, pay attention since we will see all of these concepts again in the next couple of chapters and in many cases, in later chapters as well.

2.3   Classic Crypto

In this section, we examine four classic ciphers, each of which illustrates a feature that is relevant to modern cryptosystems. First on our agenda is the simple substitution, which is one of the oldest cipher systems—dating back at least 2,000 years—and one that is good for illustrating some basic attacks. We then turn our attention to a type of double transposition cipher, which includes important concepts that are used in modern ciphers. We also discuss classic codebooks, since many modern ciphers can be viewed as the "electronic" equivalent of codebooks. Finally, we consider the so-called one-time pad, a practical cipher that is provably secure. No other cipher in this book (or in common use) is provably secure.

2.3.1   Simple Substitution Cipher

First, we consider a particularly simple implementation of a simple substitution cipher. In the simplest case, the message is encrypted by substituting the letter of the alphabet n places ahead of the current letter. For example, with $n = 3$, the substitution—which acts as the key—is

    plaintext: a b c d e f g h i j k l m n o p q r s t u v w x y z
    ciphertext: D E F G H I J K L M N O P Q R S T U V W X Y Z A B C

where we've followed the convention that the plaintext is lowercase, and the ciphertext is uppercase. In this example, the key could be given succinctly as "3" since the amount of the shift is, in effect, the key.

   Using the key 3, we can encrypt the plaintext message

$$\texttt{fourscoreandsevenyearsago} \tag{2.1}$$

by looking up each plaintext letter in the table above and then substituting the corresponding letter in the ciphertext row, or by simply replacing each letter by the letter that is three positions ahead of it in the alphabet. For the particular plaintext in (2.1), the resulting ciphertext is

$$\texttt{IRXUVFRUHDAGVHYHABHDUVDIR.}$$

To decrypt this simple substitution, we look up the ciphertext letter in the ciphertext row and replace it with the corresponding letter in the plaintext row, or we can shift each ciphertext letter backward by three. The simple substitution with a shift of three is known as the Caesar's cipher.[3]

---

[3]Historians generally agree that the Caesar's cipher was named after the Roman dictator, not the salad.

There is nothing magical about a shift by three—any shift will do. If we limit the simple substitution to shifts of the alphabet, then the possible keys are $n \in \{0, 1, 2, ..., 25\}$. Suppose Trudy intercepts the ciphertext message

```
CSYEVIXIVQMREXIH
```

and she suspect that it was encrypted with a simple substitution cipher using a shift by n. Then she can try each of the 26 possible keys, "decrypting" the message with each putative key and checking whether the resulting putative plaintext makes sense. If the message really was encrypted via a shift by n, Trudy can expect to find the true plaintext—and thereby recover the key—after 13 tries, on average.

This brute force attack is something that Trudy can always attempt. Provided that Trudy has enough time and resources, she will eventually stumble across the correct key and break the message. This most elementary of all crypto attacks is known as an *exhaustive key search*. Since this attack is always an option, it's necessary (although far from sufficient) that the number of possible keys be too large for Trudy to simply try them all in any reasonable amount of time.

How large of a keyspace is large enough? Suppose Trudy has a fast computer (or group of computers) that's able to test 2^{40} keys each second.[4] Then a keyspace of size 2^{56} can be exhausted in 2^{16} seconds, or about 18 hours, whereas a keyspace of size 2^{64} would take more than half a year for an exhaustive key search, and a keyspace of size 2^{128} would require more than nine quintillion years. For modern symmetric ciphers, the key is typically 128 bits or more, giving a keyspace of size 2^{128} or more.

Now, back to the simple substitution cipher. If we only allow shifts of the alphabet, then the number of possible keys is far too small, since Trudy can do an exhaustive key search very quickly. Is there any way that we can increase the number of keys? In fact, there is no need not to limit the simple substitution to a shifting by n, since any permutation of the 26 letters will serve as a key. For example, the following permutation, which is not a shift of the alphabet, gives us a key for a simple substitution cipher:

```
plaintext:  a b c d e f g h i j k l m n o p q r s t u v w x y z
ciphertext: Z P B Y J R G K F L X Q N W V D H M S U T O I A E C
```

In general, a simple substitution cipher can employ any permutation of the alphabet as a key, which implies that there are $26! \approx 2^{88}$ possible keys. With

---

[4]In 1998 the Electronic Frontier Foundation (EFF) built a special-purpose key cracking machine for attacking the Data Encryption Standard (DES, which we'll discuss in the next chapter). This machine, which cost $220,000, consisted of about 43,200 processors, each of which ran at 40 MHz and, overall, it was capable of testing about 2.5 million keys per second [156]. Extrapolating this to a state-of-the-art PC with a single 4 GHz processor, Trudy could test fewer than 2^{30} keys per second on one such machine. So, if she had access to 1000 such machines, she could test about 2^{40} keys per second.

Trudy's superfast computer that tests 2^{40} keys per second, trying all possible keys for the simple substitution would take more than 8900 millennia. Of course, she would expect to find the correct key half that time, or just 4450 millennia. Since 2^{88} keys is far more than Trudy can try in any reasonable amount of time, this cipher passes the crucial first requirement of any practical cipher, namely, the keyspace is big enough so that an exhaustive key search is infeasible. Does this mean that a simple substitution cipher is secure? The answer is a resounding no, as the attack described in the next section clearly illustrates.

2.3.2   Cryptanalysis of a Simple Substitution

Suppose Trudy intercepts the following ciphertext, which she suspects was produced by a simple substitution cipher, where the key could be any permutation of the alphabet:

```
PBFPVYFBQXZTYFPBFEQJHDXXQVAPTPQJKTOYQWIPBVWLXTOXBTFXQWA
XBVCXQWAXFQJVWLEQNTOZQGGQLFXQWAKVWLXQWAEBIPBFXFQVXGTVJV
WLBTPQWAEBFPBFHCVLXBQUFEVWLXGDPEQVPQGVPPBFTIXPFHXZHVFAG
FOTHFEFBQUFTDHZBQPOTHXTYFTODXQHFTDPTOGHFQPBQWAQJJTODXQH
FOQPWTBDHHIXQVAPBFZQHCFWPFHPBFIPBQWKFABVYYDZBOTHPBQPQJT
QOTOGHFQAPBFEQJHDXXQVAVXEBQPEFZBVFOJIWFFACFCCFHQWAUVWFL
QHGFXVAFXQHFUFUHILTTAVWAFFAWTEVOITDHFHFQAITITFTQVTIXPFHX
QWGFLVWPTOFFA
```
(2.2)

Since it's too much work for Trudy to try all 2^{88} possible keys, can she be more clever? Assuming the plaintext is English, Trudy can make use of the English letter frequency counts in Figure 2.2 together with the frequency counts for the ciphertext in (2.2), which appear in Figure 2.3.

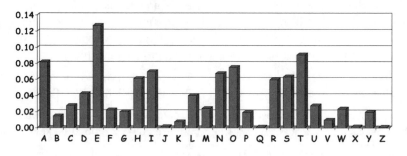

Figure 2.2: English Letter Frequency Counts

From the ciphertext frequency counts in Figure 2.3, we see that "F" is the most common letter in the encrypted message and, according to Figure 2.2, "E" is the most common letter in the English language. Trudy therefore

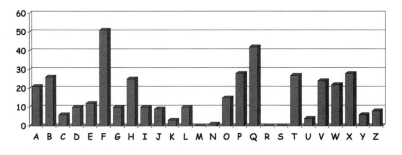

Figure 2.3: Ciphertext Frequency Counts

surmises that it's likely that "F" has been substituted for "E." Continuing in this manner, Trudy can try likely substitutions until she recognizes words, at which point she can be confident in her guesses.

Initially, the easiest word to determine might be the first word, since Trudy doesn't know where inter-word spaces belong in the text. Since the third plaintext letter appears to be "e," and given the high frequency counts of the first two letter, Trudy might reasonably guess (correctly, as it turns out) that the first word of the plaintext is "the." Making these substitutions into the remaining ciphertext, she will be able to guess more letters and the puzzle will begin to unravel. Trudy will likely make some missteps along the way, but with sensible use of the statistical information available, she will find the plaintext in considerably less time than 4450 millennia.

This attack on the simple substitution shows that a large keyspace is not sufficient to ensure security. This attack also shows that cipher designers must guard against clever attacks. But how can we protect against all such attacks, since new attacks are developed all the time? The answer is that we can't and, as a result, a cipher must be subjected to extensive analysis by skilled cryptographers before we can trust it—the more skilled cryptographers who have tried to break a cipher and failed, the more confidence we have in the system.

2.3.3 Definition of Secure

There are several reasonable definitions of a secure cipher. Ideally, we would like to have a rigorous mathematical proof that there is no feasible attack on a system, but such ciphers are few and far between and provably secure ciphers are impractical for most uses.

Lacking a proof that a cipher is secure, we could require that the best-known attack on the system is impractical, in the sense of being computationally infeasible. While this would seem to be the most crucial property, we'll use a slightly different definition. We say that a cryptosystem is *secure* if the best-known attack requires as much work as an exhaustive key search. In other words, no shortcut attack is known.

Note that by our definition, a secure cipher with a small number of keys could be easier to break than an insecure one with a large number of keys. While this may seem counterintuitive, there is a method to the madness. The rationale for our definition is that a cipher can never offer more security than an exhaustive key search, so the key size could be considered its "advertised" level of security. If a shortcut attack is known, the algorithm fails to provide its advertised level of security, as indicated by the key length. In short, a shortcut attack indicates that the cipher has a design flaw.

Note also that in practice, we must select a cipher that is secure (in the sense of our definition) and has a large enough key space so that an exhaustive key search is impractical. Both factors are necessary when choosing a cipher to protect sensitive data.

2.3.4 Double Transposition Cipher

In this section we discuss another classic cipher that illustrates some important basic concepts. The double transposition presented in this section is a weaker form of the usual double transposition cipher. We use this form of the cipher since it provides a slightly simpler means of illustrating all of the points that we want to make.

To encrypt with a double transposition cipher, we first write the plaintext into an array of a given size and then permute the rows and columns according to specified permutations. For example, suppose we write the plaintext `attackatdawn` into a 3×4 array:

$$\begin{bmatrix} a & t & t & a \\ c & k & a & t \\ d & a & w & n \end{bmatrix}.$$

Now if we transpose (or permute) the rows according to $(1, 2, 3) \rightarrow (3, 2, 1)$ and then transpose the columns according to $(1, 2, 3, 4) \rightarrow (4, 2, 1, 3)$, we obtain

$$\begin{bmatrix} a & t & t & a \\ c & k & a & t \\ d & a & w & n \end{bmatrix} \longrightarrow \begin{bmatrix} d & a & w & n \\ c & k & a & t \\ a & t & t & a \end{bmatrix} \longrightarrow \begin{bmatrix} n & a & d & w \\ t & k & c & a \\ a & t & a & t \end{bmatrix}.$$

The ciphertext is then read from the final array:

$$NADWTKCAATAT \tag{2.3}$$

For the double transposition, the key consists of the size of the matrix and the row and column permutations. Anyone who knows the key can simply put the ciphertext into the appropriate sized matrix and undo the permutations to recover the plaintext For example, to decrypt (2.3), the ciphertext is first put into a 3×4 array. Then the columns are numbered as $(4, 2, 1, 3)$ and rearranged to $(1, 2, 3, 4)$, and the rows are numbered $(3, 2, 1)$ and rearranged into $(1, 2, 3)$,

$$
\begin{bmatrix} N & A & D & W \\ T & K & C & A \\ A & T & A & T \end{bmatrix} \longrightarrow \begin{bmatrix} D & A & W & N \\ C & K & A & T \\ A & T & T & A \end{bmatrix} \longrightarrow \begin{bmatrix} A & T & T & A \\ C & K & A & T \\ D & A & W & N \end{bmatrix}
$$

and we see that we have recovered the plaintext, namely, `attackatdawn`.

The bad news is that, unlike a simple substitution, the double transposition does nothing to disguise the letters that appear in the message. The good news is that the double transposition appears to thwart an attack that relies on the statistical information contained in the plaintext, since the plaintext statistics are disbursed throughout the ciphertext.

Even this simplified version of the double transposition is not a trivial cipher to break. The idea of smearing plaintext information through the ciphertext is so useful that it is employed by modern block ciphers, as we will see in the next chapter.

2.3.5 One-Time Pad

The one-time pad, which is also known as the Vernam cipher, is a provably secure cryptosystem. Historically it has been used in various times and places, but it's not practical for most situations. However, it does nicely illustrate some important concepts that we'll see again later.

For simplicity, let's consider an alphabet with only eight letters. Our alphabet and the corresponding binary representation of letters appear in Table 2.1. It's important to note that the mapping between letters and bits is not secret. This mapping serves a similar purpose as, say, the ASCII code, which is not much of a secret either.

Table 2.1: Abbreviated Alphabet

letter	e	h	i	k	l	r	s	t
binary	000	001	010	011	100	101	110	111

Suppose that Alice, who recently got a job as a spy, wants to use a one-time pad to encrypt the plaintext message

`heilhitler.`

She first consults Table 2.1 to convert the plaintext letters to the bit string

$$001\ 000\ 010\ 100\ 001\ 010\ 111\ 100\ 000\ 101.$$

The one-time pad key consists of a randomly selected string of bits that is the same length as the message. The key is then XORed with the plaintext to yield the ciphertext. For the mathematically inclined, a fancier way to say this is that we add the plaintext and key bits modulo 2.

We denote the XOR of bit x with bit y as $x \oplus y$. Since $x \oplus y \oplus y = x$, decryption is accomplished by XOR-ing the same key with the ciphertext. Modern symmetric ciphers utilize this magical property of the XOR in various ways, as we'll see in the next chapter.

Now suppose that Alice has the key

$$111\ 101\ 110\ 101\ 111\ 100\ 000\ 101\ 110\ 000$$

which is of the proper length to encrypt her message above. Then to encrypt, Alice computes the ciphertext as

	h	e	i	l	h	i	t	l	e	r
plaintext:	001	000	010	100	001	010	111	100	000	101
key:	111	101	110	101	111	100	000	101	110	000
ciphertext:	110	101	100	001	110	110	111	001	110	101
	s	r	l	h	s	s	t	h	s	r

Converting these ciphertext bits back into letters, the ciphertext message to be transmitted is srlhssthsr.

When her fellow spy, Bob, receives Alice's message, he decrypts it using the same shared key and thereby recovers the plaintext:

	s	r	l	h	s	s	t	h	s	r
ciphertext:	110	101	100	001	110	110	111	001	110	101
key:	111	101	110	101	111	100	000	101	110	000
plaintext:	001	000	010	100	001	010	111	100	000	101
	h	e	i	l	h	i	t	l	e	r

Let's consider a couple of scenarios. First, suppose that Alice has an enemy, Charlie, within her spy organization. Charlie claims that the actual key used to encrypt Alice's message is

$$101\ 111\ 000\ 101\ 111\ 100\ 000\ 101\ 110\ 000.$$

Bob decrypts the ciphertext using the key given to him by Charlie and obtains

	s	r	l	h	s	s	t	h	s	r
ciphertext:	110	101	100	001	110	110	111	001	110	101
"key":	101	111	000	101	111	100	000	101	110	000
"plaintext":	011	010	100	100	001	010	111	100	000	101
	k	i	l	l	h	i	t	l	e	r

Bob, who doesn't really understand crypto, orders that Alice be brought in for questioning.

Now let's consider a different scenario. Suppose that Alice is captured by her enemies, who have also intercepted the ciphertext. The captors are eager to read the message and Alice is "encouraged" to provide the key for this super-secret message. Alice claims that she is actually a double agent and to prove it she provides the "key"

$$111\ 101\ 000\ 011\ 101\ 110\ 001\ 011\ 101\ 101.$$

When Alice's captors "decrypt" the ciphertext using this "key," they find

	s	r	l	h	s	s	t	h	s	r
ciphertext:	110	101	100	001	110	110	111	001	110	101
"key":	111	101	000	011	101	110	001	011	101	101
"plaintext":	001	000	100	010	011	000	110	010	011	000
	h	e	l	i	k	e	s	i	k	e

Alice's captors, who are not very knowledgeable about crypto, congratulate Alice for her patriotism and release her.

While not a proof, these examples do indicate why the one-time pad is provably secure. The bottom line is that if the key is chosen at random, and used only once, then an attacker who sees the ciphertext has no information about the message itself (other than its length, which could be padded). That is, given the ciphertext, any "plaintext" of the same length can be generated by a suitable choice of "key," and all possible plaintexts are equally likely. So the ciphertext provides no meaningful information at all about the plaintext. From a cryptographer's point of view, it doesn't get any better than that.

Of course, we are assuming that the one-time pad cipher is used correctly. The key (or pad) must be chosen at random, used only once, and must be known only to the Alice and Bob.

Since we can't do better than provable security, why don't we always use the one-time pad? Unfortunately, the cipher is impractical for most applications. Why is this the case? The crucial problem is that the pad is the same length as the message and since the pad is the key, it must be securely shared with the intended recipient before the ciphertext can be decrypted. If we can securely transmit the pad, why not simply transmit the plaintext by the same means and do away with the encryption?

Below, we'll see an historical example where it actually did make sense to use a one-time pad—in spite of its limitations. However, for modern high data-rate systems, a one-time pad cipher would be totally impractical.

While we're at it, why is it that the one-time pad can only be used once? Suppose we have two plaintext messages P_1 and P_2 and we encrypted these as as $C_1 = P_1 \oplus K$ and $C_2 = P_2 \oplus K$, that is, we have two messages encrypted with the same "one-time" pad K. In the cryptanalysis business, this is known as a *depth*. With one-time pad ciphertexts in depth, we see that

$$C_1 \oplus C_2 = P_1 \oplus K \oplus P_2 \oplus K = P_1 \oplus P_2$$

and the key has disappeared from the problem. In this case, the ciphertext does yield some information about the underlying plaintext. Another way to see this is consider an exhaustive key search. If the pad is only used once, then the attacker has no way to know whether the guessed key is correct or not. But if two messages are in depth, for the correct key, both putative plaintexts must make sense. This provides the attacker with a means to distinguish the correct key from incorrect guesses. The problem only gets worse (or better, from Trudy's perspective) the more times the key is reused.

Let's consider an example of one-time pad encryptions that are in depth. Using the same bit encoding as in Table 2.1, suppose we have

$$P_1 = \texttt{like} = 100\,010\,011\,000 \quad \text{and} \quad P_2 = \texttt{kite} = 011\,010\,111\,000$$

and both are encrypted with the same key $K = 110\,011\,101\,111$. Then

	l	i	k	e
P_1:	100	010	011	000
K:	110	011	101	111
C_1:	010	001	110	111
	i	h	s	t

and

	k	i	t	e
P_2:	011	010	111	000
K:	110	011	101	111
C_2:	101	001	010	111
	r	h	i	t

If Trudy the cryptanalyst knows that the messages are in depth, she immediately sees that the second and fourth letters of P_1 and P_2 are the same, since the corresponding ciphertext letters are identical. But far more devastating is the fact that Trudy can now guess a putative message P_1 and check her results using P_2. Suppose that Trudy (who only has C_1 and C_2) suspects that $P_1 = \texttt{kill} = 011\,010\,100\,100$. Then she can find the corresponding putative key:

	k	i	l	l
putative P_1:	011	010	100	100
C_1:	010	001	110	111
putative K:	001	011	010	011

and she can then use this K to "decrypt" C_2 and obtain

$$
\begin{array}{rcccc}
C_2: & 101 & 001 & 010 & 111 \\
\text{putative } K: & 001 & 011 & 010 & 011 \\
\hline
\text{putative } P_2: & 100 & 010 & 000 & 100 \\
& \texttt{l} & \texttt{i} & \texttt{e} & \texttt{l}
\end{array}
$$

Since this K does not yield a sensible decryption for P_2, Trudy can safely assume that her guess for P_1 was incorrect. When Trudy eventually guesses $P_1 = \texttt{like}$ she will obtain the correct key K and decrypt to find $P_2 = \texttt{kite}$, thereby confirming the correctness of the key and, therefore, the correctness of both decryptions.

2.3.6 Project VENONA

The so-called VENONA project [315] provides an interesting example of a real-world use of the one-time pad. In the 1930s and 1940s, spies from the Soviet Union who entered the United States brought with them one-time pad keys. When it was time to report back to their handlers in Moscow, these spies used their one-time pads to encrypt their messages, which could then be safely sent back to Moscow. These spies were extremely successful, and their messages dealt with the most sensitive U.S. government secrets of the time. In particular, the development of the first atomic bomb was a focus of much of the espionage. The Rosenbergs, Alger Hiss, and many other well-known traitors—and many who were never identified—figure prominently in VENONA messages.

The Soviet spies were well trained and never reused the key, yet many of the intercepted ciphertext messages were eventually decrypted by American cryptanalysts. How can that be, given that the one-time pad is provably secure? In fact, there was a flaw in the method used to generate the pads, so that, in effect, long stretches of the keys were repeated. As a result, many messages were in depth, which enabled the successful cryptanalysis of much VENONA traffic.

Part of one interesting VENONA decrypt is given in Table 2.2. This message refers to David Greenglass and his wife Ruth. LIBERAL is Julius Rosenberg who, along with his wife Ethyl, was eventually executed for his role in nuclear espionage.[5] The Soviet codename for the atomic bomb was, appropriately, ENORMOUS. For any World War II-era history buff, the VENONA decrypts at [315] make for fascinating reading.

---

[5]David Greenglass served ten years of a fifteen year sentence for his part in the crime. He later claimed that he lied in crucial testimony about Ethyl Rosenberg's level of involvement—testimony that was probably decisive in her being sentenced to death.

Table 2.2: VENONA Decrypt of Message of September 21, 1944

```
[C% Ruth] learned that her husband [v] was called up by the army
but he was not sent to the front.  He is a mechanical engineer
and is now working at the ENORMOUS [ENORMOZ] [vi] plant in
SANTA FE, New Mexico.

[45 groups unrecoverable]

detain VOLOK [vii] who is working in a plant on ENORMOUS. He is a
FELLOWCOUNTRYMAN [ZEMLYaK] [viii].  Yesterday he learned that
they had dismissed him from his work.  His active work in
progressive organizations in the past was cause of his dismissal.

In the FELLOWCOUNTRYMAN line LIBERAL is in touch with CHESTER [ix].
They meet once a month for the payment of dues.  CHESTER is
interested in whether we are satisfied with the collaboration and
whether there are not any misunderstandings.  He does not inquire
about specific items of work [KONKRETNAYa RABOTA]. In as much
as CHESTER knows about the role of LIBERAL's group we beg consent
to ask C. through LIBERAL about leads from among people who are
working on ENOURMOUS and in other technical fields.
```

2.3.7   Codebook Cipher

A classic codebook cipher is, literally, a dictionary-like book containing (plaintext) words and their corresponding (ciphertext) codewords. To encrypt a given word, the cipher clerk would simply look up the word in the codebook and replace it with the corresponding codeword. Decryption, using the inverse codebook, was equally straightforward. Table 2.3 contains an excerpt from a famous codebook used by Germany during World War I.

For example, to use the codebook in Table 2.3 to encrypt the German word **Februar**, the entire word would be replaced with the 5-digit codeword 13605. This codebook was used for encryption, while the corresponding inverse codebook, arranged with the 5-digit codewords in numerical order, was used for decryption. A codebook is a form of a substitution cipher, but the substitutions are far from simple, since substitutions are for entire words, or in some cases, entire phrases.

The codebook illustrated in Table 2.3 was used to encrypt the famous Zimmermann telegram. At the height of World War I in 1917, the German Foreign Minister, Arthur Zimmermann, sent an encrypted telegram to the German ambassador in Mexico City. The ciphertext message, which appears in Figure 2.4 [227], was intercepted by the British. At the time, the British and French were at war with Germany, but the U.S. was neutral [307].

Table 2.3: Excerpt from a German Codebook

Plaintext	Ciphertext
Februar	13605
fest	13732
finanzielle	13850
folgender	13918
Frieden	17142
Friedenschluss	17149
⋮	⋮

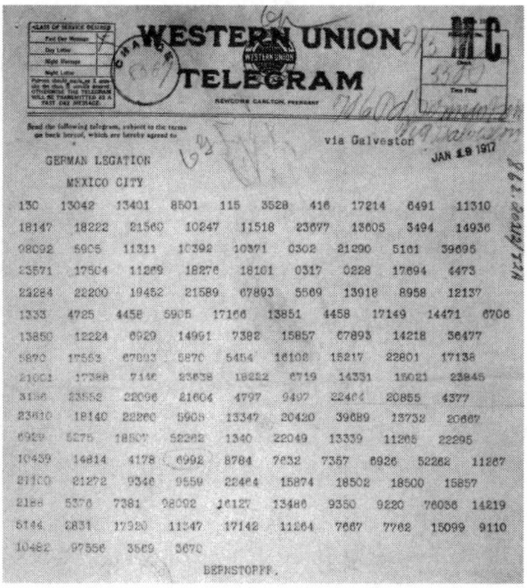

Figure 2.4: The Zimmermann Telegram

The Russians had recovered a damaged version of the German code-book, and the partial codebook had been passed on to the British. Through painstaking analyses, the British were able to fill in the gaps in the codebook so that by the time they obtained the Zimmermann telegram, they could decrypt it [83]. The telegram stated that the German government was planning to begin unrestricted submarine warfare and had concluded that this would likely lead to war with the United States. As a result, Zimmermann told his ambassador that Germany should try to recruit Mexico as an ally to fight against the United States. The incentive for Mexico was that it would "reconquer the lost territory in Texas, New Mexico and Arizona." When the Zimmermann telegram was released in the U.S., public opinion turned against Germany and, after the sinking of the Lusitania, the U.S. declared war.

The British were initially hesitant to release the Zimmermann telegram since they feared that the Germans would realize that their cipher was broken and, presumably, stop using it. However, after decrypting the Zimmermann telegram, the British took a closer look at other intercepted messages that had been sent at about the same time. To their amazement, they found that a variant of the incendiary telegram had been sent unencrypted.[6] The version of the Zimmermann telegram that the British subsequently released closely matched the unencrypted version of the telegram. As the British hoped, the Germans concluded that their codebook had not been compromised and continued to use it for sensitive messages throughout the war.

The security of a classic codebook cipher depends primarily on the physical security of the book itself. That is, the book must be protected from capture by the enemy. In addition, statistical attacks analogous to those used to break a simple substitution cipher apply to codebooks, although the amount of data required is much larger. The reason that a statistical attack on a codebook is more difficult is due to the fact that the size of the "alphabet" is much larger, and consequently far more data must be collected before the statistical information can rise above the noise.

As late as World War II, codebooks were in widespread use. Cryptographers realized that these ciphers were subject to statistical attack, so codebooks needed to be periodically replaced with new codebooks. Since this was an expensive and risky process, techniques were developed to extend the life of a codebook. To accomplish this, a so-called *additive* was generally used.

Suppose that for a particular codebook cipher, the codewords are all 5-digit numbers. Then the corresponding additive book would consist of a long list of randomly generated 5-digit numbers. After a plaintext message had been converted to a series of 5-digit codewords, a starting point in the additive book would be selected and beginning from that point, the sequence of 5-digit additives would be added to the codewords to create the ciphertext. To decrypt, the same additive sequence would be subtracted from the ciphertext before looking up the codeword in the codebook. Note that the additive book—as well as the codebook itself—is required to encrypt or decrypt a message.

Often, the starting point in the additive book was selected at random by the sender and sent in the clear (or in a slightly obfuscated form) at the start of the transmission. This additive information was part of the *message indicator*, or MI. The MI included any non-secret information needed by the intended recipient to decrypt the message.

If the additive material was only used once, the resulting cipher would be equivalent to a one-time pad and therefore, provably secure. However, in

---

[6]Apparently, the message had not initially attracted attention because it was not encrypted. The lesson here is that, ironically, encryption with a weak cipher may be worse than no encryption at all. We have more to say about this issue in Chapter 10.

practice, the additive was reused many times and, therefore, any messages sent with overlapping additives would have their codewords encrypted with the same key, where the key consists of the codebook and the specific additive sequence. Therefore, any messages with overlapping additive sequences could be used to gather the statistical information needed to attack the underlying codebook. In effect, the additive book dramatically increased the amount of ciphertext required to mount a statistical attack on the codebook, which is precisely the effect the cryptographers had hoped to achieve.

Modern block ciphers use complex algorithms to generate ciphertext from plaintext (and vice versa), but at a higher level, a block cipher can be viewed as a codebook, where each key determines a distinct codebook. That is, a modern block cipher consists of an enormous number of distinct codebooks, with the codebooks indexed by the key. The concept of an additive also lives on, in the form of an initialization vector, or IV, which is often used with block ciphers (and sometimes with stream ciphers as well). Block ciphers are discussed in detail in the next chapter.

2.3.8 Ciphers of the Election of 1876

The U.S. presidential election of 1876 was a virtual dead heat. At the time, the Civil War was still fresh in people's minds, Radical Reconstruction was ongoing in the former Confederacy, and the nation was still bitterly divided.

The contestants in the election were Republican Rutherford B. Hayes and Democrat Samuel J. Tilden. Tilden had obtained a slight plurality of the popular vote, but it is the Electoral College that determines the winner of the presidency. In the Electoral College, each state sends a delegation and for almost every state, the entire delegation is supposed to vote for the candidate who received the largest number of votes in that particular state.[7]

In 1876, the electoral college delegations of four states[8] were in dispute, and these held the balance. A commission of 15 members was appointed to determine which state delegations were legitimate, and thus determine the presidency. The commission decided that all four states should go to Hayes and he became president of the United States. Tilden's supporters immediately charged that Hayes' people had bribed officials to turn the vote in his favor, but no evidence was forthcoming.

Some months after the election, reporters discovered a large number of encrypted messages that had been sent from Tilden's supporters to officials in the disputed states. One of the ciphers used was a partial codebook together

---

[7]However, there is no legal requirement for an Electoral College delegate to vote for a particular candidate, and on occasion a "faithless elector" will vote contrary to the popular vote in his or her state.

[8]Foreshadowing the election of 2000, one of these four disputed states was, believe it or not, Florida.

Table 2.4: Election of 1876 Codebook

Plaintext	Ciphertext
Greenbacks	Copenhagen
Hayes	Greece
votes	Rochester
Tilden	Russia
telegram	Warsaw
⋮	⋮

with a transposition on the words. The codebook was only applied to important words and the transposition was a fixed permutation for all messages of a given length. The allowed message lengths were 10, 15, 20, 25, and 30 words, with all messages padded to one of these lengths. A snippet of the codebook appears in Table 2.4.

The permutation used for a message of 10 words was

$$9, 3, 6, 1, 10, 5, 2, 7, 4, 8.$$

One actual ciphertext message was

`Warsaw they read all unchanged last are idiots can't situation`

which was decrypted by undoing the permutation and substituting `telegram` for `Warsaw` to obtain

```
Can't read last telegram.
Situation unchanged.
They are all idiots.
```

The cryptanalysis of this weak cipher was relatively easy to accomplish [124]. Since a permutation of a given length was used repeatedly, many messages of particular length were in depth—with respect to the permutation as well as the codebook. A cryptanalyst could therefore compare all messages of the same length, making it relatively easy to discover the fixed permutation, even without knowledge of the partial codebook. Of course, the analyst first had to be clever enough to consider the possibility that all messages of a given length were using the same permutation, but, with this insight, the permutations were easily recovered. The codebook was then deduced from context and also with the aid of some unencrypted messages that provided context for the ciphertext messages.

And what did these decrypted messages reveal? The reporters who broke the messages were amused to discover that Tilden's supporters had tried to bribe officials in the disputed states. The irony here—or not, depending on your perspective—is that Tilden's people were guilty of precisely the same crime of which they had accused Hayes.

By any measure, this cipher was poorly designed and weak. One lesson is that the overuse of a key can be an exploitable flaw. In this case, each time a permutation was reused, it gave the cryptanalyst more information that could be collated to recover the permutation. In modern cipher systems, we try to limit the use of a key so that we do not allow a cryptanalyst to accumulate too much information and to limit the damage if a particular key is exposed.

2.4   Modern Crypto History

Don't let yesterday take up too much of today.
— Abraham Lincoln

Throughout the 20th century, cryptography played an important role in major world events. Late in the 20th century, cryptography became a critical technology for commercial and business communications as well, and it remains so today.

The Zimmermann telegram is one of the first examples from the last century of the role that cryptanalysis has had in political and military affairs. In this section, we mention a few other historical highlights from the past century. For more on the history of cryptography, the best source is Kahn's book [159].

In 1929, Secretary of State Henry L. Stimson ended the U.S. government's official cryptanalytic activity, justifying his actions with the immortal line, "Gentlemen do not read each other's mail" [291]. This would prove to be a costly mistake in the run-up to the attack on Pearl Harbor.

Prior to the Japanese attack of December 7, 1941, the United States had restarted its cryptanalytic programs. The successes of allied cryptanalysts during the World War II era were remarkable, and this period is often seen as the golden age of cryptanalysis. Virtually all significant Axis cryptosystems were broken by the Allies and the value of the intelligence obtained from these systems is difficult to overestimate.

In the Pacific theatre, the so-called Purple cipher was used for high level Japanese government communication. This cipher was broken by American cryptanalysts before the attack on Pearl Harbor, but the intelligence gained (code named MAGIC) provided no clear indication of the impending attack [82]. The Japanese Imperial Navy used a cipher known as JN-25, which was also broken by the Americans. The intelligence from JN-25 was almost certainly decisive in the extended battle of Coral Sea and Midway, where an inferior American force was able to to halt the advance of the Japanese in the Pacific for the first time. The Japanese Navy was never able to recover from the losses inflicted during this crucial battle.

In Europe, the German Enigma cipher (code named ULTRA) was a major source of intelligence for the Allies during the war [104, 118]. It is often claimed that the ULTRA intelligence was so valuable that Churchill decided not to inform the British city of Coventry of an impending attack by the German Luftwaffe, since the primary source of information on the attack came from Enigma decrypts [69]. Churchill was supposedly concerned that a warning might tip off the Germans that their cipher had been broken. That this did not occur has been well documented. Nevertheless, it was a challenge to utilize valuable ULTRA intelligence without giving away the fact that the Enigma had been broken [42].

The Enigma was initially broken by Polish cryptanalysts. After the fall of Poland, these cryptanalysts escaped to France, but shortly thereafter France fell to the Nazis. The Polish cryptanalysts eventually made their way to England, where they provided their knowledge to British cryptanalysts.[9] A British team that included the computing pioneer, Alan Turing, developed improved attacks on the Enigma [104].

A picture of the Enigma appears in Figure 2.5. Additional details on the inner workings of the Enigma are given in the problems at the end of this chapter and a cryptanalytic attack is presented in Chapter 6.

Figure 2.5: An Enigma Cipher (Courtesy of T. B. Perera and the Enigma Museum)

---

[9]Remarkably, the Polish cryptanalysts were not allowed to continue their work on the Enigma in Britian.

In the post-World War II era, cryptography slowly moved from a black art into the realm of science. The publication of Claude Shannon's seminal 1949 paper, *Information Theory of Secrecy Systems* [267], marks the turning point. Shannon proved that the one-time pad is secure and he also offered two fundamental cipher design principles: *confusion* and *diffusion*. These two principles have guided symmetric cipher design ever since.

In Shannon's use, confusion is, roughly speaking, defined as obscuring the relationship between the plaintext and ciphertext. On the other hand, diffusion is the idea of spreading the plaintext statistics through the cipher-text. A simple substitution cipher and a one-time pad employ only confusion, whereas a double transposition is a diffusion-only cipher. Since the one-time pad is provably secure, evidently confusion alone is enough, while it appears that diffusion alone is not.

These two concepts—confusion and diffusion—are as relevant today as they were on the day that they were originally published. In subsequent chapters, it will become clear that these concepts remain crucial to modern block cipher design.

Until recently, cryptography was primarily the domain of the government and military. That changed dramatically in the 1970s, due in large part to the computer revolution which led to the need to protect large amounts of electronic data. By the mid-1970s, even the U.S. government realized that there was a legitimate commercial need for secure cryptography. Furthermore, it was clear that the commercial products of the day were severely lacking. So, the National Bureau of Standards, or NBS,[10] issued a request for cryptographic algorithms. The idea was that NBS would select an algorithm that would then become an official U.S. government standard. The ultimate result of this ill-conceived process was a cipher known as the Data Encryption Standard, or DES.

It's impossible to overemphasize the role that DES has played in the modern crypto history. We'll have much more to say about DES in the next chapter.

Post-DES, academic interest in cryptography grew rapidly. Public key cryptography was discovered (or, more precisely, rediscovered) shortly after the arrival of DES. By the 1980s there were annual CRYPTO conferences, which are a consistent source of high-quality work in the field. In the 1990s the Clipper Chip and the development of a replacement for the aging DES were two of the many crypto highlights.

Governments continue to fund major organizations that work in crypto and related fields. However, it's clear that the crypto genie has escaped from its classified bottle, never to be put back.

---

[10]NBS has since been rechristened as the National Institute of Standards and Technology, or NIST, perhaps in an effort to recycle three-letter acronyms and thereby delay their eventual exhaustion by government agencies.

2.5   A Taxonomy of Cryptography

In the next three chapters, we'll focus on three broad categories of ciphers: *symmetric* ciphers, *public key* cryptosystems, and *hash functions*. Here, we give a very brief overview of these different categories.

Each of the classic ciphers discussed above is a symmetric cipher. Modern symmetric ciphers can be subdivided into *stream ciphers* and *block ciphers*. Stream ciphers generalize the one-time pad approach, sacrificing provable security for a key that is manageable. Block ciphers are, in a sense, the generalization of classic codebooks. In a block cipher, the key determines the codebook, and as long as the key remains fixed, the same codebook is used. Conversely, when the key changes, a different codebook is selected.

While stream ciphers dominated in the post-World War II era, today block ciphers are the kings of the symmetric crypto world—with a few notable exceptions. Generally speaking, block ciphers are easier to optimize for software implementations, while stream ciphers are usually most efficient in hardware.

As the name suggests, in public key crypto, encryption keys can be made public. For each public key, there is a corresponding decryption key that is known as a private key. Not surprisingly, the private key is not public—it must remain private.

If you post your public key on the Internet, anyone with an Internet connection can encrypt a message for you, without any prior arrangement regarding the key. This is in stark contrast to a symmetric cipher, where the participants must agree on a key in advance. Prior to the adoption of public key crypto, secure delivery of symmetric keys was the Achilles heel of modern cryptography. A spectacular case of a failed symmetric key distribution system can be seen in the exploits of the Walker family spy ring. The Walker family sold cryptographic keys used by the U.S. military to the Soviet Union for nearly two decades before being discovered [81, 96]. Public key cryptography does not completely eliminate the key distribution problem, since the private key must be in the hands of the appropriate user, and no one else.

Public key cryptography has another somewhat surprising and extremely useful feature, for which there is no parallel in the symmetric key world. Suppose a message is "encrypted" with the private key instead of the public key. Since the public key is public, anyone can decrypt this message. At first glance such encryption might seem pointless. However, it can serve as a digital form of a handwritten signature—anyone can verify the signature, but only the signer could have created the signature. As with all of these topics, we'll have much more to say about *digital signatures* in a later chapter.

Anything we can do with a symmetric cipher we can also accomplish with a public key cryptosystem. Public key crypto also enables us to do things that cannot be accomplished with a symmetric cipher. So why not use public key crypto for everything? The primary reason is efficiency—symmetric key crypto is orders of magnitude faster than public key. As a result, symmetric crypto is used to encrypt the vast majority of data today. Yet public key crypto has several critical roles to play in modern information security.

The third major crypto category we'll consider is cryptographic hash functions.[11] These functions take an input of any size and produce an output of a fixed size. In addition, hash functions must satisfy some very stringent requirements. For example, if the input changes in one or more bits, the output should change in about half of its bits. For another, it must be computationally infeasible to find *any* two inputs that hash to the same output. It may not be obvious that such a function is useful—or that such functions actually exist—but we'll see that they do exist and that they turn out to be extremely useful for a surprisingly wide array of problems.

2.6   A Taxonomy of Cryptanalysis

The goal of cryptanalysis is to recover the plaintext, the key, or both. By Kerckhoffs' Principle, we assume that Trudy, the cryptanalyst, has complete knowledge of the inner workings of the algorithm. Another basic assumption is that Trudy has access to the ciphertext—otherwise, why would we bother to encrypt? If Trudy only knows the algorithms and the ciphertext, then she must conduct a *ciphertext only* attack. This is the most disadvantageous possible scenario from Trudy's perspective.

Trudy's chances of success might improve if she has access to *known plaintext*. That is, Trudy might know some of the plaintext and observe the corresponding ciphertext. These matched plaintext-ciphertext pairs might provide information about the key. Of course, if all of the plaintext were known, there would be little point in recovering the key. But it's often the case that Trudy has access to (or can guess) some of the plaintext. For example, many kinds of data include stereotypical headers (email being a good example). If such data is encrypted, the attacker can likely guess some of the plaintext that corresponds to some of the ciphertext.

Surprisingly often, Trudy can actually choose the plaintext to be encrypted and see the corresponding ciphertext. Not surprisingly, this goes by the name of *chosen plaintext* attack. How is it possible for Trudy to choose the plaintext? In later chapters, we'll see that some security protocols encrypt anything that is sent and return the corresponding ciphertext. It's also possible that Trudy could have limited access to a cryptosystem, allowing her to encrypt plaintext of her choice. For example, Alice might forget to log out of her computer when she takes her lunch break. Trudy could then encrypt

---

[11]Not to be confused with hash functions that you may have seen in other computing contexts.

some selected messages before Alice returns. This type of "lunchtime attack" takes many forms.

Potentially more advantageous for the attacker is an *adaptively chosen plaintext* attack. In this scenario, Trudy chooses the plaintext, views the resulting ciphertext, and chooses the next plaintext based on the observed ciphertext. In some cases, this can make Trudy's job significantly easier.

Related key attacks are also significant in some applications. The idea here is to look for a weakness in the system when the keys are related in some special way.

There are other types of attacks that cryptographers occasionally worry about—mostly when they feel the need to publish another academic paper. In any case, a cipher can only be considered secure if no successful shortcut attack is known.

Finally, there is one particular attack scenario that applies to public key cryptography, but not the symmetric key case. Suppose Trudy intercepts a ciphertext that was encrypted with Alice's public key. If Trudy suspects that the plaintext message was either "yes" or "no," then she can encrypt both of these putative plaintexts with Alice's public key. If either matches the ciphertext, then the message has been broken. This is known as a *forward search*. Although a forward search is not applicable against a symmetric cipher, we'll see that this approach can be used to attack hash functions in some applications.

We've previously seen that the size of the keyspace must be large enough to prevent an attacker from trying all possible keys. The forward search attack implies that in public key crypto, we must also ensure that the size of the plaintext message space is large enough so that the attacker cannot simply encrypt all possible plaintext messages. In practice, this is easy to achieve, as we'll see in Chapter 4.

2.7   Summary

In this chapter we covered several classic cryptosystems, including the simple substitution, the double transposition, codebooks, and the one-time pad. Each of these illustrates some important points that we'll return to again in later chapters. We also discussed some elementary aspects of cryptography and cryptanalysis.

In the next chapter we'll turn our attention to modern symmetric key ciphers. Subsequent chapters cover public key cryptography, hash functions, and cryptanalysis. Cryptography will appear again in later parts of the book. In particular, cryptography is a crucial ingredient in security protocols. Contrary to some authors' misguided efforts, the fact is that there's no avoiding cryptography in information security.

2.8 Problems

1. In the field of information security, Kerckhoffs' Principle is like motherhood and apple pie, all rolled up into one.

   a. Define Kerckhoffs' Principle in the context of cryptography.

   b. Give a real-world example where Kerckhoffs' Principle has been violated. Did this cause any security problems?

   c. Kerckhoffs' Principle is sometimes applied more broadly than its strict cryptographic definition. Give a definition of Kerckhoffs' Principle that applies more generally.

2. Edgar Allan Poe's 1843 short story, "The Gold Bug," features a cryptanalytic attack.

   a. What type of cipher is broken and how?

   b. What happens as a result of this cryptanalytic success?

3. Given that the Caesar's cipher was used, find the plaintext that corresponds to the following ciphertext:

   VSRQJHEREVTXDUHSDQWU.

4. Find the plaintext and the key, given the ciphertext

   CSYEVIXIVQMREXIH.

   Hint: The key is a shift of the alphabet.

5. Suppose that we have a computer that can test 2^{40} keys each second.

   a. What is the expected time (in years) to find a key by exhaustive search if the keyspace is of size 2^{88}?

   b. What is the expected time (in years) to find a key by exhaustive search if the keyspace is of size 2^{112}?

   c. What is the expected time (in years) to find a key by exhaustive search if the keyspace is of size 2^{256}?

6. The weak ciphers used during the election of 1876 employed a fixed permutation of the words for a given length sentence. To see that this is weak, find the permutation of $(1, 2, 3, \ldots, 10)$ that was used to produce the scrambled sentences below, where "San Francisco" is treated as a single word. Note that the same permutation was used for all three sentences.

first try try if you and don't again at succeed
only you you you as believe old are are as
winter was in the I summer ever San Francisco coldest spent

7. The weak ciphers of the election of 1876 used a partial codebook and
   a permutation of the words. Modify this approach so that it is more
   secure.

8. This problem deals with the concepts of confusion and diffusion

   a. Define the terms confusion and diffusion as used in cryptography.

   b. Which classic cipher discussed in this chapter employs only confusion?

   c. Which classic cipher discussed in this chapter employs only diffusion?

   d. Which cipher discussed in this chapter employs both confusion and
      diffusion?

9. Recover the plaintext and key for the simple substitution example that
   appears in (2.2) on page 24.

10. Determine the plaintext and key for the ciphertext that appears in
    the *Alice in Wonderland* quote at the beginning of this chapter. Hint:
    The message was encrypted with a simple substitution cipher and the
    plaintext has no spaces or punctuation.

11. Decrypt the following message that was encrypted using a simple sub-
    stitution cipher:

    ```
    GBSXUCGSZQGKGSQPKQKGLSKASPCGBGBKGUKGCEUKUZKGGBSQEICA
    CGKGCEUERWKLKUPKQQGCIICUAEUVSHQKGCEUPCGBCGQOEVSHUNSU
    GKUZCGQSNLSHEHIEEDCUOGEPKHZGBSNKCUGSUKUASERLSKASCUGB
    SLKACRCACUZSSZEUSBEXHKRGSHWKLKUSQSKCHQTXKZHEUQBKZAEN
    NSUASZFENFCUOCUEKBXGBSWKLKUSQSKNFKQQKZEHGEGBSXUCGSZQ
    GKGSQKUZBCQAEIISKOXSZSICVSHSZGEGBSQSAHSGKHMERQGKGSKR
    EHNKIHSLIMGEKHSASUGKNSHCAKUNSQQKOSPBCISGBCQHSLIMQGKG
    SZGBKGCGQSSZNSZXQSISQQGEAEUGCUXSGBSSJCQGCUOZCLIENKGCA
    USOEGCKGCEUQCGAEUGKCUSZUEGBHSKGEHBCUGERPKHEHKHNSZKGGKAD
    ```

12. Write a program to help an analyst decrypt a simple substitution cipher.
    Your program should take the ciphertext as input, compute letter fre-
    quency counts, and display these for the analyst. The program should
    then allow the analyst to guess a key and display the results of the
    corresponding "decryption" with the putative key.

13. Extend the program described in Problem 12 so that it initially tries to decrypt the message. One sensible way to proceed is to use the computed letter frequencies and the known frequencies of English for an initial guess at the key. Then from the resulting putative decryption, count the number of dictionary words that appear and use this as a score. Next, for each letter in the key, try swapping it with the letter that is adjacent (with respect to frequency counts) and recompute the score. If the score improves, update the key; if not, don't change the putative key. Iterate this process until the score does not improve for an entire pass through the alphabet. At this point you will give your putative decryption to the analyst. To aid the analyst in the manual phase, your program must maintain all of the functionality of the program in Problem 12.

14. Encrypt the message

    we are all together

    using a double transposition cipher (of the type described in the text) with 4 rows and 4 columns, using the row permutation

    $$(1, 2, 3, 4) \longrightarrow (2, 4, 1, 3)$$

    and the column permutation

    $$(1, 2, 3, 4) \longrightarrow (3, 1, 2, 4).$$

15. Decrypt the ciphertext

    IAUTMOCSMNIMREBOTNELSTRHEREOAEVMWIH
    TSEEATMAEOHWHSYCEELTTEOHMUOUFEHTRFT

    This message was encrypted with a double transposition (of the type discussed in the text) using a matrix of 7 rows and 10 columns. Hint: The first word is "there."

16. Outline an automated attack on a double transposition cipher (of the type discussed in the text), assuming that the size of the matrix is known.

17. A double transposition cipher can be made much stronger by using the following approach. First, the plaintext is put into an $n \times m$ array, as described in the text. Next, permute the columns, and then write out the intermediate ciphertext column by column. That is, column 1 gives the first n ciphertext letters, column 2 gives the next n, and so on. Then repeat the process, that is, put the intermediate ciphertext

into an $n \times m$ array, permute the columns, and write out the ciphertext column by column. Use this approach, with a 3×4 array, and permutations $(2, 3, 1, 4)$ and $(4, 2, 1, 3)$ to encrypt the plaintext `attackatdawn`.

18. Using the letter encodings in Table 2.1, the following two ciphertext messages were encrypted with the same one-time pad:

    KHHLTK and KTHLLE.

    Find all possible plaintexts for each message and the corresponding one-time pad.

19. Using the letter encodings in Table 2.1, the following ciphertext message was encrypted with a one-time pad:

    KITLKE.

    a. If the plaintext is "thrill," what is the key?
    b. If the plaintext is "tiller," what is the key?

20. Suppose that you have a message consisting of 1024 bits. Design a method that will extend a key that is 64 bits long into a string of 1024 bits, so that the resulting 1024 bits can be XORed with the message, just like a one-time pad. Is the resulting cipher as secure as a one-time pad? Is it possible for any such cipher to be as secure as a one-time pad?

21. Design a codebook cipher that can encrypt any block of bits, not just specific words. Your cipher should include many possible codebooks, with a key used to determine which codebook will be employed to encrypt (or decrypt) a particular message. Discuss some possible attacks on your cipher.

22. Suppose that the following is an excerpt from the decryption codebook for a classic codebook cipher.

123	once
199	or
202	maybe
221	twice
233	time
332	upon
451	a

    Decrypt the following ciphertext:

    242, 554, 650, 464, 532, 749, 567

assuming that the following additive sequence was used to encrypt the message:

$$119, \ 222, \ 199, \ 231, \ 333, \ 547, \ 346$$

23. An affine cipher is a type of simple substitution where each letter is encrypted according to the rule $c = (a \cdot p + b) \bmod 26$ (see the Appendix for a discussion of mod). Here, p, c, a, and b are each numbers in the range 0 to 25, where p represents the plaintext letter, c the ciphertext letter, and a and b are constants. For the plaintext and ciphertext, 0 corresponds to "a," 1 corresponds to "b," and so on. Consider the ciphertext QJKES REOGH GXXRE OXEO, which was generated using an affine cipher. Determine the constants a and b and decipher the message. Hint: Plaintext "t" encrypts to ciphertext "H" and plaintext "o" encrypts to ciphertext "E."

24. A Vigenère cipher uses a sequence of "shift-by-n" simple substitutions, where the shifts are indexed using a keyword, with "A" representing a shift-by-0, "B" representing a shift-by-1, etc. For example, if the keyword is "DOG," then the first letter is encrypted using a simple substitution with a shift-by-3, the second letter is encrypted using a shift-by-14, the third letter is encrypted using a shift-by-6, and the pattern is repeated—the fourth letter is encrypted using a shift-by-3, the fifth letter is encrypted using a shift-by-14, and so on. Cryptanalyze the following ciphertext, i.e., determine the plaintext and the key. This particular message was encrypted using a Vigenère cipher with a 3-letter English keyword:

```
CTMYR DOIBS RESRR RIJYR EBYLD IYMLC CYQXS RRMLQ FSDXF
OWFKT CYJRR IQZSM X
```

25. Suppose that on the planet Binary, the written language uses an alphabet that contains only two letters X and Y. Also, suppose that in the Binarian language, the letter X occurs 75% of the time, while Y occurs 25% of the time. Finally, assume that you have two messages in the Binary language, and the messages are of equal length.

   a. If you compare the corresponding letters of the two messages, what fraction of the time will the letters match?

   b. Suppose that one of the two messages is encrypted with a simple substitution, where X is encrypted as Y and Y is encrypted as X. If you now compare the corresponding letters of the two messages—one encrypted and one not—what fraction of the time will the letters match?

  c. Suppose that both of the messages are encrypted with a simple substitution, where X is encrypted as Y and Y is encrypted as X. If you now compare the corresponding letters of the two messages—both of which are encrypted—what fraction of the time will the letters match?

  d. Suppose instead that you are given two randomly generated "messages" that use only the two letters X and Y. If you compare the corresponding letters of the two messages, what fraction of the time will the letters match?

  e. What is the index of coincidence (IC)? Hint: See, for example, [148].

  f. How can the index of coincidence be used to determine the length of the keyword in a Vigenère cipher (see Problem 24 for the definition of a Vigenère cipher)?

26. In the this chapter, we discussed a forward search attack.

  a. Explain how to conduct a forward search attack.

  b. How can you prevent a forward search attack against a public key cryptosystem?

  c. Why can't a forward search attack be used to break a symmetric cipher?

27. Consider a "one-way" function h. Then, given the value $y = h(x)$, it is computationally infeasible to find x directly from y.

  a. Suppose that Alice computes $y = h(x)$, where x is Alice's salary, in dollars. If Trudy obtains y, how can she determine Alice's salary x? Hint: Adapt the forward search attack to this problem.

  b. Why does your attack not violate the one-way property of h?

  c. How could Alice prevent this attack ? We assume that Trudy has access to the output of the function h, Trudy knows that the input includes Alice's salary, and Trudy knows the format of the input. Also, no keys are available, so Alice cannot encrypt the output value.

28. Suppose that a particular cipher uses a 40-bit key, and the cipher is secure (i.e., there is no known shortcut attack).

  a. How much work, on average, is an exhaustive search attack?

  b. Outline an attack, assuming that known plaintext is available.

  c. How would you attack this cipher in the ciphertext-only case?

29. Suppose that Alice encrypted a message with a secure cipher that uses a 40-bit key. Trudy knows the ciphertext and Trudy knows the algorithm, but she does not know the plaintext or the key. Trudy plans to do an exhaustive search attack, that is, she will try each possible key until she finds the correct key.

    a. How many keys, on average, must Trudy try before she finds the correct one?

    b. How will Trudy know when she has found the correct key? Note that there are too many solutions for Trudy to manually examine each one—she must have some automated approach to determining whether a putative key is correct or not.

    c. How much work is your automated test in part b?

    d. How many false alarms do you expect from your test in part b? That is, how often will an incorrect key produce a putative decrypt that will pass your test?

Chapter 3

Symmetric Key Crypto

The chief forms of beauty are order and symmetry...
— Aristotle

"You boil it in sawdust: you salt it in glue:
You condense it with locusts and tape:
Still keeping one principal object in view—
To preserve its symmetrical shape."
— Lewis Carroll, *The Hunting of the Snark*

3.1 Introduction

In this chapter, we discuss the two branches of the symmetric key crypto family tree: stream ciphers and block ciphers. Stream ciphers generalize the idea of a one-time pad, except that we trade provable security for a relatively small (and manageable) key. The key is stretched into a long stream of bits, which is then used just like a one-time pad. Like their one-time pad brethren, stream ciphers employ (in Shannon's terminology) confusion only.

Block ciphers can be viewed as the modern successors to the classic codebook ciphers, where the key determines the codebook. The internal workings of block cipher algorithms can be fairly intimidating, so it is useful to keep in mind that a block cipher is really just an "electronic" version of a codebook. Internally, block ciphers employ both confusion and diffusion.

We'll take a fairly close look at two stream cipher algorithms, A5/1 and RC4, both of which have been widely deployed. The A5/1 algorithm (used in GSM cell phones) is a good representative of a large class of stream ciphers that are based in hardware. RC4 is used in many places, including the SSL and WEP protocols. RC4 is virtually unique among stream ciphers since it is designed for efficient implementation in software.

51

In the block cipher realm, we'll look closely at DES, since it's relatively simple (by block cipher standards) and it's the granddaddy of them all, making it the block cipher to which all others are compared. We'll also take a brief look at a few other popular block ciphers. Then we'll examine some of the many ways that block ciphers are used for confidentiality and we'll consider the role of block ciphers in the equally important area of data integrity.

Our goal in this chapter is to introduce symmetric key ciphers and gain some familiarity with their inner workings and their uses. That is, we'll focus more on the "how" than the "why." To understand why block ciphers are designed the way they are, some aspects of advanced cryptanalysis are essential. We cover the ideas behind such cryptanalysis in Chapter 6.

3.2   Stream Ciphers

A stream cipher takes a key K of n bits in length and stretches it into a long *keystream*. This keystream is then XORed with the plaintext P to produce ciphertext C. Through the magic of the XOR, the same keystream is used to recover the plaintext P from the ciphertext C. Note that the use of the keystream is identical to the use of the pad (or key) in a one-time pad cipher. An excellent introduction to stream ciphers can be found in Rueppel's book [254], and for leads into some very challenging research problems in the field, see [153].

The function of a stream cipher can be viewed simply as

$$\texttt{StreamCipher}(K) = S,$$

where K is the key and S represents the resulting keystream. Remember, the keystream is not ciphertext, but is instead simply a string of bits that we use like a one-time pad.

Now, given a keystream $S = s_0, s_1, s_2 \ldots$, and plaintext $P = p_0, p_1, p_2 \ldots$ we generate the ciphertext $C = c_0, c_1, c_2 \ldots$ by XOR-ing the corresponding bits, that is,

$$c_0 = p_0 \oplus s_0, \ c_1 = p_1 \oplus s_1, \ c_2 = p_2 \oplus s_2, \ldots.$$

To decrypt ciphertext C, the keystream S is again used, that is,

$$p_0 = c_0 \oplus s_0, \ p_1 = c_1 \oplus s_1, \ p_2 = c_2 \oplus s_2, \ldots.$$

Provided that both the sender and receiver have the same stream cipher algorithm and that both know the key K, this system provides a practical generalization of the one-time pad. However, the resulting cipher is not provably secure (as discussed in the problems at the end of the chapter), so we have traded provable security for practicality.

3.2.1 A5/1

The first stream cipher that we'll examine is A5/1, which is used for confidentiality in GSM cell phones (GSM is discussed in Chapter 10). This algorithm has an algebraic description, but it also can be illustrated via a relatively simple wiring diagram. We give both descriptions here.

A5/1 employs three linear feedback *shift registers* [126], or LFSRs, which we'll label X, Y, and Z. Register X holds 19 bits, $(x_0, x_1, \ldots, x_{18})$. The register Y holds 22 bits, $(y_0, y_1, \ldots, y_{21})$, and Z holds 23 bits, $(z_0, z_1, \ldots, z_{22})$. Of course, all computer geeks love powers of two, so it's no accident that the three LFSRs hold a total of 64 bits.

Not coincidentally, the A5/1 key K is also 64 bits. The key is used as the *initial fill* of the three registers, that is, the key is used as the initial values in the three registers. After these three registers are filled with the key,[1] we are ready to generate the keystream. But before we can describe how the keystream is generated, we need to say a little more about the registers X, Y, and Z.

When register X *steps*, the following series of operations occur:

$$t = x_{13} \oplus x_{16} \oplus x_{17} \oplus x_{18}$$
$$x_i = x_{i-1} \text{ for } i = 18, 17, 16, \ldots, 1$$
$$x_0 = t$$

Similarly, for registers Y and Z, each step consists of

$$t = y_{20} \oplus y_{21}$$
$$y_i = y_{i-1} \text{ for } i = 21, 20, 19 \ldots, 1$$
$$y_0 = t$$

and

$$t = z_7 \oplus z_{20} \oplus z_{21} \oplus z_{22}$$
$$z_i = z_{i-1} \text{ for } i = 22, 21, 20, \ldots, 1$$
$$z_0 = t$$

respectively.

Given three bits x, y, and z, define $\text{maj}(x, y, z)$ to be the majority vote function, that is, if the majority of x, y, and z are 0, the function returns 0; otherwise it returns 1. Since there are an odd number of bits, there cannot be a tie, so this function is well defined.

---

[1]We've simplified things a little. In reality, the registers are filled with the key, and then there is an involved run up (i.e., initial stepping procedure) that is used before we generate any keystream bits. Here, we ignore the runup process.

In A5/1, for each keystream bit that we generate, the following takes place. First, we compute

$$m = \text{maj}(x_8, y_{10}, z_{10}).$$

Then the registers X, Y, and Z step (or not) as follows:

- If $x_8 = m$ then X steps.

- If $y_{10} = m$ then Y steps.

- If $z_{10} = m$ then Z steps.

Finally, a single keystream bit s is generated as

$$s = x_{18} \oplus y_{21} \oplus z_{22},$$

which can then be XORed with the plaintext (if encrypting) or XORed with the ciphertext (if decrypting). We then repeat the entire process to generate as many key stream bits as are required.

Note that when a register steps, its fill changes due to the bit shifting. Consequently, after generating one keystream bit, the fills of at least two of the registers X, Y, Z have changed, which implies that new bits are in positions x_8, y_{10}, and z_{10}. Therefore, we can repeat this process and generate a new keystream bit.

Although this may seem like a complicated way to generate a single keystream bit, A5/1 is easily implemented in hardware and can generate bits at a rate proportional to the clock speed. Also, the number of keystream bits that can be generated from a single 64-bit key is virtually unlimited—although eventually the keystream will repeat. The wiring diagram for the A5/1 algorithm is illustrated in Figure 3.1. See, for example, [33] for a more detailed discussion of A5/1.

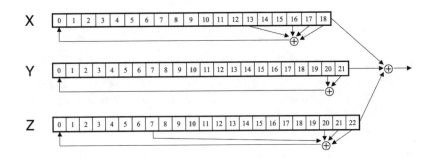

Figure 3.1: A5/1 Keystream Generator

The A5/1 algorithm is our representative example of a large class of stream ciphers that are based on shift registers and implemented in hardware. These systems were once the kings of symmetric key crypto, but in recent years the block cipher has clearly taken the crown. And where a stream cipher is needed today, it is likely to be RC4, which we'll discuss below.

Why has there been a mass migration away from stream ciphers towards block ciphers? In the bygone era of slow processor speeds, shift register based stream ciphers were necessary to keep pace with relatively high data-rate systems (such as audio). In the past, software-based crypto could not generate bits fast enough for such applications. Today, however, there are few applications for which software-based crypto is not appropriate. In addition, block ciphers are relatively easy to design and they can do everything stream ciphers can do, and more. These are the primary reasons why block ciphers are on the ascendancy.

3.2.2 RC4

RC4 is a stream cipher, but it's a completely different beast than A5/1. The RC4 algorithm is optimized for software implementation, whereas A5/1 is designed for hardware, and RC4 produces a keystream byte at each step, whereas A5/1 only produces a single keystream bit. All else being equal (which, of course, it never is), generating a byte at each step is much better than generating a single bit.

The RC4 algorithm is remarkably simple, because it is essentially just a lookup table containing a permutation of all possible 256 byte values. The crucial trick that makes it a strong cipher is that each time a byte of keystream is produced, the lookup table is modified in such a way that the table always contains a permutation of $\{0, 1, 2, \ldots, 255\}$. Because of this constant updating, the lookup table—and hence the cipher itself—presents the cryptanalyst with a moving target.

The entire RC4 algorithm is byte based. The first phase of the algorithm initializes the lookup table using the key. We'll denote the key as $\text{key}[i]$, for $i = 0, 1, \ldots, N - 1$, where each $\text{key}[i]$ is a byte. We denote the lookup table as $S[i]$, where each $S[i]$ is also a byte. Pseudo-code for the initialization of the permutation S appears in Table 3.1. One interesting feature of RC4 is that the key can be of any length from 1 to 256 bytes. And again, the key is only used to initialize the permutation S. Note that the 256-byte array K is filled by simply repeating the key until the array is full.

After the initialization phase, each keystream byte is generated following the algorithm that appears in Table 3.2. The output, which we've denoted here as `keystreamByte`, is a single byte that can be XORed with plaintext (to encrypt) or XORed with ciphertext (to decrypt). We'll mention another possible application for RC4 keystream bytes in Chapter 5.

Table 3.1: RC4 Initialization

---

for $i = 0$ to 255
   S[i] = i
   K[i] = key[i mod N]
next i
$j = 0$
for $i = 0$ to 255
   $j = (j + S[i] + K[i])$ mod 256
   swap($S[i],S[j]$)
next i
$i = j = 0$

The RC4 algorithm—which can be viewed as a self-modifying lookup table—is elegant, simple, and efficient in software. However, there is an attack that is feasible against certain uses of RC4 [112, 195, 294], but the attack is infeasible if we discard the first 256 keystream bytes that are generated. This could be achieved by simply adding an extra 256 steps to the initialization phase, where each additional step generates—and discards—a keystream byte following the algorithm in Table 3.2. As long as Alice and Bob both implement these additional steps, they can use RC4 to communicate securely.

Table 3.2: RC4 Keystream Byte

$i = (i + 1)$ mod 256
$j = (j + S[i])$ mod 256
swap($S[i], S[j]$)
$t = (S[i] + S[j])$ mod 256
keystreamByte $= S[t]$

RC4 is used in many applications, including SSL and WEP. However, the algorithm is fairly old and is not optimized for 32-bit processors (in fact, it's optimized for ancient 8-bit processors). Nevertheless, RC4 is sure to be a major player in the crypto arena for many years to come.

Stream ciphers were once king of the hill, but they are now relatively rare, in comparison to block ciphers. Some have even gone so far as to declare the death of stream ciphers [74] and, as evidence, they point to the fact that there has been almost no serious effort to develop new stream ciphers in recent years. However, today there are an increasing number of significant applications where dedicated stream ciphers are more appropriate than block ciphers. Examples of such applications include wireless devices, severely resource-constrained devices, and extremely high data-rate systems. Undoubtedly, the reports of the death of stream ciphers have been greatly exaggerated.

3.3 Block Ciphers

An iterated block cipher splits the plaintext into fixed-sized blocks and generates fixed-sized blocks of ciphertext. In most designs, the ciphertext is obtained from the plaintext by iterating a function F over some number of *rounds*. The function F, which depends on the output of the previous round and the key K, is known as the *round function*, not because of its shape, but because it is applied over multiple rounds.

The design goals for block ciphers are security and efficiency. It's not too difficult to develop a reasonably secure block cipher or an efficient block cipher, but to design one that is secure and efficient requires a high form of the cryptographer's art.

3.3.1 Feistel Cipher

A *Feistel cipher*, named after block cipher pioneer Horst Feistel, is a general cipher design principle, not a specific cipher. In a Feistel cipher, the plaintext block P is split into left and right halves,

$$P = (L_0, R_0),$$

and for each round $i = 1, 2, \ldots, n$, new left and right halves are computed according to the rules

$$L_i = R_{i-1} \tag{3.1}$$
$$R_i = L_{i-1} \oplus F(R_{i-1}, K_i) \tag{3.2}$$

where K_i is the *subkey* for round i. The subkey is derived from the key K according to a specified *key schedule* algorithm. Finally, the ciphertext C is the output of the final round, namely,

$$C = (L_n, R_n).$$

Instead of trying to memorize equations (3.1) and (3.2), it's much easier to simply remember how each round of a Fiestel cipher works. Note that equation (3.1) tells us that the "new" left half is the "old" right half. On the other hand, equation (3.2) says that the new right half is the old left half XORed with a function of the old right half and the key.

Of course, it's necessary to be able to decrypt the ciphertext. The beauty of a Feistel cipher is that we can decrypt, regardless of the particular round function F. Thanks to the magic of the XOR, we can solve equations (3.1) and (3.2) for R_{i-1} and L_{i-1}, respectively, which allows us to run the process backwards. That is, for $i = n, n-1, \ldots, 1$, the decryption rule is

$$R_{i-1} = L_i$$
$$L_{i-1} = R_i \oplus F(R_{i-1}, K_i).$$

The final result of this decryption process is the plaintext $P = (L_0, R_0)$, as desired.

Again, any round function F will work in a Feistel cipher, provided that the output of F produces the correct number of bits. It is particularly nice that there is no requirement that the function F be invertible. However, a Feistel cipher will not be secure for all possible choices of F. For example, the round function

$$F(R_{i-1}, K_i) = 0 \ \text{ for all } \ R_{i-1} \ \text{ and } \ K_i \qquad\qquad (3.3)$$

is a legitimate round function since we can encrypt and decrypt with this F. However, Trudy would be very happy if Alice and Bob decide to use a Feistel cipher with the round function in (3.3).

Note that all questions about the security of a Feistel cipher boil down to questions about the round function and the key schedule. The key schedule is usually not a major issue, so most of the analysis can be focused on F.

3.3.2   DES

> Now there was an algorithm to study;
> one that the NSA said was secure.
> — Bruce Schneier, in reference to DES

The Data Encryption Standard, affectionately known as DES,[2] was developed way back in the computing dark ages of the 1970s. The design is based on the so-called Lucifer cipher, a Feistel cipher developed by a team at IBM. DES is a surprisingly simple block cipher, but the story of how Lucifer became DES is anything but simple.

By the mid 1970s, it was clear even to U.S. government bureaucrats that there was a legitimate commercial need for secure crypto. At the time, the

---

[2]People "in the know" pronounce DES so as to rhyme with "fez" or "pez," not as the three letters D-E-S. Of course, you can say Data Encryption Standard, but that would be very uncool.

computer revolution was underway, and the amount—and sensitivity—of digital data was rapidly increasing.

In the mid 1970s, crypto was poorly understood outside of classified military and government circles, and they weren't talking (and, for the most part, that's still the case). The upshot was that businesses had no way to judge the merits of a crypto product and the quality of most such products was very poor.

Into this environment, the National Bureau of Standards, or NBS (now known as NIST) issued a request for cipher proposals. The winning submission would become a U.S. government standard and almost certainly a *de facto* industrial standard. Very few reasonable submissions were received, and it quickly became apparent that IBM's Lucifer cipher was the only serious contender.

At this point, NBS had a problem. There was little crypto expertise at NBS, so they turned to the government's crypto experts, the super-secret National Security Agency, or NSA.[3] The NSA designs and builds the crypto that is used by the U.S. military and government for highly sensitive information. However, the NSA also wears a black hat, since it conducts signals intelligence, or SIGINT, where it tries to obtain intelligence information from foreign sources.

The NSA was reluctant to get involved with DES but, under pressure, eventually agreed to study the Lucifer design and offer an opinion, provided its role would not become public. When this information came to public light [273] (as is inevitable in the United States[4]) many were suspicious that NSA had placed a backdoor into DES so that it alone could break the cipher. Certainly, the black hat SIGINT mission of NSA and a general climate of distrust of government fueled such fears. In the defense of NSA, it's worth noting that 30 years of intense cryptanalysis has revealed no backdoor in DES. Nevertheless, this suspicion tainted DES from its inception.

Lucifer eventually became DES, but not before a few subtle—and a few not so subtle—changes were made. The most obvious change was that the key length was apparently reduced from 128 bits to 64 bits. However, upon careful analysis, it was found that 8 of the 64 key bits were effectively discarded, so the actual key length is a mere 56 bits. As a result of this modification, the expected work for an exhaustive key search was reduced from 2^{127} to 2^{55}. By this measure, DES is 2^{72} times easier to break than Lucifer.

---

[3]NSA is so super-secret that its employees joke that the acronym NSA stands for No Such Agency.

[4]Your secretive author once attended a public talk by the Director of NSA, aka DIRNSA. At this talk the DIRNSA made a comment to the effect, "Do you want to know what problems we're working on now?" Of course, the audience gave an enthusiastic "Yes!" hoping that they might be about to hear the deepest darkest secrets of the super-secret spy agency. The DIRNSA responded, "Read the front page of the New York Times."

Understandably, the suspicion was that NSA had had a hand in purposely weakening DES. However, subsequent cryptanalysis of the algorithm has revealed attacks that require slightly less work than trying 2^{55} keys and, as a result, DES is probably just about as strong with a key of 56 bits as it would be with the longer Lucifer key.

The subtle changes to Lucifer involved the substitution boxes, or *S-boxes*, which are described below. These changes in particular fueled the suspicion of a backdoor. But it has become clear over time that the modifications to the S-boxes actually strengthened the algorithm by offering protection against cryptanalytic techniques that were unknown (at least outside of NSA, and they're not talking) until many years later. The inescapable conclusion is that whoever modified the Lucifer algorithm (NSA, that is) knew what they were doing and, in fact, significantly strengthened the algorithm. See [215, 273] for more information on the role of NSA in the development of DES.

Now it's time for the nitty gritty details of the DES algorithm. DES is a Feistel cipher with the following numerology:

- 16 rounds

- 64-bit block length

- 56-bit key

- 48-bit subkeys

Each round of DES is relatively simple—at least by the standards of block cipher design. The DES S-boxes are one of its most important security features. We'll see that S-boxes (or similar) are a common feature of modern block cipher designs. In DES, each S-box maps 6 bits to 4 bits, and DES employs eight distinct S-boxes. The S-boxes, taken together, map 48 bits to 32 bits. The same S-boxes are used at each round of DES and each S-box is implemented as a lookup table.

Since DES is a Feistel cipher, encryption follows the formulas given in equations (3.1) and (3.2). A single round of DES is illustrated in the wiring diagram in Figure 3.2, where each number indicates the number of bits that follow a particular "wire."

Unravelling the diagram in Figure 3.2, we see that the DES round function F can be written as

$$F(R_{i-1}, K_i) = \text{P-box}(\text{S-boxes}(\text{Expand}(R_{i-1}) \oplus K_i)). \qquad (3.4)$$

With this round function, DES can be seen to be a Feistel cipher as defined in equations (3.1) and (3.2). As required by equation (3.1), the new left half is simply the old right half. The round function F is the composition of the expansion permutation, addition of subkey, S-boxes, and P-box, as given in equation (3.4).

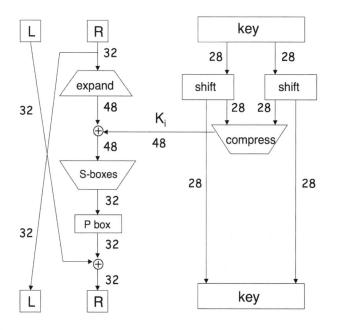

Figure 3.2: One Round of DES

The expansion permutation expands its input from 32 to 48 bits, and the subkey is XORed with the result. The S-boxes then compress these 48 bits down to 32 bits before the result is passed through the P-box. The P-box output is XORed with the old left half to obtain the new right half.

Next, we'll describe each of the components of F in precise detail, as well as the algorithm used to calculate the subkey K_i. But it's important to keep the big picture in mind and to realize that the overall structure of DES is actually fairly simple. In fact, some of the DES operations are of no security benefit whatsoever, and if these were stripped away to reveal the essential security features, the algorithm becomes even simpler.

Throughout this discussion—and elsewhere in this book—we'll adopt the convention that bits are numbered from left to right, beginning with the index zero.[5] The 48-bit output of the DES expansion permutation consists of the following bits.

31	0	1	2	3	4	3	4	5	6	7	8
7	8	9	10	11	12	11	12	13	14	15	16
15	16	17	18	19	20	19	20	21	22	23	24
23	24	25	26	27	28	27	28	29	30	31	0

---

[5]Your author is not a dinosaur (i.e., FORTRAN programmer), so the indexing starts at 0, not 1.

where the 32-bit input is, according to our convention, numbered as

$$
\begin{array}{cccccccccccccccc}
0 & 1 & 2 & 3 & 4 & 5 & 6 & 7 & 8 & 9 & 10 & 11 & 12 & 13 & 14 & 15 \\
16 & 17 & 18 & 19 & 20 & 21 & 22 & 23 & 24 & 25 & 26 & 27 & 28 & 29 & 30 & 31
\end{array}
$$

Each of the eight DES S-boxes maps 6 bits to 4 bits, and, consequently, each can be viewed as an array of 4 rows and 16 columns, with one nibble (4-bit value) stored in each of the 64 positions. When viewed in this way, each S-box has been constructed so that each of its four rows is a permutation of the hexadecimal digits $0, 1, 2, \ldots, E, F$. The DES S-box number 1 appears in Table 3.3, where the six-bit input to the S-box is denoted $b_0 b_1 b_2 b_3 b_4 b_5$. Note that the first and last input bits are used to index the row, while the middle four bits index the column. Also note that we've given the output in hex. For those who just can't get enough of S-boxes, all eight DES S-boxes can be found on the textbook website.

Table 3.3: DES S-box 1

$b_0 b_5$	$b_1 b_2 b_3 b_4$															
	0	1	2	3	4	5	6	7	8	9	A	B	C	D	E	F
0	E	4	D	1	2	F	B	8	3	A	6	C	5	9	0	7
1	0	F	7	4	E	2	D	1	A	6	C	B	9	5	3	8
2	4	1	E	8	D	6	2	B	F	C	9	7	3	A	5	0
3	F	C	8	2	4	9	1	7	5	B	3	E	A	0	6	D

The DES permutation box, or P-box, contributes little to the security of the cipher and its real purpose seems to have been lost to the mists of history. One plausible explanation is that the designers wanted to make DES more difficult to implement in software since the original design called for hardware-based implementation. It was apparently hoped that DES would remain a hardware-only algorithm, perhaps in the belief that this would allow the algorithm to remain secret. In fact, the S-boxes themselves were originally classified, so undoubtedly the goal was to keep them secret. But, predictably, the DES S-boxes were reverse engineered and they became public knowledge almost immediately. For the record, the P-box permutation is

$$
\begin{array}{cccccccccccccccc}
15 & 6 & 19 & 20 & 28 & 11 & 27 & 16 & 0 & 14 & 22 & 25 & 4 & 17 & 30 & 9 \\
1 & 7 & 23 & 13 & 31 & 26 & 2 & 8 & 18 & 12 & 29 & 5 & 21 & 10 & 3 & 24
\end{array}
$$

The only significant remaining part of DES is the key schedule algorithm, which is used to generate the subkeys. This is a somewhat convoluted process, but the ultimate result is simply that 48 of the 56 bits of key are selected at each round. The details are relevant, since block cipher designs have been attacked due flawed key schedule algorithms.

As usual, we'll number the 56-bit DES key from left-to-right, beginning with 0. We first extract 28 of the DES key bits, permute them, and call the result LK. Initially, LK consists of the following DES key bits:

$$
\begin{array}{ccccccc}
49 & 42 & 35 & 28 & 21 & 14 & 7 \\
0 & 50 & 43 & 36 & 29 & 22 & 15 \\
8 & 1 & 51 & 44 & 37 & 30 & 23 \\
16 & 9 & 2 & 52 & 45 & 38 & 31
\end{array}
$$

The remaining 28 bits of the DES key are permuted and assigned to the variable RK. Initially, RK consists of the following DES key bits:

$$
\begin{array}{ccccccc}
55 & 48 & 41 & 34 & 27 & 20 & 13 \\
6 & 54 & 47 & 40 & 33 & 26 & 19 \\
12 & 5 & 53 & 46 & 39 & 32 & 25 \\
18 & 11 & 4 & 24 & 17 & 10 & 3
\end{array}
$$

Before we can precisely state the key schedule algorithm, we need a few more items. Define the permutation LP as

$$
\begin{array}{cccccccccccc}
13 & 16 & 10 & 23 & 0 & 4 & 2 & 27 & 14 & 5 & 20 & 9 \\
22 & 18 & 11 & 3 & 25 & 7 & 15 & 6 & 26 & 19 & 12 & 1
\end{array}
$$

and RP as

$$
\begin{array}{cccccccccccc}
12 & 23 & 2 & 8 & 18 & 26 & 1 & 11 & 22 & 16 & 4 & 19 \\
15 & 20 & 10 & 27 & 5 & 24 & 17 & 13 & 21 & 7 & 0 & 3
\end{array}
$$

Finally, define

$$
r_i = \begin{cases} 1 & \text{if } i \in \{1, 2, 9, 16\} \\ 2 & \text{otherwise.} \end{cases}
$$

The DES key schedule algorithm, which is used to generate the 48-bit subkeys, appears in Table 3.4.

Note that when writing code to implement DES, we would probably not want to implement the key schedule algorithm as it appears in Table 3.4. It would be more efficient to use the key schedule algorithm to determine each K_i (in terms of the original DES key) and simply hardcode these values into our program.

For completeness, there are two other features of DES that we should mention. An initial permutation is applied to the plaintext before round one, and its inverse is applied after the final round. Also, when encrypting, the halves are swapped after last round, so the actual ciphertext is (R_{16}, L_{16}), not (L_{16}, R_{16}). Neither of these quirks serve any security purpose and we'll

Table 3.4: DES Key Schedule Algorithm

---

for each round $i = 1, 2, \ldots, n$
    LK = cyclically left shift LK by r_i bits
    RK = cyclically left shift RK by r_i bits
    The left half of subkey K_i consists of bits LP of LK
    The right half of subkey K_i consists of bits RP of RK
next i

---

ignore them in the remaining discussion. However, these are part of the DES algorithm, so they must be implemented if you want to call the resulting cipher DES.

A few words on the security of DES may be enlightening. First, mathematicians are very good at solving linear equations, and the only part of DES that is not linear is the S-boxes. Due to those annoying mathematicians, linear ciphers are inherently weak, so the S-boxes are fundamental to the security of DES. Actually, the expansion permutation has an important security role to play and, to a lesser extent, so does the key schedule. All of this will become clearer after we discuss linear and differential cryptanalytic attacks in Chapter 6. For more details on the design of the DES cipher, see [258].

Despite the concern over the design of DES—particularly the role of the NSA in the process—DES has clearly stood the test of time [181]. Today, DES is vulnerable simply because the key is too small, not because of any noteworthy shortcut attack. Although some attacks have been developed that, in theory, require somewhat less work than an exhaustive key search, all practical DES crackers[6] built to date simply try all keys until they stumble across the correct one, that is, an exhaustive key search. The inescapable conclusion is that the designers of DES knew what they were doing.

We'll have more to say about DES when we study advanced cryptanalysis in Chapter 6. In fact, the historic importance of DES is hard to overstate. DES can be viewed as the impetus behind the development of modern symmetric crypto, which makes it all the more ironic that NSA was the unwilling godfather of DES.

Next, we describe triple DES, which is often used to effectively extend the key length of DES. We'll follow this with a quick overview of a few other block ciphers. Then we discuss one truly simple block cipher in a bit more detail.

---

[6]Not to be confused with Ritz crackers.

3.3.3 Triple DES

Before moving on to other block ciphers, we discuss a popular variant of DES known as triple DES, or 3DES. But before that, we need some notation. Let P be a block of plaintext, K a key, and C the corresponding block of ciphertext. For DES, C and P are each 64 bits, while K is 56 bits, but our notation applies in general. The notation that we'll adopt for the encryption of P with key K is

$$C = E(P, K)$$

while the corresponding decryption is denoted

$$P = D(C, K).$$

Note that for the same key, encryption and decryption are inverse operations, that is,

$$P = D(E(P, K), K) \text{ and } C = E(D(C, K), K).$$

However, in general,

$$P \neq D(E(P, K_1), K_2) \text{ and } C \neq E(D(C, K_1), K_2),$$

when $K_1 \neq K_2$.

At one time, DES was nearly ubiquitous, but its key length is insufficient today. But for DES-philes, all is not lost—there is a clever way to use DES with a larger key length. Intuitively, it seems that double DES might be the thing to do, that is,

$$C = E(E(P, K_1), K_2). \tag{3.5}$$

This would seem to offer the benefits of a 112 bit key (two 56-bit DES keys), with the only drawback being a loss of efficiency due to the two DES operations.

However, there is a meet-in-the-middle attack on double DES that renders it more or less equivalent to single DES. Although the attack may not be entirely practical, it's too close for comfort. This attack is a chosen plaintext attack, meaning that we assume the attacker can always choose a specific plaintext P and obtain the corresponding ciphertext C.

So, suppose Trudy selects a particular plaintext P and obtains the corresponding ciphertext C, which for double DES is $C = E(E(P, K_1), K_2)$. Trudy's goal is to find the keys K_1 and K_2. Toward this goal, Trudy first pre-computes a table of size 2^{56} containing the pairs $E(P, K)$ and K for all possible key values K. Trudy sorts this table on the values $E(P, K)$. Now using her table and the ciphertext value C, Trudy decrypts C with keys $\tilde{K}$ until she finds a value $X = D(C, \tilde{K})$ that is in table. Then, because of the way the table was constructed, we have $X = E(P, K)$ for some K and Trudy now has

$$D(C, \tilde{K}) = E(P, K),$$

where $\tilde{K}$ and K are known. That Trudy has found the 112-bit key can be seen by encrypting both sides with the key $\tilde{K}$, which gives

$$C = E(E(P, K), \tilde{K}),$$

that is, in equation (3.5), we have $K_1 = K$ and $K_2 = \tilde{K}$.

This attack on double DES requires that Trudy pre-compute, sort, and store an enormous table of 2^{56} elements. But the table computation is one-time work,[7] so if we use this table many times (by attacking double DES many times) the work for computing the table can be amortized over the number of attacks. Neglecting the work needed to pre-compute the table, the work consists of computing $D(C, K)$ until we find a match in the table. This has an expected work of 2^{55}, just as in an exhaustive key search attack on single DES. So, in a sense, double DES is no more secure than single DES.

Since double DES isn't secure, will triple DES fare any better? Before worrying about attacks, we need to define triple DES. It seems that the logical approach to triple DES would be

$$C = E(E(E(P, K_1), K_2), K_3)$$

but this is not the way it's done. Instead, triple DES is defined as

$$C = E(D(E(P, K_1), K_2), K_1).$$

Note that triple DES only uses two keys, and encrypt-decrypt-encrypt, or EDE, is used instead of encrypt-encrypt-encrypt, or EEE. The reason for only using two keys is that 112 bits is sufficient, and three keys does not add much security (see Problem 42). But why EDE instead of EEE? Surprisingly, the answer is backwards compatibility—if 3DES is used with $K_1 = K_2 = K$ then it collapses to single DES, since

$$C = E(D(E(P, K), K), K) = E(P, K).$$

Now, what about attacks on triple DES? We can say with certainty that a meet-in-the-middle attack of the type used against double DES is impractical since the table pre-computation is infeasible or the per attack work is infeasible—see Problem 42 for more details.

Triple DES remains fairly popular today. However, with the coming of the Advanced Encryption Standard and other modern alternatives, triple DES should, like any old soldier, slowly fade away.

---

[7]The pre-computation work is one time, provided that chosen plaintext is available. If we only have known plaintext, then we would need to compute the table each time we conduct the attack—see Problem 18.

3.3.4 AES

By the 1990s it was apparent to everyone—even the U.S. government—that DES had outlived its usefulness. The crucial problem with DES is that the key length of 56 bits is susceptible to an exhaustive key search. Special-purpose DES crackers have been built that can recover DES keys in a matter of hours, and distributed attacks using volunteer computers on the Internet have succeeded in finding DES keys [98].

In the early 1990s, NIST, which is the present incarnation of NBS, issued a call for crypto proposals for what would become the Advanced Encryption Standard, or AES. Unlike the DES call for proposals of 20 years earlier, NIST was inundated with quality proposals. The field of candidates was eventually reduced to a handful of finalists, and an algorithm known a Rijndael (pronounced something like "rain doll") was ultimately selected. See [182] for information on the AES competition and [75] for the details on the Rijndael algorithm.

The AES competition was conducted in a completely open manner and, unlike the DES competition, the NSA was openly involved as one of the judges. As a result, there are no plausible claims of a backdoor having been inserted into the AES. In fact, AES is highly regarded in the cryptographic community. Shamir has stated that he believes data encrypted with a 256-bit AES key will be "secure forever," regardless of any conceivable advances in computing technology [73].

Like DES, the AES is an iterated block cipher. Unlike DES, the AES algorithm is not a Feistel cipher. The major implication of this fact is that in order to decrypt, the AES operations must be invertible. Also unlike DES, the AES algorithm has a highly mathematical structure. We'll only give a quick overview of the algorithm—large volumes of information on all aspects of AES are readily available—and we'll largely ignore the elegant mathematical structure. In any case, it is a safe bet that no crypto algorithm in history has received as much scrutiny in as short of a period of time as the AES. See [7, 75] for more details on the Rijndael algorithm.

Some of the pertinent facts of AES are as follows.

- The block size is 128 bits.[8]

- Three key lengths are available: 128, 192, or 256 bits.

- The number of rounds varies from 10 to 14, depending on the key length.

- Each round consists of four functions, in three layers—the functions are listed below, with the layer in parentheses.

---

[8]The Rijndael algorithm actually supports block sizes of 128, 192, or 256 bits, independent of the key length. However, the larger block sizes are not part of the official AES.

- ByteSub (nonlinear layer)

- ShiftRow (linear mixing layer)

- MixColumn (nonlinear layer)

- AddRoundKey (key addition layer)

AES treats the 128-bit block as a 4×4 byte array:

$$\begin{bmatrix} a_{00} & a_{01} & a_{02} & a_{03} \\ a_{10} & a_{11} & a_{12} & a_{13} \\ a_{20} & a_{21} & a_{22} & a_{23} \\ a_{30} & a_{31} & a_{32} & a_{33} \end{bmatrix}.$$

The ByteSub operation is applied to each byte a_{ij}, that is, $b_{ij} = \text{ByteSub}(a_{ij})$. The result is the array of b_{ij} as illustrated below:

$$\begin{bmatrix} a_{00} & a_{01} & a_{02} & a_{03} \\ a_{10} & a_{11} & a_{12} & a_{13} \\ a_{20} & a_{21} & a_{22} & a_{23} \\ a_{30} & a_{31} & a_{32} & a_{33} \end{bmatrix} \longrightarrow \text{ByteSub} \longrightarrow \begin{bmatrix} b_{00} & b_{01} & b_{02} & b_{03} \\ b_{10} & b_{11} & b_{12} & b_{13} \\ b_{20} & b_{21} & b_{22} & b_{23} \\ b_{30} & b_{31} & b_{32} & b_{33} \end{bmatrix}.$$

ByteSub, which is roughly the AES equivalent of the DES S-boxes, can be viewed as a nonlinear—but invertible—composition of two mathematical functions, or it can be viewed simply as a lookup table. We'll take the latter view. The ByteSub lookup table appears in Table 3.5. For example, ByteSub(3c) = eb since eb appears in row 3 and column c of Table 3.5.

Table 3.5: AES ByteSub

	0	1	2	3	4	5	6	7	8	9	a	b	c	d	e	f
0	63	7c	77	7b	f2	6b	6f	c5	30	01	67	2b	fe	d7	ab	76
1	ca	82	c9	7d	fa	59	47	f0	ad	d4	a2	af	9c	a4	72	c0
2	b7	fd	93	26	36	3f	f7	cc	34	a5	e5	f1	71	d8	31	15
3	04	c7	23	c3	18	96	05	9a	07	12	80	e2	eb	27	b2	75
4	09	83	2c	1a	1b	6e	5a	a0	52	3b	d6	b3	29	e3	2f	84
5	53	d1	00	ed	20	fc	b1	5b	6a	cb	be	39	4a	4c	58	cf
6	d0	ef	aa	fb	43	4d	33	85	45	f9	02	7f	50	3c	9f	a8
7	51	a3	40	8f	92	9d	38	f5	bc	b6	da	21	10	ff	f3	d2
8	cd	0c	13	ec	5f	97	44	17	c4	a7	7e	3d	64	5d	19	73
9	60	81	4f	dc	22	2a	90	88	46	ee	b8	14	de	5e	0b	db
a	e0	32	3a	0a	49	06	24	5c	c2	d3	ac	62	91	95	e4	79
b	e7	c8	37	6d	8d	d5	4e	a9	6c	56	f4	ea	65	7a	ae	08
c	ba	78	25	2e	1c	a6	b4	c6	e8	dd	74	1f	4b	bd	8b	8a
d	70	3e	b5	66	48	03	f6	0e	61	35	57	b9	86	c1	1d	9e
e	e1	f8	98	11	69	d9	8e	94	9b	1e	87	e9	ce	55	28	df
f	8c	a1	89	0d	bf	e6	42	68	41	99	2d	0f	b0	54	bb	16

The ShiftRow operation is a cyclic shift of the bytes in each row of the 4×4 byte array. This operation is given by

$$
\begin{bmatrix}
a_{00} & a_{01} & a_{02} & a_{03} \\
a_{10} & a_{11} & a_{12} & a_{13} \\
a_{20} & a_{21} & a_{22} & a_{23} \\
a_{30} & a_{31} & a_{32} & a_{33}
\end{bmatrix}
\longrightarrow \text{ShiftRow} \longrightarrow
\begin{bmatrix}
a_{00} & a_{01} & a_{02} & a_{03} \\
a_{11} & a_{12} & a_{13} & a_{10} \\
a_{22} & a_{23} & a_{20} & a_{21} \\
a_{33} & a_{30} & a_{31} & a_{32}
\end{bmatrix},
$$

that is, the first row doesn't shift, the second row circular left-shifts by one byte, the third row left-shifts by two bytes, and the last row left-shifts three bytes. Note that ShiftRow is inverted by simply shifting in the opposite direction.

Next, the MixColumn operation is applied to each column of the 4×4 byte array as indicated below:

$$
\begin{bmatrix}
a_{0i} \\
a_{1i} \\
a_{2i} \\
a_{3i}
\end{bmatrix}
\longrightarrow \text{MixColumn} \longrightarrow
\begin{bmatrix}
b_{0i} \\
b_{1i} \\
b_{2i} \\
b_{3i}
\end{bmatrix}
\quad \text{for } i = 0, 1, 2, 3.
$$

MixColumn consists of shift and XOR operations, and it's most efficiently implemented as a lookup table. The overall operation is nonlinear but invertible, and, as with ByteSub, it serves a similar purpose as the DES S-boxes.

The AddRoundKey operation is straightforward. Similar to DES, a key schedule algorithm is used to generate a subkey for each round. Let k_{ij} be the 4×4 subkey array for a particular round. Then the subkey is XORed with the current 4×4 byte array a_{ij} as illustrated below:

$$
\begin{bmatrix}
a_{00} & a_{01} & a_{02} & a_{03} \\
a_{10} & a_{11} & a_{12} & a_{13} \\
a_{20} & a_{21} & a_{22} & a_{23} \\
a_{30} & a_{31} & a_{32} & a_{33}
\end{bmatrix}
\oplus
\begin{bmatrix}
k_{00} & k_{01} & k_{02} & k_{03} \\
k_{10} & k_{11} & k_{12} & k_{13} \\
k_{20} & k_{21} & k_{22} & k_{23} \\
k_{30} & k_{31} & k_{32} & k_{33}
\end{bmatrix}
=
\begin{bmatrix}
b_{00} & b_{01} & b_{02} & b_{03} \\
b_{10} & b_{11} & b_{12} & b_{13} \\
b_{20} & b_{21} & b_{22} & b_{23} \\
b_{30} & b_{31} & b_{32} & b_{33}
\end{bmatrix}.
$$

We'll ignore the AES key schedule but, as with any block cipher, it's a significant part of the security of the algorithm. Finally, as we noted above, the four functions, ByteSub, ShiftRow, MixColumn, and AddRoundKey, are all invertible. As a result, the entire algorithm is invertible, and consequently AES can decrypt as well as encrypt.

3.3.5   Three More Block Ciphers

In this section, we briefly consider three well-known block cipher algorithms, namely, the International Data Encryption Algorithm (IDEA), Blowfish, and RC6. Each of these has some particular noteworthy design feature. In the next section we'll take a closer look at the Tiny Encryption Algorithm, or TEA [323].

IDEA is the handiwork of James L. Massey, one of the great—if somewhat lesser-known—cryptographers of modern times. The most innovative feature of IDEA is its use of *mixed mode arithmetic*. The algorithm combines addition modulo two (also known as XOR) with addition modulo 2^{16} and the Lai-Massey multiplication, which is "almost" multiplication modulo 2^{16}. These operations together produce the necessary nonlinearity, and as a result no explicit S-box is required. Massey was apparently the first to use this approach, which is common today. See [201] for more details on the design of IDEA.

Blowfish is one of Bruce Schneier's favorite crypto algorithms, no doubt because he invented it. Schneier is a well-known cryptographer and an entertaining writer on all things security-related. The interesting quirk of Blowfish is its use of *key dependent S-boxes*—instead of having fixed S-boxes, Blowfish generates its S-boxes based on the key. It can be shown that typical Blowfish S-boxes are strong. See [262] for more information on Blowfish.

RC6 is due to Ron Rivest, whose crypto accomplishments are truly remarkable, including the public key system RSA and the previously mentioned RC4 stream cipher, as well as one of the most popular hash functions, MD5. The unusual aspect of RC6 is its use of data-dependent rotations [247]. It is highly unusual to rely on the data as an essential part of the operation of a crypto algorithm. RC6 was one of the AES finalists, although it ultimately lost out to Rjindael.

These three ciphers illustrate a small sample of the many variations that have been used in the quest for the ideal balance between security and performance in block ciphers. In Chapter 6 we discuss linear and differential cryptanalysis, which makes the fundamental trade-offs inherent in block cipher design more explicit.

3.3.6   TEA

The final block cipher that we'll consider is the Tiny Encryption Algorithm (TEA). The wiring diagrams that we've displayed so far might lead you to conclude that block ciphers are necessarily complex. TEA nicely illustrates that such is not the case.

TEA uses a 64-bit block length and a 128-bit key. The algorithm assumes a computing architecture with 32-bit words—all operations are implicitly modulo 2^{32} and any bits beyond the 32nd position are automatically truncated. The number of rounds is variable but must be relatively large. The conventional wisdom is that 32 rounds is secure. However, each round of TEA is more like two rounds of a Feistel cipher (such as DES), so this is roughly equivalent to 64 rounds of DES. That's a lot of rounds.

In block cipher design, there is an inherent trade-off between the complexity of each round and the number of rounds required. Ciphers such as DES try to strike a balance between these two, while AES reduces the number of rounds as much as possible, at the expense of having a more complex round function. In a sense, TEA can be seen as living at the opposite extreme of AES, since TEA uses a very simple round function. But as a consequence of its simple rounds, the number of rounds must be large to achieve a high level of security. Pseudo-code for TEA encryption—assuming 32 rounds are used—appears in Table 3.6, where "$\ll$" is a left (non-cyclic) shift and "$\gg$" is a right (non-cyclic) shift.

Table 3.6: TEA Encryption

$(K[0], K[1], K[2], K[3]) =$ 128 bit key
$(L, R) =$ plaintext (64-bit block)
delta = 0x9e3779b9
sum = 0
for $i = 1$ to 32
    sum = sum + delta
    $L = L + (((R \ll 4) + K[0]) \oplus (R + \text{sum}) \oplus ((R \gg 5) + K[1]))$
    $R = R + (((L \ll 4) + K[2]) \oplus (L + \text{sum}) \oplus ((L \gg 5) + K[3]))$
next i
ciphertext = (L, R)

One interesting thing to notice about TEA is that it's not a Feistel cipher, and so we need separate encryption and decryption routines. However, TEA is about as close to a Feistel cipher as it is possible to be without actually being one—TEA uses addition and subtraction instead of XOR. But the need for separate encryption and decryption routines is a minor concern with TEA, since so few lines of code are required, and the algorithm is reasonably efficient even with the large number of rounds. The TEA decryption algorithm, assuming 32 rounds, appears in Table 3.7.

There is a somewhat obscure related key attack on TEA [163]. That is, if a cryptanalyst knows that two TEA messages are encrypted with keys that are related to each other in some very special way, then the plaintext can be recovered. This is a low-probability attack that in most circumstances can probably safely be ignored. But in case you are worried about this attack, there is a slightly more complex variant of TEA, known as extended TEA, or XTEA [218], that overcomes this potential problem. There is also a simplified version of TEA, known as STEA, that is extremely weak and is used to illustrate certain types of attacks [208].

Table 3.7: TEA Decryption

$(K[0], K[1], K[2], K[3]) = $ 128 bit key
$(L, R) = $ ciphertext (64-bit block)
delta = 0x9e3779b9
sum = delta $\ll 5$
for $i = 1$ to 32
$\qquad R = R - (((L \ll 4) + K[2]) \oplus (L + \text{sum}) \oplus ((L \gg 5) + K[3]))$
$\qquad L = L - (((R \ll 4) + K[0]) \oplus (R + \text{sum}) \oplus ((R \gg 5) + K[1]))$
$\qquad$ sum = sum $-$ delta
next i
plaintext $= (L, R)$

3.3.7 Block Cipher Modes

Using a stream cipher is easy—you generate a keystream that is the same length as the plaintext (or ciphertext) and XOR. Using a block cipher is also easy, provided that you have exactly one block to encrypt. But how should multiple blocks be encrypted with a block cipher? It turns out that the answer is not as straightforward as it might seem.

Suppose we have multiple plaintext blocks, say,

$$P_0, P_1, P_2, \ldots.$$

For a fixed key K, a block cipher is a codebook, since it creates a fixed mapping between plaintext and ciphertext blocks. Following the codebook idea, the obvious thing to do is to use a block cipher in so-called *electronic codebook mode*, or ECB. In ECB mode, we encrypt using the formula

$$C_i = E(P_i, K) \text{ for } i = 0, 1, 2, \ldots.$$

Then we can decrypt according to

$$P_i = D(C_i, K) \text{ for } i = 0, 1, 2, \ldots.$$

This approach works, but there are serious security issues with ECB mode and, as a result, it should never be used in practice.

Suppose ECB mode is used, and an attacker observes that $C_i = C_j$. Then the attacker knows that $P_i = P_j$. Although this may seem innocent enough, there are cases where the attacker will know part of the plaintext, and any match with a known block reveals another block. But even if the attacker does not know P_i or P_j, some information has been revealed, namely, that these two plaintext blocks are the same, and we don't want to give the cryptanalyst anything for free—especially if there is an easy way to avoid it.

Massey [196] gives a dramatic illustration of the consequences of this seemingly minor weakness. We give a similar example in Figure 3.3, which shows an (uncompressed) image of Alice next to the same image encrypted in ECB mode. Every block of the right-hand image in Figure 3.3 has been encrypted,

Figure 3.3: Alice and ECB Mode

but the blocks that were the same in the plaintext are the same in the ECB-encrypted ciphertext. Note that it does not matter which block cipher is used—the curious result in Figure 3.3 only depends on the fact that ECB mode was used, not on the details of the algorithm. In this case, it's not difficult for Trudy to guess the plaintext from the ciphertext.

The ECB mode problem illustrated in Figure 3.3 is the basis for the "new ciphertext-only attack" discussed in [95]. The purveyors of this "new" version of a well-known attack have created a video in which they provide a demonstration of the results, along with a large dose of marketing hype [239].

Fortunately, there are better ways to use a block cipher, which avoid the weakness of ECB mode. We'll discuss the most common method, *cipher block chaining mode*, or CBC. In CBC mode, the ciphertext from a block is used to obscure the plaintext of the next block before it is encrypted. The encryption formula for CBC mode is

$$C_i = E(P_i \oplus C_{i-1}, K) \text{ for } i = 0, 1, 2, \ldots, \tag{3.6}$$

which is decrypted via

$$P_i = D(C_i, K) \oplus C_{i-1} \text{ for } i = 0, 1, 2, \ldots. \tag{3.7}$$

The first block requires special handling since there is no ciphertext block C_{-1}. An *initialization vector*, or IV, is used to take the place of the mythical C_{-1}. Since the ciphertext is not secret, and since the IV plays a role analogous to a ciphertext block, it need not be secret either. But the IV should be randomly selected.

Using the IV, the first block is CBC encrypted as

$$C_0 = E(P_0 \oplus \text{IV}, K),$$

with the formula in equation (3.6) used for the remaining blocks. The first block is decrypted as

$$P_0 = D(C_0, K) \oplus \text{IV},$$

with the formula in equation (3.7) used to decrypt all remaining blocks. Since the IV need not be secret, it's usually randomly generated at encryption time and sent (or stored) as the first "ciphertext" block. In any case, when decrypting, the IV must be handled appropriately.

The benefit of CBC mode is that identical plaintext will not yield identical ciphertext. This is dramatically illustrated by comparing Alice's image encrypted using ECB mode—which appears in Figure 3.3—with the image of Alice encrypted in CBC mode, which appears in Figure 3.4.

Figure 3.4: Alice Prefers CBC Mode

Due to the chaining, a possible concern with CBC mode is error propagation. When the ciphertext is transmitted, garbles can occur—a 0 bit could become a 1 bit or vice versa. If a single transmission error made the plaintext unrecoverable, then CBC would be useless in practice. Fortunately, this is not the case.

Suppose the ciphertext block C_i is garbled to, say, $G \neq C_i$. Then

$$P_i \neq D(G, K) \oplus C_{i-1} \text{ and } P_{i+1} \neq D(C_{i+1}, K) \oplus G$$

but

$$P_{i+2} = D(C_{i+2}, K) \oplus C_{i+1}$$

and all subsequent blocks are decrypted correctly. That is, each plaintext block only depends on two consecutive ciphertext blocks, so errors do not propagate beyond two blocks. However, the fact that a single-bit error can cause two entire blocks to be garbled is a serious concern in high error-rate environments such as wireless. Stream ciphers do not have this problem—a single garbled ciphertext bit results in a single garbled plaintext bit—and that is one reason why stream ciphers are often preferred in wireless applications.

Another concern with a block cipher is a *cut-and-paste attack*. Suppose the plaintext

Money␣for␣Alice␣is␣$1000
Money␣for␣Trudy␣is␣$2␣␣␣

where "␣" is a blank space, is to be encrypted with a block cipher that has a 64-bit block size. Assuming that each character requires 8 bits (e.g., 8-bit ASCII), the plaintext blocks are

$$P_0 = \text{Money␣fo}$$
$$P_1 = \text{r␣Alice␣}$$
$$P_2 = \text{is␣\$1000}$$
$$P_3 = \text{Money␣fo}$$
$$P_4 = \text{r␣Trudy␣}$$
$$P_5 = \text{is␣\$2␣␣␣}$$

Suppose this data is encrypted using ECB mode.[9] Then the ciphertext blocks are computed as $C_i = E(P_i, K)$ for $i = 0, 1, \ldots, 5$.

Now suppose that Trudy knows that ECB mode is used, she knows the general structure of the plaintext, and she knows that she will receive $2. But Trudy doesn't know how much Alice will receive—though she suspects it's much more than $2. If Trudy can rearrange the order of the ciphertext blocks to

$$C_0, C_1, C_5, C_3, C_4, C_2, \qquad (3.8)$$

then Bob will decrypt this as

---

[9]Of course, you should never use ECB mode. However, this same problem arises with other modes (and types of ciphers), but it's easiest to illustrate using ECB mode.

```
Money␣for␣Alice␣is␣$2␣␣␣
Money␣for␣Trudy␣is␣$1000
```

which is clearly a preferable outcome from Trudy's perspective.

You might think that CBC mode would eliminate the cut-and-paste attack. If so, you'd be wrong. With CBC mode, a cut-and-paste attack is still possible, although it's slightly more difficult and some data will be corrupted. This is explored further in the problems at the end of the chapter.

It is also possible to use a block cipher to generate a keystream, which can then be used just like a stream cipher keystream. There are several acceptable ways to accomplish this feat, but we'll only mention the most popular, namely, *counter mode*, or CTR. As with CBC mode, CTR mode employs an initialization vector, or IV. The CTR encryption formula is

$$C_i = P_i \oplus E(\text{IV} + i, K)$$

and decryption is accomplished via[10]

$$P_i = C_i \oplus E(\text{IV} + i, K).$$

CTR mode is often used when random access is required. While random access is also fairly straightforward with CBC mode, in some cases CBC mode would not be desirable for random access—see Problem 27.

Beyond ECB, CBC, and CTR, there are many other block cipher modes; see [258] for descriptions of the more common ones. However, the three modes discussed here certainly account for the vast majority of block cipher usage.

Finally, it is worth noting that data confidentiality comes in two slightly different flavors. On the one hand, we encrypt data so that it can be transmitted over an insecure channel. On the other hand, we encrypt data that is stored on an insecure media, such as a computer hard drive. Symmetric ciphers can be used to solve either of these two closely related problems. In addition, symmetric key crypto can also be used to protect data integrity, as we see in the next section.

3.4 Integrity

Whereas confidentiality deals with preventing unauthorized reading, integrity is concerned with detecting unauthorized writing. For example, suppose that you electronically transfer funds from one one account to another. You may not want others to know about this transaction, in which case encryption will effectively provide the desired confidential. But, whether you are concerned about confidentiality or not, you certainly want the transaction to be accurately received. This is where integrity comes into the picture.

---

[10]The use of the encryption "*E*" for both the encryption and decryption formulas is *not* a typo.

In the previous section, we studied block ciphers and their use for confidentiality. Here we show that block ciphers can also provide data integrity.

It is important to realize that confidentiality and integrity are two very different concepts. Encryption with any cipher—from the one-time pad to modern block ciphers—does not protect the data from malicious or inadvertent changes. If Trudy changes the ciphertext or if garbles occur in transmission, the integrity of the data has been lost and we want to be able to automatically detect that a change has occurred. We've seen several examples—and you should be able to give several more—to show that encryption does not assure integrity.

A *message authentication code*, or MAC, uses a block cipher to ensure data integrity. The procedure is simply to encrypt the data in CBC mode, discarding all ciphertext blocks except the final one. This final ciphertext block, which is known as the CBC residue, serves as the MAC. Then the formula for the MAC, assuming N blocks of data, $P_0, P_1, P_2, \ldots, P_{N-1}$, is given by

$$C_0 = E(P_0 \oplus \mathrm{IV}, K), \; C_1 = E(P_1 \oplus C_0, K), \ldots,$$
$$C_{N-1} = E(P_{N-1} \oplus C_{N-2}, K) = \mathrm{MAC}.$$

Note that we use an initialization vector, and that a shared symmetric key is required.

For simplicity, suppose that Alice and Bob require integrity, but they are not concerned with confidentiality. Then using a key K that Alice and Bob share, Alice computes the MAC and send the plaintext, the IV, and the MAC to Bob. Upon receiving the message, Bob computes the MAC using the key and received IV and plaintext. If his computed "MAC" matches the received MAC, then he is satisfied with the integrity of the data. On the other hand, if Bob's computed MAC does not match the received MAC, then Bob knows that something is amiss. Again, as in CBC mode, the sender and receiver must share a symmetric key K in advance.

Why does this MAC computation work? Suppose Alice sends

$$\mathrm{IV}, P_0, P_1, P_2, P_3, \mathrm{MAC}$$

to Bob. Now, if Trudy changes plaintext block P_1 to, say, Q during transmission, then when Bob attempts to verify the MAC, he computes

$$C_0 = E(P_0 \oplus \mathrm{IV}, K), \; \tilde{C}_1 = E(Q \oplus C_0, K), \; \tilde{C}_2 = E(P_2 \oplus \tilde{C}_1, K),$$
$$\tilde{C}_3 = E(P_3 \oplus \tilde{C}_2, K) = \text{"MAC"} \neq \mathrm{MAC}.$$

The reason this works is because any change to a plaintext block propagates into subsequent blocks in the process of computing the MAC.

Recall that with CBC *decryption* a change in a ciphertext block only affects two of the recovered plaintext blocks. In contrast, the MAC takes advantage of the fact that for CBC *encryption*, any change in the plaintext almost certainly propagates through to the final block. This is the crucial property that enables a MAC to provide integrity.

Often confidentiality and integrity are both required. To accomplish this, we could compute a MAC with one key, then encrypt the data with another key. However, this is twice as much work as is needed for either confidentiality or integrity alone. For the sake of efficiency, it would be useful to obtain both confidentiality and integrity protection with a single CBC encryption of the data. So, suppose we CBC encrypt the data once and send the resulting ciphertext and the computed "MAC." Then we would send the entire ciphertext, along with the final ciphertext block (again). That is, the final ciphertext block would be duplicated and sent twice. Obviously, sending the same thing twice cannot provide any additional security. Unfortunately, there is no obvious way to obtain both confidentiality and integrity with a single encryption of the data. These topics are explored further in the problems at the end of the chapter.

Computing a MAC based on CBC encryption is not the only way to provide for data integrity. A hashed MAC, or HMAC, is another standard approach to integrity and a digital signature is yet another option. We'll discuss the HMAC in Chapter 5 and digital signatures in Chapters 4 and 5.

3.5   Summary

In this chapter we've covered a great deal of material on symmetric key cryptography. There are two distinct types of symmetric ciphers: stream ciphers and block ciphers. We briefly discussed two stream ciphers, A5/1 and RC4. Recall that stream ciphers generalize the one-time pad, where provable security is traded for practicality.

Block ciphers, on the other hand, can be viewed as the "electronic" equivalent of a classic codebook. We discussed the block cipher DES in considerable detail and briefly mentioned several other block ciphers. We then considered various modes of using block ciphers (specifically, ECB, CBC, and CTR modes). We also showed that block ciphers—using CBC mode—can provide data integrity.

In later chapters we'll see that symmetric ciphers are also useful in authentication protocols. As an aside, it's interesting to note that stream ciphers, block ciphers, and hash functions (covered in a later chapter) are all equivalent in the sense that anything you can do with one, you can accomplish with the other two, although in some cases it would be fairly unnatural to actually do so. For this reason, these three are equivalent cryptographic "primitives."

Symmetric key cryptography is a big topic and we've only scratched the surface here. But, armed with the background from this chapter, we'll be prepared to tackle any issues involving symmetric ciphers that arise in later chapters.

Finally, to really understand the reasoning behind block cipher design, it's necessary to delve more deeply into the field of cryptanalysis. Chapter 6, which deals with advanced cryptanalysis, is highly recommended for anyone who wants to gain a deeper understanding of block cipher design principles.

3.6 Problems

1. A stream cipher can be viewed as a generalization of a one-time pad. Recall that the one-time pad is provably secure. Why can't we prove that a stream cipher is secure using the same argument that was used for the one-time pad?

2. This problem deals with stream ciphers.

    a. If we generate a sufficiently long keystream, the keystream must eventually repeat. Why?

    b. Why is it a security concern if the keystream repeats?

3. Suppose that Alice uses a stream cipher to encrypt plaintext P, obtaining ciphertext C, and Alice then sends C to Bob. Suppose that Trudy happens to know the plaintext P, but Trudy does not know the key K that was used in the stream cipher.

    a. Show that Trudy can easily determine the keystream that was used to encrypt P.

    b. Show that Trudy can, in effect, replace P with plaintext of her choosing, say, P'. That is, show that Trudy can create a ciphertext message C' so that when Bob decrypts C' he will obtain P'.

4. This problem deals with the A5/1 cipher. For each part, justify your answer.

    a. On average, how often does the X register step?

    b. On average, how often does the Y register step?

    c. On average, how often does the Z register step?

    d. On average, how often do all three registers step?

    e. On average, how often do exactly two registers step?

    f. On average, how often does exactly one register step?

    g. On average, how often does no register step?

5. Implement the A5/1 algorithm. Suppose that, after a particular step, the values in the registers are

$$X = (x_0, x_1, \ldots, x_{18}) = (1010101010101010101)$$
$$Y = (y_0, y_1, \ldots, y_{21}) = (1100110011001100110011)$$
$$Z = (z_0, z_1, \ldots, z_{22}) = (11100001111000011110000)$$

List the next 32 keystream bits and give the contents of X, Y, and Z after these 32 bits have been generated.

6. For bits x, y, and z, the function $\text{maj}(x, y, z)$ is defined to be the majority vote, that is, if two or more of the three bits are 0, then the function returns 0; otherwise, it returns 1. Write the truth table for this function and derive the boolean function that is equivalent to $\text{maj}(x, y, z)$.

7. The RC4 cipher consists of a lookup table S, which contains 256 byte values, and two indices, i and j.

    a. The lookup table S is initialized to contain the identity permutation $0, 1, 2, \ldots, 255$ and at each step of the algorithm, S contains a permutation. How is this achieved? That is, why does S always contain a permutation?

    b. Where is RC4 used in the real world?

8. This problem deals with the RC4 stream cipher.

    a. Find a reasonable upper bound on the size of the RC4 state space. That is, find an upper bound for the number of different states that are possible for the RC4 cipher. Hint: The RC4 cipher consists of a lookup table S, and two indices i and j. Count the number of possible distinct tables S and the number of distinct indices i and j, then compute the product of these numbers.

    b. Why is the size of the state space relevant when analyzing a stream cipher?

9. Implement the RC4 algorithm. Suppose the key consists of the following seven bytes: $(\texttt{0x1A}, \texttt{0x2B}, \texttt{0x3C}, \texttt{0x4D}, \texttt{0x5E}, \texttt{0x6F}, \texttt{0x77})$. For each of the following, give S in the form of a 16×16 array where each entry is in hex.

    a. List the permutation S and indices i and j after the initialization phase has completed.

   b. List the permutation S and indices i and j after the first 100 bytes of keystream have been generated.

   c. List the permutation S and indices i and j after the first 1000 bytes of keystream have been generated.

10. Suppose that Trudy has a ciphertext message that was encrypted with the RC4 cipher—see Tables 3.1 and 3.2. For RC4, the encryption formula is given by $c_i = p_i \oplus k_i$, where k_i is the ith byte of the keystream, p_i is the ith byte of the plaintext, and c_i is the ith byte of the ciphertext. Suppose that Trudy knows the first ciphertext byte, and the first plaintext byte, that is, Trudy knows c_0 and p_0.

   a. Show that Trudy can determine the first byte of the keystream k_0.

   b. Show that Trudy can replace c_0 with c_0', where c_0' decrypts to a byte of Trudy's choosing, say, p_0'.

   c. Suppose that a CRC [326] is used to detect errors in transmission. Can Trudy's attack in part b still succeed? Explain.

   d. Suppose that a cryptographic integrity check is used (either a MAC, HMAC, or digital signature). Can Trudy's attack in part b still succeed? Explain.

11. This problem deals with a Feistel Cipher.

   a. Give the definition of a Feistel Cipher.

   b. Is DES a Feistel Cipher?

   c. Is AES a Feistel Cipher?

   d. Why is the Tiny Encryption Algorithm, TEA, "almost" a Feistel Cipher?

12. Consider a Feistel cipher with four rounds. Then the plaintext is denoted as $P = (L_0, R_0)$ and the corresponding ciphertext is $C = (L_4, R_4)$. What is the ciphertext C, in terms of L_0, R_0, and the subkey, for each of the following round functions?

   a. $F(R_{i-1}, K_i) = 0$

   b. $F(R_{i-1}, K_i) = R_{i-1}$

   c. $F(R_{i-1}, K_i) = K_i$

   d. $F(R_{i-1}, K_i) = R_{i-1} \oplus K_i$

13. Within a single round, DES employs both confusion and diffusion.

   a. Give one source of confusion within a DES round.

   b. Give one source of diffusion within a DES round.

14. This problem deals with the DES cipher.

   a. How many bits in each plaintext block?

   b. How many bits in each ciphertext block?

   c. How many bits in the key?

   d. How many bits in each subkey?

   e. How many rounds?

   f. How many S-boxes?

   g. An S-box requires how many bits of input?

   h. An S-box generates how many bits of output?

15. DES swaps the output of the final round, that is, the ciphertext is not $C = (L_{16}, R_{16})$ but instead it is $C = (R_{16}, L_{16})$. What is the purpose of this swap?

16. Recall the attack on double DES discussed in the text. Suppose that we instead define double DES as $C = D(E(P, K_1), K_2)$. Describe a meet-in-the-middle attack on this cipher.

17. Recall that for a block cipher, a key schedule algorithm determines the subkey for each round, based on the key K. Let $K = (k_0 k_1 k_2 \ldots k_{55})$ be a 56-bit DES key.

   a. List the 48 bits for each of the 16 DES subkeys $K_1, K_2, \ldots, K_{16}$, in terms of the key bits k_i.

   b. Make a table that contains the number of subkeys in which each key bit k_i is used.

   c. Can you design a DES key schedule algorithm in which each key bit is used an equal number of times?

18. Recall the meet-in-the-middle attack on double DES discussed in this chapter. Assuming that chosen plaintext is available, this attack recovers a 112-bit key with about the same work needed for an exhaustive search to recover a 56-bit key, that is, about 2^{55}.

   a. If we only have known plaintext available, not chosen plaintext, what changes do we need to make to the double DES attack?

   b. What is the work factor for the known plaintext version of the meet-in-the-middle double DES attack?

19. AES consists of four functions in three layers.

   a. Which of the four functions are primarily for confusion and which are primarily for diffusion? Justify your answer.

b. Which of the three layers are for confusion and which are for diffusion? Justify your answer.

20. Implement the Tiny Encryption Algorithm (TEA).

    a. Use your TEA algorithm to encrypt the 64-bit plaintext block

    $$0x0123456789ABCDEF$$

    using the 128-bit key

    $$0xA56BABCD00000000FFFFFFFFABCDEF01.$$

    Decrypt the resulting ciphertext and verify that you obtain the original plaintext.

    b. Using the key in part a, encrypt and decrypt the following message using each of the three block cipher modes discussed in the text (ECB mode, CBC mode, and CTR mode).

    > Four score and seven years ago our fathers brought forth on this continent, a new nation, conceived in Liberty, and dedicated to the proposition that all men are created equal.

21. Give a diagram analogous to that in Figure 3.2 for the TEA cipher.

22. Recall that an initialization vector (IV) need not be secret.

    a. Does an IV need to be random?

    b. Discuss possible security disadvantages (or advantages) if IVs are selected in sequence instead of being generated at random.

23. Draw diagrams to illustrate encryption and decryption in CBC mode. Note that these diagrams are independent of the particular block cipher that is used.

24. The formula for counter mode encryption is

    $$C_i = P_i \oplus E(\text{IV} + i, K).$$

    Suppose instead we use the formula

    $$C_i = P_i \oplus E(K, \text{IV} + i).$$

    Is this secure? If so, why? If not, why not?

25. Suppose that we use a block cipher to encrypt according to the rule

    $$C_0 = \text{IV} \oplus E(P_0, K), \; C_1 = C_0 \oplus E(P_1, K), \; C_2 = C_1 \oplus E(P_2, K), \; \ldots$$

    a. What is the corresponding decryption rule?

    b. Give two security disadvantages of this mode as compared to CBC mode.

26. Suppose that ten ciphertext blocks are encrypted in CBC mode. Show that a cut-and-paste attack is possible. That is, show that it is possible to rearrange the blocks so that some of the blocks decrypt correctly, in spite of the fact that the blocks are not in the correct order.

27. Explain how to do random access on data encrypted in CBC mode. Are there any significant disadvantages of using CBC mode for random access as compared to CTR mode?

28. CTR mode generates a keystream using a block cipher. Devise another method for using a block cipher as a stream cipher. Does your method support random access?

29. Suppose that the ciphertext in equation (3.8) had been encrypted in CBC mode instead of ECB mode. If Trudy believes ECB mode is used and tries the same cut-and-paste attack discussed in the text, which blocks decrypt correctly?

30. Obtain the files `Alice.bmp` and `Alice.jpg` from the textbook website.

    a. Use the TEA cipher to encrypt `Alice.bmp` in ECB mode, leaving the first 10 blocks unencrypted. View the encrypted image. What do you see? Explain the result.

    b. Use the TEA cipher to encrypt `Alice.jpg` in ECB mode, leaving the first 10 blocks unencrypted. View the encrypted image. What do you see? Explain the result.

31. Suppose that Alice and Bob decide to always use the same IV instead of choosing IVs at random.

    a. Discuss a security problem this creates if CBC mode is used.

    b. Discuss a security problem this creates if CTR mode is used.

    c. If the same IV is always used, which is more secure, CBC or CTR mode?

32. Suppose that Alice and Bob use CBC mode encryption.

    a. What security problems arise if they always use a fixed initialization vector (IV), as opposed to choosing IVs at random? Explain.

b. Suppose that Alice and Bob choose IVs in sequence, that is, they first use 0 as an IV, then they use 1 as their IV, then 2, and so on. Does this create any security problems as compared to choosing the IVs at random?

33. Give two ways to encrypt a partial block using a block cipher. Your first method should result in ciphertext that is the size of a complete block, while your second method should not expand the data. Discuss any possible security concerns for your two methods.

34. Recall that a MAC is given by the CBC residue, that is, the last ciphertext block when the data is encrypted in CBC mode. Given data X, key K, and an IV, define $F(X)$ to be the MAC of X.

   a. Is F one-way, that is, given $F(X)$ is it possible to determine X?
   b. Is F collision resistant, that is, given $F(X)$ is it possible to find a value Y such that $F(Y) = F(X)$?

35. Suppose Alice uses DES to compute a MAC. She then sends the plaintext, the IV, and the corresponding MAC to Bob. If Trudy alters one block of plaintext before Bob receives it, what is the probability that Bob will not detect the change?

36. Alice has four blocks of plaintext, P_0, P_1, P_2, P_3, which she encrypts using CBC mode to obtain C_0, C_1, C_2, C_3. She then sends the IV and ciphertext to Bob. Upon receiving the ciphertext, Bob plans to verify the integrity as follows. He'll first decrypt to obtain the putative plaintext, and then he'll re-encrypt this plaintext using CBC mode and the received IV. If he obtains the same C_3 as the final ciphertext block, he will trust the integrity of the plaintext.

   a. Suppose that Trudy changes C_1 to X, leaving all other blocks and the IV unchanged. Will Bob detect that the data lacks integrity?
   b. Suppose that Trudy changes C_3 to the value Y, leaving all other blocks and the IV unchanged. Will Bob detect that the data lacks integrity?
   c. Is Bob's integrity checking method secure?

37. Using CBC mode, Alice encrypts four blocks of plaintext, P_0, P_1, P_2, P_3 and she sends the resulting ciphertext blocks, C_0, C_1, C_2, C_3, and the IV to Bob. Suppose that Trudy is able to change any of the ciphertext blocks before they are received by Bob. If Trudy knows P_1, show that she can replace P_1 with X. Hint: Determine $\tilde{C}$ so that if Trudy replaces C_0 with $\tilde{C}$, when Bob decrypts C_1, he will obtain X instead of P_1.

38. Suppose we encrypt in CBC mode using the key K and we compute a MAC using the key $K \oplus X$, where X is a known constant. Assuming the ciphertext and the MAC are sent from Alice to Bob, show that Bob will detect a cut-and-paste attack.

39. Suppose Alice has four blocks of plaintext, P_0, P_1, P_2, P_3. She computes a MAC using key K_1, and then CBC encrypts the data using key K_2 to obtain C_0, C_1, C_2, C_3. Alice sends the IV, the ciphertext, and the MAC to Bob. Trudy intercepts the message and replaces C_1 with X so that Bob receives IV$, C_0, X, C_2, C_3$, and the MAC. Bob attempts to verify the integrity of the data by decrypting (using key K_2) and then computing a MAC (using key K_1) on the putative plaintext.

    a. Show that Bob will detect Trudy's tampering.

    b. Suppose that Alice and Bob only share a single symmetric key K. They agree to let $K_1 = K$ and $K_2 = K \oplus Y$, where Y is known to Alice, Bob, and Trudy. Assuming Alice and Bob use the same scheme as above, does this create any security problem?

40. Suppose that Alice and Bob have access to two secure block ciphers, say, Cipher A and Cipher B, where Cipher A uses a 64-bit key, while Cipher B uses a 128-bit key. Alice prefers Cipher A, while Bob wants the additional security provided by a 128-bit key, so he insists on Cipher B. As a compromise, Alice proposes that they use Cipher A, but they encrypt each message twice, using two independent 64-bit keys. Assume that no shortcut attack is available for either cipher. Is Alice's approach as secure as Bob's?

41. Suppose that Alice has a secure block cipher, but the cipher only uses an 8-bit key. To make this cipher "more secure," Alice generates a random 64-bit key K, and iterates the cipher eight times, that is, she encrypts the plaintext P according to the rule

$$C = E(E(E(E(E(E(E(E(P, K_0), K_1), K_2), K_3), K_4), K_5), K_6), K_7),$$

where $K_0, K_1, \ldots, K_7$ are the bytes of the 64-bit key K.

    a. Assuming known plaintext is available, how much work is required to determine the key K?

    b. Assuming a ciphertext-only attack, how much work is required to break this encryption scheme?

42. Suppose that we define triple 3DES with a 168-bit key as

$$C = E(E(E(P, K_1), K_2), K_3).$$

Suppose that we can compute and store a table of size 2^{56}, and a chosen plaintext attack is possible. Show that this triple 3DES is no more secure than the usual 3DES, which only uses a 112-bit key. Hint: Mimic the meet-in-the-middle attack on double DES.

43. Suppose that you know a MAC value X and the key K that was used to compute the MAC, but you do not know the original message. (It may be instructive to compare this problem to Problem 16 in Chapter 5.)

 a. Show that you can construct a message M that also has its MAC equal to X. Note that we are assuming that you know the key K and the same key is used for both MAC computations.

 b. How much of the message M are you free to choose?

Chapter 4

Public Key Crypto

> *You should not live one way in private, another in public.*
> — Publilius Syrus

> *Three may keep a secret, if two of them are dead.*
> — Ben Franklin

4.1 Introduction

In this chapter, we delve into the remarkable subject of public key cryptography. Public key crypto is sometimes know as asymmetric cryptography, or two key cryptography, or even non-secret key cryptography, but we'll stick with public key cryptography.

In symmetric key cryptography, the same key is used to both encrypt and decrypt the data. In public key cryptography, one key is used to encrypt and a different key is used to decrypt and as a result, the encryption key can be made public. This eliminates one of the most vexing problems of symmetric key crypto, namely, how to securely distribute the symmetric key. Of course, there is no free lunch, so public key crypto has its own issues when it comes to dealing with keys (see the section on public key infrastructure, below). Nevertheless, public key crypto is a big "win" in many real-world applications.

Actually, public key cryptography is usually defined more broadly than the two-key encryption and decryption description given in the previous paragraph. Any system that has cryptographic application and involves some crucial information being made public is likely to be considered a public key cryptosystem. For example, one popular public key system discussed in this chapter can only be used to establish a shared symmetric, not to encrypt or decrypt anything.

Public key crypto is a relative newcomer, having been invented by cryptographers working for GCHQ (the British equivalent of NSA) in the late 1960s and early 1970s and, independently, by academic researchers shortly thereafter [191]. The government cryptographers clearly did not grasp the full potential of their discovery, and it lay dormant until the academicians pushed it into the limelight. The ultimate effect has been nothing short of a revolution in cryptography. It is amazing that public key crypto is such a recent discovery, given that humans have been using symmetric crypto for thousands of years.

In this chapter, we'll examine most of the most important and widely used public key cryptosystems. Actually, relatively few public key systems are known, and fewer still are widely used. In contrast, there exists a vast number of symmetric ciphers, and a fairly significant number of these get used in practice. Each public key system is based on a very special mathematical structure, making it extraordinarily difficult to develop new systems.[1]

A public key cryptosystem is based on a trap door one-way function. "One-way" means that the function is easy to compute in one direction but hard to compute (i.e., computationally infeasible) in the other. The "trap door" feature ensures that an attacker cannot use the public information to recover the private information. Factoring is a relevant example—it is a one-way function since it's relatively easy to, say, generate two prime numbers p and q and compute their product $N = pq$, but given a sufficiently large value of N, it is difficult to find the factors p and q. We can also build a trap door based on factoring, but we defer a discussion of that to later in this chapter (see the section on RSA).

Recall that in symmetric key crypto, the plaintext is P and the ciphertext is C. But in public key crypto, tradition has it that we encrypt a message M, although, strangely, the result is still ciphertext C. Below, we follow this tradition.

To do public key crypto, Bob must have a *key pair* consisting of a *public key* and a corresponding *private key*. Anyone can use Bob's public key to encrypt a message intended for Bob's eyes only, but only Bob can decrypt the message, since, by assumption only Bob has his private key.

Bob can also apply his *digital signature* to a message M by "encrypting" it with his private key. Note that anybody can "decrypt" the message since this only requires Bob's public key, which is public. You might reasonably wonder what possible use this could be. In fact, it is one of the most useful features of public key crypto.

A digital signature is like a handwritten signature—only more so. Bob is the only one who can digitally sign as Bob, since he is the only one with access to his private key. While in principle only Bob can write his handwritten

---

[1] Public key cryptosystems definitely do not grow on trees.

signature,[2] in practice only Bob can digitally sign as Bob. Anyone with access to Bob's public key can verify Bob's digital signature, which is much more practical than hiring a handwriting expert to verify Bob's non-digital signature.

The digital version of Bob's signature has some additional advantages over the handwritten version. For one thing, a digital signature is firmly tied to the document itself, whereas a handwritten signature can be photocopied onto another document. No photocopying attack is possible with a digital signature. Even more significant is the fact that, generally speaking, it's not feasible to forge a digital signature without the private key. In the non-digital world, a forgery of Bob's signature might only be detectable by a trained expert (if at all), while a digital signature forgery can be easily and automatically detected by anyone since verification only requires Bob's public key, and everyone has access to public keys.

Next, we'll discuss in detail several public key cryptosystems. The first one that we'll consider is the knapsack cryptosystem. This is appropriate since the knapsack was one of the first practical proposed public key systems. Although the knapsack that we'll present is known to be insecure, it's relatively easy to comprehend and nicely illustrates all of the important features of such a system. After the knapsack, we discuss the gold standard of public key crypto, namely, RSA. We'll then conclude our brief tour of public key systems with a look at the Diffie-Hellman key exchange, which is also widely used in practice.

We then discuss elliptic curve cryptography, or ECC. Note that ECC is not a cryptosystem *per se*, but instead it offers a different realm in which to do the math that arises in public key systems. The advantage of ECC is that it's more efficient (in both time and space) and so it's favored in resource-constrained environments such as wireless and handheld devices. In fact, all recent U.S. government public key standards are ECC-based.

Public key cryptography is inherently more mathematical than symmetric key. So now would be a good time to review the math topics found in the Appendix. In particular, a working knowledge of elementary modular arithmetic is assumed in this chapter.

4.2 Knapsack

In their seminal paper [90], Diffie and Hellman conjectured that public key cryptography was possible, but they "only" offered a key exchange algorithm, not a viable system for encryption and decryption. Shortly thereafter, the Merkle-Hellman knapsack cryptosystem was proposed by—believe it or not—Merkle and Hellman. We'll meet Hellman again later, but it is worth noting that Merkle was also one of the founders of public key cryptography. He wrote

---

[2]What happens in practice is a different story.

a groundbreaking paper [202] that foreshadowed public key cryptography. Merkle's paper was submitted for publication at about the same time as Diffie and Hellman's paper, although it appeared much later. For some reason, Merkle's contribution usually does not receive the attention it deserves.

The Merkle-Hellman knapsack cryptosystem is based on a problem[3] that is known to be NP-complete [119]. This seems to make it an ideal candidate for a secure public key cryptosystem.

The knapsack problem can be stated as follows. Given a set of n weights labeled as

$$W_0, W_1, \ldots, W_{n-1}$$

and a desired sum S, find $a_0, a_1 \ldots, a_{n-1}$, where each $a_i \in \{0, 1\}$, so that

$$S = a_0 W_0 + a_1 W_1 + \cdots + a_{n-1} W_{n-1},$$

provided this is possible. For example, suppose the weights are

$$85, 13, 9, 7, 47, 27, 99, 86$$

and the desired sum is $S = 172$. Then a solution to the problem exists and is given by

$$a = (a_0, a_1, a_2, a_3, a_4, a_5, a_6, a_7) = (11001100)$$

since $85 + 13 + 47 + 27 = 172$.

Although the general knapsack problem is known to be NP-complete, there is a special case that can be solved in linear time. A *superincreasing knapsack* is similar to the general knapsack except that, when the weights are arranged from least to greatest, each weight is greater than sum of all previous weights. For example,

$$3, 6, 11, 25, 46, 95, 200, 411 \tag{4.1}$$

is a superincreasing knapsack. Solving a superincreasing knapsack problem is easy. Suppose we are given the set of weights in equation (4.1) and the sum $S = 309$. To solve this, we simply start with the largest weight and work toward the smallest to recover the a_i in linear time. Since $S < 411$, we have $a_7 = 0$. Then since $S > 200$, we must have $a_6 = 1$, since the sum of all remaining weights is less than 200. Then we compute $S = S - 200 = 109$ and this is our new target sum. Since $S > 95$, we have $a_5 = 1$ and we compute $S = 109 - 95 = 14$. Continuing in this manner, we find $a = 10100110$, which we can easily verify solves the problem since $3 + 11 + 95 + 200 = 309$.

---

[3]Ironically, the knapsack cryptosystem is not based on the knapsack problem. Instead it's based on a more restricted problem, known as subset sum. Nevertheless, the cryptosystem is universally known as the knapsack. Eschewing our usual pedantic nature, we'll refer to both the cryptosystem and the underlying problem as knapsacks.

Next, we outline the steps in the procedure used to construct a knapsack cryptosystem. The process begins with a superincreasing knapsack from which we generate a public and private key pair. After listing the steps, we'll illustrate the process with a specific example.

1. Generate a superincreasing knapsack.

2. Convert the superincreasing knapsack into a general knapsack.

3. The public key is the general knapsack.

4. The private key is the superincreasing knapsack together with the conversion factors.

Below, we'll see that it's easy to encrypt using the general knapsack and, with access to the private key, it's easy to decrypt. However, without the private key, it appears that Trudy must solve an NP-complete problem—the knapsack problem—to recover the plaintext from the ciphertext.

Now we'll present a specific example. For this example, we'll follow the numbering in the steps listed above.

1. For this example, we'll choose the superincreasing knapsack

$$(2, 3, 7, 14, 30, 57, 120, 251).$$

2. To convert the superincreasing knapsack into a general knapsack, we must choose a multiplier m and a modulus n so that m and n are relatively prime and n is greater than the sum of all elements in the superincreasing knapsack. For this example, we select the multiplier $m = 41$ and the modulus $n = 491$. Then the general knapsack is computed from the superincreasing knapsack by modular multiplication:

$$2m = 2 \cdot 41 = 82 \bmod 491$$
$$3m = 3 \cdot 41 = 123 \bmod 491$$
$$7m = 7 \cdot 41 = 287 \bmod 491$$
$$14m = 14 \cdot 41 = 83 \bmod 491$$
$$30m = 30 \cdot 41 = 248 \bmod 491$$
$$57m = 57 \cdot 41 = 373 \bmod 491$$
$$120m = 120 \cdot 41 = 10 \bmod 491$$
$$251m = 251 \cdot 41 = 471 \bmod 491$$

The resulting knapsack is $(82, 123, 287, 83, 248, 373, 10, 471)$. Note that this knapsack does indeed appear to be a general knapsack.[4]

---

[4] Appearances can be deceiving...

3. The public key is the general knapsack,

$$\text{Public key: } (82, 123, 287, 83, 248, 373, 10, 471).$$

4. The private key is the superincreasing knapsack together with the multiplicative inverse of the conversion factor, i.e., $m^{-1} \bmod n$. For this example, we have

$$\text{Private key: } (2, 3, 7, 14, 30, 57, 120, 251) \text{ and } 41^{-1} \bmod 491 = 12.$$

Suppose Bob's public and private key pair are those given in step 3 and step 4, respectively. Suppose that Alice wants to encrypt the message (in binary) $M = 10010110$ for Bob. Then she uses the 1 bits in her message to select the elements of the general knapsack that are summed to give the ciphertext. In this case, Alice computes

$$C = 82 + 83 + 373 + 10 = 548.$$

To decrypt this ciphertext, Bob uses his private key to find

$$C \cdot m^{-1} \bmod n = 548 \cdot 12 \bmod 491 = 193.$$

Bob then solves the superincreasing knapsack for 193. Since Bob has the private key, this is an easy (linear time) problem from which Bob recovers the message in binary $M = 10010110$ or, in decimal, $M = 150$.

Note that in this example, we have

$$548 = 82 + 83 + 373 + 10$$

and it follows that

$$\begin{aligned}
548m^{-1} &= 82m^{-1} + 83m^{-1} + 373m^{-1} + 10m^{-1} \\
&= 2mm^{-1} + 14mm^{-1} + 57mm^{-1} + 120mm^{-1} \\
&= 2 + 14 + 57 + 120 \\
&= 193 \bmod 491.
\end{aligned}$$

This example shows that multiplying by m^{-1} transforms the ciphertext—which lives in the realm of the general knapsack—into the superincreasing realm, where it's easy for Bob to solve for the weights. Proving that the decryption formula works in general is equally straightforward.

Without the private key, attacker Trudy can break a message if she can find a subset of the elements of the public key that sum to the ciphertext value C. In the example above, Trudy must find a subset of the knapsack $(82, 123, 287, 83, 248, 373, 10, 471)$ that sums precisely to 548. This appears to be a general knapsack problem, which is known to be a very difficult problem.

The trapdoor in the knapsack cryptosystem occurs when we convert the superincreasing knapsack into the general knapsack using modular arithmetic, since the conversion factors are unavailable to an attacker. The one-way feature lies in the fact that it is easy to encrypt with the general knapsack, but it's apparently hard to decrypt without the private key. Of course, with the private key, we can convert the problem into a superincreasing knapsack problem that is easy to solve.

The knapsack appears to be just what the doctor ordered. First, it is fairly easy to construct a public and private key pair. And given the public key, it is easy to encrypt, while knowledge of the private key makes it easy to decrypt. Finally, without the private key it appears that Trudy will be forced to solve an NP-complete problem.

Alas, this clever knapsack cryptosystem is insecure. It was broken by Shamir (who else?) in 1983 using an Apple II computer [265]. The attack relies on a technique known as lattice reduction that we discuss in detail in Chapter 6. The bottom line is that the "general knapsack" that is derived from the superincreasing knapsack is not really a general knapsack—in fact, it's a very special and highly structured case of the knapsack. The lattice reduction attack is able to take advantage of this structure to easily recover the plaintext (with a high probability).

Much research has been done on the knapsack problem since the demise of the Merkle-Hellman knapsack. Today, there are knapsack variants that appear to be secure, but people are reluctant to use them since the name "knapsack" is forever tainted. For more information on knapsack cryptosystems, see [88, 179, 222].

4.3   RSA

Like any worthwhile public key cryptosystem, RSA is named after its putative inventors, Rivest, Shamir, and Adleman. We've met Rivest and Shamir previously, and we'll hear from both again. In fact, Rivest and Shamir are two of the giants of modern crypto. However, the RSA concept was actually originated by Cliff Cocks of GCHQ a few years before R, S, and A independently reinvented it [191]. This does not in any way diminish the achievement of Rivest, Shamir, and Adleman, since the GCHQ work was classified and was not even widely known within the classified crypto community—it was viewed more as a curiosity than as a practical system.[5]

If you've ever wondered why there is so much interest in factoring large numbers, it's because RSA can be broken by factoring. However, it's not known for certain that factoring is difficult in the sense that, say, the knapsack

---

[5]It is also worth noting that the spies seem to have never even considered the concept of a digital signature.

problem is difficult. In true cryptographic fashion, the factoring problem on which RSA rests is hard because lots of smart people have looked at it, and apparently nobody has found an efficient solution.

To generate an RSA public and private key pair, choose two large prime numbers p and q and form their product $N = pq$. Next, choose e relatively prime to the product $(p-1)(q-1)$. Finally, find the multiplicative inverse of e modulo $(p-1)(q-1)$ and denote this inverse as d. At this point, we have N, which is the product of the two primes p and q, as well as e and d, which satisfy $ed = 1 \bmod (p-1)(q-1)$. Now forget the factors p and q.

The number N is the *modulus*, and e is the *encryption exponent* while d is the *decryption exponent*. The RSA key pair consists of

$$\text{Public key: } (N, e)$$

and

$$\text{Private key: } d.$$

In RSA, encryption and decryption are accomplished via modular exponentiation. To encrypt with RSA, we treat the plaintext message M as a number and raise it to the power e, modulo N, that is,

$$C = M^e \bmod N.$$

To decrypt C, modular exponentiation using the decryption exponent d does the trick, that is,

$$M = C^d \bmod N.$$

It's probably not obvious that RSA decryption actually works—we'll prove that it does shortly. Assume for a moment that RSA does work. Now, if Trudy can factor the modulus N (which is public) she will obtain p and q. Then she can use the other public value e to easily find the private value d since $ed = 1 \bmod (p-1)(q-1)$ and finding modular inverses is computationally easy. In other words, factoring the modulus enables Trudy to recover the private key, which breaks RSA. However, it is not known whether factoring is the only way to break RSA.

Does RSA really work? Given $C = M^e \bmod N$, we must show that

$$M = C^d \bmod N = M^{ed} \bmod N. \tag{4.2}$$

To do so, we need the following standard result from number theory [43]:

Euler's Theorem: If x is relatively prime to n then $x^{\phi(n)} = 1 \bmod n$

Recall that e and d were chosen so that

$$ed = 1 \bmod (p-1)(q-1).$$

Repeated squaring works by building up the exponent one bit at a time. At each step we double the current exponent and if the binary expansion has a 1 in the corresponding position, we also add one to the exponent.

How can we double (and add one) to an exponent? Basic properties of exponentiation tell us that if we square x^y, we obtain $(x^y)^2 = x^{2y}$ and that $x \cdot x^y = x^{y+1}$. Consequently, we can easily double or add one to any exponent. From the basic properties of modular arithmetic (see the Appendix), we know that we can reduce any intermediate results by the modulus, and thereby avoid extremely large numbers.

An example is worth a thousand words. Consider again 5^{20}. First, note that the exponent 20 is, in binary, 10100. The exponent 10100 can be built up one bit at a time, beginning from the high-order bit, as

$$(0, 1, 10, 101, 1010, 10100) = (0, 1, 2, 5, 10, 20).$$

As a result, the exponent 20 can be constructed by a series of steps, where each step consists of doubling and, when the next bit in the binary expansion of 20 is a 1, adding one, that is,

$$1 = 0 \cdot 2 + 1$$
$$2 = 1 \cdot 2$$
$$5 = 2 \cdot 2 + 1$$
$$10 = 5 \cdot 2$$
$$20 = 10 \cdot 2$$

Now to compute 5^{20}, repeated squaring proceeds as

$$5^1 = (5^0)^2 \cdot 5^1 = 5 \bmod 35$$
$$5^2 = (5^1)^2 = 5^2 = 25 \bmod 35$$
$$5^5 = (5^2)^2 \cdot 5^1 = 25^2 \cdot 5 = 3125 = 10 \bmod 35$$
$$5^{10} = (5^5)^2 = 10^2 = 100 = 30 \bmod 35$$
$$5^{20} = (5^{10})^2 = 30^2 = 900 = 25 \bmod 35$$

Note that a modular reduction occurs at each step.

Although there are many steps in the repeated squaring algorithm, each step is simple, efficient, and we never have to deal with a number that is greater than the cube of the modulus. Compare this to equation (4.4), where we had to deal with an enormous intermediate value.

4.3.3 Speeding Up RSA

Another trick that can be employed to speed up RSA is to use the same encryption exponent e for all users. As far as anyone knows, this does not weaken RSA in any way. The decryption exponents (the private keys) of different users will be different, since different p, q, and consequently N are chosen for each key pair.

Amazingly, a suitable choice for the common encryption exponent is $e = 3$. With this choice of e, each public key encryption only requires two multiplications. However, the private key operations remain expensive since there is no special structure for d. This is often acceptable since many encryptions may be done by a central server, while the decryption is effectively distributed among the clients. Of course, if the server needs to compute digital signatures, then a small e does not reduce its workload. Although the math would work, it would certainly be a bad idea to choose a common value of d for all users.

With an encryption exponent of $e = 3$, the following *cube root attack* is possible. If the plaintext M satisfies $M < N^{1/3}$, then $C = M^e = M^3$, that is, the mod N operation has no effect. As a result, an attacker can simply compute the usual cube root of C to obtain M. In practice, this is easily avoided by padding M with enough bits so that, as a number, $M > N^{1/3}$.

If multiple users all have $e = 3$ as their encryption exponent, another type of the cube root attack exists. If the same message M is encrypted with three different users' public keys, yielding, say, ciphertext C_0, C_1, and C_2, then the Chinese Remainder Theorem [43] can be used to recover the message M. This is also easily avoided in practice by randomly padding each message M or by including some user-specific information in each M, so that the messages actually differ.

Another popular common encryption exponents is $e = 2^{16}+1$. With this e, each encryption requires only 17 steps of the repeated squaring algorithm. An advantage of $e = 2^{16} + 1$ is that the same encrypted message must be sent to $2^{16} + 1$ users before the Chinese Remainder Theorem attack can succeed.

Next, we'll examine the Diffie-Hellman key exchange algorithm, which is a very different sort of public key algorithm. Whereas RSA relies on the difficulty of factoring, Diffie-Hellman is based on the so-called discrete log problem.

4.4   Diffie-Hellman

The Diffie-Hellman key exchange algorithm, or DH for short, was invented by Malcolm Williamson of GCHQ and shortly thereafter it was independently reinvented by its namesakes, Whitfield Diffie and Martin Hellman [191].

The version of DH that we discuss here is a key exchange algorithm because it can only be used to establish a shared secret. The resulting shared secret is generally used as a shared symmetric key. It's worth emphasizing that, in this book, the words "Diffie-Hellman" and "key exchange" always go together—DH is not for encrypting or signing, but instead it allows users to establish a shared symmetric key. This is no mean feat, since this key establishment problem is one of the fundamental problems in symmetric key cryptography.

The security of DH relies on the computational difficulty of the *discrete log* problem. Suppose you are given g and $x = g^k$. Then to determine k you would compute the logarithm, $\log_g(x)$. Now given g, p, and g^k mod p, the problem of finding k is analogous to the logarithm problem, but in a discrete setting. This discrete version of the logarithm problem is, not surprisingly, known as the discrete log problem. As far as is known, the discrete log problem is very difficult to solve, although, as with factoring, it is not known to be, say, NP-complete.

The mathematical setup for DH is relatively simple. Let p be prime and let g be a *generator*, which means that for any $x \in \{1, 2, \ldots, p-1\}$ there exists an exponent n such that $x = g^n$ mod p. The prime p and the generator g are public.

For the actual key exchange, Alice randomly selects a secret exponent a and Bob randomly selects a secret exponent b. Alice computes g^a mod p and sends the result to Bob, and Bob computes g^b mod p and sends the result to Alice. Then Alice computes

$$(g^b)^a \bmod p = g^{ab} \bmod p$$

and Bob computes

$$(g^a)^b \bmod p = g^{ab} \bmod p$$

and g^{ab} mod p is the shared secret, which is typically used as a symmetric key. The DH key exchange is illustrated in Figure 4.1.

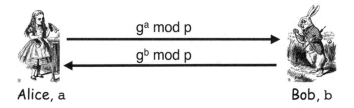

Figure 4.1: Diffie-Hellman Key Exchange

The attacker Trudy can see g^a mod p and g^b mod p, and it seems that she is tantalizingly close to knowing the secret g^{ab} mod p. However,

$$g^a \cdot g^b = g^{a+b} \neq g^{ab} \bmod p$$

Apparently, Trudy needs to find either a or b, which appears to require that she solve a difficult discrete log problem. Of course, if Trudy can find a or b

or $g^{ab} \bmod p$ by any other means, the system is broken. But, as far as is known, the only way to break DH is to solve the discrete log problem.

There is a fundamental problem with the DH algorithm—it is susceptible to a man-in-the-middle, or MiM, attack.[6] This is an active attack where Trudy places herself between Alice and Bob and captures messages from Alice to Bob and vice versa. With Trudy thusly placed, the DH exchange can be easily subverted. In the process, Trudy establishes a shared secret, say, $g^{at} \bmod p$ with Alice, and another shared secret $g^{bt} \bmod p$ with Bob, as illustrated in Figure 4.2. Neither Alice nor Bob has any clue that anything is amiss, yet Trudy is able to read or change any messages passing between Alice and Bob.[7]

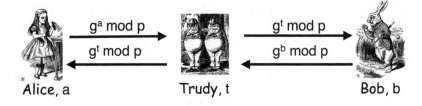

Figure 4.2: Diffie-Hellman Man-in-the-Middle Attack

The MiM attack in Figure 4.2 is a serious concern when using DH. There are several possible ways to prevent the attack, including the following:

1. Encrypt the DH exchange with a shared symmetric key.

2. Encrypt the DH exchange with public keys.

3. Sign the DH values with private keys.

At this point, you should be baffled. After all, why would we need to use DH to establish a symmetric key if we already have a shared symmetric key (as in 1) or a public key pair (as in 2 and 3)? This is an excellent question to which we'll give an excellent answer when we discuss protocols in Chapters 9 and 10.

4.5 Elliptic Curve Cryptography

Elliptic curves provide an alternative domain for performing the complex mathematical operations required in public key cryptography. So, for example, there is an elliptic curve version of Diffie-Hellman.

---

[6]Your politically incorrect author refuses to use the term "middleperson" attack.

[7]The underlying problem here is that the participants are not authenticated. In this example, Alice does not know she's talking to Bob and vice versa. It will be a few more chapters before we discuss authentication protocols.

The advantage of elliptic curve cryptography (ECC) is that fewer bits are needed to achieve the same level of security. On the down side, elliptic curve math is more complex, and consequently each mathematical operation on an elliptic curve is somewhat more expensive. Overall, elliptic curves offer a significant computational advantage over standard modular arithmetic and current U.S. government standards reflect this—all recent public key standards are ECC-based. In addition, ECC is especially important in resource-constrained environments such as handheld devices.

What is an elliptic curve? An elliptic curve E is the graph of a function of the form

$$E: \quad y^2 = x^3 + ax + b,$$

together with a special point at infinity, denoted ∞. The graph of a typical elliptic curve appears in Figure 4.3.

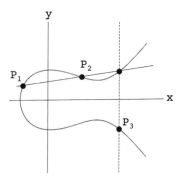

Figure 4.3: An Elliptic Curve

4.5.1 Elliptic Curve Math

Figure 4.3 also illustrates the method used to do arithmetic on an elliptic curve. The "sum" of two points on an elliptic curve has both a geometric and arithmetic interpretation. Geometrically, the sum of the points P_1 and P_2 is defined as follows: First, a line is drawn through the two points. This line usually intersects the curve in one other point. If so, this intersection point is reflected about the x axis to obtain the point P_3, which is defined to be the sum, that is,

$$P_3 = P_1 + P_2.$$

This is illustrated in Figure 4.3. Also, addition is the only mathematical operation on elliptic curves that is required.

For cryptography, we want to deal with a discrete set of points. This is easily accomplished by including a "mod p" in the generic elliptic curve

equation, that is,
$$y^2 = x^3 + ax + b \pmod{p}.$$

For example, consider the elliptic curve
$$y^2 = x^3 + 2x + 3 \pmod{5}. \tag{4.5}$$

We can list all of the points (x, y) on this curve by substituting all values for x and solving for corresponding y value or values. Since we are working modulo 5, we only need to consider $x = 0, 1, 2, 3, 4$. In this case, we obtain the following points:

$$x = 0 \implies y^2 = 3 \implies \text{no solution mod 5}$$
$$x = 1 \implies y^2 = 6 = 1 \implies y = 1, 4 \text{ mod 5}$$
$$x = 2 \implies y^2 = 15 = 0 \implies y = 0 \text{ mod 5}$$
$$x = 3 \implies y^2 = 36 = 1 \implies y = 1, 4 \text{ mod 5}$$
$$x = 4 \implies y^2 = 75 = 0 \implies y = 0 \text{ mod 5}$$

That is, we find that the points on the elliptic curve in equation (4.5) are

$$(1, 1) \ (1, 4) \ (2, 0) \ (3, 1) \ (3, 4) \ (4, 0) \text{ and } \infty. \tag{4.6}$$

Next, we again consider the problem of adding two points on a curve. We need a more computer-friendly approach than the geometric definition discussed above. The algorithm for algebraically adding two points on an elliptic curve appears in Table 4.1.

Table 4.1: Addition on an Elliptic Curve mod p

Given: curve E: $y^2 = x^3 + ax + b \pmod{p}$
$\qquad\qquad P_1 = (x_1, y_1)$ and $P_2 = (x_2, y_2)$ on E
Find: $P_3 = (x_3, y_3) = P_1 + P_2$
Algorithm:
$x_3 = m^2 - x_1 - x_2 \pmod{p}$
$y_3 = m(x_1 - x_3) - y_1 \pmod{p}$
where $m = \begin{cases} (y_2 - y_1) \cdot (x_2 - x_1)^{-1} \bmod p & \text{if } P_1 \neq P_2 \\ (3x_1^2 + a) \cdot (2y_1)^{-1} \bmod p & \text{if } P_1 = P_2 \end{cases}$
Special case 1: If $m = \infty$ then $P_3 = \infty$
Special case 2: $\infty + P = P$ for all P

Let's apply the algorithm in Table 4.1 to find the points $P_3 = (1, 4) + (3, 1)$ on the curve in equation (4.5). First, we compute

$$m = (1 - 4)/(3 - 1) = -3 \cdot 2^{-1} = -3 \cdot 3 = 1 \text{ mod 5}.$$

Then

$$x_3 = 1^2 - 1 - 3 = -3 = 2 \bmod 5$$

and

$$y_3 = 1(1 - 2) - 4 = -5 = 0 \bmod 5.$$

Therefore, on the curve $y^2 = x^3 + 2x + 3 \pmod 5$, we have $(1,4) + (3,1) = (2,0)$. Note that this sum, the point $(2,0)$, is also on the elliptic curve.

4.5.2 ECC Diffie-Hellman

Now that we can do addition on elliptic curves, let's consider the ECC version of the Diffie-Hellman key exchange. The public information consists of a curve and a point on the curve. We'll select the curve

$$y^2 = x^3 + 11x + b \pmod{167}, \tag{4.7}$$

leaving b to be determined momentarily. Next, we select any point (x, y) and determine b so that this point lies on the resulting curve. In this case, we'll choose, say, $(x, y) = (2, 7)$. Then substituting $x = 2$ and $y = 7$ into equation (4.7) we find $b = 19$. The public information is

Public: $y^2 = x^3 + 11x + 19 \pmod{167}$ and the point $(2, 7)$. $\qquad$ (4.8)

Alice and Bob each must randomly select their own secret multipliers.[8] Suppose Alice selects $A = 15$ and Bob selects $B = 22$. Then Alice computes

$$A(2, 7) = 15(2, 7) = (102, 88),$$

where all arithmetic is done on the curve in equation (4.8). Alice sends her computed result to Bob. Bob computes

$$B(2, 7) = 22(2, 7) = (9, 43),$$

which he sends to Alice. Now Alice multiplies the value she received from Bob by her secret multiplier A, that is,

$$A(9, 43) = 15(9, 43) = (131, 140).$$

Similarly, Bob computes

$$B(102, 88) = 22(102, 88) = (131, 140)$$

and Alice and Bob have established a shared secret, suitable for use as a symmetric key. Note that this elliptic curve version of Diffie-Hellman works

---

[8]Since we know how to do addition on an elliptic curve, we do multiplication as repeated addition.

since $AB \cdot P = BA \cdot P$, where A and B are multipliers and P is the specified point on the curve. The security of this method rests on the fact that, although Trudy can see $A \cdot P$ and $B \cdot P$, she (apparently) must find A or B before she can determine the shared secret. As far as is known, this elliptic curve version of DH is as difficult to break as the regular DH. Actually, for a given number of bits, the elliptic curve version is much harder to break, which allows for the use of smaller values to obtain an equivalent level of security. Since the values are smaller, the arithmetic is more efficient.

All is not lost for Trudy. She can take some comfort in the fact that the ECC version of DH is just as susceptible to a MiM attack as any other Diffie-Hellman key exchange.

4.5.3   Realistic Elliptic Curve Example

To provide some idea of the magnitude of the numbers used in real-world ECC, we present a realistic example. This example appears as part of the Certicom ECCp-109 challenge problem [52], and it is discussed in Jao's excellent survey [154]. Note that the numbers are given in decimal and no commas appear within the numbers.

Let

$$p = 564538252084441556247016902735257$$
$$a = 321094768129147601892514872825668$$
$$b = 430782315140218274262276694323197$$

and consider the elliptic curve $E : y^2 = x^3 + ax + b \pmod{p}$. Let P be the point

$$(97339010987059066523156133908935, 149670372846169285760682371978898)$$

which is on E, and let $k = 28118384031160194966820795453 0684$. Then adding the point P to itself k times, which we denote as kP, we obtain the point

$$(4464676969740586105763086188428 4, 5229680988957858880475403747790 97)$$

which is also on the curve E.

While these numbers are indeed large, they are downright puny in comparison to the numbers that must be used in a non-elliptic curve public key system. For example, a modest-sized RSA modulus has 1024 bits, which corresponds to more than 300 decimal digits. In contrast, the numbers in the elliptic curve example above only have about 1/10th as many digits.

There are many good sources of information on the hot topic of elliptic curve cryptography. For an accessible treatment see [251] or see [35] for more of the mathematical details.

4.6 Public Key Notation

Before discussing the uses of public key crypto, we need to settle on some reasonable notation. Since public key systems typically have two keys per user, adapting the notation that we used for symmetric key crypto would be awkward. In addition, a digital signature is an encryption (with the private key), but yet the same operation is a decryption when applied to ciphertext. If we're not careful, this notation thing could get complicated.

We'll adopt the following notation for public key encryption, decryption, and signing [162].

- Encrypt message M with Alice's public key: $C = \{M\}_{\text{Alice}}$.

- Decrypt ciphertext C with Alice's private key: $M = [C]_{\text{Alice}}$.

- The notation for Alice signing[9] message M is $S = [M]_{\text{Alice}}$.

Note that curly brackets represent public key operations, square brackets are for private key operations, and the subscript tells us whose key is being used. This is somewhat awkward but, in your notationally challenged author's opinion, it is the least bad of the possibilities. Finally, since public and private key operations cancel each other out,

$$[\{M\}_{\text{Alice}}]_{\text{Alice}} = \{[M]_{\text{Alice}}\}_{\text{Alice}} = M.$$

Never forget that the public key is public and, consequently, anyone can compute $\{M\}_{\text{Alice}}$. On the other hand, the private key is private, so only Alice can compute $[C]_{\text{Alice}}$ or $[M]_{\text{Alice}}$. The implication is that anyone can encrypt a message for Alice, but only Alice can decrypt the ciphertext. In terms of signing, only Alice can sign M, but, since the public key is public, anyone can verify the signature. We'll have more to say about signatures and verification after we discuss hash functions in the next chapter.

4.7 Uses for Public Key Crypto

Anything you can do with a symmetric cipher you can do with public key crypto, only slower. This includes confidentiality, in the form of transmitting data over an insecure channel or securely storing data on an insecure media. We can also use public key crypto for integrity—a signature plays the role of a MAC in the symmetric case.

In addition, there are things that we can do with public keys that have no analog in the symmetric crypto world. Specifically, public key crypto offers

---

[9]Actually, this is not the correct way to digitally sign a message; see Section 5.2 of Chapter 5.

two major advantages over symmetric key crypto. The first is that, with public key crypto, we don't need to established a shared key in advance.[10] The second major advantage is that digital signatures provide integrity (see Problem 35) and non-repudiation. We look a little closer at these two topics below.

4.7.1   Confidentiality in the Real World

The primary advantage of symmetric key cryptography over public key is efficiency.[11] In the realm of confidentiality, the primary advantage of public key cryptography is the fact that no shared key is required.

Is it possible to get the best of both worlds? That is, can we have the efficiency of symmetric key crypto and yet not have to share keys in advance? The answer is an emphatic yes. The way to achieve this highly desirable result is with a *hybrid cryptosystem*, where public key crypto is used to establish a symmetric key and the resulting symmetric key is then used to encrypt the data. A hybrid cryptosystem is illustrated in Figure 4.4.

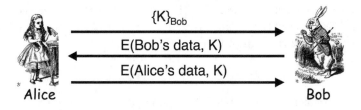

Figure 4.4: Hybrid Cryptosystem

The hybrid cryptosystem in Figure 4.4 is only for illustrative purposes. In fact, Bob has no way to know that he's talking to Alice—since anyone can do public key operations—so he would be foolish to encrypt sensitive data and send it to "Alice" following this protocol. We'll have much more to say about secure authentication and key establishment protocols in upcoming chapters. Hybrid crypto (with secure authentication) is widely used in practice today.

4.7.2   Signatures and Non-repudiation

As mentioned above, a digital signature can be used for integrity. Recall that a MAC is a way to provide integrity that uses a symmetric key. So, a signature is as good as a MAC when it comes to integrity. In addition, a digital

---

[10]Of course, we do need to get the private keys to the participants beforehand, so the key distribution problem has not been completely eliminated—it has just taken on a different form.

[11]A secondary benefit is that no public key infrastructure, or PKI, is required. We'll discuss PKI below.

signature provides *non-repudiation*, which is something that symmetric keys by their very nature cannot provide.

To understand non-repudiation, let's first consider an integrity example in the symmetric key case. Suppose Alice orders 100 shares of stock from her favorite stockbroker, Bob. To ensure the integrity of her order, Alice computes a MAC using a shared symmetric key K_{AB}. Now suppose that shortly after Alice places the order—but before she has paid any money to Bob—the stock loses all of its value. At this point Alice could claim that she did not place the order, that is, she could *repudiate* the transaction.

Can Bob prove that Alice placed the order? If all he has is the MAC, then he cannot. Since Bob also knows the symmetric key K_{AB}, he could have forged the message in which "Alice" placed the order. Note that Bob knows that Alice placed the order (since he didn't forge it), but he can't prove it in a court of law.

Now consider the same scenario, but suppose Alice uses a digital signature instead of a MAC. As with the MAC, the signature provides an integrity check. Again, suppose that the stock loses its value and Alice tries to repudiate the transaction. Can Bob prove that the order came from Alice? Yes he can, since only Alice has access to her private key.[12] Therefore, digital signatures provide integrity and non-repudiation, while a MAC can only be used for integrity. This is simply due to the fact that the symmetric key is known to both Alice and Bob, whereas Alice's private key is only known to Alice.[13] We'll have more to say about signatures and integrity in the next chapter.

4.7.3 Confidentiality and Non-repudiation

Suppose that Alice and Bob have public keys available and Alice wants to send a message M to Bob. For confidentiality, Alice would encrypt M with Bob's public key, and for integrity and non-repudiation, Alice can sign M with her private key. But suppose that Alice, who is very security conscious, wants both confidentiality and non-repudiation. Then she can't just sign M as that will not provide confidentiality, and she can't just encrypt M as that won't provide integrity. The solution seems straightforward enough—Alice can sign and encrypt the message before sending it to Bob, that is,

$$\{[M]_{\text{Alice}}\}_{\text{Bob}}.$$

---

[12]Of course, we are assuming that Alice's private key has not been lost or compromised. In any case, if the keys are in the wrong hands then all bets are off.

[13]One may be the loneliest number, but when it comes to non-repudiation, two is much worse than one.

Or would it be better for Alice to encrypt M first and then sign the result? That is, should Alice compute

$$[\{M\}_{\text{Bob}}]_{\text{Alice}}$$

instead? Can the order possibly matter? Is this something that only an anal-retentive cryptographer could care about?

Let's consider a couple of different scenarios, similar to those found in [77]. First, suppose that Alice and Bob are romantically involved. Alice decides to send the message

$$M = \text{``I love you''}$$

to Bob and she decides to use the sign and encrypt approach. So, Alice sends Bob the message

$$\{[M]_{\text{Alice}}\}_{\text{Bob}}.$$

Subsequently, Alice and Bob have a lovers' tiff and Bob, in an act of spite, decrypts the signed message to obtain $[M]_{\text{Alice}}$ and re-encrypts it using Charlie's public key, that is,

$$\{[M]_{\text{Alice}}\}_{\text{Charlie}}.$$

Bob then sends this message to Charlie, as illustrated in Figure 4.5. Of course, Charlie thinks that Alice is in love with him, which causes a great deal of embarrassment for both Alice and Charlie, much to Bob's delight.

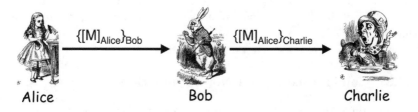

Figure 4.5: Pitfall of Sign and Encrypt

Alice, having learned her lesson from this bitter experience, vows to never sign and encrypt again. When she wants confidentiality and non-repudiation, Alice will always encrypt then sign.

Some time later, after Alice and Bob have resolved their earlier issues, Alice develops a great new theory that she wants to communicate to Bob. This time her message is [55]

$$M = \text{``Brontosauruses are thin at one end, much much thicker}$$
$$\text{in the middle, then thin again at the other end''},$$

which she dutifully encrypts then signs

$$[\{M\}_{\text{Bob}}]_{\text{Alice}}$$

before sending it to Bob.

However, Charlie, who is still angry with Bob and Alice, has set himself up as a man-in-the-middle so that he is able to intercept all traffic between Alice and Bob. Charlie knows that Alice is working on a great new theory, and he also knows that Alice only encrypts important messages. Charlie suspects that this encrypted and signed message is important and somehow related to Alice's important new theory. So, Charlie uses Alice's public key to compute $\{M\}_{\text{Bob}}$, which he then signs before sending it to Bob, that is, Charlie sends

$$[\{M\}_{\text{Bob}}]_{\text{Charlie}}$$

to Bob. This scenario is illustrated in Figure 4.6.

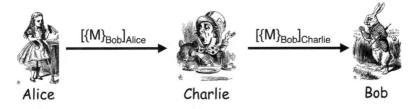

Figure 4.6: Pitfall of Encrypt and Sign

When Bob receives the message from Charlie, he assumes that this great new theory is Charlie's, and he immediately gives Charlie a promotion. When Alice learns that Charlie has taken credit for her great new theory, she swears never to encrypt and sign again.

Note that in the first scenario, Charlie assumed that $\{[M]_{\text{Alice}}\}_{\text{Charlie}}$ must have been sent from Alice to Charlie. That's not a valid assumption— Charlie's public key is public, so anyone could have done the encryption. In fact, the only thing Charlie really knows is that at some point Alice signed M. The problem here is that Charlie has apparently forgotten that public keys are public.

In the second scenario, Bob assumed that $[\{M\}_{\text{Bob}}]_{\text{Charlie}}$ must have originated with Charlie, which is also not a valid assumption. Again, since public keys are public, anybody could've encrypted M with Bob's public key. It is true that Charlie must have signed this encrypted message, but that does not imply that Charlie actually encrypted it (or even knows what the plaintext message says).

In both of these cases, the underlying problem is that the recipient does not clearly understand the way that public key cryptography works. There are some inherent limitations to public key crypto, most of which are due to the fact that anyone can do public key operations, that is, anyone can encrypt a message and anyone can verify a signature. This fact can be a source of confusion if you are not careful.

4.8   Public Key Infrastructure

A *public key infrastructure*, or PKI, is the sum total of everything required
to securely use public keys in the real world. It's surprisingly difficult and
involved to assemble all of the necessary pieces of a PKI into a working whole.
For a discussion of some of the risks inherent in PKI, see [101].

A *digital certificate* (or public key certificate or, for short, certificate)
contains a user's name along with the user's public key and this is signed by
a *certificate authority*, or CA. For example, Alice's certificate contains[14]

$$M = (\text{``Alice''}, \text{Alice's public key}) \quad \text{and} \quad S = [M]_{\text{CA}}.$$

To verify this certificate, Bob would compute $\{S\}_{\text{CA}}$ and verify that this
matches M.

The CA acts as a *trusted third party*, or TTP. By signing the certificate,
the CA is vouching for the fact it gave the corresponding private key to Alice.
That is, the CA created a public and private key pair and it put the public
key in Alice's certificate. Then the CA signed the certificate (using its private
key) and it gave the private key to Alice. If you trust the CA, you believe
that it actually gave the private key to Alice, and not to anyone else.

A subtle but important point here is that the CA is *not* vouching for the
identity of the holder of the certificate. Certificates act as public keys and,
consequently, they are public knowledge. So, for example, Trudy could send
Alice's public key to Bob and claim to be Alice. Bob must not fall for this
trick.

When Bob receives a certificate, he must verify the signature. If the
certificate is signed by a CA that Bob trusts, then he uses that CA's public
key for verification. On the other hand, if Bob does not trust the CA, then
the certificate is useless to him. Anyone can create a certificate and claim to
be anyone else. Bob must trust the CA and verify the signature before he
can assume the certificate is valid.

But what exactly does it mean for Alice's certificate to be valid? And
what useful information does this provide to Bob? Again, by signing the
certificate, the CA is vouching for the fact that it gave the private key to
Alice, and not to anyone else. In other words, the public key in the certificate
is actually Alice's public key, in the sense that Alice—and only Alice—has
the corresponding private key.

To finish beating this dead horse, after verifying the signature, Bob trusts
that Alice has the corresponding private key. It's critical that Bob does not
assume anything more than this. For example, Bob learns nothing about the

---

[14]This formula is slightly simplified. Actually, we also need to use a hash function when
we sign, but we don't yet know about hash functions. We'll give the precise formula for
digital signatures in the next chapter. Regardless, this simplified signature illustrates all of
the important concepts related to certificates.

sender of the certificate—certificates are public information, so anyone could have sent it to Bob. In later chapters we'll discuss security protocols, where we will see how Bob can use a valid certificate to verify the identity of the sender, but that requires more than simply verifying the signature on the certificate.

In addition to the required public key, a certificate could contain just about any other information that is deemed useful to the participants. However, the more information, the more likely the certificate will become invalid. For example, it might be tempting for a corporation to include the employee's department and phone number in a certificate. But then the inevitable reorganization will invalidate the certificate.

If a CA makes a mistake, the consequences can be dire. For example, VeriSign[15] once issued a signed certificate for Microsoft to someone else [136], that is, VeriSign gave the private key to someone other than Microsoft. That "someone else" could then have acted (electronically, that is) as Microsoft. This particular error was quickly detected, and the certificate was revoked, apparently before any damage was done.

This raises an important PKI issue, namely, *certificate revocation*. Certificates are usually issued with an expiration date. But if a private key is compromised, or it is discovered that a certificate was issued in error, the certificate must be revoked immediately. Most PKI schemes require periodic distribution of certificate revocation lists, or CRLs, which are supposed to be used to filter out compromised certificates. In some situations, this could place a significant burden on users, which could to lead to mistakes and security flaws.

To summarize, any PKI must deal with the following issues:

- Key generation and management

- Certificate authorities (CAs)

- Certificate revocation

Next, we'll briefly discuss a few of the many PKI *trust models* that are used today. The basic issue is deciding who you are willing to trust as a CA. Here, we follow the terminology in [162].

Perhaps the most obvious trust model is the *monopoly model*, where one universally trusted organization is the CA for the known universe. This approach is naturally favored by whoever happens to be the biggest commercial CA at the time (currently, VeriSign). Some have suggested that the government should play the role of the monopoly CA. However, believe it or not, many people don't trust the government.

---

[15]Today, VeriSign is the largest commercial source for digital certificates [316].

One major drawback to the monopoly model is that it creates a big target for attack. If the monopoly CA is ever compromised, the entire PKI system fails. And if you don't trust the CA, then the system is useless for you.

The *oligarchy model* is one step away from the monopoly model. In this model, there are multiple trusted CAs. In fact, this is the approach that is used today—a Web browser might be configured with 80 or more CA certificates. A security-conscious user such as Alice is free to decide which of the CAs she is willing to trust and which she is not. On the other hand, a more typical user like Bob will trust whatever CAs are configured in the default settings on his browser.

At the opposite extreme from the monopoly model is the *anarchy model*. In this model, anyone can be a CA, and it's up to the users to decide which CAs they want to trust. In fact, this approach is used in PGP, where it goes by the name "web of trust."

The anarchy model can place a significant burden on users. For example, suppose you receive a certificate signed by Frank and you don't know Frank, but you do trust Bob and Bob says Alice is trustworthy and Alice vouches for Frank. Should you trust Frank? This is clearly beyond the patience of the average user, who is likely to simply trust everybody or nobody so as to avoid headaches like this.

There are many other PKI trust models, most of which try to provide reasonable flexibility while putting a minimal burden on end users. The fact that there is no generally agreed upon trust model is itself one of the major problems with PKI.

4.9   Summary

In this chapter, we've covered most of the most important public key crypto topics. We began with the knapsack, which has been broken, but provides a nice introductory example. We then discussed RSA and Diffie-Hellman in some detail.

We also discussed elliptic curve cryptography (ECC), which promises to play an ever-increasing role in the future. Remember that ECC is not a particular type of cryptosystem, but instead it offers another way to do the math in public key cryptography.

We then considered signing and non-repudiation, which are major benefits of public key cryptography. And we presented the idea of a hybrid cryptosystem, which is the way that public key crypto is used in the real world for confidentiality. We also discussed the critical—and often confused—topic of digital certificates. It is important to realize exactly what a certificate does and does not provide. Finally, we took a very brief look at PKI, which is often a major roadblock to the deployment of public key crypto.

This concludes our overview of public key cryptography. We will see many applications of public key crypto in later sections of the book. In particular, many of these topics will resurface when we discuss security protocols.

4.10 Problems

1. This problem deals with digital certificates (aka public key certificates).

   a. What information must a digital certificate contain?

   b. What additional information can a digital certificate contain?

   c. Why might it be a good idea to minimize the amount of information in a digital certificate?

2. Suppose that Bob receives Alice's digital certificate from someone claiming to be Alice.

   a. Before Bob verifies the signature on the certificate, what does he know about the identity of the sender of the certificate?

   b. How does Bob verify the signature on the certificate and what useful information does Bob gain by verifying the signature?

   c. After Bob verifies the signature on the certificate, what does he know about the identity of the sender of the certificate?

3. When encrypting, public key systems operate in a manner analogous to a block cipher in ECB mode. That is, the plaintext is chopped into blocks and each block is encrypted independently.

   a. Why is ECB mode a bad idea when encrypting with a block cipher? Why is a chaining mode, such as CBC, a much better way to use a block cipher?

   b. Why is it not necessary to perform any sort of chaining mode when using public key encryption?

   c. Could your reasoning in part b be applied to block ciphers? Why or why not?

4. Suppose Alice's RSA public key is (e, N) and her private key is d. Alice wants to sign the message M, that is, she wants to compute $[M]_{\text{Alice}}$. Give the mathematical formula that she will use.

5. In equation (4.3) we proved that RSA encryption works, that is, we showed $[\{M\}_{\text{Alice}}]_{\text{Alice}} = M$. Give the analogous proof that RSA signature verification works, that is, $\{[M]_{\text{Alice}}\}_{\text{Alice}} = M$.

6. Suppose that Alice's RSA public key is $(N, e) = (33, 3)$ and her private key is $d = 7$.

   a. If Bob encrypts the message $M = 19$ using Alice's public key, what is the ciphertext C? Show that Alice can decrypt C to obtain M.

   b. Let S be the result when Alice digitally signs the message $M = 25$. What is S? If Bob receives M and S, explain the process Bob will use to verify the signature and show that in this particular case, the signature verification succeeds.

7. Why is it a bad idea to use the same RSA key pair for both signing and decryption?

8. To speed up RSA, it is possible to choose $e = 3$ for all users. However, this creates the possibility of a cube root attack as discussed in this chapter.

   a. Explain the cube root attack and how to prevent it.

   b. For $(N, e) = (33, 3)$ and $d = 7$, show that the cube root attack works when $M = 3$ but not not when $M = 4$.

9. Recall that with the RSA public key system it is possible to choose the same encryption exponent, e, for all users. For the sake of efficiency, sometimes a common value of $e = 3$ is used. Assume this is the case.

   a. What is the cube root attack on RSA and when does it succeed?

   b. Give two different ways of preventing the cube root attack. Both of your proposed fixes must still provide improved efficiency over the case where a common encryption exponent $e = 3$ is not used.

10. Consider the RSA public key cryptosystem. The best generally known attack is to factor the modulus, and the best known factoring algorithm (for a sufficiently large modulus) is the number field sieve. In terms of bits, the work factor for the number field sieve is

$$f(n) = 1.9223 n^{1/3} (\log_2 n)^{2/3},$$

where n is the number of bits in the number being factored. For example, since $f(390) \approx 60$, the work required to factor a 390-bit RSA modulus is roughly equivalent to the work needed for an exhaustive search to recover a 61-bit symmetric key.

   a. Graph the function $f(n)$ for $1 \leq n \leq 10{,}000$.

   b. A 1024-bit RSA modulus N provides roughly the same security as a symmetric key of what length?

c. A 2048-bit RSA modulus N provides roughly the same security as a symmetric key of what length?

d. What size of modulus N is required to have security roughly comparable to a 256-bit symmetric key?

11. On the diagram of the Diffie-Hellman key exchange in Figure 4.1, clearly indicate which information is public and which is private.

12. Suppose Bob and Alice share a symmetric key K. Draw a diagram to illustrate a variant of the Diffie-Hellman key exchange between Bob and Alice that prevents the man-in-the-middle attack.

13. Consider the Diffie-Hellman key exchange protocol. Suppose that Alice sends her Diffie-Hellman value, $g^a \bmod p$, to Bob. Further, suppose that Bob wants the resulting shared secret to be a specific value X. Can Bob choose his Diffie-Hellman value so that, following the protocol, Alice will compute the shared secret X? If so, provide precise details and if not, why not?

14. Suppose that Alice and Bob share a 4-digit PIN number, X. To establish a shared symmetric key, Bob proposes the following protocol: Bob will generate a random key K that he will encrypt using the PIN number X, that is, $E(K, X)$. Bob will send $E(K, X)$ to Alice, who will decrypt it using the shared PIN number X to obtain K. Alice and Bob will then use the symmetric key K to protect their subsequent conversation. However, Trudy can easily determine K by a brute force attack on the PIN number X, so this protocol is insecure. Modify the protocol to make it more secure. Note that Alice and Bob only share the 4-digit PIN number X and they do not have access to any other symmetric key or public keys. Hint: Use Diffie-Hellman.

15. A digital signature provides for data integrity and a MAC provides for data integrity. Why does a signature also provides for non-repudiation while a MAC does not?

16. A hybrid cryptosystem uses both public key and symmetric key cryptography to obtain the benefits of each.

a. Illustrate a hybrid system using Diffie-Hellman as the public key system and DES as the symmetric cipher.

b. Illustrate a hybrid system using RSA as the public key system and AES as the symmetric cipher.

17. Illustrate a man-in-the-middle attack on the ECC version of Diffie-Hellman.

18. Suppose that Alice signs the message $M =$ "I love you" and then encrypts it with Bob's public key before sending it to Bob. As discussed in the text, Bob can decrypt this to obtain the signed message and then encrypt the signed message with, say, Charlie's public key and forward the resulting ciphertext to Charlie. Could Alice prevent this "attack" by using symmetric key cryptography?

19. When Alice sends a message M to Bob, she and Bob agree to use the following protocol:

    (i) Alice computes $S = [M]_{\text{Alice}}$.

    (ii) Alice sends (M, S) to Bob.

    (iii) Bob computes $V = \{S\}_{\text{Alice}}$.

    (iv) Bob accepts the signature as valid provided $V = M$.

    With this protocol it's possible for Trudy to forge Alice's signature on a random "message" as follows. Trudy generates a value R. She then computes $N = \{R\}_{\text{Alice}}$ and sends (N, R) to Bob. Following the protocol above, Bob computes $V = \{R\}_{\text{Alice}}$ and, since $V = N$, Bob accepts the signature. Bob then believes that Alice sent him the signed nonsense "message" N. As a result, Bob gets very annoyed with Alice.

    a. Is this attack a serious concern, or just an annoyance? Justify your answer.

    b. Suppose we modify the protocol as follows:

       (i) Alice computes $S = [F(M)]_{\text{Alice}}$.

       (ii) Alice sends (M, S) to Bob.

       (iii) Bob computes $V = \{S\}_{\text{Alice}}$.

       (iv) Bob accepts the signature as valid provided $V = F(M)$.

       What conditions must the function F satisfy so as to prevent this annoying attack?

20. Suppose that Bob's knapsack private key consists of $(3, 5, 10, 23)$ along with the multiplier $m^{-1} = 6$ and modulus $n = 47$.

    a. Find the plaintext given the ciphertext $C = 20$. Give your answer in binary.

    b. Find the plaintext given the ciphertext $C = 29$. Give your answer in binary.

    c. Find m and the public key.

21. Suppose that for the knapsack cryptosystem, the superincreasing knapsack is $(3, 5, 12, 23)$ with $n = 47$ and $m = 6$.

    a. Give the public and private keys.

    b. Encrypt the message $M = 1110$ (given in binary). Give your result in decimal.

22. Consider the knapsack cryptosystem. Suppose the public key consists of $(18, 30, 7, 26)$ and $n = 47$.

    a. Find the private key, assuming $m = 6$.

    b. Encrypt the message $M = 1101$ (given in binary). Give your result in decimal.

23. Prove that for the knapsack cryptosystem, it is always possible to decrypt the ciphertext in linear time, provided that you know the private key.

24. For the knapsack example given in the text, the ciphertext was not reduced modulo n.

    a. Show that for the specific example given in this chapter, the knapsack also works if the ciphertext is reduced modulo n.

    b. Show that this is always the case, that is, show that it makes no difference to the recipient whether the ciphertext was reduced modulo n or not.

    c. Is either case (reducing the ciphertext modulo n or not) preferable from Trudy's perspective?

25. The man-in-the-middle attack on Diffie-Hellman is illustrated in Figure 4.2. Suppose that Trudy wants to establish a single Diffie-Hellman value, $g^{abt} \bmod p$, that she, Alice, and Bob all share. Does the attack illustrated below succeed? Justify your answer.

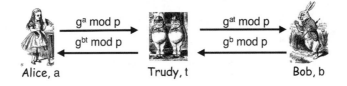

26. This problem deals with Diffie-Hellman.

    a. Why is $g = 1$ not an allowable choice for g?

    b. Why is $g = p - 1$ not an allowable choice for g?

27. In RSA, a common encryption exponent of $e = 3$ or $e = 2^{16} + 1$ is sometimes used. The RSA math will also works if we use a common decryption exponent of, say, $d = 3$. Why would it be a bad idea to use $d = 3$ as a common decryption exponent? Can you find a secure common decryption exponent d? Explain.

28. If Trudy can factor the modulus N, then she can break the RSA public key cryptosystem. The complexity class for the factorization problem is not known. Suppose that someone proves that integer factorization is a "really hard problem," in the sense that it belongs to a class of (apparently) intractable problems. What would be the practical importance of such a discovery?

29. In the RSA cryptosystem, it is possible that $M = C$, that is, the plaintext and the ciphertext may be identical.

    a. Is this a security concern in practice?

    b. For modulus $N = 3127$ and encryption exponent $e = 17$, find at least one message M that encrypts to itself.

30. Suppose that Bob uses the following variant of RSA. He first chooses N, then he finds two encryption exponents e_0 and e_1 and the corresponding decryption exponents d_0 and d_1. He asks Alice to encrypt her message M to him by first computing $C_0 = M^{e_0} \bmod N$, then encrypting C_0 to obtain the ciphertext, $C_1 = C_0^{e_1} \bmod N$. Alice then sends C_1 to Bob. Does this double encryption increase the security as compared to a single RSA encryption? Why or why not?

31. Alice receives a single ciphertext C from Bob, which was encrypted using Alice's RSA public key. Let M be the corresponding plaintext. Alice challenges Trudy to recover M under the following rules. Alice sends C to Trudy, and Alice agrees to decrypt one ciphertext that was encrypted with Alice's public key, provided that it is not C, and give the resulting plaintext to Trudy. Is it possible for Trudy to recover M?

32. Suppose that you are given the following RSA public keys, which are of the form (e, N).

User name	Public key
Alice	$(3, 5356488760553659)$
Bob	$(3, 8021928613673473)$
Charlie	$(3, 56086910298885139)$

You also know that Dave has encrypted the same message M (without padding) using each of these public keys, where the message, which contains only uppercase and lowercase English letters, is encoded with the method[16] used at [144]. Suppose that Dave's ciphertext messages are the following:

Recipient	Ciphertext
Alice	4324345136725864
Bob	2102800715763550
Charlie	46223668621385973

   a. Use the Chinese Remainder Theorem to find M.

   b. Are there other feasible ways to find M?

33. As mentioned in this chapter, "textbook" RSA is subject to a forward search attack. An easy way to prevent this attack is to pad the plaintext with random bits before encrypting. This problem shows that there is another RSA issue that is also prevented by padding the plaintext. Suppose that Alice's RSA public key is (N, e) and her private key is d. Bob encrypts the message M (without padding) using Alice's public key to obtain the ciphertext $C = M^e \bmod N$. Bob sends C to Alice and, as usual, Trudy intercepts C.

   a. Suppose that Alice will decrypt one message of Trudy's choosing, provided that it is not C. Show that Trudy can easily determine M. Hint: Trudy chooses r and asks Alice to decrypt the ciphertext $C' = Cr^e \bmod N$.

   b. Why is this "attack" prevented by padding the message?

34. Suppose that Trudy obtains two RSA ciphertext messages, both of which were encrypted with Alice's public key, that is, $C_0 = M_0^e \bmod N$ and $C_1 = M_1^e \bmod N$. Trudy does not know Alice's private key or either plaintext message.

   a. Show that Trudy can easily determine $(M_0 \cdot M_1)^e \bmod N$.

   b. Can Trudy also determine $(M_0 + M_1)^e \bmod N$?

   c. Due to the property in part a, RSA is said to be *homomorphic* with respect to multiplication. Recently, a fully homomorphic encryption scheme has been demonstrated, that is, the multiplicative homomorphic property (part a) and the additive homomorphic property (part b) both hold [67]. Discuss some significant potential uses for a practical fully homomorphic encryption scheme.

---

[16]Note that at [144], letters are encoded in the following nonstandard way: Each lowercase letter is converted to its uppercase ASCII equivalent, and uppercase letters are converted to (decimal) according to A = 33, B = 34, ..., Z = 58.

35. This problem deals with digital signatures.

    a. How and why does a digital signature provide integrity?

    b. How and why does a digital signature provide non-repudiation?

36. In the context of cryptography,

    a. Define non-repudiation.

    b. Give an example—different from the one given in this chapter—where non-repudiation is critical.

37. A digital signature or a MAC can be used to provide a cryptographic integrity check.

    a. Suppose that Alice and Bob want to use a cryptographic integrity check. Which would you recommend that they use, a MAC or a digital signature? Why?

    b. Suppose that Alice and Bob require a cryptographic integrity check and they also require non-repudiation. Which would you recommend that Alice and Bob use, a MAC or a digital signature? Why?

38. Alice wants to be "extra secure," so she proposes to Bob that they compute a MAC, then digitally sign the MAC.

    a. Does Alice's method provide a cryptographic integrity check? Why or why not?

    b. Does Alice's method provide for non-repudiation? Why or why not?

    c. Is Alice's method a good idea? Why or why not?

39. In this chapter, we showed that you can prevent a forward search attack on a public key cryptosystem by padding with random bits.

    a. Why would we like to minimize the amount of random padding?

    b. How many bits of random padding are needed? Justify your answer.

    c. Other than padding, is there another simple and practical method for preventing a forward search attack?

40. Consider the elliptic curve

$$E: \quad y^2 = x^3 + 7x + b \ (\text{mod } 11).$$

    a. Determine b so that the point $P = (4, 5)$ is on the curve E.

    b. Using the b found in part a, list all points on E.

c. Using the b found in part a, find the sum $(4, 5) + (5, 4)$ on E.

d. Using the b found in part a, find the point $3(4, 5)$.

41. Consider the elliptic curve

$$E : \quad y^2 = x^3 + 11x + 19 \pmod{167}.$$

a. Verify that the point $P = (2, 7)$ is on E.

b. Suppose this E and $P = (2, 7)$ are used in an ECC Diffie-Hellman key exchange, where Alice chooses the secret value $A = 12$ and Bob chooses the secret value $B = 31$. What value does Alice send to Bob? What does Bob send to Alice? What is the shared secret?

42. The Elgamal digital signature scheme employs a public key consisting of the triple (y, p, g) and a private key x, where these numbers satisfy

$$y = g^x \bmod p. \tag{4.9}$$

To sign a message M, choose a random number k such that k has no factor in common with $p - 1$ and compute

$$a = g^k \bmod p.$$

Then find a value s that satisfies

$$M = xa + ks \bmod (p - 1)$$

which is easy to do using the Euclidean Algorithm. The signature is verified provided that

$$y^a a^s = g^M \bmod p. \tag{4.10}$$

a. Select values (y, p, g) and x that satisfy equation (4.9). Choose a message M, compute the signature, and verify that equation (4.10) holds.

b. Prove that the math in Elgamal works, that is, prove that equation (4.10) always holds for appropriately chosen values. Hint: Use Fermat's Little Theorem, which states that if p is prime and p does not divide z, then $z^{p-1} = 1 \bmod p$.

Chapter 5

Hash Functions++

"I'm sure [my memory] only works one way." Alice remarked.
"I can't remember things before they happen."
"It's a poor sort of memory that only works backwards," the Queen remarked.
"What sort of things do you remember best?" Alice ventured to ask.
"Oh, things that happened the week after next,"
the Queen replied in a careless tone.
— Lewis Carroll, *Through the Looking Glass*

A boat, beneath a sunny sky
Lingering onward dreamily
In an evening of July —

Children three that nestle near,
Eager eye and willing ear,

$\vdots$

— Lewis Carroll, *Through the Looking Glass*

5.1   Introduction

This chapter covers cryptographic hash functions, followed by a brief discussion of a few crypto-related odds and ends. At first glance, cryptographic hash functions seem to be fairly esoteric. However, these functions turn out to be surprisingly useful in a surprisingly wide array of information security contexts. We consider the standard uses for cryptographic hash functions (digital signatures and hashed MACs), as well as a couple of non-standard but clever uses for hash functions (online bids and spam reduction). These two examples represent the tip of the iceberg when it comes to clever uses for hash functions.

There exists a semi-infinite supply of crypto-related side issues that could reasonably be covered here. To keep this chapter to a reasonable length, we only discuss a handful of these many interesting and useful topics, and each of these is only covered briefly. The topics covered include secret sharing (with a quick look at the related subject of visual cryptography), cryptographic random numbers, and information hiding (i.e., steganography and digital watermarks).

5.2   What is a Cryptographic Hash Function?

In computer science, "hashing" is an overloaded term. In cryptography, hashing has a very precise meaning, so for the time being, it would be best to forget about any other concepts of hashing that may be clouding your mind.

A *cryptographic hash function* $h(x)$ must provide all of the following.

- Compression — For any size input x, the output length of $y = h(x)$ is small. In practice, the output is a fixed size (e.g., 160 bits), regardless of the length of the input.

- Efficiency — It must be easy to compute $h(x)$ for any input x. The computational effort required to compute $h(x)$ will, of course, grow with the length of x, but it cannot grow too fast.

- One-way — Given any value y, it's computationally infeasible to find a value x such that $h(x) = y$. Another way to say this is that there is no feasible way to invert the hash.

- Weak collision resistance — Given x and $h(x)$, it's infeasible to find any y, with $y \neq x$, such that $h(y) = h(x)$. Another way to state this requirement is that it is not feasible to modify a message without changing its hash value.

- Strong collision resistance — It's infeasible to find any x and y, such that $x \neq y$ and $h(x) = h(y)$. That is, we cannot find any two inputs that hash to the same output.

Many collisions must exist since the input space is much larger than the output space. For example, suppose a particular hash function generates a 128-bit output. If we consider, say, all possible 150-bit input values then, on average, 2^{22} (that is, more than 4,000,000) of these input values hash to each possible output value. The collision resistance properties says that *all* of these collisions are computationally hard to find. This is asking a lot, and it might seem that, as a practical matter, no such function could possibly exist. Remarkably, practical cryptographic hash functions do indeed exist.

Hash functions are extremely useful in security. One particularly important use of hash functions arises in the computation of digital signatures. In the previous chapter, we said that Alice signs a message M by using her private key to "encrypt," that is, she computes $S = [M]_{\text{Alice}}$. If Alice sends M and S to Bob, then Bob can verify the signature by verifying that $M = \{S\}_{\text{Alice}}$. However, if M is large, $[M]_{\text{Alice}}$ is costly to compute—not to mention the bandwidth needed to send M and S, which are both large. In contrast, when computing a MAC, the encryption is fast and we only need to send the message along with few additional check bits (i.e., the MAC).

Suppose Alice has a cryptographic hash function h. Then $h(M)$ can be viewed as a "fingerprint" of the file M, that is, $h(M)$ is much smaller than M but it identifies M. If M' differs from M, even by just a single bit, then the hashes will almost certainly differ.[1] Furthermore, the collision resistance properties imply that it is not feasible to replace M with any different message M' such that $h(M) = h(M')$.

Now, given a cryptographic function h, Alice will sign M by first hashing M then signing the hash, that is, Alice computes $S = [h(M)]_{\text{Alice}}$. Hashes are efficient (comparable to block cipher algorithms), and only a small number of bits need to be signed, so the efficiency here is comparable to that of a MAC.

Then Alice can send Bob M and S, as illustrated in Figure 5.1. Bob verifies the signature by hashing M and comparing the result to the value obtained when Alice's public key is applied to S. That is, Bob verifies that $h(M) = \{S\}_{\text{Alice}}$. Note that only the message M and a small number of additional check bits, namely S, need to be sent from Alice to Bob. Again, this compares favorably to the overhead required when a MAC is used.

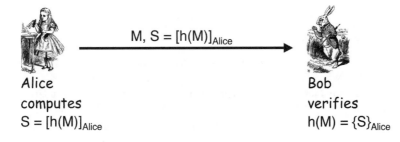

$$M, S = [h(M)]_{\text{Alice}}$$

Alice   Bob

computes   verifies

$S = [h(M)]_{\text{Alice}}$ $h(M) = \{S\}_{\text{Alice}}$

Figure 5.1: The Correct Way to Sign

Is this new-and-improved signature scheme secure? Assuming there are no collisions, signing $h(M)$ is as good as signing M. In fact, it is actually

---

[1] What if the hash values should happen to be the same? Well, then you have found a collision, which means that you've broken the hash function and you are henceforth a famous cryptographer, so it's a no-lose situation.

more secure to sign the hash than to just sign the message itself. But it is important to realize that the security of the signature now depends on the security of both the public key system and the hash function—if either is weak, the signature scheme can be broken. These and other issues are considered in the homework problems at the end of this chapter.

5.3   The Birthday Problem

The so-called birthday problem is a fundamental issue in many areas of cryptography. We discuss it here, since it's particularly relevant to hashing.

Before we get to the birthday problem, we first consider the following warm-up exercise. Suppose you are in a room with N other people. How large must N be before you expect to find at least one other person with the same birthday as you? An equivalent way to state this is: How large must N be before the probability that someone has the same birthday as you is greater than $1/2$? As with many discrete probability calculations, it's easier to compute the probability of the complement, that is, the probability that none of the N people has the same birthday as you, and subtract the result from one.

Your birthday is on one particular day of the year. If a person does not have the same birthday as you, his or her birthday must be on one of the other 364 days. Assuming all birthdays are equally likely, the probability that a randomly selected person does not have the same birthday as you is $364/365$. Then the probability that all N people do not have the same birthday as you is $(364/365)^N$ and, consequently, the probability that at least one person has the same birthday as you is

$$1 - (364/365)^N.$$

Setting this expression equal to $1/2$ and solving for N, we find $N = 253$. Since there are 365 days in a year, we might expect the answer to be on the order of 365, which it is, so this seems plausible.

Now we consider the real birthday problem. Again, suppose there are N people in a room. We want to answer the question: How large must N be before we expect two or more people will have the same birthday? In other words, how many people must be in the room so that the probability is greater than $1/2$ that two or more have the same birthday? As usual, it's easier to solve for the probability of the complement and subtract that result from one. In this case, the complement is that all N people have different birthdays.

Number the N people in the room $1, 2, 3, \ldots, N$. Person 1 has a birthday on one of the 365 days of the year. If all people have different birthdays, then person 2 must have a birthday that differs from person 1, that is, person 2 can have a birthday on any of the remaining 364 days. Similarly, person 3 can have a birthday on any of the remaining 363 days, and so on. Assuming that all birthdays are equally likely, and taking the complement, the probability of interest is

$$1 - 365/365 \cdot 364/365 \cdot 363/365 \cdots (365 - N + 1)/365.$$

Setting this expression equal to $1/2$ and solving for N, we find $N = 23$.

The birthday problem is often referred to as the *birthday paradox*, and at first glance it does seem paradoxical that with only 23 people in a room, we expect to find two or more with the same birthday. However, a few moments' thought makes the result much less paradoxical. In this problem, we are comparing the birthdays of all pairs of people. With N people in a room, the number of comparisons is $N(N-1)/2 \approx N^2$. Since there are only 365 different possible birthdays, we expect to find a match, roughly, when $N^2 = 365$, that is, when $N = \sqrt{365} \approx 19$. Viewed in this light, the birthday paradox is not so paradoxical.

What do birthdays have to do with cryptographic hash functions? Suppose that a hash function $h(x)$ produces an output that is N bits long. Then there are 2^N different possible hash values. For a good cryptographic hash function, we would expect that all output values are (more or less) equally likely. Then, since $\sqrt{2^N} = 2^{N/2}$, the birthday problem immediately implies that if we hash about $2^{N/2}$ different inputs, we can expect to find a collision, that is, we expect to find two inputs that hash to the same value. This brute force method of breaking a hash function is analogous to an exhaustive key search attack on a symmetric cipher.

The implication here is that a secure hash that generates an N-bit output can be broken with a brute force work factor of about $2^{N/2}$. In contrast, a secure symmetric key cipher with a key of length N can be broken with a work factor of 2^{N-1}. Consequently, the output of a hash function must be about twice the number of bits as a symmetric cipher key for an equivalent level of security—assuming both are secure, i.e., no shortcut attack exists for either.

5.4 A Birthday Attack

The role of hashing in digital signature computations was discussed above. Recall that if M is the message that Alice wants to sign, then she computes $S = [h(M)]_{\text{Alice}}$ and sends S and M to Bob.

Suppose that the hash function h generates an n-bit output. As discussed in [334], Trudy can, in principle, conduct a birthday attack as follows.

- Trudy selects an "evil" message E that she wants Alice to sign, but which Alice is unwilling to sign. For example, the message might state that Alice agrees to give all of her money to Trudy.

- Trudy also creates an innocent message I that she is confident Alice is willing to sign. For example, this could be a routine message of the type that Alice regularly signs.

- Then Trudy generates $2^{n/2}$ variants of the innocent message by making minor editorial changes. These innocent messages, which we denote I_i, for $i = 0, 1, \ldots, 2^{n/2} - 1$, all have the same meaning as I, but since the messages differ, their hash values differ.

- Similarly, Trudy creates $2^{n/2}$ variants of the evil message, which we denoted E_i, for $i = 0, 1, \ldots, 2^{n/2} - 1$. These messages all convey the same meaning as the original evil message E, but their hashes differ.

- Trudy hashes all of the evil messages E_i and all of the innocent messages I_i. By the birthday problem, she can expect to find a collision, say, $h(E_j) = h(I_k)$. Given such a collision, Trudy sends I_k to Alice, and asks Alice to sign it. Since this message appears to be innocent, Alice signs it and returns I_k and $[h(I_k)]_{\text{Alice}}$ to Trudy. Since $h(E_j) = h(I_k)$, it follows that $[h(E_j)]_{\text{Alice}} = [h(I_k)]_{\text{Alice}}$ and, consequently, Trudy has, in effect, obtained Alice's signature on the evil message E_j.

Note that, in this attack, Trudy has obtained Alice's signature on a message of Trudy's choosing without attacking the underlying public key system in any way. This attack is a brute force attack on the hash function h, as it is used for computing digital signatures. To prevent this attack, we could choose a hash function for which n, the size of the hash function output, is so large that Trudy cannot compute $2^{n/2}$ hashes.

5.5 Non-Cryptographic Hashes

Before looking into the inner workings of a specific cryptographic hash function, we'll first consider a few simple non-cryptographic hashes. Many non-cryptographic hashes have their uses, but none is suitable for cryptographic applications.

Consider the data

$$X = (X_0, X_1, X_2, \ldots, X_{n-1}),$$

where each X_i is a byte. We can define a hash function $h(X)$ by

$$h(X) = (X_0 + X_1 + X_2 + \cdots + X_{n-1}) \bmod 256.$$

This certainly provides compression, since any size of input is compressed to an 8-bit output. However, hash would be easy to break (in the crypto sense), since the birthday problem tells us that if we hash just $2^4 = 16$ randomly selected inputs, we can expect to find a collision. In fact, it's even worse than that, since collisions are easy to construct directly. For example, swapping two bytes will always yield a collision, such as

$$h(10101010, 00001111) = h(00001111, 10101010) = 10111001.$$

Not only is the hash output length too small, but the algebraic structure inherent in this approach is a fundamental weakness.

As another example of a non-cryptographic hash, consider the following. Again, we write the data as bytes,

$$X = (X_0, X_1, X_2, \ldots, X_{n-1}).$$

Here, we'll define the hash $h(X)$ as

$$h(X) = (nX_0 + (n-1)X_1 + (n-2)X_2 + \ldots + 2X_{n-2} + X_{n-1}) \bmod 256.$$

Is this hash secure? At least it gives different results when the byte order is swapped, for example,

$$h(10101010, 00001111) \neq h(00001111, 10101010).$$

But, again, we still have the birthday problem issue and it also happens to be relatively easy to construct collisions. For example,

$$h(00000001, 00001111) = h(00000000, 00010001) = 00010001.$$

Despite the fact that this is not a secure cryptographic hash, it's useful in a particular non-cryptographic application known as Rsync; see [253] for the details.

An example of a non-cryptographic hash that is sometimes mistakenly used as a cryptographic hash is the cyclic redundancy check, or CRC [326]. The CRC calculation is essentially long division, with the remainder acting as the CRC "hash" value. In contrast to ordinary long division, in a CRC we use XOR in place of subtraction.

In a CRC calculation, the divisor is specified as part of the algorithm and the data acts as the dividend. For example, suppose the given divisor is 10011 and the data of interest happens to be 10101011. Then we append four 0s to the data (one less than the number of bits in the divisor) and do the long division as follows:

```
                                  10110110
                        10011 ) 101010110000
                                10011
                                ─────
                                 11001
                                 10011
                                 ─────
                                  10101
                                  10011
                                  ─────
                                   11000
                                   10011
                                   ─────
                                    10110
                                    10011
                                    ─────
                                     1010
```

The CRC checksum is the remainder of the long division—in this case, 1010. For this choice of divisor, it's easy to find collisions, and in fact it's easy to construct collisions for any CRC [290].

WEP [38] mistakenly uses a CRC checksum where a cryptographic integrity check is required. This flaw opens the door to many attacks on the protocol. CRCs and similar checksum methods are only designed to detect transmission errors—not to detect intentional tampering with the data. That is, random transmission errors will almost certainly be detected (within certain parameters), but an intelligent adversary can easily change the data so that the CRC value is unchanged and, consequently, the tampering will go undetected. In cryptography, we must protect against an intelligent adversary (Trudy), not just random acts of nature.

5.6   Tiger Hash

Now we turn our attention to a specific cryptographic hash algorithm known as Tiger. While Tiger is not a particularly popular hash, it is a little easier to digest than some of the big-name hashes.

Before diving into to inner workings of Tiger, it is worth mentioning a bit about the two most popular cryptographic hashes of today. Until recently, the most popular hash in the world was undoubtedly MD5. The "MD" in MD5 does not stand for Medicinae Doctor, but instead it is an abbreviation for message digest. Believe it or not, MD5 is the successor to MD4, which itself was the successor to MD2. The earlier MDs are no longer considered secure, due to the fact that collisions have been found. In fact, MD5 collisions are easy to find—you can generate one in a few seconds on a PC [244].[2] All of the MDs were invented by crypto guru Ron Rivest. MD5 produces a 128-bit output.

---

[2]See Problem 25 for an example of an MD5 collision.

The other contender for title of world's most popular hash function is SHA–1 which is a U.S. government standard. Being a government standard, SHA is, of course, a clever 3-letter acronym—SHA stands for Secure Hash Algorithm. You might ask, why is it SHA–1 instead of just SHA? In fact, there was a SHA (now known as SHA–0), but it apparently had a minor flaw, as SHA–1 came quickly on the heels of SHA, with some minor modifications but without explanation.

The SHA–1 algorithm is actually very similar to MD5. The major practical difference between the two is that SHA–1 generates a 160-bit output, which provides a significant margin of safety over MD5. Cryptographic hash functions such as MD5 and SHA–1 hash messages in blocks, where each block passes through some number of rounds. In this sense, they're very reminiscent of block ciphers. For the details on these two hash functions, a good source is Schneier [258].

A hash function is considered secure provided no collisions have been found. As with block ciphers, efficiency is also a major concern in the design of hash functions. If, for example, it's more costly to compute the hash of M than to sign M, the hash function is not very useful, at least for digital signatures.

A desirable property of any cryptographic hash function is the so-called *avalanche effect*. The goal is that any small change in the input should cascade and cause a large change in the output—just like an avalanche. Ideally, any change in the input will result in output values that are uncorrelated, and an attacker will then be forced to conduct an exhaustive search for collisions.

The avalanche effect should occur after a few rounds, yet we would like the rounds to be as simple and efficient as possible. In a sense, the designers of hash functions face similar trade-offs as the designers of iterated block ciphers.

The MD5 and SHA–1 algorithms are not particularly enlightening, as they both seem to consist of a more-or-less random collection of transformations. Instead of discussing either of these in detail, we'll look closely at the Tiger hash. Tiger, which was developed by Ross Anderson and Eli Biham, seems to have a more structured design than SHA–1 or MD5. In fact, Tiger can be given in a form that looks very similar a block cipher [10].

Tiger was designed to be "fast and strong" and hence the name. It was also designed for optimal performance on 64-bit processors and it can serve as a replacement for MD5, SHA–1, or any other hash with an equal or smaller output.[3]

Like MD5 and SHA–1, the input to Tiger is divided into 512-bit blocks, with the input padded to a multiple of 512 bits, if necessary. Unlike MD5 or

---

[3]For any secure hash, you can truncate the output to produce a smaller hash value. There can be no shortcut attack on any subset of the bits, otherwise there would be a shortcut attack on the full-sized hash.

SHA–1, the output of Tiger is 192 bits. The numerology behind the choice of 192 is that Tiger is designed for 64-bit processors and 192 bits is exactly three 64-bit words. In Tiger, all intermediate steps also consist of 192 bit values.

Tiger's block cipher influence can be seen in the fact that it employs four S-boxes, each of which maps 8 bits to 64 bits. Tiger also employs a "key schedule" algorithm that, since there is no key, is applied to the input block, as described below.

The input X is padded to a multiple of 512 bits and written as

$$X = (X_0, X_1, \ldots, X_{n-1}), \tag{5.1}$$

where each X_i is 512 bits. The Tiger algorithm employs one *outer round* for each X_i, where one such round is illustrated in Figure 5.2. Each of a, b, and c in Figure 5.2 is 64 bits and the initial values of (a, b, c) for the first round are, in hex:

$$a = \text{0x0123456789ABCDEF}$$
$$b = \text{0xFEDCBA9876543210}$$
$$c = \text{0xF096A5B4C3B2E187}$$

The final (a, b, c) output from one round is the initial triple for the subsequent round and the final (a, b, c) from the final round is the 192-bit hash value. From this perspective, Tiger indeed looks very much like a block cipher.

Notice that the input to the first outer round F_5 is (a, b, c). Labeling the output of F_5 as (a, b, c), the input to F_7 is (c, a, b). Similarly, if we label the output of F_7 as (a, b, c), then the input to F_9 is (b, c, a). Each function F_m in Figure 5.2 consists of eight *inner rounds* as illustrated in Figure 5.3. We let W denote the 512 bit input to the inner rounds, where

$$W = (w_0, w_1, \ldots, w_7),$$

with each w_i being 64 bits. Note that all lines in Figure 5.3 represent 64 bit quantities.

The input values for the $f_{m,i}$, for $i = 0, 1, 2, \ldots, 7$, are

$$(a, b, c), (b, c, a), (c, a, b), (a, b, c), (b, c, a), (c, a, b), (a, b, c), (b, c, a),$$

respectively, where the output of $f_{m,i-1}$ is labeled (a, b, c). Each $f_{m,i}$ depends on a, b, c, w_i, and m, where w_i is the ith 64-bit sub-block of the 512-bit input W. The subscript m of $f_{m,i}$ is a multiplier, as discussed below.

We write c as

$$c = (c_0, c_1, \ldots, c_7),$$

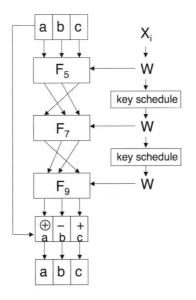

Figure 5.2: Tiger Outer Round

where each c_i is a single byte. Then $f_{m,i}$ is given by

$$c = c \oplus w_i$$
$$a = a - (S_0[c_0] \oplus S_1[c_2] \oplus S_2[c_4] \oplus S_3[c_6])$$
$$b = b + (S_3[c_1] \oplus S_2[c_3] \oplus S_1[c_5] \oplus S_0[c_7])$$
$$b = b \cdot m$$

where each S_i is an S-box (i.e., lookup table) mapping 8 bits to 64 bits. These S-boxes are large, so we won't list them here—for more details on the S-boxes, see [10].

The only remaining item to discuss is the so-called *key schedule*. Let W be the 512-bit input to the key schedule algorithm. As above, we write W as $W = (w_0, w_1, \ldots, w_7)$ where each w_i is 64 bits. Let $\bar{w}_i$ be the binary complement of w_i. Then the key schedule is given in Table 5.1, where the output is given by the final $W = (w_0, w_1, \ldots, w_7)$.

To summarize, the Tiger hash consists of 24 rounds, which can be viewed as three outer rounds, each of which has eight inner rounds. All intermediate hash values are 192 bits.

It's claimed that the S-boxes are designed so that each input bit affects each of a, b, and c after just three of the 24 rounds. Also, the key schedule algorithm is designed so that any small change in the message will affect many bits in the intermediate hash values. The multiplication in the final

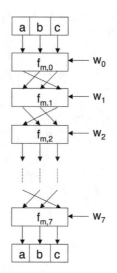

Figure 5.3: Tiger Inner Round for F_m

step of $f_{m,i}$ is also a critical feature of the design. Its purpose is to ensure that each input to an S-box in one round is mixed into many S-boxes in the next round. Together, the S-boxes, key schedule, and multiply ensure a strong avalanche effect [10].

Tiger clearly borrows many ideas from block cipher design, including S-boxes, multiple rounds, mixed mode arithmetic, a key schedule, and so on. At a higher level, we can even say that Tiger employs Shannon's principles of confusion and diffusion.

5.7 HMAC

Recall that for message integrity we can compute a message authentication code, or MAC, where the MAC is computed using a block cipher in CBC mode. The MAC is the final encrypted block, which is also known as the CBC residue. Since a hash function effectively gives us a fingerprint of a file, we should also be able to use a hash to verify message integrity.

Can Alice protect the integrity of M by simply computing $h(M)$ and sending both M and $h(M)$ to Bob? Note that if M changes, Bob will detect the change, provided that $h(M)$ has not changed (and vice versa). However, if Trudy replaces M with M' and also replaces $h(M)$ with $h(M')$, then Bob will have no way to detect the tampering. All is not lost—we can use a hash function to provide integrity protection, but it must involve a key to prevent

Table 5.1: Tiger "Key Schedule"

$$w_0 = w_0 - (w_7 \oplus \texttt{0xA5A5A5A5A5A5A5A5})$$
$$w_1 = w_1 \oplus w_0$$
$$w_2 = x_2 + w_1$$
$$w_3 = w_3 - (w_2 \oplus (\bar{w}_1 \ll 19))$$
$$w_4 = w_4 \oplus w_3$$
$$w_5 = w_5 + w_4$$
$$w_6 = w_6 - (w_5 \oplus (\bar{w}_4 \gg 23))$$
$$w_7 = w_7 \oplus w_6$$
$$w_0 = w_0 + w_7$$
$$w_1 = w_1 - (w_0 \oplus (\bar{w}_7 \ll 19))$$
$$w_2 = w_2 \oplus w_1$$
$$w_3 = w_3 + w_2$$
$$w_4 = w_4 - (w_3 \oplus (\bar{w}_2 \gg 23))$$
$$w_5 = w_5 \oplus w_4$$
$$w_6 = w_6 + w_5$$
$$w_7 = w_7 - (w_6 \oplus \texttt{0x0123456789ABCDEF})$$

Trudy from changing the hash value.[4] Perhaps the most obvious approach would be to have Alice encrypt the hash value with a symmetric cipher, $E(h(M), K)$, and send this to Bob. However, a slightly different approach is actually used to compute a *hashed MAC*, or HMAC.

Instead of encrypting the hash, we directly mix the key into M when computing the hash. How should we mix the key into the HMAC? Two obvious approaches are to prepend the key to the message, or append the key to the message: $h(K, M)$ and $h(M, K)$, respectively. Surprisingly, both of these methods create the potential for subtle attacks.

Suppose we choose to compute an HMAC as $h(K, M)$. Most cryptographic hashes hash the message in blocks—for MD5, SHA–1, and Tiger, the block size is 512 bits. As a result, if $M = (B_1, B_2)$, where each B_i is 512 bits, then

$$h(M) = F(F(A, B_1), B_2) = F(h(B_1), B_2) \qquad (5.2)$$

for some function F, where A is a fixed initial constant. For example, in the Tiger hash, the function F consists of the outer rounds illustrated in Figure 5.2, with each B_i corresponding to a 512-bit block of input and A corresponding to the 192-bit initial value (a, b, c).

If Trudy chooses M' so that $M' = (M, X)$, Trudy might be able to use equation (5.2) to find $h(K, M')$ from $h(K, M)$ without knowing K since,

---

[4]Yet another example of the "no free lunch" principle...

for K, M, and X of the appropriate size,

$$h(K, M') = h(K, M, X) = F(h(K, M), X), \qquad (5.3)$$

where the function F is known.

So, is $h(M, K)$ a better choice? It does prevent the previous attack. However, if it should happen that there is a known collision for the hash function h, that is, if there exists some M' with $h(M') = h(M)$, then by equation (5.2), we have

$$h(M, K) = F(h(M), K) = F(h(M'), K) = h(M', K) \qquad (5.4)$$

provided that M and M' are each a multiple of the block size. Perhaps this is not as serious of a concern as the previous case—if such a collision exists, the hash function is considered insecure. But we can easily eliminate any potential for this attack, so we should do so.

In fact, we can prevent both of these potential problems by using a slightly more sophisticated method to mix the key into the hash. As described in RFC 2104 [174], the approved method for computing an HMAC is as follows.[5] Let B be the block length of hash, in bytes. For all popular hashes (MD5, SHA–1, Tiger, etc.), $B = 64$. Next, define

$$\text{ipad} = \texttt{0x36} \text{ repeated } B \text{ times}$$

and

$$\text{opad} = \texttt{0x5C} \text{ repeated } B \text{ times.}$$

Then the HMAC of M is defined to be

$$\text{HMAC}(M, K) = H(K \oplus \text{opad}, H(K \oplus \text{ipad}, M)).$$

This approach thoroughly mixes the key into the resulting hash. While two hashes are required to compute an HMAC, note that the second hash will be computed on a small number of bits—the output of the first hash with the modified key appended. So, the work to compute these two hashes is only marginally more than the work needed to compute $h(M)$.

An HMAC can be used to protect message integrity, just like a MAC or digital signature. HMACs also have several other uses, some of which

---

[5]RFCs exist for a reason, as your author discovered when he was asked to implement an HMAC. After looking up the definition of the HMAC in a reputable book (which shall remain nameless) and writing code to implement the algorithm, your careful author decided to have a peek at RFC 2104. To his surprise, this supposedly reputable book had a typo, meaning that his HMAC would have failed to work with any correctly implemented HMAC. If you think that RFCs are nothing more than the ultimate cure for insomnia, you are mistaken. Yes, most RFCs do seem to be cleverly designed to maximize their sleep-inducing potential but, nevertheless, they just might save your job.

we'll mention in later chapters. It is worth noting that in some applications, some people (including your occasionally careless author) get sloppy and use a "keyed hash" instead of an HMAC. Generally, a keyed hash is of the form $h(M, K)$. But, at least for message integrity, you should definitely stick with the RFC-approved HMAC.

5.8   Uses for Hash Functions

Some standard applications that employ hash functions include authentication, message integrity (using an HMAC), message fingerprinting, error detection, and digital signature efficiency. There are a large number of additional clever and sometimes surprising uses for cryptographic hash functions. Below we'll consider two interesting examples where hash functions can be used to solve security-related problems. It also happens to be true that anything you can do with a symmetric key cipher, you can do with a cryptographic hash function, and vice versa. That is, in some abstract sense, symmetric ciphers and hash functions are equivalent. Nevertheless, as a practical matter, it is useful to have both symmetric ciphers and hash functions.

Next, we briefly consider the use of hash functions to securely place bids online. Then we'll discuss an interesting approach to spam reduction that relies on hashing.

5.8.1   Online Bids

Suppose an item is for sale online and Alice, Bob, and Charlie all want to place bids. The idea here is that these are supposed to be sealed bids, that is, each bidder gets one chance to submit a secret bid and only after all bids have been received are the bids revealed. As usual, the highest bidder wins.

Alice, Bob, and Charlie don't necessarily trust each other and they definitely don't trust the online service that accepts the bids. In particular, each bidder is understandably concerned that the online service might reveal their bid to the other bidders—either intentionally or accidentally. For example, suppose Alice places a bid of $10.00 and Bob bids $12.00. If Charlie is able to discover the values of these bids prior to placing his bid (and prior to the deadline for bidding), he could bid $12.01 and win. The point here is that nobody wants to be the first (or second) to place their bid, since there might be an advantage to bidding later.

In an effort to allay these fears, the online service proposes the following scheme. Each bidder will determine their bids, say, bid A for Alice, bid B for Bob, and C for Charlie, keeping their bids secret. Then Alice will submit $h(A)$, Bob will submit $h(B)$, and Charlie will submit $h(C)$. Once all three hashed bids have been received, the hash values will be posted online for all to see. At this point all three participants will submit their actual bids, that is, A, B, and C.

Why is this better than the naïve scheme of submitting the bids directly? If the cryptographic hash function is secure, it's one-way, so there appears to be no disadvantage to submitting a hashed bid prior to a competitor. And since it is infeasible to determine a collision, no bidder can change their bid after submitting their hash value. That is, the hash value binds the bidder to his or her original bid, without revealing any information about the bid itself. If there is no disadvantage in being the first to submit a hashed bid, and there is no way to change a bid once a hash value has been submitted, then this scheme prevents the cheating that could have resulted following the naïve approach.

However, this online bidding scheme has a problem—it is subject to a forward search attack. Fortunately, there is an easy fix that will prevent a forward search, with no cryptographic keys required (see Problem 17 at the end of this chapter).

5.8.2 Spam Reduction

Another interesting use of hashing arises in the following proposed spam reduction technique. Spam is defined as unwanted and unsolicited bulk email.[6] In this scheme, Alice will refuse to accept an email until she has proof that the sender expended sufficient effort to create the email. Here, "effort" will be measured in terms of computing resources, in particular, CPU cycles. For this to be practical, it must be easy for the recipient, Alice, to verify that a sender did indeed do the work, yet it must not be feasible for the sender to cheat by not doing the required work. Note that such a scheme would not eliminate spam, but it would limit the amount of such email that any user can send.

Let M be an email message and let T be the current time. The message M includes the sender's and intended recipient's email addresses, but does not include any additional addresses. The sender of message M must determine a value R such that

$$h(M, R, T) = (\underbrace{00\ldots0}_{N}, X). \tag{5.5}$$

That is, the sender must find a value R so that the hash in equation (5.5) has zeros in all of its first N output bits. Once this is done, the sender sends the triple (M, R, T). Before Alice, the recipient, accepts the email, she needs to verify that the time T is recent, and that $h(M, R, T)$ begins with N zeros.

Again, the sender chooses random values R and hashes each until he finds a hash value that begins with N zeros. Therefore, the sender will need to

---

[6]Spam, Spam, Spam, Spam... lovely Spam! wonderful Spam! [55]

compute, on average, about 2^N hashes. On the other hand, the recipient can verify that $h(M, R, T)$ begins with N zeros by computing a single hash— regardless of the size of N. So the work for the sender (measured in terms of hashes) is about 2^N, while the work for the recipient is always a single hash. That is, the sender's work increases exponentially in N while the recipient's work is negligible, regardless of the value of N.

To make this scheme practical, we would need to choose N so that the work level is acceptable for normal email users but unacceptably high for spammers. With this scheme, it might also be possible for users to select their own individual value of N to match their personal tolerance for spam. For example, if Alice hates spam, she could choose, say, $N = 40$. While this would likely deter spammers, it might also deter many legitimate email senders. If Bob, on the other hand, doesn't mind receiving some spam and he never wants to deter a legitimate email sender, he might set his value to, say, $N = 10$.

Spammers are sure to dislike such a scheme. Legitimate bulk emailers also might not like this scheme, since they would need to spend resources (i.e., money) to compute vast numbers of hashes. In any case, this is a plausible approach to increasing the cost of sending bulk email.

5.9 Miscellaneous Crypto-Related Topics

In this section, we discuss a few interesting[7] crypto-related topics that don't fit neatly into the categories discussed so far. First, we'll consider Shamir's secret sharing scheme. This is a conceptually simple procedure that can be used to split a secret among users. We'll also discuss the related topic of visual cryptography.

Then we consider randomness. In crypto, we often need random keys, random large primes, and so on. We'll discuss some of the problems of actually generating random numbers and we present an example to illustrate a pitfall of poor random number selection.

Finally, we'll briefly consider the topic of information hiding, where the goal is to hide information[8] in other data, such as embedding secret information in a JPEG image. If only the sender and receiver know that information is hidden in the data, the information can be passed without anyone but the participants suspecting that communication has occurred. Information hiding is a large topic and we'll only scratch the surface.

---

[7]The topics are interesting to your narcissistic author, and that's all that really matters.
[8]Duh!

5.9.1 Secret Sharing

Suppose Alice and Bob want to share a secret S in the sense that:

- Neither Alice nor Bob alone (nor anyone else) can determine S with a probability better than guessing.

- Alice and Bob together can easily determine S.

At first glance, this seems to present a difficult problem. However, it's easily solved, and the solution essentially derives from the fact that two points determine a line. Note that we call this a secret sharing scheme, since there are two participants and both must cooperate to recover the secret S.

Suppose the secret S is a real number. Draw a line L in the plane through the point $(0, S)$ and give Alice a point $A = (X_0, Y_0)$ on L and give Bob another point $B = (X_1, Y_1)$, which also lies on the line L. Then neither Alice nor Bob individually has any information about S, since an infinite number of lines pass through a single point. But together, the two points A and B uniquely determine L, and therefore the y-intercept, and hence the value S. This example is illustrated in the "2 out of 2" scheme that appears in Figure 5.4.

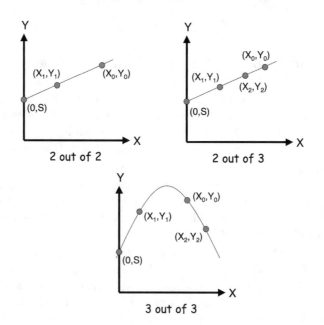

Figure 5.4: Secret Sharing Schemes

It's easy to extend this idea to an "m out of n" secret sharing scheme, for any $m \leq n$, where n is the number of participants, any m of which can cooperate to recover the secret. For $m = 2$, a line always works. For example, a "2 out of 3" scheme appears in Figure 5.4.

A line, which is a polynomial of degree one, is uniquely determined by two points, whereas a parabola, which is a polynomial of degree two, is uniquely determined by three points. In general, a polynomial of degree $m - 1$ is uniquely determined by m points. This elementary fact is what allows us to construct an m out of n secret sharing scheme for any $m \leq n$. For example, a "3 out of 3" scheme is illustrated in Figure 5.4. The general "m out of n" concept should now be clear.

Since we want to store these quantities on computers, we would like to deal with discrete quantities instead of real numbers. Fortunately, this secret sharing scheme works equally well if the arithmetic is done modulo p [264]. This elegant and secure secret sharing concept is due to the "S" in RSA (Shamir, that is). The scheme is said to be absolutely secure or information theoretic secure (see Problem 34) and it doesn't get any better than that.

5.9.1.1 Key Escrow

One particular application where secret sharing would be useful is in the *key escrow* problem [85, 86]. Suppose that we require users to store their keys with an official escrow agency. The government could then get access to keys as an aid to criminal investigations.[9] Some people (mostly in the government), once viewed key escrow as a desirable way to put crypto into a similar category as, say, traditional telephone lines, which can be tapped with a court order. At one time the U.S. government tried to promote key escrow and even went so far as to develop a system (Clipper and Capstone) that included key escrow as a feature.[10] The key escrow idea was widely disparaged, and it was eventually abandoned—see [59] for a brief history of the Clipper chip.

One concern with key escrow is that the escrow agency might not be trustworthy. It is possible to ameliorate this concern by having several escrow agencies and allow users to split the key among n of these, so that m of the n must cooperate to recover the key. Alice could, in principle, select escrow agencies that she considers most trustworthy and have her secret split among these using an m out of n secret sharing scheme.

Shamir's secret sharing scheme could be used to implement such a key escrow scheme. For example, suppose $n = 3$ and $m = 2$ and Alice's key is S. Then the "2 out of 3" scheme illustrated in Figure 5.4 could be used where, for example, Alice might choose to have the Department of Justice hold the point (X_0, Y_0), the Department of Commerce hold (X_1, Y_1), and Fred's Key

---

[9]Presumably, only with a court order.

[10]Some opponents of key escrow like to say that the U.S. government's attempt at key escrow failed because they tried to promote a security flaw as a feature.

Escrow, Inc., hold (X_2, Y_2). Then at least two of these three escrow agencies would need to cooperate to determine Alice's key S.

5.9.1.2   Visual Cryptography

Naor and Shamir [214] proposed an interesting visual secret sharing scheme. The scheme is absolutely secure, as is the polynomial-based secret sharing scheme discussed above. In visual secret sharing (aka visual cryptography), no computation is required to decrypt the underlying image.

In the simplest case, we start with a black-and-white image and create two transparencies, one for Alice and one for Bob. Each individual transparency appears to be a collection of random black and white subpixels, but if Alice and Bob overlay their transparencies, the original image appears (with some loss of contrast). In addition, either transparency alone yields no information about the underlying image.

How is this accomplished? Figure 5.5 shows various ways that an individual pixel can be split into "shares," where one share goes to Alice's transparency and the corresponding share goes to Bob's.

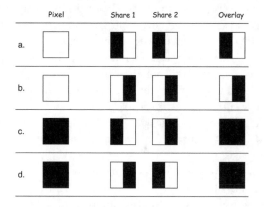

Figure 5.5: Pixel Shares

For example, if a specific pixel is white, then we can flip a coin to decide whether to use row "a" or row "b" from Figure 5.5. Then, say, Alice's transparency gets share 1 from the selected row (either a or b), while Bob's transparency gets share 2. Note that the shares are put in Alice's and Bob's transparencies at the same position corresponding to the pixel in the original image. In this case, when Alice's and Bob's transparencies are overlaid, the resulting pixel will be half-black/half-white. In the case of a black pixel, we flip a coin to select between rows "c" and "d" and we again use the selected row to determine the shares.

Note that if the original pixel was black, the overlaid shares always yield a black pixel. On the other hand, if the original pixel was white, the overlaid shares will yield a half-white/half-black pixel, which will be perceived as gray. This results in a loss of contrast (black and gray versus black and white), but the original image is still clearly discernible. For example, in Figure 5.6 we illustrate a share for Alice and a share for Bob, along with the resulting overlaying of the two shares. Note the loss of contrast, as compared to the original image.

Figure 5.6: Alice's Share, Bob's Share, and Overlay Image (Courtesy of Bob Harris)

The visual secret sharing example described here is a "2 out of 2" scheme. Similar techniques can be used to develop more general "m out of n" schemes. As mentioned above, the security of these schemes is absolute, in the same sense that secret sharing based on polynomials is absolutely secure (see Problem 36).

For a nice interactive example of visual secret sharing, see [141]. For more information on various technical aspects of visual cryptography, Stinson's website [292] is the place to go.

5.9.2   Random Numbers

In cryptography, random numbers are needed to generate symmetric keys, RSA key pairs (i.e., randomly selected large primes), and Diffie-Hellman secret exponents. In a later chapter, we'll see that random numbers have an important role to play in security protocols as well.

Random numbers are, of course, used in many non-security applications such as simulations and various statistical applications. In such cases, the random numbers usually only need to be statistically random, that is, they must be, in some statistical sense, indistinguishable from random.

However, *cryptographic random numbers* must be statistically random and they must also satisfy a much more stringent requirement—they must be unpredictable. Are cryptographers just being difficult (as usual) or is there a legitimate reason for demanding so much more of cryptographic random numbers?

To see that unpredictability is important in crypto applications, consider the following example. Suppose that a server generates symmetric keys for users. Further, suppose the following keys are generated for the listed users:

- K_A for Alice

- K_B for Bob

- K_C for Charlie

- K_D for Dave

Now, if Alice, Bob, and Charlie don't like Dave, they can pool their information to see if it will help them determine Dave's key. That is, Alice, Bob, and Charlie could use knowledge of their keys, K_A, K_B, and K_C, to see if it helps them determine Dave's key K_D. If K_D can be predicted from knowledge of the keys K_A, K_B, and K_C, then the security of the system is compromised.

Commonly used pseudo-random number generators are predictable, i.e., given a sufficient number of output values, subsequent values can be easily determined. Consequently, pseudo-random number generators are not appropriate for cryptographic applications.

5.9.2.1   Texas Hold 'em Poker

Now let's consider a real-world example that nicely illustrates the wrong way to generate random numbers. ASF Software, Inc., developed an online version of the card game known as Texas Hold 'em Poker [128]. In this game, each player is first dealt two cards, face down. Then a round of betting takes place, followed by three community cards being dealt face up—all players can see the community cards and use them in their hand. After another round of betting, one more community card is revealed, then another round of betting. Finally, a final community card is dealt, after which additional betting can occur. Of the players who remain at the end, the winner is the one who can make the best poker hand from his two cards together with the five community cards. The game is illustrated in Figure 5.7.

In an online version of the game, random numbers are required to shuffle a virtual deck of cards. The AFS poker software had a serious flaw in the way that random numbers were used to shuffle the deck of cards. As a result, the program did not produce a truly random shuffle, and it was possible for a player to determining the entire deck in real time. A player who

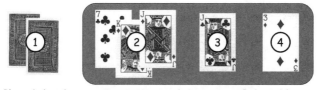

Player's hand   Community cards in center of the table

Figure 5.7: Texas Hold 'Em Poker

could take advantage of this flaw could cheat, since he would know all of the other players' hands, as well as the future community cards before they were revealed.

How was it possible to determine the shuffle? First, note that there are $52! > 2^{225}$ distinct shuffles of a 52-card deck. The AFS poker program used a "random" 32-bit integer to determine the shuffle. Consequently, the program could generate no more than 2^{32} different shuffles out of the more than 2^{225} possible. This was an inexcusable flaw, but if this was the only flaw, it would have likely remained a theoretical problem, not a practical attack.

To generate the "random" shuffle, the program used the pseudo-random number generator, or PRNG, built into the Pascal programming language. Furthermore, the PRNG was reseeded with each shuffle, with the seed value being a known function of the number of milliseconds since midnight. Since the number of milliseconds in a day is

$$24 \cdot 60 \cdot 60 \cdot 1000 < 2^{27},$$

less than 2^{27} distinct shuffles could actually occur.

Trudy, the attacker, could do even better. If she synchronized her clock with the server, Trudy could reduce the number of shuffles that needed to be tested to less than 2^{18}. These 2^{18} possible shuffles could all be generated in real time and tested against the community cards to determine the actual shuffle for the hand currently in play. In fact, after the first set of community cards were revealed, Trudy could determine the shuffle uniquely and she would then know the final hands of all other players—even before any of the other players knew their own final hand!

The AFS Texas Hold 'em Poker program is an extreme example of the ill effects of using predictable random numbers where unpredictable random numbers are required. In this example, the number of possible random shuffles was so small that it was possible to determine the shuffle and thereby break the system.

How can we generate cryptographic random numbers? Since a secure stream cipher keystream is not predictable, the keystream generated by, say, the RC4 cipher must be a good source of cryptographic random numbers. Of course, there's no free lunch, so the selection of the key—which is like the initial seed value for RC4—remains a critical issue.

5.9.2.2 Generating Random Bits

True randomness is not only hard to find, it's hard to define. Perhaps the best we can do is the concept of *entropy*, as developed by Claude Shannon. Entropy is a measure of the uncertainty or, conversely, the predictability of a sequence of bits. We won't go into the details here, but a good discussion of entropy can be found in [305].

Sources of true randomness do exist. For example, radioactive decay is random. However, nuclear computers are not very popular, so we'll need to find another source. Hardware devices are available that can be used to gather random bits based on various physical and thermal properties that are known to be unpredictable. Another source of randomness is the infamous lava lamp [200], which achieves its randomness from its chaotic behavior.

Since software is (hopefully) deterministic, true random numbers must be generated external to any code. In addition to the special devices mentioned above, reasonable sources of randomness include mouse movements, keyboard dynamics, certain network activity, and so on. It is possible to obtain some high-quality random bits by such methods, but the quantity of such bits is limited. For more information on these topics, see [134].

Randomness is an important and often overlooked topic in security. It's worth remembering that, "The use of pseudo-random processes to generate secret quantities can result in pseudo-security" [162].

5.9.3 Information Hiding

In this section we'll discuss the two faces of information hiding, namely, steganography and digital watermarking. Steganography, or hidden writing, is the attempt to hide the fact that information is being transmitted. Watermarks also generally involve hidden information, but for a slightly different purpose. For example, a copyright holder might hide a digital watermark (containing some identifying information) in digital music in a vain effort to prevent music piracy.[11]

Steganography has a long history, particularly in warfare—until modern times, steganography was used far more than cryptography. In a story related by Herodotus (circa 440 BC), a Greek general shaved the head of a slave and

---

[11]Apparently, the use of the word piracy in this context is supposed to conjure images of Blackbeard (complete with parrot and pegleg) viciously attacking copyright holders with swords and cannons. Of course, the truth is that the pirates are mostly just teenagers who—for better or for worse—have little or no concept of actually paying for music.

wrote a message on the slave's head warning of a Persian invasion. After his hair had grown back and covered the message, the slave was sent through enemy lines to deliver the message to another Greek general.[12]

The modern version of steganography involves hiding information in media such as image files, audio data, or even software [288]. This type of information hiding can also be viewed as a form of covert channel—a topic we'll return to when we discuss multilevel security in Chapter 8.

As mentioned above, digital watermarking is information hiding for a somewhat different purpose. There are several varieties of watermarks but one example consists of inserting an "invisible" identifier in the data. For example, an identifier could be added to digital music in the hope that if a pirated version of the music appears, the watermark could be read from it and the purchaser—and presumed pirate—could be identified. Such techniques have been developed for virtually all types of digital media, as well as for software. In spite of their obvious potential, digital watermarking has received only limited practical application, and there have been some spectacular failures [71].

Digital watermarks can be categorized in many different ways. For example, we can consider the following types of watermarks:

- *Invisible* — Watermarks that are not supposed to be perceptible in the media.

- *Visible* — Watermarks that are meant to be observed, such as a stamp of TOP SECRET on a document.

Watermarks can also be categorized as follows:

- *Robust* — Watermarks that are designed to remain readable even if they are attacked.

- *Fragile* — Watermarks that are supposed to be destroyed or damaged if any tampering occurs.

For example, we might like to insert a robust invisible mark in digital music in the hope of detecting piracy. Then when pirated music appears on the Internet, perhaps we can trace it back to its source. Or we might insert a fragile invisible mark into an audio file. In this case, if the watermark is unreadable, the recipient knows that tampering has occurred. This latter approach is essential an integrity check. Various other combinations of watermarks might also be considered.

Many modern currencies include (non-digital) watermarks. Several current and recent U.S. bills, including the $20 bill pictured in Figure 5.8, have

---

[12]To put this into terms that the reader will understand, the problem with this technique is that the bandwidth is too low...

visible watermarks. In this $20 bill, the image of President Jackson is embedded in the paper itself (in the right-hand section of the bill) and is visible when held up to a light. This visible watermark is designed to make counterfeiting more difficult, since special paper is required to duplicate this easily verified watermark.

Figure 5.8: Watermarked Currency

One example of an invisible watermarking scheme that has been proposed is to insert information into a photograph in such a way that if the photo were damaged it would be possible to reconstruct the entire image from a small surviving piece of the original [168]. It has been claimed that every square inch of a photo could contain enough information to reconstruct the entire photograph, without adversely affecting the quality of the image.

Now let's consider a concrete example of a simple approach to steganography. This particular example is applicable to digital images. For this approach, we'll use images that employ the well-known 24 bits color scheme—one byte each for red, green, and blue, denoted R, G, and B, respectively. For example, the color represented by $(R, G, B) = (0x7E, 0x52, 0x90)$ is much different than $(R, G, B) = (0xFE, 0x52, 0x90)$, even though the colors only differ by one bit. On the other hand, the color $(R, G, B) = (0xAB, 0x33, 0xF0)$ is indistinguishable from $(R, G, B) = (0xAB, 0x33, 0xF1)$, yet these two colors also differ by only a single bit. In fact, the low-order RGB bits are unimportant, since they represent imperceptible changes in color. Since the low-order bits don't matter, we can use them for any purposes we choose, including information hiding.

Consider the two images of Alice in Figure 5.9. The left-most Alice contains no hidden information, whereas the right-most Alice has the entire *Alice in Wonderland* book (in PDF format) embedded in the low-order RGB bits. To the human eye, the two images appear identical at any resolution. While this example is visually stunning, it's important to remember that if we compare the bits in these two images, the differences would be obvious. In particular, it's easy for an attacker to write a computer program to extract the low-order RGB bits—or to overwrite the bits with garbage and thereby destroy the hidden information, without doing any damage to the image. This example highlights one of the fundamental problems in information hiding, namely, that it is difficult to apply Kerckhoffs' Principle in a meaningful way without giving the attacker a significant advantage.

Figure 5.9: A Tale of Two Alices

Another simple steganography example might help to further demystify the concept. Consider an HTML file that contains the following text, taken from the well-known poem, "The Walrus and the Carpenter," [50] which appears in Lewis Carroll's *Through the Looking-Glass and What Alice Found There*:

"The time has come," the Walrus said,
"To talk of many things:
Of shoes and ships and sealing wax
Of cabbages and kings
And why the sea is boiling hot
And whether pigs have wings."

In HTML, the RGB font colors are specified by a tag of the form

```
<font color="#rrggbb"> ... </font>
```

where `rr` is the value of R in hexadecimal, `gg` is G in hex, and `bb` is B in hex. For example, the color black is represented by #000000, whereas white is #FFFFFF.

Since the low-order bits of R, G, and B won't affect the perceived color, we can hide information in these bits, as shown in the HTML snippet in

Table 5.2. Reading the low-order bits of the RGB colors yields the "hidden" information 110 010 110 011 000 101.

Table 5.2: Simple Steganography Example

```
<font color="#010100">"The time has come,"
                     the Walrus said,</font><br>
<font color="#000100">"To talk of many things:</font><br>
<font color="#010100">Of shoes and ships and sealing wax</font><br>
<font color="#000101">Of cabbages and kings</font><br>
<font color="#000000">And why the sea is boiling hot</font><br>
<font color="#010001">And whether pigs have wings."</font><br>
```

Hiding information in the low-order RGB bits of HTML `color` tags is obviously not as impressive as hiding *Alice in Wonderland* in Alice's image. However, the process is virtually identical in each case. Furthermore, neither method is at all robust—an attacker who knows the scheme can read the hidden information as easily as the recipient. Or an attacker could instead destroy the information by replacing the file with another one that is identical, except that the low-order RGB bits have been randomized. In the latter case, if the image is not being used to pass information, the attacker's actions are likely to go undetected since the appearance of the image contained in the file has not changed

It is tempting to hide information in bits that don't matter, since doing so will be invisible, in the sense that the content will not be affected. But relying only on the unimportant bits makes it easy for an attacker who knows the scheme to read or destroy the information. While the bits that don't matter in image files may not be as obvious to humans as low-order RGB bits in HTML tags, such bits are equally susceptible to attack by anyone who understands the image format.

The conclusion here is that for information hiding to be robust, the information must reside in bits that do matter. But this creates a serious challenge, since any changes to bits that do matter must be done very carefully for the information hiding to remain "invisible."

As noted above, if Trudy knows the information hiding scheme, she can recover the hidden information as easily as the intended recipient. Watermarking schemes therefore generally encrypt the hidden information before embedding it in a file. But even so, if Trudy understands how the scheme works, she can almost certainly damage or destroy the information. This fact has driven developers to rely on secret proprietary watermarking schemes, which runs contrary to the spirit of Kerckhoffs' Principle. This has, predictably, resulted in many approaches that fail badly when exposed to the light of day.

Further complicating the steganographer's life, an unknown watermarking scheme can often be diagnosed by a *collusion attack*. That is, the original object and a watermarked object (or several different watermarked objects) can be compared to determine the bits that carry the information and, in the process, the attacker can often learn something about how the scheme works. As a result, watermarking schemes often use spread spectrum techniques to better hide the information-carrying bits. Such approaches only make the attacker's job more difficult—they do not eliminate the threat. The challenges and perils of watermarking are nicely illustrated by the attacks on the Secure Digital Music Initiative, or SDMI, scheme, as described in [71].

The bottom line is that digital information hiding is much more difficult than it appears at first glance. Information hiding is an active research topic, and although none of the work to date has lived up to the hype, the implications of a robust scheme would be enormous. The field of information hiding is extremely old, but the digital version is relatively young, so there may still be hope for significant progress.

5.10 Summary

In this chapter, we discussed cryptographic hash functions in some detail. We described one specific hash algorithm (Tiger) and considered the correct way to compute a hashed MAC (HMAC). A couple of non-standard applications of hash functions were also discussed.

After covering hash functions, a few crypto-like topics that don't fit nicely into any of the other chapters were presented. Shamir's secret sharing scheme offers a secure method for sharing a secret in any m out of n arrangement. Naor and Shamir's visual cryptography provides a similarly secure means for sharing an image file. Random numbers, a topic that is of critical security importance, was also covered and we gave an example that illustrates the pitfalls of failing to use good random numbers.

The chapter concluded with a brief discussion of information hiding. Digital steganography and digital watermarking are both interesting and evolving fields with potential application to some very challenging security problems.

5.11 Problems

1. As discussed in this chapter, a cryptographic hash function must satisfy all of the following properties:

   - Compression
   - Efficiency
   - One-way

- Weak collision resistance
- Strong collision resistance

a. Suppose that a hash function fails to provide compression but provides all of the other required properties. Give an application where a cryptographic hash function should be used, but where this hash function would fail to be useful.

b. Repeat part a, but assume that all properties hold except for efficiency.

c. Repeat part a, but assume that all properties hold except for one-way.

d. Repeat part a, but assume that all properties hold except for the collision resistance properties.

2. Justify the following statements concerning cryptographic hash functions.

a. Strong collision resistance implies weak collision resistance.

b. Strong collision resistance does not imply one-way.

3. Suppose that a secure cryptographic hash function generates hash values that are n bits in length. Explain how a brute force attack could be implemented. What is the expected work factor?

4. How many collisions would you expect to find in the following cases?

a. Your hash function generates a 12-bit output and you hash 1024 randomly selected messages.

b. Your hash function generates an n-bit output and you hash m randomly selected messages.

5. Suppose that h is a secure hash that generates an n-bit hash value.

a. What is the expected number of hashes that must be computed to find one collision?

b. What is the expected number of hashes that must be computed to find 10 collisions? That is, what is the expected number of hashes that must be computed to find pairs (x_i, z_i) with $h(x_i) = h(z_i)$, for $i = 0, 1, 2, \ldots, 9$?

c. What is the expected number of hashes that must be computed to find m collisions?

6. A k-way collision is a set of values $x_0, x_1, \ldots, x_{k-1}$ that all hash to the same value, that is,

$$h(x_0) = h(x_1) = \cdots = h(x_{k-1}).$$

Suppose that h is a secure hash that generates an n-bit hash value.

   a. What is the expected number of hashes that must be computed to find one k-way collision?

   b. What is the expected number of hashes that must be computed to find two k-way collision?

   c. What is the expected number of hashes that must be computed to find m distinct k-way collisions?

7. Recall the digital signature birthday attack discussed in Section 5.4. Suppose we modify the hashing scheme as follows: Given a message M that Alice wants to sign, she randomly selects R, then she computes the signature as $S = [h(M, R)]_{\text{Alice}}$, and sends (M, R, S) to Bob. Does this prevent the attack? Why or why not?

8. Consider a CRC that uses the divisor 10011. Find two collisions with 10101011, that is, find two other data values that produce the same CRC checksum as 10101011.

9. Consider a CRC that uses the divisor 10011. Suppose the data value is 11010110. Trudy wants to change the data to 111*****, where "*" indicates that she doesn't care about the bit in that position, and she wants the resulting checksum to be the same as for the original data. Determine all data values Trudy could choose.

10. Fill in the number of bits on each line of the Tiger hash outer round in Figure 5.2.

11. Let h be the Tiger hash and let F be the Tiger outer round in Figure 5.2.

   a. For $M = (B_1, B_2, B_3)$, where each B_i is 512 bits, give the analog of equation (5.2).

   b. Now suppose $M = (B_1, B_2, \ldots, B_n)$ where each B_i is 512 bits. Show that $h(M) = F(h(B_1, B_2, \ldots, B_{n-1}), B_n)$.

12. A program implementing your crafty author's Bobcat hash algorithm can be found on the textbook website. This hash is essentially a scaled-down version of Tiger—whereas the Tiger hash produces a 192-bit output (three 64-bit words), the Bobcat hash produces a 48-bit value (three 16-bit words).

    a. Find a collision for the 12-bit version of Bobcat, where you truncate the 48-bit hash value to obtain a 12-bit hash. How many hashes did you compute before you found your first 12-bit collision?

    b. Find a collision for the full 48-bit Bobcat hash.

13. Alice likes to use the Tiger hash algorithm, which produces a 192-bit hash value. However, for a particular application, Alice only requires a 64-bit hash. Answer the following questions, assuming that the Tiger hash is secure.

    a. Is it safe for Alice to simply truncate the Tiger hash, that is, can she use the first 64 bits of the 192-bit output? Why or why not?

    b. Is it acceptable for Alice to take every third bit of the Tiger hash? Why or why not?

    c. Is it secure for Alice to take the three 64-bit words of the Tiger hash and XOR them together? Why or why not?

14. Consider equation (5.3).

    a. Show that the equation holds if K, M, and X are all multiples of the hash block length (commonly, 64 bytes).

    b. For which other sizes of K, M, and X does the equation hold?

    c. Show that equation (5.4) holds for any size of M, M', and K, provided that $h(M) = h(M')$.

15. Does a MAC work as an HMAC? That is, does a MAC satisfy the same properties that an HMAC satisfies?

16. Suppose that you know the output of an HMAC is X and the key is K, but you do not know the message M. Can you construct a message M' that has its HMAC equal to X, using the key K? If so, give an algorithm for constructing such a message. If not, why not? Note that we are assuming that you know the key K, and the same key is used for both HMAC computations. (It may be instructive to compare this problem to Problem 43 of Chapter 3.)

17. Recall the online bid method discussed in Section 5.8.1.

    a. What property or properties of a secure hash function h does this scheme rely on to prevent cheating?

    b. Suppose that Charlie is certain that Alice and Bob will both submit bids between $10,000 and $20,000. Describe a forward search attack that Charlie can use to determine Alice's bid and Bob's bid from their respective hash values.

    c. Is the attack in part b a practical security concern?

    d. How can the bidding procedure be modified to prevent a forward search such as that in part b?

18. Recall the spam reduction method discussed in Section 5.8.2.

    a. What property or properties of a secure hash function does this scheme rely on to reduce spam?

    b. In Section 5.8.2, it is stated that "The message M includes the sender's and intended recipient's email addresses, but does not include any additional addresses." Suppose we relax this so that we only require that the message M includes the intended recipient's email address. Find an attack on this modified spam reduction system, that is, show that a spammer could still send spam without doing a large amount of work.

19. Suppose that you have a secure block cipher, but no hash function. Also, no key is available. For simplicity, assume that the block cipher has key length and block length both equal to n.

    a. How can you use the block cipher as a cryptographic hash function, assuming that you only need to hash one block of exactly n bits?

    b. How can you use the block cipher as a cryptographic hash function when the message consists of multiple n-bit blocks?

20. Suppose that Alice wants to encrypt a message for Bob, where the message consists of three plaintext blocks, P_0, P_1, and P_2. Alice and Bob have access to a hash function and a shared symmetric key K, but no cipher is available. How can Alice securely encrypt the message so that Bob can decrypt it?

21. Alice's computer needs to have access to a symmetric key K_A. Consider the following two methods for deriving and storing the key K_A.

    (i) The key is generated as $K_A = h(\text{Alice's password})$. The key is not stored on Alice's computer. Instead, whenever K_A is required, Alice enters her password and the key is generated.

    (ii) The key K_A is initially generated at random, and it is then stored as $E(K_A, K)$, where $K = h(\text{Alice's password})$. Whenever K_A is required, Alice enters her password, which is hashed to generate K and K is then used to decrypt the key K_A.

Give one significant advantage of method (i) as compared to (ii), and one significant advantage of (ii) as compared to (i).

22. Suppose that Sally (a server) needs access to a symmetric key for user Alice and another symmetric key for Bob and another symmetric key for Charlie. Then Sally could generate symmetric keys K_A, K_B, and K_C and store these in a database. An alternative is *key diversification*, where Sally generates and stores a single key K_S. Then Sally generates the key K_A as needed by computing $K_A = h(\text{Alice}, K_S)$, with keys K_B and K_C generated in a similar manner. Give one significant advantage and one significant disadvantage of key diversification as compared to storing keys in a database.

23. We say that a function T is *incremental* if it satisfies the following property: Having once applied T to M, the time required to update the result upon modification of M is proportional to the amount of modification done to M. Suppose we have an incremental hash function H.

    a. Discuss one application where this incremental hash H would be superior to a standard (non-incremental) hash function.

    b. Suppose a message M can only be modified by appending more bits, that is, the modified message M' is $M' = (M, X)$, for some X. Given a cryptographic hash function h, define an incremental cryptographic hash function H based on h.

24. Suppose Bob and Alice want to flip a coin over a network. Alice proposes the following protocol.

    (i) Alice randomly selects a value $X \in \{0, 1\}$.

    (ii) Alice generates a 256-bit random symmetric key K.

    (iii) Using the AES cipher, Alice computes $Y = E(X, R, K)$, where R consists of 255 randomly selected bits.

    (iv) Alice sends Y to Bob.

    (v) Bob guesses a value $Z \in \{0, 1\}$ and tells Alice.

    (vi) Alice gives the key K to Bob who computes $(X, R) = D(Y, K)$.

    (vii) If $X = Z$ then Bob wins, otherwise Alice wins.

    This protocol is insecure.

    a. Explain how Alice can cheat.

    b. Using a cryptographic hash function h, modify this protocol so that Alice can't cheat.

25. The MD5 hash is considered broken, since collisions have been found and, in fact, a collision can be constructed in a few seconds on a

PC [244]. Find all bit positions where the following two messages differ.[13] Verify that the MD5 hashes of these two messages are the same.

```
00000000 d1 31 dd 02 c5 e6 ee c4   69 3d 9a 06 98 af f9 5c
00000010 2f ca b5 87 12 46 7e ab   40 04 58 3e b8 fb 7f 89
00000020 55 ad 34 06 09 f4 b3 02   83 e4 88 83 25 71 41 5a
00000030 08 51 25 e8 f7 cd c9 9f   d9 1d bd f2 80 37 3c 5b
00000040 96 0b 1d d1 dc 41 7b 9c   e4 d8 97 f4 5a 65 55 d5
00000050 35 73 9a c7 f0 eb fd 0c   30 29 f1 66 d1 09 b1 8f
00000060 75 27 7f 79 30 d5 5c eb   22 e8 ad ba 79 cc 15 5c
00000070 ed 74 cb dd 5f c5 d3 6d   b1 9b 0a d8 35 cc a7 e3
```

and

```
00000000 d1 31 dd 02 c5 e6 ee c4   69 3d 9a 06 98 af f9 5c
00000010 2f ca b5 07 12 46 7e ab   40 04 58 3e b8 fb 7f 89
00000020 55 ad 34 06 09 f4 b3 02   83 e4 88 83 25 f1 41 5a
00000030 08 51 25 e8 f7 cd c9 9f   d9 1d bd 72 80 37 3c 5b
00000040 96 0b 1d d1 dc 41 7b 9c   e4 d8 97 f4 5a 65 55 d5
00000050 35 73 9a 47 f0 eb fd 0c   30 29 f1 66 d1 09 b1 8f
00000060 75 27 7f 79 30 d5 5c eb   22 e8 ad ba 79 4c 15 5c
00000070 ed 74 cb dd 5f c5 d3 6d   b1 9b 0a 58 35 cc a7 e3
```

26. The MD5 collision in Problem 25 is said to be meaningless since the two messages appear to be random bits, that is, they do not carry any meaning. Currently, it is not possible to generate a meaningful collision using the MD5 collision attack. For this reason, it is sometimes claimed that MD5 collisions are not a significant security threat. The goal of this problem is convince you otherwise. Obtain the file MD5_collision.zip from the textbook website and unzip the folder to obtain the two Postscript files, rec2.ps and auth2.ps.

   a. What message is displayed when you view rec2.ps in a Postscript viewer? What message is displayed when you view auth2.ps in a Postscript viewer?

   b. What is the MD5 hash of rec2.ps? What is the MD5 hash of auth2.ps? Why is this a security problem? Give a specific attack that Trudy can easily conduct in this particular case. Hint: Consider a digital signature.

   c. Modify rec2.ps and auth2.ps so that they display different messages than they currently do, but they hash to the same value. What are the resulting hash values?

   d. Since it is not possible to generate a meaningful MD5 collision, how is it possible for two (meaningful) messages to have the same

---

[13]The left-most column represents the byte position (in hex) of the first byte in that row and is not part of the data. Also, the data itself is given in hexadecimal.

MD5 hash value? Hint: Postscript has a conditional statement of the form

$$(X)(Y)\text{eq}\{T_0\}\{T_1\}\text{ifelse}$$

where T_0 is displayed if the text X is identical to Y and T_1 is displayed otherwise.

27. Suppose that you receive an email from someone claiming to be Alice, and the email includes a digital certificate that contains

$$M = (\text{"Alice"}, \text{Alice's public key}) \quad \text{and} \quad [h(M)]_{\text{CA}},$$

where CA is a certificate authority.

    a. How do you verify the signature? Be precise.

    b. Why do you need to bother to verify the signature?

    c. Suppose that you trust the CA who signed the certificate. Then, after verifying the signature, you will assume that only Alice possesses the private key that corresponds to the public key contained in the certificate. Assuming that Alice's private key has not been compromised, why is this a valid assumption?

    d. Assuming that you trust the CA who signed the certificate, after verifying the signature, what do you know about the identity of the sender of the certificate?

28. Recall that we use both a public key system and a hash function when computing digital signatures.

    a. Precisely how is a digital signature computed and verified?

    b. Suppose that the public key system used to compute and verify signatures is insecure, but the hash function is secure. Show that you can forge signatures.

    c. Suppose that the hash function used to compute and verify signatures is insecure, but the public key system is secure. Show that you can forge signatures.

29. This problem deals with digital signatures.

    a. Precisely how is a digital signature computed and verified?

    b. Show that a digital signature provides integrity protection.

    c. Show that a digital signature provides non-repudiation.

30. Suppose that Alice wants to sign the message M and send the result to Bob.

    a. In terms of our standard notation, what does Alice compute?

    b. What does Alice send to Bob and how does Bob verify the signature?

31. In the previous chapter, we discussed the idea behind a forward search attack on a public key cryptosystems. In certain applications, a forward search attack can be used against a hash function.

    a. What is a forward search attack on public key encryption, and how is it prevented?

    b. Describe one plausible use for a hash function where a forward search attack is feasible.

    c. How can you prevent a forward search attack on a hash function?

32. Suppose that we have a block cipher and want to use it as a hash function. Let X be a specified constant and let M be a message consisting of a single block, where the block size is the size of the key in the block cipher. Define the hash of M as $Y = E(X, M)$. Note that M is being used in place of the key in the block cipher.

    a. Assuming that the underlying block cipher is secure, show that this hash function satisfies the collision resistance and one-way properties of a cryptographic hash function.

    b. Extend the definition of this hash so that messages of any length can be hashed. Does your hash function satisfy all of the properties of a cryptographic hash?

    c. Why must a block cipher used as a cryptographic hash be resistant to a "chosen key" attack? Hint: If not, given plaintext P, we can find two keys K_0 and K_1 such that $E(P, K_0) = E(P, K_1)$. Show that such a block cipher is insecure when used as a hash function.

33. Consider a "2 out of 3" secret sharing scheme.

    a. Suppose that Alice's share of the secret is $(4, 10/3)$, Bob's share is $(6, 2)$, and Charlie's share is $(5, 8/3)$. What is the secret S? What is the equation of the line?

    b. Suppose that the arithmetic is taken modulo 13, that is, the equation of the line is of the form $ax + by = c \pmod{13}$. If Alice's share is $(2, 2)$, Bob's share is $(4, 9)$, and Charlie's share is $(6, 3)$, what is the secret S? What is the equation of the line, mod 13?

34. Recall that we define a cipher to be secure if the best known attack is an exhaustive key search. If a cipher is secure and the key space is large, then the best known attack is computationally infeasible—for a

practical cipher, this is the ideal situation. However, there is always the possibility that a clever new attack could change a formerly secure cipher into an insecure cipher. In contrast, Shamir's polynomial-based secret sharing scheme is information theoretically secure, in the sense that there is no possibility of a shortcut attack. In other words, secret sharing is guaranteed to be secure forever.

   a. Suppose we have a "2 out of 2" secret sharing scheme, where Alice and Bob share a secret S. Why can't Alice determine any information about the secret from her share of the secret?

   b. Suppose we have an "m out of n" secret sharing scheme. Any set of $m - 1$ participants can't determine any information about the secret S. Why?

35. Obtain the file `visual.zip` from the textbook website and extract the files.

   a. Open the file `visual.html` in your favorite browser and carefully overlay the two shares. What image do you see?

   b. Use the program with a different image file to create shares. Note that the image must be a gif file. Give a screen snapshot showing the original image, the shares, and the overlaid shares.

36. Recall that we define a cipher to be secure if the best known attack is an exhaustive key search. If a cipher is secure and the key space is large, then the best known attack is computationally infeasible—for a practical cipher, this is the best possible scenario. However, there is always the possibility that a clever new attack could change a formerly secure cipher into an insecure cipher. In contrast, Naor and Shamir's visual secret sharing scheme is information theoretically secure, in the sense that there is no possibility of a shortcut attack—it is guaranteed to be secure (by our definition) forever.

   a. Consider the "2 out of 2" visual secret sharing scheme discussed in this chapter. Why can't Alice determine any information about the secret from her share of the secret?

   b. How might a more general "m out of n" visual secret sharing scheme work?

   c. For an "m out of n" visual secret sharing scheme, what would happen to the contrast of the recovered image for large m, with n a small value? For large n with m small? For large m and n?

37. Suppose that you have a text file and you plan to distribute it to several different people. Describe a simple non-digital watermarking method

that you could use to place a distinct invisible watermark in each copy of the file. Note that in this context, "invisible" does not imply that the watermark is literally invisible—instead, it means that the watermark is not obvious to the reader.

38. Suppose that you enroll in a course where the required text is a hard-copy manuscript written by the instructor. Being of simple mind, the instructor has inserted a simple-minded invisible watermark into each copy of the manuscript. The instructor claims that given any copy of the manuscript, he can easily determine who originally received the manuscript. The instructor challenges the class to solve the following problems.[14]

    (i) Determine the watermarking scheme used.

    (ii) Make the watermarks unreadable.

    Note that, in this context, "invisible" does not imply that the watermark is literally invisible—instead, it means that the watermark is not obvious to the reader.

    a. Discuss several possible methods the instructor could have used to watermark the manuscripts.

    b. How would you solve problem (i)?

    c. How would you solve (ii), assuming that you have solved (i)?

    d. Suppose that you are unable to solve (i). What could you do that would likely enable you to solve (ii) without having solved (i)?

39. Part of a Lewis Carroll poem appears in the second quote at the beginning of this chapter. Although the poem doesn't actually have a title, it's generally referenced by its opening line, *A Boat Beneath a Sunny Sky*.

    a. Give the entire poem.

    b. This poem contains a hidden message. What is it?

40. This problem deals with RGB colors.

    a. Verify that the RGB colors

    $$(\texttt{0x7E}, \texttt{0x52}, \texttt{0x90}) \ \text{ and } \ (\texttt{0x7E}, \texttt{0x52}, \texttt{0x10}),$$

    which differ in only a single bit position, are visibly different. Verify that the colors

    $$(\texttt{0xAB}, \texttt{0x32}, \texttt{0xF1}) \ \text{ and } \ (\texttt{0xAB}, \texttt{0x33}, \texttt{0xF1}),$$

---

[14]This problem is based on a true story.

which also differ in only a single bit position, are indistinguishable. Why is this the case?

b. What is the highest-order bit position that doesn't matter? That is, what is the highest bit positions can be changed without making a perceptible change in the color?

41. Obtain the image file `alice.bmp` from the textbook website.

a. Use a hex editor to hide the information `attack at dawn` in the file.

b. Provide a hex edit view showing the bits that were modified and their location in the file, as well as the corresponding unmodified bits.

c. Provide screen snapshots of the original bmp file, as well as the bmp file containing the hidden message.

42. Obtain the file `stego.zip` from the textbook website.

a. Use the program `stegoRead` to extract the hidden file contained in `aliceStego.bmp`.

b. Use the programs to insert another file into a different (uncompressed) image file and extract the information.

c. Provide screen snapshots of the image file from part b, both with and without the hidden information.

43. Obtain the file `stego.zip` from the textbook website.

a. Write a program, `stegoDestroy.c`, that will destroy any information hidden in a file, assuming that the information hiding method in `stego.c` might have been used. Your program should take a bmp file as input, and produce a bmp file as output. Visually, the output file must be identical to the input file.

b. Test your program on `aliceStego.bmp`. Verify that the output file image is undamaged. What information does `stegoRead.c` extract from your output file?

44. Obtain the file `stego.zip` from the textbook website.

a. How does the program `stego.c` hide information in an image file?

b. How could you damage the information hidden in a file without visually damaging the image, assuming the program `stego.c` was used?

c. How could this information hiding technique be made more resistant to attack?

45. Obtain the file `stego.zip` from the textbook website.

    a. Why does this information hiding method only apply to uncompressed image files?

    b. Explain how you could modify this approach to work on a compressed image format, such as jpg.

46. Write a program to hide information in an audio file and to extract your hidden information.

    a. Describe your information hiding method in detail.

    b. Compare an audio file that has no hidden information to the same file containing hidden information. Can you discern any difference in the quality of the audio?

    c. Discuss possible attacks on your information hiding system.

47. Write a program to hide information in a video file and to extract the hidden information.

    a. Describe your information hiding method in detail.

    b. Compare a video file that has no hidden information to the same file containing hidden information. Can you discern any difference in the quality of the video?

    c. Discuss possible attacks on your information hiding system.

48. This problem deals with the uses of random numbers in cryptography.

    a. Where are random numbers used in symmetric key cryptography?

    b. Where are random numbers used in RSA and Diffie-Hellman?

49. According to the text, random numbers used in cryptography must be unpredictable.

    a. Why are statistically random numbers (which are often used in simulations) not sufficient for cryptographic applications?

    b. Suppose that the keystream generated by a stream cipher is predictable in the sense that if you are given n keystream bits, you can determine all subsequent keystream bits. Is this a practical security concern? Why or why not?

Chapter 6

Advanced Cryptanalysis

For there is nothing covered, that shall not be revealed;
neither hid, that shall not be known.
— Luke 12:2

The magic words are squeamish ossifrage
— Solution to RSA challenge problem
posed in 1977 by Ron Rivest, who
estimated that breaking the message
would require 40 quadrillion years.
It was broken in 1994.

6.1 Introduction

Perhaps the best ways to gain a strong understanding of cryptography is by trying to break ciphers. As an added bonus, breaking ciphers puts us in the role of our all-purpose attacker, Trudy, and we need to think like Trudy if we are going to make our systems more secure.

In previous chapters, we've seen a few simple cryptanalytic attacks. In this chapter, we kick it up a few notches and examine some relatively involved attacks. Specifically, we'll discuss the following cryptanalytic attacks.

- An attack on the most famous World War II cipher, the Enigma

- The attack on RC4, as used in WEP

- Linear and differential cryptanalysis of a block cipher

- The lattice reduction attack on the knapsack

- A timing attack on RSA

In World War II, the Nazis believed the Enigma cipher was invincible. Polish and British cryptanalysts proved otherwise. The idea behind the attack we describe was used to break Enigma messages, and yielded invaluable intelligence during the war. The attack illustrates some of the shortcomings of pre-modern ciphers.

Next, we consider an attack on RC4. This attack is specific to the way that RC4 is used in WEP. In this case, a relatively straightforward attack exists, in spite of the fact that RC4 is considered a strong cipher. While this might seem contradictory, the problem arises from the precise details of the way that RC4 is used in WEP. This example shows that a strong cipher can be broken if it is used improperly.

Linear and differential cryptanalysis are generally not practical means of attacking ciphers directly. Instead, they are used to analyze block ciphers for design weaknesses and, as a result, modern block ciphers are built with these techniques in mind. Therefore, to understand the design principles employed in block ciphers today, it is necessary to have some understanding of linear and differential cryptanalysis.

In Chapter 4, we mentioned the attack on the knapsack public key cryptosystem. In this chapter, we'll give more details on the attack. We do not present all of the mathematical nuances, but we provide sufficient information to understand the concept behind the attack and to write a program to implement the attack. It is a relatively straightforward attack that nicely illustrates the role that mathematics and algorithms can play in breaking cryptosystems.

A side channel is an unintended source of information. Recently, it has been shown that power usage or precise timings can often reveal information about an underlying computation. Timing attacks are particularly relevant for public key systems, since the computations involved are costly, and therefore take a relatively long time. Small differences in timings can reveal information about the private key.

Side channel attacks have been used successfully against several public key systems, and we'll discuss a couple of timing attacks on RSA. These attacks are representative of some of the most interesting and surprising cryptanalytic techniques developed in the recent past.

The attacks covered in this chapter represent only a small sample of the many interesting cryptanalytic techniques that are known. For more examples, of "applied" cryptanalysis, that is, attacks that break real ciphers and produce plaintext, see the book by Stamp and Low [284]. In fact, this chapter can be viewed as a warmup exercise for [284]. In contrast, Swenson's book [295] is an excellent source for details on modern block cipher cryptanalysis, where "attacks" mostly serve the role of helping cryptographers build better ciphers, rather than breaking ciphers in the sense of producing plaintext.

6.2   Enigma

I cannot forecast to you the action of Russia.
It is a riddle wrapped in a mystery inside an enigma:
but perhaps there is a key.
— Winston Churchill

The Enigma cipher was used by Nazi Germany prior to and throughout World War II. The forerunner of the military Enigma machine was developed by Arthur Scherbius as a commercial device. The Enigma was patented in the 1920s but it continued to evolve over time and the German military versions were significantly different than the original design. In reality, "Enigma" represents a family of cipher machines, but "the Enigma" invariably refers to the specific German military cipher machine that we discuss here.[1]

It is estimated that approximately 100,000 Enigma machines were constructed, about 40,000 of those during World War II. The version of Enigma that we describe here was used by the German Army throughout World War II [104]. The device was used to send tactical battlefield messages and for high-level strategic communications.

The Enigma was broken by the Allies, and the intelligence it provided was invaluable—as evidence by its cover name, ULTRA. The Germans had an unwavering belief that the Enigma was unbreakable, and they continued to use it for vital communications long after there were clear indications that it had been compromised. Of course, it's impossible to precisely quantify the effect of Enigma decrypts on the outcome of the war, but it is not farfetched to suggest that the intelligence provided by Enigma decrypts may have shortened the war in Europe by a year, saving hundreds of thousands of lives [308].

6.2.1   Enigma Cipher Machine

A picture of an Enigma cipher machine appears in Figure 2.5 in Chapter 2. Note the keyboard—essentially, a mechanical typewriter—and the "lightboard" of letters. Analogous to an old-fashioned telephone switchboard, the front panel has cables that connect pairs of letters. This switchboard (or plugboard) is known by its German name, *stecker*. There are also three *rotors* visible near the top of the machine.

Before encrypting a message, the operator had to initialize the device. The initial settings include various rotor settings and the stecker cable pluggings. These initial settings constitute the key.

---

[1]In fact, several variants of "the Enigma" were used by the German military and government. For example, the Army version used three rotors while the Naval version had four rotors.

Once the machine had been initialized, the message was typed on the keyboard and as each plaintext letter was typed, the corresponding ciphertext letter was illuminated on the lightboard. The ciphertext letters were written down as they appeared on the lightboard and subsequently transmitted, usually by voice over radio.

To decrypt, the recipient's Enigma had to be initialize in exactly the same way as the sender's. Then when the ciphertext was typed into the keyboard, the corresponding plaintext letters would appear on the lightboard.

The cryptographically significant components of the Enigma are illustrated in Figure 6.1. These components and the ways that they interact are described below.

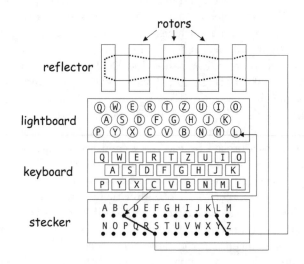

Figure 6.1: Enigma Diagram

To encrypt, a plaintext letter is entered on the keyboard. This letter first passes through the stecker, then, in turn, through each of the three rotors, through the reflector, back through each of the three rotors, back through the stecker, and finally, the resulting ciphertext letter is illuminated on the lightboard. Each rotor—as well as the reflector—consists of a hard-wired permutation of the 26 letters. Rotors as cryptographic elements are discussed in detail below in Section 6.2.3.

In the example illustrated in Figure 6.1, the plaintext letter C is typed on the keyboard, which is mapped to S due to the stecker cable connecting C to S. The letter S then passes through the rotors, the reflector, and back through the rotors. The net effect of all the rotors and the reflector is a permutation of the alphabet. In the example in Figure 6.1, S has been permuted to Z, which then becomes L due to the stecker cable between L and Z. Finally, the letter L is illuminated on the lightboard.

We use the following notation for the various permutations in the Enigma:

$$R_r = \text{rightmost rotor}$$
$$R_m = \text{middle rotor}$$
$$R_\ell = \text{leftmost rotor}$$
$$T = \text{reflector}$$
$$S = \text{stecker}$$

With this notation, from Figure 6.1 we see that

$$y = S^{-1} R_r^{-1} R_m^{-1} R_\ell^{-1} T R_\ell R_m R_r S(x)$$
$$= (R_\ell R_m R_r S)^{-1} T (R_\ell R_m R_r) S(x), \qquad (6.1)$$

where x is a plaintext letter, and y is the corresponding ciphertext letter.

If that's all there were to the Enigma, it would be nothing more than a glorified simple substitution cipher, with the initial settings determining the permutation. However, each time a keyboard letter is typed, the rightmost rotor steps one position, and the other rotors step in an odometer-like fashion—almost [48, 137].[2] That is, the middle rotor steps once for each 26 steps of the right rotor and the left rotor steps once for each 26 steps of the middle rotor. The reflector can be viewed as a fixed rotor since it permutes the letters, but it doesn't rotate. The overall effect is that the permutation changes with each letter typed. Note that, due to the odometer effect, the permutations R_r, R_m, and R_ℓ vary, but T and S do not.

Figure 6.2 illustrates the stepping of a single Engima rotor. This example shows the direction that the rotors step. From the operator's perspective, the letters appear in alphabetical order.

The Enigma is a substitution cipher where each letter is encrypted based on a permutation of the alphabet. But the Enigma is far from simple since, whenever a letter is encrypted (or decrypted), the odometer effect causes the permutation to change. Such a cipher is known as a poly-alphabetic substitution cipher. For the Enigma, the number of possible "alphabets" (i.e., permutations) is enormous.

---

[2]The "almost" is due to the mechanical system used to step the rotors, which causes the middle rotor to occasionally step twice in succession. Whenever a rotor steps, it causes the rotor to its right to also step. Suppose that the middle rotor just stepped to the position that engages the ratchet mechanism that will cause the leftmost rotor to step when the next letter is typed. Then when the next letter is typed, the left rotor will step, and this will also cause the middle rotor to step again. The middle rotor thereby steps twice in succession, violating the odometer effect. Note that this same ratcheting mechanism causes the right rotor to step whenever the middle rotor steps, but since the right rotor already steps for each letter typed, there is no noticeable effect on the right rotor.

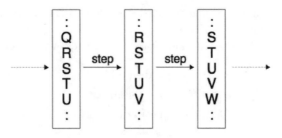

Figure 6.2: Enigma Rotor

6.2.2   Enigma Keyspace

The cryptographically significant components of the Enigma cipher are the stecker, the three rotors, and the reflector. The Enigma key consists of the initial settings for these components when the cipher is used to encrypt or decrypt a particular message. The variable settings that comprise the key are:

1. The choice of rotors.

2. The position of a movable ring on each of the two rightmost rotors. This ring allows the outer part of the rotor (labeled with the 26 letters) to rotate with respect to the inner part of the ring (where the actual permutation is wired).[3] Rotating this ring shifts the point at which the odometer effect occurs relative to the letters on the rotors.

3. The initial position of each rotor.

4. The number and plugging of the wires in the stecker.

5. The choice of reflector.

As mentioned above, each rotor implements a permutation of the 26 letters of the alphabet. The movable rings can be set to any of the 26 positions corresponding to the letters.

   Each rotor is initially set to one of the 26 positions on the rotor, which are labeled with A through Z. The stecker is similar to an old-fashioned telephone switchboard, with 26 holes, each labeled with a letter of the alphabet. The stecker can have from 0 to 13 cables, where each cable connects a pair of letters. The reflector implements a permutation of the 26 letters, with the restriction that no letter can be permuted to itself, since this would cause a short circuit. Consequently, the reflector is equivalent to a stecker with 13 cables.

---

[3]This is analogous to rotating the position of a car tire relative to the rim.

Since there are three rotors, each containing a permutation of the 26 letters, there are

$$26! \cdot 26! \cdot 26! \approx 2^{265}$$

ways to select and place rotors in the machine. In addition, the number of ways to set the two movable rings—which determine when the odometer-like effects occurs—is $26 \cdot 26 \approx 2^{9.4}$.

The initial position of each of these rotors can be set to any one of 26 positions, so there are $26 \cdot 26 \cdot 26 = 2^{14.1}$ ways to initialize the rotors. However, this number should not be included in our count, since the different initial positions are all equivalent to some other rotor in some standard position. That is, if we assume that each rotor is initially set to, say, A, then setting a particular rotor to, say, B, is equivalent to some other rotor initially set to A. Consequently, the factor of 2^{265} obtained in the previous paragraph includes all possible rotors in all possible initial positions.

Finally, we must consider the stecker. Let $F(p)$ be the number of ways to plug p cables in the stecker. From Problem 2, we have

$$F(p) = \binom{26}{2p}(2p-1)(2p-3) \cdots \cdots 1.$$

The values of $F(p)$ are tabulated in Table 6.1.

Table 6.1: Stecker Combinations

$F(0) = 2^0$	$F(1) \approx 2^{8.3}$
$F(2) \approx 2^{15.5}$	$F(3) \approx 2^{21.7}$
$F(4) \approx 2^{27.3}$	$F(5) \approx 2^{32.2}$
$F(6) \approx 2^{36.5}$	$F(7) \approx 2^{40.2}$
$F(8) \approx 2^{43.3}$	$F(9) \approx 2^{45.6}$
$F(10) \approx 2^{47.1}$	$F(11) \approx 2^{47.5}$
$F(12) \approx 2^{46.5}$	$F(13) \approx 2^{42.8}$

Summing the entries in Table 6.1, we find that there are more than $2^{48.9}$ possible stecker configurations. Note that maximum occurs with 11 cables and that $F(10) \approx 2^{47.1}$. As mentioned above, the Enigma reflector is equivalent to a stecker with 13 cables. Consequently, there are $F(13) \approx 2^{42.8}$ different reflectors.

Combining all of these results, we find that, in principle, the size of the Enigma keyspace is about

$$2^{265} \cdot 2^{9.4} \cdot 2^{48.9} \cdot 2^{42.8} \approx 2^{366}.$$

That is, the theoretical keyspace of the Enigma is equivalent to a 366 bit key. Since modern ciphers seldom employ more than a 256 bit key, this gives some indication as to why the Germans had such great—but ultimately misplaced—confidence in the Enigma.

However, this astronomical number of keys is misleading. From Problem 1, we see that under the practical limitations of actual use by the German military, only about 2^{77} Enigma keys were available. This is still an enormous number and an exhaustive key search would have been out of the question using 1940s technology. Fortunately for the civilized world, shortcut attacks exist. But before we discuss an attack, we first take a brief detour to consider rotors as cryptographic elements.

6.2.3   Rotors

Rotors were used in many cipher machines during the first half of the 20th century—the Enigma is the most famous, but there were many others. Another interesting example of a rotor cipher machine is the American World War II-era machine Sigaba. The Sigaba cipher is a fascinating design that proved to be much stronger than Enigma. For a detailed cryptanalysis of Sigaba, see [280] or for a slightly abbreviated version see [284].

From a crypto-engineering standpoint, the appeal of a rotor is that it is possible to generate a large number of distinct permutations in a robust manner from a simple electro-mechanical device. Such considerations were important in the pre-computer era. In fact, the Enigma was an extremely durable piece of hardware, which was widely used in battlefield situations.

Hardware rotors are easy to understand, but it is slightly awkward to specify the permutations that correspond to the various positions of the rotor. A good analysis of these issues can be found in [184]. Here, we briefly discuss some of the main issues.

For simplicity, consider a rotor with four letters, A through D. Assuming the signal travels from left to right, the rotor illustrated in Figure 6.3 permutes ABCD to CDBA, that is, A is permuted to C, B is permuted to D, C is permuted to B, and D is permuted to A. The inverse permutation, DCAB in our notation, can be obtained by simply passing a signal through the rotors from right-to-left instead of left-to-right. This is a useful feature, since we can decrypt with the same hardware used to encrypt. The Enigma takes this one step further.[4] That is, the Enigma machine is its own inverse, which implies that the same machine with exactly the same settings can be used to encrypt and decrypt (see Problem 5).

Suppose that the rotor in Figure 6.3 steps once. Note that only the rotor itself—represented by the rectangle—rotates, not the electrical contacts at the edge of the rotor. In this example, we assume that the rotor steps "up," that is, the contact that was at B is now at A and so on, with the contact

---

[4]No pun intended (for a change...).

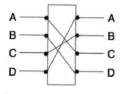

Figure 6.3: Rotor

that was at **A** wrapping around to **D**. The shift of the rotor in Figure 6.3 is illustrated in Figure 6.4. The resulting shifted permutation is **CADB**, which is, perhaps, not so obvious considering that the original permutation was **CDBA**.

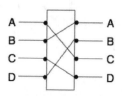

Figure 6.4: Stepped Rotor

In general, it is not difficult to determine the rotor shift of a permutation. The crucial point is that it's the offsets, or displacements, that shift. For example, in the permutation **CDBA**, the offsets are as follows: The letter **A** is permuted to **C**, which is an offset of 2 positions, the letter **B** is permuted to **D**, which is an offset of 2, the letter **C** is permuted to **B**, which is an offset of 3 (around the rotor), and **D** is permuted to **A**, which is an offset of 1. That is, the sequence of offsets for the permutation **CDBA** is $(2, 2, 3, 1)$. Cyclically shifting this sequence yields $(2, 3, 1, 2)$, which corresponds to the permutation **CADB**, and this is indeed the rotor shift that appears in Figure 6.4.

Again, physical rotors are actually very simple devices, but they are somewhat awkward to deal with in the abstract. For some additional exercise working with rotors, see Problem 12.

As mentioned above, one of the primary advantages of rotors is that they provide a simple electro-mechanical means to generate a large number of different permutations. Combining multiple rotors in series increases the number of permutations exponentially. For example, in Figure 6.5, **C** is permuted to **A**, while a shift of rotor L, denoted by $\sigma(L)$ and illustrated in Figure 6.6, causes **C** to be permuted to **B**. That is, stepping any single rotor changes the overall permutation.

With this three-rotor scheme, we can generate a cycle of 64 permutations of the letters **ABCD** by simply stepping through the 64 settings for the three

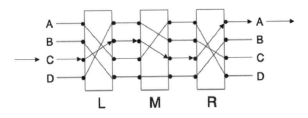

Figure 6.5: Three Rotors

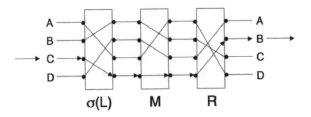

Figure 6.6: Rotor L Steps

rotors. Of course, not all of these permutations will be unique, since there are only 24 distinct permutations of the four letters ABCD. Also, by selecting different initial settings for the rotors, we can generate a different sequence of permutations. Furthermore, by selecting a different set of rotors (or reordering the given rotors), we can generate different sequences of permutations. As with a single rotor, it's easy to obtain the inverse permutations from a series of rotors by simply passing the signal through the rotors in the opposite direction. The inverse permutations are needed for decryption.

6.2.4 Enigma Attack

Polish cryptanalysts led by Marian Rejewski, Henryk Zygalski, and Jerzy Różycki were the first to successfully attack the Enigma [305]. Their challenge was greatly complicated by the fact that they did not know which rotors were in use. Through some clever mathematics, and a small but crucial piece of espionage [4], they were able to recover the rotor permutations from ciphertext. This certainly ranks as one of the greatest cryptanalytic successes of the era.

When Poland fell to the Nazis in 1939, Rejewski, Zygalski, and Różycki fled to France. After France fell under the Nazi onslaught, the Poles continued their cryptanalytic work from unoccupied Vichy France. The brilliant cryptanalytic work of Rejewski's team eventually made its way to Britain,

where the British were rightly amazed. A group of British cryptanalysts that included Gordon Welchman and computing pioneer Alan Turing took up the Enigma challenge.

The Enigma attack that we describe here is similar to one developed by Turing, but somewhat simplified. This attack requires known plaintext, which in World War II terminology was known as a *crib*.

The essential idea is that, initially, we can ignore the stecker and make a guess for the remainder of the key. From Problem 1, there are less than 2^{30} such guesses. For each of these, we use information derived from a crib (known plaintext) to eliminate incorrect guesses. This attack, which has a work factor on the order 2^{30}, could be easily implemented on a modern computer, but it would have been impractical using World War II technology.

Suppose that we have the plaintext and corresponding ciphertext that appears in Table 6.2. We make use of this data in the attack described below.

Table 6.2: Enigma Known Plaintext Example

i	0	1	2	3	4	5	6	7	8	9	10	11	12	13	14	15	16	17	18	19	20	21	22	23
Plaintext	O	B	E	R	K	O	M	M	A	N	D	O	D	E	R	W	E	H	R	M	A	C	H	T
Ciphertext	Z	M	G	E	R	F	E	W	M	L	K	M	T	A	W	X	T	S	W	V	U	I	N	Z

Let $S(x)$ be the result of the letter x passing through the stecker from the keyboard. Then $S^{-1}(x)$ is the result of x passing through the stecker in the other direction. For a given initial setting, let P_i be the permutation at step i, that is, P_i is the permutation determined by the composition of the three rotors, followed by the reflector, followed by the three rotors—in the opposite direction—at step i. Then, using the notation in equation (6.1), the overall permutation is given by

$$P_i = S^{-1} R_r^{-1} R_m^{-1} R_\ell^{-1} T R_\ell R_m R_r S,$$

where, to simplify the notation, we ignore the dependence of R_ℓ, R_m, and R_r on the step i.

Note that since P_i is a permutation, its inverse, P_i^{-1}, exists. Also, as noted above, due to the rotation of the rotors, the permutation varies with each letter typed. Consequently, P_i does indeed depend on i.

The Enigma attack we present here exploits "cycles" that occur in the known plaintext and corresponding ciphertext. Consider, for example, the column labeled 8 in Table 6.2. The plaintext letter A passes through the stecker, then through P_8 and, finally, through S^{-1} to yield the ciphertext M, that is, $S^{-1} P_8 S(\text{A}) = \text{M}$, which we can rewrite as $P_8 S(\text{A}) = S(\text{M})$.

From the known plaintext in Table 6.2, we have

$$P_8 S(\texttt{A}) = S(\texttt{M})$$
$$P_6 S(\texttt{M}) = S(\texttt{E})$$
$$P_{13} S(\texttt{E}) = S(\texttt{A}).$$

These three equations can be combined to yield the cycle

$$S(\texttt{E}) = P_6 P_8 P_{13} S(\texttt{E}). \qquad (6.2)$$

Now suppose that we select one of the possible initial settings for the machine, ignoring the stecker. Then all P_i and P_i^{-1} that correspond to this setting are known. Next, suppose that we guess, say, $S(\texttt{E}) = \texttt{G}$, that is, we guess that E and G are connected by a cable in the stecker plugboard. If it's actually true that the stecker has a wire connecting E and G, and if our guess for the initial settings of the machine is correct, then from equation (6.2) we must have

$$\texttt{G} = P_6 P_8 P_{13}(\texttt{G}). \qquad (6.3)$$

If we try all 26 choices for $S(\texttt{E})$ and equation (6.2) is never satisfied, then we know that our guess for the rotor settings is incorrect and we can eliminate this choice. We would like to use this observation to reduce the number of rotor settings, ideally, to just one. However, if we find any guess for $S(\texttt{E})$ for which equation (6.2) holds, then we cannot rule out the current rotor settings. Unfortunately, there are 26 possible guesses for $S(\texttt{E})$ and, for each, there is a $1/26$ chance that equation (6.2) holds at random. Consequently, we obtain no reduction in the number of possible keys when using just one cycle.

Fortunately, all is not lost. If we can find an additional cycle involving $S(\texttt{E})$, then we can use this in combination with equation (6.2) to reduce the number of possible rotor settings. We're in luck, since we can combine the four equations,

$$S(\texttt{E}) = P_3 S(\texttt{R})$$
$$S(\texttt{W}) = P_{14} S(\texttt{R})$$
$$S(\texttt{W}) = P_7 S(\texttt{M})$$
$$S(\texttt{E}) = P_6 S(\texttt{M})$$

to obtain

$$S(\texttt{E}) = P_3 P_{14}^{-1} P_7 P_6^{-1} S(\texttt{E}).$$

Now if we guess, say, $S(\texttt{E}) = \texttt{G}$, we have two equations that must hold if this guess is correct. There are still 26 choices for $S(\texttt{E})$, but with two cycles, there is only a $(1/26)^2$ chance that they both hold at random. Therefore, with two cycles in $S(\texttt{E})$, we can reduce the number of viable machine settings (that

is, keys) by a factor of 26. We can easily develop an attack based on these observations.

To reiterate, the crucial observation here is that, once we specify the rotor settings, all permutations $P_0, P_1, P_2, \ldots$ and $P_0^{-1}, P_1^{-1}, P_2^{-1}, \ldots$ are known. Then if we substitute a putative value for $S(\mathrm{E})$, we can immediately check the validity of all cycle equations that are available. For an incorrect guess of $S(\mathrm{E})$ (or incorrect rotor settings) there is a $1/26$ chance any given cycle will hold true. But with n cycles, there is only a $(1/26)^n$ chance that all cycle equations will hold true. Consequently, with n cycles involving $S(\mathrm{E})$, we can reduce the number of possible initial rotor settings by a factor of 26^{n-1}. Since there are only about 2^{30} rotor settings, with enough cycles, we can reduce the number of possible rotor settings to one, which is the key.

Amazingly, by recovering the initial rotor settings in this manner, stecker values are also recovered—essentially for free. However, any stecker values that do not contribute to a cycle will remain unknown, but once the rotor settings have been determined, the remaining unknown stecker settings are easy to determine (see Problem 7). It is interesting to note that, in spite of an enormous number of possible settings, the stecker contributes virtually nothing to the security of the Enigma.

It is important to realize that the attack described here would have been impractical using 1940s technology. The practical attacks of World War II required that the cryptanalyst reduce the number of cases to be tested to a much smaller number than 2^{30}. Many clever techniques were developed to squeeze as much information as possible from ciphertext. In addition, much effort was expended finding suitable cribs (i.e., known plaintext) since all of the practical attacks required known plaintext.

6.3   RC4 as Used in WEP

Suddenly she came upon a little three-legged table, all made of solid glass:
there was nothing on it but a tiny golden key...
— *Alice in Wonderland*

RC4 is described in Section 3.2.2 of Chapter 3 and WEP is described in Section 10.6 of Chapter 10. Here, we provide a detailed description of the cryptanalytic attack that is mentioned in Section 10.6. Note that the RC4 algorithm is considered secure when used properly. However, WEP, which is widely viewed as the "Swiss cheese" of security protocols, somehow managed to implement nearly all of its security functions insecurely, including RC4. As a result, there is a feasible attack on RC4 encryption as used in WEP. Before studying this attack, you might want to preview Section 10.6.

WEP encrypts data with the stream cipher RC4 using a long-term key that seldom (if ever) changes. To avoid repeated keystreams, an initialization vector, or IV, is sent in the clear with each message, where each packet is treated as a new message. The IV is mixed with the long-term key to produce the message key. The upshot is that the cryptanalyst, Trudy, gets to see the IVs, and any time an IV repeats, Trudy knows that the same keystream is being used to encrypt the data. Since the IV is only 24 bits, repeated IVs occur relatively often. A repeated IV implies a repeated keystream, and a repeated keystream is bad—at least as bad as reuse of a one-time pad. That is, a repeated keystream provides statistical information to the attacker who could then conceivably liberate the keystream from the ciphertext. Once the keystream for a packet is known, it can be used to decrypt any packet that uses the same IV.

However, in WEP, there are several possible shortcuts that make an attacker's life easier, as discussed in Section 10.6. Here, we discuss a cryptanalytic attack on the RC4 stream cipher as it is used in WEP. Again, this attack is only possible due to the specific way that WEP uses RC4—specifically, the way that it creates the session key from an initialization vector IV and the long-term key.[5]

This cryptanalytic attack has a small work factor, and it will succeed provided that a sufficient number of IVs are observed. This clever attack, which can be considered a type of *related key* attack, is due to Fluhrer, Mantin, and Shamir [112].

6.3.1   RC4 Algorithm

RC4 is simplicity itself. At any given time, the state of the cipher consists of a lookup table S containing a permutation of all byte values, $0, 1, 2, \ldots, 255$, along with two indices i and j. When the cipher is initialized, the permutation is scrambled using a key, denoted key$[i]$, for $i = 0, 1, \ldots, N - 1$, which can be of any length from 0 to 256 bytes. In the initialization routine, the lookup table S is modified (based on the key) in such a way that S always contains a permutation of the the byte values. The RC4 initialization algorithm appears in Table 6.3.

The RC4 keystream is generated one byte at a time. An index is determined based on the current contents of S, and the indexed byte is selected as the keystream byte. Similar to the initialization routine, at each step the permutation S is modified so that S always contains a permutation of $\{0, 1, 2, \ldots, 255\}$. The keystream generation algorithm appears in Table 6.4. For more details on the RC4 algorithm, see Section 3.2.2.

---

[5]The attack does highlight a shortcoming in the RC4 initialization process—a shortcoming that can be fixed without modifying the underlying RC4 algorithm.

Table 6.3: RC4 Initialization

for $i = 0$ **to** 255
$\quad S_i = i$
$\quad K_i = \text{key}[i \ (\text{mod } N)]$
next i
$j = 0$
for $i = 0$ **to** 255
$\quad j = (j + S_i + K_i) \ (\text{mod } 256)$
$\quad \text{swap}(S_i, S_j)$
next i
$i = j = 0$

Table 6.4: RC4 Keystream Generator

$i = (i + 1) \ (\text{mod } 256)$
$j = (j + S_i) \ (\text{mod } 256)$
$\text{swap}(S_i, S_j)$
$t = (S_i + S_j) \ (\text{mod } 256)$
$\text{keystreamByte} = S_t$

6.3.2 RC4 Cryptanalytic Attack

In 2000, Fluhrer, Mantin, and Shamir [112] published a practical attack on RC4 encryption as it is used in WEP. In WEP, a non-secret 24-bit initialization vector, denoted as IV, is prepended to a long-term key and the result is used as the RC4 key. Note that the role of the IV in WEP encryption is somewhat similar to the role that an IV plays in various block cipher encryption modes (see Section 3.3.7 of Chapter 3). The WEP IV is necessary to prevent messages from being sent in depth. Recall that two ciphertext messages are in depth if they were encrypted using the same key. Messages in depth are a serious threat to a stream cipher.

We assume that Trudy, the cryptanalyst, knows many WEP ciphertext messages (packets) and their corresponding IVs. Trudy would like to recover the long-term key. The Fluhrer-Mantin-Shamir attack provides a clever, efficient, and elegant way to do just that. This attack has been successfully used to break real WEP traffic [294].

Suppose that for a particular message, the three-byte initialization vector is of the form

$$\text{IV} = (3, 255, V), \tag{6.4}$$

where V can be any byte value. Then these three IV bytes become K_0, K_1, and K_2 in the RC4 initialization algorithm of Table 6.3, while K_3 is the first byte of the unknown long-term key. That is, the message key is

$$K = (3, 255, V, K_3, K_4, \ldots), \qquad (6.5)$$

where V is known to Trudy, but $K_3, K_4, K_5, \ldots$ are unknown. To understand the attack, we need to carefully consider what happens to the table S during the RC4 initialization phase when K is of the form in equation (6.5).

In the RC4 initialization algorithm, which appears in Table 6.3, we first set S to the identity permutation, so that we have

i	0	1	2	3	4	5	...
S_i	0	1	2	3	4	5	...

Suppose that K is of the form in (6.5). Then at the $i = 0$ initialization step, we compute the index $j = 0 + S_0 + K_0 = 3$ and elements i and j are swapped, resulting in the table

i	0	1	2	3	4	5	...
S_i	3	1	2	0	4	5	...

At the next step, $i = 1$ and $j = 3 + S_1 + K_1 = 3 + 1 + 255 = 3$, since the addition is modulo 256. Elements i and j are again swapped, giving

i	0	1	2	3	4	5	...
S_i	3	0	2	1	4	5	...

At step $i = 2$ we have $j = 3 + S_2 + K_2 = 3 + 2 + V = 5 + V$ and after the swap,

i	0	1	2	3	4	5	...	$5 + V$	...
S_i	3	0	$5 + V$	1	4	5	...	2	...

At the next step, $i = 3$ and $j = 5 + V + S_3 + K_3 = 6 + V + K_3$, where K_3 is unknown. After swapping, the lookup table is

i	0	1	2	3	4	5	...
S_i	3	0	$5 + V$	$6 + V + K_3$	4	5	...

i	...	$5 + V$	...	$6 + V + K_3$	...
S_i	...	2	...	1	...

assuming that, after reduction modulo 256, we have $6 + V + K_3 > 5 + V$. If this is not the case, then $6 + V + K_3$ will appear to the left of $5 + V$, which has no effect on the success of the attack.

Now suppose for a moment that the RC4 initialization algorithm were to stop after the $i = 3$ step. Then, if we generate the first byte of the keystream according to the algorithm in Table 6.4, we find $i = 1$ and $j = S_i = S_1 = 0$, so that $t = S_1 + S_0 = 0 + 3 = 3$. Then the first keystream byte would be

$$\text{keystreamByte} = S_3 = (6 + V + K_3) \pmod{256}. \tag{6.6}$$

Assuming that Trudy knows (or can guess) the first byte of the plaintext, she can determine the first byte of the keystream. If this is the case, Trudy can simply solve equation (6.6) to obtain the first unknown key byte, since

$$K_3 = (\text{keystreamByte} - 6 - V) \pmod{256}. \tag{6.7}$$

Unfortunately (for Trudy), the initialization phase is 256 steps instead of just four. But notice that as long as S_0, S_1 and S_3 are not altered in any subsequent initialization step, then equation (6.7) will hold. What is the chance that these three elements remain unchanged? The only way that an element can change is if it is swapped for another element. From $i = 4$ to $i = 255$ of the initialization, the i index will not affect any of these elements since it steps regularly from 4 to 255. If we treat the j index as random, then at each step the probability that the three indices of concern are all unaffected is $253/256$. The probability that this holds for all of the final 252 initialization steps is, therefore,

$$\left(\frac{253}{256}\right)^{252} \approx 0.0513.$$

Consequently, we expect equation (6.7) to hold slightly more than 5% of the time. Then with a sufficient number of IVs of the form in equation (6.4) Trudy can determine K_3 from equation (6.7), assuming she knows the first keystream byte in each case.

What is a sufficient number of IVs to recover K_3? If we observe n encrypted packets, each with an IV of the form in equation (6.4), then we expect to solve for the actual K_3 using equation (6.7) for about $0.05n$ of these. For the remaining $0.95n$ of the cases, we expect the result of the subtraction in equation (6.7) to be a random value in $\{0, 1, 2, \ldots, 255\}$. Then the expected number of times that any particular value other than K_3 appears is about $0.95n/256$, and the correct value will have an expected count of $0.05n + 0.95n/256 \approx 0.05n$. We need to choose n large enough so that we can, with high probability, distinguish K_3 from the random "noise." If we choose $n = 60$, then we expect to see K_3 three times, while it is unlikely that we will see any random value more than twice (see also Problem 13).

This attack is easily extended to recover the remaining unknown key bytes. We illustrate the next step—assuming that Trudy has recovered K_3, we show that she can recover the key byte K_4. In this case, Trudy will look for initialization vectors of the form

$$\text{IV} = (4, 255, V), \tag{6.8}$$

where V can be any value. Then, at the $i = 0$ step of the initialization, $j = 0 + S_0 + K_0 = 4$ and elements i and j are swapped, resulting in

i	0	1	2	3	4	5	...
S_i	4	1	2	3	0	5	...

At the next step, $i = 1$ and $j = 4 + S_1 + K_1 = 4$ (since the addition is mod 256) and elements S_1 and S_4 are swapped, giving

i	0	1	2	3	4	5	...
S_i	4	0	2	3	1	5	...

At step $i = 2$ we have $j = 4 + S_2 + K_2 = 6 + V$, and after the swap

i	0	1	2	3	4	5	...	$6 + V$	...
S_i	4	0	$6 + V$	3	1	5	...	2	...

At the next step, $i = 3$ and $j = 5 + V + S_3 + K_3 = 9 + V + K_3$, and K_3 is known. After swapping

i	0	1	2	3	4	5	...
S_i	4	0	$6 + V$	$9 + V + K_3$	1	5	...

i	...	$6 + V$	...	$9 + V + K_3$	...
S_i	...	2	...	3	...

assuming that $9 + V + K_3 > 6 + V$ when the sums are taken mod 256.

Carrying this one step further, we have $i = 4$ and

$$j = 9 + V + K_3 + S_4 + K_4 = 10 + V + K_3 + K_4,$$

where only K_4 is unknown. After swapping, the table S is of the form

i	0	1	2	3	4	5	...
S_i	4	0	$6 + V$	$9 + V + K_3$	$10 + V + K_3 + K_4$	5	...

i	...	$6 + V$	...	$9 + V + K_3$	...	$10 + V + K_3 + K_4$	...
S_i	...	2	...	3	...	1	...

If the initialization were to stop at this point (after the $i = 4$ step) then for first byte of the keystream we would find $i = 1$ and $j = S_i = S_1 = 0$, so that $t = S_1 + S_0 = 4 + 0 = 4$. The resulting keystream byte would be

$$\text{keystreamByte} = S_4 = (10 + V + K_3 + K_4) \pmod{256},$$

where the only unknown is K_4. As a result,

$$K_4 = (\text{keystreamByte} - 10 - V - K_3) \pmod{256}. \tag{6.9}$$

Of course, the initialization does not stop after the $i = 4$ step, but, as in the K_3 case, the chance that equation (6.9) holds is about 0.05. Consequently, with a sufficient number of IVs of the form in equation (6.8), Trudy can determine K_4. Continuing, any number of key bytes can be recovered, provided enough IVs of the correct form are available and Trudy knows the first keystream byte of each corresponding packet.

This same technique can be extended to recover additional key bytes, $K_5, K_6, \ldots$. In fact, if a sufficient number of packets are available, a key of any length can be recovered with a trivial amount of work. This is one reason why WEP is said to be "unsafe at any key size" [321].

Consider once again the attack to recover the first unknown key byte K_3. It is worth noting that some IVs that are not of the form $(3, 255, V)$ will be useful to Trudy. For example, suppose the IV is $(2, 253, 0)$. Then after the $i = 3$ initialization step, the array S is

i	0	1	2	3	4	$\ldots$	$3 + K_3$	$\ldots$
S_i	0	2	1	$3 + K_3$	4	$\ldots$	3	$\ldots$

If S_1, S_2, and S_3 are not altered in the remaining initialization steps, the first keystream byte will be $3 + K_3$, from which Trudy can recover K_3. Notice that for a given three-byte IV, Trudy can compute the initialization up through the $i = 3$ step and, by doing so, she can easily determine whether a given IV will be useful for her attack. Similar comments hold for subsequent key bytes. By using all of the useful IVs, Trudy can reduce the number of packets she must observe before recovering the key.

Finally, it is worth noting that it is also possible to recover the RC4 key if the IV is appended to the unknown key instead of being prepended (as in WEP); see [195] for the details.

6.3.3 Preventing Attacks on RC4

There are several possible ways to prevent attacks on RC4 that target its initialization phase. The standard suggestion is to, in effect, add 256 steps to the initialization process. That is, after the initialization in Table 6.3 has run its course, generate 256 keystream bytes according to the RC4 keystream generation algorithm in Table 6.4, discarding these bytes. After this process has completed, generate the keystream in the usual way. If the sender and receiver follow this procedure, the attack discussed in this section is not feasible. Note that no modification to the inner workings of RC4 is required.

Also, there are many alternative ways to combine the key and IV that would effectively prevent the attack described in this section; Problem 17 asks for such methods. As with so many other aspects of WEP, its designers managed to choose one of the most insecure possible approaches to using the RC4 cipher.

6.4   Linear and Differential Cryptanalysis

> *We sent the [DES] S-boxes off to Washington.*
> *They came back and were all different.*
> — Alan Konheim, one of the designers of DES

> *I would say that, contrary to what some people believe, there is no evidence*
> *of tampering with the DES so that the basic design was weakened.*
> — Adi Shamir

As discussed in Section 3.3.2, the influence of the Data Encryption Standard (DES) on modern cryptography can't be overestimated. For one thing, both linear and differential cryptanalysis were developed to attack DES. As mentioned above, these techniques don't generally yield practical attacks. Instead, linear and differential "attacks" point to design weaknesses in block ciphers. These techniques have become basic analytic tools that are used to analyze all block ciphers today.

Differential cryptanalysis is, at least in the unclassified realm, due to Biham and Shamir (yes, that Shamir, yet again) who introduced the technique in 1990. Subsequently, it has become clear that someone involved in the design of DES (that is, someone at the National Security Agency) was aware of differential cryptanalysis prior to the mid 1970s. Note that differential cryptanalysis is a chosen plaintext attack, which makes it somewhat difficult to actually apply in the real world.

Linear cryptanalysis was apparently developed by Matsui in 1993. Since DES was not designed to offer optimal resistance to a sophisticated linear cryptanalysis attacks, either NSA did not know about the technique in the 1970s, or they were not concerned about such an attack on the DES cipher. Linear cryptanalysis is slightly more realistic as a real-world attack than differential cryptanalysis, primarily because it is a known plaintext attack instead of a chosen plaintext attack.

6.4.1   Quick Review of DES

We don't require all of the details of DES here, so we'll give a simplified overview that only includes the essential facts that we'll need below. DES has eight S-boxes, each of which maps six input bits, denoted $x_0x_1x_2x_3x_4x_5$, to four output bits, denoted $y_0y_1y_2y_3$. For example, DES S-box number one, in hexadecimal notation, appears in Table 6.5.

Figure 6.7 gives a much simplified view of DES, which is sufficient for our purposes. Below, we are mostly interested in analyzing the nonlinear parts of DES, so the diagram highlights the fact that the S-boxes are the only

Table 6.5: DES S-box Number One

x_0x_5	$x_1x_2x_3x_4$															
	0	1	2	3	4	5	6	7	8	9	A	B	C	D	E	F
0	E	4	D	1	2	F	B	8	3	A	6	C	5	9	0	7
1	0	F	7	4	E	2	D	1	A	6	C	B	9	5	3	4
2	4	1	E	8	D	6	2	B	F	C	9	7	3	A	5	0
3	F	C	8	2	4	9	1	7	5	B	3	E	A	0	6	D

nonlinearity in DES. Figure 6.7 also illustrates the way that the subkey K_i enters into a DES round. This will also be important in the discussion to follow.

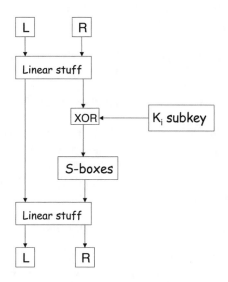

Figure 6.7: Simplified View of DES

Next, we'll present a quick overview of differential cryptanalysis followed by a similar overview of linear cryptanalysis. We'll then present a simplified version of DES, which we've called Tiny DES, or TDES. We'll present both linear and differential attacks on TDES.

6.4.2   Overview of Differential Cryptanalysis

Since differential cryptanalysis was developed to analyze DES, let's discuss it in the context of DES. Recall that all of DES is linear except for the

S-boxes. We'll see that the linear parts of DES play a significant role in its security, however, from a cryptanalytic point of view, the linear parts are easy. Mathematicians are good at solving linear equations, so it is the nonlinear parts that represent the major cryptanalytic hurdles. As a result, both differential and linear cryptanalysis are focused on dealing with the nonlinear parts of DES, namely, the S-boxes.

The idea behind a differential attack is to compare input and output differences. For simplicity, we'll first consider a simplified S-box. Suppose that a DES-like cipher uses the 3-bit to 2-bit S-box

$$
\begin{array}{c}
\text{column} \\
\begin{array}{c|cccc}
\text{row} & 00 & 01 & 10 & 11 \\
\hline
0 & 10 & 01 & 11 & 00 \\
1 & 00 & 10 & 01 & 11
\end{array}
\end{array}
\tag{6.10}
$$

where, for input bits $x_0 x_1 x_2$, the bit x_0 indexes the row, while $x_1 x_2$ indexes the column. Then, for example, $\texttt{Sbox}(010) = 11$, since the bits in row 0 and column 10 are 11.

Consider the two inputs, $X_1 = 110$ and $X_2 = 010$, and suppose the key is $K = 011$. Then $X_1 \oplus K = 101$ and $X_2 \oplus K = 001$ and we have

$$
\texttt{Sbox}(X_1 \oplus K) = 10 \text{ and } \texttt{Sbox}(X_2 \oplus K) = 01. \tag{6.11}
$$

Now suppose that K in equation (6.11) is unknown, but the inputs, namely, $X_1 = 110$ and $X_2 = 010$, are known as well as the corresponding outputs $\texttt{Sbox}(X_1 \oplus K) = 10$ and $\texttt{Sbox}(X_2 \oplus K) = 01$. Then from the S-box in (6.10) we see that $X_1 \oplus K \in \{000, 101\}$ and $X_2 \oplus K \in \{001, 110\}$. Since X_1 and X_2 are known, we have that

$$
K \in \{110, 011\} \cap \{011, 100\}
$$

which implies that $K = 011$. This "attack" is essentially a known plaintext attack on the single S-box in (6.10) for the key K. The same approach will work on a single DES S-box.

However, attacking one S-box in one round of DES does not appear to be particularly useful. In addition, the attacker will not know the input to any round except for the first, and the attacker will not know the output of any round but the last. The intermediate rounds appear to be beyond the purview of the cryptanalyst.

For this approach to prove useful in analyzing DES, we must be able to extend the attack to one complete round, that is, we must take into account all eight S-boxes simultaneously. Once we have extended the attack to one round, we must then extend the attack to multiple rounds. On the surface, both of these appear to be daunting tasks.

However, we'll see that by focusing on input and output differences, it becomes easy to make some S-boxes "active" and others "inactive." As a result, we can, in some cases, extend the attack to a single round. To then extend the attack to multiple rounds, we must choose the input difference so that the output difference is in a useful form for the next round. This is challenging and depends on the specific properties of the S-boxes, as well as the linear mixing that occurs at each round.

The crucial point here is that we'll focus on input and output differences. Suppose we know inputs X_1 and X_2. Then for input X_1, the actual input to the S-box is $X_1 \oplus K$ and for input X_2 the actual input to S-box is $X_2 \oplus K$, where the key K is unknown. Differences are defined modulo 2, implying that the difference operation is the same as the sum operation, namely, XOR. Then the S-box input difference is

$$(X_1 \oplus K) \oplus (X_2 \oplus K) = X_1 \oplus X_2. \tag{6.12}$$

Note that the input difference is independent of the key K. This is the fundamental observation that enables differential cryptanalysis to work.

Let $Y_1 = \texttt{Sbox}(X_1 \oplus K)$ and let $Y_2 = \texttt{Sbox}(X_2 \oplus K)$. Then the output difference $Y_1 \oplus Y_2$ is almost the input difference to next round. The goal is to carefully construct the input difference, so that we can "chain" differences through multiple rounds. Since the input difference is independent of the key—and since differential cryptanalysis is a chosen plaintext attack—we have the freedom to choose the inputs so that the output difference has any particular form that we desire.

Another crucial element of a differential attack is that an S-box input difference of zero always results in an output difference of zero. Why is this the case? An input difference of zero simply means that the input values, say, X_1 and X_2, are the same, in which case the output values Y_1 and Y_2 must be the same, that is, $Y_1 \oplus Y_2 = 0$. The importance of this elementary observation is that we can make S-boxes "inactive" with respect to differential cryptanalysis by choosing their input differences to be zero.

A final observation is that it is not necessary that things happen with certainty. In other words, if an outcome only occurs with some nontrivial probability, then we may be able to develop a probabilistic attack that will still prove useful in recovering the key.

Given any S-box, we can analyze it for useful input differences as follows. For each possible input value X, find all pairs X_1 and X_2 such that

$$X = X_1 \oplus X_2$$

and compute the corresponding output differences

$$Y = Y_1 \oplus Y_2,$$

where

$$Y_1 = \text{Sbox}(X_1) \text{ and } Y_2 = \text{Sbox}(X_1).$$

By tabulating the resulting counts, we can find the most biased input values. For example for the S-box in (6.10), this analysis yields the results in Table 6.6.

Table 6.6: S-box Difference Analysis

	$\text{Sbox}(X_1) \oplus \text{Sbox}(X_2)$			
$X_1 \oplus X_2$	00	01	10	11
000	8	0	0	0
001	0	0	4	4
010	0	8	0	0
011	0	0	4	4
100	0	0	4	4
101	4	4	0	0
110	0	0	4	4
111	4	4	0	0

For any S-box, an input difference of 000 is not interesting—the input values are the same and the S-box is "inactive" (with respect to differences), since the output values must be the same. For the example in Table 6.6, an input difference of 010 always gives an output of 01, which is the most biased possible result. And, as noted in equation (6.12), by selecting, say, $X_1 \oplus X_2 = 010$, the actual input difference to the S-box would be 010 since the key K drops out of the difference.

Differential cryptanalysis of DES is fairly complex. To illustrate the technique more concretely, but without all of the complexity inherent in DES, we'll present a scaled-down version of DES that we call Tiny DES, or TDES. Then we'll perform differential and linear cryptanalysis on TDES. But first we present a quick overview of linear cryptanalysis.

6.4.3 Overview of Linear Cryptanalysis

Ironically, linear cryptanalysis—like differential cryptanalysis—is focused on the nonlinear part of a block cipher. Although linear cryptanalysis was developed a few years after differential cryptanalysis, it's conceptually simpler, it's more effective on DES, and it only requires known plaintext—as opposed to chosen plaintext.

In differential cryptanalysis, we focused on input and output differences. In linear cryptanalysis, the objective is to approximate the nonlinear part of a cipher with linear equations. Since mathematicians are good at solving linear equations, if we can find such approximations, it stands to reason that we can use these to attack the cipher. Since the only nonlinear part of DES is its S-boxes, linear cryptanalysis will be focused on the S-boxes.

Consider again the simple S-box in (6.10). We denote the three input bits as $x_0 x_1 x_2$ and the two output bits as $y_0 y_1$. Then x_0 determines the row, and $x_1 x_2$ determines the column. In Table 6.7, we've tabulated the number of values for which each possible linear approximation holds. Note that any table entry that is not 4 indicates a nonrandom output.

Table 6.7: S-box Linear Analysis

input bits	output bits		
	y_0	y_1	$y_0 \oplus y_1$
0	4	4	4
x_0	4	4	4
x_1	4	6	2
x_2	4	4	4
$x_0 \oplus x_1$	4	2	2
$x_0 \oplus x_2$	0	4	4
$x_1 \oplus x_2$	4	6	6
$x_0 \oplus x_1 \oplus x_2$	4	6	2

The results in Table 6.7 show that, for example, $y_0 = x_0 \oplus x_2 \oplus 1$ with probability 1 and $y_0 \oplus y_1 = x_1 \oplus x_2$ with probability $3/4$. Using information such as this, in our analysis we can replace the S-boxes by linear functions. The result is that, in effect, we've traded the nonlinear S-boxes for linear equations, where the linear equations do not hold with certainty, but instead the equations hold with some nontrivial probability.

For these linear approximations to be useful in attacking a block cipher such as DES, we'll try to extend this approach so that we can solve linear equations for the key. As with differential cryptanalysis, we must somehow "chain" these results through multiple rounds.

How well can we approximate a DES S-box with linear functions? Each DES S-boxes was designed so that no linear combination of inputs is a good approximation to a single output bit. However, there are linear combinations of output bits that can be approximated by linear combinations of input bits. As a result, there is potential for success in the linear cryptanalysis of DES.

As with differential cryptanalysis, the linear cryptanalysis of DES is complex. To illustrate a linear attack, we'll next describe TDES, a scaled-down DES-like cipher. Then we'll perform differential and linear cryptanalysis on TDES.

6.4.4   Tiny DES

Tiny DES, or TDES, is a DES-like cipher that is simpler and easier to analyze than DES. TDES was designed by your contriving author to make linear and differential attacks easy to study—it is a contrived cipher that is trivial to break. Yet it's similar enough to DES to illustrate the principles.

TDES is a much simplified version of DES with the following numerology.

- A 16-bit block size

- A 16-bit key size

- Four rounds

- Two S-boxes, each mapping 6 bits to 4 bits

- A 12-bit subkey in each round

TDES has no P-box, initial or final permutation. Essentially, we have eliminated all features of DES that contribute nothing to its security, while at the same time scaling down the block and key sizes.

Note that the small key and block sizes imply that TDES cannot offer any real security, regardless of the underlying algorithm. Nevertheless, TDES will be a useful design for illustrating linear and differential attacks, as well as the larger issues of block cipher design.

TDES is a Feistel cipher and we denote the plaintext as (L_0, R_0). Then for $i = 1, 2, 3, 4$,

$$L_i = R_{i-1}$$
$$R_i = L_{i-1} \oplus F(R_{i-1}, K_i)$$

where the ciphertext is (L_4, R_4). A single round of TDES is illustrated in Figure 6.8, where the numbers of bits are indicated on each line. Next, we'll completely describe all of the pieces of the TDES algorithm.

TDES has two S-boxes, denoted $\texttt{SboxLeft}(X)$ and $\texttt{SboxRight}(X)$. Both S-boxes map 6 bits to 4 bits, as in standard DES. The parts of TDES that we'll be most interested in are the S-boxes and their input. To simplify the notation, we'll define the function

$$F(R, K) = \texttt{Sboxes}(\texttt{expand}(R) \oplus K), \tag{6.13}$$

where

$$\texttt{Sboxes}(x_0 x_1 x_2 \ldots x_{11}) = (\texttt{SboxLeft}(x_0 x_1 \ldots x_5), \texttt{SboxRight}(x_6 x_7 \ldots x_{11})).$$

The expansion permutation is given by

$$\texttt{expand}(R) = \texttt{expand}(r_0 r_1 \ldots r_7) = (r_4 r_7 r_2 r_1 r_5 r_7 r_0 r_2 r_6 r_5 r_0 r_3). \tag{6.14}$$

then from Table 6.8 we almost certainly have $L_3 \oplus \tilde{L}_3 = 0000\ 0000$, that is, $L_3 = \tilde{L}_3$. It follows that

$$R_4 \oplus F(L_4, K_4) = \tilde{R}_4 \oplus F(\tilde{L}_4, K_4)$$

which we rewrite as

$$R_4 \oplus \tilde{R}_4 = F(L_4, K_4) \oplus F(\tilde{L}_4, K_4). \qquad (6.23)$$

Note that, in equation (6.23), the only unknown is the subkey K_4. Next, we show how to use this result to recover some of the bits of K_4.

For a chosen plaintext pair that satisfies equation (6.19), if the resulting ciphertext pairs satisfy equation (6.22), then we know that equation (6.23) holds. Then since

$$C \oplus \tilde{C} = (L_4, R_4) \oplus (\tilde{L}_4, \tilde{R}_4) = \texttt{0x0202},$$

we have

$$R_4 \oplus \tilde{R}_4 = 0000\ 0010 \qquad (6.24)$$

and we also have

$$L_4 \oplus \tilde{L}_4 = 0000\ 0010. \qquad (6.25)$$

Let

$$L_4 = \ell_0\ell_1\ell_2\ell_3\ell_4\ell_5\ell_6\ell_7 \quad \text{and} \quad \tilde{L}_4 = \tilde{\ell}_0\tilde{\ell}_1\tilde{\ell}_2\tilde{\ell}_3\tilde{\ell}_4\tilde{\ell}_5\tilde{\ell}_6\tilde{\ell}_7.$$

Then equation (6.25) implies that $\ell_i = \tilde{\ell}_i$ for $i = 0, 1, 2, 3, 4, 5, 7$ and $\ell_6 \neq \tilde{\ell}_6$. Now substituting equation (6.24) into equation (6.23) and expanding the definition of F, we find

$$0000\ 0010 = \Big(\texttt{SboxLeft}(\ell_4\ell_7\ell_2\ell_1\ell_5\ell_7 \oplus k_0k_2k_3k_4k_5k_7),$$

$$\texttt{SboxRight}(\ell_0\ell_2\ell_6\ell_5\ell_0\ell_3 \oplus k_{13}k_{14}k_{15}k_9k_{10}k_{11})\Big)$$

$$\oplus \Big(\texttt{SboxLeft}(\tilde{\ell}_4\tilde{\ell}_7\tilde{\ell}_2\tilde{\ell}_1\tilde{\ell}_5\tilde{\ell}_7 \oplus k_0k_2k_3k_4k_5k_7),$$

$$\texttt{SboxRight}(\tilde{\ell}_0\tilde{\ell}_2\tilde{\ell}_6\tilde{\ell}_5\tilde{\ell}_0\tilde{\ell}_3 \oplus k_{13}k_{14}k_{15}k_9k_{10}k_{11})\Big). \qquad (6.26)$$

The left four bits of equation (6.26) give us

$$0000 = \texttt{SboxLeft}(\ell_4\ell_7\ell_2\ell_1\ell_5\ell_7 \oplus k_0k_2k_3k_4k_5k_7)$$

$$\oplus \texttt{SboxLeft}(\tilde{\ell}_4\tilde{\ell}_7\tilde{\ell}_2\tilde{\ell}_1\tilde{\ell}_5\tilde{\ell}_7 \oplus k_0k_2k_3k_4k_5k_7),$$

which holds for any choice of the bits $k_0k_2k_3k_4k_5k_7$, since $\ell_i = \tilde{\ell}_i$ for all $i \neq 6$. Therefore, we gain no information about the subkey K_4 from the left S-box.

On the other hand, the right four bits of equation (6.26) give us

$$0010 = \texttt{SboxRight}(\ell_0\ell_2\ell_6\ell_5\ell_0\ell_3 \oplus k_{13}k_{14}k_{15}k_9k_{10}k_{11})$$
$$\oplus \texttt{SboxRight}(\tilde{\ell}_0\tilde{\ell}_2\tilde{\ell}_6\tilde{\ell}_5\tilde{\ell}_0\tilde{\ell}_3 \oplus k_{13}k_{14}k_{15}k_9k_{10}k_{11}), \qquad (6.27)$$

which must hold for the correct choice of subkey bits $k_{13}k_{14}k_{15}k_9k_{10}k_{11}$ and will only hold with some probability for an incorrect choice of these subkey bits. Since the right S-box and the bits of L_4 and $\tilde{L}_4$ are known, we can determine the unknown subkey bits that appear in equation (6.27). The algorithm for recovering these key bits is given in Table 6.9.

Table 6.9: Algorithm to Recover Subkey Bits

```
count[i] = 0, for i = 0, 1, ..., 63
for i = 1 to iterations
    Choose P and P̃ with P ⊕ P̃ = 0x0002
    Obtain corresponding C = c₀c₁...c₁₅ and C̃ = c̃₀c̃₁...c̃₁₅
    if C ⊕ C̃ = 0x0202 then
        ℓᵢ = cᵢ and ℓ̃ᵢ = c̃ᵢ for i = 0, 1, ..., 7
        for K = 0 to 63
            if 0010 == (SboxRight(ℓ₀ℓ₂ℓ₆ℓ₅ℓ₀ℓ₃ ⊕ K)
                        ⊕ SboxRight(ℓ̃₀ℓ̃₂ℓ̃₆ℓ̃₅ℓ̃₀ℓ̃₃ ⊕ K)) then
                increment count[K]
            end if
        next K
    end if
next i
```

Each time the **for** loop in Table 6.9 is executed, count$[K]$ will be incremented for the correct subkey bits, that is, for $K = k_{13}k_{14}k_{15}k_9k_{10}k_{11}$, while for other indices K the count will be incremented with some probability. Consequently, the maximum counts indicate possible subkey values. There may be more than one such maximum count, but with a sufficient number of iterations, the number of such counts should be small.

In one particular test case of the algorithm in Table 6.9, we generated 100 pairs P and $\tilde{P}$ that satisfy $P \oplus \tilde{P} = \texttt{0x0002}$. We found that 47 of the resulting ciphertext pairs satisfied $C \oplus \tilde{C} = \texttt{0x0202}$, and for each of these we tried all 64 possible 6-bit subkeys as required by the algorithm in Table 6.9. In this experiment, we found that each of the four putative subkeys 000001, 001001, 110000, and 000111 had the maximum count of 47, while no other had a count greater than 39. We conclude that subkey K_4 must be one of these four values. Then from the definition of K_4 we have

$$k_{13}k_{14}k_{15}k_9k_{10}k_{11} \in \{000001, 001001, 110000, 111000\},$$

which is equivalent to

$$k_{13}k_{14}k_9k_{10}k_{11} \in \{00001, 11000\}. \qquad (6.28)$$

In this case, the key is

$$K = 1010\ 1001\ 1000\ 0111,$$

so that $k_{13}k_{14}k_9k_{10}k_{11} = 11000$, which appears in equation (6.28), as expected.

Of course, if we're the attacker, we don't know the key, so, to complete the recovery of K, we could exhaustively search over the remaining 2^{11} unknown key bits, and for each of these try both of the possibilities in equation (6.28). For each of these 2^{12} putative keys K, we would try to decrypt the ciphertext, and for the correct key, we will recover the plaintext. We expect to try about half of the possibilities—about 2^{11} keys—before finding the correct key K.

The total expected work to recover the entire key K by this method is about 2^{11} encryptions, plus the work required for the differential attack, which is insignificant in comparison. As a result, we can recover the entire 16-bit key with a work factor of about 2^{11} encryptions, which is much better than an exhaustive key search, since an exhaustive search has an expected work of 2^{15} encryptions. This shows that a shortcut attack exists, and as a result TDES is insecure.

6.4.6   Linear Cryptanalysis of TDES

The linear cryptanalysis of TDES is simpler than the differential cryptanalysis. Whereas the differential cryptanalysis of TDES focused on the right S-box, our linear cryptanalysis attack will focus on the left S-box, which appears above in (6.15).

With the notation

$$y_0y_1y_2y_3 = \texttt{SboxLeft}(x_0x_1x_2x_3x_4x_5),$$

it's easy to verify that for the left S-box of TDES, the linear approximations

$$y_1 = x_2 \text{ and } y_2 = x_3 \qquad (6.29)$$

each hold with probability 3/4. To develop a linear attack based on these equations, we must be able to chain these results through multiple rounds.

Denote the plaintext by $P = (L_0, R_0)$ and let $R_0 = r_0 r_1 r_2 r_3 r_4 r_5 r_6 r_7$. Then the expansion permutation is given by

$$\text{expand}(R_0) = \text{expand}(r_0 r_1 r_2 r_3 r_4 r_5 r_6 r_7) = r_4 r_7 r_2 r_1 r_5 r_7 r_0 r_2 r_6 r_5 r_0 r_3. \quad (6.30)$$

From the definition of F in equation (6.13), we see that the input to the S-boxes in round one is given by $\text{expand}(R_0) \oplus K_1$. Then, from equation (6.30) and the definition of subkey K_1, we see that the input to the left S-box in round one is

$$r_4 r_7 r_2 r_1 r_5 r_7 \oplus k_2 k_4 k_5 k_6 k_7 k_1.$$

Let $y_0 y_1 y_2 y_3$ be the round-one output of the left S-box. Then equation (6.29) implies that

$$y_1 = r_2 \oplus k_5 \quad \text{and} \quad y_2 = r_1 \oplus k_6, \quad (6.31)$$

where each equality holds with probability $3/4$. In other words, for the left S-box, output bit number 1 is input bit number 2, XORed with a bit of key, and output bit number 2 is input bit number 1, XORed with a key bit, where each of these hold with probability $3/4$.

In TDES (as in DES) the output of the S-boxes is XORed with the bits of the old left half. Let $L_0 = \ell_0 \ell_1 \ell_2 \ell_3 \ell_4 \ell_5 \ell_6 \ell_7$ and let $R_1 = \tilde{r}_0 \tilde{r}_1 \tilde{r}_2 \tilde{r}_3 \tilde{r}_4 \tilde{r}_5 \tilde{r}_6 \tilde{r}_7$. Then the the output of the left S-box from round one is XORed with $\ell_0 \ell_1 \ell_2 \ell_3$ to yield $\tilde{r}_0 \tilde{r}_1 \tilde{r}_2 \tilde{r}_3$. Combining this notation with equation (6.31), we have

$$\tilde{r}_1 = r_2 \oplus k_5 \oplus \ell_1 \quad \text{and} \quad \tilde{r}_2 = r_1 \oplus k_6 \oplus \ell_2, \quad (6.32)$$

where each of these equations holds with probability $3/4$. An analogous result holds for subsequent rounds, where the specific key bits depend on the subkey K_i.

As a result of equation (6.32), we can chain the linear approximation in equation (6.29) through multiple rounds. This is illustrated in Table 6.10. Since linear cryptanalysis is a known plaintext attack, the attacker knows the plaintext $P = p_0 p_1 p_2 \ldots p_{15}$ and corresponding ciphertext $C = c_0 c_1 c_2 \ldots c_{15}$.

The final row in Table 6.10 follows from the fact $L_4 = c_0 c_1 c_2 c_3 c_4 c_5 c_6 c_7$. We can rewrite these equations as

$$k_0 \oplus k_1 = c_1 \oplus p_{10} \quad (6.33)$$

and

$$k_7 \oplus k_2 = c_2 \oplus p_9 \quad (6.34)$$

where both hold with probability $(3/4)^3$. Since c_1, c_2, p_9, and p_{10} are all known, we have obtained some information about the key bits k_0, k_1, k_2, and k_7.

Table 6.10: Linear Cryptanalysis of TDES

$(L_0, R_0) = (p_0 \ldots p_7, p_8 \ldots p_{15})$	Bits 1 and 2 (numbered from 0)	Probability
$L_1 = R_0$	p_9, p_{10}	1
$R_1 = L_0 \oplus F(R_0, K_1)$	$p_1 \oplus p_{10} \oplus k_5, \ p_2 \oplus p_9 \oplus k_6$	3/4
$L_2 = R_1$	$p_1 \oplus p_{10} \oplus k_5, \ p_2 \oplus p_9 \oplus k_6$	3/4
$R_2 = L_1 \oplus F(R_1, K_2)$	$p_2 \oplus k_6 \oplus k_7, \ p_1 \oplus k_5 \oplus k_0$	$(3/4)^2$
$L_3 = R_2$	$p_2 \oplus k_6 \oplus k_7, \ p_1 \oplus k_5 \oplus k_0$	$(3/4)^2$
$R_3 = L_2 \oplus F(R_2, K_3)$	$p_{10} \oplus k_0 \oplus k_1, \ p_9 \oplus k_7 \oplus k_2$	$(3/4)^3$
$L_4 = R_3$	$p_{10} \oplus k_0 \oplus k_1, \ p_9 \oplus k_7 \oplus k_2$	$(3/4)^3$
$R_4 = L_3 \oplus F(R_3, K_4)$		
$C = (L_4, R_4)$	$c_1 = p_{10} \oplus k_0 \oplus k_1, \ c_2 = p_9 \oplus k_7 \oplus k_2$	$(3/4)^3$

It's easy to implement a linear attack based on the results in Table 6.10. We are given the known plaintexts $P = p_0 p_1 p_2 \ldots p_{15}$ along with the corresponding ciphertext $C = c_0 c_1 c_2 \ldots c_{15}$. For each such pair, we increment a counter depending on whether

$$c_1 \oplus p_{10} = 0 \quad \text{or} \quad c_1 \oplus p_{10} = 1$$

and another counter depending on whether

$$c_2 \oplus p_9 = 0 \quad \text{or} \quad c_2 \oplus p_9 = 1.$$

Using 100 known plaintexts the following results were obtained:

$$c_1 \oplus p_{10} = 0 \quad \text{occurred 38 times}$$
$$c_1 \oplus p_{10} = 1 \quad \text{occurred 62 times}$$
$$c_2 \oplus p_9 = 0 \quad \text{occurred 62 times}$$
$$c_2 \oplus p_9 = 1 \quad \text{occurred 38 times.}$$

In this case, we conclude from equation (6.33) that

$$k_0 \oplus k_1 = 1$$

and from equation (6.34) that

$$k_7 \oplus k_2 = 0.$$

In this example, the actual key is

$$K = 1010\ 0011\ 0101\ 0110,$$

and it's easily verified that $k_0 \oplus k_1 = 1$ and $k_7 \oplus k_2 = 0$ as we determined via the linear attack.

In this linear attack, we have only recovered the equivalent of two bits of information. To recover the entire key K, we could do an exhaustive key search for the remaining unknown bits. This would require an expected work of about 2^{13} encryptions and the work for the linear attack, which is negligible in comparison. While this may not seem too significant, it is a shortcut attack, and so it shows that TDES is insecure according to our definition.

6.4.7 Implications Block Cipher Design

Since there is no way to prove that a practical cipher is secure and since it's difficult to protect against unknown attacks, cryptographers focus on preventing known attacks. For block ciphers, the known attacks are, primarily, linear and differential cryptanalysis—and variations on these approaches. Thus the primary goal in block cipher design is to make linear and differential attacks infeasible.

How can cryptographers make linear and differential attacks more difficult? For an iterated block cipher, there is a fundamental trade-off between the number of rounds and the complexity of each round. That is, a simple round function will generally require a larger number of rounds to achieve the same degree of confusion and diffusion as a more complex function could achieve in fewer iterations.

In both linear and differential attacks, any one-round success probability that is less than 1 will almost certainly diminish with each subsequent round. Consequently, all else being equal, a block cipher with more rounds will be more secure from linear and differential attacks.

Another way to make linear and differential attacks more difficult is to have a high degree of confusion. That is, we can strive to reduce the success probability per round. For a DES-like cipher, this is equivalent to building better S-boxes. All else being equal—which it never is—more confusion means more security.

On the other hand, better diffusion will also tend to make linear and differential attacks harder to mount. In both types of attacks, it is necessary to chain results through multiple rounds, and better diffusion will make it harder to connect one-round successes into usable chains.

In TDES, the number of rounds is small, and, as a result, the one-round success probabilities are not sufficiently diminished during encryption. Also, the TDES S-boxes are poorly designed, resulting in limited confusion. Finally, the TDES `expand` permutation—the only source of diffusion in the cipher—does a poor job of mixing the bits of one round into the next round. All of these combine to yield a cipher that is highly susceptible to both linear and differential attacks.

To complicate the lives of block cipher designers, they must construct ciphers that are secure and efficient. One of the fundamental issues that block cipher designers must contend with is the inherent trade-off between the number of rounds and the complexity of each round. That is, a block cipher with a simple round structure will tend to provide limited mixing (diffusion) and limited nonlinearity (confusion), and consequently more rounds will be required.

The Tiny Encryption Algorithm (TEA) is a good example of a block cipher with a simple round structure. Since each round of TEA is extremely simple, the resulting confusion and diffusion properties are fairly weak, which necessitates a large number of rounds. At the other extreme, each round of the Advanced Encryption Standard (AES) has strong linear mixing and excellent nonlinear properties. So a relatively small number of AES rounds are needed, but each AES round is more complex than a round of TEA. Finally, DES could be viewed as residing in between these two extremes.

6.5 Lattice Reduction and the Knapsack

Every private in the French army carries a Field Marshal wand in his knapsack.
— Napoleon Bonaparte

In this section we present the details of the attack on the original Merkle-Hellman knapsack cryptosystem. This knapsack cryptosystem is discussed in Section 4.2 of Chapter 4. For a more rigorous (but still readable) presentation of the attack discussed here, see [175]. Note that some elementary linear algebra is required in this section. The Appendix contains a review of the necessary material.

Let $b_1, b_2, \ldots, b_n$ be vectors in $\mathbf{R}^m$, that is, each b_i is a (column) vector consisting of exactly m real numbers. A *lattice* is the set of all multiples of the vector b_i of the form

$$\alpha_1 b_1 + \alpha_2 b_2 + \cdots + \alpha_n b_n,$$

where each α_i in an integer.

For example, consider the vectors

$$b_1 = \begin{bmatrix} -1 \\ 1 \end{bmatrix} \text{ and } b_2 = \begin{bmatrix} 1 \\ 2 \end{bmatrix}. \tag{6.35}$$

Since b_1 and b_2 are linearly independent, any point in the plane can be written as $\alpha_1 b_1 + \alpha_2 b_2$ for some real numbers α_1 and α_2. We say that the plane $\mathbf{R}^2$ is *spanned* by the pair (b_1, b_2). If we restrict α_1 and α_2 to integers, then the resulting span, that is, all points of the form $\alpha_1 b_1 + \alpha_2 b_2$, is a *lattice*. A lattice

consists of a discrete set of points. For example, the lattice spanned by the
the vectors in equation (6.35) is illustrated in Figure 6.9.

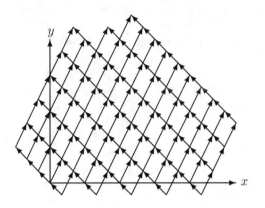

Figure 6.9: A Lattice in the Plane

Many combinatorial problems can be reduced to the problem of finding a
"short" vector in a lattice. The knapsack is one such problem. Short vectors
in a lattice can be found using a technique known as *lattice reduction*.

Before discussing the lattice reduction attack on the knapsack, let's first
consider another combinatorial problem that can be solved using this technique. The problem that we'll consider is the *exact cover*, which can be stated
as follows. Given a set S and a collection of subsets of S, find a collection
of these subsets where each element of S is in exactly one subset. It's not
always possible to find such a collection of subsets, but if it is, we'll see that
the solution is a short vector in a particular lattice.

Consider the following example of the exact cover problem. Let

$$S = \{0, 1, 2, 3, 4, 5, 6\}$$

and suppose we are given 13 subsets of S, which we label s_0 through s_{12} as
follows:

$$s_0 = \{0, 1, 3\}, s_1 = \{0, 1, 5\}, s_2 = \{0, 2, 4\}, s_3 = \{0, 2, 5\},$$
$$s_4 = \{0, 3, 6\}, s_5 = \{1, 2, 4\}, s_6 = \{1, 2, 6\}, s_7 = \{1, 3, 5\},$$
$$s_8 = \{1, 4, 6\}, s_9 = \{1\}, s_{10} = \{2, 5, 6\}, s_{11} = \{3, 4, 5\}, s_{12} = \{3, 4, 6\}.$$

Denote the number of elements of S by m and the number of subsets by n.
In this example, we have $m = 7$ and $n = 13$. Can we find a collection of
these 13 subsets where each element of S is in exactly one subset?

There are 2^{13} different collections of the 13 subsets, so we could exhaustively search through all possible collections until we find such a collection—or

until we've tried them all, in which case we would conclude that no such collection exists. But if there are too many subsets, then we need an alternative approach.

One alternative is to try a *heuristic search* technique. There are many different types of heuristic search strategies, but what they all have in common is that they search through the set of possible solutions in a nonrandom manner. The goal of such a search strategy is to search in a "smart" way to improve the odds of finding a solution sooner than an exhaustive search.

Lattice reduction can be viewed as a form of heuristic search. As a result, we are not assured of finding a solution using lattice reduction, but for many problems this techniques yields a solution with a high probability, yet the work required is small in comparison to an exhaustive search.

Before we can apply the lattice reduction method, we first need to rewrite the exact cover problem in matrix form. We define an $m \times n$ matrix A, where $a_{ij} = 1$ if element i of S is in subset s_j and otherwise $a_{ij} = 0$. Also, we define B to be a vector of length m consisting of all 1s. Then, if we can solve the matrix equation $AU = B$ for a vector U of 0s and 1s, we have solved the exact cover problem.

For the exact cover example above, the matrix equation $AU = B$ has the form

$$
\begin{bmatrix}
1 & 1 & 1 & 1 & 1 & 0 & 0 & 0 & 0 & 0 & 0 & 0 & 0 \\
1 & 1 & 0 & 0 & 0 & 1 & 1 & 1 & 1 & 1 & 0 & 0 & 0 \\
0 & 0 & 1 & 1 & 0 & 1 & 1 & 0 & 0 & 0 & 1 & 0 & 0 \\
1 & 0 & 0 & 0 & 1 & 0 & 0 & 1 & 0 & 0 & 0 & 1 & 1 \\
0 & 0 & 1 & 1 & 0 & 1 & 1 & 0 & 0 & 0 & 1 & 0 & 0 \\
0 & 1 & 0 & 1 & 0 & 0 & 0 & 1 & 0 & 0 & 1 & 1 & 0 \\
0 & 0 & 0 & 0 & 1 & 0 & 1 & 0 & 1 & 0 & 1 & 0 & 1
\end{bmatrix}
\begin{bmatrix}
u_0 \\ u_1 \\ u_2 \\ u_3 \\ u_4 \\ u_5 \\ u_6 \\ u_7 \\ u_8 \\ u_9 \\ u_{10} \\ u_{11} \\ u_{12}
\end{bmatrix}
=
\begin{bmatrix}
1 \\ 1 \\ 1 \\ 1 \\ 1 \\ 1 \\ 1
\end{bmatrix}
$$

and we seek a solution U where each $u_i \in \{0,1\}$, that is, $u_i = 1$ if the subset s_i is in the exact cover and $u_i = 0$ if subset s_i is not in the exact cover. In this particular case, it's easy to verify that a solution is given by $U = [0001000001001]$, that is, s_3, s_9, and s_{12} form an exact cover of the set S.

We have shown that the exact cover problem can be restated as finding a solution U to a matrix equation $AU = B$, where U consists entirely of 0s and 1s. This is not a standard linear algebra problem, since solutions to linear equations are not restricted to contain only 0s and 1s. This turns out to be a problem that can be solved using lattice reduction techniques. But first we need an elementary fact from linear algebra.

Suppose $AU = B$, where A is a matrix and U and B are column vectors. Let $a_1, a_2, \ldots, a_n$ denote the columns of A and $u_1, u_2, \ldots, u_n$ the elements of U. Then

$$B = u_1 a_1 + u_2 a_2 + \cdots + u_n a_n. \tag{6.36}$$

For example,

$$\begin{bmatrix} 3 & 4 \\ 1 & 5 \end{bmatrix} \begin{bmatrix} 2 \\ 6 \end{bmatrix} = 2 \begin{bmatrix} 3 \\ 1 \end{bmatrix} + 6 \begin{bmatrix} 4 \\ 5 \end{bmatrix} = \begin{bmatrix} 30 \\ 32 \end{bmatrix}.$$

Now given $AU = B$, consider the matrix equation

$$\begin{bmatrix} I_{n \times n} & 0_{n \times 1} \\ A_{m \times n} & -B_{m \times 1} \end{bmatrix} \begin{bmatrix} U_{n \times 1} \\ 1_{1 \times 1} \end{bmatrix} = \begin{bmatrix} U_{n \times 1} \\ 0_{m \times 1} \end{bmatrix},$$

which we denote as $MV = W$. Multiplying, we find that $U = U$ (which is not very informative) and the nontrivial equation $AU - B = 0$. Therefore, finding a solution V to $MV = W$ is equivalent to finding a solution U to the original equation $AU = B$.

The benefit of rewriting the problem as $MV = W$ is that the columns of M are linearly independent. This is easily seen to be the case, since the $n \times n$ identity matrix appears in the upper left, and the final column begins with n zeros.

Let $c_0, c_1, c_2, \ldots, c_n$ be the $n + 1$ columns of M and let $v_0, v_1, v_2, \ldots, v_n$ be the elements of V. Then, by the observation in equation (6.36),

$$W = v_0 c_0 + v_1 c_1 + \cdots + v_n c_n. \tag{6.37}$$

Let **L** be the lattice spanned by $c_0, c_1, c_2, \ldots, c_n$, the columns of M. Then **L** consists of all integer multiples of the columns of M. Recall that $MV = W$, where

$$W = \begin{bmatrix} u_0 \\ u_1 \\ \vdots \\ u_{n-1} \\ 0 \\ \vdots \\ 0 \end{bmatrix}.$$

Our goal is to find U. However, instead of solving linear equations for V, we can solve for U by finding W. By equation (6.37), this desired solution W is in the lattice **L**.

The Euclidean length of a vector $Y = (y_0, y_1, \ldots, y_{n-1}) \in \mathbf{R}^n$ is given by the formula

$$\|Y\| = \sqrt{y_0^2 + y_1^2 + \cdots + y_{n-1}^2}$$

Then the length of W is

$$||W|| = \sqrt{u_0^2 + u_1^2 + \cdots + u_{n-1}^2} \leq \sqrt{n}.$$

Since most vectors in L will have a length far greater than $\sqrt{n}$, we see that W is a short vector in the lattice L. Furthermore, W has a very special form, with its first n entries all equal to 0 or 1 and its last m entries all equal to 0. These facts distinguish W from typical vectors in L. Can we use this information to find W, which would give us a solution to the exact cover problem?

In fact, there is an algorithm known as the LLL algorithm [169, 189] (because it was invented by three guys whose names start with "L") to efficiently find short vectors in a lattice. Our strategy will be to use LLL to find short vectors in L, the lattice spanned by the columns of M. Then we'll examine these short vectors to see whether any have the special form of W. If we find such a vector, then it is highly probably that we have found a solution U to the original problem.

Pseudo-code for the LLL algorithm appears in Table 6.11, where the $(n + m) \times (n + 1)$ matrix M has columns $b_0, b_1, b_2, \ldots, b_n$ and the columns of matrix X are denoted $x_0, x_1, x_2 \ldots, x_n$ and the elements of Y are denoted as y_{ij}. Note that the y_{ij} can be negative, so care must be taken when implementing the floor function in $\lfloor y_{ij} + 1/2 \rfloor$.

For completeness, we've given the Gram-Schmidt orthogonalization algorithm in Table 6.12. Combined, these two algorithms only require about 30 lines of pseudo-code.

It's important to realize there is no guarantee that the LLL algorithm will find the desired vector W. But for certain types of problems, the probability of success is high.

By now, you may be wondering what any of this has to do with the knapsack cryptosystem. Next, we'll show that we can attack the knapsack via lattice reduction.

Let's consider the superincreasing knapsack

$$S = [s_0, s_1, \ldots, s_7] = [2, 3, 7, 14, 30, 57, 120, 251]$$

and choose the multiplier $m = 41$ and modulus $n = 491$ (note that this is the same knapsack example that appears in Section 4.2 of Chapter 4). Next, we observe that $m^{-1} = 12 \bmod 491$. Now to find the corresponding public knapsack, we compute $t_i = 41s_i \bmod 491$ for $i = 0, 1, \ldots, 7$, and the result is

$$T = [t_0, t_1, \ldots, t_7] = [82, 123, 287, 83, 248, 373, 10, 471].$$

This yields the knapsack cryptosystem defined by

Public key: T

Table 6.11: LLL Algorithm

// find short vectors in the lattice spanned
// by columns of $M = (b_0, b_1, \ldots, b_n)$
loop forever
    $(X, Y) = \text{GS}(M)$
    for $j = 1$ to n
        for $i = j - 1$ to 0
            if $|y_{ij}| > 1/2$ then
                $b_j = b_j - \lfloor y_{ij} + 1/2 \rfloor b_i$
            end if
        next i
    next j
    $(X, Y) = \text{GS}(M)$
    for $j = 0$ to $n - 1$
        if $\|x_{j+1} + y_{j,j+1}x_j\|^2 < \frac{3}{4}\|x_j\|^2$
            $\text{swap}(b_j, b_{j+1})$
            goto abc
        end if
    next j
    return(M)
abc: continue
end loop

---

and
$$\text{Private key: } S \text{ and } m^{-1} \bmod n.$$

For example, 10010110 is encrypted as

$$1 \cdot t_0 + 0 \cdot t_1 + 0 \cdot t_2 + 1 \cdot t_3 + 0 \cdot t_4 + 1 \cdot t_5 + 1 \cdot t_6 + 0 \cdot t_7$$
$$= 82 + 83 + 373 + 10$$
$$= 548.$$

To decrypt the ciphertext 548, the holder of the private key computes

$$548 \cdot 12 = 193 \bmod 491$$

and then uses the superincreasing knapsack S to easily solve for the plaintext 10010110.

In this particular example, the attacker Trudy knows the public key T and the ciphertext 548. Trudy can break the system if she can find $u_i \in \{0, 1\}$ so that

$$82u_0 + 123u_1 + 287u_2 + 83u_3 + 248u_4 + 373u_5 + 10u_6 + 471u_7 = 548. \quad (6.38)$$

Table 6.12: Gram-Schmidt Algorithm

// Gram-Schmidt $M = (b_0, b_1, \ldots, b_n)$
GS(M)
$\quad x_0 = b_0$
$\quad$ for $j = 1$ to n
$\quad\quad x_j = b_j$
$\quad\quad$ for $i = 0$ to $j - 1$
$\quad\quad\quad y_{ij} = (x_i \cdot b_j)/||x_i||^2$
$\quad\quad\quad x_j = x_j - y_{ij}x_i$
$\quad\quad$ next i
$\quad$ next j
$\quad$ return(X,Y)
end GS

To put this problem into the correct framework for lattice reduction, we rewrite the problem in matrix form as

$$T \cdot U = 548,$$

where T is the public knapsack and $U = [u_0, u_1, \ldots, u_7]$ appears in equation (6.38). This has the same form as $AU = B$ discussed above, so we rewrite this to put it into the form $MV = W$, which is then suitable for the LLL algorithm. In this case, we have

$$M = \begin{bmatrix} I_{8\times8} & 0_{8\times1} \\ T_{1\times8} & -C_{1\times1} \end{bmatrix} = \left[\begin{array}{cccccccc|c} 1 & 0 & 0 & 0 & 0 & 0 & 0 & 0 & 0 \\ 0 & 1 & 0 & 0 & 0 & 0 & 0 & 0 & 0 \\ 0 & 0 & 1 & 0 & 0 & 0 & 0 & 0 & 0 \\ 0 & 0 & 0 & 1 & 0 & 0 & 0 & 0 & 0 \\ 0 & 0 & 0 & 0 & 1 & 0 & 0 & 0 & 0 \\ 0 & 0 & 0 & 0 & 0 & 1 & 0 & 0 & 0 \\ 0 & 0 & 0 & 0 & 0 & 0 & 1 & 0 & 0 \\ 0 & 0 & 0 & 0 & 0 & 0 & 0 & 1 & 0 \\ 82 & 123 & 287 & 83 & 248 & 373 & 10 & 471 & -548 \end{array}\right].$$

We can now apply LLL to the matrix M to find short vectors in the lattice spanned by the columns of M. The output of LLL, which we denote by M' is a matrix of short vectors in the lattice spanned by the columns of M. In this example, LLL yields

$$M' = \begin{bmatrix} -1 & -1 & 0 & 1 & 0 & 1 & 0 & 0 & 1 \\ 0 & -1 & 1 & 0 & 1 & -1 & 0 & 0 & 0 \\ 0 & 1 & -1 & 0 & 0 & 0 & -1 & 1 & 2 \\ 1 & -1 & -1 & 1 & 0 & -1 & 0 & -1 & 0 \\ 0 & 0 & 1 & 0 & -2 & -1 & 0 & 1 & 0 \\ 0 & 0 & 0 & 1 & 1 & 1 & 1 & -1 & 1 \\ 0 & 0 & 0 & 1 & 0 & 0 & -1 & 0 & -1 \\ 0 & 0 & 0 & 0 & 0 & 0 & 1 & 1 & -1 \\ 1 & -1 & 1 & 0 & 0 & 1 & -1 & 2 & 0 \end{bmatrix}.$$

The 4th column of M' has the correct form to be a solution to the knapsack problem. For this column, Trudy obtains the putative solution

$$U = [1, 0, 0, 1, 0, 1, 1, 0]$$

and using the public key and the ciphertext, she can then easily verify that the putative solution 10010110 is, in fact, the correct solution. One interesting aspect of this particular attack is that Trudy can find the plaintext from the ciphertext without recovering the private key.

The lattice reduction attack on the knapsack is fast and efficient—it was originally demonstrated using an Apple II computer in 1983 [265]. Although the attack is not always successful, the probability of success against the original Merkle-Hellman knapsack is high.

Lattice reduction was a surprising method of attack on the knapsack cryptosystem. The lesson here is that clever mathematics (and algorithms) can sometimes break cryptosystems.

6.6   RSA Timing Attacks

> *All things entail rising and falling timing.*
> *You must be able to discern this.*
> — Miyamoto Musashi

Often it's possible to attack a cipher without directly attacking the algorithm [89]. Many processes produce unintended "side channels" that leak information. This incidental information can arise due to the way that a computation is performed, the media used, the power consumed, electromagnetic emanations, and so on. In some cases, this information can be used to recover a cryptographic key.

Paul Kocher, the father of side channel attacks [166], originally developed the technique as a way to demonstrate the vulnerablity of smartcards. Kocher singlehandedly delayed the widespread acceptance of smartcards by several years.

A large potential source of side channel information arises from so-called unintended emanations. There is an entire branch of security devoted to emissions security, or EMSEC, which also goes by the name of TEMPEST [199]. For example, Anderson [14] describes how electromagnetic fields, or EMF, from a computer screen can allow the screen image to be reconstructed at a distance.

Smartcards have been attacked via their EMF emanations as well as by *differential power analysis*, or DPA, which exploits the fact that some computations require more energy consumption than others [167]. Attacks on EMF emissions and DPA attacks are passive. More active attacks often go by the name of *differential fault analysis*, or DFA, where faults are induced with the goal of recovering information [11]. For example, excessive power may be put into a device to induce a fault. Such attacks may or may not be destructive. A smartcard used in some GSM cell phones could be attacked using DFA techniques [228].

In this section, we'll examine two timing attack on RSA. The first approach is impractical, but provides a relatively simple illustration of the concept, while the second attack has been used in the real world to break real systems.

Timing attacks exploit the fact that some computations in RSA take longer than others. By carefully measuring the time that an operation takes, we can determine the RSA private key, or at least some bits of the key [329]. More advanced versions of timing attacks have been used to successfully attack the RSA implementation in OpenSSL over a network connection [41]. For a discussion of timing attacks that apply to more general RSA implementations, see [284].

6.6.1 A Simple Timing Attack

Let M be a message that Alice is to sign using her private key d. Suppose that Alice signs M itself,[6] that is, Alice computes $M^d \bmod N$. As usual, Trudy's goal is to recover d. We'll assume that d is $n + 1$ bits in length, with n unknown bits, and we'll denote the bits of d as

$$d = d_0 d_1 \ldots d_n \quad \text{where} \quad d_0 = 1.$$

Recall that the method of repeated squaring provides an efficient means of computing modular exponentiation. Suppose repeated squaring is used

---

[6]The astute reader will recall that in Chapter 5 we said that Alice signs $h(M)$, not M. However, in security protocols, it's common to sign a random challenge without any hash being used—see Chapters 9 and 10. Many timing attacks arise in the context of security protocols, so here we'll consider the case where the message M is signed, without any hash.

to compute $M^d \bmod N$. Pseudo-code for the repeated squaring algorithm appears in Table 6.13.

Table 6.13: Repeated Squaring

```
x = M
for j = 1 to n
    x = mod(x², N)
    if dⱼ == 1 then
        x = mod(xM, N)
    end if
next j
return x
```

Suppose that the $\bmod(x, N)$ function in Table 6.13 is implemented as shown in Table 6.14. For efficiency, the expensive mod operation, denoted by "%," is only executed if a modular reduction is actually required.

Table 6.14: Efficient Mod Function

```
function mod(x, N)
if x >= N
    x = x % N
end if
return x
```

Now consider the repeated squaring algorithm in Table 6.13. If $d_j = 0$, then $x = \bmod(x^2, N)$, but if $d_j = 1$ then two operations occur, namely, $x = \bmod(x^2, N)$ and $x = \bmod(xM, N)$. As a result, the computation times might differ when $d_j = 0$ compared with when $d_j = 1$. Can Trudy take advantage of this to recover Alice's private key?

We'll assume that Trudy can conduct a "chosen plaintext" attack, that is, Alice will sign messages of Trudy's choosing. Suppose clever Trudy chooses two values, Y and Z, with $Y^3 < N$ and $Z^2 < N < Z^3$ and Alice signs both.

Let $x = Y$ and consider the $j = 1$ step in the repeated squaring algorithm of Table 6.13. We have

$$x = \bmod(x^2, N)$$

and since $x^2 = Y^2 < Y^3 < N$, the "%" operation does not occur. Then, if $d_1 = 1$, we have

$$x = \bmod(xY, N),$$

and since $xY = Y^3 < N$, again the "%" operation does not occur. Of course, if $d_1 = 0$, this "%" operation does not occur either.

Now let $x = Z$ and consider the $j = 1$ step in the algorithm of Table 6.13. In this case, we have

$$x = \mathrm{mod}(x^2, N)$$

and, since $x^2 = Z^2 < N$, the "%" operation does not occur. But if $d_1 = 1$, we have

$$x = \mathrm{mod}(xZ, N)$$

and the "%" operation occurs, since $xZ = Z^3 > N$. However, if $d_1 = 0$, then this "%" operation does not occur. That is, an additional "%" operation occurs only if $d_1 = 1$. As a result, if $d_1 = 1$ then the $j = 1$ step requires more computation and will take longer to complete for Z than for Y. If, on the other hand, $d_1 = 0$, the $j = 1$ computation step will take about the same amount of time for both Z and Y. Using this fact, can Trudy recover the bit d_1 of the private key d?

The problem for Trudy is that the repeated squaring algorithm does not stop after the $j = 1$ step. So, any timing difference in the $j = 1$ step might be swamped by timing differences that occur at later steps. But suppose Trudy can repeat this experiment many times with distinct Y and Z values, all of which satisfy the conditions given above, namely, $Y^3 < N$ and $Z^2 < N < Z^3$. Then if $d_1 = 0$, on average, Trudy would expect the Y and Z signatures to take about the same time. On the other hand, if $d_1 = 1$, then Trudy would expect the Z signatures to take longer than the Y signatures, on average. That is, timing differences for later steps in the algorithm would tend to cancel out, allowing the timing difference (or not) for the $j = 1$ step show through the noise. The point is that Trudy will need to rely on statistics gathered over many test cases to make this attack reliable.

Trudy can use the following algorithm to determine the unknown private key bit d_1. For $i = 0, 1, \ldots, m - 1$, Trudy chooses Y_i with $Y_i^3 < N$. Let y_i be the time required for Alice to sign Y_i, that is, the time required to compute $Y_i^d \bmod N$, for $i = 0, 1, \ldots, m - 1$. Then Trudy computes the average timing

$$y = (y_0 + y_1 + \cdots + y_{m-1})/m.$$

Next, for $i = 0, 1, \ldots, m - 1$, Trudy chooses Z_i with $Z_i^2 < N < Z_i^3$. Let z_i be the time required to compute $Z_i^d \bmod N$, for $i = 0, 1, \ldots, m - 1$. Again, Trudy computes the average timing

$$z = (z_0 + z_1 + \cdots + z_{m-1})/m.$$

Now if $z > y + \varepsilon$ then Trudy would assume that $d_1 = 1$, and otherwise she would assume $d_1 = 0$, where an appropriate value for ε could be determined by experimentation.

Once d_1 has been recovered, Trudy can use an analogous process to find d_2, although for this next step the Y and Z values will need to be chosen to satisfy different criteria. And once d_2 is known, Trudy can proceed to d_3 and so on—see Problem 31.

The attack discussed in this section is only practical for recovering the first few bits of the private key. Next, we discuss a more realistic timing attack that has been used to recover RSA private keys from smartcards and other resource-constrained devices.

6.6.2 Kocher's Timing Attack

The basic idea behind Kocher's timing attack [166] is elegant, yet reasonably straightforward. Suppose that the repeated squaring algorithm in Table 6.15 is used for modular exponentiation in RSA. Also, suppose that the time taken by the multiplication operation, $s = s \cdot x \pmod{N}$ in Table 6.15, varies depending on the values of s and x. Furthermore, we assume the attacker is able to determine the timings that will occur, given particular values of s and x.

Table 6.15: Repeated Squaring

```
// Compute y = x^d (mod N),
// where d = d_0 d_1 d_2 ... d_n in binary, with d_0 = 1
s = x
for i = 1 to n
    s = s^2 (mod N)
    if d_i == 1 then
        s = s · x (mod N)
    end if
next i
return(s)
```

Kocher views this as a signal detection problem, where the "signal" consists of the timing variations, which are dependent on the unknown private key bits d_i, for $i = 1, 2, \ldots, n$. The signal is corrupted by "noise," which is the result of the unknown private key bits, d_i. The objective is to recover the bits d_i one (or a few) at a time, beginning with the first unknown bit d_1. In practice, it is not necessary to recover all of the bits, since an algorithm due to Coppersmith [68] is feasible once a sufficient number of the high-order bits of d are known.

Suppose we have successfully determined bits $d_0, d_1, \ldots, d_{k-1}$ and we want to determine bit d_k. Then we randomly select several ciphertexts, say, C_j, for $j = 0, 1, 2, \ldots, m - 1$, and for each we obtain the timing $T(C_j)$ for the decryption (or signature) $C_j^d \pmod{N}$. For each of these ciphertext values, we can precisely emulate the repeated squaring algorithm in Table 6.15 for $i = 1, 2, \ldots, k - 1$, and at the $i = k$ step we can emulate both of the possible bit values, $d_k = 0$ and $d_k = 1$. Then we tabulate the differences between the measured timing and both of the emulated results. Kocher's crucial observation is that the statistical variance of the differences will be smaller for the correct choice of d_k than for the incorrect choice.

For example, suppose we are trying to obtain a private key that is only eight bits in length. Then

$$d = (d_0, d_1, d_2, d_3, d_4, d_5, d_6, d_7) \quad \text{with} \quad d_0 = 1.$$

Furthermore, suppose that we are certain that

$$d_0 d_1 d_2 d_3 \in \{1010, 1001\}.$$

Then we generate some number of random ciphertexts C_j, and for each we obtain the corresponding timing $T(C_j)$. We can emulate the first four steps of the repeated squaring algorithm for both

$$d_0 d_1 d_2 d_3 = 1010 \quad \text{and} \quad d_0 d_1 d_2 d_3 = 1001$$

for each of these ciphertexts. For a given timing $T(C_j)$, let t_ℓ be the actual time taken in step ℓ for the squaring and multiplying steps of the repeated squaring algorithm. That is, t_ℓ includes the timing of $s = s^2 \pmod{N}$ and, if $d_\ell = 1$, it also includes $s = s \cdot C_j \pmod{N}$ (see the algorithm in Table 6.15). Also, let $\tilde{t}_\ell$ be the time obtained when emulating the square and multiply steps for an assumed private exponent bit ℓ. For $m > \ell$, define the shorthand notation

$$\tilde{t}_{\ell \ldots m} = \tilde{t}_\ell + \tilde{t}_{\ell+1} + \cdots + \tilde{t}_m.$$

Of course, $\tilde{t}_\ell$ depends on the precise bits emulated, but to simplify the notation we do not explicitly state this dependence (it should be clear from context).

Now suppose we select four ciphertexts, C_0, C_1, C_2, C_3, and we obtain the timing results in Table 6.16. In this example we see that for $d_0 d_1 d_2 d_3 = 1010$ we have a mean timing of

$$E(T(C_j) - \tilde{t}_{0 \ldots 3}) = (7 + 6 + 6 + 5)/4 = 6,$$

while the corresponding variance is

$$\text{var}(T(C_j) - \tilde{t}_{0 \ldots 3}) = (1^2 + 0^2 + 0^2 + (-1)^2)/4 = 1/2.$$

On the other hand, for $d_0 d_1 d_2 d_3 = 1001$, we have

$$E(T(C_j) - \tilde{t}_{0 \ldots 3}) = 6,$$

but the variance is

$$\mathrm{var}(T(C_j) - \tilde{t}_{0...3}) = ((-1)^2 + 1^2 + (-1)^2 + 1^2)/4 = 1.$$

Although the mean is the same in both cases, Kocher's attack tells us that the smaller variance indicates that $d_0 d_1 d_2 d_3 = 1010$ is the correct answer. But this begs the question of why we should observe a smaller variance in case of a correct guess for $d_0 d_1 d_2 d_3$.

Table 6.16: Timings

j	$T(C_j)$	Emulate 1010		Emulate 1001	
		$\tilde{t}_{0...3}$	$T(C_j) - \tilde{t}_{0...3}$	$\tilde{t}_{0...3}$	$T(C_j) - \tilde{t}_{0...3}$
0	12	5	7	7	5
1	11	5	6	4	7
2	12	6	6	7	5
3	13	8	5	6	7

Consider $T(C_j)$, the timing of a particular computation $C_j^d \pmod{N}$ in Table 6.16. As above, for this $T(C_j)$, let $\tilde{t}_\ell$ be the emulated timing for the square and multiply steps corresponding to the ℓth bit of the private exponent. Also, let t_ℓ be the actual timing of the square and multiply steps corresponding to the ℓth bit of the private exponent. Let u include all timing not accounted for in the t_ℓ. The value u can be viewed as representing the measurement "error." In the example above, we assumed the private exponent d is eight bits, so for this case

$$T(C_j) = t_0 + t_1 + t_2 + \cdots + t_7 + u.$$

Now suppose that the high-order bits of d are $d_0 d_1 d_2 d_3 = 1010$. Then for the timing $T(C_j)$ we have

$$\mathrm{var}(T(C_j) - \tilde{t}_{0...3}) = \mathrm{var}(t_4) + \mathrm{var}(t_5) + \mathrm{var}(t_6) + \mathrm{var}(t_7) + \mathrm{var}(u),$$

since $\tilde{t}_\ell = t_\ell$, for $\ell = 0, 1, 2, 3$ and, consequently, there is no variance due to these emulated timings $\tilde{t}_\ell$. Note that here we are assuming the t_ℓ are independent and that the measurement error u is independent of the t_ℓ, which appear to be valid assumptions. If we denote the common variance of each t_ℓ by $\mathrm{var}(t)$, we have

$$\mathrm{var}(T(C_j) - \tilde{t}_{0...3}) = 4\,\mathrm{var}(t) + \mathrm{var}(u).$$

However, if $d_0 d_1 d_2 d_3 = 1010$, but we emulate $d_0 d_1 d_2 d_3 = 1001$, then from the point of the first d_j that is in error, our emulation will fail, giving us essentially random timing results. In this case, the first emulation error occurs at d_2 so that we find

$$\text{var}(T - \tilde{t}_{0\ldots3}) = \text{var}(t_2 - \tilde{t}_2) + \text{var}(t_3 - \tilde{t}_3) + \text{var}(t_4) + \text{var}(t_5)$$
$$+ \text{var}(t_6) + \text{var}(t_7) + \text{var}(u)$$
$$\approx 6\,\text{var}(t) + \text{var}(u)$$

since the emulated timings $\tilde{t}_2$ and $\tilde{t}_3$ can vary from the actual timings t_2 and t_3, respectively. That is, we see a larger variance when our guess for the private key bits is incorrect.

Although conceptually simple, Kocher's technique gives a powerful and practical approach to conducting a timing attack on an RSA implementation that uses repeated squaring (but not more advanced techniques). For the attack to succeed, the variance of the error term u must not vary too greatly between the different cases that are tested. Assuming that a simple repeated squaring algorithm is employed, this would almost certainly be the case since u only includes loop overhead and timing error. For more advanced modular exponentiation techniques, $\text{var}(u)$ could differ greatly for different emulated bits, effectively masking the timing information needed to recover the bits of d.

The amount of data required for Kocher's attack (that is, the number of chosen decryptions that must be timed) depends on the error term u. However, the timings can be reused as bits of d are determined, since, given additional bits of d, only the emulation steps need to change. Therefore, the required number of timings is not nearly as daunting as it might appear at first blush. Again, this attack has been used to break real systems.

The major limitation to Kocher's attack is that it has only been successfully applied to RSA implementations that only use repeated squaring. Most RSA implementations also use various other techniques (Chinese Remainder Theorem, Montgomery multiplication, Karatsuba multiplication) to speed up the modular exponentiations. Only in highly resource-constrained environments (such as smartcards) is repeated squaring used without any of these other techniques.

In [166], Kocher argues that his timing attack should work for RSA implementations that employ techniques other than repeated squaring. However, Schindler [257] (among others) disputes this assertion. In any case, different timing techniques have been developed that succeed against more highly optimized RSA implementations. As previously noted, the RSA implementation in a recent version of OpenSSL was broken using a timing attack due to Brumley and Boneh [41].

The lesson of side channel attacks is an important one that extends far beyond the details of any particular attack. Side channels demonstrate that even if crypto is secure in theory, it may not be so in practice. That is, it's not sufficient to analyze a cipher in isolation—for a cipher to be considered secure in practice, it must be analyzed in the context of a specific implementation and the larger system in which it resides. Many of these factors don't directly relate to the mathematical properties of the cipher itself. Schneier has a good article that addresses some of these issues [261].

Side channel attacks nicely illustrate that attackers don't always play by the (presumed) rules. Attackers will try to exploit the weakest link in any security system. The best way to protect against such attacks is to think like an attacker and find these weak links before Trudy does.

6.7 Summary

In this chapter, we presented several advanced cryptanalytic attacks and techniques. We started with a classic World War II cipher, the Enigma, where the attack illustrated a "divide and conquer" approach. That is, an important component of the device (the stecker) could be split off from the rest of the cipher with devastating consequences. Then we considered a stream cipher attack, specifically, RC4 as used in WEP. This attack showed that even a strong cipher can be broken if used incorrectly.

In the block cipher realm, we discussed differential and linear cryptanalysis and these attacks were applied to TDES, a simplified version of DES. Some knowledge of these topics is necessary to understand the fundamental trade-offs in block cipher design.

Next, we presented a classic attack on the Merkle-Hellman knapsack public key cryptosystem. This attack nicely illustrates the impact that mathematical advances and clever algorithms can have on cryptography.

Side channel attacks have become important in recent years. It's crucial to be aware of such attacks, which go beyond the traditional concept of cryptanalysis, since they represent a real threat to otherwise secure ciphers. We discussed specific side channel attacks on RSA.

As usual, we've only scratched the surface in this chapter. Many other cryptanalytic attacks and techniques have been developed, and cryptanalysis remains an active area of research. The cryptanalytic attacks discussed here provide a reasonably representative sample of the methods that are used to attack and analyze ciphers.

6.8 Problems

1. In World War II, the German's usually used 10 cables on the stecker, only five different rotors were in general use, one reflector was in common use, and the reflector and five rotors were known to the Allies.

a. Under these restrictions, show that there are only about 2^{77} possible Enigma keys.

b. Show that if we ignore the stecker, under these restrictions there are fewer than 2^{30} settings.

2. Let $F(p)$, for $p = 0, 1, 2, \ldots, 13$, be the number of ways to plug p cables into the Enigma stecker. Show that

$$F(p) = \binom{26}{2p} \cdot (2p - 1) \cdot (2p - 3) \cdot \cdots \cdot 1.$$

3. Recall that for the Enigma attack described in Section 6.2.4, we found the cycles

$$S(\text{E}) = P_6 P_8 P_{13} S(\text{E})$$

and

$$S(\text{E}) = P_6 P_{14}^{-1} P_7 P_6^{-1} S(\text{E}).$$

Find two more independent cycles involving $S(\text{E})$ that can be obtained from the matched plaintext and ciphertext in Table 6.2.

4. How many pairs of cycles are required to uniquely determine the Enigma rotor settings?

5. In the text, we mentioned that the Enigma cipher is its own inverse.

a. Prove that the Enigma is its own inverse. Hint: Suppose that the ith plaintext letter is x, and that the corresponding ith ciphertext letter is y. This implies that when the ith letter typed into the keyboard is x, the letter y is illuminated on the lightboard. Show that for the same key settings, if the ith letter typed into the keyboard is y, then the letter x is illuminated on the lightboard.

b. What is the advantage of a cipher machine that is its own inverse (such as the Enigma), as compared to a cipher that is not (such as Purple and Sigaba)?

6. This problem deals with the Enigma cipher.

a. Show that a ciphertext letter cannot be the same as the corresponding plaintext letter.

b. Explain how the restriction in part a gives the cryptanalyst an advantage when searching for a crib.[7]

---

[7]In modern parlance, a crib is known as known plaintext.

7. Consider the Enigma attack discussed in the text and suppose that only cycles of $S(\text{E})$ are used to recover the correct rotor settings. Then, after the attack is completed, only the stecker value of $S(\text{E})$ is known. Using only the matched plaintext and ciphertext in Table 6.2, how many additional stecker values can be recovered?

8. Write a program to simulate the Enigma cipher. Use your program to answer the following questions, where the rotor and reflector permutations are known to be

$$R_\ell = \text{EKMFLGDQVZNTOWYHXUSPAIBRCJ}$$
$$R_m = \text{BDFHJLCPRTXVZNYEIWGAKMUSQO}$$
$$R_r = \text{ESOVPZJAYQUIRHXLNFTGKDCMWB}$$
$$T = \text{YRUHQSLDPXNGOKMIEBFZCWVJAT}$$

where R_ℓ is the left rotor, R_m is the middle rotor, R_r is the right rotor, and T is the reflector. The "notch" that causes the odometer effect is at position Q for R_ℓ, V for R_m, and J for R_r. For example, the middle rotor steps when the right rotor steps from V to W.

    a. Recover the initial rotor settings given the following matched plaintext and ciphertext.

i	0	1	2	3	4	5	6	7	8	9	10	11	12	13	14	15	16	17	18	19	20	21
Plaintext	A	D	H	O	C	A	D	L	O	C	Q	U	I	D	P	R	O	Q	U	O	S	O
Ciphertext	S	W	Z	S	O	F	C	J	M	D	C	V	U	G	E	L	H	S	M	B	G	G

i	22	23	24	25	26	27	28	29	30	31	32	33	34	35	36	37	38	39	40	41	42	43
Plaintext	L	I	T	T	L	E	T	I	M	E	S	O	M	U	C	H	T	O	K	N	O	W
Ciphertext	N	B	S	M	Q	T	Q	Z	I	Y	D	D	X	K	Y	N	E	W	J	K	Z	R

    b. Recover as many of the stecker settings as is possible from the known plaintext.

9. Suppose that the same Enigma rotors (in the same order) and reflector are used as in Problem 8, and the stecker has no cables connected. Solve for the initial rotor settings and recover the plaintext given the following ciphertext.

```
ERLORYROGGPBIMYNPRMHOUQYQETRQXTYUGGEZVBFPRIJGXRSSCJTXJBMW
JRRPKRHXYMVVYGNGYMHZURYEYYXTTHCNIRYTPVHABJLBLNUZATWXEMKRI
WWEZIZNBEOQDDDCJRZZTLRLGPIFYPHUSMBCAMNODVYSJWKTZEJCKPQYYN
ZQKKJRQQHXLFCHHFRKDHHRTYILGGXXVBLTMPGCTUWPAIXOZOPKMNRXPMO
AMSUTIFOWDFBNDNLWWLNRWMPWWGEZKJNH
```

Hint: The plaintext is English.

10. Develop a ciphertext-only attack on the Enigma, assuming that all you know about the plaintext is that it is English. Analyze the work factor of your proposed attack and also estimate the minimum amount of ciphertext necessary for your attack to succeed. Assume that Enigma rotors, the rotor order, the movable ring positions, and the reflector are all known. Then you need to solve for the initial settings of the three rotors and the stecker. Hint: Since E is the most common letter in English, guess that the plaintext is EEEEEE... and use this "noisy" plaintext to solve for the rotor and stecker settings.

11. Suggest modifications to the Enigma design that would make the attack discussed in Section 6.2 infeasible. Your objective is to make minor modifications to the design.

12. Consider a rotor with a hardwired permutation of $\{0, 1, 2, \ldots, n-1\}$. Denote this permutation as $P = (p_0, p_1, \ldots, p_{n-1})$, where P permutes i to p_i. Let d_i be the displacement of p_i, that is, $d_i = p_i - i \pmod{n}$. Find a formula for the elements of the kth rotor shift of P, which we denote P_k, where the shift is in the same direction as the rotors described in Section 6.2.3. Your formula must be in terms of p_i and d_i.

13. In the RC4 attack, suppose that 60 IVs of the form $(3, 255, V)$ are available. Empirically determine the probability that the key byte K_3 can be distinguished. What is the smallest number of IVs for which this probability is greater than $1/2$?

14. In equations (6.7) and (6.9) we showed how to recover RC4 key bytes K_3 and K_4, respectively.

    a. Assuming that key bytes K_3 through K_{n-1} have been recovered, what is the desired form of the IVs that will be used to recover K_n?

    b. For K_n, what is the formula corresponding to (6.7) and (6.9)?

15. For the attack on RC4 discussed in Section 6.3, we showed that the probability that (6.7) holds is $(253/256)^{252}$. What is the probability that equation (6.9) holds? What is the probability that the corresponding equation holds for K_n?

16. In the discussion of the attack on RC4 keystream byte K_3 we showed that IVs of the form $(3, 255, V)$ are useful to the attacker. We also showed that IVs that are not of this form are sometimes useful to the attacker, and we gave the specific example of the $(2, 253, 0)$. Find an IV of yet another form that is useful in the attack on K_3.

17. The attack on RC4 discussed in this chapter illustrates that prepending an IV to a long-term key is insecure. In [112] it is shown that appending

the IV to the long-term key is also insecure. Suggest more secure ways to combine a long-term key with an IV for use as an RC4 key.

18. Suppose that Trudy has a ciphertext message that was encrypted with the RC4 cipher. Since RC4 is a stream cipher, the actual encryption formula is given by $c_i = p_i \oplus k_i$, where k_i is the ith byte of the keystream, p_i is the ith byte of the plaintext, c_i is the ith byte of the ciphertext. Suppose that Trudy knows the first ciphertext byte, and the first plaintext byte, that is, Trudy knows c_0 and p_0.

   a. Show that Trudy also knows the first byte of the keystream used to encrypt the message, that is, she knows k_0.

   b. Suppose that Trudy also happens to know that the first three bytes of the key are $(K_0, K_1, K_2) = (2, 253, 0)$. Show that Trudy can determine the next byte of the key, K_3, with a probability of success of about 0.05. Note that from part a, Trudy knows the first byte of the keystream. Hint: Suppose that the RC4 initialization algorithm were to stop after the $i = 3$ step. Write an equation that you could solve to determine the first byte of the key. Then show that this equation holds with a probability of about 0.05 when the entire 256-step initialization algorithm is used.

   c. If Trudy sees several messages encrypted with the same key that was used in part b, how can Trudy improve on the attack to recover K_3? That is, how can Trudy recover the key byte K_3 with a much higher probability of success (ideally, with certainty)?

   d. Assuming that the attack in part b (or part c) succeeds, and Trudy recovers K_3, extend the attack so that Trudy can recover K_4, with some reasonable probability of success. What is the probability that this step of the attack succeeds?

   e. Extend the attack in part d to recover the remaining key bytes, that is, $K_5, K_6, \ldots$. Show that this attack has essentially the same work factor regardless of the length of the key.

   f. Show that the attack in part a (and hence, the attack in parts a through e) also works if the first three key bytes are of the form $(K_0, K_1, K_2) = (3, 255, V)$ for any byte V.

   g. Why is this attack relevant to the (in)security of WEP?

19. The file `outDiff` (available at the textbook website) contains 100 chosen plaintext pairs P and $\tilde{P}$ that satisfy $P \oplus \tilde{P} = $ 0x0002, along with the corresponding TDES-encrypted ciphertext pairs C and $\tilde{C}$. Use this information to determine the key bits $k_{13}, k_{14}, k_{15}, k_9, k_{10}, k_{11}$ using the differential cryptanalysis attack on TDES that is described in this chapter. Then use your knowledge of these key bits to exhaustively search

for the remaining key bits. Give the key as $K = k_0 k_1 k_2 \cdots k_{15}$ in hexadecimal.

20. The file `outLin`, which is available at the textbook website, contains 100 known plaintext P along with the corresponding TDES-encrypted ciphertext C. Use this information to determine the value of $k_0 \oplus k_1$ and $k_2 \oplus k_7$ using the linear cryptanalysis attack on TDES that is described in this chapter. Then use your knowledge of these key bits to exhaustively search for the remaining key bits. Give the key in hexadecimal as $K = k_0 k_1 k_2 \cdots k_{15}$.

21. Find a 16-bit key that encrypts

$$\text{plaintext} = \texttt{0x1223} = 0001001000100011$$

to

$$\text{ciphertext} = \texttt{0x5B0C} = 0101101100001100$$

using the cipher TDES.

22. Suppose that a DES-like cipher uses the S-box below.

	0	1	2	3	4	5	6	7	8	9	A	B	C	D	E	F
00	4	6	8	9	E	5	A	C	0	2	F	B	1	7	D	3
01	6	4	A	B	3	0	7	E	2	C	8	9	D	5	F	1
10	8	5	0	B	D	6	E	C	F	7	4	9	A	2	1	3
11	A	2	6	9	F	4	0	E	D	5	7	C	8	B	3	1

If the input to this S-box is 011101, what is the output? If inputs X_0 and X_1 yield outputs Y_0 and Y_1, respectively, and $X_0 \oplus X_1 = 000001$, what is the most likely value for $Y_0 \oplus Y_1$ and what is its probability?

23. Consider the S-box below. For the input $x_0 x_1 x_2$, the bit x_0 indexes the row, while $x_1 x_2$ is the column index. We denote the output by $y_0 y_1$.

	00	01	10	11
0	10	01	00	11
1	11	00	01	10

Find the best linear approximation to y_1 in terms of x_0, x_1, and x_2. With what probability does this approximation hold?

24. Construct a difference table analogous to that in Table 6.6 for S-box 1 of DES. The DES S-box 1 appears in Table 3.3 of Chapter 3. What is the most biased difference and what is the bias?

25. Construct a difference table analogous to that in Table 6.6 for the right S-box of TDES. Verify the results in equation (6.17). What is the second most biased difference, and what is the bias?

26. Construct a linear approximation table analogous to that in Table 6.7 for S-box 1 of DES. The DES S-box 1 appears in Table 3.3 of Chapter 3. Note that your table will have 64 rows and 15 columns. What is the best linear approximation, and how well does it approximate?

27. Construct a linear approximation table analogous to that in Table 6.7 for the left S-box of TDES. Verify the results in equation (6.29). What is the next best linear approximation and how well does it approximate?

28. Recall the linear cryptanalysis of TDES discussed in Section 6.4.6. Assume that equation (6.33) holds with probability $(3/4)^3 \approx 0.42$. Also assume that the key satisfies $k_0 \oplus k_1 = 0$. Then if we conduct the attack using 100 known plaintexts, what are the expected counts for $c_1 \oplus p_{10} = 0$ and $c_1 \oplus p_{10} = 1$? Compare your answer with the empirical results presented in the text. Why do you think the theoretical and empirical results differ?

29. Suppose that Bob's knapsack public key is

$$T = [168, 280, 560, 393, 171, 230, 684, 418].$$

Suppose that Alice encrypts a message with Bob's public key and the resulting ciphertext is $C_1 = 1135$. Implement the LLL attack and use your program to solve for the plaintext P_1. For the same public key, find the plaintext P_2 for the ciphertext $C_2 = 2055$. Can you determine the private key?

30. Suppose that Bob's knapsack public key is

$$T = [2195, 4390, 1318, 2197, 7467, 5716, 3974, 3996, 7551, 668].$$

Suppose that Alice encrypts a message with Bob's public key and the resulting ciphertext is $C_1 = 8155$. Implement the LLL attack and use your program to solve for the plaintext P_1. For the same public key, find the plaintext P_2 for the ciphertext $C_2 = 14748$. Can you determine the private key?

31. Consider the "simple" timing attack on RSA discussed in Section 6.6.1.

   a. Extend the timing attack to recover the bit d_2. That is, assuming that bit d_1 has been recovered, what conditions must Y and Z satisfy so that the attack presented in the text can be used to determine d_2?

b. Extend the attack to recover d_3, assuming that d_1 and d_2 have been recovered.

c. In practice, we need to recover about half of the private key bits. Why is this attack not a practical means for recovering such a large number of private key bits?

32. Suppose that in Kocher's timing attack, we obtain the timings $T(C_j)$ and the emulated timings $\tilde{t}_{0...2}$ for $d_0 d_1 d_2 \in \{100, 101, 110, 111\}$, as given in the table below.

		$\tilde{t}_{0...2}$			
j	$T(C_j)$	100	101	110	111
0	20	5	7	5	8
1	21	4	7	4	1
2	19	1	6	4	7
3	22	2	8	5	2
4	24	10	6	8	8
5	23	11	5	7	7
6	21	1	1	6	5
7	19	7	1	2	3

a. What is the most likely value of $d_0 d_1 d_2$ and why?

b. Why does this attack not succeed if CRT or Montgomery multiplication is used?

33. Write a program to recover the 64-bit key for STEA (Simplified TEA) given one known plaintext block and the corresponding ciphertext block. The STEA algorithm and a description of the attack on STEA can be found at [208].

34. If DES were a *group* [117], then given keys K_1 and K_2, there would exist a key K_3 such that

$$E(P, K_3) = E(E(P, K_1), K_2) \text{ for all plaintext } P, \qquad (6.39)$$

and we could also find such a key K_3 if any of the encryptions were replaced by decryptions. If equation (6.39) holds, then triple DES is no more secure than single DES. It was established in [45] that DES is not a group and, consequently, triple DES is more secure than single DES. Show that TDES is not a group. Hint: Select TDES keys K_1 and K_2. You will be finished if you can verify that there does not exist any key K_3 for which $E(P, K_3) = E(E(P, K_1), K_2)$ for all possible choices of P.

Part II

Access Control

Chapter 7

Authentication

Guard: *Halt! Who goes there?*
Arthur: *It is I, Arthur, son of Uther Pendragon,*
from the castle of Camelot. King of the Britons,
defeater of the Saxons, sovereign of all England!
— Monty Python and the Holy Grail

Then said they unto him, Say now Shibboleth:
and he said Sibboleth: for he could not frame to pronounce it right.
Then they took him, and slew him at the passages of Jordan:
and there fell at that time of the Ephraimites forty and two thousand.
— Judges 12:6

7.1 Introduction

We'll use the term *access control* as an umbrella for any security issues related to access of system resources. Within this broad definition, there are two areas of primary interest, namely, authentication and authorization.

Authentication is the process of determining whether a user (or other entity) should be allowed access to a system. In this chapter, our focus is on the methods used by humans to authenticate to local machines. Another type of authentication problem arises when the authentication information must pass through a network. While it might seem that these two authentication problems are closely related, in fact, they are almost completely different. When networks are involved, authentication is almost entirely an issue of security protocols. We'll defer our discussion of protocols to Chapters 9 and 10.

By definition, authenticated users are allowed access to system resources. However, an authenticated user is generally not given carte blanche access to all system resources. For example, we might only allow a privileged user—

such as an administrator—to install software on a system. How do we restrict the actions of authenticated users? This is the field of authorization, which is covered in the next chapter. Note that authentication is a binary decision—access is granted or it is not—while authorization is all about a more fine-grained set of restrictions on access to various system resources.

In security, terminology is far from standardized. In particular, the term access control is often used as a synonym for authorization. However, in our usage, access control is more broadly defined, with both authentication and authorization falling under the heading of access control. These two parts of access control can be summarized as follows.

- Authentication: Are you who you say you are?[1]

- Authorization: Are you allowed to do that?

7.2 Authentication Methods

In this chapter we address various methods that are commonly used to authenticate a human to a machine. That is, we want to convince a dumb machine that someone or something claiming to be Alice is indeed Alice and not, say, Trudy. That is, we want to answer the question, "Are you who you say you are?" Of course, we'd like to do this in as secure manner as possible.

A human can be authenticated to a machine based on any of the following[2] "somethings" [14].

- Something you know

- Something you have

- Something you are

A password is an example of "something you know." We'll spend some time discussing passwords, and in the process show that passwords represent a weak link in many modern information security systems.

An example of "something you have" is an ATM card or a smartcard. The "something you are" category is synonymous with the rapidly expanding field of biometrics. For example, today you can purchase a laptop that scans your thumbprint and uses the result for authentication. We'll discuss a few biometric methods later in this chapter. But first up are passwords.

---

[1] Try saying that three times, fast.

[2] Additional "somethings" are sometimes proposed. For example, one wireless access point authenticates a user by the fact that the user pushes a button on the device. This shows that the user has physical access to the device, and could be viewed as authentication by "something you do."

7.3 Passwords

*Your password must be at least 18770 characters
and cannot repeat any of your previous 30689 passwords.*
— Microsoft Knowledge Base Article 276304

An ideal password is something that you know, something that a computer can verify that you know, and something nobody else can guess—even with access to unlimited computing resources. We'll see that in practice it's difficult to even come close to this ideal.

Undoubtedly you are familiar with passwords. It's virtually impossible to use a computer today without accumulating a significant number of passwords. You probably log into your computer by entering a username and password, in which case you have obviously used a password. In addition, many other things that we don't call "password" act as passwords. For example, the PIN number used with an ATM card is, in effect, a password. And if you forget your password, a user-friendly website might authenticate you based on your social security number, your mother's maiden name, or your date of birth, in which case, these things are acting as passwords. A problem with such passwords is that they are often not secret.

If left to their own devices, users tend to select bad passwords, which makes password cracking surprisingly easy. In fact, we'll provide some basic mathematical arguments to show that it's inherently difficult to achieve security via passwords.

From a security perspective, a solution to the password problem would be to instead use randomly generated cryptographic keys. The work of cracking such a "password" would be equivalent to an exhaustive key search, in which case our passwords could be made at least as strong as our cryptography. The problem with such an approach is that humans must remember their passwords and we're not good at remembering randomly selected bits.

We're getting ahead of ourselves. Before discussing the numerous problems with passwords, we consider why passwords are so popular. Why is authentication based on "something you know" so much more popular than the more secure "somethings" (i.e., "something you have" and "something you are")? The answer, as always, is cost[3] and, secondarily, convenience. Passwords are free, while smartcards and biometric devices cost money. Also, it's more convenient for an overworked system administrator to reset a password than to provide a new smartcard or issue a user a new thumb.

---

[3]Students claim that when your Socratic author asks a question in his security class, the correct answer is invariably either "money" or "it depends."

7.3.1 Keys Versus Passwords

We've already claimed that cryptographic keys would solve the password problem. To see why this is so, let's compare keys to passwords. On the one hand, suppose our generic attacker, Trudy, is confronted with a 64-bit cryptographic key. Then there are 2^{64} possible keys, and, if the key was chosen at random (and assuming there is no shortcut attack), Trudy must on average try 2^{63} keys before she expects to find the correct one.

On the other hand, suppose Trudy is confronted with a password that is known to be eight characters long, with 256 possible choices for each character. Then there are $256^8 = 2^{64}$ possible passwords. At first glance, cracking such passwords might appear to be equivalent to the key search problem. Unfortunately (or, from Trudy's perspective, fortunately) users don't select passwords at random, because users must remember their passwords. As a result, a user is far more likely to choose an 8-character dictionary word such as

password

than, say,

kf&Yw!a[

So, in this case Trudy can make far fewer than 2^{63} guesses and have a high probability of successfully cracking a password. For example, a carefully selected dictionary of $2^{20} \approx 1,000,000$ passwords would likely give Trudy a reasonable probability of cracking a given password. On the other hand, if Trudy attempted to find a randomly generated 64-bit key by trying only 2^{20} possible keys, her chance of success would be a mere $2^{20}/2^{64} = 1/2^{44}$, or less than 1 in 17 trillion. The bottom line is that the non-randomness of password selection is at the root of the problems with passwords.

7.3.2 Choosing Passwords

Not all passwords are created equal. For example, everyone would probably agree that the following passwords are weak:

- Frank

- Pikachu

- 10251960

- AustinStamp

especially if your name happens to be Frank, or Austin Stamp, or your birthday is on 10/25/1960.

Security often rests on passwords and, consequently, users should have passwords that are difficult to guess. However, users must be able to remember their passwords. With that in mind, are the following passwords better than the weak passwords above?

- `jfIej(43j-EmmL+y`

- `09864376537263`

- `POkemON`

- `FSa7Yago`

The first password, `jfIej(43j-EmmL+y`, would certainly be difficult for Trudy to guess, but it would also be difficult for Alice to remember. Such a password is likely to end up on the proverbial post-it note stuck to the front of Alice's computer. This could make Trudy's job much easier than if Alice had selected a "less secure" password.

The second password on the list above is also probably too much for most users to remember. Even the highly trained U.S. military personal responsible for launching nuclear missiles are only required to remember 12-digit firing codes [14].

The password `POkemON` might be difficult to guess, since it's not a standard dictionary word due to the digits and the upper case letters. However, if the user were known to be a fan of Pokémon, this password might be relatively easy prey.

The final password, `FSa7Yago`, might appear to reside in the difficult to guess, but too difficult to remember category. However, there is a trick to help the user remember it—it's based on a *passphrase*. That is, `FSa7Yago` is derived from the phrase "four score and seven years ago." Consequently, this password should be relatively easy for Alice to remember, and yet relatively difficult for Trudy to guess.

An interesting password experiment is described in [14]. Users were divided into three groups, and given the following advice regarding password selection:

- Group A — Select passwords consisting of at least six characters, with at least one non-letter. This is fairly typical password selection advice.

- Group B — Select passwords based on passphrases.

- Group C — Select passwords consisting of eight randomly selected characters.

The experimenters tried to crack the resulting passwords for each of the three groups. The results were as follows:

- Group A — About 30% of passwords were easy to crack. Users in this group found their passwords easy to remember.

- Group B — About 10% of the passwords were cracked, and, as with users in Group A, users in this group found their passwords easy to remember.

- Group C — About 10% of the passwords were cracked. Not surprisingly, the users in this group found their passwords difficult to remember.

These results clearly indicate that passphrases provide the best option for password selection, since the resulting passwords are relatively difficult to crack yet easy to remember.

This password experiment also demonstrated that user compliance is hard to achieve. In each of groups A, B, and C, about one-third of the users did not comply with the instructions. Assuming that non-compliant users tend to select passwords similar to Group A, about one-third of these passwords would be easy to crack. The bottom line is that nearly 10% of passwords are likely to be easy to crack, regardless of the advice given.

In some situations, it makes sense to assign passwords, and if this is the case, noncompliance with the password policy is a non-issue. The trade-off here is that users are likely to have a harder time remembering assigned passwords as compared to passwords they select themselves.

Again, if users are allowed to choose passwords, then the best advice is to choose passwords based on passphrases. In addition, system administrators should use a password-cracking tool to test for weak passwords, since attackers certainly will.

It is also sometimes suggested that periodic password changes should be required. However, users can be very clever at avoiding such requirements, invariably to the detriment of security. For example, Alice might simply "change" her password without changing it. In response to such users, the system could remember, say, five previous passwords. But a clever user like Alice will soon learn that she can cycle through five password changes and then reset her password to its original value. Or, if Alice is required to choose a new password each month she might select, say, `frank01` in January, `frank02` in February, and so on. Forcing reluctant users to choose reasonably strong passwords is not as simple as it might seem.

7.3.3   Attacking Systems via Passwords

Suppose that Trudy is an outsider, that is, she has no access to a particular system. A common attack path for Trudy would be

$$\text{outsider} \longrightarrow \text{normal user} \longrightarrow \text{administrator}.$$

In other words, Trudy will initially seek access to any account on the system and then attempt to upgrade her level of privilege. In this scenario, one weak password on a system—or in the extreme, one weak password on an entire network—could be enough for the first stage of the attack to succeed. The bottom line is that one weak password may be one too many.

Another interesting issue concerns the proper response when attempted password cracking is detected. For example, systems often lock users out after three bad passwords attempts. If this is the case, how long should the system lock? Five seconds? Five minutes? Until the administrator manually resets the service? Five seconds might be insufficient to deter an automated attack. If it takes more than five seconds for Trudy to make three password guesses for every user on the system, then she could simply cycle through all accounts, making three guesses on each. By the time she returns to a particular user's account, more than five seconds will have elapsed and she will be able to make three more guesses without any delay. On the other hand, five minutes might open the door to a denial of service attack, where Trudy is able to lock accounts indefinitely by periodically making three password guesses on an account. The correct answer to this dilemma is not readily apparent.

7.3.4 Password Verification

Next, we consider the important issue of verifying that an entered password is correct. For a computer to determine the validity of a password, it must have something to compare against. That is, the computer must have access to the correct password in some form. But it's probably a bad idea to simply store the actual passwords in a file, since this would be a prime target for Trudy. Here, as in many other areas in information security, cryptography provides a sound solution.

It might be tempting to encrypt the password file with a symmetric key. However, to verify passwords, the file must be decrypted, so the decryption key must be as accessible as the file itself. Consequently, if Trudy can steal the password file, she can probably steal the key as well. Consequently, encryption is of little value here.

So, instead of storing raw passwords in a file or encrypting the password file, it's more secure to store hashed passwords. For example, if Alice's password is FSa7Yago, we could store

$$y = h(\text{FSa7Yago})$$

in a file, where h is a secure cryptographic hash function. Then when someone claiming to be Alice enters a password x, it is hashed and compared to y, and if $y = h(x)$ then the entered password is assumed to be correct and the user is authenticated.

The advantage of hashing passwords is that if Trudy obtains the password file, she does not obtain the actual passwords—instead she only has the hashed passwords. Note that we are relying on the one-way property of cryptographic hash functions to protect the passwords. Of course, if Trudy knows the hash value y, she can conduct a forward search attack by guessing likely passwords x until she finds an x for which $y = h(x)$, at which point she will have cracked the password. But at least Trudy has work to do after she has obtained the password file.

Suppose Trudy has a dictionary containing N common passwords, say,

$$d_0, d_1, d_2, \ldots, d_{N-1}.$$

Then she could precompute the hash of each password in the dictionary,

$$y_0 = h(d_0), y_1 = h(d_1), \ldots, y_{N-1} = h(d_{N-1}).$$

Now if Trudy gets access to a password file containing hashed passwords, she only needs to compare the entries in the password file to the entries in her precomputed dictionary of hashes. Furthermore, the precomputed dictionary could be reused for each password file, thereby saving Trudy the work of recomputing the hashes. And if Trudy is feeling particularly generous, she could post her dictionary of common passwords and their corresponding hashes online, saving all other attackers the work of computing these hashes. From the good guy's point of view, this is a bad thing, since the work of computing the hashes has been largely negated. Can we prevent this attack, or at least make Trudy's job more difficult?

Recall that to prevent a forward search attack on public key encryption, we append random bits to the message before encrypting. We can accomplish a similar effect with passwords by appending a non-secret random value, known as a *salt*, to each password before hashing. A password salt is analogous to the initialization vector, or IV, in, say, cipher block chaining (CBC) mode encryption. Whereas an IV is a non-secret value that causes identical plaintext blocks to encrypt to different ciphertext values, a salt is a non-secret value that causes identical password to hash to different values.

Let p be a newly entered password. We generate a random salt value s and compute $y = h(p, s)$ and store the pair (s, y) in the password file. Note that the salt s is no more secret than the hash value. Now to verify an entered password x, we retrieve (s, y) from the password file, compute $h(x, s)$, and compare this result with the stored value y. Note that salted password verification is just as easy as it was in the unsalted case. But Trudy's job has become much more difficult. Suppose Alice's password is hashed with salt value s_a and Bob's password is hashed with salt value s_b. Then, to test Alice's password using her dictionary of common passwords, Trudy must compute the hash of each word in her dictionary with salt value s_a, but to attack

Bob's password, Trudy must recompute the hashes using salt value s_b. For a password file with N users, Trudy's work has just increased by a factor of N. Consequently, a precomputed file of hashed passwords is no longer useful for Trudy. She can't be pleased with this turn of events.[4]

7.3.5 Math of Password Cracking

Now we'll take a look at the math behind password cracking. Throughout this section, we'll assume that all passwords are eight characters in length and that there are 128 choices for each character, which implies there are

$$128^8 = 2^{56}$$

possible passwords. We'll also assume that passwords are stored in a password file that contains 2^{10} hashed passwords, and that Trudy has a dictionary of 2^{20} common passwords. From experience, Trudy expects that any given password will appear in her dictionary with a probability of about $1/4$. Also, work is measured by the number of hashes computed. Note that comparisons are free—only hash calculations count as work.

Under these assumptions, we'll determine the probability of successfully cracking a password in each of the following four cases.

I. Trudy wants to determine Alice's password (perhaps Alice is the administrator). Trudy does not use her dictionary of likely passwords.

II. Trudy wants to determine Alice's password. Trudy does use her dictionary of common passwords.

III. Trudy will be satisfied to crack any password in the password file, without using her dictionary.

IV. Trudy wants to find any password in the hashed password file, using her dictionary.

In each case, we'll consider both salted and unsalted passwords.

Case I: Trudy has decided that she wants to crack Alice's password. Trudy, who is somewhat absent-minded, has forgotten that she has a password dictionary available. Without a dictionary of common passwords, Trudy has no choice other than a brute force approach. This is precisely equivalent to an exhaustive key search and hence the expected work is

$$2^{56}/2 = 2^{55}.$$

---

[4]Salting password hashes is as close to a free lunch as you'll come in information security. Maybe the connection with a free lunch is why it's called a salt?

The result here is the same whether the passwords are salted or not, unless someone has precomputed, sorted, and stored the hashes of all possible passwords. If the hashes of all passwords are already known, then in the unsalted case, there is no work at all—Trudy simply looks up the hash value and finds the corresponding password. But, if the passwords are salted, there is no benefit to having the password hashes. In any case, precomputing all possible password hashes is a great deal of work, so for the remainder of this discussion, we'll assume this is infeasible.

Case II: Trudy again wants to recover Alice's password, and she is going to use her dictionary of common passwords. With probability 1/4, Alice's password is in Trudy's dictionary. Suppose the passwords are salted. Furthermore, suppose Alice's password is in Trudy's dictionary. Then Trudy would expect to find Alice's password after hashing half of the words in the dictionary, that is, after 2^{19} tries. With probability 3/4 the password is not in the dictionary, in which case Trudy would expect to find it after about 2^{55} tries. Combining these cases gives Trudy an expected work of

$$\frac{1}{4}\left(2^{19}\right) + \frac{3}{4}\left(2^{55}\right) \approx 2^{54.6}.$$

Note that the expected work here is almost the same as in Case I, where Trudy did not use her dictionary. However, in practice, Trudy would simply try all the words in her dictionary and quit if she did not find Alice's password. Then the work would be at most 2^{20} and the probability of success would be 1/4.

If the passwords are unsalted, Trudy could precompute the hashes of all 2^{20} passwords in her dictionary. Then this small one-time work could be amortized over the number of times that Trudy uses this attack. That is, the larger the number of attacks, the smaller the average work per attack.

Case III: In this case, Trudy will be satisfied to determine any of the 1024 passwords in the hashed password file. Trudy has again forgotten about her password dictionary.

Let $y_0, y_1, \ldots, y_{1023}$ be the password hashes. We'll assume that all 2^{10} passwords in the file are distinct. Let $p_0, p_1, \ldots, p_{2^{56}-1}$ be a list of all 2^{56} possible passwords. As in the brute force case, Trudy needs to make 2^{55} distinct comparisons before she expects to find a match.

If the passwords are not salted, then Trudy can compute $h(p_0)$ and compare it with each y_i, for $i = 0, 1, 2, \ldots, 1023$. Next she computes $h(p_1)$ and compares it with all y_i and so on. The point here is that each hash computation provides Trudy with 2^{10} comparisons. Since work is measured in terms of hashes, not comparisons, and 2^{55} comparisons are needed, the expected work is

$$2^{55}/2^{10} = 2^{45}.$$

Now suppose the passwords are salted. Let s_i denote the salt value corresponding to hash password y_i. Then Trudy computes $h(p_0, s_0)$ and compares it with y_0. Next, she computes $h(p_0, s_1)$ and compares it with y_1, she computes $h(p_0, s_2)$ and compares it with y_2, and she continues in this manner up to $h(p_0, s_{1023})$. Then Trudy must repeat this entire process with password p_1 in place of p_0, and then with password p_2 and so on. The bottom line is that each hash computation only yields one comparison and consequently the expected work is 2^{55}, which is the same as in Case I above.

This case illustrates the benefit of salting passwords. However, Trudy has not made use of her password dictionary, which is unrealistic.

Case IV: Finally, suppose that Trudy will be satisfied to recover any one of the 1024 passwords in the hashed password file, and she will make use of her password dictionary. First, note that the probability that at least one of the 1024 passwords in the file appears in Trudy's dictionary is

$$1 - \left(\frac{3}{4}\right)^{1024} \approx 1.$$

Therefore, we can safely ignore the case where no password from the file is in Trudy's dictionary.

If the passwords are not salted, then Trudy could simply hash all password in her dictionary and compare the results to all 1024 hashes in the password file. Since we are certain that at least one of these passwords is in the dictionary, Trudy's work is 2^{20} and she is assured of finding at least one password. However, if Trudy is a little more clever, she can greatly reduce this meager work factor. Again, we can safely assume that at least one of the passwords is in Trudy's dictionary. Consequently, Trudy only needs to make about 2^{19} comparisons—half the size of her dictionary—before she expects to find a password. As in Case III, each hash computation yields 2^{10} comparisons, so the expected work is only

$$2^{19}/2^{10} = 2^9.$$

Finally, note that in this unsalted case, if the hashes of the dictionary passwords have been precomputed, no additional work is required to recover one (or more) passwords. That is, Trudy simply compares the hashes in the file to the hashes of her dictionary passwords and, in the process, she recovers any passwords that appear in her dictionary.

Now we consider the most realistic case—Trudy has a dictionary of common passwords, she will be happy to recover any password from the password file, and the passwords in the file are salted. For this case, we let $y_0, y_1, \ldots, y_{1023}$ be the password hashes and $s_0, s_1, \ldots, s_{1023}$ be the corresponding salt values. Also, let $d_0, d_1, \ldots, d_{2^{20}-1}$ be the dictionary words. Suppose that Trudy first computes $h(d_0, s_0)$ and compares it to y_0, then she compute $h(d_1, s_0)$ and compares it to y_0, then she compute $h(d_2, s_0)$ and compares it to y_0, and so on. That is, Trudy first compares y_0 to all of her (hashed) dictionary words. Of course, she must use salt s_0 for these hashes. If she does not recover the password corresponding to y_0, then she repeats the process using y_1 and s_1, and so on.

Note that if y_0 is in the dictionary (which has probability $1/4$), Trudy expects to find it after about 2^{19} hashes, while if it is not in the dictionary (probability $3/4$) Trudy will compute 2^{20} hashes. If Trudy finds y_0 in the dictionary, then she's done. If not, Trudy will have computed 2^{20} hashes before she moves on to consider y_1. Continuing in this manner, we find that the expected work is about

$$\frac{1}{4}\left(2^{19}\right) + \frac{3}{4} \cdot \frac{1}{4}\left(2^{20} + 2^{19}\right) + \left(\frac{3}{4}\right)^2 \frac{1}{4}\left(2 \cdot 2^{20} + 2^{19}\right) + \cdots$$
$$+ \left(\frac{3}{4}\right)^{1023} \frac{1}{4}\left(1023 \cdot 2^{20} + 2^{19}\right) < 2^{22}.$$

This is somewhat disappointing, since it shows that, for very little work, Trudy can expect to crack at least one password.

It can be shown (see Problems 24 and 25) that, under reasonable assumptions, the work needed to crack a (salted) password is approximately equal to size of the dictionary divided by the probability that a given password is in the dictionary. In our example here, the size of the dictionary is 2^{20} while the probability of finding a password is $1/4$. So, the expected work should be about

$$\frac{2^{20}}{1/4} = 2^{22}$$

which is consistent with the calculation above. Note that this approximation implies that we can increase Trudy's work by forcing her to have a larger dictionary or by decreasing her probability of success (or both), which makes intuitive sense. Of course, the obvious way to accomplish this is to choose passwords that are harder to guess.

The inescapable conclusion is that password cracking is too easy, particularly in situations where one weak password is sufficient to break the security of an entire system. Unfortunately, when it comes to passwords, the numbers strongly favor the bad guys.

7.3.6   Other Password Issues

As bad as it is, password cracking is only the tip of the iceberg when it comes to problems with passwords. Today, most users need multiple passwords, but users can't (or won't) remember a large number of passwords. This results in a significant amount of password reuse, and any password is only as secure as the least secure place it's used. If Trudy finds one of your passwords, she would be wise to try it (and slight variations of it) in other places where you use a password.

Social engineering is also a major concern with passwords.[5] For example, if someone calls you, claiming to be a system administrator who needs your password to correct a problem with your account, would you give away your password? According to a recent survey, 34% of users will give away their password if you ask for it, and the number increases to 70% if you offer a candy bar as incentive [232].

Keystroke logging software and similar spyware are also serious threats to password-based security [22]. The failure to change default passwords is a major source of attacks as well [339].

An interesting question is, who suffers from bad passwords? The answer is that it depends. If you choose your birthday for your ATM PIN number, only you stand to lose.[6] On the other hand, if you choose a weak password at work, the entire company stands to lose. This explains why banks usually let users choose any PIN number they desire for their ATM cards, but companies generally try to force users to select reasonably strong passwords.

There are many popular password cracking tools including L0phtCrack [2] (for Windows) and John the Ripper [157] (for Unix). These tools come with preconfigured dictionaries, and it is easy to produce customized dictionaries. These are good examples of the types of tools that are available to hackers.[7] Since virtually no skill is required to leverage these powerful tools, the door to password cracking is open to all, regardless of ability.

Passwords are one of the most severe real-world security problems today, and this is unlikely to change any time soon. The bad guys clearly have the advantages when it comes to passwords. In the next section, we'll look at biometrics, which—together with smartcards ad similar devices—are often touted as the best way to escape from the multitude of problems inherent with passwords.

---

[5]Actually, social engineering is a major concern in all aspects of information security where humans play a role. Your all-too-human author heard a talk about penetration testing, where the tester was paid to probe the security of a major corporation. The tester lied and forged a (non-digital) signature to obtain entry into corporate headquarters, where he posed as a system administrator trainee. Secretaries and other employees were more than happy to accept "help" from this fake SA trainee. As a result, the tester claimed to have obtained almost all of the company's intellectual property (including such sensitive information as the design of nuclear power plants) within two days. This attack consisted almost entirely of social engineering.

[6]Perhaps the bank will lose too, but only if you live in the United States and you have a very good lawyer.

[7]Of course, almost every hacker tool has legitimate uses. For example, password cracking tools are valuable for system administrators, since they can use these tools to test the strength of the passwords on their system.

7.4   Biometrics

> *You have all the characteristics of a popular politician:*
> *a horrible voice, bad breeding, and a vulgar manner.*
> — Aristophanes

Biometrics represent the "something you are" method of authentication or, as Schneier so aptly puts it, "you are your key" [260]. There are many different types of biometrics, including such long-established methods as fingerprints. Recently, biometrics based on speech recognition, gait (walking) recognition, and even a digital doggie (odor recognition) have been developed. Biometrics are currently a very active topic for research [151, 176].

In the information security arena, biometrics are seen as a more secure alternative to passwords. For biometrics to be a practical replacement for passwords, cheap and reliable systems are needed. Today, usable biometric systems exist, including laptops using thumbprint authentication, palm print systems for secure entry into restricted facilities, the use of fingerprints to unlock car doors, and so on. But given the potential of biometrics—and the well-known weaknesses of password-based authentication—it's perhaps surprising that biometrics are not more widely used.

An ideal biometric would satisfy all of the following:

- Universal — A biometric should apply to virtually everyone. In reality, no biometric applies to everyone. For example, a small percentage of people do not have readable fingerprints.

- Distinguishing — A biometric should distinguish with virtual certainty. In reality, we can't hope for 100% certainty, although, in theory, some methods can distinguish with very low error rates.

- Permanent — Ideally, the physical characteristic being measured should never change. In practice, it's sufficient if the characteristic remains stable over a reasonably long period of time.

- Collectable — The physical characteristic should be easy to collect without any potential to cause harm to the subject. In practice, collectability often depends heavily on whether the subject is cooperative or not.

- Reliable, robust, and user-friendly — These are just some of the additional real-world considerations for a practical biometric system. Some biometrics that have shown promise in laboratory conditions have subsequently failed to deliver similar performance in practice.

Biometrics are also applied in various *identification* problems. In the identification problem we are trying to answer the question "Who are you?," while for the authorization problem, we want to answer the question, "Are you who you say you are?" That is, in identification, the goal is to identify the subject from a list of many possible subjects. This occurs, for example, when a suspicious fingerprint from a crime scene is sent to the FBI fingerprint database for comparison with all of the millions of fingerprint records currently on file.

In the identification problem, the comparison is one-to-many whereas for authentication, the comparison is one-to-one. For example, if someone claiming to be Alice uses a thumbprint mouse biometric, the captured thumbprint image is only compared with the stored thumbprint of Alice. The identification problem is inherently more difficult and subject to a much higher error rate due to the larger number of comparisons that must be made. That is, each comparison carries with it a probability of an error, so the more comparisons required, the higher the error rate.

There are two phases to a biometric system. First, there is an *enrollment phase*, where subjects have their biometric information gathered and entered into a database. Typically, during this phase very careful measurement of the pertinent physical information is required. Since this is one-time work (per subject), it's acceptable if the process is slow and multiple measurements are required. In some fielded systems, enrollment has proven to be a weak point since it may be difficult to obtain results that are comparable to those obtained under laboratory conditions.

The second phase in a biometric system is the *recognition phase*. This occurs when the biometric detection system is used in practice to determine whether (for the authentication problem) to authenticate the user or not. This phase must be quick, simple, and accurate.

We'll assume that subjects are cooperative, that is, they're willing to have the appropriate physical characteristic measured. This is a reasonable assumption in the authentication case, since authentication is generally required for access to certain information resources or for entry into an otherwise restricted area.

For the identification problem, it is often the case that subjects are uncooperative. For example, consider a facial recognition system used for identification. Las Vegas casinos use such systems to detect known cheaters as they attempt to enter a casino [300]. Another fanciful proposed use of facial recognition is to spot terrorists in airports.[8] In such cases, the enrollment conditions may be far from ideal, and in the recognition phase, the subjects are certainly uncooperative as they likely do everything possible to avoid detection. Of course, uncooperative subjects can only serve to make the underlying biometric problem more difficult. For the remainder of this discussion we'll focus on the authentication problem and we'll assume that the subjects are cooperative.

---

[8]Apparently, terrorists are welcome in casinos, as long as they don't cheat.

7.4.1   Types of Errors

There are two types of errors that can occur in biometric recognition. Suppose Bob poses as Alice and the system mistakenly authenticates Bob as Alice. The rate at which such misauthentication occurs is the *fraud rate*. Now suppose that Alice tries to authenticate as herself, but the system fails to authenticate her. The rate at which this type of error occurs is the *insult rate* [14].

For any biometric, we can decrease the fraud or insult rate at the expense of the other. For example, if we require a 99% voiceprint match, then we can obtain a low fraud rate, but the insult rate will be high, since a speaker's voice will naturally change slightly from time to time. On the other hand, if we set the threshold at a 30% voiceprint match, the the fraud rate will likely be high, but the system will have a low insult rate.

The *equal error rate* is the rate for which the fraud and insult rates are the same. That is, the parameters of the system are adjusted until the fraud rate and insult rate are precisely in balance. This is a useful measure for comparing different biometric systems.

7.4.2   Biometric Examples

In this section, we'll briefly discuss three common biometrics. First, we'll consider fingerprints, which, in spite of their long history, are relative newcomers in computing applications. Then we'll discuss palm prints and iris scans.

7.4.2.1   Fingerprints

Fingerprints were used in ancient China as a form of signature, and they have served a similar purpose at other times in history. But the use of fingerprints as a scientific form of identification is a much more recent phenomenon.

A significant analysis of fingerprints occurred in 1798 when J. C. Mayer suggested that fingerprints might be unique. In 1823, Johannes Evangelist Purkinje discussed nine fingerprint patterns, but this work was a biological treatise and did not suggest using fingerprints as a form of identification. The first modern use of fingerprints for identification occurred in 1858 in India, when Sir William Hershel used palm prints and fingerprints as forms of signatures on contracts.

In 1880, Dr. Henry Faulds published an article in *Nature* that discussed the use of fingerprints for identification purposes. In Mark Twain's *Life on the Mississippi*, which was published in 1883, a murderer is identified by a fingerprint. However, the widespread use of fingerprinting only became possible in 1892 when Sir Francis Galton developed a classification system based on "minutia" that enabled efficient searching, and he verified that fingerprints do not change over time [188].

Examples of the different types of minutia in Galton's classification system appear in Figure 7.1. Galton's system allowed for an efficient solution to the identification problem in the pre-computer era.[9]

Loop (double)   **Whorl**   **Arch**

Figure 7.1: Examples of Galton's Minutia

Today, fingerprints are routinely used for identification, particularly in criminal cases. It is interesting to note that the standard for determining a match varies widely. For example, in Britain fingerprints must match in 16 points, whereas in the United States, no fixed number of points are required to match.[10]

A fingerprint biometric works by first capturing an image of the fingerprint. The image is then enhanced using various image-processing techniques, and various points are identified and extracted from the enhanced image. This process is illustrated in Figure 7.2.

Figure 7.2: Automatic Extraction of Minutia

The points extracted by the biometric system are compared in a manner that is somewhat analogous to the manual analysis of fingerprints. For authentication, the extracted points are compared with the claimed user's stored

---

[9]Fingerprints were classified into one of 1024 "bins." Then, given a fingerprint from an unknown subject, a binary search based on the minutia quickly focused the effort of matching the print on one of these bins. Consequently, only a very small subset of recorded fingerprints needed to be carefully compared to the unknown fingerprint.

[10]This is a fine example of the way that the U.S. generously ensures full employment for lawyers—they can always argue about whether fingerprint evidence is admissible or not.

information, which was previously captured during the enrollment phase. The system then determines whether a statistical match occurs, with some predetermined level of confidence. This fingerprint comparison process is illustrated in Figure 7.3.

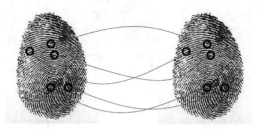

Figure 7.3: Minutia Comparison

7.4.2.2 Hand Geometry

Another popular biometric is hand geometry, which is particularly popular for entry into secure facilities [138, 256]. In this system, the shape of the hand is carefully measured, including the width and length of the hand and fingers.[11] The paper [152] describes 16 such measurements, of which 14 are illustrated in Figure 7.4 (the other two measure the thickness of the hand). Human hands are not nearly as unique as fingerprints, but hand geometry is easy and quick to measure, while being sufficiently robust for many authentication uses. However, hand geometry would probably not be suitable for identification, since the number of false matches would be high.

One advantage of hand geometry systems is that they are fast, taking less than one minute in the enrollment phase and less than five seconds in the recognition phase. Another advantage is that human hands are symmetric, so if the enrolled hand is, say, in a cast, the other hand can be used by placing it palm side up. Some disadvantages of hand geometry include that it cannot be used on the young or the very old, and, as we'll discuss in a moment, the system has a relatively high equal error rate.

7.4.2.3 Iris Scan

A biometric that is, in theory, one of the best for authentication is the iris scan. The development of the iris (the colored part of the eye) is chaotic, which implies that minor variations lead to large differences. There is little or no genetic influence on the iris pattern, so that the measured pattern

---

[11]Note that palm print systems do not read your palm. For that, you'll have to see your local chiromancer.

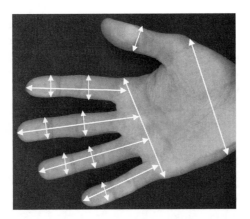

Figure 7.4: Hand Geometry Measurements

is uncorrelated for identical twins and even for the two eyes of one individual. Another desirable property is that the pattern is stable throughout a lifetime [149].

The development of iris scan technology is relatively new. In 1936, the idea of using the human iris for identification was suggested by Frank Burch. In the 1980s, the idea resurfaced in James Bond films, but it was not until 1986 that the first patents appeared—a sure sign that people foresaw money to be made on the technology. In 1994, John Daugman, a researcher at Cambridge University, patented what is generally accepted as the best approach currently available [76].

Iris scan systems require sophisticated equipment and software. First, an automated iris scanner locates the iris. Then a black and white photo of the eye is taken. The resulting image is processed using a two-dimensional wavelet transform, the result of which is a 256-byte (that is, 2048-bit) iris code.

Two iris codes are compared based on the Hamming distance between the codes. Suppose that Alice is trying to authenticate using an iris scan. Let x be the iris code computed from Alice's iris in the recognition phase, while y is Alice's iris code stored in the scanner's database, which was gathered during the enrollment phase. Then x and y are compared by computing the distance $d(x, y)$ defined by

$$d(x, y) = \frac{\text{number of non-match bits}}{\text{number of bits compared}}. \tag{7.1}$$

For example, $d(0010, 0101) = 3/4$ and $d(101111, 101001) = 1/3$.

For an iris scan, $d(x, y)$ is computed on the 2048-bit iris code. A perfect match yields $d(x, y) = 0$, but we can't expect perfection in practice. Under laboratory conditions, for the same iris the expected distance is 0.08, and for different irises the expect distance is 0.50. The usual thresholding scheme is to accept the comparison as a match if the distance is less than 0.32 and otherwise consider it a non-match [76]. An image of an iris appears in Figure 7.5.

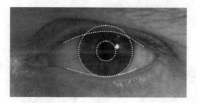

Figure 7.5: An Iris Scan

Define the *match* cases to be those where, for example, Alice's data from the enrollment phase is compared to her scan data from the recognition phase. Define the *no-match* cases to be when, for example, Alice's enrollment data is compared to Bob's recognition phase data (or vice versa). Then the left histogram in Figure 7.6 represents match data, while the right histogram represents no-match data. Note that the match data provides information relevant to the insult rate, whereas the no-match data provides information relevant to the fraud rate.

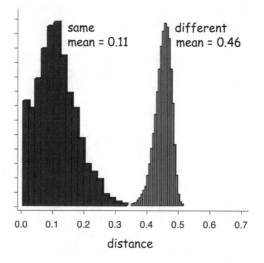

Figure 7.6: Histogram of Iris Scan Results [149]

The iris scan is often cited as the ultimate biometric for authentication. The histogram in Figure 7.6, which is based on 2.3 million comparisons, tends to support this view, since the overlapping region between the "same" (match) and "different" (no-match) cases appears to be virtually nonexistent. Note that the overlap represents the region where an error can occur. In reality, there is some overlap between the histograms in in Figure 7.6, but the overlap is extremely small.

The iris scan distances for the match data in Table 7.1 provide a more detailed view of the same histogram marked as "same" in Figure 7.6. From Figure 7.6, we see that the equal error rate (which corresponds to the crossover point between the two graphs) occurs somewhere near distance 0.34. From Table 7.1, this implies an equal error rate of about 10^{-5}. For this biometric, we would certainly be willing to tolerate a slightly higher insult rate since that would further reduce the fraud rate. Hence, the typical threshold used is 0.32, as mentioned above.

Table 7.1: Iris Scan Match Scores and Error Rates [149]

Score	Probability
0.29	1 in 1.3×10^{10}
0.30	1 in 1.5×10^{9}
0.31	1 in 1.8×10^{8}
0.32	1 in 2.6×10^{7}
0.33	1 in 4.0×10^{6}
0.34	1 in 6.9×10^{5}
0.35	1 in 1.3×10^{5}

Is it possible to attack an iris-scanning system? Suppose Bob has a good photo of Alice's eye. Then he can claim to be Alice and try to use the photo to trick the system into authenticating him as Alice. This attack is not at all far fetched. In fact, an Afghan woman whose photo appeared on a famous *National Geographic* magazine cover in 1984 was positively identified 17 years later by comparing her then-current iris scan with an iris scan taken from the 1984 photo. The woman had never seen the magazine, but she did recall being photographed. The magazine cover with the woman's photo and the fascinating story of finding this person after years of war and chaos in Afghanistan can be found at [28].

To prevent attacks based on a photo, an iris-scanning system could first shine a light on the "eye" and verify that the pupil contracts before proceeding with the iris scan. While this eliminates an attack that relies on a static photo, it also might significantly increase the cost of the system. Given that biometrics are in competition with passwords, and passwords are free, cost is always an issue.

7.4.3   Biometric Error Rates

Recall that the equal error rate—the point at which the fraud rate equals the insult rate—is generally considered the best measure for comparing different biometric systems. The equal error rates for several popular biometrics are given in Table 7.2.

Table 7.2: Biometric Equal Error Rates [32]

Biometric	Equal error rate
fingerprint	2.0×10^{-3}
hand geometry	2.0×10^{-3}
voice recognition	2.0×10^{-2}
iris scan	7.6×10^{-6}
retina scan	1.0×10^{-7}
signature recognition	2.0×10^{-2}

For fingerprint biometric systems, the equal error rate may seem high. However, most fingerprint biometrics are relatively cheap devices that do not achieve anything near the theoretical potential for fingerprint matching. On the other hand, hand geometry systems are relatively expensive and sophisticated devices, so they probably do achieve something close to the theoretical potential.

In theory, iris scanning has an equal error rate of about 10^{-5}. But to achieve such spectacular results, the enrollment phase must be extremely accurate. If the real-world enrollment environment is not up to laboratory standards, then the results might not be so impressive.

Undoubtedly many inexpensive biometrics systems fare worse than the results given in Table 7.2. And biometrics in general have a very poor record with respect to the inherently difficult identification problem.

7.4.4   Biometric Conclusions

Biometrics clearly have many potential advantages over passwords. In particular, biometrics are difficult, although not impossible, to forge. In the case of fingerprints, Trudy could steal Alice's thumb, or, in a less gruesome attack, Trudy might be able to use a copy of Alice's fingerprint. Of course, a more sophisticated system might be able to detect such an attack, but then the system will be more costly, thereby reducing its desirability as a replacement for passwords.[12]

---

[12]Unfortunately for security, passwords are likely to remain free for the foreseeable future.

There are also many potential software-based attacks on authentication. For example, it may be possible to subvert the software that does the comparison or to manipulate the database that contains the enrollment data. Such attacks apply to most authentication systems, regardless of whether they are based on biometrics, passwords, or other techniques.

While a broken cryptographic key or password can be revoked and replaced, it's not clear how to revoke a broken biometric. This and other biometric pitfalls are discussed by Schneier [260].

Biometrics have a great deal of potential as a substitute for passwords, but biometrics are not foolproof. And given the enormous problems with passwords and the vast potential of biometrics, it's perhaps surprising that biometrics are not more widely used today. This should change in the future as biometrics become more robust and inexpensive.

7.5 Something You Have

Smartcards or other hardware tokens can be used for authentication. Such authentication is based on the "something you have" principle. A smartcard is a credit card sized device that includes a small amount of memory and computing resources, so that it is able to store cryptographic keys or other secrets, and perhaps even do some computations on the card. A special-purpose smartcard reader, as shown in Figure 7.7, is used to read the key stored on the card. Then the key can be used to authenticate the user. Since a key is used, and keys are selected at random, password guessing attacks can be eliminated.[13]

Figure 7.7: A Smartcard Reader (Courtesy of Athena, Inc.)

There are several other examples of authentication based on "something you have," including a laptop computer (or its MAC address), an ATM card, or a password generator. Here, we give an example of a password generator.

---

[13]Well, a PIN might be required to access the key, so password issues might still arise.

A password generator is a small device that the user must have (and use) to log in to a system. Suppose that Alice has a password generator, and she wants to authenticate herself to Bob. Bob sends a random "challenge" R to Alice, which Alice then inputs into the password generator along with her PIN number. The password generator then produces a response, which Alice transmits to Bob. If the response is correct, Bob is convinced that he's indeed talking to Alice, since only Alice is supposed to have the password generator. This process is illustrated in Figure 7.8.

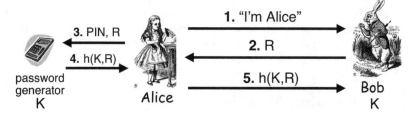

Figure 7.8: Password Generator

For a challenge-response authentication scheme to work, Bob must be able to verify that Alice's response is correct. For the example in Figure 7.8, Bob and the password generator must both have access to the key K, since the password generator needs the key to compute the hash, and Bob needs the key to verify Alice's response. Alice accesses the key K only indirectly—by entering her PIN into the key generator. We'll see more examples of the use of challenge-response mechanisms in the upcoming chapters on security protocols.

7.6   Two-Factor Authentication

In fact, the password generator scheme in Figure 7.8 requires both "something you have" (the password generator) and "something you know" (the PIN). Any authentication method that requires two out of the three "somethings" is known as *two-factor authentication*. Another example of a two-factor authentication is an ATM card, where the user must have the card and know the PIN number. Other examples of two-factor authentication include a credit card together with a signature, a biometric thumbprint system that also requires a password, and a cell phone that requires a PIN.

7.7   Single Sign-On and Web Cookies

Before concluding this chapter, we briefly mention two additional authentication topics. First, we discuss *single sign-on*, which is a topic of considerable practical importance. We'll also briefly mention *Web cookies*, which are often used as a weak form of authentication.

Users find it troublesome to enter their authentication information (typically, passwords) repeatedly. For example, when browsing the Web, it is not uncommon that many different websites require passwords. While this is sensible from a security perspective, it places a burden on users who must either remember different passwords for many different websites or compromise their security by reusing passwords.

A more convenient solution would be to have Alice authenticate once and then have a successful result automatically "follow" her wherever she goes on the Internet. That is, the initial authentication would require Alice's participation, but subsequent authentications would happen behind the scenes. This is known as single sign-on, and single sign-on for the Internet has been a topic of some interest for several years.

As with many computing topics, there are competing and incompatible approaches to single sign-on for the Internet. As is often the case, there is the Microsoft way, and the "everybody else" way. The approach favored by Microsoft goes by the name of Passport [171, 203], while the method preferred by (nearly) everybody else is the Liberty Alliance [100, 192]. The latter approach is based on the Security Assertion Markup Language, or SAML [78].

Certainly, a secure single sign-on for the Internet would be a major convenience. However, it does not appear that any such method is likely to gain widespread acceptance any time soon. It is worth noting that we will see a single sign-on architecture in Chapter 10 when we discuss the Kerberos security protocol.

Finally, we mention Web cookies, which have some interesting security implications. When Alice is surfing the Web, websites often provide Alice's browser with a Web cookie, which is simply a numerical value that is stored and managed by Alice's browser. The website also stores the cookie, which is used to index a database that retains information about Alice.

When Alice returns to a website for which she has a cookie, the cookie is automatically passed by her browser to the website. The website can then access its database to remember important information about Alice. In this way, cookies maintain state across sessions. Since the Web uses HTTP, which is a stateless protocol, cookies are also used to maintain state within a session.

In a sense, cookies can act as a single sign-on method for a website. That is, a website can authenticate "Alice" based on the possession of Alice's Web cookie. Or, in a slightly stronger version, a password is used to initially authenticate Alice, after which the cookie is considered sufficient. Either way, this is a fairly weak form of authentication, but it illustrates the often irresistible temptation to use whatever is available and convenient as a security mechanism, whether it is secure or not.

7.8   Summary

You can authenticate to a machine based on "something you know," "something you have," or "something you are." Passwords are synonymous with the "something you know" method of authentication. In this chapter, we discussed passwords at length. The bottom line is that passwords are far from an ideal method of authentication, but they are likely to remain popular for the foreseeable future, since passwords are the lowest cost option.

We also discussed authentication based on "something you are," i.e., biometrics. It is clear that biometrics offer the potential for much higher security than passwords. However, biometrics cost money, and they are not entirely without problems.

We briefly mentioned "something you have" methods of authentication, as well as two-factor authentication, which combines any two of the three methods. Finally, we briefly discussed single sign-on and Web cookies.

In the next chapter, we'll discuss authorization, which deals with restrictions placed on authenticated users. The authentication problem returns to the fore in Chapters 9 and 10, where we cover security protocols. We'll see that authentication over a network is a whole nother can of worms.

7.9   Problems

1. As discussed in this chapter, relatively strong passwords can be derived from passphrases.

   a. Give two passwords derived from the passphrase "Gentlemen do not read other gentlemen's mail."

   b. Give two passwords derived from the passphrase "Are you who you say you are?"

2. For each of the following passwords, give a passphrase that the password could have been derived from.

   a. PokeGCTall

   b. 4s&7yrsa

   c. gimmeliborD

   d. IcntgetNOsat

3. In the context of biometrics, define the terms *fraud rate* and *insult rate*. In statistics, which of these is a Type I error and which is a Type II error?

4. In some applications, a passcode consisting of some number of digits is required (for example, a PIN). Using the number-to-letter conversion on a telephone,

   a. What passcode corresponds to the password "hello"?

   b. Find as many passwords as you can that correspond to the passcode 5465, where each password is an English dictionary word.

5. Suppose that on a particular system, all passwords are 10 characters, there are 64 choices for each character, and the system has a password file containing 512 hashed passwords. Furthermore, Trudy has a dictionary of 2^{20} common passwords. Provide pseudo-code for an efficient attack on the password file in the following cases.

   a. The password hashes are not salted.

   b. The password hashes are salted.

6. This problem deals with storing passwords in a file.

   a. Why is it a good idea to hash passwords that are stored in a file?

   b. Why is it a much better idea to hash passwords stored in a file than to encrypt the password file?

   c. What is a salt and why should a salt be used whenever passwords are hashed?

7. On a particular system, all passwords are 8 characters, there are 128 choices for each character, and there is a password file containing the hashes of 2^{10} passwords. Trudy has a dictionary of 2^{30} passwords, and the probability that a randomly selected password is in her dictionary is 1/4. Work is measured in terms of the number of hashes computed.

   a. Suppose that Trudy wants to recover Alice's password. Using her dictionary, what is the expected work for Trudy to crack Alice's password, assuming the passwords are not salted?

   b. Repeat part a, assuming the passwords are salted.

   c. What is the probability that at least one of the passwords in the password file appears in Trudy's dictionary?

8. Suppose you are a merchant and you decide to use a biometric fingerprint device to authenticate people who make credit card purchases at your store. You can choose between two different systems: System A has a fraud rate of 1% and an insult rate of 5%, while System B has a fraud rate of 5% and an insult rate of 1%.

   a. Which system is more secure and why?

    b. Which system is more user-friendly and why?

    c. Which system would you choose and why?

9. Research has shown that most people cannot accurately identify an individual from a photo. For example, one study found that most people will accept an ID with any photo that has a picture of a person of the same gender and race as the presenter.

    a. It has also been demonstrated that when photos are included on credit cards, the fraud rate drops significantly. Explain this apparent contradiction.

    b. Your easily amused author frequents an amusement park that provides each season passholder with a plastic card similar to a credit card. The park takes a photo of each season passholder, but the photo does not appear on the card. Instead, when the card is presented for admission to the park, the photo appears on a screen that is visible to the park attendant. Why might this approach be better than putting the photo on the card?

10. Suppose all passwords on a given system are 8 characters and that each character can be any one of 64 different values. The passwords are hashed (with a salt) and stored in a password file. Now suppose Trudy has a password cracking program that can test 64 passwords per second. Trudy also has a dictionary of 2^{30} common passwords and the probability that any given password is in her dictionary is 1/4. The password file on this system contains 256 password hashes.

    a. How many different passwords are possible?

    b. How long, on average, will it take Trudy to crack the administrator's password?

    c. What is the probability that at least one of the 256 passwords in the password file is in the dictionary?

    d. What is the expected work for Trudy to recover any one of the passwords in the password file?

11. Let h be a secure cryptographic hash function. For this problem, a password consists of a maximum of 14-characters and there are 32 possible choices for each character. If a password is less than 14 characters, it's padded with nulls until it is exactly 14 characters. Let P be the resulting 14 character password. Consider the following two password hashing schemes.

    (i) The password P is split into two parts, with X equal to the first 7 characters and Y equal to the last 7 characters. The password is stored as $(h(X), h(Y))$. No salt is used.

(ii) The password is stored as $h(P)$. Again, no salt is used.

Note that the method in scheme (i) is used in Windows to store the so-called LANMAN password.

    a. Assuming a brute force attack, how much easier is it to crack the password if scheme (i) is used as compared with scheme (ii)?

    b. If scheme (i) is used, why might a 10-character password be *less* secure than a 7-character password?[14]

12. Suppose that passwords are stored as follows, where there are 128 possible choices for each character: If a password exceeds 16 characters, it is truncated to 16 characters. If a password is less than 16 characters, it is padded with "A" until it is exactly 16 characters. The resulting 16-character password is split into two parts, X_0 and X_1, where X_0 consists of the first six characters and X_1 consists of the last 10 characters. The password is hashed as $Y_0 = h(X_0, S_0)$ and $Y_1 = h(X_1, S_1)$, where S_0 and S_1 are each 64-bit salt values. The values (Y_0, S_0) and (Y_1, S_1) are stored for use in password verification.

    a. Precisely how are (Y_0, S_0) and (Y_1, S_1) used to verify an entered password?

    b. What is the expected work for an exhaustive search to recover one particular password (for example, the administrator's password)?

    c. How would you attack a password in a way that could provide a significant shortcut over an exhaustive search or a standard dictionary attack? Explain.

13. Many websites require users to register before they can access information or services. Suppose that you register at such a website, but when you return later you've forgotten your password. The website then asks you to enter your email address, which you do. Later, you receive your original password via email.

    a. Discuss several security concerns with this approach to dealing with forgotten passwords.

    b. The correct way to deal with passwords is to store salted hashes of passwords. Does this website use the correct approach? Justify your answer.

---

[14]In fact, the standard advice for LANMAN passwords is that users should choose either a 7-character password, or a 14-character password, since anything in between these two lengths is less secure.

14. Alice forgets her password. She goes to the system administrator's office, and the admin resets her password and gives Alice the new password.

    a. Why does the SA reset the password instead of giving Alice her previous (forgotten) password?

    b. Why should Alice re-reset her password immediately after the SA has reset it?

    c. Suppose that after the SA resets Alice's password, she remembers her previous password. Alice likes her old password, so she resets it to its previous value. Would it be possible for the SA to determine that Alice has chosen the same password as before? Why or why not?

15. Consider the password generator in Figure 7.8.

    a. If R is repeated, is the protocol secure?

    b. If R is predictable, is the protocol secure?

16. Describe attacks on an authentication scheme based on Web cookies.

17. Briefly outline the most significant technical differences between Passport and Liberty Alliance.

18. MAC address are globally unique and they don't change except in rare instances where hardware changes.

    a. Explain how the MAC address on your computer could be used as a "something you have" form of authentication.

    b. How could you use the MAC address as part of a two-factor authentication scheme?

    c. How secure is your authentication scheme in part a? How much more secure is your authentication scheme in part b?

19. Suppose you have six accounts, each of which requires a password, and you choose distinct passwords for each account.

    a. If the probability that any given password is in Trudy's password dictionary is $1/4$, what is the probability that at least one of your passwords is in Trudy's dictionary?

    b. If the probability that any one of your passwords is in Trudy's dictionary is reduced to $1/10$, what is the probability that at least one of your passwords is in Trudy's dictionary?

20. Suppose that you have n accounts, each of which requires a password. Trudy has a dictionary and the probability that a password appears in Trudy's dictionary is p.

    a. If you use the same password for all n accounts, what is the probability that your password appears in Trudy's dictionary?

    b. If you use distinct passwords for each of your n accounts, what is the probability that at least one of your passwords appears in Trudy's dictionary? Show that if $n = 1$, your answer agrees with your answer to part a.

    c. Which is more secure, choosing the same password for all accounts, or choosing different passwords for each account? Why? See also Problem 21.

21. Suppose that Alice uses two distinct passwords—one strong password for sites where she believes security is important (e.g., her online bank), and one weak password for sites where she does not care much about security (e.g., social networking sites).

    a. Alice believes this is a reasonable compromise between security and convenience. What do you think?

    b. What are some practical difficulties that might arise with such an approach?

22. Suppose Alice requires passwords for eight different accounts. She could choose the same password for all of these accounts. With just a single password to remember, Alice might be more likely to choose a strong password. On the other hand, Alice could choose different passwords for each account. With distinct passwords, she might be tempted to choose weaker passwords since this might make it easier for her to remember all of her passwords.

    a. What are the trade-offs between one well-chosen password versus several weaker passwords?

    b. Is there a third approach that is more secure than either of these options?

23. Consider Case I from Section 7.3.5.

    a. If the passwords are unsalted, how much work is it for Trudy to precompute all possible hash values?

    b. If each password is salted with a 16-bit value, how much work is it for Trudy to precompute all possible hash values?

    c. If each password is salted with a 64-bit value, how much work is it for Trudy to precompute all possible hash values?

24. Suppose that Trudy has a dictionary of 2^n passwords and the probability that a given password is in her dictionary is p. If Trudy obtains a file containing a large number of salted password hashes, show that the expected work to recover a password is bounded by $2^{n-1}(1+2(1-p)/p)$. Hint: As in Section 7.3.5, Case IV, ignore the highly improbable case where none of the passwords in the file appears in Trudy's dictionary. Then make use of the fact that $\sum_{k=0}^{\infty} x^k = 1/(1-x)$ and also $\sum_{k=1}^{\infty} kx^k = x/(1-x)^2$, provided $|x| < 1$.

25. For password cracking, generally the most realistic situation is Case IV of Section 7.3.5. In this case, the amount of work that Trudy must do to determine a password depends on the size of the dictionary, the probability that a given password is in the dictionary, and the size of the password file. Suppose Trudy's dictionary is of size 2^n, the probability that a password is in the dictionary is p, and the password file is of size M. Show that if p is small and M is sufficiently large, then Trudy's expected work is about $2^n/p$. Hint: Use the result of Problem 24.

26. Suppose that when a fingerprint is compared with one other (non-matching) fingerprint, the chance of a false match is 1 in 10^{10}, which is approximately the error rate when 16 points are required to determine a match (the British legal standard). Suppose that the FBI fingerprint database contains 10^7 fingerprints.

    a. How many false matches will occur when 100,000 suspect fingerprints are each compared with the entire database?

    b. For any individual suspect, what is the chance of a false match?

27. Suppose DNA matching could be done in real time.

    a. Describe a biometric for secure entry into a restricted facility based on this technique.

    b. Discuss one security concern and one privacy concern with your proposed system in part a.

28. This problem deals with biometrics.

    a. What is the difference between the authentication problem and the identification problem?

    b. Which is the inherently easier problem, authentication or identification? Why?

29. This problem deals with biometrics.

    a. Define fraud rate.

    b. Define insult rate.

    c. What is the equal error rate, how is it determined, and why is it useful?

30. Gait recognition is a biometric that distinguishes based on the way a person walks, whereas a digital doggie is a biometric that distinguishes based on odor.

    a. Describe an attack on gait recognition when it's used for identification.

    b. Describe an attack on a digital doggie when it's used for identification.

31. Recently, facial recognition has been touted as a possible method for, say, identifying terrorists in airports. As mentioned in the text, facial recognition is used by Las Vegas casinos in an attempt to detect cheaters. Note that in both of these cases the biometric is being used for identification (not authentication), presumably with uncooperative subjects.

    a. Discuss an attack on facial recognition when used by a casino to detect cheaters.

    b. Discuss a countermeasure that casinos might employ to reduce the effectiveness of your attack in part a.

    c. Discuss a counter-countermeasure that attackers might employ to reduce the effectiveness of your countermeasure in b.

32. In one episode of the television show *MythBusters*, three successful attacks on fingerprint biometrics are demonstrated [213].

    a. Briefly discuss each of these attacks.

    b. Discuss possible countermeasures for each of the attacks in part a. That is, discuss ways that the biometric systems could be made more robust against the specific attacks.

33. This problem deals with possible attacks on a hand geometry biometric system.

    a. Discuss analogous attacks to those in Problem 32 but for a hand geometry biometric system.

    b. In your judgment, which would be more difficult to break, the fingerprint door lock in Problem 32, or an analogous system based on hand geometry? Justify your answer.

34. A retina scan is an example of a well-known biometric that was not discussed in this chapter.

    a. Briefly outline the history and development of the retina scan biometric. How does a modern retina scan system work?

    b. Why, in principle, can a retina scan be extremely effective?

    c. List several pros and cons of retina scanning as compared to a fingerprint biometric.

    d. Suppose that your company is considering installing a biometric system that every employee will use every time they enter their office building. Your company will install either a retina scan or an iris scan system. Which would you prefer that they choose? Why?

35. A sonogram is a visual representation of sound. Obtain and install a speech analysis tool that can generate sonograms.[15]

    a. Examine several sonograms of your voice, each time saying "open sesame." Qualitatively, how similar are the sonograms?

    b. Examine several sonograms of someone else saying "open sesame." How similar are these sonograms to each other?

    c. In what ways do your sonograms from part a differ from those in part b?

    d. How would you go about trying to develop a reliable biometric based on voice recognition? What characteristics of the sonograms might be useful for distinguishing speakers?

36. This problem deals with possible attacks on an iris scan biometric system.

    a. Discuss analogous attacks to those in Problem 32 on an iris scan biometric system.

    b. Why would it be significantly more difficult to break an iris scan system than the fingerprint door lock in Problem 32?

    c. Given that an iris scan biometric is inherently stronger than a fingerprint-based biometric system, why are fingerprint biometrics far more popular?

---

[15]Your audacious author uses Audacity [20] to record speech and Sonogram [272] to generate sonograms and analyze the resulting audio files. Both of these are freeware.

37. Suppose that a particular iris scan systems generates 64-bit iris codes instead of the standard 2048-bit iris codes mentioned in this chapter. During the enrollment phase, the following iris codes (in hex) are determined.

User	Iris code
Alice	BE439AD598EF5147
Bob	9C8B7A1425369584
Charlie	885522336699CCBB

During the recognition phase, the following iris codes are obtained.

User	Iris code
U	C975A2132E89CEAF
V	DB9A8675342FEC15
W	A6039AD5F8CFD965
X	1DCA7A54273497CC
Y	AF8B6C7D5E3F0F9A

Use the iris codes above to answer the following questions.

    a. Use the formula in equation (7.1) to compute the following distances:

$$d(\text{Alice}, \text{Bob}), \quad d(\text{Alice}, \text{Charlie}), \quad d(\text{Bob}, \text{Charlie}).$$

    b. Assuming that the same statistics apply to these iris codes as the iris codes discussed in Section 7.4.2.3, which of the users, U,V,W,X,Y, is most likely Alice? Bob? Charlie? None of the above?

38. A popular "something you have" method of authentication is the RSA SecurID [252]. The SecureID system is often deployed as a USB key. The algorithm used by SecurID is similar to that given for the password generator illustrated in Figure 7.8. However, no challenge R is sent from Bob to Alice; instead, the current time T (typically, to a resolution of one minute) is used. That is, Alice's password generator computes $h(K, T)$ and this is sent directly to Bob, provided Alice has entered the correct PIN (or password).

    a. Draw a diagram analogous to that in Figure 7.8 illustrating the SecurID algorithm.

    b. Why do we need T? That is, why is the protocol insecure if we remove T?

c. What are the advantages and disadvantages of using the time T as compared to using a random challenge R?

d. Which is more secure, using a random challenge R or the time T? Why?

39. A password generator is illustrated in Figure 7.8.

    a. Discuss possible cryptanalytic attacks on the password generator scheme in Figure 7.8.

    b. Discuss network-based attacks on the password generator scheme in Figure 7.8.

    c. Discuss possible non-technical attacks on the password generator scheme in Figure 7.8.

40. In addition to the holy trinity of "somethings" discussed in this chapter (something you know, are, or have), it is also possible to base authentication on "something you do." For example, you might need to press a button on your wireless access point to reset it, proving that you have physical access to the device.

    a. Give another real-world example where authentication could be based on "something you do."

    b. Give an example of two-factor authentication that includes "something you do" as one of the factors.

Chapter 8

Authorization

> *It is easier to exclude harmful passions than to rule them,*
> *and to deny them admittance than to control them after they have been admitted.*
> — Seneca

> *You can always trust the information given to you by people who are crazy;*
> *they have an access to truth not available through regular channels.*
> — Sheila Ballantyne

8.1 Introduction

Authorization is the part of access control concerned with restrictions on the actions of authenticated users. In our terminology, authorization is one aspect of access control and authentication is another. Unfortunately, some authors use the term "access control" as a synonym for authorization.

In the previous chapter we discussed authentication, where the issue is one of establishing identity. In its most basic form, authorization deals with the situation where we've already authenticated Alice and we want to enforce restrictions on what she is allowed to do. Note that while authentication is binary (either a user is authenticated or not), authorization can be a much more fine grained process.

In this chapter, we'll extend the traditional notion of authorization to include a few non-traditional topics. We'll discuss CAPTCHAs, which are designed to restrict access to humans (as opposed to computers), and we'll consider firewalls, which can be viewed as a form of access control for networks. We'll follow up the section on firewalls with a discussion of intrusion detection systems, which come into play when firewalls fail to keep the bad guys out.

8.2   A Brief History of Authorization

History is ... bunk.
— Henry Ford

Back in the computing dark ages,[1] authorization was often considered the heart of information security. Today, that seems like a rather quaint notion. In any case, it is worth briefly considering the historical context from which modern information security has arisen.

While cryptography has a long and storied history, other aspects of modern information security are relative newcomers. Here, we take a brief look at the history of system certification, which, in some sense, represents the modern history of authorization. The goal of such certification regimes is to give users some degree of confidence that the systems they use actually provide a specified level of security. While this is a laudable goal, in practice, system certification is often laughable. Consequently, certification has never really become a significant piece of the security puzzle—as a rule, only those products that absolutely must be certified are. And why would any product need to be certified? Governments, which created the certification regimes, require certification for certain products that they purchase. So, as a practical matter, certification is generally only an issue if you are trying to sell your product to the government.[2]

8.2.1   The Orange Book

The Trusted Computing System Evaluation Criteria (TCSEC), or "orange book" [309] (so called because of the color of its cover) was published in 1983. The orange book was one of a series of related books developed under the auspices of the National Security Agency. Each book had a different colored cover and collectively they are known as the "rainbow series." The orange book primarily deals with system evaluation and certification and, to some extent, multilevel security—a topic discussed later in this chapter.

Today, the orange book is of little, if any, practical relevance. Moreover, in your opinionated author's opinion, the orange book served to stunt the growth of information security by focusing vast amounts of time and resources on some of the most esoteric and impractical aspects of security.[3]

Of course, not everyone is as enlightened as your humble author, and, in some circles, there is still something of a religious fervor for the orange book

---

[1]That is, before the Apple Macintosh was invented.

[2]It's tempting to argue that certification is an obvious failure simply because there is no evidence that the government is any more secure than anybody else, in spite of its use of certified security products. However, your certifiable author will, for once, refrain from making such a smug and unsubstantiated (but oddly satisfying) claim.

[3]Other than that, the orange book was a smashing success.

Criteria, which is another reason why it will never evoke more than a yawn from the masses.

Next, we consider the classic view of authorization. Then we look at multilevel security (and related topics) before considering a few cutting-edge topics, including firewalls, IDS, and CAPTCHAs.

8.3 Access Control Matrix

The classic view of authorization begins with Lampson's access control matrix [5]. This matrix contains all of the relevant information needed by an operating system to make decisions about which users are allowed to do what with the various system resources.

We'll define a *subject* as a user of a system (not necessarily a human user) and an *object* as a system resource. Two fundamental constructs in the field of authorization are *access control lists*, or ACLs, and *capabilities*, or C-lists. Both ACLs and C-lists are derived from Lampson's *access control matrix*, which has a row for every subject and a column for every object. Sensibly enough, the access allowed by subject S to object O is stored at the intersection of the row indexed by S and the column indexed by O. An example of an access control matrix appears in Table 8.1, where we use UNIX-style notation, that is, x, r, and w stand for execute, read, and write privileges, respectively.

Table 8.1: Access Control Matrix

	OS	Accounting program	Accounting data	Insurance data	Payroll data
Bob	rx	rx	r	—	—
Alice	rx	rx	r	rw	rw
Sam	rwx	rwx	r	rw	rw
Accounting program	rx	rx	rw	rw	r

Notice that in Table 8.1, the accounting program is treated as both an object and a subject. This is a useful fiction, since we can enforce the restriction that the accounting data is only modified by the accounting program. As discussed in [14], the intent here is to make corruption of the accounting data more difficult, since any changes to the accounting data must be done by software that, presumably, includes standard accounting checks and balances. However, this does not prevent all possible attacks, since the system administrator, Sam, could replace the accounting program with a faulty (or fraudulent) version and thereby break the protection. But this trick does allow Alice and Bob to access the accounting data without allowing them to corrupt it—either intentionally or unintentionally.

8.3.1   ACLs and Capabilities

Since all subjects and all objects appear in the access control matrix, it contains all of the relevant information on which authorization decisions can be based. However, there is a practical issue in managing a large access control matrix. A system could have hundreds of subjects (or more) and tens of thousands of objects (or more), in which case an access control matrix with millions of entries (or more) would need to be consulted before any operation by any subject on any object. Dealing with such a large matrix could impose a significant burden on the system.

To obtain acceptable performance for authorization operations, the access control matrix can be partitioned into more manageable pieces. There are two obvious ways to split the access control matrix. First, we could split the matrix into its columns and store each column with its corresponding object. Then, whenever an object is accessed, its column of the access control matrix would be consulted to see whether the operation is allowed. These columns are known as access control lists, or ACLs. For example, the ACL corresponding to insurance data in Table 8.1 is

$$(\text{Bob}, -), (\text{Alice}, \texttt{rw}), (\text{Sam}, \texttt{rw}), (\text{accounting program}, \texttt{rw}).$$

Alternatively, we could store the access control matrix by row, where each row is stored with its corresponding subject. Then, whenever a subject tries to perform an operation, we can consult its row of the access control matrix to see if the operation is allowed. This approach is know as capabilities, or C-lists. For example, Alice's C-list in Table 8.1 is

$$(\text{OS}, \texttt{rx}), (\text{accounting program}, \texttt{rx}), (\text{accounting data}, \texttt{r}),$$
$$(\text{insurance data}, \texttt{rw}), (\text{payroll data}, \texttt{rw}).$$

It might seem that ACLs and C-lists are equivalent, since they simply provide different ways of storing the same information. However, there are some subtle differences between the two approaches. Consider the comparison of ACLs and capabilities illustrated in Figure 8.1.

Note that the arrows in Figure 8.1 point in opposite directions, that is, for ACLs, the arrows point from the resources to the users, while for capabilities, the arrows point from the users to the resources. This seemingly trivial difference has real significance. In particular, with capabilities, the association between users and files is built into the system, while for an ACL-based system, a separate method for associating users to files is required. This illustrates one of the inherent advantages of capabilities. In fact, capabilities have several security advantages over ACLs and, for this reason, C-lists are

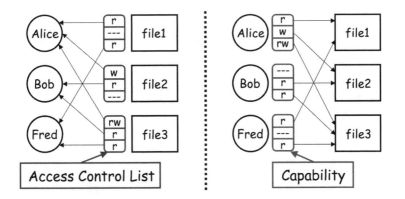

Figure 8.1: ACLs versus Capabilities

much beloved within the academic research community [206]. In the next section, we discuss one potential security advantage of capabilities over ACLs. Then we move on to the topic of multilevel security.

8.3.2 Confused Deputy

The *confused deputy* is a classic security problem that arises in many contexts [139]. For our illustration of this problem, we consider a system with two resources, a compiler and a file named BILL that contains critical billing information, and one user, Alice. The compiler can write to any file, while Alice can invoke the compiler and she can provide a filename where debugging information will be written. However, Alice is not allowed to write to the file BILL, since she might corrupt the billing information. The access control matrix for this scenario appears in Table 8.2.

Table 8.2: Access Control Matrix for Confused Deputy Example

	Compiler	BILL
Alice	x	—
Compiler	rx	rw

Now suppose that Alice invokes the compiler, and she provides BILL as the debug filename. Alice does not have the privilege to access the file BILL, so this command should fail. However, the compiler, which is acting on Alice's behalf, does have the privilege to overwrite BILL. If the compiler acts with its privilege, then a side effect of Alice's command will be the trashing of the BILL file, as illustrated in Figure 8.2.

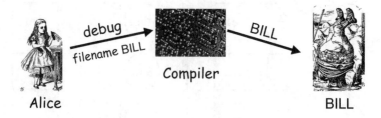

Figure 8.2: Confused Deputy

Why is this problem known as the confused deputy? The compiler is acting on Alice's behalf, so it is her deputy. The compiler is confused since it is acting based on its own privileges when it should be acting based on Alice's privileges.

With ACLs, it's more difficult (but not impossible) to avoid the confused deputy. In contrast, with capabilities it's relatively easy to prevent this problem, since capabilities are easily delegated, while ACLs are not. In a capabilities-based system, when Alice invokes the compiler, she can simply give her C-list to the compiler. The compiler then consults Alice's C-list when checking privileges before attempting to create the debug file. Since Alice does not have the privilege to overwrite BILL, the situation in Figure 8.2 can be avoided.

A comparison of the relative advantages of ACLs and capabilities is instructive. ACLs are preferable when users manage their own files and when protection is data oriented. With ACLs, it's also easy to change rights to a particular resource. On the other hand, with capabilities it's easy to delegate (and sub-delegate and sub-sub-delegate, and so on), and it's easier to add or delete users. Due to the ability to delegate, it's easy to avoid the confused deputy when using capabilities. However, capabilities are more complex to implement and they have somewhat higher overhead—although it may not be obvious, many of the difficult issues inherent in distributed systems arise in the context of capabilities. For these reasons, ACLs are used in practice far more often than capabilities.

8.4 Multilevel Security Models

In this section we briefly discuss security modeling in the context of multilevel security. Security models are often presented at great length in information security textbooks, but here we'll only mention two of the best-known models, and we only present an overview of these models. For a more thorough introduction to MLS and related security models, see [283] or Gollmann's book [125].

In general, security models are descriptive, not proscriptive. That is, these models tell us what needs to be protected, but they don't answer the real question, that is, how to provide such protection. This is not a flaw in the models, as they are designed to set a framework for protection, but it is an inherent limitation on the practical utility of security modeling.

Multilevel security, or MLS, is familiar to all fans of spy novels, where classified information often figures prominently. In MLS, the subjects are the users (generally, human) and the objects are the data to be protected (for example, documents). Furthermore, *classifications* apply to objects while *clearances* apply to subjects.

The U.S. Department of Defense, or DoD, employs four levels of classifications and clearances, which can be ordered as

$$\text{TOP SECRET} > \text{SECRET} > \text{CONFIDENTIAL} > \text{UNCLASSIFIED}. \qquad (8.1)$$

For example, a subject with a SECRET clearance is allowed access to objects classified SECRET or lower but not to objects classified TOP SECRET. Apparently to make them more visible, security levels are generally rendered in upper case.

Let O be an object and S a subject. Then O has a classification and S has a clearance. The security *level* of O is denoted $L(O)$, and the security level of S is similarly denoted $L(S)$. In the DoD system, the four levels shown above in (8.1) are used for both clearances and classifications. Also, for a person to obtain a SECRET clearance, a more-or-less routine background check is required, while a TOP SECRET clearance requires an extensive background check, a polygraph exam, a psychological profile, etc.

There are many practical problems related to the classification of information. For example, the proper classification is not always clear, and two experienced users might have widely differing views. Also, the level of granularity at which to apply classifications can be an issue. It's entirely possible to construct a document where each paragraph, when taken individually, is UNCLASSIFIED, yet the overall document is TOP SECRET. This problem is even worse when source code must be classified, which is sometimes the case within the DoD. The flip side of granularity is aggregation—an adversary might be able to glean TOP SECRET information from a careful analysis of UNCLASSIFIED documents.

Multilevel security is needed when subjects and objects at different levels use the same system resources. The purpose of an MLS system is to enforce a form of access control by restricting subjects so that they only access objects for which they have the necessary clearance.

Military and government have long had an interest in MLS. The U.S. government, in particular, has funded a great deal of research into MLS and, as a consequence, the strengths and weaknesses of MLS are relatively well understood.

Today, there are many potential uses for MLS outside of its traditional classified government setting. For example, most businesses have information that is restricted to, say, senior management, and other information that is available to all management, while still other proprietary information is available to everyone within the company and, finally, some information is available to everyone, including the general public. If this information is stored on a single system, the company must deal with MLS issues, even if they don't realize it. Note that these categories correspond directly to the TOP SECRET, SECRET, CONFIDENTIAL, and UNCLASSIFIED classifications discussed above.

There is also interest in MLS in such applications as network firewalls. The goal in such a case is to keep an intruder, Trudy, at a low level to limit the damage that she can inflict after she breaches the firewall. Another MLS application that we'll examine in more detail below deals with private medical information.

Again, our emphasis here is on MLS models, which explain what needs to be done but do not tell us how to implement such protection. In other words, we should view these models as high-level descriptions, not as security algorithms or protocols. There are many MLS models—we'll only discuss the most elementary. Other models can be more realistic, but they are also more complex and harder to analyze and verify.

Ideally, we would like to prove results about security models. Then any system that satisfies the assumptions of the model automatically inherits all of the results that have been proved about the model. However, we will not delve so deeply into security models in this book.

8.4.1   Bell-LaPadula

The first security model that we'll consider is Bell-LaPadula, or BLP, which, believe it or not, was named after its inventors, Bell and LaPadula. The purpose of BLP is to capture the minimal requirements, with respect to confidentiality, that any MLS system must satisfy. BLP consists of the following two statements:

> **Simple Security Condition**: Subject S can read object O if and only if $L(O) \leq L(S)$.
>
> ***-Property** (Star Property): Subject S can write object O if and only if $L(S) \leq L(O)$.

The simple security condition merely states that Alice, for example, cannot read a document for which she lacks the appropriate clearance. This condition is clearly required of any MLS system.

The star property is somewhat less obvious. This property is designed to prevent, say, TOP SECRET information from being written to, say, a SECRET document. This would break MLS security since a user with a SECRET clearance could then read TOP SECRET information. The writing could occur intentionally or, for example, as the result of a computer virus. In his groundbreaking work on viruses, Cohen mentions that viruses could be used to break MLS security [60], and such attacks remain a very real threat to MLS systems today.

The simple security condition can be summarized as "no read up," while the star property implies "no write down." Consequently, BLP is sometimes succinctly stated as "no read up, no write down." It's difficult to imagine a security model that's any simpler.

Although simplicity in security is a good thing, BLP may be too simple. At least that is the conclusion of McLean, who states that BLP is "so trivial that it is hard to imagine a realistic security model for which it does not hold" [198]. In an attempt to poke holes in BLP, McLean defined a "system Z" in which an administrator is allowed to temporarily reclassify objects, at which point they can be "written down" without violating BLP. System Z clearly violates the spirit of BLP, but, since it is not expressly forbidden, it is apparently allowed.

In response to McLean's criticisms, Bell and LaPadula fortified BLP with a *tranquility property*. Actually, there are two versions of this property. The strong tranquility property states that security labels can never change. This removes McLean's system Z from the BLP realm, but it's also impractical in the real world, since security labels must sometimes change. For example, the DoD regularly declassifies documents, which would be impossible under strict adherence to the strong tranquility property. For another example, it is often desirable to enforce *least privilege*. If a user has, say, a TOP SECRET clearance but is only browsing UNCLASSIFIED Web pages, it is desirable to only give the user an UNCLASSIFIED clearance, so as to avoid accidentally divulging classified information. If the user later needs a higher clearance, his active clearance can be upgraded. This is known as the *high water mark principle*, and we'll see it again when we discuss Biba's model, below.

Bell and Lapadula also offered a *weak tranquility property* in which a security label can change, provided such a change does not violate an "established security policy." Weak tranquility can defeat system Z, and it can allow for least privilege, but the property is so vague as to be nearly meaningless for analytic purposes.

The debate concerning BLP and system Z is discussed thoroughly in [34], where the author points out that BLP proponents and McLean are each making fundamentally different assumptions about modeling. This debate gives rise to some interesting issues concerning the nature—and limits—of modeling.

The bottom line regarding BLP is that it's very simple, and as a result it's one of the few models for which it's possible to prove things about systems. Unfortunately, BLP may be too simple to be of any practical benefit.

BLP has inspired many other security models, most of which strive to be more realistic. The price that these systems pay for more reality is more complexity. This makes most other models more difficult to analyze and more difficult to apply, that is, it's more difficult to show that a real-world system satisfies the requirements of the model.

8.4.2   Biba's Model

In this section, we'll look briefly at Biba's model. Whereas BLP deals with confidentiality, Biba's model deals with integrity. In fact, Biba's model is essentially an integrity version of BLP.

If we trust the integrity of object O_1 but not that of object O_2, then if object O is composed of O_1 and O_2, we cannot trust the integrity of object O. In other words, the integrity level of O is the minimum of the integrity of any object contained in O. Another way to say this is that for integrity, a low water mark principle holds. In contrast, for confidentiality, a high water mark principle applies.

To state Biba's model formally, let $I(O)$ denote the integrity of object O and $I(S)$ the integrity of subject S. Biba's model is defined by the two statements:

> **Write Access Rule**: Subject S can write object O if and only if $I(O) \leq I(S)$.

> **Biba's Model**: A subject S can read the object O if and only if $I(S) \leq I(O)$.

The write access rule states that we don't trust anything that S writes any more than we trust S. Biba's model states that we can't trust S any more than the lowest integrity object that S has read. In essence, we are concerned that S will be "contaminated" by lower integrity objects, so S is forbidden from viewing such objects.

Biba's model is actually very restrictive, since it prevents S from ever viewing an object at a lower integrity level. It's possible—and, in many cases, perhaps desirable—to replace Biba's model with the following:

> **Low Water Mark Policy**: If subject S reads object O, then $I(S) = \min(I(S), I(O))$.

Under the low water mark principle, subject S can read anything, under the condition that the integrity of subject S is downgraded after accessing an object at a lower level.

Figure 8.3 illustrates the difference between BLP and Biba's model. Of course the fundamental difference is that BLP is for confidentiality, which implies a high water mark principle, while Biba is for integrity, which implies a low water mark principle.

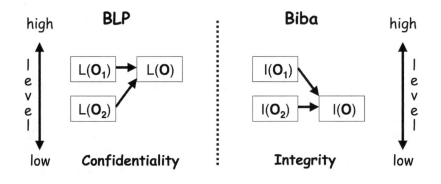

Figure 8.3: BLP versus Biba

8.5 Compartments

Multilevel security systems enforce access control (or information flow) "up and down," where the security levels are ordered in a hierarchy, such as (8.1). Usually, a simple hierarchy of security labels is not flexible enough to deal with a realistic situation. In practice, it is usually necessary to also use *compartments* to further restrict information flow "across" security levels.

We use the notation

SECURITY LEVEL {COMPARTMENT}

to denote a security level and its associated compartment or compartments. For example, suppose that we have compartments CAT and DOG within the TOP SECRET level. Then we would denote the resulting compartments as TOP SECRET {CAT} and TOP SECRET {DOG}. Note that there is also a TOP SECRET {CAT,DOG} compartment. While each of these compartments is TOP SECRET, a subject with a TOP SECRET clearance can only access a compartment if he or she is specifically allowed to do so. As a result, compartments have the effect of restricting information flow across security levels.

Compartments serve to enforce the *need to know* principle, that is, subjects are only allowed access to the information that they must know for their work. If a subject does not have a legitimate need to know everything at, say, the TOP SECRET level, then compartments can be used to limit the TOP SECRET information that the subject can access.

Why create compartments instead of simply creating a new classification level? It may be the case that, for example, TOP SECRET {CAT} and TOP SECRET {DOG} are not comparable, that is, neither

$$\text{TOP SECRET \{CAT\}} \leq \text{TOP SECRET \{DOG\}}$$

nor

$$\text{TOP SECRET \{CAT\}} \geq \text{TOP SECRET \{DOG\}}$$

holds. Using a strict MLS hierarchy, one of these two conditions must hold true.

Consider the compartments in Figure 8.4, where the arrows represent "$\geq$" relationships. In this example, a subject with a TOP SECRET {CAT} clearance does not have access to information in the TOP SECRET {DOG} compartment. In addition, a subject with a TOP SECRET {CAT} clearance has access to the SECRET {CAT} compartment but not to the compartment SECRET {CAT,DOG}, even though the subject has a TOP SECRET clearance. Again, compartments provide a means to enforce the need to know principle.

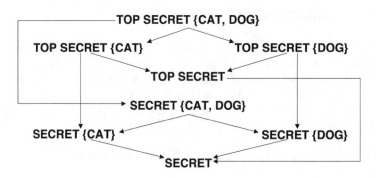

Figure 8.4: Compartments Example

Multilevel security can be used without compartments and vice versa, but the two are usually used together. An interesting example described in [14] concerns the protection of personal medical records by the British Medical Association, or BMA. The law that required protection of medical records mandated a multilevel security system—apparently because lawmakers were familiar with MLS. Certain medical conditions, such as AIDS, were considered to be the equivalent of TOP SECRET, while other less sensitive information, such as drug prescriptions, was considered SECRET. But if a subject had been prescribed AIDS drugs, anyone with a SECRET clearance could easily deduce TOP SECRET information. As a result, all information tended to be classified at the highest level, and consequently all users required the highest level of clearance, which defeated the purpose of the system. Eventually, the BMA system was changed to a system using only compartments, which effectively solved the problem. Then, for example, AIDS prescription information could be compartmented from general prescription information, thereby enforcing the desired need to know principle.

In the next two sections we'll discuss covert channels and inference control. Both of these topics are related to MLS, but covert channels, in particular, arise in many different contexts.

8.6 Covert Channel

A *covert channel* is a communication path not intended as such by the system's designers. Covert channels exist in many situations, but they are particularly prevalent in networks. Covert channels are virtually impossible to eliminate, so the emphasis is instead on limiting the capacity of such channels.

MLS systems are designed to restrict legitimate channels of communication. But a covert channel provides another way for information to flow. It is not difficult to give an example where resources shared by subjects at different security levels can be used to pass information, and thereby violate the security of an MLS system.

For example, suppose Alice has a TOP SECRET clearance while Bob only has a CONFIDENTIAL clearance. If the file space is shared by all users, then Alice and Bob can agree that if Alice wants to send a 1 to Bob, she will create a file named, say, `FileXYzW`, and if she wants to send a 0 she will not create such a file. Bob can check to see whether file `FileXYzW` exists, and if it does, he knows Alice has sent him a 1, while if it does not, Alice has sent him a 0. In this way, a single bit of information has been passed through a covert channel, that is, through a means that was not intended for communication by the designers of the system. Note that Bob cannot look inside the file `FileXYzW` since he does not have the required clearance, but we are assuming that he can query the file system to see if such a file exists.

A single bit leaking from Alice to Bob is not a concern, but Alice could leak any amount of information by synchronizing with Bob. That is, Alice and Bob could agree that Bob will check for the file `FileXYzW` once each minute. As before, if the file does not exist, Alice has sent 0, and if it does exists, Alice has sent a 1. In this way Alice can (slowly) leak TOP SECRET information to Bob. This process is illustrated in Figure 8.5.

Covert channels are everywhere. For example, the print queue could be used to signal information in much the same way as in the example above. Networks are a rich source of covert channels, and several hacking tools exist that exploit these covert channels—we'll mention one later in this section.

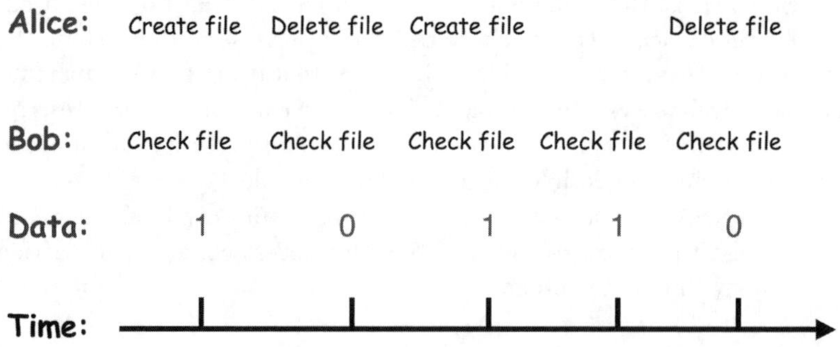

Alice: Create file   Delete file   Create file   Delete file

Bob: Check file   Check file   Check file   Check file   Check file

Data: 1   0   1   1   0

Time:

Figure 8.5: Covert Channel Example

Three things are required for a covert channel to exist. First, the sender and receiver must have access to a shared resource. Second, the sender must be able to vary some property of the shared resource that the receiver can observe. Finally, the sender and receiver must be able to synchronize their communication. From this description, it's apparent that potential covert channels really are everywhere. Of course, we can eliminate all covert channels—we just need to eliminate all shared resources and all communication. Obviously such a system would generally be of little use.

The conclusion here is that it's virtually impossible to eliminate all covert channels in any useful system. The DoD apparently agrees, since their guidelines merely call for reducing covert channel capacity to no more than one bit per second [131]. The implication is that DoD has given up trying to eliminate covert channels.

Is a limit of one bit per second sufficient to prevent damage from covert channels? Consider a TOP SECRET file that is 100 MB in size. Suppose the plaintext version of this file is stored in a TOP SECRET file system, while an encrypted version of the file—encrypted with, say, AES using a 256-bit key—is stored in an UNCLASSIFIED location. Following the DoD guidelines, suppose that we have reduced the covert channel capacity of this system to 1 bit per second. Then it would take more than 25 years to leak the entire 100 MB TOP SECRET document through a covert channel. However, it would take less than 5 minutes to leak the 256-bit AES key through the same covert channel. The conclusion is that reducing covert channel capacity might be useful, but it will not be sufficient in all cases.

Next, we consider a real-world example of a covert channel. The Transmission Control Protocol (TCP) is widely used on the Internet. The TCP header, which appears in the Appendix in Figure A-3, includes a "reserved" field which is reserved for future use, that is, it is not used for anything. This field can easily be used to pass information covertly.

It's also easy to hide information in the TCP sequence number or ACK field and thereby create a more subtle covert channel. Figure 8.6 illustrates the method used by the tool `Covert_TCP` to pass information in the sequence number. The sender hides the information in the sequence number X and the packet—with its source address forged to be the address of the intended recipient—is sent to an innocent server. When the server acknowledges the packet, it unwittingly completes the covert channel by passing the information contained in X to the intended recipient. Such stealthy covert channels are often employed in network attacks [270].

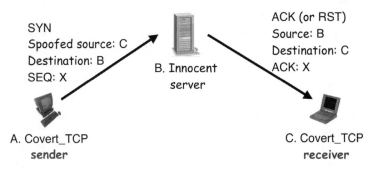

Figure 8.6: Covert Channel Using TCP Sequence Number

8.7 Inference Control

Consider a database that includes information on college faculty in California. Suppose we query the database and ask for the average salary of female computer science professors at San Jose State University (SJSU) and we find the answer is $100,000. We then query the database and ask for the number of female computer science professors at SJSU, and the answer is one. Then we could go to the SJSU computer science department website and determine the identity of this person.[8] In this example, specific information has leaked from responses to general questions. The goal of inference control is to prevent such leaks from happening, or at least minimize the leakage.

A database containing medical records would be of considerable interest to researchers. For example, by searching for statistical correlations, it may be possible to determine causes or risk factors for certain diseases. But patients want to keep their medical information private. How can we allow access to the statistically significant data while protecting privacy?

---

[8]In this case, no harm was done, since state employee salaries are public information in California.

An obvious first step is to remove names and addresses from the medical records. But this is not sufficient to ensure privacy as the college professor example above clearly demonstrates. What more can be done to provide stronger inference control while leaving the data accessible for legitimate research uses?

Several techniques used in inference control are discussed in [14]. One such technique is *query set size control*, in which no response is returned if the size of the set it too small. This approach would make it more difficult to determine the college professor's salary in the example above. However, if medical research is focused on a rare disease, query set size control could also prevent or distort important research.

Another technique is known as the *N-respondent, k% dominance rule*, whereby data is not released if $k\%$ or more of the result is contributed by N or fewer subjects. For example, we might query the census database and ask for the average net worth of individuals in Bill Gates' neighborhood. With any reasonable setting for N and k no results would be returned. In fact, this technique is actually applied to information collected by the United States Census Bureau.

Another approach to inference control is randomization, that is, a small amount of random noise is added to the data. This is problematic in situations such as research into rare medical conditions, where the noise might swamp legitimate data.

Many other methods of inference control have been proposed, but none are completely satisfactory. It appears that strong inference control may be impossible to achieve in practice, yet it seems obvious that employing some inference control, even if it's weak, is better than no inference control at all. Inference control will make Trudy's job more difficult, and it will almost certainly reduce the amount of information that leaks, thereby limiting the damage.

Does this same logic hold for crypto? That is, is it better to use weak encryption or no encryption at all? Surprisingly, for crypto, the answer is that, in most cases, you'd be better off not encrypting rather than using a weak cipher. Today, most information is not encrypted, and encryption tends to indicate important data. If there is a lot of data being sent and most of it is plaintext (e.g., email sent over the Internet), then Trudy faces an enormous challenge in attempting to filter interesting messages from this mass of uninteresting data. However, if your data is encrypted, it would be much easier to filter, since encrypted data looks random, whereas unencrypted data tends to be highly structured.[9] That is, if your encryption is weak, you may have just solved Trudy's difficult filtering problem for her, while providing no significant protection from a cryptanalytic attack [14].

---

[9]For one way around this problem, see [287].

8.8 CAPTCHA

The Turing test was proposed by computing pioneer (and breaker of the Enigma) Alan Turing in 1950. The test has a human ask questions to a human and a computer. The questioner, who can't see either the human or the computer, can only submit questions by typing on a keyboard, and responses are received on a computer screen. The questioner does not know which is the computer and which is the human, and the goal is to distinguish the human from the computer, based solely on the questions and answers. If the human questioner can't solve this puzzle with a probability better than guessing, the computer passes the Turing test. This test is the gold standard in artificial intelligence, and no computer has yet passed the Turing test, but occasionally some claim to be getting close.

A "completely automated public Turing test to tell computers and humans apart," or *CAPTCHA*,[10] is a test that a human can pass, but a computer can't pass with a probability better than guessing [319]. This could be considered as a sort of inverse Turing test. The assumptions here are that the test is generated by a computer program and graded by a computer program, yet no computer can pass the test, even if that computer has access to the source code used to generate the test. In other words, a "CAPTCHA is a program that can generate and grade tests that it itself cannot pass, much like some professors" [319].

At first blush, it seems paradoxical that a computer can create and score a test that it cannot pass. However, this becomes less of a paradox when we look more closely the details of the process.

Since CAPTCHAs are designed to prevent non-humans from accessing resources, a CAPTCHA can be viewed as a form of access control. According to folklore, the original motivation for CAPTCHAs was an online poll that asked users to vote for the best computer science graduate school. In this version of reality, it quickly become obvious that automated responses from MIT and Carnegie-Mellon were skewing the results [320] and researchers developed the idea of a CAPTCHA to prevent automated "bots" from stuffing the ballot box. Today, CAPTCHAs are used in a wide variety of applications. For example, free email services use CAPTCHAs to prevent spammers from automatically signing up for large numbers of email accounts.

The requirements for a CAPTCHA include that it must be easy for most humans to pass and it must be difficult or impossible for a machines to pass, even if the machine has access to the CAPTCHA software. From the attacker's perspective, the only unknown is some randomness that is used to generate the specific CAPTCHA. It is also desirable to have different types

---

[10]CAPTCHAs are also known as "human interactive proofs," or HIPs. While CAPTCHA may well rank as the worst acronym in the history of the universe, HIP is, well, just not hip.

of CAPTCHAs in case some person cannot pass one particular type. For example, many websites allow users to choose an audio CAPTCHA as an alternative to the usual visual CAPTCHA.

An example of a CAPTCHA from [320] appears in Figure 8.7. In this case, a human might be asked to find three words that appear in the image. This is a relatively easy problem for humans and today it is also a fairly easy problem for computers to solve—much stronger CAPTCHAs exist.

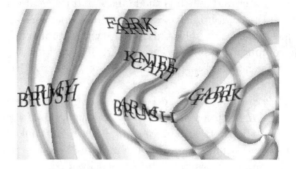

Figure 8.7: CAPTCHA (Courtesy of Luis von Ahn [320])

Perhaps surprisingly, in [56] it is shown that computers are actually better than humans at solving all of the fundamental visual CAPTCHA problems, with one exception—the so-called segmentation problem, i.e., the problem of separating the letters from each other. Consequently, strong CAPTCHAs tend to look more like Figure 8.8 than Figure 8.7.

Figure 8.8: A Strong CAPTCHA [47]

For a word-based visual CAPTCHA, we assume that Trudy knows the set of possible words that could appear and she knows the general format of the image, as well as the types of distortions that can be applied. From Trudy's perspective, the only unknown is a random number that is used to select the word or words and to distort the resulting image.

There are several types of visual CAPTCHAs of which Figures 8.7 and 8.8 are representative examples. There are also audio CAPTCHAs in which the audio is distorted in some way. The human ear is very good at removing such distortion, while automated methods are not so good. Currently, there are no text-based CAPTCHAs.

The computing problems that must be solved to break CAPTCHAs can be viewed as difficult problems from the domain of artificial intelligence, or AI.

For example, automatic recognition of distorted text is an AI problem, and the same is true of problems related to distorted audio. If attackers are able to break such CAPTCHAs, they have, in effect, solved a hard AI problem. As a result, attacker's efforts are being put to good use.

Of course, the attackers may not play by the rules—so-called CAPTCHA farming is possible, where humans are paid to solve CAPTCHAs. For example, it has been widely reported that the lure of free pornography has been successfully used to get humans to solve vast numbers of CAPTCHAs at minimal cost to the attacker [172].

8.9 Firewalls

Suppose you want to meet with the chairperson of your local computer science department. First, you will probably need to contact the computer science department secretary. If the secretary deems that a meeting is warranted, she will schedule it; otherwise, she will not. In this way, the secretary filters out many requests that would otherwise occupy the chair's time.

A *firewall* acts a lot like a secretary for your network. The firewall examines requests for access to your network, and it decides whether they pass a reasonableness test. If so, they are allowed through, and, if not, they are refused.

If you want to meet the chair of the computer science department, the secretary does a certain level of filtering; however, if you want to meet the President of the United States,[11] his secretary will perform a much different level of filtering. This is somewhat analogous to firewalls, where some simple firewalls only filter out obviously bogus requests and other types of firewalls make a much greater effort to filter anything suspicious.

A network firewall, as illustrated in Figure 8.9, is placed between the internal network, which might be considered relatively safe,[12] and the external network (the Internet), which is known to be unsafe. The job of the firewall is to determine what to let into and out of the internal network. In this way, a firewall provides access control for the network.

As with most of information security, for firewalls there is no standard terminology. But whatever you choose to call them, there are essentially three types of firewalls—marketing hype from firewall vendors not withstanding. Each type of firewall filters packets by examining the data up to a particular layer of the network protocol stack. If you are not familiar with networking (and even if you are), now would be a good time to review the networking material in the Appendix.

---

[11]POTUS, that is.

[12]This is almost certainly not a valid assumption. It's estimated that about 80% of all significant computer attacks are due to insiders [49].

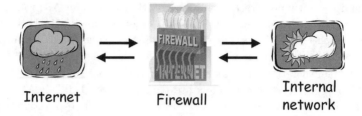

Figure 8.9: Firewall

We'll adopt the following terminology for the classification of firewalls.

- A *packet filter* is a firewall that operates at the network layer.

- A *stateful packet filter* is a firewall that lives at the transport layer.

- An *application proxy* is, as the name suggests, a firewall that operates at the application layer where it functions as a proxy.

8.9.1   Packet Filter

A packet filter firewall examines packets up to the network layer, as indicated in Figure 8.10. As a result, this type of firewall can only filter packets based on the information that is available at the network layer. The information at this layer includes the source IP address, the destination IP address, the source port, the destination port, and the TCP flag bits (SYN, ACK, RST, etc.).[13] Such a firewall can filter packets based on ingress or egress, that is, it can have different filtering rules for incoming and outgoing packets.

The primary advantage of a packet filter is efficiency. Since packets only need to be processed up to the network layer and only header information is examined, the entire operation is inherently efficient. However, there are several disadvantages to the simple approach employed by a packet filter. First, the firewall has no concept of state, so each packet is treated independently of all others. In particular, a packet filter can't examine a TCP connection. We'll see in a moment that this is a serious limitation. In addition, a packet filter firewall is blind to application data, which is where viruses and other malware resides.

Packet filters are configured using access control lists, or ACLs. In this context, "ACL" has a completely different meaning than in Section 8.3.1. An example of a packet filter ACL appears in Table 8.3. Note that the purpose of the ACL in Table 8.3 is to restrict incoming packets to Web responses,

---

[13]Yes, we're cheating. TCP is part of the transport layer, so the TCP flag bits are not visible if we follow a strict definition of network layer. Nevertheless, it's OK to cheat sometimes, especially in a security class.

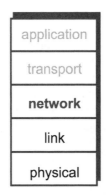

Figure 8.10: Packet Filter

Table 8.3: Example ACL

Action	Source IP	Dest IP	Source Port	Dest Port	Protocol	Flag Bits
Allow	Inside	Outside	Any	80	HTTP	Any
Allow	Outside	Inside	80	> 1023	HTTP	ACK
Deny	All	All	All	All	All	All

which should have source port 80. The ACL allows all outbound Web traffic, which should be destined to port 80. All other traffic is forbidden.

How might Trudy take advantage of the inherent limitations of a packet filter firewall? Before we can answer this question, we need a couple of fun facts. Usually, a firewall (of any type) drops packets sent to most incoming ports. That is, the firewall filters out and drops packets that are trying to access services that should not be accessed. Because of this, the attacker, Trudy, wants to know which ports are open through the firewall. These open ports are where Trudy will concentrate her attack. So, the first step in any attack on a firewall is usually a *port scan*, where Trudy tries to determine which ports are open through the firewall.

Now suppose Trudy wants to attack a network that is protected by a packet filter. How can Trudy conduct a port scan of the firewall? She could, for example, send a packet that has the ACK bit set, without the prior two steps of the TCP three-way handshake. Such a packet violates the TCP protocol, since the initial packet in any connection must have the SYN bit set. Since the packet filter has no concept of state, it will assume that this packet is part of an established connection and let it through—provided that it is sent to an open port. Then when this forged packet reaches a host on the internal network, the host will realize that there is a problem (since the packet is not part of an established connection) and respond with a RST packet, which is supposed to tell the sender to terminate the connection. While this process may seem harmless, it allows Trudy to scan for open ports through the firewall. That is, Trudy can send an initial packet with the ACK flag set to a particular port p. If no response is received, then the firewall is not forwarding packets sent to port p. However, if a RST packet is received, then the packet was allowed through port p into the internal network. This technique, which is known as a TCP ACK scan, is illustrated in Figure 8.11.

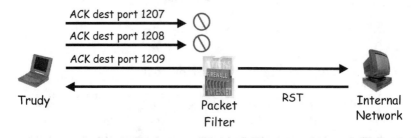

Figure 8.11: TCP ACK Scan

From the ACK scan in Figure 8.11, Trudy has learned that port 1209 is open through the firewall. To prevent this attack, the firewall would need to remember existing TCP connections, so that it will know that the ACK scan packets are not part of any legitimate connection. Next, we'll discuss stateful packet filters, which keep track of connections and are therefore able to prevent this ACK scan attack.

8.9.2   Stateful Packet Filter

As the name implies, a stateful packet filter adds state to a packet filter firewall. This means that the firewall keeps track of TCP connections, and it can remember UDP "connections" as well. Conceptually, a stateful packet filter operates at the transport layer, since it is maintaining information about connections. This is illustrated in Figure 8.12.

The primary advantage of a stateful packet filter is that, in addition to all of the features of a packet filter, it also keeps track of ongoing connection. This prevents many attacks, such as the TCP ACK scan discussed in the previous section. The disadvantages of a stateful packet filter are that it cannot examine application data, and, all else being equal, it's slower than a packet filtering firewall since more processing is required.

application
transport
network
link
physical

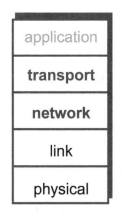

Figure 8.12: Stateful Packet Filter

8.9.3 Application Proxy

A proxy is something that acts on your behalf. An application proxy firewall processes incoming packets all the way up to the application layer, as indicated in Figure 8.13. The firewall, acting on your behalf, is then able to verify that the packet appears to be legitimate (as with a stateful packet filter) and, in addition, that the actual data inside the packet is safe.

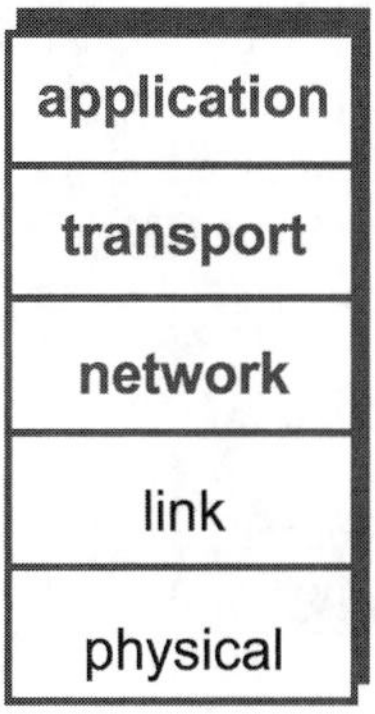

application
transport
network
link
physical

Figure 8.13: Application Proxy

The primary advantage of an application proxy is that it has a complete view of connections and application data. Consequently, it can have as comprehensive of a view as the host itself could have. As a result, the application proxy is able to filter bad data at the application layer (such as viruses) while also filtering bad packets at the transport layer. The disadvantage of an application proxy is speed or, more precisely, the potential lack thereof. Since the firewall is processing packets to the application layer, examining the resulting data, maintaining state, etc., it is doing a great deal more work than packet filtering firewalls.

One interesting feature of an application proxy is that the incoming packet is destroyed and a new packet is created in its place when the data passes through the firewall. Although this might seem like a minor and insignificant point, it's actually a security feature. To see why creating a new packet is beneficial, we'll consider the tool known as `Firewalk`, which is designed to scan for open ports through a firewall. While the purpose of `Firewalk` is the same as the TCP ACK scan discussed above, the implementation is completely different.

The time to live, or TTL, field in an IP packet header contains the number of hops that the packet will travel before it is terminated. When a packet is terminated due to the TTL field, an ICMP "time exceeded" error message is sent back to the source.[14]

Suppose Trudy knows the IP address of the firewall, the IP address of one system on the inside network, and the number of hops to the firewall. Then she can send a packet to the IP address of the known host inside the firewall, with the TTL field set to one more than the number of hops to the firewall. Suppose Trudy sets the destination port of such a packet to p. If the firewall does not let data through on port p, there will be no response. If, on the other hand, the firewall does let data through on port p, Trudy will receive a time exceeded error message from the first router inside the firewall that receives the packet. Trudy can then repeat this process for different ports p to determine open ports through the firewall. This port scan is illustrated in Figure 8.14. `Firewalk` will succeed if the firewall is a packet filter or a stateful packet filter. However, `Firewalk` won't succeed if the firewall is an application proxy (see Problem 29).

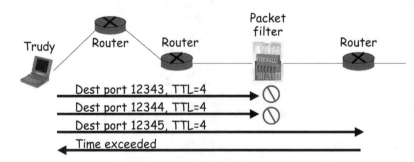

Figure 8.14: Firewalk

---

[14]And what happens to terminated packets? Of course, they die and go to packet heaven.

The net effect of an application proxy is that it forces Trudy to talk to the proxy and convince it to forward her messages. Since the proxy is likely to be well configured and carefully managed—compared with a typical host—this may prove difficult.

8.9.4 Personal Firewall

A personal firewall is used to protect a single host or a small network, such as a home network. Any of the three methods discussed above (packet filter, stateful packet filter, or application proxy) could be used, but generally such firewalls are relatively simple for the sake of efficiency and ease of configuration.

8.9.5 Defense in Depth

Finally, we consider a network configuration that includes several layers of protection. Figure 8.15 gives a schematic for a network that includes a packet filter firewall, an application proxy, and personal firewalls, as well as a demilitarized zone, or DMZ.

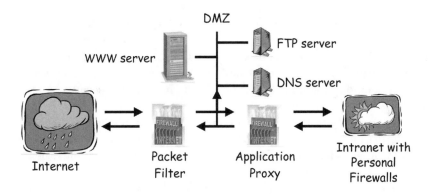

Figure 8.15: Defense in Depth

The packet filter in Figure 8.15 is used to prevent common attacks on the systems in the DMZ. The systems in the DMZ are those that must be exposed to the outside world. These systems receive most of the outside traffic, so a simple packet filter is used for the sake of efficiency. The systems in the DMZ must be carefully maintained by the administrator since they are the most exposed to attack. However, if an attack succeeds on a system in the DMZ, the consequences for the company are annoying, but they will probably not be life threatening, since the internal network is largely unaffected.

In Figure 8.15, an application proxy firewall sits between the internal network and the DMZ. This provides the strongest possible firewall protection for the internal network. The amount of traffic into the internal network is likely to be relatively small, so an application proxy in this position will not create a bottleneck. As a final layer of protection, personal firewalls could be deployed on the individual hosts inside the corporate network.

The architecture in Figure 8.15 is an example of *defense in depth*, which is a good security strategy in general—if one layer of the defense is breached, there are more layers that the attacker must overcome. If Trudy is skilled enough to break through one level, then she may have the necessary skills to penetrate other levels. But it's likely to take her some time to do so and the longer it takes, the more time an administrator has to detect Trudy's attack in progress.

Regardless of the strength of the firewall (or firewalls), some attacks by outsiders will succeed. In addition, attacks by insiders are a serious threat and firewalls are of limited value against such attacks. In any case, when an attack succeeds, we would like to detect it as soon as possible. In the next section we'll discuss this intrusion detection problem.

8.10   Intrusion Detection Systems

The primary focus of computer security tends to be *intrusion prevention*, where the goal is to keep the Trudys of the world out of your system or network. Authentication can be viewed as a means to prevent intrusions, and firewalls are certainly a form of intrusion prevention, as are most types of virus protection. Intrusion prevention is the information security analog of locking the doors on your car.

But even if you lock the doors on your car, it might still get stolen. In information security, no matter how much effort you put into intrusion prevention, occasionally the bad guys will be successful and an intrusion will occur.

What should we do when intrusion prevention fails? *Intrusion detection systems*, or IDSs, are a relatively recent development in information security. The purpose of such a system is to detect attacks before, during, and after they occur.

The basic approach employed by IDSs is to look for "unusual" activity. In the past, an administrator would scan through log files looking for signs of unusual activity—automated intrusion detection is a natural outgrowth of manual log file analysis.

It is also worth noting that intrusion detection is currently an active research topic. As with any relatively new technology, there are many claims in the field that have yet to be substantiated. At this point, it's far from clear how successful or useful some of these techniques will prove, particularly in the face of increasingly sophisticated attacks.

Before discussing the main threads in IDS, we mention in passing that *intrusion response* is a related topic of practical importance. That is, once an intrusion is detected, we want to respond to it. In some cases we obtain specific information and a reasonable response is fairly obvious. For example, we might detect a password guessing attack aimed at a specific account, in which case we could respond by locking the account. However, it's not always so straightforward. We'll see below that in some cases IDSs provide little specific information on the nature of an attack. In such cases, determining the proper response is not easy, since we may not be sure of the specifics of the attack. In any case, we won't deal further with intrusion response here.

Who are the intruders that an IDS is trying to detect? An intruder could be a hacker who got through your network defenses and is now launching an attack on the internal network. Or, even more insidious, the intrusion could be due to an evil insider, such as a disgruntled employee.

What sorts of attacks might an intruder launch? An intruder with limited skills (i.e., a "script kiddie") would likely attempt a well-known attack or a slight variation on such an attack. A more skilled attacker might be capable of launching a significant variation on a well-known attack, or a little-known attack or an entirely new attack. Often, the attacker will simply use the breached system as a base from which to launch attacks on other systems.

Broadly speaking, there are two approaches to intrusion detection.

- *Signature-based IDSs* detect attacks based on specific known signatures or patterns. This is analogous to signature-based virus detection, which we'll discuss in Chapter 11.

- *Anomaly-based IDSs* attempt to define a baseline of normal behavior and provide a warning whenever the system strays too far from this baseline.

We'll have more to say about signature-based and anomaly-based intrusion detection below.

There are also two basic architectures for IDSs.

- *Host-based IDSs* apply their detection method or methods to activity that occurs on hosts. These systems have the potential to detect attacks that are visible at hosts (e.g., buffer overflows or escalation of privilege). However, host-based systems have little or no view of network activities.

- *Network-based IDSs* apply their detection methods to network traffic. These systems are designed to detect attacks such as denial of service, port scans, probes involving malformed packets, etc. Such systems have some obvious overlap with firewalls. Network-based systems have little or no direct view of host-based attacks.

Of course, various combinations of these categories of IDSs are possible. For example a host-based system could use both signature-based and anomaly-based techniques, or a signature-based system might employ aspects of both host-based and network-based detection.

8.10.1   Signature-Based IDS

Failed login attempts may be indicative of a password cracking attack, so an IDS might consider "N failed login attempts in M seconds" an indication, or *signature*, of an attack. Then anytime that N or more failed login attempts occur within M seconds, the IDS would issue a warning that a password cracking attack is suspected to be in progress.

If Trudy happens to know that Alice's IDS issues a warning whenever N or more failed logins occur within M seconds, then Trudy can safely guess $N-1$ passwords every M seconds. In this case, the signature detection would slow Trudy's password guessing attack, but it would not completely prevent the attack. Another concern with such a scheme is that N and M must be set so that the number of false alarms is not excessive.

Many techniques are used to make signature-based detection more robust, where the usual approach is to detect "almost" signatures. For example, if about N login attempts occur in about M seconds, then the system could warn of a possible password cracking attack, perhaps with a degree of confidence based on the number of attempts and the time interval. But it's not always easy to determine reasonable values for "about." Statistical analysis and heuristics are useful, but much care must be taken to minimize the false alarm rate. False alarms will quickly undermine confidence in any security system—like the boy who cried wolf, the security system that screams "attack" when none is present, will soon be ignored.

The advantages of signature-based detection include simplicity, efficiency (provided the number of signatures is not excessive), and an excellent ability to detect known attacks. Another major benefit is that the warning that is issued is specific, since the signature matches a specific attack pattern. With a specific warning, an administrator can quickly determine whether the suspected attack is real or a false alarm and, if it is real, the admin can usually respond appropriately.

The disadvantages of signature detection include the fact that the signature file must be current, the number of signatures may become large thereby reducing efficiency, and most importantly, the system can only detect known attacks. Even slight variations on known attack will likely be missed by signature-based systems.

Anomaly-based IDSs attempt to overcome the shortcomings of signature-based schemes. But no anomaly-based scheme available today could reasonably claim to be a replacement for signature-based detection. That is, an anomaly-based system can supplement the performance of a signature-based system, but it is not a replacement for signature detection.

8.10.2 Anomaly-Based IDS

Anomaly-based IDSs look for unusual or abnormal behavior. There are several major challenges inherent in such an approach. First, we must determine what constitutes normal behavior for a system, and this must occur when the system is behaving normally. Second, the definition of normal must adapt as system usage changes and evolves, otherwise the number of false alarms will grow. Third, there are difficult statistical thresholding issues involved. For example, we must have a good idea of how far abnormal is away from normal.

Statistics are obviously necessary in the development of an anomaly-based IDS. Recall that the *mean* defines the statistical norm while the *variance* gives us a way to measure the distribution of the data about the mean. The mean and variance together gives us a way to determine abnormal behavior.

How can we measure normal system behavior? Whatever characteristics we decide to measure, we must take the measurements during times of representative behavior. In particular, we must not set the baseline measurements during an attack or else an attack will be considered normal. Measuring abnormal or, more precisely, determining how to separate normal variations in behavior from an attack, is an equally challenging problem. Abnormal must be measured relative to some specific value of normal. We'll consider abnormal as synonymous with attack, although in reality there are other possible causes of abnormal behavior, which further complicates the situation.

Statistical discrimination techniques are used to separate normal from abnormal. Examples of such techniques include Bayesian analysis, linear discriminant analysis (LDA), quadratic discriminant analysis (QDA), neural nets, and hidden Markov models (HMM), among others. In addition, some anomaly detection researchers employ advanced modeling techniques from the fields of artificial intelligence and artificial immune systems. Such approaches are beyond the scope of our discussion here.

Next, we'll consider two simplified examples of anomaly detection. The first example is simple, but not very realistic, whereas the second is slightly less simple and correspondingly more realistic.

Suppose that we monitor the use of the three commands

`open, read, close.`

We find that under normal use, Alice uses the series of commands

`open, read, close, open, open, read, close.`

For our statistic, we'll consider pairs of consecutive commands and try to devise a measure of normal behavior for Alice. From Alice's series of commands, we observe that, of the six possible ordered pairs or commands, four pairs appear to be normal for Alice, namely,

(open,read), (read,close), (close,open), (open,open),

while the other two pairs,

(read,open), (close,read),

are not normally used by Alice. We can use this observation to identify potentially unusual behavior by "Alice" that might indicate an intruder is posing as Alice. We can then monitor the use of these three commands by Alice. If the ratio of abnormal to normal pairs is "too high," we would warn the administrator that an attack may be in progress.

This simple anomaly detection scheme can be improved. For example, we could include the expected frequency of each normal pair in the calculation, and if the observed pairs differ significantly from the expected distribution, we would warn of a possible attack. We might also try to improve the anomaly detection by using more than two consecutive commands, or by including more commands, or by including other user behavior in the model, or by using a more sophisticated statistical discrimination technique.

For a slightly more plausible anomaly detection scheme, let's focus on file access. Suppose that, over an extended period of time, Alice has accessed four files, F_0, F_1, F_2, F_3, at the rates H_0, H_1, H_2, H_3, respectively, where the observed values of the H_i are given in Table 8.4.

Table 8.4: Alice's Initial File Access Rates

H_0	H_1	H_2	H_3
0.10	0.40	0.40	0.10

Now suppose that, over a recent time interval, Alice has accessed file F_i at the rate A_i, for $i = 0, 1, 2, 3$, as given in Table 8.5. Do Alice's recent file access rates represent normal use? To decide, we need some way to compare her long-term access rates to the current rates. To answer this question, we'll employ the statistic

$$S = (H_0 - A_0)^2 + (H_1 - A_1)^2 + (H_2 - A_2)^2 + (H_3 - A_3)^2, \qquad (8.2)$$

where we define $S < 0.1$ as normal. In this example, we have

$$S = (0.1 - 0.1)^2 + (0.4 - 0.4)^2 + (0.4 - 0.3)^2 + (0.1 - 0.2)^2 = 0.02,$$

and we conclude that Alice's recent use is normal—at least according to this one statistic.

Table 8.5: Alice's Recent File Access Rates

A_0	A_1	A_2	A_3
0.10	0.40	0.30	0.20

Alice's file access rates can be expected to vary over time, and we need to account for this in our IDS. We'll do so by updating Alice's long-term history values H_i according to the formula

$$H_i = 0.2 \cdot A_i + 0.8 \cdot H_i \ \text{ for } i = 0, 1, 2, 3. \tag{8.3}$$

That is, we update the historical access rates based on a moving average that combines the previous values with the recently observed rates—the previous values are weighted at 80%, while the current values are weighted 20%. Using the data in Tables 8.4 and 8.5, we find that the updated values of H_0 and H_1 are unchanged, whereas

$$H_2 = 0.2 \cdot 0.3 + 0.8 \cdot 0.4 = 0.38 \ \text{ and } \ H_3 = 0.2 \cdot 0.2 + 0.8 \cdot 0.1 = 0.12.$$

These updated values appear in Table 8.6.

Table 8.6: Alice's Updated File Access Rates

H_0	H_1	H_2	H_3
0.10	0.40	0.38	0.12

Suppose that over the next time interval Alice's measured access rates are those given in Table 8.7. Then we compute the statistic S using the values in Tables 8.6 and 8.7 and the formula in equation (8.2) to find

$$S = (0.1 - 0.1)^2 + (0.4 - 0.3)^2 + (0.38 - 0.3)^2 + (0.12 - 0.3)^2 = 0.0488.$$

Since $S = 0.0488 < 0.1$ we again conclude that this is normal use for Alice. Again, we update Alice's long-term averages using the formula in (8.3) and

Table 8.7: Alice's More Recent File Access Rates

A_0	A_1	A_2	A_3
0.10	0.30	0.30	0.30

Table 8.8: Alice's Second Updated Access Rates

H_0	H_1	H_2	H_3
0.10	0.38	0.364	0.156

the data in Tables 8.6 and 8.7. In this case, we obtain the results that appear in Table 8.8.

Comparing Alice's long-term file access rates in Table 8.4 with her long-term averages after two updates, as given in Table 8.8, we see that the rates have changed significantly over time. Again, it is necessary that an anomaly-based IDS adapts over time, otherwise we will have a large number of false alarms (and a very annoyed system administrator) as Alice's actual behavior changes. However, this also presents an opportunity for the attacker, Trudy.

Since the H_i values slowly evolve to match Alice's behavior, Trudy can pose as Alice and remain undetected, provided she doesn't stray too far from Alice's usual behavior. But even more worrisome is the fact that Trudy can eventually convince the anomaly detection algorithm that her evil behavior is normal for Alice, provided Trudy has enough patience. For example, suppose that Trudy, posing as Alice, wants to always access file F_3. Then, initially, she can access file F_3 at a slightly higher rate than is normal for Alice. After the next update of the H_i values, Trudy will be able to access file F_3 at an even higher rate without triggering a warning from the anomaly detection software, and so on. By going slowly, Trudy will eventually convince the anomaly detector that it's normal for "Alice" to only access file F_3.

Note that $H_3 = 0.1$ in Table 8.4 and, two iterations later, $H_3 = 0.156$ in Table 8.8. These changes did not trigger a warning by the anomaly detector. Does this change represent a new usage pattern by Alice, or does it indicate an attempt by Trudy to trick the anomaly detector by going slow?

To make this anomaly detection scheme more robust, we should also incorporate the variance. In addition, we would certainly need to measure more than one statistic. If we measured N different statistics, $S_1, S_2, \ldots S_N$, we might combine them according to a formula such as

$$T = (S_1 + S_2 + S_3 + \ldots + S_N)/N$$

and make the determination of normal or abnormal based on the statistic T. This would provide a more comprehensive view of normal behavior and make it more difficult for Trudy, as she would need to approximate more of Alice's normal behavior. A similar—although much more sophisticated—approach is used in a popular IDS known as NIDES [9, 155]. NIDES incorporates both anomaly-based and signature-based IDSs. A good elementary introduction to NIDES, as well as several other IDSs, can be found in [304].

Robust anomaly detection is a difficult problem for a number of reasons. For one, system usage and user behavior constantly evolves and, therefore, so must the anomaly detector. Without allowing for such changes in behavior, false alarms would soon overwhelm the administrator, who would quickly lose confidence in the system. But an evolving anomaly detector means that it's possible for Trudy to slowly convince the anomaly detector that an attack is normal.

Another fundamental issue with anomaly detection is that a warning of abnormal behavior may not provide any useful specific information to the administrator. A vague warning that the system may be under attack could make it difficult to take concrete action. In contrast, a signature-based IDS will provide the administrator with precise information about the nature of the suspected attack.

The primary potential advantage of anomaly detection is that there is a chance of detecting previously unknown attacks. It's also sometimes argued that anomaly detection can be more efficient than signature detection, particularly if the signature file is large. In any case, the current generation of anomaly detectors must be used in combination with a signature-based IDS since they are not sufficiently robust to act as standalone systems.

Anomaly-based intrusion detection is an active research topic, and many security professionals have high hopes for its ultimate success. Anomaly detection is often cited as key future security technology [120]. But it appears that the hackers are not convinced, at least based on the title of a talk presented at a recent Defcon[15] conference: "Why anomaly-based intrusion detection systems are a hacker's best friend" [79].

The bottom line is that anomaly detection is a difficult and tricky problem. It also appears to have parallels with the field of artificial intelligence. Nearly a third of a century has passed since we were promised "robots on your doorstep" [327] and such predictions appear no more plausible today than at the time they were originally made. If anomaly-based intrusion detection proves to be anywhere near as challenging as AI, it may never live up to its claimed potential.

8.11 Summary

In this chapter we reviewed some of the history of authorization, with the focus on certification regimes. Then we covered the basics of traditional authorization, namely, Lampson's access control matrix, ACLs, and capabilities. The confused deputy problem was used to highlight the differences between ACLs and capabilities. We then presented some of the security issues re-

---

[15]Defcon is the oldest, largest, and best-known hackers convention. It's held in Las Vegas each August, and it's inexpensive, totally chaotic, lots of fun, and hot (literally).

lated to multilevel security (MLS) and compartments, as well as the topics of covert channels and inference control. MLS naturally led us into the rarified air of security modeling, where we briefly considered Bell-LaPadula and Biba's Model.

After covering the basics of security modeling, we pulled our heads out of the clouds, put our feet back on *terra firma*, and proceeded to discuss a few important non-traditional access control topics, including CAPTCHAs and firewalls. We concluded the chapter by stretching the definition of access control to cover intrusion detection systems (IDS). Many of the issues we discussed with respect to IDSs will resurface when we cover virus detection in Chapter 11.

8.12   Problems

1. On page 269 there is an example of orange book guidelines for testing at the so-called C division. Your skeptical author implies that these guidelines are somewhat dubious.

   a. Why might the guidelines that appear on page 269 not be particularly sensible or useful?

   b. Find three more examples of useless guidelines that appear in Part II of the orange book [309]. For each of these, summarize the guideline and give reasons why you feel it is not particularly sensible or useful.

2. The seven Common Criteria EALs are listed in Section 8.2.2. For each of these seven levels, summarize the testing required to achieve that level of certification.

3. In this chapter we discussed access control lists (ACLs) and capabilities (aka C-lists).

   a. Give two advantaged of capabilities over ACLs.

   b. Give two advantages of ACLs over capabilities.

4. In the text, we argued that it's easy to delegate using capabilities.

   a. It is also possible to delegate using ACLs. Explain how this would work.

   b. Suppose Alice delegates to Bill who then delegates to Charlie who, in turn, delegates to Dave. How would this be accomplished using capabilities? How would this be accomplished using ACLs? Which is easier and why?

   c. Which is better for delegation, ACLs or capabilities? Why?

5. Suppose Alice wants to temporarily delegate her C-list (capabilities) to Bob. Alice decides that she will digitally sign her C-list before giving it to Bob.

   a. What are the advantages, if any, of such an approach?

   b. What are the disadvantages, if any, of such an approach?

6. Briefly discuss one real-world application not mentioned in the text where multilevel security (MLS) would be useful.

7. What is the "need to know" principle and how can compartments be used to enforce this principle?

8. Suppose that you work in a classified environment where MLS is employed and you have a TOP SECRET clearance.

   a. Describe a potential covert channel involving the User Datagram Protocol (UDP).

   b. How could you minimize your covert channel in part a, while still allowing network access and communication by users with different clearances?

9. The *high water mark principle* and *low water mark principle* both apply in the realm of multilevel security.

   a. Define the high water mark principle and the low water mark principle in the context of MLS.

   b. Is BLP consistent with a high water mark principle, a low water mark principle, both, or neither? Justify your answer.

   c. Is Biba's Model consistent with a high water mark principle, a low water mark principle, both, or neither? Justify your answer.

10. This problem deals with covert channels.

   a. Describe a covert channel involving the print queue and estimate the realistic capacity of your covert channel.

   b. Describe a subtle covert channel involving the TCP network protocol.

11. We briefly discussed the following methods of inference control: query set size control; N-respondent, $k\%$ dominance rule; and randomization.

   a. Explain each of these three methods of inference control.

   b. Briefly discuss the relative strengths and weaknesses of each of these methods.

12. Inference control is used to reduce the amount of private information that can leak as a result of database queries.

    a. Discuss one practical method of inference control not mentioned in the book.

    b. How could you attack the method of inference control given in your solution to part a?

13. A *botnet* consists of a number of compromised machines that are all controlled by an evil botmaster [39, 146].

    a. Most botnets are controlled using the Internet Relay Chat (IRC) protocol. What is IRC and why is it particularly useful for controlling a botnet?

    b. Why might a covert channel be useful for controlling a botnet?

    c. Design a covert channel that could provide a reasonable means for a botmaster to control a botnet.

14. Read and briefly summarize each of the following sections from the article on covert channels at [131]: 2.2, 3.2, 3.3, 4.1, 4.2, 5.2, 5.3, 5.4.

15. Ross Anderson claims that "Some kinds of security mechanisms may be worse than useless if they can be compromised" [14].

    a. Does this statement hold true for inference control? Why or why not?

    b. Does this hold true for encryption? Why or why not?

    c. Does this hold true for methods that are used to reduce the capacity of covert channels? Why or why not?

16. Combine BLP and Biba's Model into a single MLS security model that covers both confidentiality and integrity.

17. BLP can be stated as "no read up, no write down." What is the analogous statement for Biba's Model?

18. Consider the visual CAPTCHA known as Gimpy [249].

    a. Explain how EZ Gimpy and Hard Gimpy work.

    b. How secure is EZ Gimpy compared to Hard Gimpy?

    c. Discuss the most successful known attack on each type of Gimpy.

19. This problem deals with visual CAPTCHAs.

a. Describe an example of a real-world visual CAPTCHA not discussed in the text and explain how this CAPTCHA works, that is, explain how a program would generate the CAPTCHA and score the result, and what a human would need to do to pass the test.

b. For the CAPTCHA in part a, what information is available to an attacker?

20. Design and implement your own visual CAPTCHA. Outline possible attacks on your CAPTCHA. How secure is your CAPTCHA?

21. This problem deals with audio CAPTCHAs.

a. Describe an example of a real-world audio CAPTCHA and explain how this CAPTCHA works, that is, explain how a program would generate the CAPTCHA and score the result, and what a human would need to do to pass the test.

b. For the CAPTCHA in part a, what information is available to an attacker?

22. Design and implement your own audio CAPTCHA. Outline possible attacks on your CAPTCHA. How secure is your CAPTCHA?

23. In [56] it is shown that computers are better than humans at solving all of the fundamental visual CAPTCHA problems, with the exception of the segmentation problem.

a. What are the fundamental visual CAPTCHA problems?

b. With the exception of the segmentation problem, how can computers solve each of these fundamental problems?

c. Intuitively, why is the segmentation problem more difficult for computers to solve?

24. The reCAPTCHA project is an attempt to make good use of the effort humans put into solving CAPTCHAs [322]. In reCAPTCHA, a user is shown two distorted words, where one of the words is an actual CAPTCHA, but the other is a word—distorted to look like a CAPTCHA—that an optical character recognition (OCR) program was unable to recognize. If the real CAPTCHA is solved correctly, then the reCAPTCHA program assumes that the other word was also solved correctly. Since humans are good at correcting OCR errors, reCAPTCHA can be used, for example, to improve the accuracy of digitized books.

a. It is estimated that about 200,000,000 CAPTCHAs are solved daily. Suppose that each of these is a reCAPTCHA and each requires about 10 seconds to solve. Then, in total, about how much time would be spent by users solving OCR problems each day? Note that we assume two CAPTCHAs are solved for one reCAPTCHA, so 200,000,000 CAPTCHAs represents 100,000,000 reCAPTCHAs.

b. Suppose that when digitizing a book, on average, about 10 hours of human effort is required to fix OCR problems. Under the assumptions in part a, how long would it take to correct all of the OCR problems created when digitizing all books in the Library of Congress? The Library of Congress has about 32,000,000 books, and we assume that every CAPTCHA in the world is a reCAPTCHA focused on this specific problem.

c. How could Trudy attack a reCAPTCHA system? That is, what could Trudy do to make the results obtained from a reCAPTCHA less reliable?

d. What could the reCAPTCHA developer do to minimize the effect of attacks on the system?

25. It has been widely reported that spammers sometimes pay humans to solve CAPTCHAs [293].

a. Why would spammers want to solve lots of CAPTCHAs?

b. What is the current cost, per CAPTCHA solved (in U.S. dollars), to have humans solve CAPTCHAs?

c. How might you entice humans to solve CAPTCHAs for you without paying them any money?

26. In this chapter, we discussed three types of firewalls: packet filter, stateful packet filter, and application proxy.

a. At which layer of the Internet protocol stack does each of these firewalls operate?

b. What information is available to each of these firewalls?

c. Briefly discuss one practical attack on each of these firewalls.

27. Commercial firewalls do not generally use the terminology packet filter, stateful packet filter, or application proxy. However, any firewall must be one of these three types, or a combination thereof. Find information on a commercial firewall product and explain (using the terminology of this chapter) which type of firewall it really is.

28. If a packet filter firewall does not allow reset (RST) packets out, then the TCP ACK scan described in the text will not succeed.

a. What are some drawbacks to this approach?

     b. Could the TCP ACK scan attack be modified to work against such a system?

29. In this chapter it's stated that `Firewalk`, a port scanning tool, will succeed if the firewall is a packet filter or a stateful packet filter, but it will fail if the firewall is an application proxy.

     a. Why is this the case? That is, why does `Firewalk` succeed when the firewall is a packet filter or stateful packet filter, but fail when the firewall is an application proxy?

     b. Can `Firewalk` be modified to work against an application proxy?

30. Suppose that a packet filter firewall resets the TTL field to 255 for each packet that it allows through the firewall. Then the `Firewalk` port scanning tool described in the this chapter will fail.

     a. Why does `Firewalk` fail in this case?

     b. Does this proposed solution create any problems?

     c. Could `Firewalk` be modified to work against such a firewall?

31. An application proxy firewall is able to scan all incoming application data for viruses. It would be more efficient to have each host scan the application data it receives for viruses, since this would effectively distribute the workload among the hosts. Why might it still be preferable to have the application proxy perform this function?

32. Suppose incoming packets are encrypted with a symmetric key that is known only to the sender and the intended recipient. Which types of firewall (packet filter, stateful packet filter, application proxy) will work with such packets and which will not? Justify your answers.

33. Suppose that packets sent between Alice and Bob are encrypted and integrity protected by Alice and Bob with a symmetric key known only to Alice and Bob.

     a. Which fields of the IP header can be encrypted and which cannot?

     b. Which fields of the IP header can be integrity protected and which cannot?

     c. Which of the firewalls—packet filter, stateful packet filter, application proxy—will work in this case, assuming all IP header fields that can be integrity protected are integrity protected, and all IP header fields that can be encrypted are encrypted? Justify your answer.

34. Suppose that packets sent between Alice and Bob are encrypted and integrity protected by Alice's firewall and Bob's firewall with a symmetric key known only to Alice's firewall and Bob's firewall.

    a. Which fields of the IP header can be encrypted and which cannot?

    b. Which fields of the IP header can be integrity protected and which cannot?

    c. Which of the firewalls—packet filter, stateful packet filter, application proxy—will work in this case, assuming all IP header fields that can be integrity protected are integrity protected, and all IP header fields that can be encrypted are encrypted? Justify your answer.

35. Defense in depth using firewalls is illustrated in Figure 8.15. List other security applications where defense in depth is a sensible strategy.

36. Broadly speaking, there are two distinct types of intrusion detection systems, namely, signature-based and anomaly-based.

    a. List the advantages of signature-based intrusion detection, as compared to anomaly-based intrusion detection.

    b. List the advantages of an anomaly-based IDS, in contrast to a signature-based IDS.

    c. Why is effective anomaly-based IDS inherently more challenging than signature-based detection?

37. A particular vendor uses the following approach to intrusion detection.[16] The company maintains a large number of honeypots distributed across the Internet. To a potential attacker, these honeypots look like vulnerable systems. Consequently, the honeypots attract many attacks and, in particular, new attacks tend to show up on the honeypots soon after— sometimes even during—their development. Whenever a new attack is detected at one of the honeypots, the vendor immediately develops a signature and distributes the resulting signature to all systems using its product. The actual derivation of the signature is generally a manual process.

    a. What are the advantages, if any, of this approach as compared to a standard signature-based system?

    b. What are the advantages, if any, of this approach as compared to a standard anomaly-based system?

---

[16]This problem is based on a true story, just like many Hollywood movies...

    c. Using the terminology given in this chapter, the system outlined in this problem would be classified as a signature-based IDS, not an anomaly-based IDS. Why?

    d. The definition of signature-based and anomaly-based IDS are not standardized.[17] The vendor of the system outlined in this problem refers to it as an anomaly-based IDS. Why might they insist on calling it an anomaly-based IDS, when your well-nigh infallible author would classify it as a signature-based system?

38. The anomaly-based intrusion detection example presented in this chapter is based on file-use statistics.

    a. Many other statistics could be used as part of an anomaly-based IDS. For example, network usage would be a sensible statistic to consider. List five other statistics that could reasonably be used in an anomaly-based IDS.

    b. Why might it be a good idea to combine several statistics rather than relying on just a few?

    c. Why might it not be a good idea to combine several statistics rather than relying on just a few?

39. Recall that the anomaly-based IDS example presented in this chapter is based on file-use statistics. The expected file use percentages (the H_i values in Table 8.4) are periodically updated using equation (8.3), which can be viewed as a moving average.

    a. Why is it necessary to update the expected file use percentages?

    b. When we update the expected file use percentages, it creates a potential avenue of attack for Trudy. How and why is this the case?

    c. Discuss a different generic approach to constructing and updating an anomaly-based IDS.

40. Suppose that at the time interval following the results in Table 8.8, Alice's file-use statistics are given by $A_0 = 0.05$, $A_1 = 0.25$, $A_2 = 0.25$, and $A_3 = 0.45$.

    a. Is this normal for Alice?

---

[17]Lack of standard terminology is a problem throughout most of the fields in information security (crypto being one of the few exceptions). It's important to be aware of this situation, since differing definitions is a common source of confusion. Of course, this problem is not unique to information security—differing definitions also cause confusion in many other fields of human endeavor. For proof, ask any two randomly selected economists about the current state of the economy.

      b. Compute the updated values of H_0 through H_3.

41. Suppose that we begin with the values of H_0 through H_3 that appear in Table 8.4.

    a. What is the minimum number of iterations required until it is possible to have $H_2 > 0.9$ without the IDS triggering a warning at any step?

    b. What is the minimum number of iterations required until it is possible to have $H_3 > 0.9$ without the IDS triggering a warning at any step?

42. Consider the results given in Table 8.6.

    a. For the subsequent time interval, what is the largest possible value for A_3 that will not trigger a warning from the IDS?

    b. Give values for A_0, A_1, and A_2 that are compatible with the solution to part a.

    c. Compute the statistic S, using the solutions from parts a and b, and the H_i values in Table 8.6.

Part III

Protocols

Chapter 9

Simple Authentication Protocols

*"I quite agree with you," said the Duchess; "and the moral of that is—
'Be what you would seem to be'—or,
if you'd like it put more simply—'Never imagine yourself not to be
otherwise than what it might appear to others that what you were
or might have been was not otherwise than what you
had been would have appeared to them to be otherwise.' "*
— Lewis Carroll, *Alice in Wonderland*

Seek simplicity, and distrust it.
— Alfred North Whitehead

9.1 Introduction

Protocols are the rules that are followed in some particular interaction. For example, there is a protocol that you follow if you want to ask a question in class, and it goes something like this:

1. You raise your hand.

2. The teacher calls on you.

3. You ask your question.

4. The teacher says, "I don't know."[1]

There are a vast number of human protocols, some of which can be very intricate, with numerous special cases to consider.

---

[1] Well, at least that's the way it works in your oblivious author's classes.

In the context of networking, protocols are the rules followed in networked communication systems. Examples of formal networking protocols include HTTP, FTP, TCP, UDP, PPP, and there are many, many more. In fact, the study of networks is largely the study of networking protocols.

Security protocols are the communication rules followed in security applications. In Chapter 10 we'll look closely at several real-world security protocols including SSH, SSL, IPSec, WEP, and Kerberos. In this chapter, we'll consider simplified authentication protocols so that we can better understand the fundamental security issues involved in the design of such protocols. If you want to delve a little deeper than the material presented in this chapter, the paper [3] has a discussion of some security protocol design principles.

In Chapter 7, we discussed methods that are used, primarily, to authenticate humans to a machines. In this chapter, we'll discuss authentication protocols. Although it might seem that these two authentication topics must be closely related, in fact, they are almost completely different. Here, we'll deal with the security issues related to the messages that are sent over a network to authenticate the participants. We'll see examples of well-known types of attacks on protocols and we'll show how to prevent these attacks. Note that our examples and analysis are informal and intuitive. The advantage of this approach is that we can cover all of the basic concepts quickly and with minimal background, but the price we pay is that some rigor is sacrificed.

Protocols can be subtle—often, a seemingly innocuous change makes a significant difference. Security protocols are particularly subtle, since the attacker can actively intervene in the process in a variety of ways. As an indication of the challenges inherent in security protocols, many well-known security protocols—including WEP, GSM, and even IPSec—have significant security issues. And even if the protocol itself is not flawed, a particular implementation can be.

Obviously, a security protocol must meet some specified security requirements. But we also want protocols to be efficient, both in computational cost and bandwidth usage. An ideal security protocol would not be too fragile, that is, the protocol would function correctly even when an attacker actively tries to break it. In addition, a security protocol should continue to work even if the environment in which it's deployed changes. Of course, it's impossible to protect against every possible eventuality, but protocol developers can try to anticipate likely changes in the environment and build in protections. Some of the most serious security challenges today are due to the fact that protocols are being used in environments for which they were not initially designed. For example, many Internet protocols were designed for a friendly, academic environment, which is about as far from the reality of the modern Internet as possible. Ease of use and ease of implementation are also desirable features of security protocols. Obviously, it's going to be difficult to design an ideal protocol.

9.2   Simple Security Protocols

The first security protocol that we consider is a protocol that could be used for entry into a secure facility, such as the National Security Agency. Employees are given a badge that they must wear at all times when in the secure facility. To enter the building, the badge is inserted into a card reader and the employee must provide a PIN number. The secure entry protocol can be described as follows.

1. Insert badge into reader.

2. Enter PIN.

3. Is the PIN correct?

   - Yes: Enter the building.
   - No: Get shot by a security guard.[2]

When you withdraw money from an ATM machine, the protocol is virtually identical to the secure entry protocol above, but without the violent ending:

1. Insert ATM card into reader

2. Enter PIN

3. Is the PIN correct?

   - Yes: Conduct your transactions
   - No: Machine eats your ATM card

The military has a need for many specialized security protocols. One example is an *identify friend or foe* (IFF) protocol. These protocols are designed to help prevent friendly-fire incidents—where soldiers accidentally attack soldiers on their own side—while not seriously hampering the fight against the enemy.

A simple example of an IFF protocol appears in Figure 9.1. This protocol was reportedly used by the South African Air Force, or SAAF, when fighting in Angola in the mid-1970s [14]. The South Africans were fighting Angola for control of Namibia (known as Southwest Africa at the time). The Angolan side was flying Soviet MiG aircraft, piloted by Cubans.[3]

---

[2]Of course, this is an exaggeration—you get three tries before being shot by the security guard.

[3]This was one of the hot wars that erupted during the Cold War. Early in the war, the South Africans were amazed by the skill of the "Angolan" pilots. They eventually realized the pilots were actually Cuban when satellite photos revealed baseball diamonds.

The IFF protocol in Figure 9.1 works as follows. When the SAAF radar detects an aircraft approaching its base, a random number, or *challenge*, N is sent to the aircraft. All SAAF aircraft have access to a key K that they use to encrypt the challenge, $E(N, K)$, which is computed and sent back to the radar station. Time is of the essence, so all of this happens automatically, without human intervention. Since enemy aircraft do not know K, they cannot send back the required response. It would seem that this protocol gives the radar station a simple way to determine whether an approaching aircraft is a friend (let it land) or foe (shoot it down).

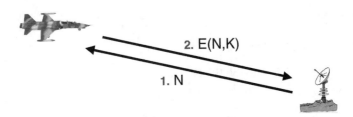

Figure 9.1: Identify Friend or Foe (IFF)

Unfortunately for those manning the radar station, there is a clever attack on the IFF system in Figure 9.1. Anderson has dubbed this attack the MiG-in-the-middle [14], which is a pun on man-in-the-middle. The scenario for the attack, which is illustrated in Figure 9.2, is as follows. While an SAAF Impala fighter is flying a mission over Angola, a Cuban-piloted MiG aircraft (the foe of the SAAF) loiters just outside of the range of the SAAF radar. When the Impala fighter is within range of a Cuban radar station in Angola, the MiG is told to move within range of the SAAF radar. As specified by the protocol, the SAAF radar sends the challenge N to the MiG. To avoid being shot down, the MiG needs to respond with $E(N, K)$, and quickly. Because the MiG does not know the key K, its situation appears hopeless. However, the MiG can forward the challenge N to its radar station in Angola, which, in turn, forwards the challenge to the SAAF Impala. The Impala fighter—not realizing that it has received the challenge from an enemy radar site—responds with $E(N, K)$. At this point, the Cuban radar relays the response $E(N, K)$ to the MiG, which can then provide it to the SAAF radar. Assuming this all happens fast enough, the SAAF radar will signal that the MiG is a friend, with disastrous consequences for the SAAF radar station and its operators.

Although it nicely illustrates an interesting security failure, it seems that this MiG-in-the-middle attack never actually occurred [15]. In any case, this is our first illustration of a security protocol failure, but it certainly won't be the last.

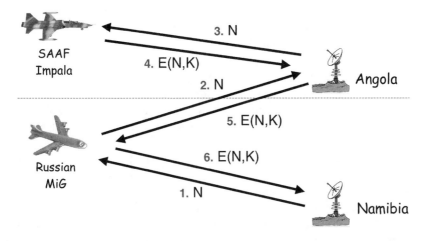

Figure 9.2: MiG-in-the-Middle

9.3   Authentication Protocols

> *"I can't explain myself, I'm afraid, Sir," said Alice,*
> *"because I'm not myself you see."*
> — Lewis Carroll, *Alice in Wonderland*

Suppose that Alice must prove to Bob that she's Alice, where Alice and Bob are communicating over a network. Keep in mind that Alice can be a human or a machine, and ditto for Bob. In fact, in this networked scenario, Alice and Bob will almost invariably be machines, which has important implications that we'll consider in a moment.

In many cases, it's sufficient for Alice to prove her identity to Bob, without Bob proving his identity to Alice. But sometimes *mutual authentication* is necessary, that is, Bob must also prove his identity to Alice. It seems obvious that if Alice can prove her identity to Bob, then precisely the same protocol can be used in the other direction for Bob to prove his identity to Alice. We'll see that, in security protocols, the obvious approach is not always secure.

In addition to authentication, a *session key* is inevitably required. A session key is a symmetric key that will be used to protect the confidentiality and/or integrity of the current session, provided the authentication succeeds. Initially, we'll ignore the session key so that we can concentrate on authentication.

In certain situations, there may be other requirements placed on a security protocol. For example, we might require that the protocol use public keys, or symmetric keys, or hash functions. In addition, some situations might call for a protocol that provides anonymity or plausible deniability (discussed below) or other not-so-obvious features.

We've previously considered the security issues associated with authentication on standalone computer systems. While such authentication presents its own set of challenges (hashing, salting, etc.), from the protocol perspective, it's straightforward. In contrast, authentication over a network requires very careful attention to protocol issues. When a network is involved, numerous attacks are available to Trudy that are generally not a concern on a standalone computer. When messages are sent over a network, Trudy can passively observe the messages and she can conduct various active attacks such as replaying old messages, inserting, deleting, or changing messages. In this book, we haven't previously encountered anything comparable to these types of attacks.

Our first attempt at authentication over a network is the protocol in Figure 9.3. This three-message protocol requires that Alice (the client) first initiate contact with Bob (the server) and state her identity. Then Bob asks for proof of Alice's identity, and Alice responds with her password. Finally, Bob uses Alice's password to authenticate Alice.

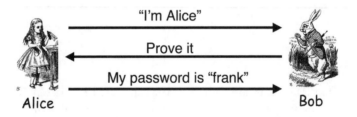

Figure 9.3: Simple Authentication

Although the protocol in Figure 9.3 is certainly simple, it has some major flaws. For one thing, if Trudy is able to observe the messages that are sent, she can later replay the messages to convince Bob that she is Alice, as illustrated in Figure 9.4. Since we are assuming these messages are sent over a network, this replay attack is a serious threat.

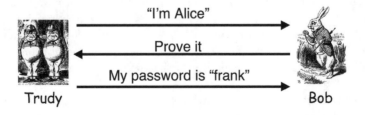

Figure 9.4: Replay Attack

Another issue with the too-simple authentication in Figure 9.3 is that Alice's password is sent in the clear. If Trudy observes the password when it is sent from Alice's computer, then Trudy knows Alice's password. This is even worse than a replay attack since Trudy can then pose as Alice on any site where Alice has reused this particular password. Another password issue with this protocol is that Bob must know Alice's password before he can authenticate her.

This simple authentication protocol is also inefficient, since the same effect could be accomplished in a single message from Alice to Bob. So, this protocol is a loser in every respect. Finally, note that the protocol in Figure 9.3 does not attempt to provide mutual authentication, which may be required in some cases.

For our next attempt at an authentication protocol, consider Figure 9.5. This protocol solves some of the problems of our previous simple authentication protocol. In this new-and-improved version, a passive observer, Trudy, will not learn Alice's password and Bob no longer needs to know Alice's password—although he must know the hash of Alice's password.

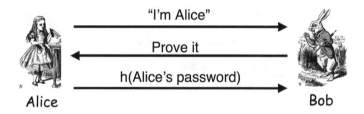

Figure 9.5: Simple Authentication with a Hash

The major flaw in the protocol of Figure 9.5 is that it's still subject to a replay attack, where Trudy records Alice's messages and later replays them to Bob. In this way, Trudy could be authenticated as Alice, without knowledge of Alice's password.

To authenticate Alice, Bob will need to employ a *challenge-response* mechanism. That is, Bob will send a challenge to Alice, and the response from Alice must be something that only Alice can provide and that Bob can verify. To prevent a replay attack, Bob can incorporate a "number used once," or *nonce*, in the challenge. That is, Bob will send a unique challenge each time, and the challenge will be used to compute the appropriate response. Bob can thereby distinguish the current response from a replay of a previous response. In other words, the nonce is used to ensure the freshness of the response. This approach to authentication with replay prevention is illustrated in Figure 9.6.

First, we'll design an authentication protocol using Alice's password. A password is something only Alice should know and Bob can verify—assuming that Bob knows Alice's password, that is.

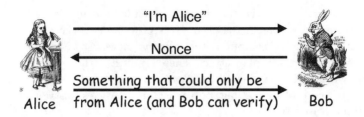

Figure 9.6: Generic Authentication

Our first serious attempt at an authentication protocol that is resistant to replay appears is Figure 9.7. In this protocol, the nonce sent from Bob to Alice is the challenge. Alice must respond with the hash of her password together with the nonce, which, assuming Alice's password is secure, serves to prove that the response was generated by Alice. Note that the nonce proves that the response is fresh and not a replay.

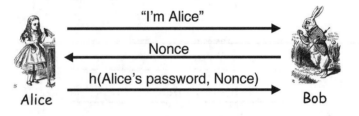

Figure 9.7: Challenge-Response

One problem with the protocol in Figure 9.7 is that Bob must know Alice's password. Furthermore, Alice and Bob typically represent machines rather than users, so it makes no sense to use passwords. After all, passwords are little more than a crutch used by humans because we are incapable of remembering keys. That is, passwords are about the closest thing to a key that humans can remember. So, if Alice and Bob are actually machines, they should be using keys instead of passwords.

9.3.1 Authentication Using Symmetric Keys

Having liberated ourselves from passwords, let's design a secure authentication protocol based on symmetric key cryptography. Recall that our notation for encrypting is $C = E(P, K)$ where P is plaintext, K is the key, and C is the ciphertext, while the notation for decrypting is $P = D(C, K)$. When discussing protocols, we are primarily concerned with attacks on protocols, not attacks on the cryptography used in protocols. Consequently, in this chapter we'll assume that the underlying cryptography is secure.

Suppose that Alice and Bob share the symmetric key K_{AB}. As in symmetric cryptography, we assume that nobody else has access to K_{AB}. Alice will authenticate herself to Bob by proving that she knows the key, without revealing the key to Trudy. In addition, the protocol must provide protection against a replay attack.

Our first symmetric key authentication protocol appears in Figure 9.8. This protocol is analogous to our previous password-based challenge-response protocol, but instead of hashing a nonce with a password, we've encrypted the nonce R with the shared symmetric key K_{AB}.

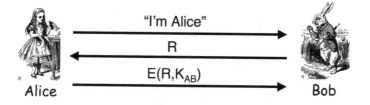

Figure 9.8: Symmetric Key Authentication Protocol

The symmetric key authentication protocol in Figure 9.8 allows Bob to authenticate Alice, since Alice can encrypt R with K_{AB}, Trudy cannot, and Bob can verify that the encryption was done correctly—Bob knows K_{AB}. This protocol prevents a replay attack, thanks to the nonce R, which ensures that each response is fresh. The protocol lacks mutual authentication, so our next task will be to develop a mutual authentication protocol based on symmetric keys.

Our first attempt at mutual authentication appears in Figure 9.9. This protocol is certainly efficient, and it does use symmetric key cryptography, but it has an obvious flaw. The third message in this protocol is simply a replay of the second, and consequently it proves nothing about the sender, be it Alice or Trudy.

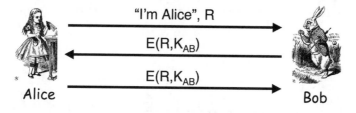

Figure 9.9: Mutual Authentication?

A more plausible approach to mutual authentication would be to use the secure authentication protocol in Figure 9.8 and repeat the process twice, once for Bob to authenticate Alice and once more for Alice to authenticate Bob. We've illustrated this approach in Figure 9.10, where we've combined some messages for the sake of efficiency.

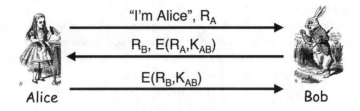

Figure 9.10: Secure Mutual Authentication?

Perhaps surprisingly, the protocol in Figure 9.10 is insecure—it is subject to an attack that is analogous to the MiG-in-the-middle attack discussed previously. In this attack, which is illustrated in Figure 9.11, Trudy initiates a conversation with Bob by claiming to be Alice and sends a challenge R_A to Bob. Following the protocol, Bob encrypts the challenge R_A and sends it, along with his challenge R_B, to Trudy. At this point Trudy appears to be stuck, since she doesn't know the key K_{AB}, and therefore she can't respond appropriately to Bob's challenge. However, Trudy cleverly opens a new connection to Bob where she again claims to be Alice and this time sends Bob his own "random" challenge R_B. Bob, following the protocol, responds with $E(R_B, K_{AB})$, which Trudy can now use to complete the first connection. Trudy can leave the second connection to time out, since she has—in the first connection—convinced Bob that she is Alice.

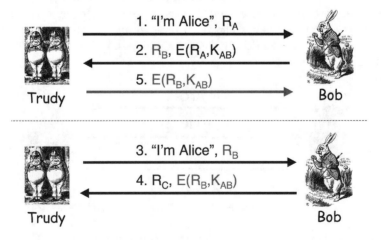

Figure 9.11: Trudy's Attack

The conclusion is that a non-mutual authentication protocol may not be secure for mutual authentication. Another conclusion is that protocols (and attacks on protocols) can be subtle. Yet another conclusion is that "obvious" changes to protocols can cause unexpected security problems.

In Figure 9.12, we've made a couple of minor changes to the insecure mutual authentication protocol of Figure 9.10. In particular, we've encrypted the user's identity together with the nonce. This change is sufficient to prevent Trudy's previous attack since she cannot use a response from Bob for the third message—Bob will realize that he encrypted it himself.

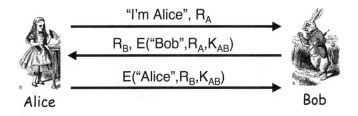

"I'm Alice", R_A

R_B, $E(\text{"Bob"}, R_A, K_{AB})$

$E(\text{"Alice"}, R_B, K_{AB})$

Alice   Bob

Figure 9.12: Strong Mutual Authentication Protocol

One lesson here is that it's a bad idea to have the two sides in a protocol do exactly the same thing, since this might open the door to an attack. Another lesson is that small changes to a protocol can result in big changes in its security.

9.3.2 Authentication Using Public Keys

In the previous section we devised a secure mutual authentication protocol using symmetric keys. Can we accomplish the same thing using public key cryptography? First, recall our public key notation. Encrypting a message M with Alice's public key is denoted $C = \{M\}_{\text{Alice}}$ while decrypt C with Alice's private key, and thereby recovering the plaintext M, is denoted $M = [C]_{\text{Alice}}$. Signing is also a private key operation. Of course, encryption and decryption are inverse operation, as are signing and signature verification, that is

$$[\{M\}_{\text{Alice}}]_{\text{Alice}} = M \ \text{ and } \ \{[M]_{\text{Alice}}\}_{\text{Alice}} = M.$$

It's always important to remember that in public key cryptography, anybody can do public key operations, while only Alice can use her private key.[4]

Our first attempt at authentication using public key cryptography appears in Figure 9.13. This protocol allows Bob to authenticate Alice, since only Alice can do the private key operation that is necessary to reply with R in the third message. Also, assuming that the nonce R is chosen (by Bob) at

---

[4]Repeat to yourself 100 times: The public key is public.

random, a replay attack is not feasible. That is, Trudy cannot replay R from a previous iteration of the protocol, since the random challenge will almost certainly not be the same in a subsequent iteration.

However, if Alice uses the same key pair to encrypt as she uses for authentication, then there is a potential problem with the protocol in Figure 9.13. Suppose Trudy has previously intercepted a message encrypted with Alice's public key, say, $C = \{M\}_{\text{Alice}}$. Then Trudy can pose as Bob and send C to Alice in message two, and Alice will decrypt it and send the plaintext back to Trudy. From Trudy's perspective, it doesn't get any better than that. The moral of the story is that you should not use the same key pair for signing as you use for encryption.

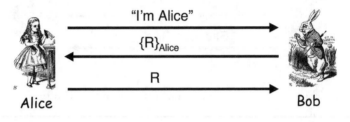

Figure 9.13: Authentication with Public Key Encryption

The authentication protocol in Figure 9.13 uses public key encryption. Is it possible to accomplish the same feat using digital signatures? In fact, it is, as illustrated in Figure 9.14.

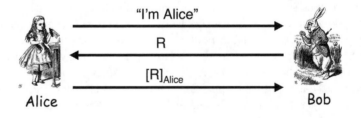

Figure 9.14: Authentication via Digital Signature

The protocol in Figure 9.14 has similar security issues as the public key encryption protocol in Figure 9.13. In Figure 9.14, if Trudy can pose as Bob, she can get Alice to sign anything. Again, the solution to this problem is to always use different key pairs for signing and encryption. Finally, note that, from Alice's perspective, the protocols in Figures 9.13 and 9.14 are identical, since in both cases she applies her private key to whatever shows up in message two.

9.3.3 Session Keys

Along with authentication, we invariably require a session key. Even when a symmetric key is used for authentication, we want to use a distinct session keys to encrypt data within each connection. The purpose of a session key is to limit the amount of data encrypted with any one particular key, and it also serves to limit the damage if one session key is compromised. A session key is used to provide confidentiality or integrity protection (or both) to the messages.

We want to establish the session key as part of the authentication protocol. That is, when the authentication is complete, we will also have securely established a shared symmetric key. Therefore, when analyzing an authentication protocol, we need to consider attacks on the authentication itself, as well as attacks on the session key.

Our next goal is to design an authentication protocol that also provides a shared symmetric key. It looks to be straightforward to include a session key in our secure public key authentication protocol. Such a protocol appears in Figure 9.15.

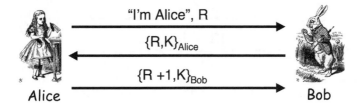

Figure 9.15: Authentication and a Session Key

One possible concern with the protocol of Figure 9.15 is that it does not provide for mutual authentication—only Alice is authenticated.[5] But before we tackle that issue, can we modify the protocol in Figure 9.15 so that it uses digital signatures instead of public key encryption? This also seems straightforward, and the result appears in Figure 9.16.

However, there is a fatal flaw in the protocol of Figure 9.16. Since the key is signed, anybody can use Bob's (or Alice's) public key and find the session key K. A session key that is public knowledge is definitely not secure. But before we dismiss this protocol entirely, note that it does provide mutual authentication, whereas the public key encryption protocol in Figure 9.15 does not. Can we combine these protocols so as to achieve both mutual

---

[5]One strange thing about this protocol is that the key K acts as Bob's challenge to Alice and the nonce R is useless. But there is a method to the madness, which will become clear shortly.

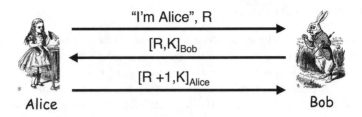

Figure 9.16: Signature-Based Authentication and Session Key

authentication and a secure session key? The answer is yes, and there are a couple of ways to do so.

Suppose that, instead of signing or encrypting the messages, we sign and encrypt the messages. Figure 9.17 illustrates such a sign and encrypt protocol. This appears to provide the desired secure mutual authentication and a secure session key.

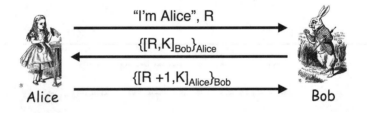

Figure 9.17: Mutual Authentication and Session Key

Since the protocol in Figure 9.17 provides mutual authentication and a session key using sign and encrypt, surely encrypt and sign must work, too. An encrypt and sign protocol appears in Figure 9.18.

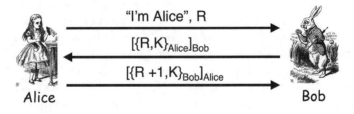

Figure 9.18: Encrypt and Sign Mutual Authentication

Note that the values $\{R, K\}_{\text{Alice}}$ and $\{R + 1, K\}_{\text{Bob}}$ in Figure 9.18 are available to anyone who has access to Alice's or Bob's public keys (which, by assumption, is anybody who wants them). Since this is not the case in Figure 9.17, it might seem that sign and encrypt somehow reveals less information than encrypt and sign. However, it appears that an attacker must break the public key encryption to recover K in either case and, if so, there is no security difference between the two. Recall that when analyzing protocols, we assume all crypto is strong, so breaking the encryption is not an option for Trudy.

9.3.4 Perfect Forward Secrecy

Now that we have conquered mutual authentication and session key establishment (using public keys), we turn our attention to *perfect forward secrecy*, or PFS. What is PFS? Rather than answer directly, we'll look at an example that illustrates what PFS is not. Suppose that Alice encrypts a message with a shared symmetric key K_{AB} and sends the resulting ciphertext to Bob. Trudy can't break the cipher to recover the key, so out of desperation she simply records all of the messages encrypted with the key K_{AB}. Now suppose that at some point in the future Trudy manages to get access to Alice's computer, where she finds the key K_{AB}. Then Trudy can decrypt the recorded ciphertext messages. While such an attack may seem unlikely, the problem is potentially significant since, once Trudy has recorded the ciphertext, the encryption key remains a vulnerability into the future. To avoid this problem, Alice and Bob must both destroy all traces of K_{AB} once they have finished using it. This might not be as easy as it seems, particularly if K_{AB} is a long-term key that Alice and Bob will need to use in the future. Furthermore, even if Alice is careful and properly manages her keys, she would have to rely on Bob to do the same (and vice versa).

PFS makes such an attack impossible. That is, even if Trudy records all ciphertext messages and she later recovers all long-term secrets (symmetric keys and/or private keys), she cannot decrypt the recorded messages. While it might seem that this is an impossibility, it is not only possible, but actually fairly easy to achieve in practice.

Suppose Bob and Alice share a long-term symmetric key K_{AB}. Then if they want PFS, they definitely can't use K_{AB} as their encryption key. Instead, Alice and Bob must agree on a session key K_S and forget K_S after it's no longer needed, i.e., after the current session ends. So, as in our previous protocols, Alice and Bob must find a way to agree on a session key K_S, by using their long-term symmetric key K_{AB}. However, for PFS we have the added condition that if Trudy later finds K_{AB}, she cannot determine K_S, even if she recorded all of the messages exchanged by Alice and Bob.

Suppose that Alice generates a session key K_S and sends $E(K_S, K_{AB})$ to Bob, that is, Alice simply encrypts the session key and sends it to Bob. If we are not concerned with PFS, this would be a sensible way to establish a session key in conjunction with an authentication protocol. However, this approach, which is illustrated in Figure 9.19, does not provide PFS. If Trudy records all of the messages and later recovers K_{AB}, she can decrypt $E(K_S, K_{AB})$ to recover the session key K_S, which she can then use to decrypt the recorded ciphertext messages. This is precisely the attack that PFS is supposed to prevent.

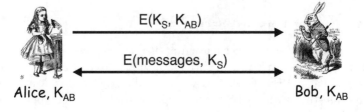

$$E(K_S, K_{AB})$$

$$E(\text{messages}, K_S)$$

Alice, K_{AB} Bob, K_{AB}

Figure 9.19: Naïve Attempt at PFS

There are actually several ways to achieve PFS, but the most elegant approach is to use an *ephemeral Diffie-Hellman* key exchange. As a reminder, the standard Diffie-Hellman key exchange protocol appears in Figure 9.20. In this protocol, g and p are public, Alice chooses her secret exponent a and Bob chooses his secret exponent b. Then Alice sends $g^a \bmod p$ to Bob and Bob sends $g^b \bmod p$ to Alice. Alice and Bob can each compute the shared secret $g^{ab} \bmod p$. Recall that the crucial weakness with Diffie-Hellman is that it is subject to a man-in-the-middle attack, as discussed in Section 4.4 of Chapter 4.

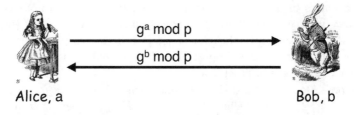

$$g^a \bmod p$$

$$g^b \bmod p$$

Alice, a Bob, b

Figure 9.20: Diffie-Hellman

If we are to use Diffie-Hellman for PFS,[6] we must prevent the man-in-the-middle attack, and, of course, we must somehow assure PFS. The aforementioned ephemeral Diffie-Hellman can accomplish both. To prevent the MiM attack, Alice and Bob can use their shared symmetric key K_{AB} to encrypt the Diffie-Hellman exchange. Then to get PFS, all that is required is that, once Alice has computed the shared session key $K_S = g^{ab} \bmod p$, she must forget

---

[6]Your acronym-loving author was tempted to call this protocol DH4PFS or maybe EDH4PFS but, for once, he showed restraint.

her secret exponent a and, similarly, Bob must forget his secret exponent b. This protocol is illustrated in Figure 9.21.

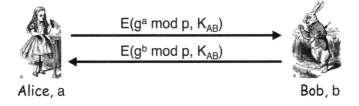

$$E(g^a \bmod p, K_{AB})$$
$$E(g^b \bmod p, K_{AB})$$

Alice, a   **Bob, b**

Figure 9.21: Ephemeral Diffie-Hellman for PFS

One interesting feature of the PFS protocol in Figure 9.21 is that once Alice and Bob have forgotten their respective secret exponents, even they can't reconstruct the session key K_S. If Alice and Bob can't recover the session key, certainly Trudy can be no better off. If Trudy records the conversation in Figure 9.21 and later is able to find K_{AB}, she will not be able to recover the session key K_S unless she can break Diffie-Hellman. Assuming the underlying crypto is strong, we have satisfied our requirements for PFS.

9.3.5 Mutual Authentication, Session Key, and PFS

Now let's put it all together and design a mutual authentication protocol that establishes a session key with PFS. The protocol in Figure 9.22, which is a slightly modified form of the encrypt and sign protocol from Figure 9.18, appears to fill the bill. It is a good exercise to give convincing arguments that Alice is actually authenticated (explaining exactly where and how that happens and why Bob is convinced he's talking to Alice), that Bob is authenticated, that the session key is secure, that PFS is provided, and that there are no obvious attacks.

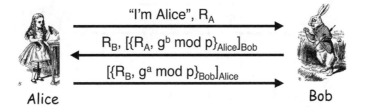

"I'm Alice", R_A

$R_B, [\{R_A, g^b \bmod p\}_{Alice}]_{Bob}$

$[\{R_B, g^a \bmod p\}_{Bob}]_{Alice}$

Alice   **Bob**

Figure 9.22: Mutual Authentication, Session Key and PFS

Now that we've developed a protocol that satisfies all of our security requirements, we can turn our attention to questions of efficiency. That is, we'll try to reduce the number of messages in the protocol or increase the efficiency in some other way, such as by reducing the number of public key operations.

9.3.6 Timestamps

A *timestamp T* is a time value, typically expressed in milliseconds. With some care, a timestamp can be used in place of a nonce, since a current timestamp ensures freshness. The benefit of a timestamp is that we don't need to waste any messages exchanging nonces, assuming that the current time is known to both Alice and Bob. Timestamps are used in many real-world security protocols, such as Kerberos, which we discuss in the next chapter.

Along with the potential benefit of increased efficiency, timestamps create some security issues as well.[7] For one thing, the use of timestamps implies that time is a security-critical parameter. For example, if Trudy can attack Alice's system clock (or whatever Alice relies on for the current time), she may cause Alice's authentication to fail. A related problem is that we can't rely on clocks to be perfectly synchronized, so we must allow for some *clock skew*, that is, we must accept any timestamp that is close to the current time. In general, this can open a small window of opportunity for Trudy to conduct a replay attack—if she acts within the allowed clock skew a replay will be accepted. It is possible to close this window completely, but the solution puts an additional burden on the server (see Problem 27). In any case, we would like to minimize the clock skew without causing excessive failures due to time inconsistencies between Alice and Bob.

To illustrate the benefit of a timestamp, consider the authentication protocol in Figure 9.23. This protocol is essentially the timestamp version of the sign and encrypt protocol in Figure 9.17. Note that by using a timestamp, we're able to reduce the number of messages by a third.

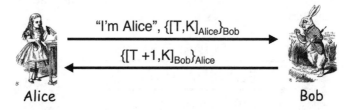

Figure 9.23: Authentication Using a Timestamp

The authentication protocol in Figure 9.23 uses a timestamp together with sign and encrypt and it appears to be secure. So it would seem obvious that the timestamp version of encrypt and sign must also be secure. This protocol is illustrated in Figure 9.24.

---

[7]This is yet another example of the "no free lunch" principle.

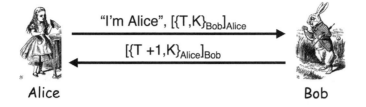

Figure 9.24: Encrypt and Sign Using a Timestamp

Unfortunately, with protocols, the obvious is not always correct. In fact, the protocol in Figure 9.24 is subject to attack. Trudy can recover $\{T, K\}_{\text{Bob}}$ by applying Alice's public key. Then Trudy can open a connection to Bob and send $\{T, K\}_{\text{Bob}}$ in message one, as illustrated in Figure 9.25. Following the protocol, Bob will then send the key K to Trudy in a form that Trudy can decrypt. This is not good, since K is the session key shared by Alice and Bob.

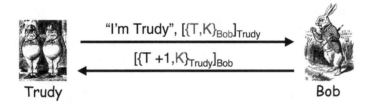

Figure 9.25: Trudy's Attack on Encrypt and Sign

The attack in Figure 9.25 shows that our encrypt and sign protocol is not secure when we use a timestamp. But our sign and encrypt protocol is secure when a timestamp is used. In addition, the nonce versions of both sign and encrypt as well as encrypt and sign are secure (see Figures 9.17 and 9.18). These examples nicely illustrate that, when it comes to security protocols, we should never take anything for granted.

Is the flawed protocol in Figure 9.24 fixable? In fact, there are several minor modifications that will make this protocol secure. For example, there's no reason to return the key K in the second message, since Alice already knows K and the only purpose of this message is to authenticate Bob. The timestamp in message two is sufficient to authenticate Bob. This secure version of the protocol is illustrated in Figure 9.26 (see also Problem 21).

In the next chapter, we'll discuss several well-known, real-world security protocols. These protocols use the concepts that we've presented in this chapter. But before moving on to the real world of Chapter 10, we briefly look at a couple of additional protocol topics. First, we'll consider a weak

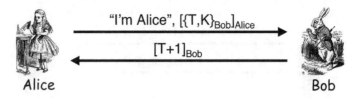

Figure 9.26: Secure Encrypt and Sign with a Timestamp

form of authentication that relies on TCP which, unfortunately, is sometimes used in practice. Finally, we discuss the Fiat-Shamir zero knowledge protocol. We'll encounter Fiat-Shamir again in the final chapter.

9.4   Authentication and TCP

In this section we'll take a quick look at how TCP is sometimes used for authentication. TCP was not designed to be used in this manner and, not surprisingly, this authentication method is not secure. But it does illustrate some interesting network security issues.

There is an undeniable temptation to use the IP address in a TCP connection for authentication.[8] If we could make this work, then we wouldn't need any of those troublesome keys or pesky authentication protocols.

Below, we'll give an example of TCP-based authentication and we illustrate an attack on the scheme. But first we briefly review the TCP three-way handshake, which is illustrated in Figure 9.27. The first message is a synchronization request, or SYN, whereas the second message, which acknowledges the synchronization request, is a SYN-ACK, and the third message—which can also contain data—acknowledges the previous message, and is simply known as an ACK.

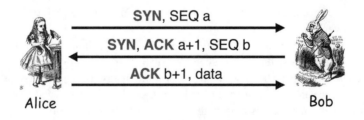

Figure 9.27: TCP 3-Way Handshake

---

[8]As we'll see in the next chapter, the IPSec protocol relies on the IP address for user identity in one of its modes. So, even people who should know better cannot always resist the temptation.

Suppose that Bob decides to rely on the completed three-way handshake to verify that he is connected to a specific IP address, which he knows belongs to Alice. Then, in effect, he is using the TCP connection to authenticate Alice. Since Bob sends the SYN-ACK to Alice's IP address, it's tempting to assume that the corresponding ACK must have come from Alice. In particular, if Bob verifies that ACK $b + 1$ appears in message three, he has some reason to believe that Alice, at her known IP address, has received message two and responded, since message two contains SEQ b and nobody else should know b. An underlying assumption here is that Trudy can't see the SYN-ACK packet—otherwise she would know b and she could easily forge the ACK. Clearly, this is not a strong form of authentication. However, as a practical matter, it might actually be difficult for Trudy to intercept the message containing b. So, if Trudy cannot see b, is the protocol secure?

Even if Trudy cannot see the initial SEQ number b, she might be able to make a reasonable guess. If so, the attack scenario illustrated in Figure 9.28 may be feasible. In this attack, Trudy first sends an ordinary SYN packet to Bob, who responds with a SYN-ACK. Trudy examines the SEQ value b_1 in this SYN-ACK packet. Suppose that Trudy can use b_1 to predict Bob's next initial SEQ value b_2.[9] Then Trudy can send a packet to Bob with the source IP address forged to be Alice's IP address. Bob will send the SYN-ACK to Alice's IP address which, by assumption, Trudy can't see. But, if Trudy can guess b_2, she can complete the three-way handshake by sending ACK $b_2 + 1$ to Bob. As a result, Bob will believe that data received from Trudy on this particular TCP connection actually came from Alice.

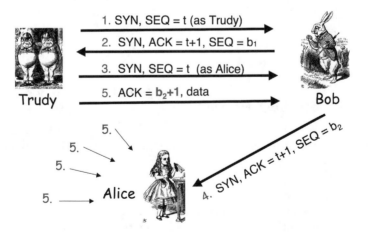

Figure 9.28: TCP "Authentication" Attack

[9]In practice, Trudy could send many SYN packets to Bob, trying to diagnose his initial sequence number generation scheme before actually attempting to guess a value.

Note that Bob always responds to Alice's IP address and, by assumption, Trudy cannot see his responses. But Bob will accept data from Trudy, thinking it came from Alice, as long as the connection remains active. However, when the data sent by Bob to Alice's IP address reaches Alice, Alice will terminate the connection since she has not completed the three-way handshake. To prevent this from happening, Trudy could mount a denial of service attack on Alice by sending enough messages so that Bob's messages can't get through—or, even if they do get through, Alice can't respond. This denial of service is illustrated Figure 9.28. Of course, if Alice happens to be offline, Trudy could conduct the attack without having to do this denial of service on Alice.

This attack is well known, and as a result initial SEQ numbers are supposed to be generated at random. So, how random are initial SEQ numbers? Surprisingly, they're often not very random at all. For example, Figure 9.29 provides a visual comparison of random initial SEQ numbers versus the highly biased initial SEQ numbers generated under an early version of Mac OS X. The Mac OS X numbers are biased enough that the attack in Figure 9.28 would have a reasonable chance of success. Many other vendors fail to generate random initial SEQ numbers, as can be seen from the fascinating pictures at [335].

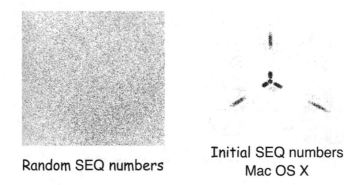

Figure 9.29: Plots of Initial SEQ Numbers (Courtesy of Michal Zalewski [335])

Even if initial SEQ numbers are random, it's a bad idea to rely on a TCP connection for authentication. A much better approach would be to employ a secure authentication protocol after the three-way handshake has completed. Even a simple password scheme would be far superior to relying on TCP. But, as often occurs in security, the TCP authentication method is sometimes used in practice simply because it's there, it's convenient, and it doesn't annoy users—not because it's secure.

9.5   Zero Knowledge Proofs

In this section we'll discuss a fascinating authentication scheme developed by Fiege, Fiat, and Shamir [111] (yes, that Shamir), but usually known simply as Fiat-Shamir. We'll mention this method again in Chapter 13 when we discuss Microsoft's trusted operating system.

In a *zero knowledge proof*,[10] or ZKP, Alice wants to prove to Bob that she knows a secret without revealing any information about the secret—neither Trudy nor Bob can learn anything about the secret. Bob must be able to verify that Alice knows the secret, even though he gains no information about the secret. On the face of it, this sounds impossible. However, there is an interactive probabilistic process whereby Bob can verify that Alice knows a secret to an arbitrarily high probability. This is an example of an interactive proof system.

Before describing such a protocol, we first consider Bob's Cave,[11] which appears in Figure 9.30. Suppose that Alice claims to know the secret phrase ("open sarsaparilla"[12]) that opens the door between R and S in Figure 9.30. Can Alice convince Bob that she knows the secret phrase without revealing any information about it?

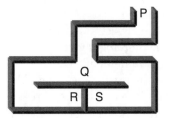

Figure 9.30: Bob's Cave

Consider the following protocol. Alice enters Bob's Cave and flips a coin to decide whether to position herself at point R or S. Bob then enters the cave and proceeds to point Q. Suppose that Alice happens to be positioned at point R. This situation is illustrated in Figure 9.31.

Then Bob flips a coin to randomly select one side or the other and asks Alice to appear from that side. With the situation as in Figure 9.31, if Bob happens to select side R, then Alice would appear at side R whether she knows the secret phrase or not. But if Bob happens to choose side S, then Alice can only appear on side S if she knows the secret phrase that opens

---

[10]Not to be confused with a "zero knowledge Prof."

[11]Traditionally, Ali Baba's Cave is used here.

[12]Traditionally, the secret phrase is "open says me," which sounds a lot like "open sesame." In the cartoon world, "open sesame" somehow became "open sarsaparilla" [242].

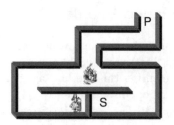

Figure 9.31: Bob's Cave Protocol

the door between R and S. In other words, if Alice doesn't know the secret phrase, the probability that she can trick Bob into believing that she does is $\frac{1}{2}$. This does not seem particularly useful, but if the protocol is repeated n times, then the probability that Alice can trick Bob every time is only $(\frac{1}{2})^n$. So, Alice and Bob will repeat the protocol n times and Alice must pass every time before Bob will believe she knows the secret phrase.

Note that if Alice (or Trudy) does not know the secret phrase, there is always a chance that she can trick Bob into believing that she does. However, Bob can make this probability as small as he desires by choosing n appropriately. For example, with $n = 20$ there is less than a 1 in 1,000,000 chance that "Alice" would convince Bob that she knows the phrase when she does not. Also, Bob learns nothing about the secret phrase in this protocol. Finally, it is critical that Bob randomly chooses the side where he asks Alice to appear—if Bob's choice is predictable, then Alice (or Trudy) would have a better chance of tricking Bob and thereby breaking the protocol.

While Bob's Cave indicates that zero knowledge proofs are possible in principle, cave-based protocols are not particularly popular. Can we achieve the same effect without the cave? The answer is yes, thanks to the Fiat-Shamir protocol.

Fiat-Shamir relies on the fact that finding a square root modulo N is as difficult as factoring. Suppose $N = pq$, where p and q are prime. Alice knows a secret S, which, of course, she must keep secret. The numbers N and $v = S^2 \bmod N$ are public. Alice must convince Bob that she knows S without revealing any information about S.

The Fiat-Shamir protocol, which is illustrated in Figure 9.32, works as follows. Alice randomly selects a value r, and she computes $x = r^2 \bmod N$. In message one, Alice sends x to Bob. In message two, Bob chooses a random value $e \in \{0, 1\}$, which he sends to Alice who, in turn, then computes the quantity $y = rS^e \bmod N$. In the third message Alice sends y to Bob. Finally, Bob needs to verify that

$$y^2 = xv^e \bmod N,$$

which, if everyone has followed the protocol, holds true since

$$y^2 = r^2 S^{2e} = r^2(S^2)^e = xv^e \bmod N. \tag{9.1}$$

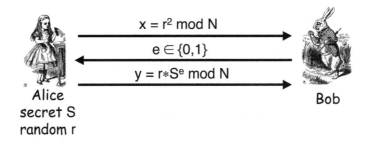

Figure 9.32: Fiat-Shamir Protocol

In message two, Bob sends either $e = 0$ or $e = 1$. Let's consider these cases separately. If Bob sends $e = 1$, then Alice responds with $y = r \cdot S \bmod N$ in the third message, and equation (9.1) becomes

$$y^2 = r^2 \cdot S^2 = r^2 \cdot (S^2) = x \cdot v \bmod N.$$

Note that in this case, Alice must know the secret S.

On the other hand, if Bob sends $e = 0$ in message two, then Alice responds in the third message with $y = r \bmod N$ and equation (9.1) becomes

$$y^2 = r^2 = x \bmod N.$$

Note that in this case, Alice does not need to know the secret S. This may seem strange, but it's roughly equivalent to the situation in Bob's Cave where Alice did not need to open the secret passage to come out on the correct side. Regardless, it is tempting to have Bob always send $e = 1$. However, we'll see in a moment that that this would not be wise.

The first message in the Fiat-Shamir protocol is the *commitment* phase, since Alice commits to her choice of r by sending $x = r^2 \bmod N$ to Bob. That is, Alice cannot change her mind (she is committed to r), but she has not revealed r, since finding modular square roots is hard. The second message is the *challenge* phase—Bob is challenging Alice to provide the correct response. The third message is the *response* phase, since Alice must respond with the correct value. Bob then verifies the response using equation (9.1). These phases correspond to the three steps in Bob's Cave protocol in Figure 9.31, above.

The mathematics behind the Fiat-Shamir protocol works, that is, assuming everyone follows the protocol, Bob can verify $y^2 = xv^e \bmod N$ from the information he receives. But this does not establish the security of the protocol. To do so, we must determine whether an attacker, Trudy, can convince Bob that she knows Alice's secret S and thereby convince Bob that she is Alice.

Suppose Trudy expects Bob to send the challenge $e = 0$ in message two. Then Trudy can send $x = r^2 \bmod N$ in message one and $y = r \bmod N$ in message three. That is, Trudy simply follows the protocol in this case, since she does not need to know the secret S.

On the other hand, if Trudy expects Bob to send $e = 1$, then she can send $x = r^2 v^{-1} \bmod N$ in message one and $y = r \bmod N$ in message three. Following the protocol, Bob will compute $y^2 = r^2$ and $xv^e = r^2 v^{-1} v = r^2$ and he will find that equation (9.1) holds. Bob therefore accepts the result as valid.

The conclusion here is that Bob must choose $e \in \{0, 1\}$ at random (as specified by the protocol). If so, then Trudy can only trick Bob with probability $\frac{1}{2}$, and, as with Bob's Cave, after n iterations, the probability that Trudy can fool Bob is only $(\frac{1}{2})^n$.

So, Fiat-Shamir requires that Bob's challenge $e \in \{0, 1\}$ be unpredictable. In addition, Alice must generate a random r at each iteration of the protocol or her secret S will be revealed (see Problem 40 at the end of this chapter).

Is the Fiat-Shamir protocol really zero knowledge? That is, can Bob—or anyone else—learn anything about Alice's secret S? Recall that v and N are public, where $v = S^2 \bmod N$. In addition, Bob sees $r^2 \bmod N$ in message one, and, assuming $e = 1$, Bob sees $rS \bmod N$ in message three. If Bob can find r from $r^2 \bmod N$, then he can find S. But finding modular square roots is computationally infeasible. If Bob were somehow able to find such square roots, he could obtain S directly from the public value v without bothering with the protocol at all. While this is not a rigorous proof that Fiat-Shamir is zero knowledge, it does indicate that there is nothing obvious in the protocol itself that helps Bob (or anyone else) to determine Alice's secret S.

Is there an security benefit of Fiat-Shamir, or is it just fun and games for mathematicians? If public keys are used for authentication, then each side must know the other side's public key. At the start of the protocol, typically Alice would not know Bob's public key, and vice versa. So, in many public key-based protocols Bob sends his certificate to Alice. But the certificate identifies Bob, and consequently this exchange would tell Trudy that Bob is a party to the transaction. In other words, public keys make it hard for the participants to remain anonymous.

A potential advantage of zero knowledge proofs is that they allow for authentication with anonymity. In Fiat-Shamir, both sides must know the public value v, but there is nothing in v that identifies Alice, and there is nothing in the messages that are passed that must identify Alice. This is an advantage that has led Microsoft to include support for zero knowledge proofs in its Next Generation Secure Computing Base, or NGSCB, which we'll discuss in Chapter 13. The bottom line is that Fiat-Shamir does have some potential practical utility.

9.6 The Best Authentication Protocol?

In general there is no "best" authentication protocol. What is best for a particular situation will depend on many factors. At a minimum, we need to consider the following questions.

- What is the sensitivity of the application?

- How much delay is tolerable?

- Do we want to deal with time as a security critical parameter?

- What type of crypto is supported—public key, symmetric key, or hash functions?

- Is mutual authentication required?

- Is a session key required?

- Is perfect forward secrecy desired?

- Is anonymity a concern?

In the next chapter, we'll see that there are additional issues that can influence our choice of protocol.

9.7 Summary

In this chapter we discussed several different ways to authenticate and establish a session key over an insecure network. We can accomplish these feats using symmetric keys, public keys, or hash functions (with symmetric keys). We also learned how to achieve perfect forward secrecy, and we considered the benefits (and potential drawbacks) of using timestamps.

Along the way, we came across many security pitfalls. You should now have some appreciation for the subtle issues that can arise with security protocols. This will be useful in the next chapter where we look closely at several real-world security protocols. We'll see that, despite extensive development effort by lots of smart people, such protocols are not immune to some of the security flaws highlighted in this chapter.

9.8   Problems

1. Modify the authentication protocol in Figure 9.12 so that it uses a hash function instead of symmetric key encryption. The resulting protocol must be secure.

2. The insecure protocol in Figure 9.24 was modified in Figure 9.26 to be secure. Find two other distinct ways to slightly modify the protocol in Figure 9.24 so that the resulting protocol is secure. Your protocols must use a timestamp and "encrypt and sign."

3. We want to design a secure mutual authentication protocol based on a shared symmetric key. We also want to establish a session key, and we want perfect forward secrecy.

   a. Design such a protocol that uses three messages.

   b. Design such a protocol that uses two messages.

4. Consider the following mutual authentication protocol, where K_{AB} is a shared symmetric key.

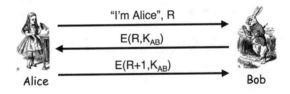

Alice   Bob

Give two different attacks that Trudy can use to convince Bob that she is Alice.

5. Consider the attack on TCP authentication illustrated in Figure 9.28. Suppose that Trudy cannot guess the initial sequence number b_2 exactly. Instead, Trudy can only narrow b_2 down to one of, say, 1,000 possible values. How can Trudy conduct an attack so that she is likely to succeed?

6. Timestamps can be used in place of nonces in security protocols.

   a. What is the primary advantage of using timestamps?

   b. What is the primary disadvantage of using timestamps?

7. Consider the following protocol, where CLNT and SRVR are constants, and the session key is $K = h(S, R_A, R_B)$.

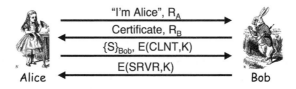

    a. Does Alice authenticate Bob? Justify your answer.

    b. Does Bob authenticate Alice? Justify your answer.

8. Consider the following protocol, where K_{AB} is a shared symmetric key, CLNT and SRVR are constants, and $K = h(S, R_A, R_B)$ is the session key.

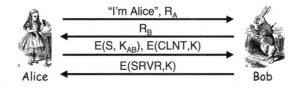

    a. Does Alice authenticate Bob? Justify your answer.

    b. Does Bob authenticate Alice? Justify your answer.

9. The following two-message protocol is designed for mutual authentication and to establish a session key K. Here, T is a timestamp.

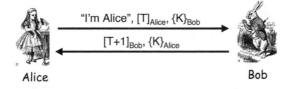

    This protocol is insecure. Illustrate a successful attack by Trudy.

10. Suppose R is a random challenge sent in the clear from Alice to Bob and K is a symmetric key known only to Alice and Bob. Which of the following are secure session keys and which are not? Justify your answers.

    a. $R \oplus K$

    b. $E(R, K)$

    c. $E(K, R)$

d. $h(K, R)$

e. $h(R, K)$

11. Design a secure two-message authentication protocol that provides mutual authentication and establishes a session key K. Assume that Alice and Bob know each other's public keys beforehand. Does your protocol protect the anonymity of Alice and Bob from a passive attacker (i.e., an attacker who can only observe messages sent between Alice and Bob)? If not, modify your protocol so that it does provide anonymity.

12. For some particular security protocol, suppose that Trudy can construct messages that appear to any observer (including Alice and/or Bob) to be valid messages between Alice and Bob. Then the protocol is said to provide *plausible deniability*. The idea here is that Alice and Bob can (plausibly) argue that any conversation they had using the protocol never actually occurred—it could have been faked by Trudy. Consider the following protocol, where $K = h(R_A, R_B, S)$.

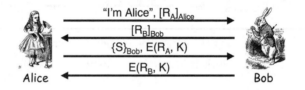

Does this protocol provide plausible deniability? If so, why? If not, slightly modify the protocol so that it does, while still providing mutual authentication and a secure session key.

13. Consider the following protocol where $K = h(R_A, R_B)$.

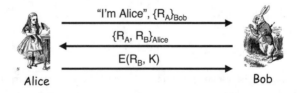

Does this protocol provide for plausible deniability (see Problem 12)? If so, why? If not, slightly modify the protocol so that it does, while still providing mutual authentication and a secure session key.

14. Design a mutual authentication protocol that employs digital signatures for authentication and provides plausible deniability (see Problem 12).

15. Is plausible deniability (see Problem 12) a feature or a security flaw? Explain.

16. The following mutual authentication protocol is based on a shared symmetric key K_{AB}.

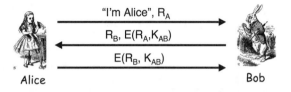

Show that Trudy can attack the protocol to convince Bob that she is Alice, where, as usual, we assume that the cryptography is secure. Modify the protocol to prevent such an attack by Trudy.

17. Consider the following mutual authentication and key establishment protocol, which employs a timestamp T and public key cryptography.

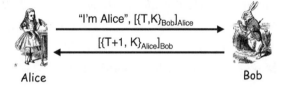

Show that Trudy can attack the protocol to discover the key K where, as usual, we assume that the cryptography is secure. Modify the protocol to prevent such an attack by Trudy.

18. Consider the following mutual authentication and key establishment protocol, which uses a timestamp T and public key cryptography.

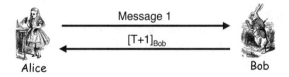

For each of the following cases, explain whether or not the resulting protocol provides an effective means for secure mutual authentication and a secure session key K. Ignore replay attacks based solely on the clock skew.

a. Message 1: $\{[T, K]_{\text{Alice}}\}_{\text{Bob}}$

    b. Message 1: $\{$ "Alice", $[T, K]_{\text{Alice}}\}_{\text{Bob}}$

    c. Message 1: "Alice", $\{[T, K]_{\text{Alice}}\}_{\text{Bob}}$

    d. Message 1: T, "Alice", $\{[K]_{\text{Alice}}\}_{\text{Bob}}$

    e. Message 1: "Alice", $\{[T]_{\text{Alice}}\}_{\text{Bob}}$ and let $K = h(T)$

19. Consider the following three-message mutual authentication and key establishment protocol, which is based on a shared symmetric key K_{AB}.

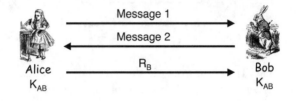

For each of the following cases, briefly explain whether or not the resulting protocol provides an effective means for secure mutual authentication and a secure session key K.

    a. Message 1: $E(\text{"Alice"}, K, R_A, K_{AB})$, Message 2: $R_A,\ E(R_B, K_{AB})$

    b. Message 1: "Alice", $E(K, R_A, K_{AB})$, Message 2: $R_A,\ E(R_B, K)$

    c. Message 1: "Alice", $E(K, R_A, K_{AB})$, Message 2: $R_A,\ E(R_B, K_{AB})$

    d. Message 1: "Alice", R_A, Message 2: $E(K, R_A, R_B, K_{AB})$

20. Consider the following three-message mutual authentication and key establishment protocol, which is based on public key cryptography.

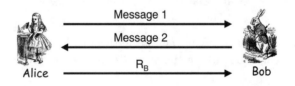

For each of the following cases, briefly explain whether or not the resulting protocol provides an effective means for secure mutual authentication and a secure session key K.

    a. Message 1: $\{$ "Alice", $K, R_A\}_{\text{Bob}}$, Message 2: $R_A,\ R_B$

    b. Message 1: "Alice", $\{K, R_A\}_{\text{Bob}}$, Message 2: $R_A,\ \{R_B\}_{\text{Alice}}$

    c. Message 1: "Alice", $\{K\}_{\text{Bob}}, [R_A]_{\text{Alice}}$, Message 2: $R_A,\ [R_B]_{\text{Bob}}$

    d. Message 1: R_A, $\{$ "Alice", $K\}_{\text{Bob}}$, Message 2: $[R_A]_{\text{Bob}},\ \{R_B\}_{\text{Alice}}$

    e. Message 1: $\{$ "Alice", $K, R_A, R_B\}_{\text{Bob}}$, Message 2: $R_A,\ \{R_B\}_{\text{Alice}}$

21. Consider the following mutual authentication and key establishment protocol (it may be instructive to compare this protocol to the protocol in Figure 9.26).

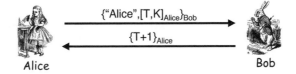

{"Alice",[T,K]$_{Alice}$}$_{Bob}$

{T+1}$_{Alice}$

Alice   Bob

Suppose that Trudy pretends to be Bob. Further, suppose that Trudy can guess the value of T to within 5 minutes, and the resolution of T is to the nearest millisecond.

   a. What is the probability that Trudy can send a correct response in message two, causing Alice to erroneously authenticate Trudy as Bob?

   b. Give two distinct modifications to the protocol, each of which make Trudy's attack more difficult, if not impossible.

22. Consider the following mutual authentication and key establishment protocol, where the session key is given by $K = g^{ab} \bmod p$.

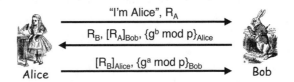

"I'm Alice", R$_A$

R$_B$, [R$_A$]$_{Bob}$, {g^b mod p}$_{Alice}$

[R$_B$]$_{Alice}$, {g^a mod p}$_{Bob}$

Alice   Bob

Suppose that Alice attempts to initiate a connection with Bob using this protocol.

   a. Show that Trudy can attack the protocol so that both of the following will occur.

      i. Alice and Bob authenticate each other.

      ii. Trudy knows Alice's session key.

      Hint: Consider a man-in-the-middle attack.

   b. Is this attack of any use to Trudy?

23. For each of the following cases, design a mutual authentication and key establishment protocol that uses public key cryptography and minimizes the number of messages.

    a. Use a timestamp to authenticate Alice and a nonce to authenticate Bob.

    b. Use a nonce to authenticate Alice and a timestamp to authenticate Bob.

24. Suppose we replace the third message of the protocol in Figure 9.22 with

$$\{R_B\}_{\text{Bob}}, \quad g^a \bmod p.$$

    a. How can Trudy convince Bob that she is Alice, that is, how can Trudy break the authentication?

    b. Can Trudy convince Bob that she is Alice and also determine the session key that Bob will use?

25. Suppose we replace the second message of the protocol in Figure 9.22 with

$$R_B, \ [R_A]_{\text{Bob}}, \quad g^b \bmod p,$$

and we replace the third message with

$$[R_B]_{\text{Alice}}, \quad g^a \bmod p.$$

    a. Can Trudy convince Bob that she is Alice, that is, can Trudy break the authentication?

    b. Can Trudy determine the session key that Alice and Bob will use?

26. In the text, it is claimed that the protocol in Figure 9.18 is secure, while the similar protocol in Figure 9.24 is not. Why does the attack on the latter protocol not succeed against the former?

27. A timestamp-based protocol may be subject to a replay attack, provided that Trudy can act within the clock skew. Reducing the acceptable clock skew might make the attack more difficult, but it will not prevent the attack unless the skew is zero, which is impractical. Assuming a non-zero clock skew, what can Bob, the server, do to prevent attacks based on the clock skew?

28. Modify the identify friend or foe (IFF) protocol discussed at the beginning of the chapter so that it's no longer susceptible to the MiG-in-the-middle attack.

29. Consider the authentication protocol below, which is based on knowledge of a shared 4-digit PIN number. Here, $K_{\text{PIN}} = h(\text{PIN}, R_A, R_B)$.

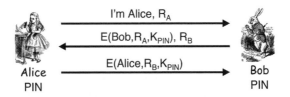

a. Suppose that Trudy passively observes one iteration of the protocol. Can she determine the 4-digit PIN number? Justify your answer.

b. Suppose that the PIN number is replaced by a 256-bit shared symmetric key. Is the protocol secure? Why or why not?

30. Consider the authentication protocol below, which is based on knowledge of a shared 4-digit PIN number. Here, $K_{PIN} = h(PIN)$.

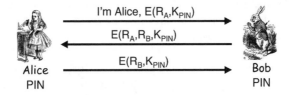

Suppose that Trudy passively observes one iteration of the protocol. Can she then determine the 4-digit PIN? Justify your answer.

31. Consider the authentication protocol below, which is based on knowledge of a shared 4-digit PIN number and uses Diffie-Hellman. Here, $K_{PIN} = h(PIN)$ and $K = g^{ab} \bmod p$.

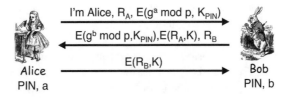

a. Suppose that Trudy passively observes one iteration of the protocol. Can she then determine the 4-digit PIN number? Justify your answer.

b. Suppose that Trudy can actively attack the protocol. Can she determine the 4-digit PIN? Explain.

32. Describe a way to provide perfect forward secrecy that does not use Diffie-Hellman.

33. Can you achieve an effect similar to perfect forward secrecy (as described in this chapter) using only symmetric key cryptography? If so, give such a protocol and, if not, why not?

34. Design a zero knowledge protocol analogy that uses Bob's Cave and only requires one iteration for Bob to determine with certainty whether or not Alice knows the secret phrase.

35. The analogy between Bob's Cave and the Fiat-Shamir protocol is not entirely accurate. In the Fiat-Shamir protocol, Bob knows which value of e will force Alice to use the secret value S, assuming Alice follows the protocol. That is, if Bob chooses $e = 1$, then Alice must use the secret value S to construct the correct response in message three, but if Bob chooses $e = 0$, then Alice does not use S. As noted in the text, Bob must choose e at random to prevent Trudy from breaking the protocol. In the Bob's Cave analogy, Bob does not know whether Alice was required to use the secret phrase or not (again, assuming that Alice follows the protocol).

   a. Modify the cave analogy so that Bob knows whether Alice used the secret phrase or not, assuming that Bob is not allowed to see which side Alice actually chooses. Bob's New-and-Improved Cave protocol must still resist an attack by someone who does not know the secret phrase.

   b. Does your new cave analogy differ from the Fiat-Shamir protocol in any significant way?

36. Suppose that in the Fiat-Shamir protocol in Figure 9.32 we have $N = 63$ and $v = 43$. Recall that Bob accepts an iteration of the protocol if he verifies that $y^2 = x \cdot v^e \bmod N$.

   a. In the first iteration of the protocol, Alice sends $x = 37$ in message one, Bob sends $e = 1$ in message two, and Alice sends $y = 4$ in message three. Does Bob accept this iteration of the protocol? Why or why not?

   b. In the second iteration of the protocol, Alice sends $x = 37$, Bob sends $e = 0$, and Alice sends $y = 10$. Does Bob accept this iteration of the protocol? Why or why not?

   c. Find Alice's secret value S. Hint: $10^{-1} = 19 \bmod 63$.

37. Suppose that in the Fiat-Shamir protocol in Figure 9.32 we have $N = 77$ and $v = 53$.

a. Suppose that Alice sends $x = 15$ in message one, Bob sends $e = 1$ in message two, and Alice sends $y = 5$ in message three. Show that Bob accepts this iteration of the protocol.

b. Suppose Trudy knows in advance that Bob will select $e = 1$ in message two. If Trudy selects $r = 10$, what can she send for x in message one and y in message three so that Bob accepts this iteration of the protocol? Using your answer, show that Bob actually accepts this iteration. Hint: $53^{-1} = 16 \bmod 77$.

38. Suppose that in the Fiat-Shamir protocol in Figure 9.32 we have $N = 55$ and Alice's secret is $S = 9$.

   a. What is v?

   b. If Alice chooses $r = 10$, what does Alice send in the first message?

   c. Suppose Alice chooses $r = 10$ and Bob sends $e = 0$ in message two. What does Alice send in the third message?

   d. Suppose Alice chooses $r = 10$ and Bob sends $e = 1$ in message two. What does Alice send in the third message?

39. Consider the Fiat-Shamir protocol in Figure 9.32. Suppose that the public values are $N = 55$ and $v = 5$. Suppose Alice sends $x = 4$ in the first message, Bob sends $e = 1$ in the second message, and Alice sends $y = 30$ in message three. Show that Bob will verify Alice's response in this case. Can you find Alice's secret S?

40. In the Fiat-Shamir protocol in Figure 9.32, suppose that Alice gets lazy and she decides to use the same "random" r for each iteration.

   a. Show that Bob can determine Alice's secret S.

   b. Why is this a security concern?

41. Suppose that in the Fiat-Shamir protocol, as illustrated in Figure 9.32, we have $N = 27{,}331$ and $v = 7339$.

   a. In the first iteration, Alice sends $x = 21{,}684$ in message one, Bob sends $e = 0$ in message two, and Alice sends $y = 657$ in the third message. Show that Bob verifies Alice's response in this case.

   b. At the next iteration, Alice again sends $x = 21{,}684$ in message one, but Bob sends $e = 1$ in message two, and Alice responds with $y = 26{,}938$ in message three. Show that Bob again verifies Alice's response.

   c. Determine Alice's secret S. Hint: $657^{-1} = 208 \bmod 27{,}331$.

Chapter 10

Real-World Security Protocols

> The wire protocol guys don't worry about security because
> that's really a network protocol problem. The network protocol
> guys don't worry about it because, really, it's an application problem.
> The application guys don't worry about it because,
> after all, they can just use the IP address and trust the network.
> — Marcus J. Ranum

> In the real world, nothing happens at the right place at the right time.
> It is the job of journalists and historians to correct that.
> — Mark Twain

10.1   Introduction

In this chapter, we'll discuss several widely used real-world security protocols. First on the agenda is the Secure Shell, or SSH, which is used for a variety of purposes. Next, we consider the Secure Socket Layer, or SSL, which is currently the most widely used security protocol for Internet transactions. The third protocol that we'll consider in detail is IPSec, which is a complex protocol with some significant security issues. Then we will discuss Kerberos, a popular authentication protocol based on symmetric key cryptography and timestamps.

We conclude the chapter with two wireless protocols, WEP and GSM. WEP is a seriously flawed security protocols, and we'll consider several well-known attacks. The final protocol we'll cover is GSM, which is used to secure mobile communications. The GSM protocol is provides an interesting case study due to the large number and wide variety of known attacks.

10.2   SSH

The Secure Shell, SSH, creates a 'secure tunnel which can be used to secure otherwise insecure commands. For example, in UNIX, the `rlogin` command is used for a remote login, that is, to log into a remote machine over a network. Such a login typically requires a password and `rlogin` simply sends the password in the clear, which might be observed by a snooping Trudy. By first establishing an SSH session, any inherently insecure command such as `rlogin` will be secure. That is, an SSH session provides confidentiality and integrity protection, thereby eliminating Trudy's ability to obtain passwords and other confidential information that would otherwise be sent unprotected.

SSH authentication can be based on public keys, digital certificates, or passwords. Here, we give a slightly simplified version of SSH using digital certificates.[1] The other authentication options are covered in various homework problems at the end of this chapter.

SSH is illustrated in Figure 10.1, using the following notation:

$$\text{certificate}_A = \text{Alice's certificate}$$
$$\text{certificate}_B = \text{Bob's certificate}$$
$$CP = \text{crypto proposed}$$
$$CS = \text{crypto selected}$$
$$H = h(\text{Alice}, \text{Bob}, CP, CS, R_A, R_B, g^a \bmod p, g^b \bmod p, g^{ab} \bmod p)$$
$$S_B = [H]_{\text{Bob}}$$
$$K = g^{ab} \bmod p$$
$$S_A = [H, \text{Alice}, \text{certificate}_A]_{\text{Alice}}$$

As usual, h is a cryptographic hash function.

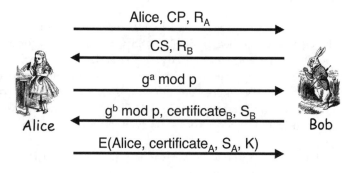

Figure 10.1: Simplified SSH

---

[1]In our simplified version, a few parameters have been omitted and a couple of bookkeeping messages have been eliminated.

10.4   IPSec

Figure 10.7 illustrates the primary logical difference between SSL and IPSec, that is, one lives at the socket layer (SSL), while the other resides at the network layer (IPSec). As mentioned above, the major advantage of IPSec is that it's essentially transparent to applications. However, IPSec is a complex protocol, which can perhaps best be described as over-engineered.

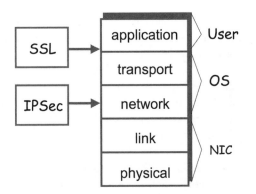

Figure 10.7: IPSec

IPSec has many dubious features, which makes implementation difficult. Also, IPSec has some flaws, probably as a direct result of its complexity. In addition, there are interoperability issues, due to the complexity of the IPSec specification, which seems to run contrary to the point of having a standard. Another complicating factor is that the IPSec specification is split into three pieces, to be found in RFC 2407 [237], RFC 2408 [197], and RFC 2409 [140], and these RFCs were written by disjoint sets of authors using different terminology.

The two main parts to IPSec are

- The Internet Key Exchange, or IKE, which provides for mutual authentication and a session key. There are two phases of IKE, which are analogous to SSL sessions and connections.

- The Encapsulating Security Payload and Authentication Header, or ESP/AH, which together make up the second part of IPSec. ESP[5] provides encryption and integrity protection to IP packets, whereas AH provides integrity only.

Technically, IKE is a standalone protocol that could live a life separate from ESP/AH. However, since IKE's only application in the real world seems to

---

[5]Contrary to what you are thinking, this protocol cannot read your mind.

be in conjunction with IPSec, we lump them together under the name IPSec. The comment about IPSec being over-engineered applies primarily to IKE. The developers of IKE apparently thought they were creating the Swiss army knife of security protocols—a protocol that would be used to solve every conceivable authentication problem. This explains the multitude of options and features built into IKE. However, since IKE is only used with IPSec, any features or options that are not directly relevant to IPSec are simply extraneous.

First, we'll consider IKE, then ESP/AH. IKE, the more complex of the two, consists of two phases—cleverly called Phase 1 and Phase 2. Phase 1 is the more complex of the two. In Phase 1, a so-called IKE security association, or IKE-SA, is established, while in Phase 2, an IPSec security association, IPSec-SA, is established. Phase 1 corresponds to an SSL session, whereas Phase 2 is comparable to an SSL connection. In IKE, both Phase 1 and Phase 2 must occur before we can do ESP/AH.

Recall that SSL connections serve a specific and useful purpose—they make SSL more efficient when HTTP 1.0 is used. But, unlike SSL, in IPSec there is no obvious need for two phases. And if multiple Phase 2s do not occur (and they typically do not), then it would be more efficient to just require Phase 1 with no Phase 2. However, this is not an option. Apparently, the developers of IKE believed that their protocol was so self-evidently wonderful that users would want to do multiple Phase 2s (one for IPSec, another for something else, another for some other something else, and so on). This is our first example of over-engineering in IPSec, and it won't be the last.

In IKE Phase 1, there are four different key options:

- Public key encryption (original version)

- Public key encryption (improved version)

- Digital signature

- Symmetric key

For each of these key options there is a main mode and an aggressive mode. As a result, there are a staggering eight different versions of IKE Phase 1. Do you need any more evidence that IPSec is over-engineered?

You may be wondering why there are public key encryption and digital signature options in Phase 1. Surprisingly, the answer is not over-engineering. Alice always knows her own private key, but she may not know Bob's public key. With the signature version of IKE Phase 1, Alice does not need to have Bob's public key in hand to start the protocol. In any protocol that uses public key crypto, Alice will need Bob's public key to complete the protocol, but in the signature mode, she can simultaneously begin the protocol and search for Bob's public key. In contrast, in the public key encryption modes,

Alice needs Bob's public key immediately, so she must first find Bob's key before she can begin the protocol. So, there could be an efficiency gain with the signature option.

We'll discuss six of the eight Phase 1 variants, namely, digital signatures (main and aggressive modes), symmetric key (main and aggressive modes), and public key encryption (main and aggressive). We'll consider the original version of public key encryption, since it's slightly simpler, although less efficient, than the improved version.

Each of the Phase 1 variants use an ephemeral Diffie-Hellman key exchange to establish a session key. The benefit of this approach is that it provides perfect forward secrecy (PFS). For each of the variants we discuss, we'll use the following Diffie-Hellman notation. Let a be Alice's (ephemeral) Diffie-Hellman exponent and let b be Bob's (ephemeral) Diffie-Hellman exponent. Let g be the generator and p the prime. Recall that p and g are public.

10.4.1 IKE Phase 1: Digital Signature

The first Phase 1 variant that we'll consider is digital signature, main mode. This six message protocol is illustrated in Figure 10.8, where

$$CP = \text{crypto proposed}$$
$$CS = \text{crypto selected}$$
$$IC = \text{initiator cookie}$$
$$RC = \text{responder cookie}$$
$$K = h(\text{IC}, \text{RC}, g^{ab} \bmod p, R_A, R_B)$$
$$\text{SKEYID} = h(R_A, R_B, g^{ab} \bmod p)$$
$$\text{proof}_A = [h(\text{SKEYID}, g^a \bmod p, g^b \bmod p, \text{IC}, \text{RC}, \text{CP}, \text{"Alice"})]_{\text{Alice}}$$

Here, h is a hash function and proof_B is analogous to proof_A.

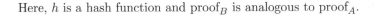

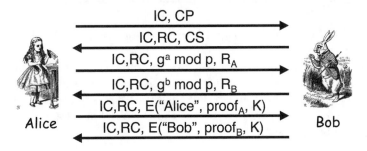

Figure 10.8: Digital Signature, Main Mode

Let's briefly consider each of the six messages that appear in Figure 10.8. In the first message, Alice provides information on the ciphers that she supports and other crypto related information, along with a so-called cookie.[6] In message two, Bob selects from Alice's crypto proposal and sends the cookies, which serve as an identifier for the remainder of the messages in the protocol. The third message includes a nonce and Alice's Diffie-Hellman value. Bob responds similarly in message four, providing a nonce and his Diffie-Hellman value. In the final two messages, Alice and Bob authenticate each other using digital signatures.

Recall that an attacker, Trudy, is said to be passive if she can only observe messages sent between Alice and Bob. In contrast, if Trudy is an active attacker, she can also insert, delete, alter, and replay messages. For the protocol in Figure 10.8, a passive attacker cannot discern Alice or Bob's identity. So this protocol provides anonymity, at least with respect to passive attacks. Does this protocol also provide anonymity in the case of an active attack? This question is considered in Problem 27, which means that the answer is not to be found here.

Each key option has a main mode and an aggressive mode. The main modes are supposed to provide anonymity, while the aggressive modes are not. Anonymity comes at a price—aggressive mode only requires three messages, as opposed to six messages for main mode.

The aggressive mode version of the digital signature key option appears in Figure 10.9. Note that there is no attempt to hide the identities of Alice or Bob, which simplifies the protocol considerably. The notation in Figure 10.9 is the same as that used in Figure 10.8.

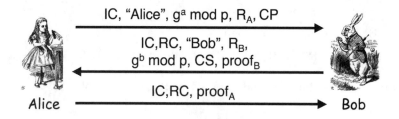

Figure 10.9: Digital Signature, Aggressive Mode

One subtle difference between digital signature main and aggressive modes is that in main mode it is possible to negotiate the values of g and p as part of the "crypto proposed" and "crypto accepted" messages. However, this is not the case in aggressive mode, since the Diffie-Hellman value $g^a \bmod p$ is sent in the first message.

---

[6]Not to be confused with Web cookies or chocolate chip cookies. We have more to say about these IPSec cookies in Section 10.4.4, below.

As per the appropriate RFCs, for each key option main mode MUST be implemented, while aggressive mode SHOULD be implemented. In [162], the authors interpret this to mean that if aggressive mode is not implemented, "you should feel guilty about it."

10.4.2 IKE Phase 1: Symmetric Key

The next version of Phase 1 that we'll consider is the symmetric key option— both main mode and aggressive mode. As above, the main mode is a six-message protocol, where the format is formally the same as in Figure 10.8, above, except that the notation is interpreted as follows.

$$K_{AB} = \text{symmetric key shared in advance}$$
$$K = h(\text{IC}, \text{RC}, g^{ab} \bmod p, R_A, R_B, K_{AB})$$
$$\text{SKEYID} = h(K, g^{ab} \bmod p)$$
$$\text{proof}_A = h(\text{SKEYID}, g^a \bmod p, g^b \bmod p, \text{IC}, \text{RC}, \text{CP}, \text{Alice})$$

Again, the purported advantage of the complex six-message main mode over the corresponding aggressive mode is that main mode is supposed to provide anonymity. But there is a Catch-22 in this main mode. Note that in message five Alice sends her identity, encrypted with key K. But Bob has to use the key K_{AB} to determine K. So Bob has to know to use the key K_{AB} *before* he knows that he's talking to Alice. However, Bob is a busy server who deals with lots of users (Alice, Charlie, Dave, . . .). How can Bob possibly know that he is supposed to use the key he shares with Alice before he knows he's talking to Alice? The answer is that he cannot, at least not based on any information available within the protocol itself.

The developers of IPSec recognized this snafu. And their solution? Bob is to rely on the IP address to determine which key to use. So, Bob must use the IP address of incoming packets to determine who he's talking to before he knows who he's talking to (or something like that. . .). The bottom line is that Alice's IP address acts as her identity.

There are a couple of problems with this approach. First, Alice must have a static IP address—this mode fails if Alice's IP address changes. A more fundamental issue is that the protocol is complex and uses six messages, presumably to hide identities. But the protocol fails to hide identities, unless you consider a static IP address to be secret. So it would seem pointless to use symmetric key main mode instead of the simpler and more efficient aggressive mode, which we describe next.[7]

IPSec symmetric key aggressive mode follows the same format as the digital signature aggressive mode in Figure 10.9, with the key and signature

---

[7]Of course, main mode MUST be implemented, while aggressive mode SHOULD be implemented. Go figure.

computed as in symmetric key main mode. As with the digital signature variant, the main difference from main mode is that aggressive mode does not attempt to hide identities. Since symmetric key main mode also fails to effectively hide Alice's identity, this is not a serious limitation of aggressive mode in this case.

10.4.3   IKE Phase 1: Public Key Encryption

Next, we'll consider the public key encryption version of IKE Phase 1, both main and aggressive modes. We've already seen the digital signature versions. In the main mode of the encryption version, Alice must know Bob's public key in advance and vice versa. Although it would be possible to exchange certificates, that would reveal the identities of Alice and Bob, defeating the primary advantage of main mode. So an assumption here is that Alice and Bob have access to each other's certificates, without sending them over the network.

The public key encryption main mode protocol is given in Figure 10.10, where the notation is as in the previous modes, except

$$K = h(\text{IC}, \text{RC}, g^{ab} \bmod p, R_A, R_B)$$

$$\text{SKEYID} = h(R_A, R_B, g^{ab} \bmod p)$$

$$\text{proof}_A = h(\text{SKEYID}, g^a \bmod p, g^b \bmod p, \text{IC}, \text{RC}, \text{CP}, \text{``Alice''})$$

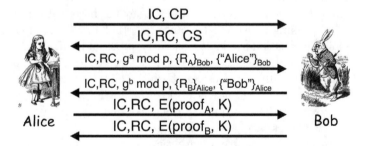

Figure 10.10: Public Key Encryption, Main Mode

Public key encryption, aggressive mode, appears in Figure 10.11, where the notation is similar to main mode. Interestingly, unlike the other aggressive modes, public key encryption aggressive mode allows Alice and Bob to remain anonymous. Since this is the case, is there any possible advantage of main mode over aggressive mode? The answer is yes, but it's a minor issue (see Problem 25 at the end of the chapter).

There is an interesting security quirk that arises in the public key encryption versions—both main and aggressive modes. For simplicity, let's consider

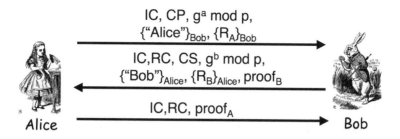

Figure 10.11: Public Key Encryption, Aggressive Mode

aggressive mode. Suppose Trudy generates Diffie-Hellman exponents a and b and random nonces R_A and R_B. Then Trudy can compute all of the remaining quantities that appear in the protocol in Figure 10.11, namely, $g^{ab} \bmod p$, K, SKEYID, proof$_A$, and proof$_B$. The reason that Trudy can do this is because the public keys of Alice and Bob are public.

Why would Trudy go to the trouble of generating all of these values? Once Trudy has done so, she can create an entire conversation that appears to be a valid IPSec transaction between Alice and Bob, as indicated in Figure 10.12. Amazingly, this conversation appears to be valid to any observer, including Alice and/or Bob!

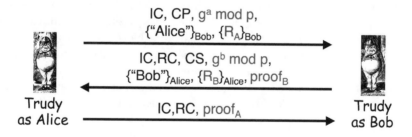

Figure 10.12: Trudy Making Mischief

Note that in Figure 10.12, Trudy is playing the roles of both Alice and Bob. Here, Trudy does not convince Bob that she's Alice, she does not convince Alice that she's Bob, nor does she determine a session key used by Alice and Bob. So, this is a very different kind of attack than we have previously seen. Or maybe it's not an attack at all.

But surely, the fact that Trudy can create a fake conversation that appears to be a legitimate connection between Alice and Bob is a security flaw. Surprisingly, in this mode of IPSec it is considered a security feature, which goes by the name of *plausible deniability*. A protocol that includes plausible deniability allows Alice and Bob to deny that a conversation ever took place, since anyone could have faked the whole thing. In some situations, this could be a desirable feature. On the other hand, in some situations it might be a problem. For example, if Alice makes a purchase from Bob, she could later repudiate it, unless Bob also required a digital signature from Alice.

10.4.4   IPSec Cookies

The cookies IC and RC that appear in the IPSec protocols above are officially known as "anti-clogging tokens" in the relevant RFCs. These IPSec cookies have no relation to Web cookies, which are used to maintain state across HTTP sessions. Instead, the stated purpose of IPSec cookies is to make denial of service, or DoS, attacks more difficult.

Consider TCP SYN flooding, which is a prototypical DoS attack. Each TCP SYN request causes the server to do a little work (create a SEQ number, for example) and to keep some amount of state. That is, the server must remember the so-called half-open connection so that it can complete the connection when the corresponding ACK arrives in the third step of the three-way handshake. It is this keeping of state that an attacker can exploit to create a DoS. If the attacker bombards a server with a large number of SYN packets and never completes the resulting half-open connections, the server will eventually deplete its resources. When this occurs, the server cannot handle legitimate SYN requests and a DoS results.

To reduce the threat of DoS in IPSec, the server Bob would like to remain stateless as much as possible. The IPSec cookies are supposed to help Bob remain stateless. However, they clearly fail to achieve their design goal. In each of the main mode protocols, Bob must remember the crypto proposal, CP, from message one, since it is required in message six when Bob computes proof_B. Consequently, Bob must keep state beginning with the first message. The IPSec cookies therefore offer no significant DoS protection.

10.4.5   IKE Phase 1 Summary

Regardless of which of the eight versions is used, successful completion of IKE Phase 1 results in mutual authentication and a shared session key. This is known an an IKE Security Association (IKE-SA).

IKE Phase 1 is computationally expensive in any of the public key modes, and the main modes also require six messages. Developers of IKE assumed that it would be used for lots of things, not just IPSec (which explains the over-engineering). So they included an inexpensive Phase 2, which must be used after the IKE-SA has been established in Phase 1. That is, a separate Phase 2 is required for each different application that will make use of the IKE-SA. However, if IKE is only used for IPSec (as is the case in practice), the potential efficiency provided by multiple Phase 2s is not realized.

IKE Phase 2 is used to establish a so-called IPSec Security Association, or IPSec-SA. The IKE Phase 1 is more or less equivalent to establishing an SSL session, whereas IKE Phase 2 is more or less equivalent to establishing an SSL connection. Again, the designers of IPSec wanted to make it as flexible as possible, since they assumed it would be used for lots of things other than IPSec. In fact, IKE could conceivably be used for lots of things other than IPSec, however, in practice, it's not.

10.4.6 IKE Phase 2

IKE Phase 2 is mercifully simple—at least in comparison to Phase 1. Before IKE Phase 2 can occur, IKE Phase 1 must be completed, in which case a shared session key K, the IPSec cookies, IC, RC, and the IKE-SA have all been established and are known to Alice and Bob. Given that this is the case, the IKE Phase 2 protocol appears in Figure 10.13, where the following holds true.

- The crypto proposal includes ESP or AH (discussed below). This is where Alice and Bob decide whether to use ESP or AH.

- SA is an identifier for the IKE-SA established in Phase 1.

- The hashes numbered 1, 2, and 3 depend on SKEYID, R_A, R_B, and the IKE SA from Phase 1.

- The keys are derived from KEYMAT $= h(\text{SKEYID}, R_A, R_B, \text{junk})$, where the "junk" is known to all (including an attacker).

- The value of SKEYID depends on the Phase 1 key method.

- Optionally, PFS can be employed, using an ephemeral Diffie-Hellman exchange.

Note that R_A and R_B in Figure 10.13 are not the same as those from IKE Phase 1. As a result, the keys generated in each Phase 2 differ from the Phase 1 key and from each other.

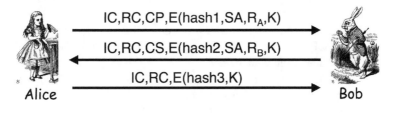

Figure 10.13: IKE Phase 2

After completing IKE Phase 1, we have established an IKE-SA, and after completing IKE Phase 2, we have established an IPSec-SA. After Phase 2, both Alice and Bob have been authenticated and they have a shared session key for use in the current connection.

Recall that in SSL, once we completed mutual authentication and had established a session key, we were done. Since SSL deals with application layer data, we simply encrypt and integrity protect in a standard way. In SSL, the network is transparent to Alice and Bob because SSL lives at the socket layer—which is really part of the application layer. This is one advantage to dealing with application layer data.

In IPSec, protecting the data is not so straightforward. Assuming IPSec authentication succeeds and we establish a session key, then we need to protect IP datagrams. The complication here is that protection must occur at the network layer. But before we discuss this issue in detail, we need to consider IP datagrams from the perspective of IPSec.

10.4.7   IPSec and IP Datagrams

An IP datagram consists of a header and data. The IP header is illustrated in the Appendix in Figure A-5. If the `options` field is empty (as it usually is), then the IP header consists of 20 bytes. For the purposes of IPSec, one important point is that routers must see the destination address in the IP header so that they can route the packet. Most other header fields are also used in conjunction with routing the packet. Since the routers do not have access to the session key, we cannot encrypt the IP header.

A second crucial point is that some of the fields in the IP header change as the packet is forwarded. For example, the TTL field—which contains the number of hops remaining before the packet dies—is decremented by each router that handles the packet. Since the session key is not known to the routers, any header fields that change cannot be integrity protected. In IPSec-speak, the header fields that can change are known as mutable fields.

Next, we look inside an IP datagram. Consider, for example, a Web browsing session. The application layer protocol for such traffic is HTTP, and the transport layer protocol is TCP. In this case, IP encapsulates a TCP packet, which encapsulates an HTTP packet as is illustrated in Figure 10.14. The point here is that, from the perspective of IP (and hence, IPSec), the data includes more than application layer data. In this example, the "data" includes the TCP and HTTP headers, as well as the application layer data. We'll see why this is relevant below.

As previously mentioned, IPSec uses either ESP or AH to protect an IP datagram. Depending on which is selected, an ESP header or an AH header is included in an IPSec-protected datagram. This header tells the recipient to treat this as an ESP or AH packet, not as a standard IP datagram.

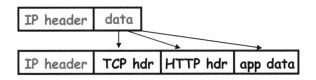

Figure 10.14: IP Datagram

10.4.8 Transport and Tunnel Modes

Independent of whether ESP or AH is used, IPSec employs either *transport mode* or *tunnel mode*. In transport mode, as illustrated in Figure 10.15, the new ESP/AH header is sandwiched between the IP header and the data. Transport mode is more efficient since it adds a minimal amount of additional header information. Note that in transport mode the original IP header remains intact. The downside of transport mode is that a passive attacker can see the headers. So, if Trudy observes an IPSec protected conversation between Alice and Bob where transport mode is used, the headers will reveal that Alice and Bob are communicating.[8]

Transport mode is designed for host-to-host communication, that is, when Alice and Bob are communicating directly with each other using IPSec. This is illustrated in Figure 10.16.

Figure 10.15: IPSec Transport Mode

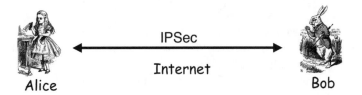

Figure 10.16: IPSec from Host-to-Host

In tunnel mode, as illustrated in Figure 10.17, the entire IP packet is encapsulated in a new IP packet. One advantage of this approach is that the

---

[8]Recall that we cannot encrypt the header.

original IP header is no longer visible to an attacker—assuming the packet is encrypted. However, if Alice and Bob are communicating directly with each other, the new IP header will be the same as the encapsulated IP header, so hiding the original header would be pointless. However, IPSec is often used from firewall to firewall, not from host to host. That is, Alice's firewall and Bob's firewall communicate using IPSec, not Alice and Bob directly. Suppose IPSec is being used from firewall to firewall. Using tunnel mode, the new IP header will only reveal that the packet is being sent between Alice's firewall and Bob's firewall. So, if the packet is encrypted, Trudy would know that Alice's and Bob's firewalls are communicating, but she would not know which specific hosts behind the firewalls are communicating.

Tunnel mode was designed for firewall-to-firewall communication. Again, when tunnel mode is used from firewall to firewall—as illustrated in Figure 10.18—Trudy does not know which hosts are communicating. The disadvantage of tunnel mode is the overhead of an additional IP header.

Figure 10.17: IPSec Tunnel Mode

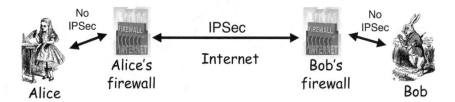

Figure 10.18: IPSec from Firewall to Firewall

Technically, transport mode is not necessary, since we could encapsulate the original IP packet in a new IPSec packet, even in the host-to-host case. For firewall-to-firewall protected traffic, tunnel mode is necessary, as we must preserve the original IP header so that the destination firewall can route the packet to the destination host. But transport mode is more efficient, which makes it preferable when traffic is protected from host to host.

10.4.9 ESP and AH

Once we've decided whether to use transport mode or tunnel mode, then we must (finally) consider the type of protection we actually want to apply to the IP datagrams. The choices are confidentiality, integrity, or both. But we also must consider the protection, if any, to apply to the header. In IPSec, the only choices are AH and ESP. So, what protection options do each of these provide?

AH, the Authentication Header, provides integrity only, that is, AH provides no encryption. The AH integrity protection applies to everything beyond the IP header and some fields of the header. As previously mentioned, not all fields of the IP header can be integrity protected (TTL, for example). AH classifies IP header fields as mutable or immutable, and it applies its integrity protection to all of the immutable fields.

In ESP, the Encapsulating Security Payload, both integrity and confidentiality are required. Both the confidentiality and integrity protection are applied to everything beyond the IP header, that is, the "data" from the perspective of IP. No protection is applied to the IP header

Encryption is required in ESP. However, there is a trick whereby ESP can be used for integrity only. In ESP, Alice and Bob negotiate the cipher that they will use. One of the ciphers that MUST be supported is the NULL cipher, described in RFC 2410 [123]. Here are some excerpts from this unusual RFC.

- NULL encryption is a block cipher, the origins of which appear to be lost in antiquity.

- Despite rumors, there is no evidence that NSA suppressed publication of this algorithm.

- Evidence suggests it was developed in Roman times as an exportable version of Caesar's cipher.

- NULL encryption can make use of keys of varying length.

- No IV is required.

- NULL encryption is defined by $\mathrm{Null}(P, K) = P$ for any plaintext P and any key K.

This RFC proves that security people are strange.[9]

In ESP, if the NULL cipher is selected then no encryption is applied, but the data is integrity protected. This case looks suspiciously similar to AH. So, why does AH exist?

There are three reasons given to justify the existence of AH. As previously noted, the IP header can't be encrypted since routers must see the header to route packets. But AH does provide integrity protection to the immutable

---

[9]As if you didn't already know that.

fields in the IP header, whereas ESP provides no protection to the header. That is, AH provides slightly more integrity protection than ESP/NULL.

A second reason for the existence of AH is that ESP encrypts everything beyond the IP header, provided a non-NULL cipher is selected. If ESP is used and the packet is encrypted, a firewall can't look inside the packet to, for example, examine the TCP header. Perhaps surprisingly, ESP with NULL encryption doesn't solve this problem. When the firewall sees the ESP header, it will know that ESP is being used. However, the header does not tell the firewall that the NULL cipher is used—that was negotiated between Alice and Bob and is not included in the header. So, when a firewall sees that ESP is used, it has no way to know whether the TCP header is encrypted or not. In contrast, when a firewall sees that AH is used, it knows that nothing is encrypted.

Neither of these reasons for the existence of AH is particularly persuasive. The designers of AH/ESP could have made minor modifications to the protocol so that ESP alone could overcome these drawbacks. But there is a more convincing reason given for the existence of AH. At one meeting where the IPSec standard was being developed, "someone from Microsoft gave an impassioned speech about how AH was useless ..." and "... everyone in the room looked around and said, Hmm. He's right, and we hate AH also, but if it annoys Microsoft let's leave it in since we hate Microsoft more than we hate AH" [162]. So now you know the rest of the story.

10.5   Kerberos

In Greek mythology, Kerberos is a three-headed dog that guards the entrance to Hades.[10] In security, Kerberos is a popular authentication protocol that uses symmetric key cryptography and timestamps. Kerberos originated at MIT and is based on work by Needham and Schroeder [217]. Whereas SSL and IPSec are designed for the Internet, Kerberos is designed for a smaller scale, such as on a local area network (LAN) or within a corporation.

Suppose we have N users, where each pair needs to be able to authenticate each other. If our authentication protocol is based on public key cryptography, then each user requires a public-private key pair and, consequently, N key pairs are needed. On the other hand, if our authentication protocol is based on symmetric keys, it would appear that each pair of users must share a symmetric key, in which case $N(N-1)/2 \approx N^2$ keys are required. Consequently, authentication based on symmetric keys doesn't scale. However, by relying on a Trusted Third Party (TTP), Kerberos only requires N symmetric keys for N users. Users do not share keys with each other. Instead each user shares one key with the KDC, that is, Alice and the KDC share K_A, Bob

---

[10]The authors of [162] ask, "Wouldn't it make more sense to guard the exit?"

and the KDC share K_B, Carol and the KDC share K_C, and so on. Then, the KDC acts as a go-between that enables any pair of users to communicate securely with each other. The bottom line is that Kerberos uses symmetric keys in a way that does scale.

The Kerberos TTP is a security critical component that must be protected from attack. This is certainly a security issue, but in contrast to a system that uses public keys, no public key infrastructure (PKI) is required.[11] In essence, the Kerberos TTP plays a similar role as a certificate authority in a public key system.

The Kerberos TTP is known as the *key distribution center*, or KDC.[12] Since the KDC acts as a TTP, if it's compromised, the security of the entire system is compromised.

As noted above, the KDC shares a symmetric key K_A with user Alice, and it shares a symmetric key K_B with Bob, and so on. The KDC also has a master key K_{KDC}, which is known only to the KDC. Although it might seem senseless to have a key that only the KDC knows, we'll see that this key plays a critical role. In particular, the key K_{KDC} allows the KDC to remain stateless, which eliminates most denial of service attacks. A stateless KDC is a major security feature of Kerberos.

Kerberos is used for authentication and to establish a session key that can subsequently be used for confidentiality and integrity. In principle, any symmetric cipher can be used with Kerberos. However, in practice, it seems the crypto algorithm of choice is the Data Encryption Standard (DES).

In Kerberos-speak, the KDC issues various types of *tickets*. Understanding these tickets is critical to understanding Kerberos. A ticket contains the keys and other information required to access network resource. One special ticket that the KDC issues is the all-important *ticket-granting ticket*, or TGT. A TGT, which is issued when a user initially logs into the system, acts as the user's credentials. The TGT is then used to obtain (ordinary) tickets that enable access to network resources. The use of TGTs is crucial to the statelessness of Kerberos.

Each TGT contains a session key, the user ID of the user to whom the TGT is issued, and an expiration time. For simplicity, we'll ignore the expiration time, but it's worth noting that TGTs don't last forever. Every TGT is encrypted with the key K_{KDC}. Recall that only the KDC knows the key K_{KDC}. As a result, a TGT can only be read by the KDC.

Why does the KDC encrypt a user's TGT with a key that only the KDC knows and then send the result to the user? The alternative would be for the KDC to maintain a database of which users are logged in, their session keys, etc. That is, the TGT would have to maintain state. In effect, TGTs

---

[11] As we discussed in Chapter 4, PKI presents a substantial challenge in practice.

[12] The most difficult part about Kerberos is keeping track of all of the acronyms. There are a lot more acronyms to come—we're just getting warmed up.

provides a simple, effective, and secure way to distribute this database to the users. Then when, say, Alice presents her TGT to the KDC, the KDC can decrypt it and, voila, it remembers everything it needs to know about Alice.[13] The role of the TGT will become clear below. For now, just note that TGTs are a clever design feature of Kerberos.

10.5.1 Kerberized Login

To understand Kerberos, let's first consider how a "Kerberized" login works, that is, we'll examine the steps that occur when Alice logs in to a system where Kerberos is used for authentication. As on most systems, Alice first enters her username and password. In Kerberos, Alice's computer then derives the key K_A from Alice's password, where K_A is the key that Alice and the KDC share. Alice's computer uses K_A to obtain Alice's TGT from the KDC. Alice can then use her TGT (i.e., her credentials) to securely access network resources. Once Alice has logged in, all of the security is automatic and takes place behind the scenes, without any additional involvement by Alice.

A Kerberized login is illustrated in Figure 10.19, where the following notation is used.

- The key K_A is derived as $K_A = h(\text{Alice's password})$

- The KDC creates the session key S_A

- Alice's computer uses K_A to obtain S_A and the TGT; then Alice's computer forgets K_A

- $\text{TGT} = E(\text{"Alice"}, S_A; K_{\text{KDC}})$

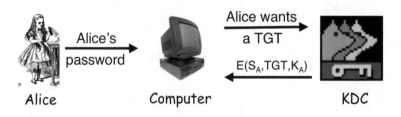

Figure 10.19: Kerberized Login

---

[13]Your hapless author's ill-fated startup company had a similar situation, i.e., a database of customer security-related information that had to be maintained (assuming the company had ever actually had any customers, that is). Instead of creating a security-critical database, the company chose to encrypt each user's information with a key known only to the company, then distribute this encrypted data to the appropriate user. Users then had to present this encrypted data before they could access any security-related features of the system. This is essentially the same trick used in Kerberos TGTs.

One major advantage to the Kerberized login is that the entire security process (beyond the password entry) is transparent to Alice. The major disadvantage is that the reliance on the security of the KDC is total.

10.5.2 Kerberos Ticket

Once Alice's computer receives its TGT, it can then use the TGT to request access to network resources. For example, suppose that Alice wants to talk to Bob. Then Alice's computer presents its TGT to the KDC, along with an authenticator. The authenticator is an encrypted timestamp that serves to avoid a replay. After the KDC verifies Alice's authenticator, it responds with a "ticket to Bob." Alice's computer then uses this ticket to Bob to securely communicate directly with Bob's computer. Alice's acquisition of the ticket to Bob is illustrated in Figure 10.20, where the following notation is used.

$$\text{REQUEST} = (\text{TGT}, \text{authenticator})$$
$$\text{authenticator} = E(\text{timestamp}, S_A)$$
$$\text{REPLY} = E(\text{``Bob''}, K_{AB}, \text{ticket to Bob}; S_A)$$
$$\text{ticket to Bob} = E(\text{``Alice''}, K_{AB}; K_B)$$

In Figure 10.20, the KDC obtains the key S_A from the TGT and uses this key to verify the timestamp. Also, the key K_{AB} is the session key that Alice and Bob will use for their session.

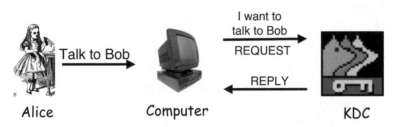

Figure 10.20: Alice Gets Ticket to Bob

Once Alice has obtained the "ticket to Bob," she can then securely communicate with Bob. This process is illustrated in Figure 10.21, where the ticket to Bob is as above and

$$\text{authenticator} = E(\text{timestamp}, K_{AB}).$$

Note that Bob decrypts "ticket to Bob" with his key K_B to obtain K_{AB}, which he then uses to verify the timestamp. The key K_{AB} is also used to protect the confidentiality and integrity of the subsequent conversation between Alice and Bob.

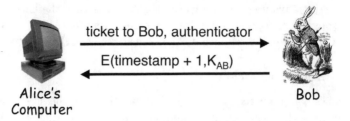

Figure 10.21: Alice Contacts Bob

Since timestamps are used for replay prevention, Kerberos minimizes the number of messages that must be sent. As we mentioned in the previous chapter, the primary drawback to using timestamps is that time becomes a security-critical parameter. Another issue with timestamps is that we can't expect all clocks to be perfectly synchronized and therefore some clock skew must be tolerated. In Kerberos, this clock skew is by default set to five minutes, which seems like an eternity in a networked world.

10.5.3   Kerberos Security

Recall that, when Alice logs in, the KDC sends $E(S_A, \text{TGT}; K_A)$ to Alice, where $\text{TGT} = E(\text{``Alice''}, S_A; K_{\text{KDC}})$. Since the TGT is encrypted with the key K_{KDC}, why is the TGT encrypted again with the key K_A? The answer is that this is a minor flaw in Kerberos, since it's extra work that provides no additional security. If the key K_{KDC} is compromised, the entire security of the system is broken, so there is no added benefit to encrypting the TGT again after it's already encrypted with K_{KDC}.

Notice that, in Figure 10.20, Alice remains anonymous in the REQUEST. This is a nice security feature that is a side benefit of the fact that the TGT is encrypted with the key K_{KDC}. That is, the KDC does not need to know who is making the REQUEST before it can decrypt the TGT, since all TGTs are encrypted with K_{KDC}. Anonymity with symmetric keys can be difficult, as we saw with the IPSec symmetric key main mode. But, in this part of Kerberos, anonymity is easy.

In the Kerberos example above, why is "ticket to Bob" sent to Alice, when Alice simply forwards it on to Bob? Apparently, it would be more efficient to have the KDC send the ticket directly to Bob, and the designers of Kerberos were certainly concerned with efficiency (e.g., they use timestamps instead of nonces). However, if the ticket to Bob arrives at Bob before Alice initiates contact, then Bob would have to remember the key K_{AB} until it's needed. That is, Bob would need to maintain state. Statelessness is an important feature of Kerberos.

Finally, how does Kerberos prevent replay attacks? Replay prevention relies on the timestamps that appear in the authenticators. But there is still an issue of replay within the clock skew. To prevent such replay attacks, the KDC would need to remember all timestamps received within the clock skew interval. However, most Kerberos implementations apparently don't bother to do this [162].

Before departing the realm of Kerberos, we consider a design alternative. Suppose we have the KDC remember session keys instead of putting these in the TGT. This design would eliminate the need for TGTs. But it would also require the KDC to maintain state, and a stateless KDC is one of the most impressive design features in Kerberos.

10.6 WEP

Wired Equivalent Privacy, or WEP, is a security protocol that was designed to make a wireless local area network (LAN) as secure as a wired LAN. By any measure, WEP is a seriously flawed protocol. As Tanenbaum so aptly puts it [298]:

> The 802.11 standard prescribes a data link-level security protocol called WEP (Wired Equivalent Privacy), which is designed to make the security of a wireless LAN as good as that of a wired LAN. Since the default for a wired LAN is no security at all, this goal is easy to achieve, and WEP achieves it as we shall see.

10.6.1 WEP Authentication

In WEP, a wireless access point shares a single symmetric key with all users. While it is not ideal to share one key among many users, it certainly does simplify things for the access point. In any case, the actual WEP authentication protocol is a simple challenge-response, as illustrated in Figure 10.22, where Bob is the access point, Alice is a user, and K is the shared symmetric key.

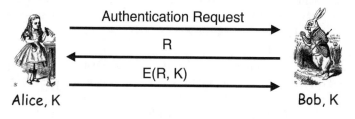

Figure 10.22: WEP Authentication

10.6.2   WEP Encryption

Once Alice has been authenticated, packets are encrypted using the RC4 stream cipher (see Section 3.2.2 for details on the RC4 algorithm), as illustrated in Figure 10.23. Each packet is encrypted with a key $K_{IV} = (IV, K)$, where IV is a 3-byte initialization vector that is sent in the clear with the packet, and K is the same key used for authentication. The goal here is to encrypt packets with distinct keys, since reuse of the key would be a bad idea (see Problem 36). Note that, for each packet, Trudy knows the 3-byte IV, but she does not know K. So the encryption key varies and it's not known by Trudy.

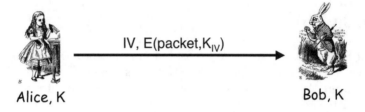

IV, E(packet,K_{IV})

Alice, K   Bob, K

Figure 10.23: WEP Encryption

Since the IV is only three bytes long, and the key K seldom changes, the encryption key $K_{IV} = (IV, K)$ will repeat often (see Problems 37). Furthermore, whenever the key K_{IV} repeats, Trudy will know it, since the IV is visible (assuming K has not changed). RC4 is a stream cipher, so a repeated key implies reuse of the keystream, which is a serious problem. Further repeats of the same IV make Trudy's job even easier.

The number of repeated encryption keys could be reduced if K was changed regularly. Unfortunately, the long-term key K seldom changes since, in WEP, such a change is a manual process and the access point and all hosts must update their keys. That is, there is no key update procedure built into WEP.

The bottom line is that, whenever Trudy sees a repeated IV, she can safely assume the same keystream was used. Since the IV is only 24 bits, repeats will occur relatively often. And, since a stream cipher is used, a repeated keystream is at least as bad as reuse of a one-time pad.

In addition to this small-IV problem, there is another distinct cryptanalytic attack on WEP encryption. While RC4 is considered a strong cipher when used correctly, there is a practical attack that can be used to recover the RC4 key from WEP ciphertext. This clever attack, which can be considered a type of related key attack, is due to Fluhrer, Mantin, and Shamir [112]. This attack is discussed in detail in Section 6.3 of Chapter 6, or see [284] for more information.

10.6.3 WEP Non-Integrity

WEP has numerous security problems, but one of the most egregious is that it uses a cyclic redundancy check (CRC) for "integrity" protection. Recall that a cryptographic integrity check is supposed to detect malicious tampering with the data—not just transmission errors. While a CRC is a good error detection method, it is useless for cryptographic integrity, since an intelligent adversary can alter the data and, simultaneously, the CRC value so that the integrity check is passed. This is precisely the attack that a true cryptographic integrity check, such as a MAC, HMAC, or digital signature, will prevent.

This integrity problem is made worse by the fact that the data is encrypted with a stream cipher. Because a stream cipher is used, WEP encryption is linear, which allows Trudy to make changes directly to the ciphertext and change the corresponding CRC value so that the receiver will not detect the tampering. That is, Trudy does not need know the key or plaintext to make undetectable changes to the data. Under this scenario, Trudy won't know what changes she has made, but the point is that the data can be corrupted in a way that neither Alice nor Bob can detect.

The problems only get worse if Trudy should happen to know some of the plaintext. For example, suppose that Trudy knows the destination IP address of a given WEP-encrypted packet. Then without any knowledge of the key, Trudy can change the destination IP address to an IP address of her choosing (for example, her own IP address), and change the CRC integrity check so that her tampering will go undetected. Since WEP traffic is only encrypted from the host to the wireless access point (and vice versa), when the altered packet arrives at the access point, it will be decrypted and forwarded to Trudy's preferred IP address. From the perspective of a lazy cryptanalyst, it doesn't get any better than this. Again, this attack is made possible by the lack of any real integrity check. The bottom line is that the WEP "integrity check" provides no cryptographic integrity whatsoever.

10.6.4 Other WEP Issues

There are many more WEP security vulnerabilities. For example, if Trudy can send a message over the wireless link and intercept the ciphertext, then she will know the plaintext and the corresponding ciphertext, which enables her to immediately recover the keystream. This same keystream will be used to encrypt any message that uses the same IV, provided the long-term key has not changed (which, as pointed out above, it seldom does).

Would Trudy ever know the plaintext of an encrypted message sent over the wireless link? Perhaps Trudy could send an email message to Alice and ask her to forward it to another person. If Alice does so, then Trudy could intercepted the ciphertext message corresponding to the known plaintext.

Another issue is that, by default, a WEP access point broadcasts its SSID (the Service Set Identifier), which acts as its ID. The client must use the SSID when authenticating to the access point. One security feature of WEP makes it possible to configure the access point so that it does not broadcast the SSID, in which case the SSID acts something like a password that users must know to authenticate to the access point. However, users send the SSID in the clear when contacting the access point, and Trudy only needs to intercept one such packet to discover the SSID "password." Even worse, there are tools that will force WEP clients to de-authenticate, in which case the clients will then automatically attempt to re-authenticate, in the process, sending the SSID in the clear. Consequently, as long as there is at least one active user, it's a fairly simple process for Trudy to obtain the SSID.

10.6.5 WEP: The Bottom Line

It's difficult—if not impossible—to view WEP as anything but a security disaster. However, in spite of all of its multiple security problems, in some circumstances it may be possible to make WEP moderately secure in practice. Ironically, this has more to do with the inherent insecurity of WEP than with any inherent security of WEP. Suppose that you configure your WEP access points so that it encrypts the data, it does not broadcast its SSID, and you use access control (i.e., only machines with specified MAC addresses are allowed to use the access point). Then an attacker must expend some effort to gain access—at a minimum, Trudy must break the encryption, spoof her MAC address, and probably force users to de-authenticate so that she can obtain the SSID. While there are tools to help with all of these tasks, it would likely be much simpler for Trudy to find an unprotected WEP network. Like most people, Trudy generally chooses the path of least resistance. Of course, if Trudy has reason to specifically target your WEP installation (as opposed to simply wanting free network access), you will be vulnerable as long as you rely on WEP.

Finally, we note that there are more secure alternatives to WEP. For example, Wi-Fi Protected Access (WPA) is significantly stronger, but it was designed to use the same hardware as WEP, so some security compromises were necessary. A few attacks on WPA are known but, as a practical matter, it seems to be secure. There is also a WPA2 which, in principle, is somewhat stronger than WPA, but it requires more powerful hardware. As with WPA, there are some claimed attacks on WPA2, but these also appear to be of little practical significance. Today, WEP can be broken in minutes whereas the only serious threats against WPA and WPA2 are password cracking attacks. If reasonably strong passwords are chosen, WPA and WPA2 both would be considered practically secure, by any conceivable definition. In any case, both WPA and WPA2 are vast improvements over WEP [325].

10.7 GSM

To date, many wireless protocols, such as WEP, have a poor track record with respect to security [17, 38, 93]. In this section we'll discuss the security of GSM cell phones. GSM illustrates some of the unique security problems that arise in a wireless environment. It's also an excellent example of how mistakes at the design phase are extremely difficult to correct later. But before we delve into to GSM security, we need some background information on the development of cell phone technology.

Back in the computing stone age (prior to the 1980s, that is) cell phones were expensive, completely insecure, and as large as a brick. These *first-generation* cell phones were analog, not digital, and there were few standards and little or no thought was given to security.

The biggest security issue with early cell phones was their susceptibility to *cloning*. These cell phones would send their identity in the clear when a phone call was placed, and this identity was used to determine who to bill for the phone call. Since the ID was sent over a wireless media, it could easily be captured and then used to make a copy or clone, of the phone. This allowed the bad guys to make free phone calls, which did not please cellular phone companies, who ultimately had to bear the cost. Cell phone cloning became a big business, with fake base stations created simply to harvest IDs [14].

Into this chaotic environment came GSM, which began in 1982 as Groupe Spéciale Mobile, but in 1986 it was formally rechristened as Global System for Mobile Communications.[14] The founding of GSM marks the official beginning of *second-generation* cell phone technology [142]. We'll have much more to say about GSM security below.

Recently, *third-generation* cell phones have become popular. The 3rd Generation Partnership Project, or 3GPP [1], is the trade group behind 3G phones. We'll briefly mention the security architecture promoted by the 3GPP after we complete our survey of GSM security.

10.7.1 GSM Architecture

The general architecture of GSM is illustrated in Figure 10.24, where the following terminology is used.

- The *mobile* is the cell phone.

- The *air interface* is where the wireless transmission from the cell phone to a base station occurs.

- The *visited network* typically includes multiple base stations and a *base station controller*, which acts as a hub for connecting the base stations

---

[14]This is a tribute to the universality of three-letter acronyms.

under its control to the rest of the GSM network. The base station controller includes a *visitor location registry*, or VLR, which is used to keep tabs on all mobiles currently active in the VLR's network.

- The *public switched telephone network*, or PSTN, is the ordinary (non-cellular) telephone system. The PSTN is sometimes referred to as "land lines" to distinguish it from the wireless network.

- The *home network* is the network where the mobile is registered. Each mobile is associated with a unique home network. The home network includes a *home location registry*, or HLR, which keeps track of the most recent location of all mobiles listed in the HLR. The *authentication center*, or AuC, maintains the crucial billing information for all mobiles that belong to the corresponding HLR.

We'll discuss these pieces of the GSM puzzle in more detail below.

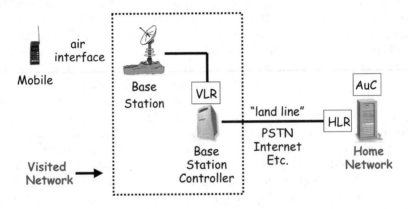

Figure 10.24: GSM Overview

Each GSM mobile phone contains a Subscriber Identity Module, or SIM, which is a tamper-resistant smartcard. The SIM contains an International Mobile Subscriber ID, or IMSI, which, not surprisingly, is used to identify the mobile. The SIM also contains a 128-bit key that is known only by the mobile and its home network. This key is universally know as Ki, so we'll follow the standard notation.

The purpose of using a smartcard for the SIM is to provide an inexpensive form of tamper-resistant hardware. The SIM card also provides two-factor authentication, relying on "something you have" (the mobile containing the SIM) and "something you know" in the form of a four-digit PIN. However, the PIN is usually treated as an annoyance, and it's often not used.

Again, the visited network is the network where the mobile is currently located. A base station is one cell in the cellular system, whereas the base station controller manages a collection of cells. The VLR has information on all mobiles currently visiting the base station controller's territory.

The home network stores a given mobile's crucial information, namely, its IMSI and key Ki. Note that the IMSI and Ki are, in effect, the username and "password" for the mobile when it wants to access the network to make a call. The HLR keeps track of the most recent location of each of it's registered mobiles, while the AuC contains each registered mobile's IMSI and key Ki.

10.7.2 GSM Security Architecture

Now we're ready to take a close look at the GSM security architecture. The primary security goals set forth by the designers of GSM were the following.

- Make GSM as secure as ordinary telephones (the PSTN)

- Prevent cell phone cloning

Note that GSM was not designed to resist an active attack. At the time, active attacks were considered infeasible, since the necessary equipment was costly. However, today the cost of such equipment is little more than that of a good laptop computer, so neglecting active attacks was probably shortsighted. The designers of GSM considered the biggest threats to be insecure billing, corruption, and similar low-tech attacks.

GSM attempts to deal with three security issues: anonymity, authentication, and confidentiality. In GSM, the anonymity is supposed to prevent intercepted traffic from being used to identify the caller. Anonymity is not particularly important to the phone companies, except to the extent that it is important for customer confidence. Anonymity is something users might reasonably expect from non-cellular phone calls.

Authentication, on the other hand, is of paramount importance to phone companies, since correct authentication is necessary for proper billing. The first-generation cloning problems can be viewed as an authentication failure. As with anonymity, confidentiality of calls over the air interface is important to customers, and so, to that extent, it's important to phone companies.

Next, we'll look at GSM's approach to anonymity, authentication, and confidentiality in more detail. Then we'll discuss some of the many security flaws in GSM.

10.7.2.1 Anonymity

GSM provides a very limited form of anonymity. The IMSI is sent in the clear over the air interface at the start of a call. Then a random Temporary Mobile Subscriber ID, or TMSI, is assigned to the caller, and the TMSI is subsequently used to identify the caller. In addition, the TMSI changes frequently. The net effect is that, if an attacker captures the initial part of a call, the caller's anonymity will be compromised. But if the attacker misses the initial part of the call, then the anonymity is, in a practical sense, reasonably well protected. Although this is not a strong form of anonymity, it may be sufficient for real-world situations where an attacker could have difficulty filtering the IMSIs out of a large volume of traffic. It seems that the GSM designers did not take anonymity too seriously.

10.7.2.2   Authentication

From the phone company's perspective, authentication is the most critical aspect of the GSM security architecture. Authenticating the user to the base station is necessary to ensure that the phone company will get paid for the service they provide. In GSM, the caller is authenticated to the base station, but the authentication is not mutual. That is, the GSM designers decided that it was not necessary to verify the identity of the base station. We'll see that this was a significant security oversight.

GSM authentication uses a simple challenge-response mechanism. The caller's IMSI is received by the base station, which then passes it to the caller's home network. Recall that the home network knows the caller's IMSI and key Ki. The home network generates a random challenge, RAND, and computes the "expected response," $XRES = A3(RAND, Ki)$, where A3 is a hash function. Then the pair $(RAND, XRES)$ is sent from the home network to the base station. The base station sends the challenge, RAND, to the mobile. The mobile's response is denoted SRES, where SRES is computed by the mobile as $SRES = A3(RAND, Ki)$. To complete the authentication, the mobile sends SRES to the base station which verifies that $SRES = XRES$. Note that in this authentication protocol, the caller's key Ki never leaves its home network or the mobile. It's important that Trudy cannot obtain Ki, since that would enable her to clone the caller's phone.

10.7.2.3   Confidentiality

GSM uses a stream cipher to encrypt the data. The reason for this choice is due to the relatively high error rate in the cell phone environment, which is typically about 1 in 1000 bits. With a block cipher, each transmission error causes one or two plaintext blocks to be garbled (depending on the mode), while a stream cipher garbles only those plaintext bits corresponding to the specific ciphertext bits that are in error.[15]

The GSM encryption key is universally denoted as Kc, so we'll follow that convention. When the home network receives the IMSI from the base station controller, the home network computes $Kc = A8(RAND, Ki)$, where A8 is

---

[15]It is possible to use error correcting codes to minimize the effects of transmission errors, making block ciphers feasible. However, this adds another layer of complexity to the process.

a. What does Bob need to know so that he can authenticate Alice?

b. Based on Problem 1, part b, we see that Trudy, as an active attacker, can establish a shared symmetric key K with Alice. Assuming this is the case, can Trudy then use K to determine Alice's password?

c. What are the significant advantages and disadvantages of this version of SSH, as compared to the version in Figure 10.1, which is based on certificates?

3. Consider the SSH protocol in Figure 10.1. One variant of the protocol allows us to replace certificate$_A$ with Alice's public key. In this version of the protocol, Alice must have a public/private key pair, but she is not required to have a certificate. It is also possible to replace certificate$_B$ with Bob's public key.

a. Suppose that Bob has a certificate, but Alice does not. What must Bob do so that he can authenticate Alice?

b. Suppose that Alice has a certificate, but Bob does not. What must Alice do so that she can authenticate Bob?

c. What are the significant advantages and disadvantages of this public key version of SSH, as compared to the certificate version in Figure 10.1?

4. Use Wireshark [328] to capture SSH authentication packets.

a. Identify the packets that correspond to the messages shown in Figure 10.1.

b. What other SSH packets do you observe, and what do these packets contain?

5. Consider the SSH specification, which can be found in RFC 4252 [331] and RFC 4253 [333].

a. Which message or messages in Figure 10.1 correspond to the message or messages labeled as SSH_MSG_KEXINIT in the protocol specification?

b. Which message or messages in Figure 10.1 correspond to the message or messages labeled as SSH_MSG_NEWKEYS in the protocol specification?

c. Which message or messages in Figure 10.1 correspond to the message or messages labeled as SSH_MSG_USERAUTH in the protocol specification?

    d. In the actual SSH protocol, there are two additional messages that would come between the fourth and fifth messages in Figure 10.1. What are these messages and what purpose do they serve?

6. Consider the SSL protocol in Figure 10.4.

    a. Suppose that the nonces R_A and R_B are removed from the protocol and we define $K = h(S)$. What effect, if any, does this have on the security of the authentication protocol?

    b. Suppose that we change message four to

$$\mathrm{HMAC}(\mathrm{msgs}, \mathrm{SRVR}, K).$$

    What effect, if any, does this have on the security of the authentication protocol?

    c. Suppose that we change message three to

$$\{S\}_{\mathrm{Bob}}, \ h(\mathrm{msgs}, \mathrm{CLNT}, K).$$

    What effect, if any, does this have on the security of the authentication protocol?

7. Consider the SSL protocol in Figure 10.4. Modify the protocol so that the authentication is based on a digital signature. Your protocol must provide secure authentication of the server Bob, and a secure session key.

8. Consider the SSL protocol in Figure 10.4. This protocol does not allow Bob to remain anonymous, since his certificate identifies him.

    a. Modify the SSL session protocol so that Bob can remain anonymous with respect to a passive attacker.

    b. Can you solve part a without increasing the number of messages?

9. The SSL protocol discussed in Section 10.3 uses public key cryptography.

    a. Design a variant of SSL that is based on symmetric key cryptography.

    b. What is the primary disadvantage of using symmetric keys for an SSL-like protocol?

10. Use Wireshark [328] to capture SSL authentication packets.

    a. Identify the packets that correspond to the messages shown in Figure 10.4.

b. What do the other SSL packets contain?

11. SSL and IPSec are both designed to provide security over the network.

    a. What are the primary advantages of SSL over IPSec?

    b. What are the primary advantages of IPSec over SSL?

12. SSL and IPSec are both designed to provide security over the network.

    a. What are the significant similarities between the two protocols?

    b. What are the significant differences between the two protocols?

13. Consider a man-in-the-middle attack on an SSL session between Alice and Bob.

    a. At what point should this attack fail?

    b. What mistake might Alice reasonably make that would allow this attack to succeed?

14. In Kerberos, Alice's key K_A, which is shared by Alice and the KDC, is computed (on Alice's computer) as $K_A = h(\text{Alice's password})$. Alternatively, this could have been implemented as follows. Initially, the key K_A is randomly generated on Alice's computer. The key is stored on Alice's computer as $E(K_A, K)$ where the key K is computed as $K = h(\text{Alice's password})$. The key K_A is also stored on the KDC.

    a. What are the advantages to this alternate approach of generating and storing K_A?

    b. Are there any disadvantages to computing and storing $E(K_A, K)$?

15. Consider the Kerberos interaction discussed in Section 10.5.2.

    a. Why is the ticket to Bob encrypted with K_B?

    b. Why is "Alice" included in the (encrypted) ticket to Bob?

    c. In the REPLY message, why is the ticket to Bob encrypted with the key S_A?

    d. Why is the ticket to Bob sent to Alice (who must then forward it to Bob) instead of being sent directly to Bob?

16. Consider the Kerberized login discussed in this chapter.

    a. What is a TGT and what is its purpose?

    b. Why is the TGT sent to Alice instead of being stored on the KDC?

    c. Why is the TGT encrypted with K_{KDC}?

    d. Why is the TGT encrypted with K_A when it is sent from the KDC to Alice's computer?

17. This problem deals with Kerberos.

    a. Why can Alice remain anonymous when requesting a ticket to Bob?

    b. Why can Alice not remain anonymous when requesting a TGT from the KDC?

    c. Why can Alice remain anonymous when she sends the "ticket to Bob" to Bob?

18. Suppose we use symmetric keys for authentication and each of N users must be able to authenticate any of the other $N-1$ users. Evidently, such a system requires one symmetric key for each pair of users, or on the order of N^2 keys. On the other hand, if we use public keys, only N key pairs are required, but we must then deal with PKI issues.

    a. Kerberos authentication uses symmetric keys, yet only N keys are required for N users. How is this accomplished?

    b. In Kerberos, no PKI is required. But, in security, there is no free lunch, so what's the tradeoff?

19. Dog race tracks often employ Automatic Betting Machines (ABMs),[18] which are somewhat analogous to ATM machines. An ABM is a terminal where Alice can place her own bets and scan her winning tickets. An ABM does not accept or dispense cash. Instead, an ABM only accepts and dispenses *vouchers*. A voucher can also be purchased from a special voucher machine for cash, but a voucher can only be redeemed for cash by a human teller.

A voucher includes 15 hexadecimal digits, which can be read by a human or scanned by a machine—the machine reads a bar code on the voucher. When a voucher is redeemed, the information is recorded in a voucher database and a paper receipt is printed. For security reasons, the (human) teller must submit the paper receipt which serves as the physical record that the voucher was cashed.

A voucher is valid for one year from its date of issue. However, the older that a voucher is, the more likely that it has been lost and will never be redeemed. Since vouchers are printed on cheap paper, they are often damaged to the point where they fail to scan, and they can even be difficult for human tellers to process manually.

---

[18]Not to be confused with anti-ballistic missiles.

A list of all outstanding vouchers is kept in a database. Any human teller can read the first 10 hex digits from this database for any outstanding voucher. But, for security reasons, the last five hex digits are not available to tellers.

If Ted, a teller, is asked to cash a valid voucher that doesn't scan, he must manually enter its hex digits. Using the database, it's generally easy for Ted to match the first 10 hex digits. However, the last five hex digits must be determined from the voucher itself. Determining these last five hex digits can be difficult, particularly if the voucher is in poor condition.

To help overworked tellers, Carl, a clever programmer, added a wildcard feature to the manual voucher entry program. Using this feature, Ted (or any other teller) can enter any of the last five hex digits that are readable and "*" for any unreadable digits. Carl's program will then inform Ted whether an outstanding voucher exists that matches in the digits that were entered, ignoring any position with a "*." Note that this program does not give Ted the missing digits, but instead, it simply returns a yes or no answer.

Suppose that Ted is given a voucher for which none of the last five hex digits can be read.

   a. Without the wildcard feature, how many guesses must Ted make, on average, to recover the last five hex digits of this particular voucher?

   b. Using the wildcard feature, how many guesses, on average, must Ted make to recover the last 5 hex digits of this voucher?

   c. How could Dave, a dishonest teller, exploit the wildcard feature to cheat the system?

   d. What is the risk for Dave? That is, how might Dave get caught under the current system?

   e. Modify the current system so that it allows tellers to securely and efficiently deal with vouchers that fail to scan automatically, but also makes it impossible (or at least more difficult) for Dave to cheat the system.

20. IPSec is a much more complex protocol than SSL, which is often attributed to the fact that IPSec is over-engineered. Suppose that IPSec was not over-engineered. Then would IPSec still be more complex than SSL? In other words, is IPSec inherently more complex than SSL, or not?

21. IKE has two phases, Phase 1 and Phase 2. In IKE Phase 1, there are four key options and, for each of these, there is a main mode and an aggressive mode.

    a. What are the primary differences between main mode and aggressive mode?

    b. What is the primary advantage of the Phase 1 digital signature key option over Phase 1 public key encryption?

22. IKE has two phases, Phase 1 and Phase 2. In IKE Phase 1, there are four key options and, for each of these, there is a main mode and an aggressive mode.

    a. Explain the difference between Phase 1 and Phase 2.

    b. What is the primary advantage of Phase 1 public key encryption main mode over Phase 1 symmetric key encryption main mode?

23. IPSec cookies are also known as anti-clogging tokens.

    a. What is the intended security purpose of IPSec cookies?

    b. Why do IPSec cookies fail to fulfill their intended purpose?

    c. Redesign the IPSec Phase 1 symmetric key signing main mode so that the IPSec cookies do serve their intended purpose.

24. In IKE Phase 1 digital signature main mode, $proof_A$ and $proof_B$ are signed by Alice and Bob, respectively. However, in IKE Phase 1, public key encryption main mode, $proof_A$ and $proof_B$ are neither signed nor encrypted with public keys. Why is it necessary to sign these values in digital signature mode, yet it is not necessary to public key encrypt (or sign) them in public key encryption mode?

25. As noted in the text, IKE Phase 1 public key encryption aggressive mode[19] allows Alice and Bob to remain anonymous. Since anonymity is usually given as the primary advantage of main mode over aggressive mode, is there any reason to ever use public key encryption main mode?

26. IKE Phase 1 uses ephemeral Diffie–Hellman for perfect forward secrecy (PFS). Recall that in our example of PFS in Section 9.3.4 of Chapter 9, we encrypted the Diffie–Hellman values with a symmetric key to prevent the man-in-the-middle attack. However, the Diffie–Hellman values are not encrypted in IKE. Is this a security flaw? Explain.

---

[19]Don't try saying "IKE Phase 1 public key encryption aggressive mode" all at once or you might give yourself a hernia.

27. We say that Trudy is a *passive attacker* if she can only observe the messages sent between Alice and Bob. If Trudy is also able to insert, delete, or modify messages, we say that Trudy is an *active attacker*. If, in addition to being an active attacker, Trudy is able to establish a legitimate connection with Alice or Bob, then we say that Trudy is an *insider*. Consider IKE Phase 1 digital signature main mode.

    a. As a passive attacker, can Trudy determine Alice's identity?

    b. As a passive attacker, can Trudy determine Bob's identity?

    c. As an active attacker, can Trudy determine Alice's identity?

    d. As an active attacker, can Trudy determine Bob's identity?

    e. As an insider, can Trudy determine Alice's identity?

    f. As an insider, can Trudy determine Bob's identity?

28. Repeat Problem 27 for symmetric key encryption, main mode.

29. Repeat Problem 27 for public key encryption, main mode.

30. Repeat Problem 27 for public key encryption, aggressive mode.

31. Recall that IPSec transport mode was designed for host-to-host communication, while tunnel mode was designed for firewall-to-firewall communication.

    a. Why does IPSec tunnel mode fail to hide the header information when used from host to host?

    b. Does IPSec tunnel mode also fail to hide the header information when used from firewall to firewall? Why or why not?

32. Recall that IPSec transport mode was designed for host-to-host communication, while tunnel mode was designed for firewall-to-firewall communication.

    a. Can transport mode be used for firewall-to-firewall communication? Why or why not?

    b. Can tunnel mode be used for host-to-host communication? Why or why not?

33. ESP requires both encryption and integrity, yet it is possible to use ESP for integrity only. Explain this apparent contradiction.

34. What are the significant differences, if any, between AH and ESP with NULL encryption?

35. Suppose that IPSec is used from host to host as illustrated in Figure 10.16, but Alice and Bob are both behind firewalls. What problems, if any, does IPSec create for the firewalls under the following assumptions.

    a. ESP with non-NULL encryption is used.

    b. ESP with NULL encryption is used.

    c. AH is used.

36. Suppose that we modify WEP so that it encrypts each packet using RC4 with the key K, where K is the same key that is used for authentication.

    a. Is this a good idea? Why or why not?

    b. Would this approach be better or worse than $K_{IV} = (IV, K)$, as is actually done in WEP?

37. WEP is supposed to protect data sent over a wireless link. As discussed in the text, WEP has many security flaws, one of which involves its use of initialization vectors, or IVs. WEP IVs are 24 bits long. WEP uses a fixed long-term key K. For each packet, WEP sends an IV in the clear along with the encrypted packet, where the packet is encrypted with a stream cipher using the key $K_{IV} = (IV, K)$, that is, the IV is pre-pended to the long-term key K. Suppose that a particular WEP connection sends packets containing 1500 bytes over an 11 Mbps link.

    a. If the IVs are chosen at random, what is the expected amount of time until the first IV repeats? What is the expected amount of time until some IV repeats?

    b. If the IVs are not selected at random but are instead selected in sequence, say, $IV_i = i$, for $i = 0, 1, 2, \ldots, 2^{24} - 1$, what is the expected amount of time until the first IV repeats? What is the expected amount of time until some IV is repeated?

    c. Why is a repeated IV a security concern?

    d. Why is WEP "unsafe at any key length" [321]? That is, why is WEP no more secure if K is 256 bits than if K is 40 bits? Hint: See [112] for more information.

38. On page 379 it is claimed that if Trudy knows the destination IP address of a WEP-encrypted packet, she can change the IP address to any address of her choosing, and the access point will send the packet to Trudy's selected IP address.

    a. Suppose that C is the encrypted IP address, P is the plaintext IP address (which is known to Trudy), and X is the IP address where

Trudy wants the packet sent. In terms of C, P, and X, what will Trudy insert in place of C?

b. What else must Trudy do for this attack to succeed?

39. WEP also incorporates a couple of security features that were only briefly mentioned in the text. In this problem, we consider two of these features.

    a. By default, a WEP access point broadcasts its SSID, which acts as the name (or ID) of the access point. A client must send the SSID to the access point (in the clear) before it can send data to the access point. It is possible to set WEP so that it does not broadcast the SSID, in which case the SSID is supposed to act like a password. Is this a useful security feature? Why or why not?

    b. It is possible to configure the access point so that it will only accept connections from devices with specified MAC addresses. Is this a useful security feature? Why or why not?

40. After the terrorist attacks of September 11, 2001, it was widely reported that the Russian government ordered all GSM base stations in Russia to transmit all phone calls unencrypted.

    a. Why would the Russian government have given such an order?

    b. Are these news reports consistent with the technical description of the GSM security protocol given in this chapter?

41. Modify the GSM security protocol, which appears in Figure 10.25, so that it provides mutual authentication.

42. In GSM, each home network has an AuC database containing user keys Ki. Instead, a process known as *key diversification* could be used. Key diversification works as follows. Let h be a secure cryptographic hash function and let K_M be a master key known only to the AuCs. In GSM, each user has a unique ID known as an IMSI. In this key diversification scheme, a user's key Ki would be given by $Ki = h(K_M, \text{IMSI})$, and this key would be stored on the mobile. Then given any IMSI, the AuC would compute the key as $Ki = h(K_M, \text{IMSI})$.

    a. What is the primary advantage of key diversification?

    b. What is the primary disadvantage of key diversification?

    c. Why do you think the designers of GSM chose not to employ key diversification?

43. Give a secure one-message protocol that prevents cell phone cloning and establishes a shared encryption key. Mimic the GSM protocol.

44. Give a secure two-message protocol that prevents cell phone cloning, prevents a fake base station attack, and establishes a shared session key. Mimic the GSM protocol.

Part IV

Software

Chapter 11

Software Flaws and Malware

If automobiles had followed the same development cycle as the computer,
a Rolls-Royce would today cost $100, get a million miles per gallon,
and explode once a year, killing everyone inside.
— Robert X. Cringely

My software never has bugs. It just develops random features.
— Anonymous

11.1 Introduction

Why is software an important security topic? Is it really on par with crypto, access control, and protocols? For one thing, virtually all of information security is implemented in software. If your software is subject to attack, all of your other security mechanisms are vulnerable. In effect, software is the foundation on which all other security mechanisms rest. We'll see that software provides a poor foundation on which to build security—comparable to building your house on quicksand.[1]

In this chapter, we'll discuss several software security issues. First, we consider unintentional software flaws that can cause security problems [183]. Then we consider malicious software, or malware, which is intentionally designed to be bad. We'll also discuss the future of malware, and we'll mention a few other types of software-based attacks.

Software is a big subject, so we continue with software-related security topics in the next two chapters. Even with three chapters worth of material we can, as usual, do little more than scratch the surface.

---

[1]Or, in an analogy that is much closer to your fearless author's heart, it's like building a house on a hillside in earthquake country.

11.2   Software Flaws

Bad software is everywhere [143]. For example, the NASA Mars Lander, which cost $165 million, crashed into Mars due to a software error related to converting between English and metric units of measure [150]. Another infamous example is the Denver airport baggage handling system. Bugs in this software delayed the airport opening by 11 months at a cost of more than $1 million per day [122].[2] Software failures also plagued the MV-22 Osprey, an advanced military aircraft—lives were lost due to this faulty software [178]. Attacks on smart electric meters, which have the potential to incapacitate the power grid, have been blamed on buggy software [127]. There are many many more examples of such problems.

In this section, we're interested in the security implications of software flaws. Since faulty software is everywhere, it shouldn't be surprising that the bad guys have found ways to take advantage of this situation.

Normal users find software bugs and flaws more or less by accident. Such users hate buggy software, but out of necessity, they've learned to live with it. Users are surprisingly good at making bad software work.

Attackers, on the other hand, look at buggy software as an opportunity, not a problem. They actively search for bugs and flaws in software, and they like bad software. Attackers try to make software misbehave, and flaws can prove very useful in this regard. We'll see that buggy software is at the core of many (if not most) attacks.

It's generally accepted among computer security professionals that complexity is the enemy of security [74], and modern software is extremely complex. In fact, the complexity of software has far outstripped the abilities of humans to manage the complexity. The number of lines of code (LOC) in a piece of software is a crude measure of its complexity—the more lines of code, the more complex. The numbers in Table 11.1 highlight the extreme complexity of large-scale software projects.

Conservative estimates place the number of bugs in commercial software at about 0.5 per 1,000 LOC [317]. A typical computer might have 3,000 executable files, each of which contains the equivalent of, perhaps, 100,000 LOC, on average. Then, on average, each executable has 50 bugs, which implies about 150,000 bugs living in a single computer.

If we extend this calculation to a a medium-sized corporate network with 30,000 nodes, we'd expect to find about 4.5 billion bugs in the network. Of

---

[2]The automated baggage handling system proved to be an "unmitigated failure" [87] and it was ultimately abandoned in 2005. As an aside, it's interesting to note that this expensive failure was only the tip of the iceberg in terms of cost overruns and delays for the overall airport project. And, you might be wondering, what happened to the person responsible for this colossal waste of taxpayer money? He was promoted to U.S. Secretary of Transportation [170].

Table 11.1: Approximate Lines of Code

System	LOC
Netscape	17 million
Space shuttle	10 million
Linux kernel 2.6.0	5 million
Windows XP	40 million
Mac OS X 10.4	86 million
Boeing 777	7 million

course, many of these bugs would be duplicates, but 4.5 billion is still a staggering number.

Now suppose that only 10% of bugs are security critical and that only 10% of these are remotely exploitable. Then our typical corporate network "only" has 4.5 million serious security flaws that are directly attributable to bad software!

The arithmetic of bug counting is good news for the bad guys and very bad news for the good guys. We'll return to this topic later, but the crucial point is that we are not going to eliminate software security flaws any time soon—if ever. We'll discuss ways to reduce the number and severity of flaws, but many flaws will inevitably remain. The best we can realistically hope for is to effectively manage the security risk created by buggy and complex software. In almost any real-world situation, absolute security is often unobtainable, and software is definitely no exception.[3]

In this section, we'll focus on program flaws. These are unintentional software bugs that can have security implications. We'll consider the following specific classes of flaws.

- Buffer overflow

- Race conditions

- Incomplete mediation

After covering these unintentional flaws, we'll turn our attention to malicious software, or malware. Recall that malware is designed to do bad things.

A programming mistake, or bug, is an *error*. When a program with an error is executed, the error might (or might not) cause the program to reach

---

[3]One possible exception is cryptography—if you use strong crypto, and use it correctly, you are as close to absolutely secure as you will ever be. However, crypto is usually only one part of a security system, so even if your crypto is perfect, many vulnerabilities will likely remain. Unfortunately, people often equate crypto with information security, which leads some to mistakenly expect absolute security.

an incorrect internal state, which is known as a *fault*. A fault might (or might not) cause the system to depart from its expected behavior, which is a *failure* [235]. In other words, an error is a human-created bug, while a fault is internal to the software, and a failure is externally observable.

For example, the C program in Table 11.2 has an error, since `buffer[20]` has not been allocated. This error might cause a fault, where the program reaches an incorrect internal state. If a fault occurs, it might lead to a failure, where the program behaves incorrectly (e.g., the program crashes). Whether a fault occurs, and whether this leads to a failure, depends on what resides in the memory location where `buffer[20]` is written. If that particular memory location is not used for anything important, the program might execute normally, which makes debugging challenging.

Table 11.2: A Flawed Program

```
int main(){
    int buffer[10];
    buffer[20] = 37;}
```

Distinguishing between errors, faults, and failures is a little too pedantic for our purposes. So, for the remainder of this section, we use the term *flaw* as a synonym for all three. The severity should be apparent from context.

One of the primary goals in software engineering is to ensure that a program does what it's supposed to do. However, for software to be secure, a much higher standard is required—secure software software must do what it's supposed to do *and nothing more* [317]. It's difficult enough just trying to ensure that a program does what it's supposed to do. Trying to ensure that a program does "nothing more" is asking for a lot more.

Next, we'll consider three specific types of program flaws that can create significant security vulnerabilities. The first of these is the infamous stack-based *buffer overflow*, also known as *smashing the stack*. Stack smashing has been called the attack of the decade for the 1990s [14] and it's likely to be the attack of the decade for the current decade, regardless of which decade happens to be current. There are several variants of the buffer overflow attack we discuss. These variants are considered in problems at the end of the chapter.

The second class of software flaws we'll consider are *race conditions*. These are common, but generally much more difficult to exploit than buffer overflows. The third major software vulnerability that we consider is *incomplete mediation*. This is the flaw that often makes buffer overflow conditions exploitable. There are other types of software flaws, but these three represent the most common sources of problems.

11.2.1 Buffer Overflow

> *Alice says, "My cup runneth over, what a mess."*
> *Trudy says, "Alice's cup runneth over, what a blessing."*
> — Anonymous

Before we discuss buffer overflow attacks in detail, let's consider a scenario where such an attack might arise. Suppose that a Web form asks the user to enter data, such as name, age, date of birth, and so on. The entered information is then sent to a server and the server writes the data entered in the "name" field to a buffer[4] that can hold N characters. If the server software does not verify that the length of the name is at most N characters, then a buffer overflow might occur.

It's reasonably likely that any overflowing data will overwrite something important and cause the computer to crash (or thread to die). If so, Trudy might be able to use this flaw to launch a denial of service (DoS) attack. While this could be a serious issue, we'll see that a little bit of cleverness on Trudy's part can turn a buffer overflow into a much more devastating attack. Specifically, it is sometimes possible for Trudy to execute code of her choosing on the affected machine. It's remarkable that a common programming bug can lead to such an outcome.

Consider again the C source code that appears in Table 11.2. When this code is executed, a buffer overflow occurs. The severity of this particular buffer overflow depends on what resided in memory at the location corresponding to `buffer[20]` before it was overwritten. The buffer overflow might overwrite user data or code, or it could overwrite system data or code, or it might overwrite unused space.

Consider, for example, software that is used for authentication. Ultimately, the authentication decision resides in a single bit. If a buffer overflow overwrites this authentication bit, then Trudy can authenticate herself as, say, Alice. This situation is illustrated in Figure 11.1, where the "F" in the position of the boolean flag indicates failed authentication.

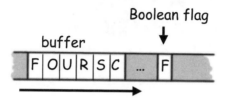

Figure 11.1: Buffer and a Boolean Flag

---

[4]Why is it a "buffer" and not an "array"? Obviously, it's because we're talking about buffer overflow, not array overflow...

If a buffer overflow overwrites the memory position where the boolean flag is stored, Trudy can overwrite "F" (i.e., a 0 bit) with "T" (i.e., a 1 bit), and the software will believe that Trudy has been authenticated. This attack is illustrated in Figure 11.2.

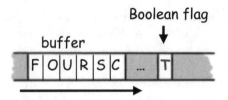

Figure 11.2: Simple Buffer Overflow

Before we can discuss the more sophisticated forms of the buffer overflow attack, we give a quick overview of memory organization for a typical modern processor. A simplified view of memory—which is sufficient for our purposes—appears in Figure 11.3. The *text* section is for code, while the *data* section holds static variables. The *heap* is for dynamic data, while the *stack* can be viewed as "scratch paper" for the processor. For example, dynamic local variables, parameters to functions, and the return address of a function call are all stored on the stack. The *stack pointer*, or SP, indicates the top of the stack. Notice that the stack grows up from the bottom in Figure 11.3, while the heap grows down.

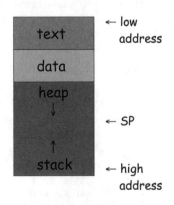

Figure 11.3: Memory Organization

11.2.1.1   Smashing the Stack

Smashing the stack refers to a particularly devastating attack that relies on a buffer overflow. For a stack smashing attack, Trudy is interested in the stack during a function call. To see how the stack is used during a function call, consider the simple example in Table 11.3.

Table 11.3: Code Example

```
void func(int a, int b){
    char buffer[10];
}
void main(){
    func(1,2);
}
```

When the function `func` in Table 11.3 is called, the values that are pushed onto the stack appear in Figure 11.4. Here, the stack is being used to provide space for the array `buffer` while the function executes. The stack also holds the return address where control will resume after the function finishes executing. Note that `buffer` is positioned above the return address on the stack, that is, `buffer` is pushed onto the stack after the return address. As a result, if the buffer overflows, the overflowing data will overwrite the return address. This is the crucial fact that makes the buffer overflow attack so lethal.

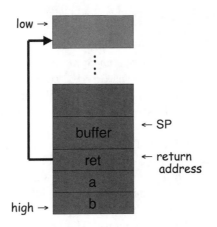

Figure 11.4: Stack Example

The `buffer` in Table 11.3 holds 10 characters. What happens if we put more than 10 characters into `buffer`? The buffer will overflow, analogous to the way that a 5-gallon gas tank will overflow if we try to add 10 gallons of gas. In both cases, the overflow will likely cause a mess. In the buffer overflow case, Figure 11.4 shows that the buffer will overflow into the space where the return address is located, thereby "smashing" the stack. Our assumption here is that Trudy has control over the bits that go into `buffer` (e.g., the "name" field in a Web form).

If Trudy overflows `buffer` so that the return address is overwritten with random bits, the program will jump to a random memory location when the function has finished executing. In this case, which is illustrated in Figure 11.5, the most likely outcome is that the program crashes.

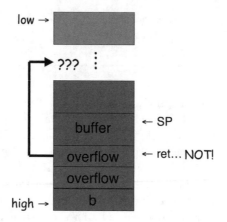

Figure 11.5: Buffer Overflow Causes a Problem

Trudy might be satisfied with simply crashing a program. But Trudy is clever enough to realize that there's much more potential to cause trouble in this situation. Since Trudy can overwrite the return address with a random address, can she also overwrite it with a specific address of her choosing? Often, the answer is yes. If so, what specific address might Trudy want to choose?

With some trial and error, Trudy can probably overwrite the return address with the address of the start of `buffer`. Then the program will try to "execute" the data stored in the buffer. Why might this be useful to Trudy? Recall that Trudy can choose the data that goes into the buffer. So, if Trudy can fill the buffer with "data" that is valid executable code, Trudy can execute this code on the victim's machine. The bottom line is that Trudy gets to execute code of her choosing on the victim's computer. This has to be bad for security. This clever version of the stack smashing attack is illustrated in Figure 11.6.

It's worth reflecting on the buffer overflow attack illustrated in Figure 11.6. Due to an unintentional programming error, Trudy can, in some cases, overwrite the return address, causing code of her choosing to execute on a remote machine. The security implications of such an attack are mind-boggling.

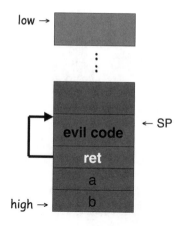

Figure 11.6: Evil Buffer Overflow

From Trudy's perspective, there are a couple of difficulties with this stack smashing attack. First, Trudy may not know the precise address of the evil code she has inserted into buffer, and second, she may not know the precise location of the return address on the stack. Neither of these presents an insurmountable obstacle.

Two simple tricks make a buffer overflow attack much easier to mount. For one, Trudy can precede the injected evil code with a NOP "landing pad" and, for another, she can insert the desired return address repeatedly. Then, if any of the multiple return addresses overwrite the actual return address, execution will jump to the specified address. And if this specified address lands on any of the inserted NOPs, the evil code will be executed immediately after the last NOP in the landing pad. This improved stack smashing attack is illustrated in Figure 11.7.

For a buffer overflow attack to succeed, obviously the program must contain a buffer overflow flaw. Not all buffer overflows are exploitable, but those that are enable Trudy to inject code into the system. That is, if Trudy finds an exploitable buffer overflow, she can execute code of her choosing on the affected system. Trudy will probably have some work to do to develop a useful attack, but it certainly can be done. And there are plenty of sources available online to help Trudy hone her skills—the standard reference is [8].

11.2.1.2   Stack Smashing Example

In this section, we'll examine code that contains an exploitable buffer overflow and we'll demonstrate an attack. Of course, we'll be working from Trudy's perspective.

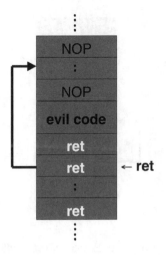

Figure 11.7: Improved Evil Buffer Overflow

Suppose that Trudy is confronted with a program that asks for a serial number—a serial number that Trudy doesn't know. Trudy wants to use the program, but she's too cheap to pay money to obtain a valid serial number.[5] Trudy does not have access to the source code, but she does possess the executable.

When Trudy runs the program and enters an incorrect serial number, the program halts without providing any further information, as indicated in Figure 11.8. Trudy proceeds to try a few different serial numbers, but, as expected, she is unable to guess the correct serial number.

Figure 11.8: Serial Number Program

Trudy then tries entering unusual input values to see how the program reacts. She is hoping that the program will misbehave in some way and that she might have a chance of exploiting the incorrect behavior. Trudy realizes she's in luck when she observes the result in Figure 11.9. This result indicates

---

[5]In the real world, Trudy would be wise to Google for a serial number. But let's assume that Trudy can't find a valid serial number online.

that the program has a buffer overflow. Note that 0x41 is the ASCII code for the character "A." By carefully examining the error message, Trudy realizes that she has overwritten exactly two bytes of the return address with the character A.

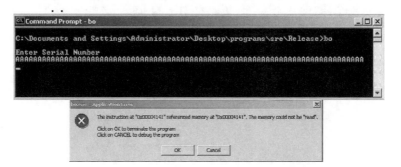

Figure 11.9: Buffer Overflow in Serial Number Program

Trudy then disassembles[6] the **exe** file and obtains the assembly code that appears in Figure 11.10. The significant information in this code is the "Serial number is correct" string, which appears at address 0x401034. If Trudy can overwrite the return address with the address 0x401034, then the program will jump to "Serial number is correct" and she will have obtained access to the code, without having any knowledge of the correct serial number.

```
.text:00401000
.text:00401000                 sub     esp, 1Ch
.text:00401003                 push    offset aEnterSerialNum ; "\nEnter Serial Number\n"
.text:00401008                 call    sub_40109F
.text:0040100D                 lea     eax, [esp+20h+var_1C]
.text:00401011                 push    eax
.text:00401012                 push    offset aS        ; "%s"
.text:00401017                 call    sub_401088
.text:0040101C                 push    8
.text:0040101E                 lea     ecx, [esp+2Ch+var_1C]
.text:00401022                 push    offset aS123n456 ; "S123N456"
.text:00401027                 push    ecx
.text:00401028                 call    sub_401050
.text:0040102D                 add     esp, 18h
.text:00401030                 test    eax, eax
.text:00401032                 jnz     short loc_401041
.text:00401034                 push    offset aSerialNumberIs ; "Serial number is correct.\n"
.text:00401039                 call    sub_40109F
.text:0040103E                 add     esp, 4
```

Figure 11.10: Disassembled Serial Number Program

But Trudy can't directly enter a hex address for the serial number, since the input is interpreted as ASCII text. Trudy consults an ASCII table where she finds that 0x401034 is "@^P4" in ASCII, where "^P" is control-P. Confident of success, Trudy starts the program, then enters just enough characters

---

[6]We'll have more to say about disassemblers in the next chapter when we cover software reverse engineering.

so that she is poised to overwrite the return address, and then she enters
"@^P4." To her surprise, Trudy obtains the results in Figure 11.11.

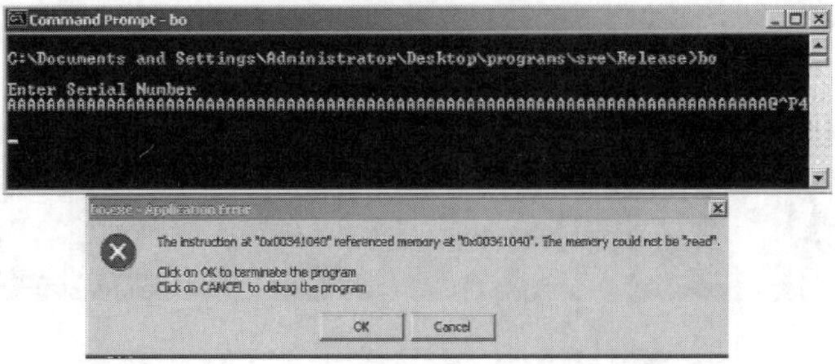

Figure 11.11: Failed Buffer Overflow Attack

A careful examination of the error message shows that the address where
the error arose was 0x341040. Apparently, Trudy caused the program to
jump to this address instead of her intended address of 0x401034. Trudy
notices that the intended address and the actual address are byte-reversed.
The problem here is that the machine Trudy is dealing with uses the little
endian convention, so that the low-order byte is first and the high-order byte
comes last. That is, the address that Trudy wants, namely, 0x401034, is
stored internally as 0x341040. So Trudy changes her attack slightly and
overwrites the return address with 0x341040, which in ASCII is "4^P@."
With this change, Trudy is successful, as shown in Figure 11.12.

Figure 11.12: Successful Buffer Overflow Attack

The point of this example is that without knowledge of the serial number,
and without access to the source code, Trudy was able to break the security
of the software. The only tool she used was a disassembler to determine the
address that she needed to use to overwrite the return address. In principle,
this address could be found by trial and error, although that would be tedious,
at best. If Trudy has the executable in her possession, she would be foolish
not to employ a disassembler—and Trudy is no fool.

For the sake of completeness, we provide the C source code, bo.c, corresponding to the executable, bo.exe. This source code appears in Table 11.4.

Table 11.4: Source Code for Serial Number Example

```
main()
{
    char in[75];
    printf("\nEnter Serial Number\n");
    scanf("%s", in);
    if(!strncmp(in, "S123N456", 8))
    {
        printf("Serial number is correct.\n");
    }
}
```

Again, Trudy was able to complete her buffer overflow attack without access to the source code in Table 11.4. We provide the source code here for reference.

Finally, note that in this buffer overflow example, Trudy did not execute code on the stack. Instead, she simply overwrote the return address, which caused the program to execute code that already existed at the specified address. That is, no code injection was employed, which greatly simplfies the attack. This version of stack smashing is usually referred to as a *return-to-libc* attack.

11.2.1.3 Stack Smashing Prevention

There are several possible ways to prevent stack smashing attacks. One approach is to eliminate all buffer overflows from software. However, this is more difficult than it sounds and even if we eliminate all such bugs from new software, there is a huge base of existing software that is riddled with buffer overflows.

Another option is to detect buffer overflows as they occur and respond accordingly. Some programming languages do this automatically. Yet another option is to not allow code to execute on the stack. Finally, if we randomize the location where code is loaded into memory, then the attacker cannot know the address where the `buffer` or other code is located, which would prevent most buffer overflow attacks. In this section, we'll briefly discuss these various options.

An easy way to minimize the damage caused by many stack-based buffer overflows is to make the stack non-executable, that is, do not allow code to execute on the stack. Some hardware (and many operating systems) support this *no execute*, or NX bit [129]. Using the NX bit, memory can be flagged so that code can't execute in specified locations. In this way the stack (as well as the heap and data sections) can be protected from many buffer overflow attacks. Recent versions of Microsoft Windows support the NX bit [311].

As the NX approach becomes more widely deployed and used, we should see a decline in the number and severity of buffer overflow attacks. However, NX will not prevent all buffer overflow attacks. For example, the return-to-libc attack discussed in the previous section would not be affected. For more information on NX and its security implications, see [173].

Using safe programming languages such as Java or C# will eliminate most buffer overflows at the source. These languages are safe because at runtime they automatically check that all memory accesses are within the declared array bounds. Of course, there is a performance penalty for such checking, and for that reason much code will continue to be written in C, particularly for applications destined for resource-constrained devices. In contrast to these safe languages, there are several C functions that are known to be unsafe and these functions are the source of the vast majority of buffer overflow attacks. There are safer alternatives to all of the unsafe C functions, so the unsafe functions should never be used—see the problems at the end of the chapter for more details.

Runtime stack checking can be used to prevent stack smashing attacks. In this approach, when the return address is popped off of the stack, it's checked to verify that it hasn't changed. This can be accomplished by pushing a special value onto the stack immediately after the return address. Then when Trudy attempts to overwrite the return address, she must first overwrite this special value, which provides a means for detecting the attack. This special value is usually known as a *canary*, in reference to the coal miner's canary.[7] The use of a canary for stack smashing detection is illustrated in Figure 11.13.

Note that if Trudy can overwrite an anti-stack-smashing canary with itself, then her attack will go undetected. Can we prevent the canary from being overwritten with itself?

A canary can be a constant, or a value that depends on the return address. A specific constant that is sometimes used is 0x000aff0d. This constant includes 0x00 as the first byte since this is the string terminating byte. Any string that overflows a buffer and includes 0x00 will be terminated at that point and no more of the stack will be overwritten. Consequently, an attacker can't use a string input to overwrite the constant 0x000aff0d with itself, and any other value that overwrites the canary will be detected. The other bytes in this constant serve to prevent other types of buffer overflow attacks.

---

[7]Coal miners would take a canary with them underground into the mine. If the canary died, the coal miners knew there was a problem with the air and they needed to get out of the mine as soon as possible.

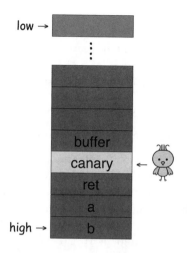

Figure 11.13: Canary

Microsoft recently added a canary feature to its C++ compiler based on the approach discussed in [246]. Any program compiled with the /GS compiler flag will use a canary—or, in Microsoft-speak, a "security cookie"—to detect buffer overflows at runtime. But the initial Microsoft implementation was apparently flawed. When the canary died, the program passed control to a user-supplied handler function. It was discovered that an attacker could specify this handler function, thereby executing arbitrary code on the victim machine [245], although the severity of this attack was disputed by Microsoft [187]. Assuming the claimed attack was valid, then all buffer overflows compiled under the /GS option were exploitable, even those that would not have been exploitable without the /GS option. In other words, the cure was worse than the disease.

Another option for minimizing the effectiveness of buffer overflow attacks is Address Space Layout Randomization, or ASLR [105]. This technique is used in recent Windows operating systems and several other modern OSs. ASLR relies on the fact that buffer overflow attacks are fairly delicate. That is, to execute code on the stack, Trudy usually overwrites the return address with a hard-coded specific address that causes execution to jump to the specified location. When ASLR is used, programs are loaded into more or less random locations in memory, so that any address that Trudy has hard-coded into her attack is only likely to be correct a small percentage of the time. Then Trudy's attack will only succeed a correspondingly small percentage of the time.

However, in practice, only a relatively small number of "random" layouts are used. Vista, for example, uses 256 distinct layouts and, consequently,

a given buffer overflow attacks should have a natural success probability of
about 1/256. However, due to a weakness in the implementation, Vista does
not choose from these 256 possible layouts uniformly, which results in a significantly greater chance of success for a clever attacker [324]. In addition, a
so-called de-randomization attack on certain specific ASLR implementations
is discussed in [263].

11.2.1.4 Buffer Overflow: The Last Word

Buffer overflow was unquestionably the attack of the decade for each of the
past several decades. For example, buffer overflow has been the enabling
vulnerability in many major malware outbreaks. This, in spite of the fact
that buffer overflow attacks have been well known since the 1970s, and it's
possible to prevent most such attacks by using the NX bit approach and/or
safe programming languages and/or ASLR. Even with an unsafe language
such as C, buffer overflow attacks can be greatly reduced by using the safer
versions of the unsafe functions.

Can we hope to relegate buffer overflow attacks to the scrapheap of history? Developers must be educated, and tools for preventing and detecting
buffer overflow conditions must be used. If it's available on a given platform, the NX bit should certainly be employed and ASLR is a very promising
technology. Unfortunately, buffer overflows will remain a problem for the foreseeable future because of the large amount of legacy code and older machines
that will continue to be in service.

11.2.2 Incomplete Mediation

The C function `strcpy(buffer, input)` copies the contents of the input
string `input` to the array `buffer`. As we discovered above, a buffer overflow
will occur if the length of `input` is greater than the length of `buffer`. To prevent such a buffer overflow, the program must validate the input by checking
the length of `input` before attempting to write it to `buffer`. Failure to do so
is an example of *incomplete mediation.*

As a somewhat more subtle example, consider data that is input to a Web
form. Such data is often transferred to the server by embedding it in a URL,
so that's the method we'll employ here. Suppose the input is validated on
the client before constructing the required URL.

For example, consider the following URL:

```
http://www.things.com/orders/final&custID=112&
        num=55A&qty=20&price=10&shipping=5&total=205
```

On the server, this URL is interpreted to mean that the customer with ID
number 112 has ordered 20 of item number 55, at a cost of $10 each, with

a \$5 shipping charge, giving a total cost of \$205. Since the input was checked on the client, the developer of the server software believes it would be wasted effort to check it again on the server.

However, instead of using the client software, Trudy can directly send a URL to the server. Suppose Trudy sends the following URL to the server:

```
http://www.things.com/orders/final&custID=112&
        num=55A&qty=20&price=10&shipping=5&total=25
```

If the server doesn't bother to validate the input, Trudy can obtain the same order as above, but for the bargain basement price of \$25 instead of the legitimate price of \$205.

Recent research [79] revealed numerous buffer overflows in the Linux kernel, and most of these were due to incomplete mediation. This is perhaps somewhat surprising since the Linux kernel is usually considered to be very good software. After all, it is open source, so anyone can look for flaws in the code (we'll have more to say about this in the next chapter) and it is the kernel, so it must have been written by experienced programmers. If these software flaws are common in such code, they are undoubtedly more common in most other code.

There are tools available to help find likely cases of incomplete mediation. These tools should be more widely used, but they are not a cure-all since this problem can be subtle, and therefore difficult to detect automatically. As with most security tools, these tools can also be useful for the bad guys.

11.2.3 Race Conditions

Ideally, security processes should be *atomic*, that is, they should occur all at once. So-called race conditions can arise when a security-critical process occurs in stages. In such cases, an attacker may be able to make a change between the stages and thereby break the security. The term race condition refers to a "race" between the attacker and the next stage of the process, although it's not so much a race as a matter of careful timing for the attacker.

The race condition that we'll consider occurs in an outdated version of the Unix command `mkdir`, which creates a new directory. With this version of `mkdir`, the directory is created in stages—there is a stage that determines authorization followed by a stage that transfers ownership. If Trudy can make a change after the authorization stage but before the transfer of ownership, then she can, for example, become the owner of some directory that she should not be able to access.

The way that this version of `mkdir` is supposed to work is illustrated in Figure 11.14. Note that `mkdir` is not atomic and that is the source of the race condition.

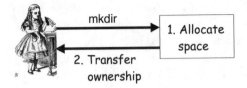

Figure 11.14: How `mkdir` is Supposed to Work

Trudy can exploit this particular `mkdir` race condition if she can somehow implement the attack that is illustrated in Figure 11.15. In this attack scenario, after the space for the new directory is allocated, a link is established from the the password file (which Trudy is not authorized to access) to this newly created space, before ownership of the new directory is transferred to Trudy. Note that this attack is not really a race, but instead it requires careful (or lucky) timing by Trudy.

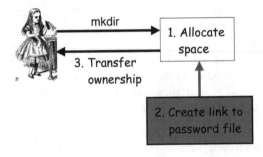

Figure 11.15: Attack on `mkdir` Race Condition

Today, race conditions are probably fairly common and with the trend towards increased parallelism, they are sure to become even more prevalent. However, real-world attacks based on race conditions are rare—attackers clearly favor buffer overflows.

Why are attacks based on race conditions a rarity? For one thing, exploiting a race condition requires careful timing. In addition, each race condition is unique, so there is no standard formula for such an attack. In comparison to, say, buffer overflow attacks, race conditions are certainly more difficult to exploit. Consequently, as of today buffer overflows are the low hanging fruit and are therefore favored by attackers. However, if the number of buffer overflows is reduced, or buffer overflows are made sufficiently difficult to exploit, it's a safe bet that we will see a corresponding increase in attacks based on race conditions. This is yet another illustration of Stamp's Principle: there is job security in security.

11.3   Malware

> *Solicitations malefactors!*
> — Plankton

In this section, we'll discuss software that is designed to break security. Since such software is malicious in its intent, it goes by the name of *malware*. Here, we mostly just cover the basics—for more details, the place to start is Aycock's fine book [21].

Malware can be subdivided into many different categories. We'll use the following classification system, although there is considerable overlap between the various types.

- A *virus* is malware that relies on someone or something else to propagate from one system to another. For example, an email virus attaches itself to an email that is sent from one user to another. Until recently, viruses were the most popular form of malware.[8]

- A *worm* is like a virus except that it propagates by itself without the need for outside assistance. This definition implies that a worm uses a network to spread its infection.

- A *trojan horse*, or trojan, is software that appears to be one thing but has some unexpected functionality. For example, an innocent-looking game could do something malicious while the victim is playing.

- A *trapdoor* or *backdoor* allows unauthorized access to a system.

- A *rabbit* is a malicious program that exhausts system resources. Rabbits could be implemented using viruses, worms, or other means.

- *Spyware* is a type of malware that monitors keystrokes, steals data or files, or performs some similar function [22].

Generally, we won't be too concerned with placing a particular piece of malware into its precise category. We'll use the term virus as shorthand for a virus, worm, or other such malware. It is worth noting that many "viruses" (in popular usage of the term) are not viruses in the technical sense.

Where do viruses live on a system? It should come as no surprise that *boot sector* viruses live in the boot sector, where they are able to take control early in the boot process. Such a virus can then take steps to mask its presence before it can be detected. From a virus writer's perspective, the boot sector is a good place to be.

---

[8]The term "virus" is sometimes reserved for parasitic malware, that is, malware that relies on other code to perform its intended function.

Another class of viruses are *memory resident*, meaning that they stay in memory. Rebooting the system may be necessary to flush these viruses out. Viruses also can live in applications, macros, data, library routines, compilers, debuggers, and even in virus checking software.

By computing standards, malware is ancient. The first substantive work on viruses was done by Fred Cohen in the 1980s [62], who clearly demonstrated that malware could be used to attack computer systems.[9]

Arguably, the first virus of any significance to appear in the wild was the so-called Brain virus of 1986. Brain did nothing malicious, and it was considered little more than a curiosity. As a result, it did not awaken people to the security implications of malware. That complacency was shaken in 1988 when the Morris Worm appeared. In spite of its early date, the Morris Worm remains one of the more interesting pieces of malware to date, and we'll have more to say about it below. The other examples of malware that we'll discuss in some detail are Code Red, which appeared in 2001, and SQL Slammer, which appeared in January of 2003. We'll also present a simple example of a trojan and we'll discuss the future of malware. For more details on many aspects of malware—including good historical insights—see [66].

11.3.1   Brain

The Brain virus of 1986 was more annoying than harmful. Its importance lies in the fact that it was first, and as such it became a prototype for many later viruses. But because it was not malicious, there was little reaction by users. In retrospect, Brain provided a clear warning of the potential for malware to cause damage, but at the time that warning was mostly ignored. In any case, computing systems remained extremely vulnerable to malware.

Brain placed itself in the boot sector and other places on the system. It then screened all disk access so as to avoid detection and to maintain its infection. Each time the disk was read, Brain would check the boot sector to see if it was infected. If not, it would reinstall itself in the boot sector and elsewhere. This made it difficult to completely remove the virus. For more details on Brain, see Chapter 7 of Robert Slade's excellent history of viruses [66].

11.3.2   Morris Worm

Information security changed forever when the eponymous Morris Worm attacked the Internet in 1988 [37, 229]. It's important to realize that the Internet of 1988 was nothing like the Internet of today. Back then, the Internet was populated by academics who exchanged email and used `telnet` for remote

---

[9]Cohen credited Len Adleman (the "A" in RSA) with coining the term "virus."

access to supercomputers. Nevertheless, the Internet had reached a critical mass that made it vulnerable to self-sustaining worm attacks.

The Morris Worm was a cleverly designed and sophisticated piece of software that was written by a lone graduate student at Cornell University.[10] Morris claimed that his worm was a test gone bad. In fact, the most serious consequence of the worm was due to a flaw (according to Morris). In other words, the worm had a bug.

The Morris Worm was apparently supposed to check whether a system was already infected before trying to infect it. But this check was not always done, and so the worm tried to re-infect already infected systems, which led to resource exhaustion. So the (unintended) malicious effect of the Morris Worm was essentially that of a so-called rabbit.

Morris' worm was designed to do the following three things.

- Determine where it could spread its infection

- Spread its infection wherever possible

- Remain undiscovered

To spread its infection, the Morris worm had to obtain remote access to machines on the network. To gain access, the worm attempted to guess user account passwords. If that failed, it tried to exploit a buffer overflow in `fingerd` (part of the Unix `finger` utility), and it also tried to exploit a trapdoor in `sendmail`. The flaws in `fingerd` and `sendmail` were well known at the time but not often patched.

Once access had been obtained to a machine, the worm sent a bootstrap loader to the victim. This loader consisted of 99 lines of C code that the victim machine compiled and executed. The bootstrap loader then fetched the rest of the worm. In this process, the victim machine even authenticated the sender.

The Morris worm went to great lengths to remain undetected. If the transmission of the worm was interrupted, all of the code that had been transmitted was deleted. The code was also encrypted when it was downloaded, and the downloaded source code was deleted after it was decrypted and compiled. When the worm was running on a system, it periodically changed its name and process identifier (PID), so that a system administrator would be less likely to notice anything unusual.

It's no exaggeration to say that the Morris Worm shocked the Internet community of 1988. The Internet was supposed to be able to survive a nuclear attack, yet it was brought to its knees by a graduate student and a few

---

[10]As if to add a conspiratorial overtone to the the entire affair, Morris' father worked at the super-secret National Security Agency at the time [248].

hundred lines of C code. Few, if any, had imagined that the Internet was so vulnerable to such an attack.

The results would have been much worse if Morris had chosen to have his worm do something truly malicious. In fact, it could be argued that the greatest damage was caused by the widespread panic the worm created—many users simply pulled the plug, believing it to be the only way to protect their system. Those who stayed online were able to receive some information and therefore recovered more quickly than those who chose to rely on the infallible "air gap" firewall.

As a direct result of the Morris Worm, the Computer Emergency Response Team (CERT) [51] was established, which continues to be a primary clearinghouse for timely computer security information. While the Morris Worm did result in increased awareness of the vulnerability of the Internet, curiously, only limited actions were taken to improve security. This event should have served as a wakeup call and could well have led to a complete redesign of the security architecture of the Internet. At that point in history, such a redesign effort would have been relatively easy, whereas today it is completely infeasible. In that sense, the Morris Worm can be seen as a missed opportunity.

After the Morris Worm, viruses became the mainstay of malware writers. Only relatively recently have worms reemerged in a big way. Next, we'll consider two worms that indicate some of the trends in malware.

11.3.3 Code Red

When Code Red appeared in July of 2001, it infected more than 300,000 systems in about 14 hours. Before Code Red had run its course, it infected several hundred thousand more, out of an estimated 6,000,000 susceptible systems worldwide. To gain access to a system, the Code Red worm exploited a buffer overflow in Microsoft IIS server software. It then monitored traffic on port 80, looking for other potential targets.

The action of Code Red depended on the day of the month. From day 1 to 19, it tried to spread its infection, then from day 20 to 27 it attempted a distributed denial of service (DDoS) attack on www.whitehouse.gov. There were many copycat versions of Code Red, one of which included a trapdoor for remote access to infected systems. After infection, this variant flush all traces of the worm, leaving only the trapdoor.

The speed at which Code Red infected the network was something new and, as a result, it generated a tremendous amount of hype [72]. For example, it was claimed that Code Red was a "beta test for information warfare" [235]. However, there was (and still is) no evidence to support such claims or any of the other general hysteria that surrounded the worm.

11.3.4   SQL Slammer

The SQL Slammer worm burst onto the scene in January of 2003, when it infected at least 75,000 systems within 10 minutes. At its peak, the number of Slammer infections doubled every 8.5 seconds [209].

The graphs in Figure 11.16 show the increase in Internet traffic as a result of Slammer. The graph on the bottom shows the increase over a period of hours (note the initial spike), while the graph on the top shows the increase over the first five minutes.

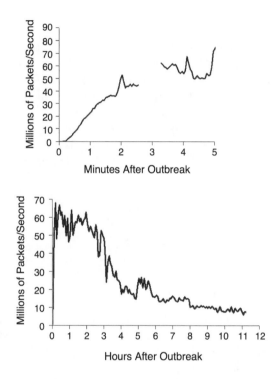

Figure 11.16: Slammer and Internet Traffic

The reason that Slammer created such a spike in Internet traffic is that each infected site searched for new susceptible sites by randomly generating IP addresses. A more efficient search strategy would have made more effective use of the available bandwidth. We'll return to this idea below when we discuss the future of malware.

It's been claimed (with good supporting evidence) that Slammer spread too fast for its own good, and effectively burned out the available bandwidth on the Internet [92]. In other words, if Slammer had been able to throttle itself slightly, it could have ultimately infected more systems and it might have caused significantly more damage.

Why was Slammer so successful? For one thing, the entire worm fit into a single 376-byte UDP packet. Firewalls are often configured to let sporadic packets through, on the theory that a single small packet can do no harm by itself. The firewall then monitors the "connection" to see whether anything unusual occurs. Since it was generally expected that much more that 376 bytes would be required for an attack, Slammer succeeded in large part by defying the assumptions of the security experts.

11.3.5 Trojan Example

In this section, we'll present a trojan, that is, a program that has some unexpected function. This trojan comes from the Macintosh world, and it's totally harmless, but its creator could just as easily have had this program do something malicious [103]. In fact, the program could have done anything that a user who executed the program could do.

This particular trojan appears to be audio data, in the form of an mp3 file that we'll name `freeMusic.mp3`. The icon for this file appears in Figure 11.17. A user would expect that double clicking on this file would automatically launch iTunes, and play the music contained in the mp3 file.

Figure 11.17: Icon for `freeMusic.mp3`

After double-clicking on the icon in Figure 11.17, iTunes launches (as expected) and an mp3 file titled "Wild Laugh" is played (probably not expected). Simultaneously, and unexpectedly, the message window in Figure 11.18 appears.

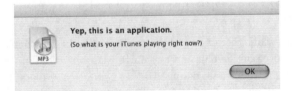

Figure 11.18: Unexpected Effect of `freeMusic.mp3` Trojan

What just happened? This "mp3" file is a wolf in sheep's clothing—the file `freeMusic.mp3` is not an mp3 file at all. Instead it's an application (that is, an executable file) that has had its icon changed so that it appears to be an mp3 file. A careful look at `freeMusic.mp3` reveals this fact, as shown in Figure 11.19.

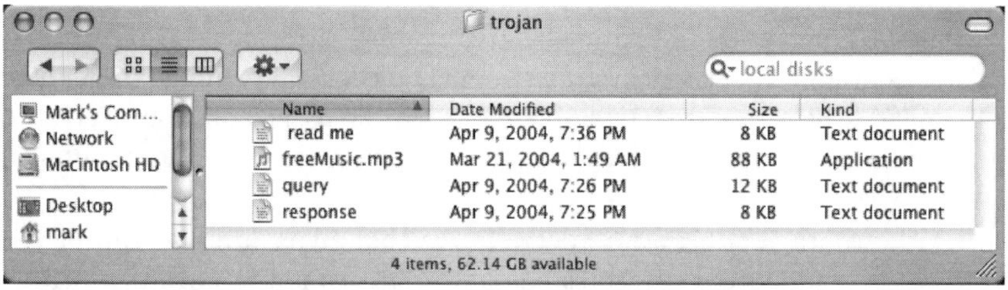

⊖ ⊖ ⊖		🗀 trojan			⊜
◀ ▶	🔡 ☰ ▥ ✿▾			Q▾ local disks	

Name	▲	Date Modified	Size	Kind
📄 read me		Apr 9, 2004, 7:36 PM	8 KB	Text document
🎵 freeMusic.mp3		Mar 21, 2004, 1:49 AM	88 KB	Application
📄 query		Apr 9, 2004, 7:26 PM	12 KB	Text document
📄 response		Apr 9, 2004, 7:25 PM	8 KB	Text document

4 items, 62.14 GB available

Mark's Com... / Network / Macintosh HD / Desktop / mark

Figure 11.19: Trojan Revealed

Most users are unlikely to give a second thought to opening a file that appears to be an mp3. This trojan only issues a harmless warning, but that's because the author had no malicious intent and instead simply wanted to illustrate a point [160].

11.3.6 Malware Detection

There are three general approaches that are used to detect malware. The first, and most common, is *signature detection*, which relies on finding a pattern or signature that is present in a particular piece of malware. A second approach is *change detection*, which detects files that have changed. A file that has unexpectedly changed might indicate an infection. The third approach is *anomaly detection*, where the goal is to detect unusual or virus-like files or behavior. We'll briefly discuss each of these approaches and consider their relative advantages and disadvantages.

In Chapter 8, we discussed signature-based and anomaly-based intrusion detection systems (IDSs). There are many parallels between IDSs and the corresponding virus detection methods.

11.3.6.1 Signature Detection

A signature is generally a string of bits found in a file, which might include wildcards. A hash value could also serve as a signature, but it would be less flexible and easier for virus writers to defeat.

For example, according to [296], the signature used for the W32/Beast virus is `83EB 0274 EB0E 740A 81EB 0301 0000`. We can search for this signature in all files on a system. However, if we find the signature, we can't be certain that we've found the virus, since other innocent files could contain the same string of bits. If the bits in searched files were random, the chance of such a false match would be $1/2^{112}$, which is negligible. However, computer software and data is far from random, so there is probably some realistic chance of a false match. This means that if a matching signature is found, further testing may be required to be certain that it actually represents the W32/Beast virus.

Signature detection is highly effective on malware that is known and for which a common signature can be extracted. Another advantage of signature detection is that it places a minimal burden on users and administrators, since all that is required is to keep signature files up to date and periodically scan for viruses.

A disadvantage of signature detection is that signature files can become large—tens or hundreds of thousands of signatures is the norm—which can make scanning slow. Also, the signature files must be kept up to date. A more fundamental problem is that we can only detect known signatures. Even a slight variant of a known virus might be missed.

Today, signature detection is by far the most popular malware detection method. As a result, virus writers have developed some sophisticated means for avoiding signature detection. We'll have more to say about this below.

11.3.6.2   Change Detection

Since malware must reside somewhere, if we detect a change somewhere on a system, then it may indicate an infection. That is, if we detect that a file has changed, it may be infected with a virus. We'll refer to this approach as change detection.

How can we detect changes? Hash functions are useful in this regard. Suppose we compute hashes of all files on a system and securely store these hash values. Then at regular intervals we can recompute the hashes and compare the new values with the stored values. If a file has changed in one or more bits—as it will in the case of a virus infection—we'll find that the computed hash does not match the previously computed hash value.

One advantage of change detection is that there are virtually no false negatives, that is, if a file has been infected, we'll detect a change. Another major advantage is that we can detect previously unknown malware (a change is a change, whether it's caused by a known or unknown virus).

However, the disadvantages to change detection are many. Files on a system often change and as a result there will be many false positives, which places a heavy burden on users and administrators. If a virus is inserted into a file that changes often, it will be more likely to slip through a change detection regimen. And what should be done when a suspicious change is detected? A careful analysis of log files might prove useful. But, in the end, it might be necessary to fall back to a signature scan, in which case the advantages of change detection have been largely negated.

11.3.6.3 Anomaly Detection

Anomaly detection is aimed at finding any unusual or virus-like or other potentially malicious activity or behavior. We discussed this idea in detail Chapter 8 when we covered intrusion detection systems (IDSs), so we only briefly discuss the concepts here.

The fundamental challenge with anomaly detection lies in determining what is normal and what is unusual, and being able to distinguish between the two. Another serious difficulty is that the definition of normal can change, and the system must adapt to such changes, or it will likely overwhelm users with false alarms.

The major advantage of anomaly detection is that there is some hope of detecting previously unknown malware. But, as with change detection, the disadvantages are many. For one, anomaly detection is largely unproven in practice. Also, as discussed in the IDS section of Chapter 8, a patient attacker may be able to make an anomaly appear to be normal. In addition, anomaly detection is not robust enough to be used as a standalone detection system, so it is usually combined with a signature detection system.

In any case, many people have very high hopes for the ultimate success of anomaly detection. However, today anomaly detection is primarily a challenging research problem rather than a practical security solution.

Next, we'll discuss some aspects of the future of malware. This discussion should make it clear that better malware detection tools will be needed, and sooner rather than later.

11.3.7 The Future of Malware

What does the future hold for malware? Below, we'll briefly consider a few possible attacks. Given the resourcefulness of malware developers, we can expect to see attacks based on these or similar ideas in the future [24, 289].

But before we discuss the future, let's briefly consider the past. Virus writers and virus detectors have been locked in mortal combat since the first virus detection software appeared. For each advance in detection, virus writers have responded with strategies that make their handiwork harder to detect.

One of the first responses of virus writers to the success of signature detection systems was *encrypted* malware. If an encrypted worm uses a different key each time it propagates, there will be no common signature. Often the encryption is extremely weak, such as a repeated XOR with a fixed bit pattern. The purpose of the encryption is not confidentiality, but to simply mask any possible signature.

The Achilles heel of encrypted malware is that it must include decryption code, and this code is subject to signature detection. The decryption routine typically includes very little code, making it more difficult to obtain a signature, and yielding more cases requiring secondary testing. The net result is that signature scanning can be applied, but it will be slower than for unencrypted malware.

The next step in the evolution of malware was the use of *polymorphic* code. In a polymorphic virus the body is encrypted and the decryption code is morphed. Consequently, the signature of the virus itself (i.e., the body) is hidden by encryption, while the decryption code has no common signature due to the morphing.

Polymorphic malware can be detected using emulation. That is, suspicious code can be executed in an emulator. If the code is malware, it must eventually decrypt itself, at which point standard signature detection can be applied to the body. This type of detection will be much slower than a simple signature scan due to the emulation.

Metamorphic malware takes polymorphism to the limit. A metamorphic worm mutates before infecting a new system.[11] If the mutation is sufficient, such a worm can likely avoid any signature-based detection system. Note that the mutated worm must do the same thing as the original worm, but yet its internal structure must be different enough to avoid detection. Detection of metamorphic software is currently a challenging research problem [297].

Let's consider how a metamorphic worm might replicate [79]. First, the worm could disassemble itself and then strip the resulting code to a base form. Randomly selected blocks of code could be inserted into the assembly. These variations could include, for example, rearranging jumps and inserting dead code. The resulting code would then be assembled to obtain a worm with the same functionality as the original, but it would be unlikely to have a common signature.

While the metamorphic generator described in the previous paragraph sounds plausible, in reality it is surprisingly difficult to produce highly metamorphic code. As of the time of this writing, the hacker community has produce a grand total of one reasonably metamorphic generator. These and related topics are discussed in the series of papers [193, 279, 312, 330].

Another distinct approach that virus writers have pursued is speed. That is, viruses such as Code Red and Slammer have tried to infect as many machines as possible in as short of a time as possible. This can also be viewed as an attack aimed at defeating signature detection, since a rapid attack would not allow time for signatures to be extracted and distributed.

According to the late pop artist Andy Warhol, "In the future everybody will be world-famous for 15 minutes" [301]. A *Warhol worm* is designed to infect the entire Internet in 15 minutes or less. Recall that Slammer infected a large number of systems in 10 minutes. Slammer burned out the available

---

[11]Metamorphic malware is sometimes called "body polymorphic," since polymorphism is applied to the entire virus body.

bandwidth due to the way that it searched for susceptible hosts, and as a result, Slammer was too bandwidth-intensive to have infected the entire Internet in 15 minutes. A true Warhol worm must do "better" than Slammer. How is this possible?

One plausible approach is the following. The malware developer would do preliminary work to develop an initial "hit list" of sites that are susceptible to the particular exploit used by the worm. Then the worm would be seeded with this hit list of vulnerable IP addresses. Many sophisticated tools exist for identifying systems and these could help to pinpoint systems that are susceptible to a given attack.

When this Warhol worm is launched, each of the sites on its initial hit list will be infected since they are all known to be vulnerable. Then each of these infected sites can scan a predetermined part of IP address space looking for additional victims. This approach would avoid duplication and the resulting wasted bandwidth that caused Slammer to bog down.

Depending on the size of the initial hit list, the approach described above could conceivably infect the entire Internet in 15 minutes or less. No worm this sophisticated has yet been seen in the wild. Even Slammer relied on randomly generated IP addresses to spread its infection.

Is it possible to do "better" than a Warhol worm? That is, can the entire Internet be infected in significantly less than 15 minutes? A *flash worm* is designed to infect the entire Internet almost instantly.

Searching for vulnerable IP addresses is the slow part of any worm attack. The Warhol worm described above uses a smarter search strategy, where it relies on an initial list of susceptible systems. A flash worm could take this approach to the limit by embedding all susceptible IP addresses into the worm.

A great deal of work would be required to predetermine all vulnerable IP addresses, but there are hacker tools available that would significantly reduce the burden. Once all vulnerable IP addresses are known, the list could be partitioned between several initial worm variants. This would still result in large worms [79], but each time the worm replicates, it would split the list of addresses embedded within it, as illustrated in Figure 11.20. Within a few generations the worm would be reduced to a reasonable size. The strength of this approach is that it results in virtually no wasted time or bandwidth.

It has been estimated that a well-designed flash worm could infect the entire Internet in as little as 15 seconds! Since this is much faster than humans could possibly respond, any defense against such an attack must be automated. A conjectured defense against flash worms [79] would be to deploy many personal intrusion detection systems and to have a master IDS monitor these personal IDSs. When the master IDS detects unusual activity, it can let it proceed on a few nodes, while temporarily blocking it elsewhere. If the sacrificial nodes are adversely affected, then an attack is in progress,

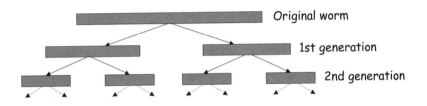

Figure 11.20: A Flash Worm

and it can be blocked elsewhere. On the other hand, if it's a false alarm, the other nodes are only delayed slightly. This defensive strategy shares many of the challenges associated with anomaly-based intrusion detection systems, as discussed in Chapter 8.

11.3.8 Cyber Diseases Versus Biological Diseases

It's currently fashionable to make biological analogies with computing. There are many such analogies that are applied to the field of security. In the field of malware and in particular, computer viruses, the analogy is fairly obvious.

There clearly are similarities between biological and computer "diseases." For example, in nature, if there are too few susceptible individuals, a disease will die out. A somewhat similar situation exists on the Internet, where too few susceptible systems may not allow a worm to become self-sustaining, particularly if the worm is randomly searching for vulnerable IP addresses.

There are, however, some significant differences between cyber diseases and biological diseases. For example, there is virtually no sense of distance on the Internet, so many of the models developed for biological diseases don't apply to cyber diseases.[12] Also, in nature, diseases attack more or less at random, while in computer systems hackers often specifically target the most desirable or vulnerable systems. As a result, computer attacks are potentially more focused and damaging than biological diseases. The important point here is that, although the biological analogy is useful, it cannot be taken too literally.

Finally, we note in passing that cell phones have not been plagued with malware to nearly the same degree as computer systems. Various explanations for this phenomenon have been given, with two of the more plausible being the relative diversity of mobile systems and inherently stronger security architectures. For a discussion of the Android security architecture and some of the difficulties of mounting a successful attack, see [211].

---

[12]However, with some cell phone attacks, proximity is required (e.g., attacks that rely on Bluetooth) while network-based attacks are also possible. So, cell phone attacks could include aspects of both biological viruses and computer viruses.

11.4 Botnets

A *botnet* is a collection of a large number of compromised machines under the control of a *botmaster*. The name derives from the fact that individual compromised machines are known as *bots* (shorthand for robots). In the past, such machines were often known as zombies.

Until recently, botmasters typically employed the Internet Relay Chat (IRC) protocol to manage their bots. However, newer botnets often use Peer-to-Peer (P2P) architectures since these are more difficult for authorities to track and shut down.

Botnets have proven ideal tools for sending spam and for launching distributed denial of service (DDoS) attacks. For example, a botnet was used in a highly-publicized denial of service attack on Twitter that was apparently aimed at silencing one well-known blogger from the Republic of Georgia [207].[13]

Botnets are a hot security topic, but at this point in time their activities in the wild are not completely understood. For example, there are wildly differing estimates for the sizes of various botnets [224].

Finally, it is often claimed that in the past most attacks were conducted primarily for fame within the hacker community, or for ideological reasons, or by script kiddies with little knowledge of what they were actually doing. That is, attacks were essentially just malicious pranks. In contrast (or so the claim goes), today attacks are primarily for profit. Some even believe that organized crime is behind most current attacks. The profit motive is plausible since earlier widespread attacks (Code Red, Slammer, etc.) were first and foremost designed to make headlines, whereas botnets strive to remain undetected. In addition, botnets are ideal for use in various subtle attack-for-hire scenarios. Of course, you should always be skeptical of those who hype any supposed threat, especially when they have a vested interest in the hype becoming conventional wisdom.[14]

11.5 Miscellaneous Software-Based Attacks

In this section we'll consider a few software-based attacks that don't fit neatly into any of our previous discussion. While there are numerous such attacks, we'll restrict our attention to a few representative examples. The topics we'll discuss are *salami attacks*, *linearization attacks*, *time bombs*, and the general issue of trusting software.

---

[13]Of course, this raised suspicion that Russian government intelligence agencies were behind the attack. However, the attack accomplished little, other than greatly increasing the fame of the attackee, so it's difficult to believe that any intelligence agency would be so stupid. On the other hand, "government intelligence" is an oxymoron.

[14]Or, more succinctly, "Beware the prophet seeking profit" [205].

11.5.1 Salami Attacks

In a salami attack, a programmer slices off a small amount of money from individual transactions, analogous to the way that you might slice off thin pieces from a salami.[15] These slices must be difficult for the victim to detect. For example, it's a matter of computing folklore that a programmer at a bank can use a salami attack to slice off fractional cents leftover from interest calculations. These fractional cents—which are not noticed by the customers or the bank—are deposited in the programmer's account. Over time, such an attack could prove highly lucrative for the dishonest programmer.

There are many confirmed cases of salami attacks. The following examples all appear in [158]. In one documented case, a programmer added a few cents to every employee payroll tax withholding calculation, but credited the extra money to his own tax. As a result, this programmer got a hefty tax refund. In another example, a rent-a-car franchise in Florida inflated gas tank capacity so it could overcharge customers for gas. An employee at a Taco Bell location reprogrammed the cash register for the late-night drive-through line so that $2.99 specials registered as $0.01. The employee then pocketed the $2.98 difference—a rather large slice of salami!

In a particularly clever salami attack, four men who owned a gas station in Los Angeles hacked a computer chip so that it overstated the amount of gas pumped. Not surprisingly, customers complained when they had to pay for more gas than their tanks could hold. But this scam was hard to detect, since the gas station owners were clever. They had programmed the chip to give the correct amount of gas whenever exactly 5 or 10 gallons was purchased, because they knew from experience that inspectors usually ask for 5 or 10 gallons. It took multiple inspections before they were caught.

11.5.2 Linearization Attacks

Linearization is an approach that is applicable in a wide range of attacks, from traditional lock picking to state-of-the-art cryptanalysis. Here, we consider an example related to breaking software, but it is important to realize that this concept has wide application.

Consider the program in Table 11.5, which checks an entered number to determine whether it matches the correct serial number. In this case, the correct serial number happens to be S123N456. For efficiency, the programmer decided to check one character at a time and to quit checking as soon as one incorrect character is found. From a programmer's perspective, this is a perfectly reasonable way to check the serial number, but it might open the door to an attack.

---

[15]Or the name might derive from the fact that a salami consists of bunch of small undesirable pieces that are combined to yield something of value.

Table 11.5: Serial Number Program

```
int main(int argc, const char *argv[])
{
    int i;
    char serial[9]="S123N456\n";
    if(strlen(argv[1]) < 8)
    {
        printf("\nError---try again.\n\n");
        exit(0);
    }
    for(i = 0; i < 8; ++i)
    {
        if(argv[1][i] != serial[i]) break;
    }
    if(i == 8)
    {
        printf("\nSerial number is correct!\n\n");
    }
}
```

How can Trudy take advantage the code in Table 11.5? Note that the correct serial number will take longer to process than any incorrect serial number. More precisely, the more leading characters that are correct, the longer the program will take to check the number. So, a putative serial number that has the first character correct will take longer than any that has an incorrect first character. Therefore, Trudy can select an eight-character string and vary the first character over all possibilities. If she can time the program precisely enough, she will find that the string beginning with S takes the most time. Trudy can then fix the first character as S and vary the second character, in which case she will find that a second character of 1 takes the longest. Continuing, Trudy can recover the serial number one character at a time. That is, Trudy can attack the serial number in linear time, instead of searching an exponential number of cases.

How great is the advantage for Trudy in this linearization attack? Suppose the serial number is eight characters long and each character has 128 possible values. Then there are $128^8 = 2^{56}$ possible serial numbers. If Trudy must randomly guess complete serial numbers, she would obtain the serial number in about 2^{55} tries, which is an enormous amount of work. On the other hand, if she can use a linearization attack, an average of only $128/2 = 64$ guesses

are required for each letter, for a total expected work of about $8 \cdot 64 = 2^9$. This makes an otherwise infeasible attack into a trivial attack.

A real-world example of a linearization attack occurred in TENEX [235], a timeshare system used in ancient times.[16] In TENEX, passwords were verified one character at a time, so the system was subject to a linearization attack similar to the one described above. However, careful timing was not even necessary. Instead, it was possible to arrange for a "page fault" to occur when the next unknown character was guessed correctly. Then a user-accessible page fault register would tell the attacker that a page fault had occurred and, therefore, that the next character had been guessed correctly. This attack could be used to crack any password in seconds.

11.5.3   Time Bombs

Time bombs are another interesting class of software-based attacks. We'll illustrate the concept with an infamous example. In 1986, Donald Gene Burleson told his employer to stop withholding taxes from his paycheck. Since this isn't legal, the company refused. Burleson, a tax protester, made it known that he planned to sue his company. Burleson used company time and resources to prepare his legal case against his company. When the company discovered what Burleson was doing, they fired him [240].

It later came to light that Burleson had been developing malicious software. After he was fired, Burleson triggered his "time bomb" software, which proceeded to delete thousands of records from the company's computer.

The Burleson story doesn't end here. Out of fear of embarrassment, the company was reluctant to pursue a legal case, despite their losses. Then in a bizarre twist, Burleson sued his former employer for back pay, at which point the company finally sued Burleson. The company eventually won, and in 1988 Burleson was fined $11,800. The case took two years to prosecute at a cost of tens of thousands of dollars and resulted in little more than a slap on the wrist. The light sentence was likely due to the fact that laws regarding computer crime were unclear at that early date. In any case, this was one of the first computer crime cases in the United States, and many cases since have followed a similar pattern. In particular, companies are often reluctant to pursue such cases for fear that it will damage their reputation.

11.5.4   Trusting Software

Finally, we consider a philosophical question with practical significance: Can you ever trust software? In the fascinating article [303], the following thought experiment is discussed. Suppose that a C compiler has a virus. When

---

[16]The 1960s and 1970s, that is. In computing, that's the age when dinosaurs roamed the earth.

compiling the `login` program, this virus creates a backdoor in the form of an account with a known password. Also, if the C compiler is recompiled, the virus incorporates itself into the newly compiled C compiler.

Now suppose that you suspect that your system is infected with a virus. You want to be absolutely certain that you fix the problem, so you decide to start over from scratch. You recompile the C compiler, then use it to recompile the operating system, which includes the `login` program. You haven't gotten rid of the problem, since the backdoor was once again compiled into the `login` program.

Analogous situations could arise in the real world. For example, imagine that an attacker is able to hide a virus in your virus scanning software. Or consider the damage that could be done by a successful attack on online virus signature updates—or other automated software updates.

Software-based attacks might not be obvious, even to an expert who examines the source code line by line. For example, in the Underhanded C Contest, the rules state in part that [70]

> ...in this contest you must write code that is as readable, clear, innocent and straightforward as possible, and yet it must fail to perform at its apparent function. To be more specific, it should do something subtly evil.

Some of the programs submitted to this contest are extremely subtle and they demonstrate that it is possible to make evil code look innocent.

We'll return to the theme of trusting software when we discuss operating systems in Chapter 13. Specifically, we will outline an ambitious design for a trusted operating system.

11.6 Summary

In this chapter, we discussed some of the security threats that arise from software. The threats considered here come in two basic flavors. The plain vanilla flavor consists of unintentional software flaws that attackers can sometimes exploit. The classic example of such a flaw is the buffer overflow, which we discussed in some detail. Another common flaw with security implications is a race condition.

The more exotic flavor of software security threats arise from intentionally malicious software, or malware. Such malware includes the viruses and worms that plague users today, as well as trojans and backdoors. Malware writers have developed highly sophisticated techniques for avoiding detection, and they appear set to push the envelope much further in the near future. Whether detection tools are up to the challenge posed by the next generation of malware is an open question.

11.7   Problems

1. With respect to security, it's been said that complexity, extensibility, and connectivity are the "trinity of trouble" [143]. Define each of these terms and explain why each represents a potential security problem.

2. What is a validation error, and how can such an error lead to a security flaw?

3. Provide a detailed discussion of one real-world virus or worm that was not covered in the text.

4. What is a race condition? Discuss an example of a real-world race condition, other than the `mkdir` example presented in the text.

5. One type of race condition is known as a time-of-check-to-time-of-use, or TOCTTOU (pronounced "TOCK too").

    a. What is a TOCTTOU race condition and why is it a security issue?

    b. Is the `mkdir` race condition discussed in this chapter an example of a TOCTTOU race condition?

    c. Give two real-world examples of TOCTTOU race conditions.

6. Recall that a canary is a special value that is pushed onto the stack after the return address.

    a. How is a canary used to prevent stack smashing attacks?

    b. How was Microsoft's implementation of this technique, the `/GS` compiler option, flawed?

7. Discuss one real-world example of a buffer overflow that was exploited as part of a successful attack.

8. Explain how a heap-based buffer overflow works, in contrast to the stack-based buffer overflow discussed in this chapter.

9. Explain how an integer overflow works, in contrast to the stack-based buffer overflow discussed in this chapter.

10. Read the article [311] and explain why the author views the NX bit as only one small part of the solution to the security problems that plague computers today.

11. As discussed in the text, the C function `strcpy` is unsafe. The C function `strncpy` is a safer version of `strcpy`. Why is `strncpy` safer but not safe?

12. Suppose that Alice's system employs the NX bit method of protecting against buffer overflow attacks. If Alice's system uses software that is known to harbor multiple buffer overflows, would it be possible for Trudy to conduct a denial of service attack against Alice by exploiting one of these buffer overflows? Explain.

13. Suppose that the NX bit method of protecting against buffer overflow attacks is employed.

    a. Will the buffer overflow illustrated in Figure 11.5 succeed?

    b. Will the attack in Figure 11.6 succeed?

    c. Why will the return-to-libc buffer overflow example discussed in Section 11.2.1.2 succeed?

14. List all unsafe C functions and explain why each is unsafe. List the safer alternative to each and explain whether each is safe or only safer, as compared to its unsafe alternative.

15. In addition to stack-based buffer overflow attacks (i.e., smashing the stack), heap overflows can also be exploited. Consider the following C code, which illustrates a heap overflow.

```
int main()
{
    int diff, size = 8;
    char *buf1, *buf2;
    buf1 = (char *)malloc(size);
    buf2 = (char *)malloc(size);
    diff = buf2 - buf1;
    memset(buf2, '2', size);
    printf("BEFORE: buf2 = %s ", buf2);
    memset(buf1, '1', diff + 3);
    printf("AFTER: buf2 = %s ", buf2);
    return 0;
}
```

    a. Compile and execute this program. What is printed?

    b. Explain the results you obtained in part a.

    c. Explain how a heap overflow might be exploited by Trudy.

16. In addition to stack-based buffer overflow attacks (i.e., smashing the stack), integer overflows can also be exploited. Consider the following C code, which illustrates an integer overflow [36].

```
int copy_something(char *buf, int len)
{
    char kbuf[800];
    if(len > sizeof(kbuf))
    {
        return -1;
    }
    return memcpy(kbuf, buf, len);
}
```

a. What is the potential problem with this code? Hint: The last argument to the function memcpy is interpreted as an unsigned integer.

b. Explain how an integer overflow might be exploited by Trudy.

17. Obtain the file overflow.zip from the textbook website and extract the Windows executable.

    a. Exploit the buffer overflow so that you bypass its serial number check. Turn in a screen capture to verify your success.

    b. Determine the correct serial number.

18. Consider the following protocol for adding money to a debit card.

   (i) User inserts debit card into debit card machine.

   (ii) Debit card machine determines current value of card (in dollars), which is stored in variable x.

   (iii) User inserts dollars into debit card machine and the value of the inserted dollars is stored in variable y.

   (iv) User presses **enter** button on debit card machine.

   (v) Debit card machine writes value of $x + y$ dollars to debit card and ejects card.

Recall the discussion of race conditions in the text. This particular protocol has a race condition.

    a. What is the race condition in this protocol?

    b. Describe a possible attack that exploits the race condition.

    c. How could you change the protocol to eliminate the race condition, or at least make it more difficult to exploit?

19. Recall that a trojan horse is a program that has unexpected functionality.

a. Write your own trojan horse, where the unexpected functionality is completely harmless.

b. How could your trojan program be modified to do something malicious?

20. Recall that a computer virus is malware that relies on someone or something (other than itself) to propagate from one system to another.

    a. Write your own computer virus, where the "malicious" activity is completely harmless.

    b. Explain how your virus could be modified to do something malicious.

21. Recall that a worm is a type of malware similar to a virus except that a worm propagates by itself.

    a. Write your own worm, where the "malicious" activity is completely harmless.

    b. Explain how your worm could be modified to do something malicious.

22. Virus writers use encryption, polymorphism, and metamorphism to evade signature detection.

    a. What are the significant differences between encrypted worms and polymorphic worms?

    b. What are the significant differences between polymorphic worms and metamorphic worms?

23. This problem deals with metamorphic software.

    a. Define metamorphic software.

    b. Why would a virus writer employ metamorphic techniques?

    c. How might metamorphic software be used for good instead of evil?

24. Suppose that you are asked to design a metamorphic generator. Any assembly language program can be given as input to your generator, and the output must be a metamorphic version of the input program. That is, your generator must produce a morphed version of the input program and this morphed code must be functionally equivalent to the input program. Furthermore, each time your generator is applied to the same input program, it must, with high probability, produce a distinct metamorphic copy. Finally, the more variation in the metamorphic copies, the better. Outline a plausible design for such a metamorphic generator.

25. Suppose that you are asked to design a metamorphic worm, where each time the worm propagates, it must first produce a morphed version of itself. Furthermore, all morphed versions must, with high probability, be distinct, and the more variation within the metamorphic copies, the better. Outline a plausible design for such a metamorphic worm.

26. A metamorphic worm that generates its own morphed copies is sometimes said to "carry its own metamorphic engine" (see Problem 25). In some situations it might be possible to instead use a standalone metamorphic generator (see Problem 24) to produce the metamorphic copies, in which case the worm would not need to carry its own metamorphic engine.

   a. Which of these two types of metamorphic worms would be easier to implement and why?

   b. Which of these two types of metamorphic worms would likely be easier to detect and why?

27. A polymorphic worm uses code morphing techniques to obfuscate its decryption code while a metamorphic worm uses code morphing techniques to obfuscate the entire worm. Apart than the amount of code that must be morphed, why is it more difficult to develop a metamorphic worm than a polymorphic worm? Assume that in either case the worm must carry its own morphing engine (see Problems 25 and 26).

28. In the paper [330] several metamorphic malware generators are tested. Curiously, all but one of the generators fail to produce any significant degree of metamorphism. Viruses from each of these weak metamorphic generators are easily detected using standard signature detection techniques. However, one metamorphic generator, known as NGVCK, is shown to produce highly metamorphic viruses, and these successfully evade signature detection by commercial virus scanners. Finally, the authors show that, in spite of the high degree of metamorphism, NGVCK viruses are relatively easy to detect using machine learning techniques—specifically, hidden Markov models [278].

   a. These results tend to indicate that the hacker community has, with rare exception, failed to produce highly metamorphic malware. Why do you suppose this is the case?

   b. It might seem somewhat surprising that the highly metamorphic NGVCK viruses can be detected. Provide a plausible explanation as to why these viruses can be detected.

   c. Is it possible to produce undetectable metamorphic viruses? If so, how? If not, why not?

29. In contrast to a flash worm, a slow worm is designed to slowly spread its infection while remaining undetected. Then, at a preset time, all of the slow worms could emerge and do something malicious. The net effect would be similar to that of a flash worm.

    a. Discuss one weakness (from Trudy's perspective) of a slow worm as compared with a flash worm.

    b. Discuss one weakness (also from Trudy's perspective) of a flash worm compared with a slow worm.

30. It has been suggested that from the perspective of signature detection, malware now far outnumbers goodware. That is, the number of signatures required to detect malicious programs exceeds the number of legitimate programs.

    a. Is it plausible that there could be more malware than legitimate programs? Why or why not?

    b. Assuming there is more malware than goodware, design an improved signature-based detection system.

31. Provide a brief discussion of each of the following botnets. Include a description of the command and control architecture and provide reasonable estimates for the maximum size and current size of each.

    a. Mariposa

    b. Conficker

    c. Kraken

    d. Srizbi

32. Phatbot, Agobot, and XtremBot all belong to the same botnet family.

    a. Pick one of these variants and discuss its command and control structure.

    b. These botnets are open source projects that are distributed under the GNU General Public License (GPL). This is highly unusual for malware—most malware writers are arrested and jailed if they are caught. Why do you suppose that the authors of these botnets are not punished?

33. In this chapter, the claim is made that "botnets are ideal for use in various attack-for-hire scenarios." Spam and various DoS attacks are the usual examples given for the uses of botnets. Give examples of other types of attacks (other than spam and DoS, that is) for which botnets would be useful.

34. After infecting a system, some viruses take steps to cleanse the system of any (other) malware. That is, they remove any malware that has previously infected the system, apply security patches, update signature files, etc.

    a. Why would it be in a virus writer's interest to protect a system from other malware?

    b. Discuss some possible defenses against malware that includes such anti-malware provisions.

35. Consider the code that appears in Table 11.5.

    a. Provide pseudo-code for a linearization attack on the code in Table 11.5.

    b. What is the source of the problem with this code, that is, why is the code susceptible to attack?

36. Consider the code in Table 11.5, which is susceptible to a linearization attack. Suppose that we modify the program as follows:

```
int main(int argc, const char *argv[])
{
    int i;
    boolean flag = true;
    char serial[9]="S123N456\n";
    if(strlen(argv[1]) < 8)
    {
        printf("\nError---try again.\n\n");
        exit(0);
    }
    for(i = 0; i < 8; ++i)
    {
        if(argv[1][i] != serial[i]) flag = false;
    }
    if(flag)
    {
        printf("\nSerial number is correct!\n\n");
    }
}
```

Note that we never break out of the `for` loop early, yet we can still determine whether the correct serial number was entered. Explain why this modified version of the program is still susceptible to a linearization attack.

37. Consider the code in Table 11.5, which is susceptible to a linearization attack. Suppose that we modify the program so that it computes the hash of the putative serial number and we compare this hash to the hash of the actual serial number. Is this modified program susceptible to a linearization attack? Explain.

38. Consider the code in Problem 36, which is susceptible to a linearization attack. Suppose that we modify the program so that it computes a random delay within each iteration of the loop.

    a. This program is still susceptible to a linearization attack. Why?

    b. An attack on this modified program would be more difficult than an attack on the code that appears in Problem 36. Why?

39. Consider the code in Table 11.5, which is susceptible to a linearization attack. Suppose that we modify the program as follows:

```
int main(int argc, const char *argv[])
{
    int i;
    char serial[9]="S123N456\n";
    if(strcmp(argv[1], serial) == 0)
    {
        printf("\nSerial number is correct!\n\n");
    }
}
```

Note that we are using the library function `strcmp` to compare the input string to the actual serial number.

    a. Is this version of the program immune to a linearization attack? Why or why not?

    b. How is `strcmp` implemented? That is, how does it determine whether the two strings are identical or not?

40. Obtain the Windows executable contained in `linear.zip` (available at the textbook website).

    a. Use a linearization attack to determine the correct eight-digit serial number.

    b. How many guesses did you need to find the serial number?

    c. What is the expected number of guesses that would have been required if the code was not vulnerable to a linearization attack?

41. Suppose that a bank does 1000 currency exchange transactions per day.

    a. Describe a salami attack on such transactions.

    b. How much money would Trudy expect to make using this salami attack in a day? In a week? In a year?

    c. How might Trudy get caught?

42. Consider the code in Table 11.5, which is susceptible to a linearization attack. Suppose that we modify the program as follows:

```
int main(int argc, const char *argv[])
{
    int i;
    int count = 0;
    char serial[9]="S123N456\n";
    if(strlen(argv[1]) < 8)
    {
        printf("\nError---try again.\n\n");
        exit(0);
    }
    for(i = 0; i < 8; ++i)
    {
        if(argv[1][i] != serial[i])
            count = count + 0;
        else
            count = count + 1;
    }
    if(count == 8)
    {
        printf("\nSerial number is correct!\n\n");
    }
}
```

Note that we never break out of the for loop early, yet we can still determine whether the correct serial number was entered. Is this version of the program immune to a linearization attack? Explain.

43. Modify the code in Table 11.5 so that it is immune to a linearization attack. Note that the resulting program must take exactly the same amount of time to execute for any incorrect input. Hint: Do not use any predefined functions (such as strcmp or strncmp) to compare the input with the correct serial number.

44. Read the article "Reflections on Trusting Trust" [303] and summarize the author's main points.

Chapter 12

Insecurity in Software

Every time I write about the impossibility of effectively protecting digital files
on a general-purpose computer, I get responses from people decrying the
death of copyright. "How will authors and artists get paid for their work?"
they ask me. Truth be told, I don't know. I feel rather like the physicist
who just explained relativity to a group of would-be interstellar travelers,
only to be asked: "How do you expect us to get to the stars, then?"
I'm sorry, but I don't know that, either.
— Bruce Schneier

So much time and so little to do! Strike that. Reverse it. Thank you.
— Willy Wonka

12.1   Introduction

In this chapter, we begin with software reverse engineering, or SRE. To fully
appreciate the inherent difficulty of implementing security in software, we
must look at software the way that attackers do. Serious attackers use SRE
techniques to find and exploit flaws—or create new flaws—in software.

After our brief look at SRE, we'll discuss digital rights management, or
DRM, which provides a good example of the limitation of relying on software
for security. DRM illustrates the impact of SRE on software-based security.

The last major topic of this chapter is software development. It was
tempting to label this section "secure software development," but truly secure
software is difficult to achieve in practice. We'll discuss methods to improve
the security of software, but we'll also see why most of the advantages lie
with the bad guys. Finally, we briefly consider the relative security merits of
open source versus closed source software.

12.2   Software Reverse Engineering

SRE or software reverse engineering—which is also known as reverse code engineering or, simply, reversing—can be used for good or for not so good. The good uses include understanding malware [336, 337] or legacy code [57]. Here, we're primarily interested in the not-so-good uses, which include removing usage restrictions from software, finding and exploiting software flaws, cheating at games, breaking DRM systems, and many, many other attacks on software.

We'll assume that the reverse engineer is our old friend Trudy. For the most part, we assume that Trudy only has an executable, or exe, that was generated by compiling, say, a C program. That is, Trudy does not have access to the source code. We will consider one Java reversing example, but unless obfuscation techniques have been applied, Java class files are trivial to reverse to obtain (nearly) the original source code. And even using obfuscation may not make Java significantly more difficult to reverse. On the other hand, "native code" (i.e., hardware-specific machine code) is inherently more difficult to reverse. For one thing, the best we can realistically do is disassemble an exe and, consequently, Trudy must analyze the program as assembly code, not as a higher-level language.

Of course, Trudy's ultimate goal is to break things. So, Trudy might reverse the software as a step toward finding a weakness or otherwise devising an attack. Often, however, Trudy wants to modify the software to bypass some annoying security feature. Before Trudy can modify the software, SRE is a necessary first step.

SRE is usually focused on software that runs under Microsoft Windows. Consequently, much of our discussion here is Windows-specific.

Essential reverse engineering tools include a *disassembler* and a *debugger*. A disassembler converts an executable into assembly code, as best it can, but a disassembler can't always disassemble code correctly, since, for example, it's not always possible to distinguish code from data. This implies that in general, it's not possible to disassemble an exe file and reassemble the result into a functioning executable. This will make Trudy's task slightly more challenging but by no means insurmountable.

A debugger is used to set break points, which allows Trudy to step through the code as it executes. For any reasonably complex program, a debugger is a necessary tool for understanding the code.

OllyDbg [225] includes a highly regarded debugger, disassembler, and hex editor [173]. OllyDbg is more than sufficient for all of the problems that appear in this chapter and, best of all, it's free. IDA Pro is a powerful disassembler and debugger [147]. IDA Pro costs a few hundred dollars (there is a free trial version) and it is generally considered to have the best disassembler available. Hackman [299] is an inexpensive shareware disassembler and debugger that might also be worth considering.

A hex editor can be used to directly modify, or *patch*,[1] an **exe** file. Today, all self-respecting debuggers include a built-in hex editor, so you may not need a standalone hex editor. But, if you should need a separate hex editor, UltraEdit and HIEW are among the most popular shareware choices.

Several other more specialized tools are sometimes useful for reverse engineering. Examples of such tools include Regmon, which monitors all accesses of the Windows registry, and Filemon, which, as you might have guessed, monitors all accesses of files. Both of these tools are available from Microsoft as freeware. VMWare [318]—which allows a user to set up virtual machines—is a powerful tool that is particularly useful if you want to reverse engineer malware while minimizing the risk of damaging your system.

Does Trudy really need a disassembler and a debugger? Note that the disassembler gives Trudy a static view of the code, which can be used to obtain an overview of the program logic. After perusing the disassembled code, Trudy can zero in on areas that are likely to be of interest. But without a debugger, Trudy would have a difficult time skipping over the boring parts of the code. Trudy would, in effect, be forced to mentally execute the code so that she could know the state of registers, variable values, flag bits, etc., at some particular point in the code. Trudy may be clever, but this would be an insurmountable obstacle for all but the simplest program.

As all software developers know, a debugger allows Trudy to set break points. In this way, Trudy can treat uninteresting parts of the code as a black box and skip directly to the interesting parts. Also, as we mentioned above, not all code disassembles correctly, and for such cases a debugger is required. The bottom line is that both a disassembler and a debugger are required for any serious SRE task.

The necessary technical skills required for SRE include a working knowledge of the target assembly language and some experience with the necessary tools—primarily a debugger. For Windows, some knowledge of the Windows Portable Executable, or PE, file format is also important [236]. These skills are beyond the scope of this book—see [99] or [161] for more information. Below we'll restrict our attention to simple SRE examples. These examples illustrate the concepts, but do not require any significant knowledge of assembly, any knowledge of the PE file format, etc.

Finally, SRE requires boundless patience and optimism, since the work can be extremely tedious and labor intensive. There are few automated tools, which means that SRE is essentially a manual process that requires many long hours spent slogging through assembly code. From Trudy's perspective, however, the payoff can be well worth the effort.

---

[1]Here, "patch" means that we directly modify the binary without recompiling the code. Note that this is a different meaning than "patch" in the context of security patches that are applied to code.

12.2.1   Reversing Java Bytecode

Before we consider a "real" SRE example, let's take a quick look at a Java example. When you compile Java source code, it's converted into bytecode and this bytecode is executed by the the Java virtual machine, or JVM. In comparison to, say, the C programming language, the advantage of Java's approach is that the bytecode is more or less machine independent, while the primary disadvantage is a loss of efficiency.

When it comes to reversing, Java bytecode makes Trudy's life much easier. A great deal more information is retained in bytecode than native code, so it is possible to decompile bytecode with great accuracy. There are tools available that will convert Java bytecode into Java source code, and the resulting source code is likely to be very similar to the original source code. There are tools available to obfuscate Java, thereby making Trudy's job more challenging, but none are particularly strong—even highly obfuscated Java bytecode is generally easier to reverse than un-obfuscated machine code.

For example, consider the Java program in Figure 12.1. Note that this program computes and prints the first n Fibonacci numbers, where n is specified by the user.

```java
import java.io.*;

public class Fibo
{
    /** Prompt user for a value of n, then
        print n Fibonacci numbers
     */
    public static void main(String[] args) throws IOException {
        BufferedReader rd = new BufferedReader (
                new InputStreamReader(System.in));
        System.out.print("Enter value of n: ");
        String ns = rd.readLine();
        int n = Integer.parseInt(ns);
        int p = 0, c = 1, a;
        while (n-- > 0) {
            System.out.println(c);
            a = p + c;
            p = c;
            c = a;
        }
    }
}
```

Figure 12.1: Java Program

The program in Figure 12.1 was compiled into bytecode and the resulting class file was decompiled using Fernflower, an online tool [110]. This decompiled Java file appears in Figure 12.2.

```
import java.io.BufferedReader;
import java.io.IOException;
import java.io.InputStreamReader;

public class Fibo
{
    public static void main(String[] var0) throws IOException {
        BufferedReader var1 = new BufferedReader(
                new InputStreamReader(System.in));
        System.out.print("Enter value of n: ");
        String var2 = var1.readLine();
        int var3 = Integer.parseInt(var2);
        int var4 = 0;
        int var6;
        for(int var5 = 1; var3-- > 0; var5 = var6) {
            System.out.println(var5);
            var6 = var4 + var5;
            var4 = var5;
        }
    }
}
```

Figure 12.2: Decompiled Java Program

Note that the original Java source in Figure 12.1 is almost identical to the decompiled Java code in Figure 12.2. The significant differences are that the comments have been lost and the variable names have changed. These differences make the decompiled program slightly more difficult to understand than the original. Nevertheless, Trudy would certainly prefer to decipher code like that in Figure 12.2 rather than deal with assembly code.[2]

As mentioned above, there are tools to obfuscate Java. These tools can obfuscate the control flow and data, insert junk code, and so on. It is even possible to encrypt the bytecode. However, none of these tools seem to be particularly strong—see the homework problems for some examples.

12.2.2 SRE Example

The native code SRE example that we'll consider only requires the use of a disassembler and a hex editor. We'll disassemble the executable to understand the code. Then we'll use the hex editor to patch the code to change its behavior. It's important to realize that this is a very simple example—to do SRE in the real world, a debugger would certainly be required.

For our SRE example, we'll consider code that requires a serial number. The attacker Trudy doesn't know the serial number, and when she guesses (incorrectly) she obtains the results in Figure 12.3.

---

[2]If you don't believe it, take a look at the next section.

Figure 12.3: Serial Number Program

Trudy could try to brute force guess the serial numbers but that's unlikely
to succeed. Being a dedicate reverser, Trudy decides the first thing she'll
do is to disassemble serial.exe. A small part of the resulting IDA Pro
disassembly appears in Figure 12.4.

```
.text:00401003        push    offset aEnterSerialNum ; "\nEnter Serial Number\n"
.text:00401008        call    sub_4010AF
.text:0040100D        lea     eax, [esp+18h+var_14]
.text:00401011        push    eax
.text:00401012        push    offset aS       ; "%s"
.text:00401017        call    sub_401098
.text:0040101C        push    8
.text:0040101E        lea     ecx, [esp+24h+var_14]
.text:00401022        push    offset aS123n456 ; "S123N456"
.text:00401027        push    ecx
.text:00401028        call    sub_401060
.text:0040102D        add     esp, 18h
.text:00401030        test    eax, eax
.text:00401032        jz      short loc_401045
.text:00401034        push    offset aErrorIncorrect ; "Error! Incorrect serial number.
.text:00401039        call    sub_4010AF
```

Figure 12.4: Serial Number Program Disassembly

The line at address 0x401022 in Figure 12.4 indicates that the correct
serial number is S123N456. Trudy tries this serial number and finds that it is
indeed correct, as indicated in Figure 12.5.

Figure 12.5: Correct Serial Number

But Trudy suffers from short-term memory loss, and she has particular
trouble remembering serial numbers. Therefore, Trudy would like to patch
the executable serial.exe so that she doesn't need to remember the serial
number. Trudy looks again at the disassembly in Figure 12.4, and she notices
that the test instruction at address 0x401030 is significant due to the jump
instruction, jz at 0x401032 that immediately follows. That is, if the jump
occurs, the program will jump elsewhere, bypassing the error message. This
has to be good, since Trudy doesn't want to see "Incorrect serial number."

At this point, Trudy must rely on her knowledge of assembly code (or her ability to Google for such knowledge). The instruction `test eax,eax` computes a binary AND of the `eax` register with itself. Depending on the result, this instruction causes various flag bits to be set. One of these flag bits is the zero flag, which is set if `test eax,eax` results in zero. That is, the instruction `test eax,eax` causes the zero flag to be set to one provided that `eax` AND `eax` is zero. With this in mind, Trudy might want to consider ways to force the zero flag bit to be set so that she can bypassing the dreaded "Incorrect serial number" message.

There are many possible ways for Trudy to patch the code. But, whatever approach is used, care must be taken or else the resulting code will not behave as expected. Trudy must take care to only replace bytes. In particular, Trudy cannot insert additional bytes or remove any bytes, since doing so would cause subsequent instructions to be misaligned, that is, the instructions would not align properly, which would almost certainly cause the program to crash.

Trudy decides that she will try to modify the `test` instruction so that the zero flag bit will always be set. If she can accomplish this, then the remainder of the code can be left unchanged. After some thought, Trudy realizes that if she replaces `test eax,eax` with `xor eax,eax`, then the zero flag bit will alway be set to one. This works regardless of what is in the `eax` register, since whenever something is XORed with itself, the result is zero, which will cause the zero flag bit to be set to one. Trudy should then be able to bypass the "Incorrect serial number" message, regardless of which serial number she enters at the prompt.

So, Trudy has determined that changing `test` to `xor` will cause the program to behave as she wants. However, Trudy still needs to determine whether she can actually patch the code to make this change without causing any unwanted side effect. In particular, she must be careful not to insert or delete bytes.

Trudy next examines the bits of the `exe` file (in hex) at address `0x401030` and she observes the results displayed in Figure 12.6, which tells her that `test eax,eax` is, in hex, `0x85C0`.... Relying on her favorite assembly code reference manual, Trudy learns that `xor eax,eax` is, in hex, `0x33C0`.... Trudy realizes she's in luck, since she only needs to change one byte in the executable to make her desired change. Again, it's crucial that she does not need to insert or delete any bytes, as doing so would almost certainly cause the resulting code to fail.

```
.text:00401010   04 50 68 84 80 40 00 E8-7C 00 00 00 6A 00 8D 4C
.text:00401020   24 10 68 78 80 40 00 51-E8 33 00 00 00 83 C4 18
.text:00401030   85 C0 74 11 68 4C 80 40-00 E8 71 00 00 00 83 C4
.text:00401040   04 83 C4 14 C3 68 30 80-40 00 E8 60 00 00 00 83
```

Figure 12.6: Hex View of `serial.exe`

Trudy then uses her favorite hex editor to patch `serial.exe`. Since the addresses in the hex editor won't necessarily match those in the disassembler, she searches through `serial.exe` to find the bits `0x85C07411684C`, as can be seen in Figure 12.6. Since this is the only occurrence of the bit string in the file, she knows this is the right location. She then changes the byte `0x85` to `0x33` and she saves the resulting file as `serialPatch.exe`.

Note that in OllyDbg, for example, patching the code is easier, since Trudy just needs to change the `test` instruction to `xor` in the debugger and save the result. That is, no hex editor is required. In any case, a comparison of the original and the patched executables appears in Figure 12.7.

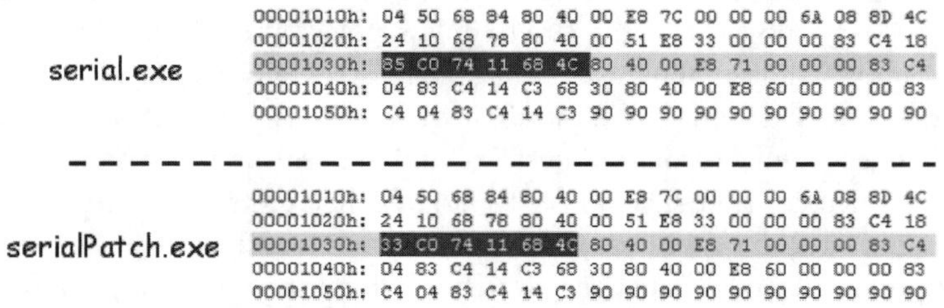
serial.exe
00001010h: 04 50 68 84 80 40 00 E8 7C 00 00 00 6A 08 8D 4C
00001020h: 24 10 68 78 80 40 00 51 E8 33 00 00 00 83 C4 18
00001030h: 85 C0 74 11 68 4C 80 40 00 E8 71 00 00 00 83 C4
00001040h: 04 83 C4 14 C3 68 30 80 40 00 E8 60 00 00 00 83
00001050h: C4 04 83 C4 14 C3 90 90 90 90 90 90 90 90 90 90
serialPatch.exe
00001010h: 04 50 68 84 80 40 00 E8 7C 00 00 00 6A 08 8D 4C
00001020h: 24 10 68 78 80 40 00 51 E8 33 00 00 00 83 C4 18
00001030h: 33 C0 74 11 68 4C 80 40 00 E8 71 00 00 00 83 C4
00001040h: 04 83 C4 14 C3 68 30 80 40 00 E8 60 00 00 00 83
00001050h: C4 04 83 C4 14 C3 90 90 90 90 90 90 90 90 90 90

Figure 12.7: Hex View of Original and Patched

Trudy then executes the patched code `serialPatch.exe` and enters an incorrect serial number. The results in Figure 12.8 show that the patched program accepted an incorrect serial number.

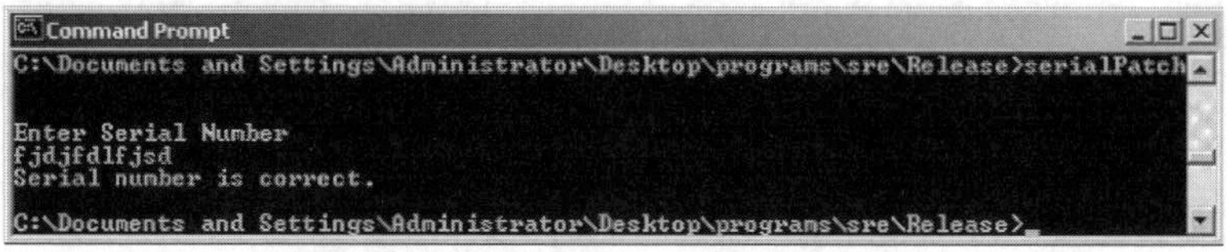
Command Prompt
C:\Documents and Settings\Administrator\Desktop\programs\sre\Release>serialPatch
Enter Serial Number
fjdjfdlfjsd
Serial number is correct.
C:\Documents and Settings\Administrator\Desktop\programs\sre\Release>_

Figure 12.8: Patched Executable

Finally, we've disassembled both `serial.exe` and `serialPatch.exe` with the comparison given in Figure 12.9. These snippets of code show that the patching achieved its desired results.

Kaspersky's book [161] is a good source for more information on SRE techniques and the book [233] has a readable introduction to some aspects of SRE. However, the best SRE book available is Eilam's [99]. There are many online SRE resources, perhaps the best of which is at [57].

Next, we'll briefly consider ways to make SRE attacks more difficult. Although it's impossible to prevent such attacks on an open system such as a PC, we can make life more difficult for Trudy. A good, but dated, source of information on anti-SRE techniques is [53].

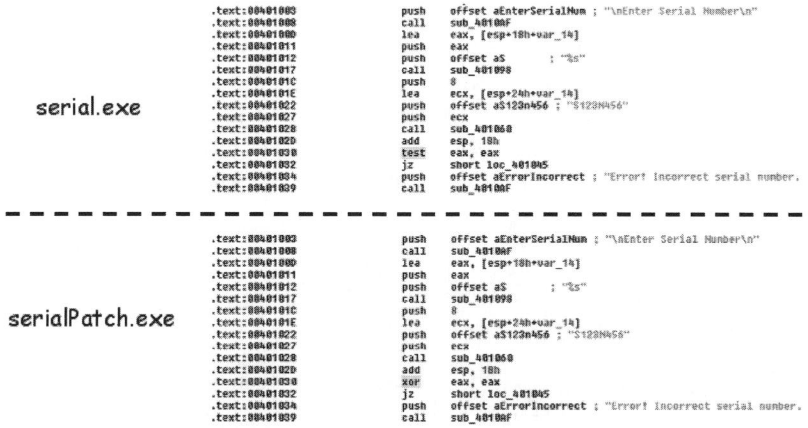

Figure 12.9: Disassembly of Original and Patched

First, we'll consider anti-disassembly techniques, that is, techniques that can be used to confuse a disassembler. Our goal here is to give the attacker an incorrect static view of the code or, better yet, no static view at all. Below, we'll also consider anti-debugging techniques that can be used to obscure the attacker's dynamic view of the code. Then in Section 12.2.5 we'll discuss some tamper-resistance techniques that can be applied to software to make the code more difficult for an attacker to understand and therefore more difficult to patch.

12.2.3 Anti-Disassembly Techniques

There are several well-known anti-disassembly methods.[3] For example, it's possible to encrypt the executable file—when the **exe** file is in encrypted form, it can't be disassembled correctly. But there is a chicken and egg problem here that is similar to the situation that occurs with encrypted viruses. That is, the code must be decrypted before it can be executed. A clever attacker can use the decryption code to gain access to the decrypted executable.

Another simple, but not too effective, anti-disassembly trick is false disassembly [317] which is illustrated in Figure 12.10. In this example, the top part of the figure indicates the actual flow of the program, while the bottom part indicates the false disassembly that will occur if the disassembler is not too smart. In the top part of Figure 12.10, the second instruction causes the program to jump over the junk, which consists of invalid instructions. If a disassembler tries to disassemble these invalid instructions, it will get confused

---

[3]Your verbose author was tempted to call this section "anti-disassemblymentarianism." Fortunately, he resisted the temptation.

and it may even incorrectly disassemble many instructions beyond the end of the junk, since the actual instructions are not aligned properly. However, if Trudy carefully studies this false disassembly, she will eventually realize that inst 2 jumps into the middle of inst 4, and she can then undo the effects. In fact, quality disassemblers will not be seriously confused by such a simple trick, but slightly more complex examples can have some limited effect.

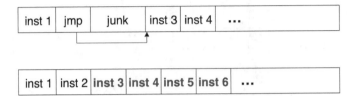

Figure 12.10: False Disassembly

A more sophisticated anti-disassembly trick is self-modifying code. As the name suggests, self-modifying code modifies its own executable in real time [61]. This is a highly effective way to confuse a disassembler, but it's also likely to confuse the developers, since it's difficult to implement, highly error prone, and well-nigh impossible to maintain. Another supposed anti-disassembly approach is discussed in [19].

12.2.4   Anti-Debugging Techniques

There are several methods that can be used to make debugging more difficult. Since debuggers use specific debug registers, a program can monitor the use of these registers and stop (or misbehave) if they are used. That is, a program can monitor for inserted breakpoints, which is a telltale sign of a debugger.

Debuggers don't handle threads well so when properly implemented, interacting threads can offer a relatively strong means for confusing a debugger. In [338] it is shown that by introducing "junk" threads and intentional deadlock among some of these, only a small percentage of the useful code is ever visible in OllyDbg.[4] Furthermore, the code that is visible varies with each run in an unpredictable way. The overhead associated with this approach is fairly high, so it would not be appropriate for the entire code base of a large application. However, this technique could be applied to protect a highly sensitive code section such as that used for entering and checking a serial number.

There are many other debugger-unfriendly tricks, most of which are highly debugger-specific. For example, one anti-debugging technique is illustrated

---

[4]This does not mean that OllyDbg is a bad debugger—this same trick confuses other popular debuggers at least as much as it confuses OllyDbg.

in Figure 12.11. The top part of the figure gives the series of instructions that are to be executed. Suppose that for efficiency, when the processor fetches `inst 1`, it also prefetches `inst 2`, `inst 3`, and `inst 4`. Also, suppose that when the debugger is running, it does not prefetch instructions. Then we can take advantage of this difference to confuse the debugger, as illustrated in the bottom half of Figure 12.11, where `inst 1` overwrites the memory location of `inst 4`. When the program is not being debugged, this causes no problem since `inst 1` through `inst 4` are all fetched at the same time. But if the debugger does not prefetch `inst 4`, it will be confused when it tries to execute the junk that has overwritten `inst 4` [317].

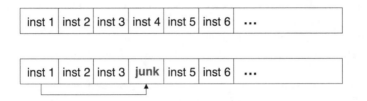

Figure 12.11: Anti-Debugging Example

There are some potential problems with the anti-debugging method in Figure 12.11. First, if the program tries to execute this segment of code more than once (say, within a loop), the junk code will be executed. Also, this code is extremely platform dependent. Finally, if Trudy has enough patience and skill, she will eventually unravel this trick and eliminate its effect.

12.2.5 Software Tamper Resistance

In this section, we discuss several methods that can be employed to make software more tamper resistant. The goal of tamper resistance is to make patching more difficult, either by making the code more difficult to understand or by making the code fail if it's patched. The techniques we'll discuss have been used in practice, but as with most software protection methods, there's little (if any) empirical evidence to support their effectiveness.

12.2.5.1 Guards

It's possible to have a program hash sections of itself as it executes and compare the computed hash values with the known hash values of the original code. If tampering (e.g., patching) occurs, a hash check will fail and the program can take evasive action. These hash checks are sometimes known as guards. Guards can be viewed as a way to make the code fragile in the sense that the code breaks when tampering occurs.

Research has shown that by using guards it's possible to obtain good coverage of software with a minimal performance penalty [54, 145]. But there are some subtle issues. For example, if all guards are identical, then it would be relatively easy for an attacker to automatically detect and remove them. For more information on some issues related to guards, see [268]. Finally, it seems that guards would be ideally suited for use with interacting threads (as discussed above in Section 12.2.4), which could provide a relatively strong defense against tampering.

12.2.5.2   Obfuscation

Another popular form of tamper resistance is code obfuscation. Here, the goal is to make the code difficult to understand. The rationale is that if Trudy can't understand the code, she will have a difficult time patching it. In a sense, code obfuscation is the opposite of good software engineering practices.

As a simple example, spaghetti code can be viewed as a form of obfuscation. There has been much research into more robust methods of obfuscation, and one of the strongest appears to be the *opaque predicate* [64]. For example, consider the following pseudo-code:

```
int x,y;
```
$$\vdots$$
$$\texttt{if}\,((x-y)\,(x-y) > (x^2 - 2xy + y^2))\{\ldots\}$$

Notice that the `if` conditional is always false, since

$$(x-y)(x-y) = x^2 - 2xy + y^2$$

for any values of x and y. But an attacker might waste a significant amount of time analyzing the dead code that follows this `if` conditional. While this particular opaque predicate is not particularly opaque, many non-obvious examples have been developed. Again, this technique will not prevent an attack, but it can substantially increase the time and effort required for a successful attack.

Code obfuscation has sometimes been promoted as a powerful general-purpose security technique. In fact, in Diffie and Hellman's original conception of public key cryptography, they suggested a "one-way compiler" (i.e., an obfuscating compiler) as a possible path toward developing such a cryptosystem [90]. However, obfuscation did not turn out to be useful in public key crypto, and recently it has been convincingly argued that obfuscation cannot provide strong protection in the same sense as, say, cryptography [25]. Nevertheless, obfuscation might still have a significant practical benefit in a field such as software protection.

For example, consider a piece of software that is used to determine authentication. Ultimately, authentication is a one-bit decision, regardless of the precise details of the method used. Therefore, somewhere in the authentication software there is, effectively, a single bit that determines whether authentication succeeds or fails. If Trudy can find this bit, she can force authentication to always succeed and thereby break the security. Obfuscation can make Trudy's job of finding this crucial bit into a challenging game of "hide and seek" in software. Obfuscation can, in effect, smear this one bit of information over a large body of code, thereby forcing Trudy to analyze a considerable amount of code. If the time and difficulty required to understand the obfuscated code is sufficiently high, Trudy might give up. If so, the obfuscation has served a useful purpose.

Obfuscation can also be combined with other methods, including any of the anti-disassembly, anti-debugging, or anti-patching techniques discussed above. All of these will tend to increase Trudy's work. However, it is unrealistic to believe that we can drive the cost so high that an army of persistent attackers cannot eventually break our code.

12.2.6 Metamorphism 2.0

The usual practice in software development is to distribute identical copies, or clones, of a particular piece of software. This has obvious benefits with regard to development, maintainability, and so on. But software cloning has some negative security implications. In particular, if an attack is found on any one copy, the exact same attack will work on all copies. That is, the software has no *break once, break everywhere* resistance, or BOBE resistance (this is sometimes rendered as "break once run anywhere," or BORA).

In the previous chapter, we saw that metamorphic software is used by virus writers in to avoid detection. Might a similar technique be used for good instead of evil? For example, suppose we develop a piece of software, but instead of distributing cloned copies, we distribute metamorphic copies. That is, each copy of our software differs internally, but all copies are functionally identical [285]. This is analogous to the metamorphic malware that we discussed in Chapter 11.

Suppose we distribute N cloned copies of a particular piece of software. Then one successful attack breaks all N clones. In other words, this software has no BOBE resistance. On the other hand, if we distribute N metamorphic copies of the software, where each of these N is functionally identical, but they differ in their internal structure, then an attack on one instance will not necessarily work against any other instances. The strength of such an approach depends heavily on how different the non-clones are, but in the best case, N times as much work is required to break all N instances. This is the best possible situation with respect to BOBE resistance.

Thanks to open platforms and SRE, we cannot prevent attacks on software. Arguably, the best we can hope for is increased BOBE resistance. Metamorphism is one possible way to achieve a reasonable level of BOBE resistance.

An analogy is often made between software diversity and genetic diversity in biological systems [61, 115, 114, 194, 221, 230, 231, 277]. For example, if all plants in a field are genetically identical, then one disease can wipe out the entire field. But if the plants are genetically diverse, then one disease will only kill some of the plants. This is essentially the same reasoning that lies behind metamorphic software.

To illustrate the potential benefits of metamorphism, suppose that our software has a common program flaw, say, an exploitable buffer overflow. If we clone this software, then one successful buffer overflow attack will work against all copies of the software. Suppose instead that the software is metamorphic. Then even if the buffer overflow exists in all instances, the same attack will almost certainly not work against many of the instances, since buffer overflow attacks are—as we saw in Chapter 11—fairly delicate.

Metamorphic software is an intriguing concept that has been used in some applications [46, 275]. The use of metamorphism raises concerns regarding software development, software upgrades, and so on. Note that metamorphism does not prevent SRE, but it can provide significant BOBE resistance. Metamorphism is best known for its use in malware, but perhaps it's not just for evil anymore.

12.3   Digital Rights Management

Digital rights management, or DRM, provides a good example of the limitations of doing security in software. Most of the topics discussed in the previous sections of this chapter are relevant to the DRM problem.

In this section, we'll discuss what DRM is, and is not. Then we'll describe an actual DRM system designed to protect PDF documents within a corporate environment. We'll also briefly outline a DRM system designed to protect streaming media, and we'll discuss a proposed peer-to-peer application that employs DRM.

12.3.1   What is DRM?

At its most fundamental level, DRM can be viewed as an attempt to provide "remote control" over digital content. That is, we would like to distribute digital content, but we want to retain some control over its use after it has been delivered [121].

Suppose Trudy wants to sell her new book, *For the Hack of It*, in digital form online. There is a huge potential market on the Internet, Trudy can keep all of the profits, and nobody will need to pay any shipping charges, so this seems like an ideal solution. However, after a few moments of reflection, Trudy realizes that there is a serious problem. What happens if, say, Alice buys Trudy's digital book and then redistributes it for free online? In the worst case, Trudy might only sell one copy [274, 276].

The fundamental problem is that it's trivial to make a perfect copy of digital content and almost as easy to redistribute it. This is a major change from the pre-digital era, when copying a book was costly and redistributing it was difficult. For an excellent discussion of the challenges faced in the digital age compared with those of the pre-digital era, see the paper [31].

In this section, we'll focus on the digital book example. However, similar comments hold for other digital media, including audio and video.

Persistent protection is a buzzword for the ideal level of DRM protection. That is, we want to protect the digital content so that the protection stays with the content after it's delivered. Examples of the kinds of persistent protection restrictions that we might want to enforce on a digital book include the following:

- No copying

- Read once

- Do not open until Christmas

- No forwarding

What can be done to enforce persistent protection? One option is to rely on the honor system, whereby we do not actually force users to obey the rules but instead simply request that they do so. Since most people are good, honest, decent, law-abiding, and trustworthy, we might expect this to work well. Or maybe not.

Perhaps surprisingly, the honor system has actually been tried. Stephen King, the horror novel writer, published his book *The Plant* online in installments [94, 250]. King said that he would only continue to publish installments if a high enough rate of readers paid.

Of the planned seven installments of *The Plant*, only the first six appeared online. Stephen King's spokesman claimed that the rate of payers had dropped so low that Mr. King would not publish the remaining part online, leaving some angry customers who had paid for 6/7ths of a book [250]. Before dismissing the honor system entirely, it's worth noting that shareware essentially follows the honor system model.

Another option is to give up on enforcing DRM on an open platform such as a PC. In the previous section, we saw that SRE attacks render software on a PC vulnerable. Consequently, if we try to enforce persistent protection through software on an open platform, we are likely doomed to failure.

However, the lure of Internet sales has created an interest in DRM, even if it can't be made perfectly robust. We'll also see that companies have an interest in DRM as a way to comply with certain government regulations.

If we decide that it's worthwhile to attempt DRM on a PC, one option is to build a weak software-based system. Several of these have been deployed, and most are extremely weak. For example, such a DRM system for protecting digital documents might be defeated by a user who is knowledgeable enough to operate a screen capture program.

Another option would be to develop a "strong" software-based DRM system. In the next section we'll describe a system that strives for just such a level of protection. This design is based on a real DRM system developed by your multifaceted author for MediaSnap, Inc., as discussed in [275].

A fairly high level of DRM protection can be achieved on a closed system, such as a game system. These systems are very good at enforcing restrictions similar to the persistent protection requirements mentioned above. There have been efforts to include closed system features in PCs. In large part, this work is motivated by the desire to provide reasonably robust DRM on the PC. We'll return to this topic in Chapter 13 when we discuss Microsoft's Next Generation Secure Computing Base, or NGSCB. In this chapter, we'll only consider software-based DRM.

It is sometimes claimed—or at least strongly implied—that cryptography is the solution to the DRM problem. That this is not the case can easily be seen by considering the generic black box crypto diagram in Figure 12.12, which illustrates a symmetric key system.

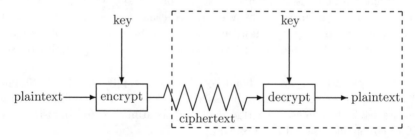

Figure 12.12: Cryptography and DRM

In the standard crypto scenario, the attacker Trudy has access to the ciphertext and perhaps some plaintext and some side-channel information. In the DRM scenario, we are trying to enforce persistent protection on a remote computer. What's more, the legitimate recipient is a potential attacker.

Suppose Trudy is the legitimate recipient of a DRM-protected document. Then Trudy has access to everything within the dashed box in Figure 12.12. In particular, Trudy has access to the key. We certainly can't expect crypto to solve our problem if we give the attacker the key!

With DRM, it's necessary to use encryption so that the data can be securely delivered, and so that Trudy can't trivially remove the persistent protection. But if Trudy is clever, she won't attack the crypto directly. Instead, she will try to find the key, which is hidden somewhere in the software (or at least available to the software at some point in the process). One of the fundamental problems in DRM can be reduced to the problem of playing hide and seek with a key in software [266].

Out of necessity, software-based DRM systems rely largely on *security by obscurity*, that is, the security resides in the fact that Trudy doesn't completely understand the system. In a sense, this is the opposite of Kerckhoffs' Principle. Security by obscurity is generally considered a derogatory term in the security field, since once the obscurity is gone, so is the security. However, in software-based DRM, there is often no other viable option.

Software obfuscation and the other techniques discussed in the previous section are examples of security by obscurity. It's always preferable not to rely on security by obscurity, but, when there is no other option, then we need to consider whether we can derive any useful measure of security from some clever application of obscurity.[5]

Current DRM systems also rely heavily on secret designs, in clear violation of the spirit of Kerckhoffs' Principle. Of course, this is partly due to the reliance on obscurity, but even a general overview of the security architecture is unavailable for most DRM systems, unless it has been provided by some outside source. For example, details on Apple's Fairplay DRM system were not available from Apple, but can be found, for example, in [313].

There is a fundamental limit on the effectiveness of any DRM system, since the so-called *analog hole* is always present. That is, when the content is rendered, it can be captured in analog form—for example, when digital music is played, it can be recorded using a microphone, regardless of the strength of the DRM protection. Similarly, a digital book can be captured in unprotected form using a digital camera to photograph the pages displayed on a computer screen. Such attacks are outside the boundaries of a DRM system.

Another interesting feature of DRM is the degree to which human nature matters. For software-based systems, it's clear that absolute DRM security is impossible, so the challenge is to develop something that might work in practice. Whether this is possible or not depends heavily on the context, as we'll see in the examples discussed below. The bottom line is that DRM is not strictly a technical problem. While this is also true of many security

---

[5]In spite of its bad name, security by obscurity is used surprisingly often in the real world. For example, system administrators often rename important system files so that they are more difficult for an attacker to locate. If Trudy breaks into the system, it will take her some time to locate these important files, and the longer it takes, the better chance we have of detecting her presence. So, it does make sense to use obscurity in situations such as this.

topics (passwords, the MiM "attack" on SSL, etc.), it's more obvious in DRM than in many other areas.

We've mentioned several times that strong software-based DRM is impossible. Let's be explicit as to why this is the case. From the previous SRE sections, it should be clear that we can't really hide a secret in software, since we can't prevent SRE. A user with full administrator privilege can eventually break any anti-SRE protection and thereby attack DRM software that is trying to enforce persistent protection. In other words, SRE is the "killer app" for attacking software-based DRM.

Next we describe a real-world DRM system designed to protect PDF documents. Then we discuss a system designed to protect streaming media, another system designed for a P2P environment, and, finally, the role of DRM within a corporate environment. Other DRM systems are described in [241] and [314].

12.3.2   A Real-World DRM System

The information in this section is based on a DRM system designed and developed by MediaSnap, Inc., a small Silicon Valley startup company. The system is intended for use with digital documents that will be distributed via email.

There are two major components to the MediaSnap DRM systems, a server component that we'll call the Secure Document Server, or SDS, and the client software, which is a software plugin to the Adobe PDF reader.

Suppose Alice wants to send a DRM-protected document to Bob. Alice first creates the document, then attaches it to an email. She selects the recipient, Bob, in the usual way, and she uses a special pull down menu on her email client to select the desired level of persistent protection. She then sends the email.

The entire email, including any attachments, is converted to PDF and it is then encrypted (using standard crypto techniques) and sent to the SDS. It is the SDS that applies the desired persistent protection to the document. The SDS then packages the document so that only Bob can access it using his client DRM software—it is the client software that will attempt to enforce the persistent protection. The resulting document is then emailed to Bob. This process is illustrated in Figure 12.13.

A key is required to access the DRM-protected document, and this key is stored on the SDS. Whenever Bob wants to access the protected document, he must first authenticate to the SDS and only then will the key be sent from the SDS to Bob. Once Bob gets the key, he can access the document, but only through the DRM software. This process is illustrated in Figure 12.14.

There are security issues both on the server side and on the client side. The SDS must protect keys and authenticate users, and it must apply the

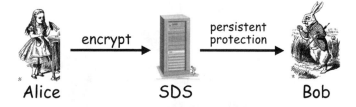

Figure 12.13: DRM for PDF Documents

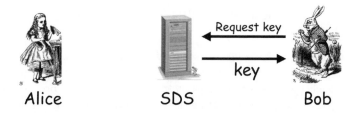

Figure 12.14: Accessing Protected Documents

required persistent protection to documents. The client software must protect keys, authenticate users, and enforce the persistent protection, all while operating in a potentially hostile environment. The SDS resides at corporate headquarters and is relatively secure. The DRM client software, on the other hand, is readily available to any attacker. The discussion below concerns the client software.

The high-level design of the client software is illustrated in Figure 12.15. The software has an outer layer that attempts to create a tamper-resistant barrier. This includes anti-disassembly and anti-debugging techniques, some of which were discussed above. For example, the executable code is encrypted, and false disassembly is used to protect the part of the code that performs the decryption. In addition, the executable code is only decrypted in small slices so that it's more difficult for an attacker to obtain the entire code in plaintext form.

The anti-debugging technique is fairly sophisticated, although the basic idea is simply to monitor for the use of the debug registers. One obvious attack on such a scheme is essentially a man-in-the-middle, where the attacker debugs the code but responds to the anti-debugging software in such a way that it appears no debugger is running.

We know from the previous section that tamper-resistance techniques can delay an attacker, but they can't prevent a persistent attacker from eventual success. The software inside the tamper-resistant layer is heavily obfuscated to further delay an attacker who has penetrated the tamper-resistant outer layer.

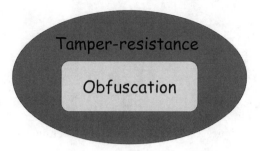

Figure 12.15: DRM Software Design

The obfuscation is applied to security critical operations, including key management, authentication, and cryptography. The authentication information is cached, since we don't want to ask the user to repeatedly enter a password (or other means of authentication). Each time the authentication data is cached, it is cached in a different location in memory and in a different form.

The digital content is encrypted using the Advanced Encryption Standard (AES) block cipher. Unfortunately, standard crypto is difficult to obfuscate since the algorithms are well known and the implementations are standardized for efficiency and to prevent implementation errors. As a result, the MediaSnap system also employs a "scrambling" algorithm, which is essentially a proprietary cipher. This scrambling is used in addition to—and not in place of—a strong cipher, so there is no violation of Kerckhoffs' Principle.

The scrambling algorithm, which is itself obfuscated, presents a much more substantial SRE challenge than a standard cipher, such as AES. The keys are also obfuscated by splitting them into multiple parts and hiding some parts in data and other parts in code. In short, the MediaSnap system employs multiple layers of obfuscation.

Another security feature implemented by the system is an anti-screen capture technique, which is somewhat analogous to the anti-debugging technique mentioned above. Digital watermarking is also employed. As we learned in Chapter 5, watermarking is designed to provide the ability to trace stolen content. However, in practice, watermarking has proven to be of relatively limited value, particularly if the attacker knows the watermarking scheme.

The MediaSnap DRM software employs metamorphism for BOBE resistance. The metamorphism is implemented in several places, most notably in the scrambling algorithms. We'll have more to say about this below when we discuss a DRM application designed to protect streaming media.

The MediaSnap DRM system employs a wide variety of software protection techniques. It is almost certainly one of the most advanced software-based DRM systems ever attempted. The only significant protection mechanism not employed is the guards or "fragilization" technique discussed above, and the only reason guards are not used is that they're not easily incorporated with encrypted executable code.

One major security concern that we did not yet mention is the role of the operating system. In particular, if we can't trust the operating system to behave correctly, then our DRM client software can be undercut by attacks on the operating system. The topic of trusted operating systems is the focus of the next chapter.

12.3.3 DRM for Streaming Media

Suppose we want to stream digital audio or video over the Internet, and this digital media is to be viewed in real time. If we want to charge money for this service, how can we protect the content from capture and redistribution? This sounds like a job for DRM. The DRM system we describe here follows the design given in [282].

Possible attacks on streaming media include spoofing the stream between the endpoints, man-in-the-middle, replay or redistribution of the data, and capturing the plaintext at the client. We are concerned primarily with the latter attack. The threat here arises from unauthorized software that is used to capture the plaintext stream on the client.

The most innovative feature of our proposed design is the use of scrambling algorithms, which are encryption-like algorithms, as described in the previous section. We'll assume that we have a large number of distinct scrambling algorithms at our disposal and we'll use these to achieve a significant degree of metamorphism.

Each instance of the client software comes equipped with a large number of scrambling algorithms included. Each client has a distinct subset of scrambling algorithms chosen from a master set of all scrambling algorithms, and the server knows this master set. The client and server must negotiate a specific scrambling algorithm to be used for a particular piece of digital content. We'll describe this negotiation process below.

We'll also encrypt the content so that we don't need to rely on the scrambling algorithm for cryptographic strength. The purpose of the scrambling is metamorphism—and BOBE resistance—not cryptographic security.

The data is scrambled and then encrypted on the server. On the client, the data must be decrypted and then de-scrambled. The de-scrambling occurs in a proprietary device driver, just prior to rendering the content. The purpose of this approach is to keep the plaintext away from the attacker, Trudy, until the last possible moment prior to rendering.

In the design discussed here, Trudy is faced with a proprietary device driver and each copy of the software has a unique set of hardcoded scrambling algorithms. Therefore, Trudy is faced with a significant SRE challenge and each copy of the client software presents a distinct challenge. Consequently, the overall system should have good BOBE resistance.

Suppose the server knows N different scrambling algorithms, denoted $s_0, s_1, \ldots, s_{N-1}$. Each client is equipped with a subset of these algorithms. For example, a particular client might have the scrambling algorithms

$$\text{LIST} = \{s_{12}, s_{45}, s_2, s_{37}, s_{23}, s_{31}\}.$$

This LIST is stored on the client as $E(\text{LIST}, K_{\text{server}})$, where K_{server} is a key that only the server knows. The primary benefit of this approach is that the database that maps clients to their scrambling algorithms is distributed among the clients, eliminating a potential burden on the server. Notice that this approach is reminiscent of the way Kerberos uses TGTs to manage security-critical information.

To negotiate a scrambling algorithm, the client sends its LIST to the server. The server then decrypts the LIST and chooses one of the algorithms that is built into the client. The server must then securely communicate its scrambling algorithm choice to the client. This process is illustrated in Figure 12.16, where the server has selected the mth scrambling algorithm on the client's LIST. Here, the key K is a session key that has been established between the client and server.

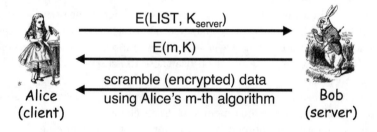

Figure 12.16: Scrambling Algorithm Selection

The metamorphism provided by the scrambling algorithms is deeply embedded in the system and tied to all of the data. Furthermore, if the server knows that a particular scrambling algorithm is broken, the server won't select it. And if a particular client has too many broken algorithms, the server will force a software upgrade before agreeing to distribute the content.

The server can also distribute the client software (or some crucial component of it) immediately prior to distributing the content. This would make it more difficult for Trudy to capture the streamed media in real time, due to the limited time available to attack the software. Of course, Trudy could record the stream and then attack the software at her leisure. However, in many situations, an attack that is not close to real time would be of little concern.

Since the scrambling algorithms are unknown to the attacker, they require a significant effort to reverse engineer, whereas a standard crypto algorithm does not need to be reverse engineered at all—the attacker only needs to find the key. As we mentioned above, it could be argued that such use of scrambling algorithms is just security by obscurity. But in this particular application, it appears to be of some value since it improves BOBE resistance.

12.3.4 DRM for a P2P Application

Today, much digital content is delivered via peer-to-peer, or P2P, networks. For example, such networks contain large amounts of illegal, or pirated, music. The following scheme is designed to gently coerce users into paying a small fee for legal content that is distributed over a P2P network. Note that this P2P network may contain large amounts of illegal content in addition to the legal content.

The scheme we describe here is based on the work of Exploit Systems [108]. But before we discuss this application in detail, let's briefly review how a P2P network works.

Suppose Alice has joined a P2P network, and she requests some music, say, "Relay" by The Who. Then a query for this song floods through the network, and any peer who has the song—and is willing to share it—responds to Alice. This is illustrated in Figure 12.17. In this example, Alice can choose to download the song from either Carol or Pat.

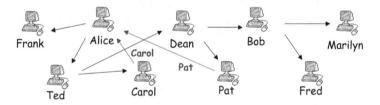

Figure 12.17: P2P Network

Figure 12.18 illustrates the same scenario in a P2P network that includes a special peer that we'll call a *peer offering service*, or POS. The POS acts much like any other peer, except that it has only legal—and DRM-protected—music.

When Alice makes her request on a P2P network with a POS, it appears to her that she has received responses from Bill, Ben, Carol, Joe, and Pat. If Alice selects to download the music from Bill, Ben, or Joe, she will receive DRM protected content for which she will be required to pay a small fee before she can listen to the music. On the other hand, if Alice selects either Carol or Pat, she receives the music for free, just as in the P2P network without the POS.

For the POS concept to work, it must not be apparent to Alice whether a peer is an ordinary peer or a POS peer. In addition, the POS must have a significant percentage of its peers appear in the top ten responses. Let's assume that these technical challenges can be resolved in favor of the POS.

Now suppose Alice first selects Bill, Ben, or Joe. Then after downloading the music and discovering that she must pay, Alice is free to select another peer and, perhaps, another, until she finds one that has pirated (i.e., free) music. But is it worth Alice's time to download the song repeatedly just to avoid paying? If the music is priced low enough, perhaps not. In addition, the legal (DRM-protected) version can offer extras that might further entice Alice to pay a small fee.

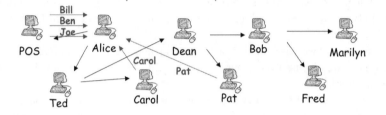

Figure 12.18: P2P Network with POS

The POS idea is clever, since it piggybacks on existing P2P networks. And in the POS scenario, relatively weak DRM is sufficient. As long as it's more trouble for Alice to break the DRM than to click and wait for another download, the DRM has served its purpose.

12.3.5   Enterprise DRM

There are government regulations that require companies to protect certain types of private information and there are similar regulations regarding many types of business records. For example, the Health Insurance Portability and Accountability Act, or HIPAA, requires that companies protect personal medical records. HIPAA stipulates fines of up to $10,000 per incident (i.e., per record) for failing to provide sufficient protection. Companies that deal with medical records often need to make such records accessible to certain employees, but, due to HIPAA, they also must be careful that these records do not leak to unauthorized recipients. DRM can help to solve this problem.

The Sarbanes-Oxley Act, or SOA, requires that companies must preserve certain documents, such as information that might be relevant to insider trading stock violations. Again, DRM could be used here to be sure that such information is protected as required by law. The bottom line is that DRM-like protections are needed by corporations for regulatory compliance.

We refer to this as *enterprise DRM* to distinguish it from the e-commerce scenarios discussed above.

From a technical point of view, the enterprise DRM security requirements are similar to those for e-commerce. But the motivation for enterprise DRM is entirely different, since the purpose is to prevent a company from losing money (due to fines) instead of being an avenue for making money (as in e-commerce). More significantly, the human dimension is completely different. In an enterprise setting the threat of reprisals (getting fired or sued) are far more plausible than in the e-commerce setting. Also, the required level of protection is different. In enterprise DRM, a corporation has likely shown due diligence and thereby complied with the regulations, provided that an active attack on the DRM system is required to break its security. A moderate level of DRM is sufficient in this case. From a technical perspective, enterprise DRM is very much a solvable problem.

In e-commerce, the strength of the DRM system is the predominate concern. But in the enterprise setting, other more mundane issues are more important [286]. For example, policy management is an important concern. That is, it must be easy for an administrator to set policies for individual users, groups, etc. Authentication issues are also significant, since the DRM system must interface with an existing corporate authentication system, and the system must prevent authentication spoofing. From a technical perspective, these are not major obstacles.

DRM for e-commerce and enterprise DRM face similar technical hurdles. But because the human dimension is so different, one is virtually unsolvable (at least for software-based systems), while the other is fairly easy.

12.3.6 DRM Failures

There are far too many examples of failed e-commerce DRM systems to list them all here, but we'll mention a few. One infamous system could be defeated by a felt-tip pen [97], while another was defeated by holding down the shift key while downloading the content [6].

The Secure Digital Music Initiative, or SDMI, is an interesting case. Prior to implementing SDMI on real-world systems, the SDMI Consortium posted a series of challenge problems online, presumably to show how secure their system would be in practice. A group of researchers was able to completely break the security of the SDMI, and for their hard work they were rewarded with the threat of multiple lawsuits. Eventually the attackers' results were published, and they make fascinating reading—particularly with respect to the inherent limitations of watermarking schemes [71].

Major corporations have put forth DRM systems that were easily broken. For example, Adobe eBooks security was defeated [23, 133], and as in the case of SDMI, the attacker's reward consisted of unenforceable legal threats [310].

Another poor DRM system was Microsoft's MS-DRM (version 2). Microsoft violated Kerckhoffs' Principle, which resulted in a fatally flawed block cipher algorithm. The attacker in this case was "Beale Screamer" [29], who avoided legal reprisals, presumably due to his anonymity.

12.3.7   DRM Conclusions

DRM illustrates the limitations of doing security in software, particularly when that software must function in a hostile environment. Such software is vulnerable to attack, and the protection options are extremely limited. In other words, the attacker has nearly all of the advantages.

Tamper-resistant hardware and a trusted operating system can make a significant difference. We'll discuss these topics more in Chapter 13.

In the next section, we shift gears to discuss security issues related to software development. Much of our discussion will be focused through the lens of the open source versus closed source software debate.

12.4   Software Development

The standard approach to software development is to develop and release a product as quickly as possible. While some testing is done, it is almost never sufficient, so the code is patched as flaws are discovered by users.[6] In security, this is known as *penetrate and patch.*

Penetrate and patch is a bad way to develop software in general, and a terrible way to develop secure software. Since it's a security liability, why is this the standard software development paradigm? There is more to it than simply an ethical failing by software developers. In software, whoever is first to market is likely to become the market leader, even if their product ultimately is inferior to the competition. And in the computing world, the market leader tends to dominate more so than in most fields. This first to market advantage creates an overwhelming incentive to sell software before it's been thoroughly tested.

There also seems to be an implicit assumption that if you patch bad software long enough it will eventually become good software. This is sometimes referred to as the *penetrate and patch fallacy* [317]. Why is this a fallacy? For one thing, there is huge body of empirical evidence to the contrary—regardless of the number of service packs applied, software continues to exhibit serious flaws. In fact, patches often add new flaws. And software is a moving target due to new versions, new features, changing environment, new uses, new attacks, and so on.

---

[6]Note that "patch" has a slightly different meaning here than in the SRE context. Here, it means "to fix bugs," whereas in SRE it refers to a change made directly to the executable code to add, remove, or modify certain features of the software.

Another contributing factor toward the current sorry state of software security is that users generally find it easier and safer to follow the leader. For example, a system administrator probably won't get fired if his system has a serious flaw, provided everybody else has the same flaw. On the other hand, that same administrator might not receive much credit if his system works normally while other systems are having problems.

Yet another major impetus for doing things like everybody else is that administrators and users have more people they can ask for support. Together, these perverse economic incentives are sometimes collectively referred to as *network economics* [14].

Secure software development is difficult and costly. Development must be done carefully, with security in mind from the beginning. And, as we'll make somewhat precise below, an extraordinarily large amount of testing is required to achieve reasonably low bug rates. It's certainly cheaper and easier to let customers do the testing, particularly when there is no serious economic disincentive to do so, and, due to network economics, there is an enormous incentive to rush to market.

Why is there no economic disincentive for flawed software? Even if a software flaw causes major losses to a corporation, the software vendor has no legal liability. Few, if any, other products enjoy a comparable legal status. In fact it's sometimes suggested that holding software vendors legally liable for the adverse effects of their products would be a market-friendly way to improve the quality of software. But software vendors have so far successfully argued that such liability would stifle innovation. In any case, it's far from certain that such an approach would have any serious impact on the overall quality of software. Even if software quality did improve, the cost might be greater than anticipated and there would certainly be some unintended negative consequences.

12.4.1   Open Versus Closed Source Software

We'll look at some of the security problems inherent in software through the prism of the open source versus closed source debate. Some of the conclusions will probably surprise you.

With open source software, the source code is available to users. For example, the Linux operating system is open source. With closed source software, on the other hand, the source code is not available to the general public. Windows is an example of closed source software. In this section, we want to examine the relative security strengths and weaknesses of open source and closed source software.

The primary claimed security advantages of open source software can be summarized as "more eyeballs," that is, more people can look at the code, so fewer flaws should remain undiscovered. This is really just a variant on

Kerckhoffs' Principle, and what self-respecting security person could possibly argue with that?

However, upon closer examination, the benefit of more eyeballs becomes more questionable, at least with respect to software security. First, how many of these eyeballs are looking for security flaws? And how many are focused on the low-level (tedious, boring) parts of the code, which are more likely to harbor security flaws? Also, how many of these eyeballs belong to people who are knowledgable about security—those who would have a realistic chance of discovering subtle security flaws?

Another issue with open source is that attackers can also look for flaws in the source code. Conceivably, an ingenious evil coder might even be able to insert a security flaw into an open source project. While this may sound far-fetched, the Underhanded C Contest shows that it's possible to write evil code that looks innocent [70].

An interesting open source case study is `wu-ftp`. This open source software is of modest size, at about 8,000 lines of code, and it implements a security-critical application (file transfer). Yet this software was widely deployed and in use for ten years before serious security flaws were discovered [317]. More generally, the open source movement appears to have done little to reduce security flaws. Perhaps the fundamental problem is that open source software also follows the penetrate and patch model of development. However, there is some evidence that open source software is significantly less buggy than closed source [84].

If open source software has its security issues, certainly closed source software is worse. Or is it? The security flaws in closed source are not as visible to attackers, which could be viewed as providing some protection (although it could be argued that this is just a form of security by obscurity). But does this provide any significant protection? Given the record of attacks on closed source software, it is clear that many exploits do not require source code—our simple SRE example in Section 12.2 illustrates why this is the case. Although it is possible to analyze closed source code, it's a lot more work than for open source software.

Advocates of open source often cite the *Microsoft fallacy* as a reason why open source software is inherently superior to closed source [317]. This fallacy can be summarized as follows.

1. Microsoft makes bad software.

2. Microsoft software is closed source.

3. Therefore all closed source software is bad.

While it is always tempting to blame everything on Microsoft, this one doesn't hold water. For one thing, it's not logically correct. Perhaps the real issue is the fact that Microsoft follows the penetrate and patch model.

Next, we'll take a little closer look at the security of open source and closed source software. But before we get to that, it's reasonable to ponder why Microsoft software is successfully attacked so often. Is there some fundamental problem with Microsoft software?

Microsoft is obviously a big target for any attacker—an attacker who wants the most bang for the buck is naturally attracted to Microsoft. While there are few exploits against, say, Mac OS X, this almost certainly has more to do with the fact that it receives less attention from hackers (and, not coincidentally, the hacker tools are much less well developed) than any inherent security advantage of OS X. An attack on OS X would do far less damage overall and therefore bring less "glory" to the attacker. Even from the perspective of stealthy attacks, such as botnets, there is much more incentive to attack a big target like Microsoft—numbers matter.

Now let's consider the security implications of open and closed source software from a slightly more theoretical angle. It can be shown that the probability of a security failure after t units of testing is about K/t, where K is a constant, and this approximation holds over a large range of values for t [12]. The constant K is a measure of the initial quality of the software—the smaller K, the better the software was initially. This formula implies that the *mean time between failure*, or MTBF, is given by

$$\text{MTBF} = t/K. \tag{12.1}$$

That is, the average amount of time until some software security flaw rears its ugly head and causes problems is t/K, where t is the amount of time that has been spent testing the software. The bottom line is that software security improves with testing, but it only improves linearly.

The implication of equation (12.1) is bad news for the good guys. For example, to achieve a level of, say, 1,000,000 hours between security failures, software must be tested for (on the order of) 1,000,000 hours.

Is it really true that software only improves linearly with testing? Empirical results have shown that this is the case, and it is the conventional wisdom of many in the software field that this is reality for large and complex software systems [14].

What does equation (12.1) imply about the security of open source versus closed source software? Consider a large and complex open source project. Then we would expect this project to satisfy equation (12.1). Now suppose this same project was instead closed source. Then it would be reasonable to expect that the flaws are harder to find than in the open source case. For simplicity, suppose the flaws are twice as hard to find in the closed source case. Then it might seem that

$$\text{MTBF} = 2t/K. \tag{12.2}$$

If this is correct, closed source software is twice as secure as open source. However, equation (12.2) is not correct, since the closed source testing is only half as effective as in the open source case, that is, we need to test twice as long to expose the same number of bugs. In other words, the closed source software has more security flaws, but they are harder to find. In fact, if the flaws are twice as hard to find, then our testing is only half as effective and we arrive back at equation (12.1). This Zen-like argument shows that, in some sense, the security of open and closed source software is indistinguishable— see [12] for more details.

It might be argued that closed source software has open source alpha testing, where flaws are found at the higher open source rate, since developers have access to the software. This alpha testing is followed by closed source beta testing and use, where customers actually use the software and, effectively, test it in the process. This combination would seem to yield the best of both worlds—fewer bugs due to the open source alpha testing with the remaining bugs harder to find due to the code being closed source. However, in the larger scheme of things, alpha testing is a small part of the total testing, particularly with the pressures to rush to market. Although this argument could, in principle, give an edge to closed source, in practice it's probably not a significant advantage. The surprising conclusion here is that open and closed source software are probably about the same from a security perspective.

12.4.2   Finding Flaws

A fundamental security problem with software testing is that the good guys must find almost all security flaws, whereas Trudy only needs to find one that the good guys haven't yet found. This implies that software reliability is far more challenging in security than in software engineering in general.

An example from [14] nicely illustrates this asymmetric warfare between attacker and defender. Recall that the mean time between faliure is given by $\text{MTBF} = t/K$. For the sake of argument, suppose there are 10^6 security flaws in a large and complex software project and assume that for each individual flaw, $\text{MTBF} = 10^9$ hours. That is, any specific flaw is expected to show up after about a billion hours of use. Then, since there are 10^6 flaws, we would expect to observe one flaw for every $10^9/10^6 = 10^3$ hours of testing or use.

Suppose that the good guys hire 10,000 testers who spend a total of 10^7 hours testing, and they find, as expected, 10^4 flaws. Evil Trudy, by herself, spends 10^3 hours testing and finds one flaw. Since the good guys found only 1% of the flaws, the chance that they found Trudy's specific bug is only 1%. This is not good. As we've seen in other areas of security, the math overwhelmingly favors the bad guys.

12.4.3 Other Software Development Issues

Software development generally includes the following steps [235]: specify, design, implement, test, review, document, manage, and maintain. Most of these topics are beyond the scope of this book, but in this section, we'll mention a few software development issues that have a significant impact on security.

Secure software development is not easy, as our previous discussion of testing indicates. And testing is only part of the development process. To improve security, much more time and effort are required throughout the entire development process. Unfortunately, there is little or no economic incentive for this today.

Next, we'll briefly discuss the following security-critical software development topics:

- Design

- Hazard analysis

- Peer review

- Testing

- Configuration management

- Postmortem for mistakes

We've already discussed testing, but we'll have more to say about some other testing-related issues below.

The design phase is critical for security since a careful initial design can avoid high-level errors that are difficult—if not impossible—to correct later. Perhaps the most important point is to design security features in from the start, since retrofitting security is difficult, if not impossible. Internet protocols offer an excellent illustration of this difficulty. IPv4, for example, has no built-in security, while the new-and-improved version, IPv6, makes IPSec mandatory. However, the transition to IPv6 is proving slow to nonexistent and, consequently, the Internet remains much less secure than it could be.

Usually an informal approach is used at the design phase, but so-called *formal methods* can sometimes be applied [40]. Using formal methods, it's possible to rigorously prove that a design is correct. Unfortunately, formal methods are generally too difficult to be practical in most real-world situations.

To build secure software, the threats must be considered in advance. This is where the field of *hazard analysis* comes into play. There are several informal ways to approach this problem, such as developing a hazard list containing potential security problems, or simply making a list of "what ifs."

A slightly more systematic approach is Schneier's *attack tree* concept, where possible attacks are organized into a tree-like structure [259]. A nice feature of this approach is that you can prune entire branches of attacks if you can prevent the attacks closer to the root of the tree.

There are several other approaches to hazard analysis, including hazard and operability studies (HAZOP), failure modes and effective analysis (FMEA), and fault tree analysis (FTA) [235]. We'll not discuss these topics here.

Peer review is also a useful tool for improving security. There are three levels of peer review which, from most informal to most formal, are sometimes called *review, walk-through,* and *inspection.* Each level of review is useful, and there is good empirical evidence that peer review is effective [235].

Next, we'll discuss testing, but from a different perspective than above in Section 12.4. Testing occurs at different levels of the development process, which can be categorize as follows:

- *Module testing* — Small sections of the code are tested individually.

- *Component testing* — A few modules are combined and tested together.

- *Unit testing* — Many components are combined for testing.

- *Integration testing* — Everything is put everything together and tested as a whole.

At each of these levels, security flaws can be uncovered. For example, features that interact in a new or unexpected way may evade detection at the component level but be exposed during integration testing.

Another way to view testing is based on its purpose. We can define categories as follows:

- *Function testing* — Here, we verify that the system functions as required.

- *Performance testing* — Requirements such as speed and resource use are verified.

- *Acceptance testing* — The customer is actively involved.

- *Installation testing* — Not surprisingly, this is testing done at install time.

- *Regression testing* — Testing that is done after any significant change to the system.

Again, security vulnerabilities can be exposed during any of these types of testing.

Another useful testing technique is *active fault detection*, where instead of simply waiting for a system to fail, the tester actively tries to make it fail. This is the approach that an attacker will follow and it might uncover security flaws that a more passive approach would miss.

An interesting concept is *fault injection*, where faults are inserted into the process, even if there is no obvious way for such a fault to occur. This might, for example, reveal buffer overflow problems that would otherwise go unnoticed if the testing is restricted to expected inputs.

Bug injection can enable testers to obtain an estimate on the number of bugs remaining in code. Suppose we insert 100 bugs into our code and our testers find 30 of these. Further, suppose that in addition to these 30 bugs, our testers find 300 other bugs. Since the testers found 30% of the inserted bugs, it might be reasonable to assume that they also found 30% of the actual bugs. If so, then roughly 700 bugs would remain, after removing all of the discovered bugs and the 70 remaining inserted bugs. Of course, this assumes that the injected bugs are similar to the naturally occurring bugs, which is probably not entirely valid. Nevertheless, bug injection may provide a useful estimate of the number of bugs and, indirectly, the number of security flaws.

A testing case history is given in [235]. In this example, the system had 184,000 lines of code. Flaws were found at the following rates:

- 17.3% were found when inspecting the system design.

- 19.1% were found inspecting component design.

- 15.1% were found during code inspection.

- 29.4% were found during integration testing.

- 16.6% were found during system and regression testing.

The conclusion is that many kinds of testing must be conducted and that overlapping testing is helpful.

Configuration management, that is, how we deal with changes to a system, can also be a security-critical issue. Several types of changes can occur, and these changes can be categorized as follows: *minor changes* are needed to maintain daily functioning, *adaptive changes* are more substantial modifications, while *perfective changes* are improvements to the software, and, finally, *preventive changes*, which are intended to prevent any loss of performance [235]. Any such changes to a system can introduce new security flaws or expose existing flaws, either directly as a result of the new software, or due to interactions with the existing software base.

After identifying and fixing any security flaw, it is important to carefully analyze the flaw. This sort of *postmortem analysis* is the best way to learn from the problem and thereby increase the odds that a similar problem will be avoided in the future. In security, we always learn more when things go wrong than when they go right. If we fail to analyze those cases where we know that things went wrong, then we've missed a significant opportunity. Postmortem analysis may be the most underutilized method in all of security engineering.

As we observed earlier in this chapter, security testing is far more demanding than non-security testing. In the latter case, we need to verify that the system does what it's supposed to, while in security testing we must verify that the system does what it is supposed to and nothing more. That is, there can be no unintended "features," since any such feature provides a potential avenue of attack.

In any realistic scenario, it's almost certainly impossible to do exhaustive testing. Furthermore, the MTBF formula discussed in Section 12.4.1 indicates that an extraordinarily large amount of testing would be required to achieve a high level of security. So, is secure software really as hopeless as it seems? Fortunately, there may be a loophole. If we can eliminate an entire class of potential security flaws with one (or a few) tests, then the statistical model that the MTBF is based on will break down [14]. For example, if we have a test (or a few tests) that enable us to find all buffer overflows, then we can eliminate this entire class of serious flaws with a relatively small amount of work. This is the holy grail of software testing in general, and security testing in particular.

The bottom line on secure software development is that network economics and penetrate and patch are the biggest enemies of secure software. Unfortunately, there is generally little incentive for secure software development, and until that changes, we probably can't expect major improvements in security. In those cases where security is a high priority, it is possible to develop reasonably secure software, but there is most definitely a cost. That is, proper development practices can minimize security flaws, but secure development is a costly and time-consuming proposition.[7] For all of these reasons (and more), you should not expect to see a dramatic improvements in software security anytime soon.

Even with the best software development practices, security flaws will still exist. Since absolute security is almost never possible in the real world, it should not be surprising that absolute security in software is not realistic. In any case, the goal of secure software development—as in most areas of security—is to minimize and manage the risks.

---

[7] As you probably realize, it's that annoying "no free lunch" thing yet again.

12.5 Summary

In this chapter we showed that security in software is difficult to achieve. We focused on three topics, namely, reverse engineering, digital rights management, and software development.

Software reverse engineering (SRE) illustrates what an attacker can do to software. Even without access to the source code, an attacker can understand and modify your code. Making very limited use of the available tools, we were able to easily defeat the security of a program. While there are things that can be done to make reverse engineering more difficult, as a practical matter, most software is wide open to SRE-based attacks.

We then discussed digital rights management (DRM), which illustrates the futility of attempting to enforce strong security measures through software. After our look at SRE, this should not have come as a surprise.

Finally, we discussed the difficulties involved in secure software development. Although we looked at the problem from the perspective of open source versus closed source software, from any perspective secure software development is extremely challenging. Some elementary math confirms that the attacker has most of the advantages. Nevertheless, it is possible—although difficult and costly—to develop reasonably secure software. Unfortunately, today secure software is the exception rather than the rule.

12.6 Problems

1. Obtain the file `SRE.zip` from the textbook website and extract the Windows executable.

   a. Patch the code so that any serial number results in the message "Serial number is correct!!!" Turn in a screen capture showing your results.

   b. Determine the correct serial number.

2. For the SRE example in Section 12.2.2, we patched the code by changing a `test` instruction to `xor`.

   a. Give at least two ways—other than changing `test` to `xor`—that Trudy could patch the code so that any serial number will work.

   b. Changing the `jz` instruction that appears at address `0x401032` in Figure 12.4 to `jnz` is not a correct solution to part a. Why not?

3. Obtain the file `unknown.zip` from the textbook website and extract the Java class file `unknown.class`.

   a. Use CafeBabe [44] to reverse this class file.

b. Analyze the code to determine what the program does.

4. Obtain the file `Decorator.zip` from the textbook website and extract the file `Decorator.jar`. This program is designed to evaluate a student's application for admission based on various test scores. Applicants applying to medical school must include their score on the MCAT test score, while applicants to law school must include their score on the LSAT test. Applicants to the graduate school (which includes Law and Medicine) must include their score on the GRE test, and foreign applicants must include their score on the TOEFL exam. An applicant is accepted if his or her GPA is above 3.5 and they exceed a set threshold for their required tests (MCAT, LSAT, GRE, TOEFL). Since the school is locate in California, the requirements are more lenient for California residents. This program creates six applicants of which two are not accepted because of their low score. Finally, the program was obfuscated using ProGuard (using only options under the "obfuscation" button, i.e., no shrinking, optimization, etc., were applied); see [58] for a detailed solution to a similar example.

   a. Patch the program so that the two applicants who were not accepted are accepted. Accomplish this by lowering the thresholds in their respective failing categories to the values of their scores.

   b. Using the result from part a, further patch the code so that a California resident who was accepted (in the original program) is now rejected.

5. Obtain the file `encrypted.zip` from the textbook website and extract the file `encrypted.jar`. This application was encrypted using SandMark [63], with the "obfuscate" tab and "Class Encryptor" option selected and, possibly, other obfuscation options.

   a. Generate a decompiled version of this program directly from the obfuscated (and encrypted) code. Hint: Do not attempt to use a cryptanalytic attack to break the encryption. Instead, look for an unencrypted class file. This is a custom class loader that decrypts the encrypted files before they are executed. Reverse this custom class loader and modify it so that it prints out the class files in plaintext.

   b. How could you make this encryption scheme more difficult to break?

6. Obtain the file `deadbeef.zip` from the textbook website and extract the C source file `deadbeef.c`.

a. Modify the program so that it tests for a debugger using the Windows function `IsDebuggerPresent`. The program should silently terminate if a debugger is detected, whether or not the correct serial number is entered.

b. Show that you can determine the serial number using a debugger, in spite of the `IsDebuggerPresent()` function. Briefly explain how you were able to bypass the `IsDebuggerPresent()` check.

7. Obtain the file `mystery.zip` from the textbook website and extract the Windows executable `mystery.exe`.

a. What is the output when you run the program with each of the following usernames, assuming an incorrect serial number in each case?

   i. mark

   ii. markstamp

   iii. markkram

b. Analyze the code to determine all restrictions, if any, on valid usernames. You will need to disassemble and/or debug the code.

c. This program uses an anti-debugging technique, namely, the Windows system function `IsDebuggerPresent()`. Analyze the code to determine what the program does in case a debugger is detected. Why is this better than simply terminating the program?

d. Patch the program so that you can debug it. That is, you need to nullify the effect of `IsDebuggerPresent()`.

e. By debugging the code, determine the corresponding valid serial number for each valid username that appears in part a. Hint: Debug the program and enter a username along with any serial number. At some point the program will compute the valid serial number corresponding to the entered username—it does this so that it can compare to the entered serial number. If you set a breakpoint at the correct location, the valid serial number will be stored in a register, which you can then observe.

f. Create a patched version of the code, `mysteryPatch.exe` that accepts any username/serial number pair.

8. Obtain `mystery.zip` from the textbook website and extract the Windows executable `mystery.exe`. As mentioned in Problem 7, part e, the program contains code that generates a valid serial number corresponding to any valid username. Such an algorithm is known as a key generator, or simply a *keygen*. If Trudy has a functioning copy of the keygen algorithm, she can generate an unlimited number of valid

username/serial number pairs. In principle, it would be possible for Trudy to analyze a keygen algorithm and write her own (functionally equivalent) standalone keygen program from scratch. However, keygen algorithms are generally complex, making such an attack difficult in practice. But all is not lost (at least from Trudy's perspective). It is often possible—and relatively simple—to "rip" the keygen algorithm from a program. That is, an attacker can extract the assembly code representing the keygen algorithm and embed it directly in a C program, thereby creating a standalone keygen utility, without having to understand the details of the algorithm.

a. Rip the keygen algorithm from `mystery.exe`, that is, extract the keygen assembly code and use it directly in your own standalone keygen program. Your program must take any valid username as input and produce the corresponding valid serial number. Hint: In Visual C++ assembly code can be embedded directly in a C program by using the `asm` directive. You may need to initialize certain register values to make the ripped code function correctly.

b. Use your program from part a to generate a serial number for the username `markkram`. Verify that your serial number is correct by testing it in the original `mystery.exe` program.

9. This problem deals with software reverse engineering (SRE).

a. Suppose debugging is impossible. Is SRE still possible?

b. Suppose disassembly is impossible. Is SRE still possible?

10. How can the the anti-debugging technique illustrated in Figure 12.11 be implemented so that it also provides anti-disassembly protection?

11. Why are guards incompatible with encrypted object code?

12. Recall that an opaque predicate is a "conditional" that is actually not a conditional. That is, the conditional always evaluates to the same result, but it is not obvious that this is the case.

a. Why is an opaque predicate a useful defense against reverse engineering attacks?

b. Give an example—different from that given in the text—of an opaque predicate based on a mathematical identity.

c. Give an example of an opaque predicate based on an input string.

13. The goal of this problem is to show that you can convert any conditional into an opaque predicate.

a. Given the conditional

```
if(a < b)
    // do something
else
    // do something else
```

slightly modify the `if` statement so that the `do something` branch always executes.

b. Explain why your solution to part a will work in general.

c. How stealthy is your approach, that is, how difficult would it be for an attacker to (automatically) detect your opaque predicates? Could you make your approach stealthier?

14. Opaque predicates have been proposed as a method for watermarking software [18, 212].

a. How might such a watermarking technique be implemented?

b. Consider possible attacks on such a watermarking scheme.

15. Describe in detail one anti-disassembly method not discussed in this chapter.

16. Describe in detail one anti-debugging method not discussed in the text.

17. Consider a DRM system implemented in software on a PC.

a. Define persistent protection.

b. Why is encryption necessary, but not sufficient, to provide persistent protection?

18. Consider a DRM system implemented in software on a PC. As discussed in the text, such systems are inherently insecure. Suppose that in an alternate universe such a system could be made highly secure.

a. How would such a system benefit copyright holders?

b. How could such a system be used to enhance privacy? Give a concrete example.

19. Suppose that it's impossible to patch some particular software that implements DRM protection. Is the DRM system then secure?

20. Some DRM systems have been implemented on open systems and some have been implemented in closed systems.

a. What is the primary advantage of implementing DRM on a closed system?

b. What is the primary advantage to implementing DRM on an open platform?

21. Once a user authenticates, it is sometimes desirable to have the program keep this authentication information available, so that we do not need to bother the user to authenticate repeatedly.[8]

a. Devise a method for a program to cache authentication information, where the information is stored in a different form each time it's cached.

b. Is there any security advantage to your approach in part a, as compared to simply storing the information the same each time?

22. Above, we discuss break-once, break-everywhere (BOBE) resistance.

a. Why is BOBE resistance desirable for software in general, and DRM systems in particular?

b. In the text, it is argued that metamorphism can increase BOBE resistance. Discuss one other method that could be used to increase BOBE resistance.

23. In [266], it's shown that keys are easy to find when hidden in data, since keys are random and most data is not.

a. Devise a more secure method for hiding a key in data.

b. Devise a method for storing a key K in data and in software. That is, both the code and the data are required to reconstruct the key K.

24. In an analogy to genetic diversity in biological systems, it is sometimes argued that metamorphism can increase the resistance of software to certain types of attacks, such as buffer overflow.

a. Why should metamorphic software be more resistant to buffer overflow attacks? Hint: See [281].

b. Discuss other types of attacks that metamorphism might help to prevent.

c. From a development perspective, what difficulties does metamorphism present?

25. The Platform for Privacy Preferences Project (P3P) is supposed to enable "smarter privacy tools for the web" [238]. Consider the P3P implementation outlined in the papers [185, 186].

---

[8]This could be viewed as a form of single sign-on.

a. Discuss the possible privacy benefits of such a system.

b. Discuss attacks on such a P3P implementation.

26. Suppose that a particular system has 1,000,000 bugs, each with MTBF of 10,000,000 hours. The good guys work for 10,000 hours and find 1,000 bugs.

   a. If Trudy works for 10 hours and finds 1 bug, what is the probability that Trudy's bug was not found by the good guys?

   b. If Trudy works for 30 hours and finds 3 bugs, what is the probability that at least one of her bugs was not found by the good guys?

27. Suppose that a large and complex piece of software has 10,000 bugs, each with an MTBF of 1,000,000 hours. Then you expect to find a particular bug after 1,000,000 hours of testing, and—since there are 10,000 bugs—you expect to find one bug for every 100 hours of testing. Suppose the good guys do 200,000 hours of testing while the bad "guy," Trudy, does 400 hours of testing.

   a. How many bugs should Trudy find? How many bugs should the good guys find?

   b. What is the probability that Trudy finds at least one bug that the good guys did not?

28. It can be shown that the probability of a security failure after t hours of testing is approximately K/t for some constant K. This implies that the mean time between failures (MTBF) is about t/K after t hours of testing. So, security improves with testing, but it only improves linearly. One implication is that to ensure an average of, say, 1,000,000 hours between security failures, we must test for (on the order of) 1,000,000 hours. Suppose that an open source software project has a MTBF of t/K. If this same project were instead closed source, we might suspect that each bug would be twice as hard for an attacker to find. If this is true, it would appear that the MTBF in the closed source case is $2t/K$ and hence the closed source project will be twice as secure for a given amount of testing t. Discuss some flaws with this reasoning.

29. This problem compares closed systems and open systems.

   a. Define "open system" and give an example of an open system.

   b. Define "closed system" and give an example of a closed system.

   c. What are the advantages of open systems, as compared to closed systems?

    d. What are the advantages of closed systems, as compared to open systems?

30. Suppose that a particular open source project has $\text{MTBF} = t/K$. Without access to the source code, you believe that bugs in the software are three times as hard to find as in the open source case. If this is true, what would the MTBF be if this project were closed source?

31. Suppose that $\text{MTBF} = t^2/K$, instead of t/K. Then would there be an advantage to closed source software over open source, or vice versa, assuming that bugs are twice as hard to find in the closed source case?

32. Suppose that there are 100 security flaws in a particular software project and we can list these flaws in such a way that security flaw i requires i hours of testing to find. That is, it takes one hour to find flaw number one, two more hours to find flaw number two, three more hours to find flaw number three, and so on. What is the MTBF for this system?

33. As a deterrent to Microsoft's new Evil Death Star [210], the citizens of planet Earth have decided to build their own Good Death Star. The good citizens of Earth are debating whether to keep their Good Death Star plans secret or make the plans public.

    a. Give several reasons that tend to support keeping the plans secret.

    b. Give several reasons that tend to support making the plans public.

    c. Which case do you find more persuasive, keeping the plans secret or making the plans public? Why?

34. Suppose that you insert 100 typos into a textbook manuscript. Your editor finds 25 of these typos and, in the process, she also finds 800 other typos.

    a. Assuming that you remove all of the discovered typos and the 75 other typos that you inserted, estimate the number of typos remaining in the manuscript.

    b. What does this have to do with software security?

35. Suppose that you are asked to approximate the number of unknown bugs that remain in a particular piece of software. You insert 100 bugs into the software and then have your QA team test the software. In testing, your team discovers 40 of the bugs that you inserted, along with 120 bugs that you did not insert.

    a. Use these results to estimate the number of undiscovered bugs that remain in the program, assuming that you remove all of the discovered bugs as well as the 60 remaining bugs that you inserted.

b. Why might this test give inaccurate results?

36. Suppose that a large software company, Software Monopoly, or SM, is about to release a new software product called Doors, affectionately known as SM-Doors. The software for Doors is estimated to have 1,000,000 security flaws. It is also estimated that each security flaw that remains in the software upon release will cost SM about $20, due to lost sales resulting from damage to its reputation. SM pays its developers $100 per hour during the alpha testing phase, and at this phase, developers find flaws at a rate of about 1 flaw for every 10 hours of testing. In effect, customers act as beta testers when they find additional flaws in Doors. Suppose that SM charges $500 per copy of Doors and the estimated market for Doors is about 2,000,000 units. What is the optimal amount of alpha testing for SM to conduct?

37. Repeat Problem 36 assuming that developers find flaws at a rate of $N/100,000$ per hour of testing, where N is the number of flaws remaining in the software, and all other parameters are the same as in Problem 36. Note that this implies it is more difficult for developers to find flaws as the number of flaws decreases, which is probably more realistic than the linear assumption in Problem 36. Hint: You may want to use the fact that

$$\sum_{k=0}^{n} \frac{a}{b-k} \approx a(\ln b - \ln(b-n)).$$

Chapter 13

Operating Systems and Security

UNIX is basically a simple operating system,
but you have to be a genius to understand the simplicity.
— Dennis Ritchie

And it is a mark of prudence never to trust wholly
in those things which have once deceived us.
— Rene Descartes

13.1 Introduction

In this chapter, we'll look at some of the security issues related to operating systems (OSs). OSs are large and complex pieces of software. Recall that in Chapter 12 we argued that there are almost certain to be security flaws in any large and complex computer program. But here we are concerned with the security protection provided by the OS, not with the very real threat of bad OS software. That is, we are concerned with the role of the OS as the security enforcer. This is a large topic that ties into many other aspects of security and we'll just barely scratch the surface.

First, we'll describe the primary security-related functions of any modern operating system. Then we'll discuss the notion of a trusted OS, and we'll conclude with a look at Microsoft's fairly recent effort to develop a trusted operating system, which goes by the catchy name of the Next Generation Secure Computing Base, or better yet, NGSCB.

13.2   OS Security Functions

An OS must deal with potential security issues whether they arise accidentally
or as part of a malicious attack. Modern OSs are designed for multi-user
environments and multi-tasking operations. Consequently, an OS must, at a
minimum, deal with *separation, memory protection*, and *access control*. We
briefly discuss each of these three topics below.

13.2.1   Separation

Arguably the most fundamental security issue for a modern OS is that of
separation. That is, the OS must keep users and processes separate from
each other.

There are several ways that separation can be enforced [235], including
the following:

- *Physical separation* — Users are restricted to separate devices. This
  provides a strong form of separation, but it is often impractical.

- *Temporal separation* — Processes are separated in time. This eliminates
  many problems that arise due to concurrency and simplifies the job of
  the OS. However, there is a loss of efficiency.

- *Logical separation* — For example, each process might be allocated its
  own "sandbox." A process is free to do almost anything within its
  sandbox, but it can do almost nothing outside of its sandbox.

- *Cryptographic separation* — Crypto can be used to make information
  unintelligible to an outsider.

Of course, various combinations of these methods can be used.

13.2.2   Memory Protection

Another fundamental issue an OS must deal with is memory protection. This
includes protection for the memory that the OS itself uses as well as the
memory of user processes. A fence, or *fence address*, is one option for memory
protection. A fence is a particular address that users and their processes
cannot cross—only the OS can operate on one side of the fence, and users are
restricted to the other side.

A fence could be static, in which case there is a fixed fence address. However, this places a strict limit on the size of the OS, which is a major drawback
(or benefit, depending on your perspective). Alternatively, a dynamic fence
can be used, which can be implemented using a fence register to specify the
current fence address.

In addition to a fence, *base* and *bounds* registers can be used. These registers contain the lower and upper address limits of a particular user (or process) space. The base and bounds register approach implicitly assumes that the user (or process) space is contiguous in memory.

The OS must determine what protection to apply to a specific memory location. In some cases it might be sufficient to apply the same protection to all of a user's (or process's) memory. At the other extreme, *tagging* specifies the protection for each individual address. While this is as fine-grained protection as possible, it introduces significant overhead. The overhead can be reduced by tagging sections of the address space instead of each individual address. In any case, another drawback to tagging is compatibility, since tagging schemes are not in common use.

The most common methods of memory protection are *segmentation* and *paging*. While these are not as flexible as tagging, they're much more efficient. We briefly discuss each of these next.

Segmentation, as illustrated in Figure 13.1, divides the memory into logical units, such as individual procedures or the data in one array. Then appropriate access control can be enforced on each segments. A benefit of segmentation is that any segment can be placed in any memory location— provided the location is large enough to hold it. Of course, the OS must keep track of the locations of all segments, which is accomplished using <segment,offset> pairs, where the cleverly named segment specifies the segment, and the offset is the starting address of the specified segment.

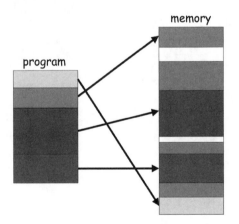

Figure 13.1: Segmentation

Other benefits of segmentation include the fact that segments can be moved to different locations in memory and they can also be moved in and out of memory. With segmentation, all address references must go through the OS, so the OS can, in this respect, achieve complete mediation. Depending

on the access control applied to particular segments, users can share access
to some segments or users can be restricted to specific segments.

One serious drawback to segmentation is that the segments are of variable
sizes. As a result, before the OS tries to reference any element of a given
`segment` it must know the size of the segment so that it can be sure that
the requested address is within the `segment`. But some segments—such as
those that include dynamic memory allocation—can grow during execution.
Consequently, the OS must keep track of dynamic segment sizes. And due
the variability of segment sizes, memory fragmentation is a potential problem.
Finally, when memory is compacted to make better use of the available space,
the segmentation tables change. In short, segmentation is complex and places
a significant burden on the OS.

Paging is like segmentation, except that all segments are of a fixed size,
as illustrated in Figure 13.2. With paging, access to a particular page uses a
pair of the form `<page,offset>`. The advantages of paging over segmentation
include no fragmentation, improved efficiency, and the fact that there are no
variable sizes to worry about. The disadvantages are that there is, in general,
no logical unity to pages, which makes it more difficult to determine the
proper access control to apply to a given page.

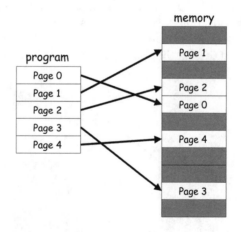

Figure 13.2: Paging

13.2.3 Access Control

OSs are the ultimate enforcers of access control. This is one reason why the
OS is such an attractive target for attack—a successful attack on the OS
can effectively nullify any protection built in at a higher level. We discussed
access control in Chapter 8 and we'll briefly return to the subject in the next
section when we discuss the concept of a trusted OS.

13.3 Trusted Operating System

> *There's none deceived but he that trusts.*
> — Benjamin Franklin

A system is *trusted* if we rely on it for security. In other words, if a trusted system fails to provide the expected security, then the security of the system is broken.

In this context, there is a distinction between trust and security. Trust implies reliance, that is, trust is binary choice—either we trust or we don't. Security, on the other hand, is a judgment of the effectiveness of a particular mechanisms. Security should be judged relative to a clearly specified policy or statement.

Note that security depends on trust. For example, a trusted component that fails to provide the expected level of security will break the overall security of the system. Ideally, we only trust secure systems, and all trust relationships are explicit.

Since a trusted system is one that we rely on for security, an untrusted system must be one that we don't rely on for security. As a consequence, if all untrusted systems are compromised, the security of the system is unaffected. A curious implication of this simple observation is that only a trusted system can break security. Hold this thought, since we'll have more to say about it in the next section.

What should a trusted OS do? Since any OS must deal with separation, memory protection, and access control, at a minimum, a trusted OS must do these things securely. Any list of generic good security principles would likely include the following: least privilege (e.g., the low watermark principle), simplicity, open design (e.g., Kerckhoffs' Principle), complete mediation, whitelisting (as opposed to blacklisting), separation, and ease of use. We might expect a trusted OS to securely deal with many of these issues. However, most commercial OSs are feature-rich, which tends to lead to complexity and poor security. Modern commercial OSs are not to be trusted.

13.3.1 MAC, DAC, and More

As mentioned above and illustrated in Figure 13.3, any OS must provide some degree of separation, memory protection, and access control. On the other hand, since we rely on a trusted OS for our security, it will almost certainly need to go beyond the minimal security operations. Specific security measures that we would like to see from a trusted OS likely include mandatory access control, discretionary access control, object reuse protection, complete mediation, trusted path, and logs. A trusted OS is illustrated in Figure 13.4.

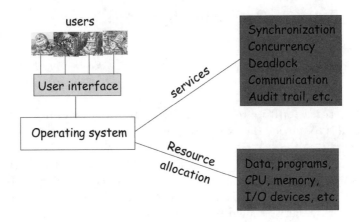

Figure 13.3: Operating System Overview

Mandatory access control, or MAC, is access that is not controlled by the owner of an object. For example, Alice does not decide who holds a TOP SECRET clearance, so she can't completely control the access to a document classified at this level. In contrast, *discretionary access control*, or DAC, is the type of access control that is determined by the owner of an object. For example, in UNIX file protection, the owner of a file controls read, write, and execute privileges.

If both DAC and MAC apply to an object, MAC is "stronger." For example, suppose Alice owns a document marked TOP SECRET. Then Alice can set the DAC since she owns the document. However, regardless of the DAC settings, if Bob only has a SECRET clearance, he can't access the document because he doesn't meet the MAC requirements. On the other hand, if the DAC is stricter than the MAC, then the DAC would determine the access.

A trusted OS must also prevent information from leaking from one user to another. Any OS will use some form of memory protection and access control, but we require strong protection from a trusted OS. For example, when the OS allocates space for a file, that same space may have previously been used by a different user's process. If the OS takes no additional precautions, the bits that remain from the previous process could be accessible and thereby leak information. A trusted OS must take steps to prevent this from occurring.

A related problem is *magnetic remanence*, where faint images of previously stored data can sometimes be read, even after the space has been overwritten by new data. To minimize the chance of this occurring, the DoD sets guidelines that require memory to be overwritten repeatedly with different bit patterns before it's considered safe to allow another process access to that space [132].

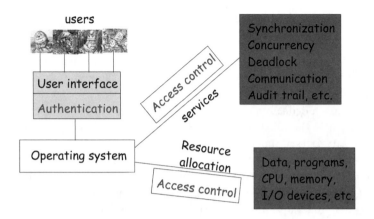

Figure 13.4: Trusted Operating System Overview

13.3.2 Trusted Path

When you enter your password at the login prompt, what happens to that password? We know what is supposed to happen to the password (hashed with a salt, etc.), but what actually happens depends on the software that is running on your system. How can you be sure that software is not doing something evil, such as writing your password to a file that will later be emailed to Trudy? This is the *trusted path* problem, and as Ross Anderson puts it in [14]:

> I don't know how to be confident even of a digital signature I make on my own PC, and I've worked in security for over fifteen years. Checking all of the software in the critical path between the display and the signature software is way beyond my patience.

Ideally, a trusted OS would provide strong assurance of a trusted path. If so, one benefit is that we could have confidence in a digital signature on a PC.

The OS is also responsible for logging security-related events. This sort of information is necessary to detect attacks and for postmortem analysis. Logging is not as simple as it might seem. In particular, it is not always obvious precisely what to log. If we log too much, then we might overwhelm any human who must examine the data, and we could even overwhelm automated systems that try to find the relevant needle in this haystack of data. For example, should we log incorrect passwords? If so, then "almost" passwords would appear in the log file, and log files would themselves be security critical. If not, it may be harder to detect when a password-guessing attack is in progress.

13.3.3   Trusted Computing Base

The *kernel* is the lowest-level part of the OS. The kernel is responsible for synchronization, inter-process communication, message passing, interrupt handling, and so on. A *security kernel* is the part of the kernel that deals with security.

Why have a dedicated security kernel? Since all accesses must go through the kernel, it's the ideal place for access control. It's also good practice to have security-critical functions in one location. By locating all such functions in one place, security functions are easier to test and modify.

One of the primary motivations for an attack on the OS is that the attacker can get below higher-level security functions and thereby bypass these security features. By putting as many security functions as possible at the OSs lowest layer, it may be more difficult for an attacker to get below these functions.

The *reference monitor* is the part of the security kernel that deals with access control. The reference monitor mediates all access between subjects and objects, as illustrated in Figure 13.5. Ideally, this crucial part of the security kernel would be tamper resistant, and it should also be analyzable, small, and simple, since an error at this level could be devastating to the security of the entire system.

Figure 13.5: Reference Monitor

The *trusted computing base*, or TCB, is everything in the OS that we rely on to enforce security. Our definition of trust implies that, if everything outside TCB were subverted, our trusted OS would still be secure.

Security-critical operations will likely occur in many places within the OS. Ideally, we would design the security kernel first and then build the OS around it. Unfortunately, reality is usually just the opposite, as security tends to be an afterthought instead of a primary design goal. However, there are examples of OSs that have been designed from scratch, with security as a main objective. One such OS is SCOMP, which was developed by Honeywell. SCOMP has less than 10,000 lines of code in its security kernel, and it strives for simplicity and analyzability [116]. Contrast this to, say, Windows XP, which has some 40,000,000 lines of code and numerous dubious (from a security point of view) features.

Ideally the TCB should gather all security functions into an identifiable layer. For example, the TCB illustrated in Figure 13.6 is a poor design, since security-critical features are spread throughout the OS. Here, any change in a security feature may have unintended consequences in other OS functionality, and the individual security operations are difficult to analyze, particularly with respect to their interactions.

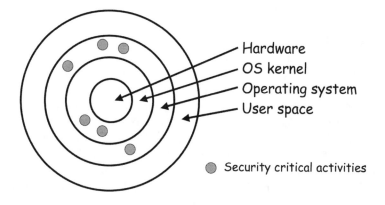

Figure 13.6: Poor TCB Design

The TCB illustrated in Figure 13.7 is preferable, since all security functions are collected in a well-defined security kernel [235]. In this design, the security impact of any change in one security function can be analyzed by studying its effect on the security kernel. Also, an attacker who subverts OS operations at a higher level will not have defeated the TCB operations.

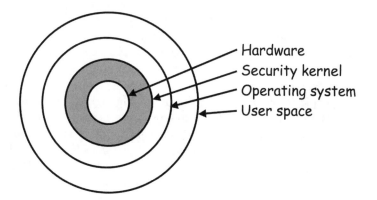

Figure 13.7: Good TCB Design

In summary, the TCB consists of everything in the OS that we rely on for security. If everything outside the TCB is subverted, we're still secure, but if anything in the TCB is subverted, then the security is likely broken.

In the next section we'll examine NGSCB, which is an ambitious effort by Microsoft to develop a trusted OS for the PC platform. DRM was the original motivation for NGSCB, but it has wide security implications [107].

13.4   Next Generation Secure Computing Base

Microsoft's Next Generation Secure Computing Base, or NGSCB (which is, strangely, pronounced "en scub"), was originally slated to be part of the "Longhorn" OS (i.e., Windows Vista). But it appears that most of the features of NGSCB won't appear until a later release, if ever.[1] Regardless, the concept is intriguing and it might yet find widespread application.

NGSCB is designed to work with special hardware, which is to be developed by the Trusted Computing Group, or TCG, led by Intel [306]. NGSCB is the part of Windows that will interface with the TCG hardware. TCG was formerly known as the Trusted Computing Platform Alliance, or TCPA, and NGSCB was formerly known as Palladium. It's been theorized that the name changes are due to bad publicity surrounding the initial discussion of TCPA/Palladium [190].

The original motivation for TCPA/Palladium was digital rights management. Due to the negative reaction this received, TCG/NGSCB now downplays the DRM connection, although it clearly remains a motivating factor. Today, TCG/NGSCB is promoted as a general security-enhancing technology, with DRM being just one of many potential applications. But, as we'll see below, not everyone is convinced that this is a good idea. Depending on who you ask, TCG/NGSCB—which is often shortened to TC—stands for "trusted computing" [219] or "treacherous computing" [13].

The underlying goal of TCG/NGSCB is to provide some of the strengths of a closed system on the open PC platform [102, 220]. Closed systems, such as game consoles and smartcards, are very good at protecting secrets, primarily due to their tamper-resistant features. As a result, closed systems are good at forcing people to pay money for the use of copyrighted information, such as game software. The drawback to closed systems is their limited flexibility. In contrast, open systems such as PCs offer incredible flexibility, but, as we have seen, they do a poor job of protecting secrets. This is primarily because open systems have no real means to defend their own software. Ron Rivest has aptly described NGSCB as a "virtual set-top box inside your PC" [74].

The TCG is supposed to provide tamper-resistant hardware that might someday be standard on PCs. Conceptually, this can be viewed as a smartcard embedded within the PC hardware. This tamper-resistant hardware

---

[1]Only one application of this technology appears to have been implemented so far. The "secure startup" feature in Vista and Windows 7 is said to use some features of NGSCB [204].

provides a secure place to store cryptographic keys or other secrets. These secrets can be secured, even from a user with full administrator privileges. To date, nothing comparable exists for PCs.

It is important to realize that the TCG tamper-resistant hardware is in addition to all of the usual PC hardware, not in place of it. To take advantage of this special hardware, the PC will have two OSs—its usual OS and a special trusted OS to deal with the TCG hardware. NGSCB is Microsoft's version of this trusted OS.

According to Microsoft, the design goals of NGSCB are twofold. First, it is to provide high assurance, that is, users can have a high degree of confidence that NGSCB will behave correctly, even when it's under attack. The second goal is to provide authenticated operation. To protect the secrets stored in the tamper-resistant hardware, it's critical that only trusted software can access the TCG hardware. By carefully validating (i.e., authenticating) all software, NGSCB can provide a high degree of trust. Protection against hardware tampering is not a design goal of NGSCB, since that is the domain of the TCG.

Specific details concerning NGSCB are sketchy, and, based on the available information, Microsoft has not yet resolved all of the fine points. As a result, the following information is somewhat speculative. The details might become clearer in the future.

The high-level architecture of NGSCB is illustrated in Figure 13.8. The "left-hand side," or LHS, is where the usual, untrusted, Windows OS lives, while the "right-hand side," or RHS, is where the trusted OS resides. The Nexus is the trusted computing base, or TCB, of the NGSCB. So-called Nexus Computing Agents, or NCAs, are the only software components that are allowed to communicate between the (trusted) Nexus and (untrusted) LHS [27]. The NCAs are a critical component of NGSCB—as critical as the Nexus.

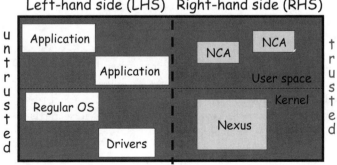

Figure 13.8: NGSCB Overview

13.4.1   NGSCB Feature Groups

NGSCB includes the following four major "feature groups."

- *Strong process isolation* — Prevents processes from interfering with each other.

- *Sealed storage* — The tamper-resistant hardware where secrets (that is, keys) can be securely stored.

- *Secure path* — Provides a protected path to and from the mouse, keyboard, and monitor.

- *Attestation* — A clever feature allows for "things" to be securely authenticated.

Attestation allows the TCB to be securely extended via NCAs. All four feature groups are primarily aimed at protecting against malicious code. Next, we'll describe each of these feature groups in a little more detail.

13.4.1.1   Process Isolation

Process isolation is enforced by "curtained memory," which appears to be little more than a buzzword. In any case, the trusted OS (the Nexus) must be protected from the untrusted OS as well as from the BIOS, device drivers, and other low-level operations that could be used to attack it. Curtained memory is the name for the memory protection scheme that provides such protection.

   Process isolation also applies to the NCAs. The NCAs must be isolated from any software that they don't trust. These trust relationships are determined by users—to an extent. That is, a user can disable a trusted NCAs, but a user cannot make an untrusted NCA trusted. If the latter were possible, then the security of the trusted OS could be easily broken.

13.4.1.2   Sealed Storage

Sealed storage contains a secret, which is most likely a key (or keys). If software X wants to access the secret, as an integrity check, a hash of X is computed. The confidentiality of the secret is protected since it can only be accessed by trusted software while the integrity of the secret is assured since it resides in the sealed storage.

13.4.1.3   Secure Path

The details of the secure path feature are also vague. It's claimed that for input, the path from the keyboard to the Nexus and the path from the mouse to the Nexus are both "secure"—but exactly how this is implemented is not entirely clear. Apparently, digital signatures are used so that the Nexus can verify the integrity of the data [302]. For output, there is a similar secure path from the Nexus to the screen, although here the signature verification would seem to be more exposed.

13.4.1.4   Attestation

The most innovative feature of NGSCB is attestation, which provides for the secure authentication of "things," such as devices, services, and, most importantly, software. This is separate from user authentication. Attestation is accomplished using public key cryptography, and it relies on a certified key pair, where the private key—which is not user accessible—lives in the sealed storage.

The TCB can be extended via attestation of NCAs. A new NCA is trusted provided that it passes the attestation check, which enables new applications to be added to an NGSCB system. This is a major feature, and we'll have more to say about it below.

One issue with attestation is that, since it uses public key cryptography, certificates must be exchanged. Since public keys reveal users' identities, anonymity is lost in this approach. To protect anonymity, NGSCB provides support for a trusted third party, or TTP. The TTP verifies the signature and vouches for it. Anonymity can be preserved in this way—although the TTP will know the signer's identity.

It is also claimed that NGSCB provides support for zero knowledge proofs. As we discussed in Chapter 9, zero knowledge proofs allow us to verify that a user knows a secret without revealing any information about the secret. According to Microsoft, when using zero knowledge proofs in NGSCB, "anonymity is preserved unconditionally" [27].

13.4.2   NGSCB Compelling Applications

What good is TCG/NGSCB? There are several compelling applications, but here we'll mention only two. First, suppose that Alice types a document on her computer. She can then move the document to the RHS (the trusted space), read the document carefully, then digitally sign the document before moving it back to the (untrusted) LHS. In this way, Alice can be confident of what she actually signed, which, as indicated by Ross Anderson's quote on page 497, is almost impossible on a non-NGSCB computer today.

A second application where NGSCB is useful is DRM. One fundamental problem that is solved by NGSCB is that of protecting a secret or key. In Chapter 12 we saw that it's impossible to securely protect a key in software.

By using tamper-resistant hardware (sealed storage) and other NGSCB features, protecting a key is much more plausible.

The NGSCB secure path also prevents certain DRM attacks. For example, with DRM-protected digital documents, an attacker could use a screen capture to scrape protected data from the screen. This would be much more difficult with the NGSCB secure path in place.

NBSCB also allows for the positive identification of users. Although this can be done without a trusted OS, there is a much higher degree of assurance with NGSCB, since the user's ID (in the form of a private key) is embedded in the secure storage.

13.4.3 Criticisms of NGSCB

> *Microsoft isn't evil, they just make really crappy operating systems.*
> — Linus Torvalds

According to Microsoft, everything you know and love about Windows will still work in the LHS of an NGSCB system. Microsoft also insists that the user is in charge, since the user determines all of the following:

- Which Nexus (if any) will run on the system

- Which NCAs are allowed to run on the system

- Which NCAs are allowed to identify the system

In addition, there is no way for an external process to enable a Nexus or NCA. This is to allay the fear that Microsoft would be in charge of an NGSCB computer. In addition, the Nexus code is open source. Finally, the Nexus does not block, delete, or censor any data—although NCAs do. For example, if a particular NCA is part of a DRM system, then it must "censor" any data for which user Alice has not paid. But each NCA on Alice's system must be authorized by Alice, so she could choose not to authorize the particular NCA that deals with DRM. Of course, she won't have access to DRM-protected content if she does not authorize the required NCA.

Microsoft goes to great lengths to argue that NGSCB is harmless. The most likely reason for this is that many people seem to be convinced that NGSCB is anything but harmless.

There are many NGSCB critics, but here we'll only consider two. The first is Ross Anderson, whose criticisms can be found at [13]. Anderson is one of the harshest TCG/NGSCB critics and perhaps the most influential. We'll then discuss the criticisms of Clark Thomborson, whose criticisms are less well known but raise some interesting fundamental issues [302].

Anderson's primary beef seems to be that when NGSCB is used, a digital object can be controlled by its creator, not by the user of the machine where it currently resides. For example, suppose Alice writes a book, *Bob in Wonderland*. With NGSCB, she can specify the NCA that must be used to access the digital form of this book. Of course, Bob can refuse to accept the NCA, but in that case his access is denied. And if Bob allows the NCA on his system, he may have restrictions placed on his actions (such as, he cannot use a screen capture, he cannot email the book, etc.).

It's worth noting that such restrictions are exactly what is needed in certain applications such as multilevel security (MLS). But Anderson's argument is that such restrictions are inappropriate as part of a general-purpose tool, such as a PC. Anderson gives the following simple example: suppose Microsoft Word encrypts all documents with a key that is only made available to Microsoft products. Then it would be even more difficult to stop using Microsoft products than it is today.

Anderson also claims that files from a compromised machine could be blacklisted (for example, to prevent music piracy). To illustrate this point, he gives an example similar to the following. Suppose that every student at San Jose State University (SJSU) uses a single pirated copy of Microsoft Word. If Microsoft blacklists this copy and thereby prevents it from working on all NGSCB machines, then SJSU students will simply avoid using NGSCB. But if Microsoft instead makes all NGSCB machines refuse to open documents created with this copy of Word, then SJSU users can't share documents with any NGSCB user. This could be a way to coerce SJSU students into using legitimate copies of Word.

Anderson makes some rather strange statements in [13], including the following:

> The Soviet Union tried to register and control all typewriters. NGSCB attempts to register and control all computers.

And there is an even more "interesting" statement:

> In 2010 President Clinton may have two red buttons on her desk—one that sends missiles to China and another that turns off all of the PCs in China. . .

Fortunately, this Orwellian prediction was way off the mark (in every respect). In any case, it's not clear to your usually paranoid author exactly how NGSCB would enable either scenario. Nevertheless, these are the kinds of concerns that an influential critic has raised.

Clark Thomborson has raised some issues that strike at the heart of the NGSCB concept [302]. In his view, NGSCB should be seen as a security guard. By passive observation, a real-world security guard can learn a great deal about the workings of the facility he or she is guarding.[2] The NGSCB security guard is similar to a human security guard, in the sense that it can learn something about a user's sensitive information by passive observation.

So, how can Alice be sure that NGSCB is not spying on her? Microsoft would probably argue that this can't happen since the Nexus software is public, the NCAs can be debugged (as required for application development), and, besides, NGSCB is strictly an "opt in" technology. But there may be a loophole here. The release versions of NCAs can't be debugged and the debug and release versions will necessarily have different hash values. Consequently, the release version of an NCA could conceivably do something that the debug version does not do—such as spy on Alice.

The bottom line with regard to TCG/NGCSB is that it's an attempt to embed a trusted OS within an open platform. Without something similar, there is a legitimate concern that the PC may lose out, particularly in entertainment-related areas, where copyright holders might insist on the security of closed-system solutions.

NGSCB critics worry that users will lose control over their PCs—or be spied on by their PC. But it could reasonably be argued that users must choose to opt in, and, if a user does not opt in, nothing has been lost. So, what's the big deal?

However, NGSCB is a trusted system, and as we noted above, only a trusted system can break your security. When put in this light, NGSCB deserves careful scrutiny.

13.5 Summary

In this chapter, we considered operating system security and, more specifically, the role of a trusted OS. We then discussed Microsoft's NGSCB, which is an attempt to build a trusted OS for the PC platform. NGSCB has implications for many security-related fields, including digital rights management, a topic we covered in some detail in Chapter 12. NGSCB has its critics and we discussed some of their criticisms. We also considered possible counterarguments to the criticisms.

13.6 Problems

1. Expand and define each of the following acronyms: TCG, TCB, PITA, MAC, DAC, NGSCB.

---

[2]Recently, a former security guard at a major apartment complex took your author's class. This student confirmed that as a security guard, he learned a lot about the residents of the apartment complex, simply by passive observation. Your puritanical author would like to share some of these observations, but he cannot since this book is rated "G."

2. This problem deals with the definition of a trusted system.

    a. What does it mean to say that a system is "trusted"?

    b. Do you agree with the statement, "Only a trusted system can break your security"? Why or why not?

3. In this chapter we discussed segmentation and paging.

    a. What are the significant differences between segmentation and paging?

    b. Give one significant security advantage of segmentation over paging.

    c. What is the primary advantage of paging over segmentation?

4. Explain how paging and segmentation could be combined in one system.

5. This problem deals with mandatory access control (MAC) and discretionary access control (DAC).

    a. Define the terms mandatory access control and discretionary access control.

    b. What are the significant differences between MAC and DAC?

    c. Give two specific examples where mandatory access control is used and give two examples where discretionary access control is used.

6. Why would Trudy almost certainly prefer to subvert the OS rather than successfully attack one particular application?

7. In this chapter we briefly compared blacklisting and whitelisting.

    a. What is blacklisting?

    b. What is whitelisting?

    c. As a general security principle, which is preferable, whitelisting or blacklisting? Why?

    d. Which is likely to be more convenient for users, blacklisting or whitelisting? Why?

8. Recall that a trusted computing base (TCB) consists of everything in the OS that we rely on to enforce security. Which parts of NBSCB comprise its TCB?

9. In this chapter, a few compelling applications of NGSCB are mentioned, including "what you see is what you sign," digital rights management (DRM), and multilevel security (MLS). Discuss one additional compelling application of a trusted OS such as NGSCB.

10. Explain how NGSCB helps to solve some of the fundamental problems in digital rights management (DRM).

11. Explain how NGSCB helps to solve some of the fundamental problems in multilevel security (MLS).

12. A trusted OS, such as NGSCB, would make multilevel security (MLS) much more feasible. Given that this is the case, the military and government are likely to be interested in NGSCB. Why might businesses also be interested in NGSCB?

13. Some people believe that businesses will find NGSCB useful and that NGSCB will become commonplace in PCs as a result. If this is the case, then most PCs will eventually have a trusted operating system, but not because consumers find it particularly useful. Do you think this is likely to occur? Why or why not?

14. It is sometimes argued that digital rights management (DRM) is, in some sense, the modern incarnation of multilevel security (MLS).

    a. List some significant similarities between DRM and MLS.

    b. List some significant differences between DRM and MLS.

15. Suppose that you happen to have a secure multilevel security (MLS) system. Could this system be used to enforce digital rights management (DRM)?

16. Suppose that you have a secure digital rights management (DRM) system. Could this system be used to enforce multilevel security (MLS)?

17. This problem deals with NGSCB.

    a. What is attestation and what is its purpose?

    b. What are NCAs and what two purposes do they serve?

18. In the text, we mentioned two critics of NGSCB, namely, Ross Anderson and Clark Thomborson.

    a. Summarize Ross Anderson's criticisms of NGSCB.

    b. Summarize Clark Thomborson's criticisms of NGSCB.

    c. Which of these two critics do you find more compelling and why?

19. In Chapter 12, we discussed software reverse engineer. It's also possible to reverse engineer most hardware. Since this is the case, would DRM be any more secure on an NGSCB system than on a non-NGSCB system?

20. Give two real-world examples of closed systems. How well does each protect its software?

21. Give two real-world examples of open systems. How well does each protect its software?

22. Is each of the following an open system or a closed system? For each system, give an example of a real-world attack that has occurred.

    a. PC

    b. Cell phone

    c. iPod

    d. Xbox

    e. Kindle (an e-book reader)

23. Find an influential critic of NGSCB (other than the critics mentioned in the text) and summarize his or her arguments against NGSCB.

24. Find a supporter of NGSCB and summarize his or her arguments in favor of NGSCB.

25. Read the discussion of "treacherous computing" at [13] and summarize the author's main points.

26. Public key crypto is used in NGSCB for attestation. One concern with this approach is that anonymity might be lost. Recall that in Kerberos, Alice's anonymity is protected (e.g., when Alice sends her TGT to the KDC, she doesn't need to identify herself). Since anonymity is a concern, would it make sense for NGSCB to use an approach similar to Kerberos?

27. Why is the NGSCB sealed storage integrity check implemented using hashing instead of public key signing?

28. Why is NGSCB attestation implemented using digital signatures instead of hashing?

29. In NGSCB, how do each of the following help to protect against malicious software?

    a. Process isolation

    b. Sealed storage

    c. Secure path

    d. Attestation

30. Give two reasons why NGSCB attestation is necessary.

31. In NGSCB, each of the four "feature groups" is, apparently, necessary but not sufficient to ensure security. Discuss a specific attack that is difficult or impossible on an NGSCB system, but is easy when the specified feature group is missing.

    a. Process isolation

    b. Sealed storage

    c. Secure path

    d. Attestation

32. Explain Rivest's comment that TCG/NGSCB is like "a virtual set-top box inside your PC."

33. Suppose that students take in-class tests on their own laptop computers. When they finish answering the questions, they email their results to the instructor using a wireless Internet connection. Assume that the wireless access point is accessible during the test.

    a. Discuss ways that students might attempt to cheat.

    b. How could NGSCB be used to make cheating more difficult?

    c. How might students attempt to cheat on an NGSCB system?

34. Google's Native Client (NaCl) is a technology designed to allow untrusted code to run securely in a Web browser [332]. The primary advantage is speed, but there are many security issues, some of which are reminiscent of issues faced by NGSCB.

    a. Outline the NaCl security architecture.

    b. NaCl uses a "trampoline" to transfer control from untrusted code to trusted code. Explain how this works.

    c. Compare and contrast the security approach used in NaCl with each of the following: Xax, CFI, Active X.

APPENDIX

This appendix includes two sections. The first section contains an abbreviated introduction to networking, with the emphasis on security issues. The second section provides a quick review of the basic math that is used in various parts of this book.

A-1 Network Security Basics

> *There are three kinds of death in this world.*
> *There's heart death, there's brain death, and there's being off the network.*
> — Guy Almes

A-1.1 Introduction

In this section, we give a condensed introduction to networking, presented through the prism of security. Networking is a large and complex topic. Here, we'll cover the minimal amount of information that is required elsewhere in this textbook, and we'll also add a few passing comments on network-specific security issues that are of independent interest.

A network consists of *hosts* and *routers*. The term host is a catchall for a wide variety of network-connected devices, including laptops, desktop computers, servers, cell phones, PDAs, etc. The purpose of the network is to transfer data between the hosts. Ideally, we'd like the network to be transparent to users. We're primarily concerned with the mother of all networks, the Internet.[1]

A network has an *edge* and a *core*. The hosts mentioned above live at the edge, while the core consists of an interconnected mesh of routers. The purpose of the core is to route data through the network from host to host. A generic network diagram appears in Figure A-1.

---

[1]And, of course, everyone knows that the Internet was invented by Al Gore.

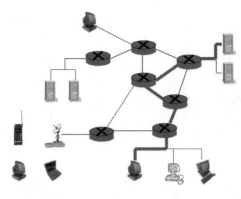

Figure A-1: Network

The Internet is a *packet switched* network, meaning that the data is sent in discrete chunks known as packets. In contrast, the traditional telephone system is a *circuit switched* network. For each telephone call, a dedicated circuit—with dedicated bandwidth—is established between the end points. Packet switched networks can make more efficient use of the available bandwidth, although there is some additional complexity, and things get particularly involved if circuit switched-like behavior is desired.

The study of modern networking is largely the study of networking protocols. Networking protocols precisely specify communication rules employed by the network. For the Internet, the details are usually spelled out in RFCs, which are, in effect, Internet standards.[2]

Protocols can be classified in many different ways, but one classification that is particularly relevant in security is *stateless* versus *stateful*. Stateless protocols don't "remember" anything, while stateful protocols do have some "memory." Many security problems are related to state. For example, denial of service, or DoS, attacks often take advantage of stateful protocols, while stateless protocols can also have their own security issues, as we'll see below.

A-1.2   The Protocol Stack

It's standard practice to view networks in terms of layers, where each layer is responsible for some particular operations. When these layers are all stacked up, the result is, not surprisingly, known as a *protocol stack*. It's important

---

[2]RFC stands for Request for Comments. However, authors of RFCs are not actually requesting comments. Instead, RFCs act as Internet standards. But curiously, most RFCs are not official Internet standards and, in fact, only a relatively few RFCs have been promoted to the level of official Internet standards. How does a lowly RFC become a high-falutin' Internet standard? Well, it's all spelled out in in RFC 2026, which is itself not an Internet standard. Confused?

to realize that a protocol stack is more conceptual than an actual physical construct. Nevertheless, the idea of a protocol stack does simplify the study of networks—although newcomers to networking are excused for not believing it. The infamous OSI reference model includes seven layers, but we'll strip it down to the layers that matter, which only leaves the following five:

- The *application layer* is responsible for handling the application data that is sent from host to host. Examples of application layer protocols include HTTP, SMTP, FTP, and Gnutella.

- The *transport layer* deals with logical end-to-end transport of the data. The transport layer protocols of interest are TCP and UDP.

- The *network layer* is responsible for routing data through the network. IP is the network layer protocol that matters most to us.

- The *link layer* handles the transferring of data over individual links within the network. There are many link layer protocols, but we'll only mention two, Ethernet and ARP.

- The *physical layer* sends the bits over the physical media. If you want to know about the physical layer, take an electrical engineering course.

Conceptually, a packet of data passes down the protocol stack (from the application layer to the physical layer) at the source and then back up the protocol stack at the destination. Routers in the core of the network must process packets up to the network layer so they can make sensible routing decisions. Layering is illustrated in Figure A-2.

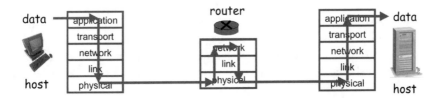

Figure A-2: Layering in Action

Suppose that X is a freshly minted packet of application data. As X goes down protocol stack, each protocol adds additional information, usually in the form of a *header*, which includes information required by the protocol being used at that particular layer. Let H_A be the header added at the application layer. Then the application layer passes (H_A, X) down the stack to the transport layer. If H_T is the transport layer header, then $(H_T, (H_A, X))$ is passed to the network layer where another header, say, H_N is added to give $(H_N, (H_T, (H_A, X)))$. Finally, the link layer adds a header, H_L, and the packet

$$(H_L, (H_N, (H_T, (H_A, X))))$$

is passed to the physical layer. In particular, note that the application layer header is the innermost header, which might seem backward until you think about it a little bit. When the packet is processed up the protocol stack at the destination (or at a router), the headers are stripped off layer by layer—like peeling an onion—and the information in each header is used to determine the proper course of action by the corresponding protocol.

Next, we'll take a brief look at each of the layers. We'll follow [177] and go down the protocol stack from the application layer to the link layer.

A-1.3   Application Layer

Typical network applications include Web browsing, email, file transfer, P2P, and so on. These are distributed applications that run on hosts. The hosts would prefer the network to be completely transparent.

As mentioned above, HTTP, SMTP, IMAP, FTP, and Gnutella are examples of application layer protocols. Note that the protocol is only one part of an application. For example, an email application includes an email client (such as Outlook or Thunderbird), a sending host, a receiving host, email servers, and various networking protocols such as SMTP and POP3.

Most applications are designed for the client-server paradigm, where the *client* is the host that requests a service and the *server* is the host that responds to the request. In other words, the client is the one who speaks first and the server is the one trying to fulfill the request. For example, if you request a Web page, you are the client and the Web server is the server, which only seems right. However, in some cases the distinction between client and server is not so obvious. For example, in a file-sharing application, your computer is a client when you request a file, and it is a server when someone downloads a file from you. Both of these events could even occur simultaneously, in which case you would be both a client and a server at the same time.

Peer-to-peer, or P2P, file sharing applications offer something of an alternative to the traditional client-server model. In the P2P model, hosts act as both clients and servers, as mentioned in the previous paragraph. But the real challenge in P2P lies in locating a "server" with the content that a client desires. There are several interesting approaches to this problem. For example, some P2P systems distribute the database that maps available content to hosts among certain special peers, whereas others simply flood each request through the network. In the latter case, hosts with the desired content respond directly to the requester. For example, KaZaA uses the distributed database approach, while Gnutella employs query flooding.

Next, we'll briefly discuss a few specific application layer protocols. First, let's consider HTTP, the HyperText Transfer Protocol, which is the application layer protocol used when you browse the Web. As mentioned above, the client requests a Web page and the server responds to the request. Since HTTP is a stateless protocol, *Web cookies* were developed as a tasty way to maintain state. When you initially contact a Web site, the Web site can choose to provide your browser with a cookie (assuming your browser is willing to accept it). A cookie is simply an identifier that is used to index a database maintained by the Web server. When your browser subsequently sends HTTP messages to the Web server, your browser will automatically pass the cookie to the server. The server can then consult its database and thereby remember information about you. In this way, Web cookies make it possible to maintain state within a single session as well as across sessions.

Web cookies are also sometimes used as a very weak form of authentication and cookies enable such modern conveniences as shopping carts and recommendation lists. However, cookies do raise some privacy concerns, since a Web site with memory (which is enabled by cookies) can learn a great deal about you. This problem only gets worse if multiple sites pool their information, since they can probably gain a fairly complete picture of your Web persona.

Another interesting application layer protocol is SMTP, the Simple Mail Transfer Protocol, which is used to transfer email from the sender to the recipient's email server. Then POP3, IMAP, or HTTP (for Web mail) is used to transfer the messages from the email server to the recipient. An SMTP email server can act as a server or a client when email is transferred over the network.

As with many application protocols, SMTP commands are human readable. For example, the commands in Table A-1 are legitimate SMTP commands that were typed as part of a telnet session—the user typed the lines beginning with C while the server responded with the lines marked as S. This particular session resulted in a spoofed email being sent to your gullible author at stamp@cs.sjsu.edu from arnold@ca.gov.

Another application layer protocol with security implications is DNS, the Domain Name Service. The primary purpose of DNS is to convert a friendly human-readable name, such as www.google.com, into its equivalent 32-bit IP address (discussed below), which computers and routers prefer. DNS is implemented as a distributed heirarchical database. There are only 13 "root" DNS servers worldwide and a successful attack on these would cripple the Internet. This is perhaps as close to a single point of failure as exits in the Internet today. Attacks on root servers have succeeded, however, because of the distributed nature of the DNS, it would be necessary for such an attack to continue for an extended period of time before it would seriously affect the Internet. No attack on DNS has had such staying power—at least not yet.

Table A-1: Spoofed email in SMTP

```
C: telnet eniac.cs.sjsu.edu 25
S: 220 eniac.sjsu.edu
C: HELO ca.gov
S: 250 Hello ca.gov, pleased to meet you
C: MAIL FROM: <arnold@ca.gov>
S: 250 arnold@ca.gov... Sender ok
C: RCPT TO: <stamp@cs.sjsu.edu>
S: 250 stamp@cs.sjsu.edu ... Recipient ok
C: DATA
S: 354 Enter mail, end with "." on a line by itself
C: It is my pleasure to inform you that you
C: are terminated
C:  .
S: 250 Message accepted for delivery
C: QUIT
S: 221 eniac.sjsu.edu closing connection
```

A-1.4   Transport Layer

The network layer (discussed below) offers unreliable, "best effort" delivery of packets. This means that the network layer attempts to get packets to their destination, but if a packet fails to arrive (or its data is corrupted or a packet arrives out of order or ...), the network takes no responsibility, much like the U.S. Postal Service. Any improved service beyond this limited best effort— such as the reliable delivery of packets—must be implemented somewhere above the network layer. Also, such additional service must be implemented on the hosts, since the core of the network only offers this best-effort delivery service. Reliable delivery of packets is the primary purpose of the transport layer.

Before we dive into the transport layer it's worth pondering why the network layer is allowed to be unreliable by design. Recall that we are dealing with a packet switched network. Consequently, it's possible that hosts will put more packets into the network than it can handle. Routers include buffers to store extra packets until they can be forwarded, but these buffers are finite— when a router's buffer is full, the router has no choice but to drop packets. The data in packets can also get corrupted in transit. And, since routing is a dynamic process, it's possible that packets in one particular connection can follow different paths. When this occurs, the packets can arrive at the destination in a different order than they were sent by the source. It's the job of the transport layer to deal with such reliability issues. The bottom line is that routing packets through the core of the network is difficult, so the designers of the Internet decided to minimize the burden at this level, and thus the minimal best effort approach at the network layer.

There are two transport layer protocols of importance: TCP and UDP. The Transmission Control Protocol, or TCP, provides for reliable delivery. TCP will make sure that your packets arrive, that they are sequenced in the correct order, and that the data has not been corrupted. To oversimplify things, the way that TCP provides these services is by including sequence numbers in packets and telling the sender to retransmit packets when problems are detected. Note that TCP runs on hosts, and all communication is over the same (unreliable) network where the data is sent. The format of the TCP header appears in Figure A-3.

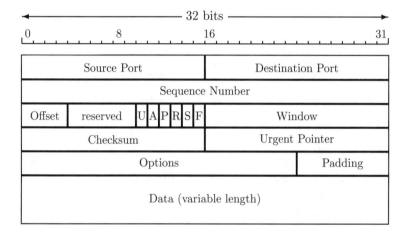

Figure A-3: TCP Header

TCP assures that packets arrive at their destination and that they are processed in order. TCP also makes sure that packets are not sent too fast for the receiver, which is known as *flow control*. In addition, TCP provides network-wide *congestion control*. This congestion control feature is complex, but one interesting aspect is that it attempts to give every host a fair share of the available bandwidth. That is, if congestion is detected, every TCP connection will get about the same amount of the available bandwidth. Of course, everyone wants more than their fair share, so hosts can (and do) try to cheat this congestion control feature by opening multiple TCP connections.

TCP is said to be connection-oriented, which means that TCP contacts the server before sending data. That is, TCP checks that the destination server is alive and listening on the appropriate port. It's important to realize that this TCP "connection" is only a logical connection—no true dedicated connection takes place.

The TCP connection establishment is of particular importance. A so-called *three-way handshake* is used, where the three messages that are exchanged are the following:

- SYN — The client requests "synchronization" with the server.

- SYN-ACK — The server acknowledges receipt of the SYN request.

- ACK — The client acknowledges the SYN-ACK. This third message can also include data. For example, if the client is Web browsing, the client could include the request for a specific Web page along with the ACK message.

The three-way handshake is illustrated in Figure A-4.

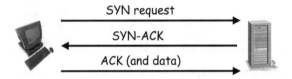

SYN request

SYN-ACK

ACK (and data)

Figure A-4: TCP 3-Way Handshake

TCP also provides for orderly tearing down of connections. Connections are terminated by a process involving a FIN (finish) packet or by a single RST (reset) packet.

The TCP three-way handshake makes denial of service, or DoS, attacks possible. Whenever a SYN packet is received, the server must remember the so-called "half-open" connection. This remembering consumes a small amount of server resources. As a result, too many half-open connections will cause server resources to be exhausted, at which point the server can no longer respond to new connections.

A straightforward DoS attack that is launched from a single machine using a single IP address is relatively easy to defend against—the intended victim can simply ignore or block any IP address that sends too many TCP requests. The attacker could make the attack difficult to block by spoofing the source IP addresses to make it appear that the requests are coming from many different machines. However, the amount of traffic needed to significantly affect the victim is likely to be more than one machine can generate. Consequently, most successful DoS attacks are actually distributed denial of service, or DDoS, attack. In a DDoS attack, many different machines are used to overwhelm the victim. If a large number of machines are used in a DDoS attack, then the generated traffic may be sufficient to prevent the victim from responding to legitimate requests. The distributed nature of such an attack makes it difficult to defend against.

The transport layer includes another protocol of note, the User Datagram Protocol, or UDP. Whereas TCP provides everything and the kitchen sink, UDP is a truly minimal no-frills service. The benefit of UDP is that it requires minimal overhead, but the tradeoff is that it provides no assurance that packets arrive, no assurance packets are in the proper order, and so on. In other words, UDP adds little to the unreliable network over which it operates.

Why does UDP exist? UDP is more efficient since it has a smaller header, but the major potential benefit derives from the fact that UDP has no flow control or congestion control. Due to the lack of these controls, there are no restrictions to slow down the sender. However, if packets are sent too fast, they will be dropped—either at an intermediate router or at the destination. So, how can UDP be a good thing? In some applications, delay is not tolerable, but it is acceptable to lose some fraction of the packets. Streaming audio and video fit this description, and for these applications UDP is generally preferable to TCP. In effect, UDP allows an application to get more than its fair share of the bandwidth, at the risk of packets getting dropped. Finally, it's worth noting that reliable data transfer over UDP is possible, but the reliability must be built in by the developer at the application layer. This would seem to provide the best of both worlds—reliability with no bandwidth limitations—at the expense of a more complex application layer protocol.

A-1.5   Network Layer

The network layer is the crucial layer for the core of network. Recall that the core is an interconnected mesh of routers, and the purpose of the network layer is to provide the information needed to route packets through this mesh. The network layer protocol of interest here is the Internet Protocol, or IP. As mentioned above, IP follows a best effort approach. Note that IP must run in every host and router in the network. The format of the IP header appears in Figure A-5.

In addition to network layer protocols, routers also run routing protocols. The purpose of a routing protocol is to determine the best path to use when sending a packet. There are many routing protocols, but the most popular are RIP, OSPF, and BGP. These protocols are very interesting, but we won't discuss them here.

Every host on the Internet must be associated with a 32-bit IP address. Unfortunately, there are not enough IP addresses for the number of hosts, and as a result many tricks are employed to effectively extend the IP address space. IP addresses are given in so-called dotted decimal notation of the form $W.X.Y.Z$, where each value is between 0 and 255. For example, 195.72.180.27 is a valid IP address. Note that a host's IP address can—and often does—change.

Although each host has a 32-bit IP address, there can be many processes

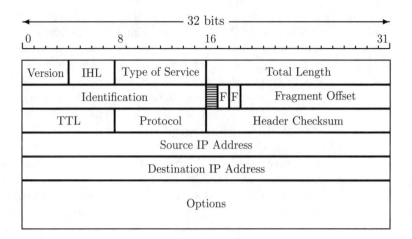

Figure A-5: IP Header

running on a single host. For example, you could browse the Web, send email, and do a file transfer all at the same time. To effectively communicate across the network, it's necessary to distinguish these processes. The way this is accomplished is by assigning each process a 16-bit *port number*. The port numbers below 1024 are said to be well known, and they're reserved for specific applications. For example, port 80 is used for HTTP and port 110 is for POP3. The port numbers from 1024 to 65535 are dynamic and assigned as needed. An IP address together with a port number defines a *socket*, and a socket uniquely identifies a process on the Internet.

The IP header is used by routers to determine the proper route for a packet through the network. The header includes fields for the source and destination IP addresses. There is also a time-to-live, or TTL, field that limits the number of hops that a packet can travel before it dies and goes to packet heaven. This prevents wayward packets from bouncing around the Internet for all of eternity. There are also fields that deal with fragmentation, which is our next topic.

Each link on the Internet limits the maximum size of packets. If a packet is too big, it's the router's job to split it into smaller packets. This process in known as *fragmentation*. To prevent multiple fragmentation and reassembly steps, the fragments are only reassembled at the their destination.

Fragmentation creates many security issues. One problem is that the actual purpose of a packet is easily disguised by breaking it into fragments. The fragments can be arranged to overlap when reassembled, which further exacerbates this problem. The result is that the receiving host can only determine the purpose of a packet after it has received all of the fragments and reassembled the pieces. A firewall has a great deal more work to do when dealing with fragmented packets. As a result, fragmentation opens the door to DoS and many other types of attacks.

Currently, we use IP version 4, that is, IPv4. It has many shortcomings, including too-small 32-bit addresses and poor security (fragmentation being just one example). As a result, a new-and-improved version, IP version 6 (IPv6), has been developed. IPv6 includes 128-bit addresses—which gives a virtually inexhaustible supply of IP addresses—and strong security in the form of IPSec. Unfortunately, IPv6 is a classic example of how not to develop a replacement protocol. There is no natural way to migrate from IPv4 to IPv6 and, consequently, IPv6 has yet to take hold on a large scale [30].

A-1.6   Link Layer

The link layer is responsible for getting the packet over each individual link in the network. That is, the link layer deals with getting a packet from a host to a router, from a router to a router, from a router to a host or, locally, from one host to another host. As a packet traverses the network, different links can be completely different. For example, a single packet might travel over Ethernet, a wired point-to-point line, and a wireless microwave link when traveling from its source to its destination.

In each host, the link layer and physical layer are implemented in a semi-autonomous adapter known as a Network Interface Card, or NIC—examples include Ethernet cards and wireless 802.11 cards. The NIC is (mostly) out of the host's control, and that's why it's said to be semi-autonomous.

One link layer protocol of particular importance is Ethernet. Ethernet is a multiple access protocol, meaning that it's used when many hosts are competing for a shared resource. Such situations occur on a local area network, or LAN. In Ethernet, if two packets are transmitted by different hosts at essentially the same time, they can collide, in which case both packets are corrupted. The packets must then be resent. The challenge is to efficiently handle collisions in a distributed environment. There are many possible ways to deal with a shared media, but Ethernet is by far the most popular method. In any respectable networking course, a significant amount of time is devoted to Ethernet, but we won't go into the details here.

While IP addresses are used at the network layer, the link layer has its own addressing scheme. We'll refer to link layer addresses as MAC addresses, but they are also known as LAN addresses, physical addresses, etc. MAC addresses are 48 bits, and they're globally unique. The MAC address is embedded in the NIC, and, unlike an IP address, it cannot change (unless a new NIC is installed). MAC addresses are used to forward packets at the link layer.

Why do we need both IP addresses and MAC addresses? An analogy is often made to home addresses and social security numbers. A home address is like an IP address, since it can change. On the other hand, even if you move, your social security number stays the same, which makes it analogous to a MAC address. However, this doesn't really answer the question. In fact, it would be conceivable to do away with MAC addresses, but it is somewhat more efficient to use these two forms of addressing. Fundamentally, the dual addressing is necessary due to layering, which requires that the link layer should work with any network layer addressing scheme. In fact, some network layer protocols (such as IPX) do not use IP addresses and the link layer requires no modification to work with such protocols. The bottom line is that a strict adherence to layering requires that we have two distinct addressing schemes.

There are many interesting and significant link layer protocols. We've mentioned Ethernet and we'll mention just one more, namely, the Address Resolution Protocol, or ARP. The primary purpose of ARP is to find the MAC address that corresponds to a given IP address for hosts on the same LAN. Each node has its own ARP table, which contains the mapping between IP addresses and MAC addresses. This ARP table—which is also known as an ARP cache—is generated automatically. The entries expire after a period of time (typically, 20 minutes) so they must be refreshed periodically. Believe it or not, ARP is the protocol used to determine ARP table entries.

How does ARP work? When a node doesn't know a particular IP-to-MAC mapping, it broadcasts an ARP request message to every node on the LAN. The appropriate node on the LAN (i.e., the node with the given IP address) responds with an ARP reply. The requesting node can then fill in the corresponding entry in its ARP cache.

ARP is a stateless protocol, and as such, a node does not maintain a record of ARP requests that it has sent. As a consequence, a node will accept any ARP reply that it receives, even if it made no corresponding ARP request. This opens the door to an attack by a malicious host on the LAN. This attack, known as *ARP cache poisoning*, is illustrated in Figure A-6. In this example, the host with MAC address CC-CC-CC-CC-CC-CC has sent a bogus ARP reply to both of the other hosts, and they have updated their ARP caches accordingly. As a result, whenever AA-AA-AA-AA-AA-AA and BB-BB-BB-BB-BB-BB send packets to each other, the packets will first pass through the hands of the evil host CC-CC-CC-CC-CC-CC, who can alter the messages, delete the messages, or simply pass them along unchanged. This type of attack is known as a man-in-the-middle, or MiM, regardless of the gender of the attacker.

Recall that TCP provides an example of a stateful protocol that is subject to attack. ARP, on the other hand, is an example of a vulnerable stateless protocol. So stateless and stateful protocols both have the potential for security vulnerabilities.

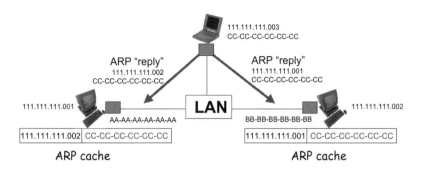

Figure A-6: ARP Cache Poisoning

A-1.7 Conclusions

In this section, we've barely scratched the surface of the vast topic that is networking. Tanenbaum [298] presents a good introduction to a wide range of networking topics, and his book is well suited to independent study. Another good introductory textbook on networking is Kurose and Ross [177]. A more detailed discussion of networking protocols can be found in [113]. If more details are needed than what is available in [113], consult the appropriate RFCs.

A-2   Math Essentials

> *7/5ths of all people don't understand fractions.*
> — Anonymous

A-2.1 Introduction

This section contains a brief overview of the math topics that are relevant to understanding the material presented in this book. First, we cover some modular arithmetic basics. Modular arithmetic figures prominently in the field of public key cryptography. We then discuss a few very basic facts about permutations. Permutations are a fundamental building block of ciphers— from classic ciphers to modern block ciphers. Next, we consider a few concepts from discrete probability and, finally, we provide a quick introduction to linear algebra. Chapter 6 contains the details of the lattice-reduction attack on the knapsack cryptosystem, and that's the only place where linear algebra is used in this book.

A-2.2 Modular Arithmetic

For integers x and n, the value of x modulo n, which is abbreviated x mod n, is defined to be the remainder when x is divided by n. Note that the remainder when a number is divided by n must be one of the values $0, 1, 2 \ldots, n-1$, so these are the only possible results when you are asked to compute x mod n.

In non-modular arithmetic, the number line is used to represent the relative positions of the numbers. For modular arithmetic, a mod n "clock" labeled with the integers $0, 1, 2 \ldots, n-1$ serves a similar purpose, and for this reason modular arithmetic can be viewed as clock arithmetic. For example, the mod 6 clock appears in Figure A-7.

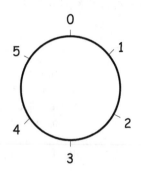

Figure A-7: Number "Line" Mod 6

The notation for modular arithmetic is flexible—we can write x mod $n = y$ or $x = y$ mod n or x (mod n) $= y$ or $x = y$ (mod n). The point here is that if a "mod n" appears anywhere in an equation, the entire equation is taken modulo n. It is common to say that we "reduce" x mod n, and if you really want to impress your friends, you can say modulo n instead of mod n.

A basic property of modular addition is

$$((a \bmod n) + (b \bmod n)) \bmod n = (a+b) \bmod n,$$

so that, for example,

$$(7+12) \bmod 6 = 19 \bmod 6 = 1 \bmod 6$$

and

$$(7+12) \bmod 6 = (1+0) \bmod 6 = 1 \bmod 6.$$

That is, we can apply the mod operations any place (or places) we please and the result will not change. Often, for computational efficiency (or convenience) we do the modular reductions in some not-so-obvious order.

The same property holds true for modular multiplication, that is,

$$((a \bmod n)(b \bmod n)) \bmod n = ab \bmod n.$$

For example,

$$(7 \cdot 4) \bmod 6 = 28 \bmod 6 = 4 \bmod 6$$

and

$$(7 \cdot 4) \bmod 6 = (1 \cdot 4) \bmod 6 = 4 \bmod 6.$$

This simple property is critical for effective modular exponentiation, and modular exponentiation is the fundamental computation used in the RSA public key cryptosystem.

Modular inverses play an important role in public key cryptography. In ordinary (non-modular) addition, the additive inverse of x is the number that we add to x to get 0. Of course, in non-modular arithmetic, that's just a fancy way of saying that the additive inverse of x is $-x$. The additive inverse of $x \bmod n$ is denoted $-x \bmod n$, but we have to use the definition to make sense of the " $-$ ". Recall that when working modulo n, the only numbers that exist are $0, 1, 2, \ldots, n-1$. Then, from the definition, $-x \bmod n$ is the number in this range that we add to x to obtain $0 \bmod n$. For example, $-2 \bmod 6 = 4$, since $2 + 4 = 0 \bmod 6$. That is, $-2 = 4 \bmod 6$, which can also be seen by starting at 0 on the mod 6 clock and going counterclockwise by 2.

In ordinary arithmetic, the multiplicative inverse of x, denoted as x^{-1}, is the number that we multiply by x to obtain 1. In the non-modular world, this is easy, since $x^{-1} = 1/x$, provided that $x \neq 0$. But in the modular case there are no fractions, so things are not as straightforward. From the definition, the multiplicative inverse of $x \bmod n$, which is denoted $x^{-1} \bmod n$, is the number that we multiply by x to obtain $1 \bmod n$. For example, $3^{-1} \bmod 7 = 5$, since $3 \cdot 5 = 1 \bmod 7$. That is, $3^{-1} = 5 \bmod 7$.

What is $2^{-1} \bmod 6$? Since we are working mod 6, the only possible choices are $0, 1, 2, 3, 4, 5$, and it's easy to verify by an exhaustive search that none of these satisfy the definition. Consequently, 2 does not have a multiplicative inverse, modulo 6, which shows that for modular arithmetic, there are numbers other than 0 that do not have multiplicative inverses.

When does a (modular) multiplicative inverse exist? To answer that, we must delve slightly deeper. A number p is said to be *prime* if it has no factors other than 1 and p. We say that two numbers x and y are *relatively prime* if they have no common factor other than 1. For example, 8 and 9 are relatively prime, although neither 8 nor 9 is prime. It can be shown that $x^{-1} \bmod y$ exists if and only if x and y are relatively prime. When the modular inverse exists, it's easy to find—in a computational sense—using the Euclidean algorithm [43]. It's also easy (computationally) to tell when a modular inverse doesn't exist, that is, it's easy to test whether x and y are relatively prime.

For our discussion of public key cryptography, we require one additional result from number theory. The *totient function* (or Euler's totient function), which is denoted as $\phi(n)$, is the number of positive integers less than n that are relatively prime to n. For example, $\phi(4) = 2$ since 4 is relatively prime to 3 and 1, but not 2. Also, $\phi(5) = 4$ since 5 is relatively prime to 1,2,3 and 4, while $\phi(12) = 4$, since the only positive integers less than 12 that are relatively prime to 12 are 1, 5, 7, and 11.

For any prime number p, it's easy to see that $\phi(p) = p - 1$. Furthermore, it is fairly easy to show that if p and q are prime, then $\phi(pq) = (p - 1)(q - 1)$; see Burton's fine book [43] for the details. These elementary properties of $\phi(n)$ are used in Section 4.3 of Chapter 4, which covers the RSA public key cryptosystem.

A-2.3   Permutations

Let S be a given set. Then a *permutation* of S is an ordered list of the elements of S, where each element appears exactly once. For example, $(3, 1, 4, 0, 5, 2)$ is a permutation of $\{0, 1, 2, 3, 4, 5\}$, but $(3, 1, 4, 0, 5)$ is not and neither is the list $(3, 1, 4, 2, 5, 2)$.

It's easy to count the number of permutations of a set of n elements: there are n ways to choose the first element of the permutation, $n - 1$ selections remain for the next element, and so on. Consequently, there are $n!$ permutations of any set of n elements. For example, there are 24 permutations of the set $\{0, 1, 2, 3\}$.

Permutations play a prominent role in cryptography. Classic ciphers are often based on permutations, while many modern block ciphers also make heavy use of permutations.

A-2.4   Probability

In this book, we only require a few elementary facts from the field of discrete probability. Let $S = \{0, 1, 2, \ldots, N - 1\}$ represent the set of all possible outcomes of some experiment. If each outcome is *equally likely*, then the probability of the *event* X, where $X \subset S$, is

$$P(X) = \text{number of elements in } X / \text{number of elements in } S.$$

For example, if we roll two dice, the set S can be taken to be the 36 equally likely ordered pairs

$$S = \{(1, 1), (1, 2), \ldots, (1, 6), (2, 1), (2, 2), \ldots, (6, 6)\}.$$

Then when we roll two dice we find, for example,

$$P(\text{sum equal } 7) = 6/36 = 1/6,$$

since 6 of the elements in S sum to 7.

Often, it's easier to compute the probability of X using the fact

$$P(X) = 1 - P(\text{complement of } X),$$

where the complement of X is the set of elements in S that are not in X. For example, when rolling two dice,

$$P(\text{sum } > 3) = 1 - P(\text{number } \leq 3) = 1 - 3/36 = 11/12.$$

Although there are many good sources of information on discrete probability, probably your author's favorite is the ancient—but excellent—book by Feller [109]. Feller covers all of the basics and many interesting and useful advanced topics, all in a very readable and engaging style.

A-2.5 Linear Algebra

In Chapter 6, the discussion of the attack on the knapsack cryptosystem requires a small amount of linear algebra. Here, we present only the minimum amount of linear algebra required to understand the material in that particular section.

We write $v \in \mathbf{R}^n$ to denote a vector containing n components, where each element is a real number. For example,

$$v = [v_1, v_2, v_3, v_4] = [4, 7/3, 13, -3/2] \in \mathbf{R}^4.$$

The *dot product* of two vectors $u, v \in \mathbf{R}^n$, is

$$u \cdot v = u_1 v_1 + u_2 v_2 + \cdots + u_n v_n.$$

Note that the dot product only applies to vectors of the same length and the result of the dot product is a number, not a vector.

A *matrix* is an $n \times m$ array of numbers. For example,

$$A = \begin{bmatrix} 3 & 4 & 2 \\ 1 & 7 & 9 \end{bmatrix} \tag{A-1}$$

is a 2×3 matrix, and we sometimes write $A_{2 \times 3}$ to emphasize the dimensions. We denote the element in the ith row and jth column of A as a_{ij}. For example, in the matrix A, above, $a_{1,2} = 4$.

To multiply a matrix by a number, we simply multiply each element of the matrix by the number. For example, for the matrix A in equation (A-1), we have

$$3A = \begin{bmatrix} 3 \cdot 3 & 3 \cdot 4 & 3 \cdot 2 \\ 3 \cdot 1 & 3 \cdot 7 & 3 \cdot 9 \end{bmatrix} = \begin{bmatrix} 9 & 12 & 6 \\ 3 & 21 & 27 \end{bmatrix}$$

Addition of matrices is only defined if the matrices have the same dimensions. If so, the corresponding elements are simply added. For example,

$$\begin{bmatrix} 3 & 2 \\ 1 & 5 \end{bmatrix} + \begin{bmatrix} -1 & 4 \\ 6 & 2 \end{bmatrix} = \begin{bmatrix} 2 & 6 \\ 7 & 7 \end{bmatrix}.$$

Matrix multiplication, on the other hand, is less intuitive than matrix addition or multiplication by a number. Given matrices $A_{m \times n}$ and $B_{k \times \ell}$, the product $C = AB$ is only defined if $n = k$, in which case the product C is $m \times \ell$. When the product is defined, the element in row i and column j of C, that is, c_{ij}, is given by the dot product of the ith row of A with the jth column of B. For example, for the matrix A in (A-1) and

$$B = \begin{bmatrix} -1 & 2 \\ 2 & -3 \end{bmatrix}$$

the product

$$BA = C_{2 \times 3} = \begin{bmatrix} [-1,2] \cdot \begin{bmatrix} 3 \\ 1 \end{bmatrix} & [-1,2] \cdot \begin{bmatrix} 4 \\ 7 \end{bmatrix} & [-1,2] \cdot \begin{bmatrix} 2 \\ 9 \end{bmatrix} \\ [2,-3] \cdot \begin{bmatrix} 3 \\ 1 \end{bmatrix} & [2,-3] \cdot \begin{bmatrix} 4 \\ 7 \end{bmatrix} & [2,-3] \cdot \begin{bmatrix} 2 \\ 9 \end{bmatrix} \end{bmatrix}$$

$$= \begin{bmatrix} -1 & 10 & 16 \\ 3 & -13 & -23 \end{bmatrix}.$$

Note that for these two matrices, the product AB is undefined, which shows that matrix multiplication is, in general, not commutative.

The *identity matrix* $I_{n \times n}$ has 1s on the main diagonal, and 0s elsewhere. Note that the identity matrix is always a square matrix, that is, a matrix with an equal numbers of rows and columns. For example, the 3×3 identity matrix is

$$I = \begin{bmatrix} 1 & 0 & 0 \\ 0 & 1 & 0 \\ 0 & 0 & 1 \end{bmatrix}.$$

For a square matrix A, the identity matrix of the appropriate size is the multiplicative identity, that is, $AI = IA = A$.

We can also define block matrices, where the elements are themselves matrices. We can multiply block matrices provided that the dimensions meet the requirements for matrix multiplications, *and* the dimensions on all of the individual blocks that are to be multiplied also are appropriate for multiplication. For example, if

$$M = \begin{bmatrix} I_{n \times n} & C_{n \times 1} \\ A_{m \times n} & B_{m \times 1} \end{bmatrix} \quad \text{and} \quad V = \begin{bmatrix} U_{n \times \ell} \\ T_{1 \times \ell} \end{bmatrix},$$

then

$$MV = \begin{bmatrix} X_{n \times \ell} \\ Y_{m \times \ell} \end{bmatrix},$$

where $X = U + CT$ and $Y = AU + BT$. You should verify that all of these operations are defined.

We'll require only one more result from linear algebra. Suppose x and y are vectors in $\mathbb{R}^n$. Then we say that x and y are *linearly independent* provided that the only scalars (i.e., numbers) α and β for which

$$\alpha x + \beta y = 0$$

are $\alpha = \beta = 0$. For example,

$$\begin{bmatrix} 1 \\ -1 \end{bmatrix} \quad \text{and} \quad \begin{bmatrix} 1 \\ 2 \end{bmatrix}$$

are linearly independent. Linear independence extends to more than two vectors. The importance of linear independence derives from the fact that if a set of vectors are linearly independent, then none of the vectors can be written as a *linear combination* of the other vectors, that is, none of the vectors can be written as a sum of multiples of the other vectors in the set. This is the sense in which the vectors are independent.

A-2.6 Conclusions

That concludes our brief review of the math used in this book. Hopefully, you're still awake. In any case, the math required in this text is minimal, so fear not if some of the details discussed here appear somewhat opaque. You can simply review this material as needed if you run into any mathematical speed bumps on your way to security enlightenment.

Annotated Bibliography

If you can't annoy somebody, there is little point in writing.
— Kingsley Amis

[1] 3GPP home page, at `www.3gpp.org/`
Cited on page 381

[2] @stake LC 5, at `en.wikipedia.org/wiki/@stake`
Cited on page 241

  • Prior to being acquired by Symantec, @stake was a leading security
    company. At one time they made news for supposedly firing a top-
    notch security expert for his implicit criticism of Microsoft (see,
    for example, `dc.internet.com/news/article.php/3083901`).

[3] M. Abadi and R. Needham, Prudent engineering practice for crypto-
    graphic protocols, *IEEE Transactions on Software Engineering*, Vol. 22,
    No. 1, pp. 6–15, January 1996.
    Cited on page 314

[4] E. Aboufadel, Work by the Poles to break the Enigma codes, at
    `faculty.gvsu.edu/aboufade/web/enigma/polish.htm`
    Cited on page 176

  • A brief description of the brilliant work by the Polish cryptana-
    lysts.

[5] Access control matrix, at
    `en.wikipedia.org/wiki/Access_Control_Matrix`
    Cited on page 271

[6] E. Ackerman, Student skirts CD's piracy guard, SiliconValley.com, at
    `technews.acm.org/articles/2003-5/1008w.html#item2`
    Cited on page 471

- The classic "hold down the shift key" attack on a DRM system.

[7] AES algorithm (Rijndael) information, at
`csrc.nist.gov/archive/aes/index1.html`
Cited on page 67

  - A good place to tap into the wealth of information available on
    Rijndael and the AES.

[8] Aleph One, Smashing the stack for fun and profit, *Phrack*, Volume
Seven, Issue Forty-Nine, File 14 of 16, at
`www.phrack.com/issues.html?issue=49&id=14&mode=txt`
Cited on page 411

  - The first widely available and hacker-friendly source of information
    on buffer overflow attacks.

[9] D. Anderson, T. Frivold, and A. Valdes, Next-generation intrusion detection expert system (NIDES): summary, at
`citeseerx.ist.psu.edu/viewdoc/summary?doi=10.1.1.121.5956`
Cited on page 300

  - This is one in a series of papers about NIDES.

[10] R. Anderson and E. Biham, Tiger: a fast new hash function, at
`www.cs.technion.ac.il/~biham/Reports/Tiger/`
Cited on pages 133 and 135

  - Two crypto experts present the details of their hash function.

[11] R. J. Anderson and M. G. Kuhn, Improved differential fault analysis,
at `jya.com/akdfa.txt`
Cited on page 211

  - Along with most other security topics under the sun, Ross Ander-
    son is an expert on side channel attacks.

[12] R. Anderson, Security in Open versus Closed Systems — The Dance of
Boltzmann, Coase and Moore, at
`www.cl.cam.ac.uk/~rja14/Papers/toulouse.pdf`
Cited on pages 475 and 476

  - This paper gives an interesting and fairly elementary argument
    that—from a security perspective—there's no significant difference
    between open and closed source software. This is Ross Anderson
    at his best.

[13] R. Anderson, TCPA/Palladium frequently asked questions, at
`www.cl.cam.ac.uk/~rja14/tcpa-faq.html`
Cited on pages 500, 505, and 509

[14] R. Anderson, *Security Engineering*, Wiley, 2001, at
`www.cl.cam.ac.uk/~rja14/book.html`
Cited on pages 9, 13, 211, 230, 233, 244, 271, 280, 284, 304, 316, 381,
406, 473, 475, 476, 480, and 497

- Ross Anderson is the reigning God of information security and
  this book is his Bible. For the nitty-gritty details, you'll have to
  go elsewhere, but for the big picture, this is very good. There is
  also a second edition that covers some new ground. However, this
  first edition is available for free at the given link.

[15] R. Anderson, *Security Engineering* Errata, at
`www.cl.cam.ac.uk/~rja14/errata.html`
Cited on page 316

- This is worth reading just for Anderson's description of the pub-
  lishing process. Here you'll also learn (among other things) that
  the MiG-in-the-middle attack never actually occurred.

[16] Z. Anderson, Warcart, at `web.mit.edu/zacka/www/warcart.html`
Cited on page 16

[17] W. A. Arbaugh, N. Shankar, and Y. C. J. Wan, Your 802.11 wireless
network has no clothes, at `www.cs.umd.edu/~waa/wireless.pdf`
Cited on page 381

- Well-written description of the many security flaws in 802.11.

[18] G. Arboit, A method for watermarking Java programs via opaque predicates, at `crypto.cs.mcgill.ca/~garboit/sp-paper.pdf`
Cited on page 485

[19] D. Aucsmith, Tamper resistant software: an implementation, *Proceedings of the First International Information Hiding Workshop, Lecture
Notes in Computer Science 1174*, Springer-Verlag, Cambridge, UK,
pp. 317–334, 1996.
Cited on pages 456 and 562

- Difficult to read and impossible for mere mortals like myself to
  comprehend. I challenge anyone to make sense of this, even with
  Aucsmith's patent as backup.

[20] Audacity, The free, cross-platform sound editor, at
`audacity.sourceforge.net/`
Cited on page 262

[21] J. Aycock, *Computer Viruses and Malware*, Advances in Information
Security, Vol. 22, Springer-Verlag, 2006.
Cited on page 421

  • A well-written, humorous, and easily accessible introduction to
    malware.

[22] J. Aycock, *Spyware and Adware*, Springer-Verlag, 2010.
Cited on pages 241 and 421

  • Another excellent malware book from John Aycock.

[23] D. V. Bailey, Inside eBook security, *Dr. Dobb's Journal*, November
2001, at `www.drdobbs.com/184404845`
Cited on page 471

  • The weakness of eBook security is exposed.

[24] I. Balepin, Superworms and cryptovirology: a deadly combination, at
`wwwcsif.cs.ucdavis.edu/~balepin/files/worms-cryptovirology.pdf`
Cited on page 429

  • The future of malware is considered.

[25] B. Barak, O. Goldreich, R. Impagliazzo, S. Rudich, A. Sahai, S. Vadhan
and K. Yang, On the (im)possibility of obfuscating programs (extended
abstract), in J. Kilian, editor, Advances in Cryptology – CRYPTO 2001,
Lecture Notes in Computer Science 2139, at
`www.iacr.org/archive/crypto2001/21390001.pdf`
Cited on page 458

  • This paper created quite a stir when published. The upshot is that,
    in some sense, obfuscation can probably never "really" be secure.
    There is some debate as to whether the model used is realistic,
    and what "really" really means.

[26] E. Barkan, E. Biham, and N. Keller, Instant ciphertext-only cryptanalysis of GSM encrypted communication, at
`cryptome.org/gsm-crack-bbk.pdf`
Cited on page 386

  • Attacks on the GSM protocol as well as attacks on A5/2 and A5/1.

[27] M. Barrett and C. Thomborson, Using NGSCB to mitigate existing software threats, at `www.cs.auckland.ac.nz/~cthombor/Pubs/cses.pdf`
Cited on pages 501 and 503

[28] BBC News, Afghan girl found after 17 years, at
`news.bbc.co.uk/1/hi/world/south_asia/1870382.stm`
Cited on page 249

[29] Beale Screamer, Microsoft's digital rights management scheme—technical details, at
`web.elastic.org/~fche/mirrors/cryptome.org/beale-sci-crypt.htm`
Cited on pages 21 and 472

  • Interesting and well written, at least by hacker standards.

[30] D. J. Bernstein, The IPv6 mess, at `cr.yp.to/djbdns/ipv6mess.html`
Cited on page 521

[31] P. Biddle et al., The darknet and the future of content distribution, at
`crypto.stanford.edu/DRM2002/darknet5.doc`
Cited on page 461

  • A true classic. Anyone interested in DRM must read this.

[32] Biometrics comparison chart, at
`ctl.ncsc.dni.us/biomet%20web/BMCompare.html`
Cited on page 250

[33] A. Biryukov, A. Shamir, and D. Wagner, Real time cryptanalysis of A5/1 on a PC, at
`home.in.tum.de/~gerold/KryptDokumente/a5_Angriff/a51-bsw.htm`
Cited on pages 54 and 386

  • An efficient attack on A5/1 that requires huge amounts of storage.

[34] M. Bishop, *Computer Security: Art and Science*, Addison Wesley, 2003.
Cited on pages 10 and 277

  • In my humble opinion, this book often crosses the line into the realm of theory for the sake of theory. The book is definitely not an easy read. The best sections are those on topics that are theoretical by their very nature. For example, the discussion of security modeling is excellent.

[35] I. Blake, G. Seroussi, and N. Smart, *Elliptic Curves in Cryptography*, Cambridge University Press, 2000.
Cited on page 106

- The mathematical results are all there but without the proofs.

[36] blexim, Basic Integer Overflows, *Phrack Magazine*, Volume 0x0b, Issue
0x3c, Phile #0x0a of 0x10, at
`www.phrack.com/issues.html?issue=60&id=10`
Cited on page 439

[37] L. Boettger, The Morris worm: how it affected computer security and
lessons learned by it, at
`hackersnews.org/hackerhistory/morrisworm.html`
Cited on page 422

[38] N. Borisov, I. Goldberg, and D. Wagner, Intercepting mobile communications: the insecurity of 802.11, at
`www.isaac.cs.berkeley.edu/isaac/wep-draft.pdf`
Cited on pages 132 and 381

  - A good source for information concerning the many flaws of WEP.

[39] Botnet, at `en.wikipedia.org/wiki/Botnet`
Cited on page 304

[40] J. Bowen, Formal methods, *The World Wide Web Virtual Library*, at
`formalmethods.wikia.com/wiki/Jonathan_Bowen`
Cited on page 477

[41] D. Brumley and D. Boneh, Remote timing attacks are practical, at
`crypto.stanford.edu/~dabo/papers/ssl-timing.pdf`
Cited on pages 211 and 217

  - A nice paper describing a side-channel attack on the RSA imple-
    mentation in OpenSSL.

[42] S. Budiansky, *Battle of Wits: The Complete Story of Codebreaking in
World War II*, The Free Press, 2000.
Cited on page 38

  - An excellent and highly readable book. The historical accuracy is
    first rate, and the author has good insight into both the technical
    aspects and the human side of intelligence gathering. My only
    quibble is that the subtitle is somewhat misleading, since the focus
    is clearly on the Enigma and the British.

[43] D. M. Burton, *Elementary Number Theory*, fourth edition, Wm.
C. Brown, 1998.
Cited on pages 96, 100, 525, and 526

[44] Cafebabe bytecode editor, at
`cafebabe.sourceforge.net/index.html`
Cited on page 481

  • If you want to see just how easy it is to reverse engineer a Java
    program, try this tool on your favorite `class` file.

[45] K. W. Campbell and M. J. Wiener, DES is not a group, *Advances in
Cryptology*, CRYPTO '92, Springer-Verlag, 1993, pp. 512–520.
Cited on page 225

  • Definitive proof—though late in coming—that triple DES really is
    more secure than single DES.

[46] P. Capitant, Software tamper-proofing deployed 2-year anniversary report, Macrovision Corporation, at
`www.cs.sjsu.edu/faculty/stamp/DRM/`
`       DRM%20papers/Software_Tamper-Proofing.ppt`
Cited on page 460

  • Some good information on DRM techniques, based on real-world
    experiences.

[47] CAPTCHA, at
`en.wikipedia.org/wiki/CAPTCHA`
Cited on page 286

[48] A. Carlson, Simulating the Enigma cypher machine, at
`homepages.tesco.net/~andycarlson/enigma/simulating_enigma.html`
Cited on page 171

  • Describes the double stepping well.

[49] J. Carr, Strategies & issues: thwarting insider attacks, *Network Magazine*, September 4, 2002.
Cited on page 287

[50] L. Carroll, *Alice's Adventures in Wonderland*, at
`www.sabian.org/alice.htm`
Cited on page 151

[51] CERT coordination center, at `www.cert.org/`
Cited on page 424

[52] Certicom Corporation, Certicom ECC Challenge, November 1997, at
`www.certicom.com/index.php/the-certicom-ecc-challenge`
Cited on page 106

[53] P. Červeň, *Crackproof Your Software: Protect Your Software Against Crackers*, No Starch Press, 2002.
Cited on page 454

- Easily the best available book for information on anti-disassembly and anti-debugging techniques. A new edition would be valuable since the material is heavily focused on Windows 98.

[54] H. Chang and M. J. Atallah, Protecting software code by guards, *Workshop on Security and Privacy in Digital Rights Management 2001.*
Cited on pages 458 and 548

- Surprisingly similar to the paper [145], which was presented at the same conference.

[55] G. Chapman et al., *The Complete Monty Python's Flying Circus: All the Words*, vols. 1 and 2, Pantheon, 1989.
Cited on pages 110 and 140

[56] K. Chellapilla, K. Larson, P. Simard, and M. Czerwinski, Computers beat Humans at Single Character Recognition in Reading based Human Interaction Proofs (HIPs), Microsoft Research, at
`www.ceas.cc/2005/papers/160.pdf`
Cited on pages 286 and 305

- A very interesting paper that shows that computers are better than humans at solving all of the basic visual CAPTCHA/HIP problems, with the exception of the segmentation problem. The obvious implication is that a strong CAPTCHA must rely primarily on the segmentation problem for its security.

[57] T. Cipresso, Software Reverse Engineering Education, Master's Thesis, Department of Computer Science, San Jose State University, 2009, at
`reversingproject.info/`
Cited on pages 448 and 454

- An excellent overview of the uses of SRE (both good and bad), along with several detailed examples (with complete, animated solutions). I've used these examples as the basis for a software reverse engineering course, and they are also ideal for self-study.

[58] T. Cipresso, Java bytecode anti-reversing exercise, at
`reversingproject.info/?page_id=65`
Cited on page 482

[59] Clipper chip, at `en.wikipedia.org/wiki/Clipper_chip`
Cited on page 143

[60] F. B. Cohen, Experiments with computer viruses, 1984, at
www.all.net/books/virus/part5.html
Cited on page 277

- Discussion of early virus experiments by the father of the computer
  virus.

[61] F. B. Cohen, Operating system protection through program evolution,
at all.net/books/IP/evolve.html
Cited on pages 456 and 460

- A fascinating idea, that has implications far beyond operating systems.

[62] F. B. Cohen, *A Short Course on Computer Viruses*, second edition,
Wiley, 1994.
Cited on page 422

- A nice book, but the material is dated.

[63] C. Collberg, SandMark: a tool for the study of software protection
mechanisms, at sandmark.cs.arizona.edu/
Cited on page 482

[64] C. S. Collberg and C. Thomborson, Watermarking, tamper-proofing
and obfuscation—tools for software protection, *IEEE Transactions on
Software Engineering*, Vol. 28, No. 8, August 2002.
Cited on page 458

- These authors are the originators of most of the sophisticated
  methods of software obfuscation.

[65] Common Criteria — The Common Criteria portal, at
www.commoncriteriaportal.org/
Cited on page 269

[66] Computer Knowledge, Virus tutorial, at
www.cknow.com/cms/vtutor/cknow-virus-tutorial.html
Cited on page 422

- A wide ranging and fairly thorough discussion of many issues related to malware. Robert Slade's history of viruses—which is current up to about the year 2000—is included.

[67] M. Cooney, IBM touts encryption innovation: New technology performs
calculations on encrypted data without decrypting it, *ComputerWorld*,
June 25, 2009, at

www.computerworld.com/action/article.do?command=viewArticle
Basic&articleId=9134823&source=CTWNLE_nlt_security_2009-06-25
Cited on page 121

[68] D. Coppersmith, Small solutions to polynomial equations, and low exponent RSA vulnerabilities, *Journal of Cryptology*, Vol. 10, 1997, pp. 233–260.
Cited on page 214

[69] Coventry blitz, at en.wikipedia.org/wiki/Coventry_Blitz
Cited on page 38

[70] S. Craver, The underhanded C contest, at
underhanded.xcott.com/
Cited on page 437

  • An amusing contest with some incredible examples of innocent-looking code doing malicious things.

[71] S. A. Craver et. al., Reading between the lines: lessons learned from the SDMI challenge, *Proceedings of the 10th USENIX Security Symposium*, Washington, DC, August 13–17, 2001, at
www.usenix.org/events/sec01/craver.pdf
Cited on pages 149, 153, and 471

  • One of the best security papers you'll ever read. The authors demolish the security of the proposed SDMI system. If you think watermarking is easy, or if you're tempted to ignore Kerckhoffs' Principle, you'll change your mind after reading this.

[72] R. X. Cringely, Calm before the storm, at
www.pbs.org/cringely/pulpit/2001/pulpit_20010730_000422.html
Cited on page 424

[73] Cryptographer's Panel, RSA Conference 2002, at
www.cs.sjsu.edu/~stamp/cv/tripreports/RSA2002.html
Cited on page 67

[74] Cryptographer's Panel, RSA Conference 2004, at
www.cs.sjsu.edu/~stamp/cv/tripreports/RSA04.html
Cited on pages 56, 404, and 500

[75] J. Daemen and V. Rijmen, The Rijndael block cipher, at
csrc.nist.gov/archive/aes/index.html
Cited on page 67

[76] J. Daugman, How iris recognition works, at
`www.cl.cam.ac.uk/users/jgd1000/irisrecog.pdf`
Cited on page 247

[77] D. Davis, Defective sign & encrypt in S/MIME, PKCS#7, MOSS, PEM, PGP, and XML, at
`world.std.com/~dtd/sign_encrypt/sign_encrypt7.html`
Cited on page 110

[78] E. X. DeJesus, SAML brings security to XML, *XML Magazine*, Volume 3, No. 1, January 11, 2002, pp. 35–37.
Cited on page 253

[79] Defcon 11, at `www.cs.sjsu.edu/~stamp/cv/tripreports/defcon11.html`
Cited on pages 301, 419, 430, and 431

   • My "trip report" about Defcon 11.

[80] Defcon 16, at `www.defcon.org/html/defcon-16/dc-16-post.html`
Cited on page 16

[81] Definition of John Anthony Walker, at
`www.wordiq.com/definition/John_Anthony_Walker`
Cited on page 40

[82] Definition of Purple code, at `www.wordiq.com/definition/Purple_code`
Cited on page 37

[83] Definition of Zimmermann Telegram, at
`www.wordiq.com/definition/Zimmermann_Telegram`
Cited on page 33

[84] M. Delio, Linux: fewer bugs than rivals, *Wired*, December 2004, at
`www.wired.com/software/coolapps/news/2004/12/66022`
Cited on page 474

[85] D. E. Denning and D. K. Branstad, A taxonomy for key escrow encryption systems, *Communications of the ACM*, Vol. 39, No. 3, March 1996, at `www.cosc.georgetown.edu/~denning/crypto/Taxonomy.html`
Cited on page 143

[86] D. E. Denning, Descriptions of key escrow systems, at
`www.cosc.georgetown.edu/~denning/crypto/Appendix.html`
Cited on page 143

[87] Denver International Airport, at
`en.wikipedia.org/wiki/Denver_International_Airport`
Cited on page 404

[88] Y. Desmedt, What happened with knapsack cryptographic schemes?, *Performance Limits in Communication, Theory and Practice*, J. K. Skwirzynski, ed., Kluwer, pp. 113–134, 1988. Cited on page 95

[89] J. F. Dhem et. al., A practical implementation of the timing attack, at `www.cs.jhu.edu/~fabian/courses/CS600.624/Timing-full.pdf` Cited on page 210

[90] W. Diffie and M. Hellman, New directions in cryptography, *IEEE Transactions on Information Theory*, Vol. IT–22, No. 6, pp. 644–654, November 1976, at `www.cs.jhu.edu/~rubin/courses/sp03/papers/diffie.hellman.pdf` Cited on pages 91, 458, and 555

   • Diffie and Hellman's classic paper, where they argue (correctly, as it turned out) that public key cryptography is possible.

[91] DI Management, RSA Algorithm, at `www.di-mgt.com.au/rsa_alg.html#pkcs1schemes` Cited on page 98

[92] I. Dubrawsky, Effects of Internet worms on routing, RSA Conference 2004, at `www.cs.sjsu.edu/faculty/stamp/cv/tripreports/RSA04.html` Cited on page 425

[93] I. Dubrawsky and L. Hayden, Wireless LANs and privacy, at `www.isoc.org/inet2002/inet-technologyprogram.shtml` Cited on page 381

[94] D. Dumars, Stephen King's The Plant withers, at `www.mania.com/stephen-kings-plant-withers_article_26476.html` Cited on page 461

[95] J. E. Dunn, Encrypted image backups open to new attack, *Techworld*, October 2008, at `www.techworld.com/security/news/index.cfm?newsid=105263` Cited on page 73

[96] P. Earley, Family of spies: The John Walker Jr. spy case, *The Crime Library*, at `www.crimelibrary.com/spies/walker/` Cited on page 40

[97] Easy solution to bypass latest CD-audio protection, at `www.cdfreaks.com/news/4068` Cited on page 471

- The classic "felt-tip pen" attack.

[98] EFF DES cracker, at
en.wikipedia.org/wiki/EFF_DES_cracker
Cited on page 67

[99] E. Eilam, *Reversing: Secrets of Reverse Engineering*, Wiley, 2005.
Cited on pages 449, 454, 548, and 558

- The best book available on reversing—at least until your humble author finishes his reverse engineering textbook...

[100] G. Ellison, J. Hodges, and S. Landau, Risks presented by single sign-on architectures, October 18, 2002, at research.sun.com/liberty/RPSSOA/
Cited on page 253

[101] C. Ellison and B. Schneier, Ten risks of PKI: what you're not being told about public key infrastructure, *Computer Security Journal*, Vol. 16, No. 1, pp. 1–7, 2000, at www.schneier.com/paper-pki.html
Cited on page 112

[102] P. England et. al., A trusted open platform, *IEEE Computer*, pp. 55–62, July 2003.
Cited on page 500

- A general description of NGSCB/TCG at an early stage in its development.

[103] A. C. Engst, Mac OS X trojan technique: beware of geeks bearing gifts, *TidBITS*, No. 726, April 2004, at
db.tidbits.com/getbits.acgi?tbart=07636
Cited on pages 426 and 549

- A proof-of-concept trojan for the Mac. See [160] for additional context.

[104] Enigma machine, at en.wikipedia.org/wiki/Enigma_machine
Cited on pages 38 and 169

[105] U. Erlingsson, Y. Younan, and F. Piessens, Low-level Software Security by Example, to appear in *Handbook of Communications Security*, Springer-Verlag, 2009.
Cited on page 417

- An excellent survey of low-level software vulnerabilities and defenses.

[106] Evaluation assurance level, at
en.wikipedia.org/wiki/Evaluation_Assurance_Level
Cited on page 270

[107] D. B. Everett, Trusted computing platforms, at
www.netproject.com/presentations/TCPA/david_everett.pdf
Cited on page 500

[108] Exploit Systems, Inc., at www.exploitsystems.com/
Cited on page 469

- An unsuccessful—yet clever—approach to making money from the
pirates who inhabit peer-to-peer networks.

[109] W. Feller, *An Introduction to Probability Theory and Its Applications*,
third edition, Wiley, 1968.
Cited on page 527

- The best source for information on discrete probability.

[110] Fernflower — Java Decompiler, at www.reversed-java.com/fernflower/
Cited on page 450

[111] U. Fiege, A. Fiat, and A. Shamir, Zero knowledge proofs of identity,
*Proceedings of the Nineteenth Annual ACM Conference on Theory of
Computing*, pp. 210–217, 1987.
Cited on page 335

[112] S. Fluhrer, I. Mantin and A. Shamir, Weaknesses in the key scheduling
algorithm of RC4, at www.drizzle.com/~aboba/IEEE/rc4_ksaproc.pdf
Cited on pages 56, 180, 221, 378, 398, 554, and 569

- Several attacks on RC4 are discussed, including a devastating attack on the encryption in WEP. This paper suffers from some typos
and a lack of detail. See Mantin's thesis [195] for a more readable
and complete version.

[113] B. A. Forouzan, *TCP/IP Protocol Suite*, second edition, McGraw Hill,
2003.
Cited on page 523

- Forouzan has digested the relevant RFCs and provides the important points in a readable form—no mean feat.

[114] S. Forrest, S. A. Hofmeyr, and A. Somayaji, Computer immunology,
Communications of the ACM, Vol. 40, No. 10, pp. 88–96, October 1997.
Cited on page 460

- A somewhat "far out" view of the role that biological analogies can play in security.

[115] S. Forrest, A. Somayaji, and D. H. Ackley, Building diverse computer systems, at `www.cs.unm.edu/~forrest/publications/hotos-97.pdf`
Cited on page 460

[116] L. Fraim, SCOMP: A solution to the multilevel security problem, *IEEE Computer*, pp. 26–34, July 1983.
Cited on page 498

- One of the few serious attempts to develop a trusted operating system.

[117] J. Fraleigh, *A First Course in Abstract Algebra*, Addison Wesley, seventh edition, 2002.
Cited on page 225

[118] K. Gaj and A. Orlowski, Facts and myths of Enigma: breaking stereotypes, at
`ece.gmu.edu/courses/ECE543/viewgraphs_F03/EUROCRYPT_2003.pdf`
Cited on page 38

[119] M. R. Garey and D. S. Johnson, *Computers and Intractability: A Guide to the Theory of NP–Completeness*, W. H. Freeman & Company, 1979.
Cited on page 92

[120] B. Gates, Keynote address, RSA Conference 2004, at
`www.cs.sjsu.edu/faculty/stamp/cv/trireports/RSA04.html`
Cited on page 301

[121] D. Geer, comments from "Who will kill online privacy first—the lawyers or the techies?", at
`www.cs.sjsu.edu/~stamp/cv/trireports/RSA2002.html`
Cited on page 460

[122] W. W. Gibbs, Software's chronic crisis, Trends in Computing, *Scientific American*, September 1994, p. 86, at
`www.cis.gsu.edu/~mmoore/CIS3300/handouts/SciAmSept1994.html`
Cited on page 404

[123] R. Glenn and S. Kent, RFC 2410 — The NULL encryption algorithm and its use with IPsec, at `www.faqs.org/rfcs/rfc2410.html`
Cited on page 371

- Good nerdy humor.

[124] D. B. Glover, *Secret Ciphers of the 1876 Presidential Election*, Aegean Park Press, 1991.
Cited on page 36

[125] D. Gollmann, *Computer Security*, Wiley, 1999.
Cited on page 274

- A fairly theoretical treatment of most topics. Includes an excellent discussion of security modeling.

[126] S. W. Golomb, *Shift Register Sequences*, Aegean Park Press, 1982.
Cited on page 53

[127] D. Goodin, Buggy 'smart meters' open door to power-grid botnet: Grid-burrowing worm only the beginning, *The Register*, at
www.theregister.co.uk/2009/06/12/smart_grid_security_risks/
Cited on page 404

[128] S. Goodwin, Internet gambling software flaw discovered by Reliable Software Technologies software security group, at
www.cigital.com/news/index.php?pg=art&artid=20
Cited on page 146

- A nice description of an attack on an online version of Texas hold 'em poker.

[129] E. Grevstad, CPU-based security: the NX bit, at
hardware.earthweb.com/chips/article.php/3358421
Cited on page 416

[130] GSM cloning, at www.isaac.cs.berkeley.edu/isaac/gsm.html
Cited on page 386

[131] A guide to understanding covert channel capacity analysis of a trusted system, National computer security center, November 1993, at
www.fas.org/irp/nsa/rainbow/tg030.htm
Cited on pages 282 and 304

[132] A guide to understanding data remanence in automated information systems, NCSC–TG–025, at
www.cerberussystems.com/INFOSEC/stds/ncsctg25.htm
Cited on page 496

[133] B. Guignard, How secure is PDF?, at
www-2.cs.cmu.edu/~dst/Adobe/Gallery/PDFsecurity.pdf
Cited on page 471

- A brief explanation of the ElcomSoft utility to remove PDF security. Correctly concludes that "your encrypted PDF files offer about as much strength as dried egg shells!"

[134] E. Guisado, Secure random numbers, at
erngui.com/articles/rng/index.html
Cited on page 148

[135] A. Guthrie, "Alice's Restaurant," lyrics at
www.arlo.net/lyrics/alices.shtml
Cited on page 2

[136] Hacker may be posing as Microsoft, *USA Today*, February 6, 2002, at
www.usatoday.com/tech/techinvestor/2001-03-22-microsoft.htm
Cited on page 113

- Discusses a Microsoft certificate that went astray.

[137] D. Hamer, Enigma: actions involved in the 'double-stepping' of the middle rotor, *Cryptologia*, Vol. 21, No. 1, January 1997, pp. 47–50, at
www.eclipse.net/~dhamer/downloads/rotorpdf.zip
Cited on page 171

[138] Hand based biometrics, *Biometric Technology Today*, pp. 9–11, July & August 2003.
Cited on page 246

[139] N. Hardy, The confused deputy (or why capabilities might have been invented), at www.skyhunter.com/marcs/capabilityIntro/confudep.html
Cited on page 273

- This paper is itself confusing, but it's worth understanding.

[140] D. Harkins and D. Carrel, RFC 2409 — The Internet key exchange (IKE), at www.faqs.org/rfcs/rfc2409.html
Cited on page 359

[141] B. Harris, Visual cryptography, two levels, personal correspondence.
Cited on page 145

[142] History of GSM, at www.cellular.co.za/gsmhistory.htm
Cited on page 381

[143] G. Hoglund and G. McGraw, *Exploiting Software*, Addison Wesley, 2004.
Cited on pages 404, 438, and 550

- In spite of some good reviews, this book is, in your author's humble opinion, not on par with Kaspersky's book [161] or Eilam's fine book [99].

[144] J. J. Holt and J. W. Jones, Discovering number theory, Section 9.4: Going farther: RSA, at
www.math.mtu.edu/mathlab/COURSES/holt/dnt/phi4.html
Cited on page 121

- A small part of an excellent set of number theory notes—all available online.

[145] B. Horne et, al., Dynamic self-checking techniques for improved tamper resistance, *Workshop on Security and Privacy in Digital Rights Management 2001.*
Cited on pages 458 and 538

- Very similar to the "guards" paper [54]. Interestingly, both papers were presented at the same conference and both are undoubtedly patented.

[146] HotBots '07, USENIX first workshop on hot topics in understanding botnets, at www.usenix.org/event/hotbots07/tech/
Cited on page 304

[147] IDA Pro disassembler, at www.hex-rays.com/idapro/
Cited on page 448

- The best disassembler in the known universe, it also includes a good debugger.

[148] Index of Coincidence, Wikipedia, at
en.wikipedia.org/wiki/Index_of_coincidence
Cited on page 48

[149] Iridian Technologies, Iris recognition: science behind the technology, at
www.l1id.com/pages/383-science-behind-the-technology
Cited on pages 247 and 248

[150] D. Isbell, M. Hardin, and J. Underwood, Mars climate team finds likely cause of loss, at
science.ksc.nasa.gov/mars/msp98/news/mco990930.html
Cited on page 404

[151] A. Jain, L. Hong, and S. Pankanti, Biometric Identification, *Communications of the ACM*, Vol. 43, No. 2, pp. 91–98, 2000.
Cited on page 242

[152] A. Jain, A. Ross, and S. Pankanti, *Proceedings of the 2nd AVBPA Conference*, Washington, DC, March 22–24, pp. 166–171, 1999.
Cited on page 246

[153] C. J. A. Jansen, *Investigations on Nonlinear Streamcipher Systems: Construction and Evaluation Methods*, PhD thesis, Technical University of Delft, 1989.
Cited on page 52

- An unusual and hard to find manuscript. Some very difficult research problems are discussed.

[154] D. Jao, Elliptic curve cryptography, in *Handbook of Communication and Information Security*, Springer-Verlag, 2009.
Cited on page 106

[155] H. S. Javitz and A. Valdes, The NIDES statistical component description and justification.
Cited on page 300

- One of many NIDES papers available online.

[156] John Gilmore on the EFF DES cracker, at
www.computer.org/internet/v2n5/w5news-des.htm
Cited on page 23

[157] John the Ripper password cracker, at www.openwall.com/john/
Cited on page 241

[158] M. E. Kabay, Salami fraud, *Network World Security Newsletter*, July 24, 2002, at
www.nwfusion.com/newsletters/sec/2002/01467137.html
Cited on page 434

[159] D. Kahn, *The Codebreakers: The Story of Secret Writing*, revised edition, Scribner, 1996.
Cited on pages 21 and 37

- *The* source for crypto history prior to its original publication date of 1967. Supposedly, it was updated in 1996, but little new information was added.

[160] L. Kahney, OS X trojan horse is a nag, at
www.wired.com/news/mac/0,2125,63000,00.html?tw=rss.TEK
Cited on pages 427 and 543

- Additional discussion of this harmless trojan can be found at [103].

[161] K. Kaspersky, *Hacker Disassembling Uncovered*, A-List, 2003.
Cited on pages 449, 454, 548, and 558

- A good resource for anyone interested in software reverse engineering. Far superior to [143], although it does suffer somewhat from poor writing, as do most "hacker" publications.

[162] C. Kaufman, R. Perlman, and M. Speciner, *Network Security*, second edition, Prentice Hall, 2002.
Cited on pages 107, 113, 148, 363, 372, and 377

- Excellent coverage of networking protocols as well as good—though brief—coverage of many relevant crypto topics. Chapter 11 alone is worth the price of the book. Overall, the content is consistently first rate, with the possible exception of the IPSec chapters.

[163] J. Kelsey, B. Schneier, and D. Wagner, Related-key cryptanalysis of 3-WAY, Biham-DES, CAST, DES-X, NewDES, RC2, and TEA, *ICICS '97 Proceedings*, Springer-Verlag, November 1997.
Cited on page 71

[164] A. Kerckhoffs, La cryptographie militaire, *Journal des Sciences Militaires*, Vol. IX, pp. 5–83, January 1883, pp. 161–191, February 1883.
Cited on page 21

[165] Kerckhoffs' law, at en.wikipedia.org/wiki/Kerckhoffs'_law
Cited on page 21

[166] P. C. Kocher, Timing attacks on implementations of Diffie-Hellman, RSA, DSS, and other systems, at
www.cryptography.com/resources/whitepapers/TimingAttacks.pdf
Cited on pages 210, 214, and 217

[167] P. Kocher, J. Jaffe, and B. Jun, Differential power analysis, *Advances in Cryptology — CRYPTO '99*, Vol. 1666 of Lecture Notes in Computer Science, M. Wiener, editor, Springer-Verlag, pp. 388–397, 1999, at
www.cryptography.com/resources/whitepapers/DPA.html
Cited on page 211

- One of the few papers written by Kocher on side channel attacks. This is curious, since he is clearly a leader in the field.

[168] Kodak research and development, at
www.kodak.com/US/en/corp/researchDevelopment/worldwide/index.jhtml
Cited on page 150

[169] F. Koeune, Some interesting references about LLL, at
`www.dice.ucl.ac.be/~fkoeune/LLL.html`
Cited on page 207

[170] D. Kopel, Pẽna's new airport still a failure, at
`davekopel.org/Misc/OpEds/op021997.htm`
Cited on page 404

[171] D. P. Kormann and A. D. Rubin, Risks of the Passport single signon
protocol, at `avirubin.com/passport.html`
Cited on page 253

[172] M. Kotadia, Spammers use free porn to bypass Hotmail protection, *ZD Net UK*, May 6, 2004, at
`news.zdnet.co.uk/internet/security/0,39020375,39153933,00.htm`
Cited on page 287

[173] J. Koziol et al., *The Shellcoder's Handbook*, Wiley, 2004.
Cited on pages 416 and 448

  • For a long time, there were few books that made any serious attempt to discuss hacking techniques. Of course, hackers knew (or could learn) about such techniques, so this lack of information only hindered the good guys while doing little or nothing to deter the bad guys. Recently, however, there has been a flood of "hacking" books and this book is among the best of the genre.

[174] H. Krawczyk, M. Bellare and R. Canetti, RFC 2104 — HMAC: Keyed-hashing for message authentication, at
`www.faqs.org/rfcs/rfc2104.html`
Cited on page 138

[175] D. L. Kreher and D. R. Stinson, *Combinatorial Algorithms*, CRC Press, 1999.
Cited on page 203

  • The best available mathematical discussion of the lattice reduction attack on the knapsack. However, be forewarned that this book has many typos, which is death for an algorithms book.

[176] M. Kuhn, Security—biometric identification, at
`www.cl.cam.ac.uk/Teaching/2003/Security/guestslides/`
`      slides-biometric-4up.pdf`
Cited on page 242

[177] J. F. Kurose and K. W. Ross, *Computer Networking*, Addison Wesley,
      2003.
      Cited on pages 514 and 523

      - A good textbook for an introduction to networking class. For self-
        study, I prefer Tanenbaum [298].

[178] P. B. Ladkin, Osprey, cont'd, *The Risks Digest*, Vol. 21, issue 41, 2001,
      at `catless.ncl.ac.uk/Risks/21.41.html#subj7`
      Cited on page 404

[179] M. K. Lai, Knapsack cryptosystems: the past and the future,
      March 2001, at `www.cecs.uci.edu/~mingl/knapsack.html`
      Cited on page 95

[180] B. W. Lampson, Computer security in the real world, *IEEE Computer*,
      pp. 37–46, June 2004.
      Cited on page 4

[181] S. Landau, Standing the test of time: the Data Encryption Standard,
      Notices of the AMS, Vol. 47, No. 3, pp. 341–349, March 2000.
      Cited on page 64

      - A good technical description of DES. As the title suggests, this
        paper should have (finally) put to rest all of the nonsense about a
        back door in DES.

[182] S. Landau, Communications security for the twenty-first century: the
      Advanced Encryption Standard, *Notices of the AMS*, Vol. 47, No. 4,
      pp. 450–459, April 2000.
      Cited on page 67

      - This paper has good detail on the Rijndael algorithm, as well as
        an overview of the other AES finalists.

[183] C. E. Landwehr et al., A taxonomy of computer program security flaws,
      with examples, *ACM Computing Surveys*, Vol. 26, No. 3, pp. 211–254,
      September 1994.
      Cited on page 403

[184] M. Lee, Cryptanalysis of the SIGABA, Master's Thesis, University of
      California, Santa Barbara, June 2003.
      Cited on page 174

      - An excellent overview of rotors as cryptographic elements and a
        good description of Sigaba. However, the cryptanalysis only covers
        reduced-rotor versions of the cipher, which are qualitatively much
        different than the full Sigaba.

[185] H.-H. Lee and M. Stamp, P3P privacy enhancing agent, *Proceedings of the 3rd ACM Workshop on Secure Web Services* (SWS'06), Alexandria, Virginia, November 3, 2006, pp. 109–110, at www.cs.sjsu.edu/faculty/stamp/papers/sws10p-lee.pdf
Cited on page 486

[186] H.-H. Lee and M. Stamp, An agent-based privacy enhancing model, *Information Management & Computer Security*, Vol. 16, No. 3, 2008, pp. 305–319, at www.cs.sjsu.edu/faculty/stamp/papers/PEA_final.doc
Cited on page 486

[187] R. Lemos, Spat over MS 'flaw' gets heated, *ZD Net UK News*, at news.zdnet.co.uk/software/developer/0,39020387,2104559,00.htm
Cited on pages 417 and 559

- The debate over the implementation of Microsoft's buffer overflow prevention technique. It is claimed that the "cure" was worse than the disease.

[188] C. J. Lennard and T. Patterson, History of fingerprinting, at www.policensw.com/info/fingerprints/finger01.html
Cited on page 244

[189] A. K. Lenstra, H. W. Lenstra, Jr., and L. Lovàsz, Factoring polynomials with rational coefficients, *Math. Ann.*, 261, 1982.
Cited on page 207

- The LLL lattice reduction algorithm.

[190] J. Lettice, Bad publicity, clashes trigger MS Palladium name change, *The Register*, at www.theregister.co.uk/content/4/29039.html
Cited on page 500

- What's in a name? That which we call NGSCB by any other name would smell like Palladium.

[191] S. Levy, The open secret, *Wired*, issue 7.04, April 1999, at www.wired.com/wired/archive/7.04/crypto_pr.html
Cited on pages 90, 95, and 100

- So you think Diffie, Hellman, Merkle, Rivest, Shamir, and Adleman invented public key cryptography? Think again.

[192] Liberty alliance project, at www.projectliberty.org/
Cited on page 253

[193] D. Lin, Hunting for undetectable metamorphic viruses, Master's Thesis, Department of Computer Science, San Jose State University, 2010, at `www.cs.sjsu.edu/faculty/stamp/students/lin_da.pdf` Cited on page 430

  • This paper gives a metamorphic generator that produces variants that cannot be detected using signature detection or the machine learning techniques discussed in [330].

[194] A. Main, Application security: building in security during the development stage, at `www.cloakware.com/downloads/news/` Cited on page 460

[195] I. Mantin, Analysis of the stream cipher RC4, at `www.wisdom.weizmann.ac.il/~itsik/RC4/Papers/Mantin1.zip` Cited on pages 56, 185, and 544

  • A clearer and more detailed description of the RC4 attacks presented in [112].

[196] J. L. Massey, Design and analysis of block ciphers, *EIDMA Minicourse 8–12 May 2000.* Cited on page 73

  • Some excellent insights by one of the lesser-known giants of cryptography.

[197] D. Maughan et al., RFC 2408 — Internet security association and key management protocol (ISAKMP), at `www.faqs.org/rfcs/rfc2408.html` Cited on page 359

[198] J. McLean, A comment on the "basic security theorem" of Bell and La-Padula, *Information Processing Letters*, Vol. 20, No. 2, February 1985. Cited on page 277

  • McLean attacks BLP.

[199] J. McNamara, The complete, unofficial TEMPEST information page, at `www.eskimo.com/~joelm/tempest.html` Cited on page 211

[200] T. McNichol, Totally random: how two math geeks with a lava lamp and a webcam are about to unleash chaos on the Internet, *Wired*, Issue 11.08, August 2003, at `www.wired.com/wired/archive/11.08/random.html` Cited on page 148

[201] A. Menezes, P. C. van Oorschot, and S. A. Vanstone, *Handbook of Applied Cryptography*, CRC Press, 1997, Chapter 7, at
www.cacr.math.uwaterloo.ca/hac/about/chap7.pdf
Cited on page 70

- More precise than Schneier's book [258], but in need of a second edition.

[202] R. Merkle, Secure communications over insecure channels, *Communications of the ACM*, April 1978, pp. 294–299 (submitted in 1975), at
www.itas.fzk.de/mahp/weber/merkle.htm
Cited on page 92

- Given its submission date, this paper should be at least as famous as Diffie and Hellman's [90]. However, due to its absurdly late publication date, it's not.

[203] Microsoft .NET Passport: one easy way to sign in online, at
www.passport.net
Cited on page 253

[204] Microsoft shared source initiative, at
www.microsoft.com/resources/ngscb/default.mspx
Cited on page 500

[205] D. Miller, Beware the prophet seeking profit, at
www.exercisereports.com/2009/11/27/
    "beware-the-prophet-seeking-profit-"/
Cited on page 433

[206] M. S. Miller, K.-P. Yee, and J. Shapiro, Capability myths demolished, at zesty.ca/capmyths/
Cited on page 273

- Capabilities are loved by academics, as this paper illustrates. However, in typical academic fashion, the paper ignores the significant practical challenges that arise when capabilities are actually implemented.

[207] E. Mills, Twitter, Facebook attack targeted one user, *CNET News*, at
news.cnet.com/8301-27080_3-10305200-245.html
Cited on page 433

[208] F. Mirza, Block ciphers and cryptanalysis
Cited on pages 71 and 225

- A good paper that uses STEA (simplified TEA) as an example to illustrate certain cryptanalytic attacks.

[209] D. Moore et al., The spread of the Sapphire/Slammer worm, at
www.caida.org/publications/papers/2003/sapphire/sapphire.html
Cited on page 425

[210] A. Muchnick, Microsoft nearing completion of Death Star, at
bbspot.com/News/2002/05/deathstar.html
Cited on page 488

- Geeky humor at its best.

[211] D. Mulani, How smart is your Android smartphone?, Master's Thesis, Department of Computer Science, San Jose State University, 2010, at
www.cs.sjsu.edu/faculty/stamp/students/mulani_deepika.pdf
Cited on page 432

[212] G. Myles and C. Collberg, Software watermarking via opaque predicates, at sandmark.cs.arizona.edu/ginger_pubs_talks/icecr7.pdf
Cited on page 485

[213] MythBusters, excerpt at
www.metacafe.com/watch/252534/myth_busters_finger_print_lock/
Cited on page 261

- A very interesting series of attacks on fingerprint biometrics, including successful attacks on a system that the manufacturer (foolishly) claimed had "never been broken."

[214] M. Naor and A. Shamir, Visual cryptography, Eurocrypt '94, at
www.wisdom.weizmann.ac.il/~naor/topic.html#Visual_Cryptography
Cited on page 144

[215] National Security Agency, at en.wikipedia.org/wiki/NSA
Cited on page 60

[216] National Security Agency, Centers of Academic Excellence, at
www.nsa.gov/ia/academic_outreach/nat_cae/index.shtml
Cited on page 269

[217] R. Needham and M. Schroeder, Using encryption for authentication in large networks of computers *Communications of the ACM*, Vol. 21, No. 12, pp. 993–999, 1978.
Cited on page 372

- This is the foundation on which Kerberos was built.

[218] R. M. Needham and D. J. Wheeler, Tea extensions, at
`www.cl.cam.ac.uk/ftp/users/djw3/xtea.ps`
Cited on page 71

  • An "extended" version of TEA that eliminates an obscure related key attack.

[219] Next-generation secure computing base, at
`www.microsoft.com/resources/ngscb/default.mspx`
Cited on page 500

[220] NGSCB: Trusted computing base and software authentication, at
`www.microsoft.com/resources/ngscb/documents/ngscb_tcb.doc`
Cited on page 500

[221] J. R. Nickerson et al., The encoder solution to implementing tamper resistant software, at
`www.cert.org/research/isw/isw2001/papers/Nickerson-12-09.pdf`
Cited on page 460

[222] A. M. Odlyzko, The rise and fall of knapsack cryptosystems, at
`www.dtc.umn.edu/~odlyzko/doc/arch/knapsack.survey.pdf`
Cited on page 95

[223] Office Space, at `en.wikipedia.org/wiki/Office_Space`
Cited on page 14

[224] G. Ollmann, Size matters — measuring a botnet operator's pinkie, *Virus Bulletin: VB2010*, at
`www.virusbtn.com/conference/vb2010/abstracts/Ollmann.xml`
Cited on page 433

[225] OllyDbg, at `www.ollydbg.de/`
Cited on page 448

[226] Optimal asymmetric encryption padding, at
`en.wikipedia.org/wiki/Optimal\_Asymmetric\_Encryption\_Padding`
Cited on page 98

[227] Our Documents—High-resolution PDFs of Zimmermann Telegram (1917), at `www.ourdocuments.gov/doc.php?flash=true&doc=60&page=pdf`
Cited on page 32

[228] P. S. Pagliusi, A contemporary foreword on GSM security, in G. Davida, Y. Frankel, and O. Rees, editors, *Infrastructure Security: International Conference—InfraSec 2002*, Bristol, UK, October 1–3, 2002, Lecture Notes in Computer Science 2437, pp. 129–144, Springer-Verlag, 2002.
Cited on pages 211, 385, and 387

- This is a comprehensive and highly readable description of the major security flaws in GSM.

[229] J. C. Panettieri, Who let the worms out? — the Morris worm, *eWeek*, March 12, 2001, at `www.eweek.com/article2/0,1759,1245602,00.asp`
Cited on page 422

[230] D. B. Parker, Automated crime, at
`www.windowsecurity.com/whitepapers/Automated_Crime_.html`
Cited on page 460

[231] D. B. Parker, Automated security, at
`www.windowsecurity.com/whitepapers/Automated_Crime_.html`
Cited on page 460

- A security guru discusses the use of metamorphism to enhance security.

[232] Passwords revealed by sweet deal, *BBC News*, April 20, 2004, at
`news.bbc.co.uk/2/hi/technology/3639679.stm`
Cited on page 241

- Most users reveal passwords for a candy bar.

[233] C. Peikari and A. Chuvakin, *Security Warrior*, O'Reilly, 2004.
Cited on page 454

- A reasonably interesting book with some real software hacking examples. However, Kaspersky's book [161] is much more thorough, and much better, as is Eilam's book [99].

[234] S. Petrovic and A. Fúster-Sabater, Cryptanalysis of the A5/2 algorithm, at `eprint.iacr.org/2000/052/`
Cited on page 386

[235] C. P. Pfleeger and S. L. Pfleeger, *Security in Computing*, third edition, Prentice Hall, 2003.
Cited on pages 406, 424, 436, 477, 478, 479, 492, and 499

- Particularly good for OS security and some software issues. However, much of the information is dated—the book is ancient by computing standards, having been originally published in 1989.

[236] M. Pietrek, An in-depth look into the Win32 portable executable file format, at `msdn.microsoft.com/en-us/magazine/cc301805.aspx`
Cited on page 449

[237] D. Piper, RFC 2407 — The Internet IP security domain of interpretation for ISAKMP, at `www.faqs.org/rfcs/rfc2407.html`
Cited on page 359

[238] Platform for Privacy Preferences Project (P3P), at `www.w3.org/p3p`
Cited on page 486

[239] PMC Ciphers, at
`www.turbocrypt.com/eng/content/TurboCrypt/Backup-Attack.html`
Cited on page 73

[240] A. Pressman, Wipe 'em out, then sue for back pay, at
`www.internetwright.com/drp/RiskAssess.htm`
Cited on page 436

- An interesting description of an insider attack. Most interesting of all is the response by the company, which probably remains fairly typical today.

[241] P. Priyadarshini and M. Stamp, Digital rights management for untrusted peer-to-peer networks, *Handbook of Research on Secure Multimedia Distribution*, IGI Global, March 2009, at
`www.cs.sjsu.edu/faculty/stamp/papers/Pallavi_paper.doc`
Cited on page 464

[242] J. Raley, Ali Baba Bunny — 1957, Jenn Raley's Bugs Bunny page, at
`www.jenn98.com/bugs/1957-1.html`
Cited on page 335

- Bugs Bunny and Daffy Duck in Ali Baba's cave.

[243] J. R. Rao, et al., Partitioning attacks: or how to rapidly clone some GSM cards, *2002 IEEE Symposium on Security and Privacy*, May 12–15, 2002.
Cited on page 387

[244] A real MD5 collision, *Educated Guesswork*, August 2004 archives, at
`www.rtfm.com/movabletype/archives/2004_08.html#001055`
Cited on pages 132 and 159

[245] C. Ren, M. Weber, and G. McGraw, Microsoft compiler flaw technical note, at `www.cigital.com/news/index.php?pg=art&artid=70`
Cited on page 417

- A discussion of an attack on Microsoft's buffer overflow prevention technique. Microsoft argued that the claimed attack was exaggerated [187].

[246] G. Richarte, Four different tricks to bypass StackShield and StackGuard protection
       Cited on page 417

[247] R. L. Rivest et al., The RC6 block cipher, at
       `www.secinf.net/cryptography/The_RC6_Block_Cipher.html`
       Cited on page 70

[248] Robert Morris, at `www.rotten.com/library/bio/hackers/robert-morris/`
       Cited on page 423

       • The creator of the Morris Worm.

[249] S. Robinson, Up to the challenge: computer scientists crack a set of AI-based puzzles, *SIAM News*, Vol. 35, No. 9, November 2002, at
       `www.siam.org/siamnews/11-02/gimpy.htm`
       Cited on page 304

[250] M. J. Rose, Stephen King's 'Plant' uprooted, *Wired*, November 28, 2000, at `www.wired.com/news/culture/0,1284,40356,00.html`
       Cited on page 461

[251] M. Rosing, *Implementing Elliptic Curve Cryptography*, Manning Publications, 1998.
       Cited on page 106

       • A good elementary introduction to elliptic curve cryptography.

[252] RSA SecurID, at `www.rsa.com/node.aspx?id=1156`
       Cited on page 263

[253] Rsync Open source software project, at `samba.anu.edu.au/rsync/`
       Cited on page 131

[254] R. A. Rueppel, *Analysis and Design of Stream Ciphers*, Springer-Verlag, 1986.
       Cited on page 52

       • This book is a classic, which Rueppel wrote when he was Massey's student.

[255] R. Ryan, Z. Anderson, and A. Chiesa, Anatomy of a subway hack, at
       `tech.mit.edu/V128/N30/subway/Defcon_Presentation.pdf`
       Cited on page 16

       • A fascinating security analysis of the Boston subway system.

[256] R. Sanchez-Reillo, C. Sanchez-Avila and Ana Gonzalez-Marcos, Bio-
      metric identification through hand geometry measurements, *IEEE
      Transactions on Pattern Analysis and Machine Intelligence*, Vol. 22,
      No. 10, pp. 1168–1171, 2000.
      Cited on page 246

[257] W. Schindler, A timing attack against RSA with the Chinese Remain-
      der Theorem, *CHES 2000*, LNCS 1965, Ç. K. Koç and C. Paar, Eds.,
      Springer-Verlag, 2000, pp. 109–124.
      Cited on page 217

[258] B. Schneier, *Applied Cryptography*, second edition, Wiley, 1996.
      Cited on pages 64, 76, 133, and 555

      • This book is, for better or for worse, the crypto bible for working
        security professionals.

[259] B. Schneier, Attack trees, *Dr. Dobb's Journal*, December 1999, at
      www.schneier.com/paper-attacktrees-ddj-ft.html
      Cited on page 478

      • A practical and intuitive approach to "hazard analysis."

[260] B. Schneier, Biometrics: truths and fictions, at
      www.schneier.com/crypto-gram-9808.html
      Cited on pages 242 and 251

[261] B. Schneier, Risks of relying on cryptography, Inside Risks 112, *Com-
      munications of the ACM*, Vol. 42, No. 10, October 1999, at
      www.schneier.com/essay-021.html
      Cited on page 218

      • Schneier, in his own inimitable style, emphasizes the point that
        attackers don't necessarily play by the rules.

[262] B. Schneier, The Blowfish encryption algorithm, at
      www.schneier.com/blowfish.html
      Cited on page 70

      • Schneier describes his favorite crypto algorithm.

[263] H. Shacham, et al, On the Effectiveness of Address-Space Randomiza-
      tion, at crypto.stanford.edu/~nagendra/papers/asrandom.ps
      Cited on page 418

[264] A. Shamir, How to share a secret, *Communications of the ACM*, Vol. 22,
      No. 11, pp. 612–613, November 1979, at

szabo.best.vwh.net/secret.html
Cited on page 143

[265] A. Shamir, A polynomial-time algorithm for breaking the basic Merkle-Hellman cryptosystem, *IEEE Transactions on Information Theory*, Vol. IT–30, No. 5, pp. 699–704, September 1984.
Cited on pages 95 and 210

- Shamir's clever attack on the original knapsack cryptosystem.

[266] A. Shamir and N. van Someren, Playing hide and seek with stored keys
Cited on pages 463 and 486

- This paper includes a simple and effective statistical test for distinguishing random from non-random.

[267] C. E. Shannon, Communication theory of secrecy systems, *Bell System Technical Journal*, Vol. 28–4, pp. 656–715, 1949.
Cited on page 39

- The paper that started it all. Most of this paper remains surprisingly relevant after more than $3/5^{\text{ths}}$ of a century.

[268] K. Skachkov, Tamper-resistant software: design and implementation, at www.cs.sjsu.edu/faculty/stamp/students/TRSDIfinal.doc
Cited on page 458

- Discusses some of the issues related to tamper-resistant software of Aucsmith [19] variety. A toy implementation is presented.

[269] S. Skorobogatov and R. Anderson, Optical fault induction attacks, *IEEE Symposium on Security and Privacy*, 2002.
Cited on page 387

[270] E. Skoudis, *Counter Hack*, Prentice Hall, 2002.
Cited on page 283

- An excellent book that includes plenty of details on how a sophisticated hacker analyzes and attacks a target. A must read for the system administrators of the world.

[271] SSL 3.0 specification, at
www.lincoln.edu/math/rmyrick/ComputerNetworks/InetReference/
    ssl-draft/3-SPEC.HTM
Cited on page 355

[272] Sonogram, Visible speech, at
www.dontcrack.com/freeware/downloads.php/id/266/software/Sonogram/
Cited on page 262

[273] Staff Report, U. S. Senate Select Committee on Intelligence, Un-
classified summary: involvement of NSA in the development of the
Data Encryption Standard, Staff Report, 98th Congress, 2nd Session,
April 1978.
Cited on pages 59 and 60

- Senate report that cleared NSA of any wrongdoing in the design
  of DES. Needless to say, this did not convince the critics.

[274] M. Stamp, Digital rights management: for better or for worse?, *Ex-
tremeTech*, May 20, 2003.
Cited on page 461

- Tries to make the case that, in spite of its technical shortcomings,
  DRM can facilitate e-commerce if the business model is right.

[275] M. Stamp, Digital rights management: the technology behind the hype,
Journal of Electronic Commerce Research, Vol. 4, No. 3, 2003, at
www.csulb.edu/web/journals/jecr/issues/20033/paper3.pdf
Cited on pages 460 and 462

- Perhaps the most detailed description of a fielded commercial
  DRM system ever published.

[276] M. Stamp, Risks of digital rights management, Inside Risks 147, *Communications of the ACM*, Vol. 45, No. 9, p. 120, September 2002, at
www.csl.sri.com/users/neumann/insiderisks.html#147
Cited on page 461

- This article highlights some of the obvious difficulties of doing
  DRM in software.

[277] M. Stamp, Risks of monoculture, Inside Risks 165, *Communications of
the ACM*, Vol. 47, No. 3, p. 120, March 2004, at
www.csl.sri.com/users/neumann/insiderisks04.html#165
Cited on page 460

- An intuitive discussion of the potential security benefits of diverse
  software.

[278] M. Stamp, A revealing introduction to hidden Markov models, at
www.cs.sjsu.edu/faculty/stamp/RUA/HMM.pdf
Cited on page 442

[279] M. Stamp, S. Attaluri, and S. McGhee, Profile hidden Markov models and metamorphic virus detection, *Journal in Computer Virology*, Vol. 5, No. 2, May 2009, pp. 151–169.
Cited on page 430

[280] M. Stamp and W. O. Chan, SIGABA: Cryptanalysis of the full keyspace, *Cryptologia*, Vol. 31, No. 3, July 2007, pp. 201–222.
Cited on page 174

[281] M. Stamp and X. Gao, Metamorphic software for buffer overflow mitigation, *Proceedings of the 2005 Conference on Computer Science and its Applications*, at
www.cs.sjsu.edu/faculty/stamp/papers/BufferOverflow.doc
Cited on page 459

[282] M. Stamp and D. Holankar, Secure streaming media and digital rights management, *Proceedings of the 2004 Hawaii International Conference on Computer Science*, January 2004, at
www.cs.sjsu.edu/~stamp/cv/papers/hawaii.pdf
Cited on page 467

  • A nice protocol (OK, I'm biased. . .) for delivering DRM-protected streaming media that includes many of the software protection tricks discussed in this book.

[283] M. Stamp and A. Hushyar, Multilevel security models, *The Handbook of Information Security*, H. Bidgoli, editor, Wiley, 2006.
Cited on page 274

  • This paper gives an overview of many different security models. It likely contains more than you'll ever want to know about security modeling.

[284] M. Stamp and R. M. Low, *Applied Cryptanalysis: Breaking Ciphers in the Real World*, Wiley, 2007.
Cited on pages 168, 174, 211, and 378

  • A personal favorite of mine. . .

[285] M. Stamp and P. Mishra, Software uniqueness: how and why, *Proceedings of the 2003 Conference on Computer Science and its Applications*, at
www.cs.sjsu.edu/~stamp/cv/papers/iccsaPuneet.html
Cited on page 459

[286] M. Stamp and E. J. Sebes, Enterprise digital rights management:
Ready for primetime?, *Business Communications Review*, pp. 52–55,
March 2004.
Cited on page 471

- Makes the case that DRM within an enterprise is a much different
beast than DRM for e-commerce.

[287] M. Stamp, M. Simova, and C. Pollett, Stealthy ciphertext, *Proceedings
of 3rd International Conference on Internet Computing (ICOMP'05)*,
Las Vegas, Nevada, June 27–30, 2005, at
`www.cs.sjsu.edu/faculty/stamp/papers/stealthy.pdf`
Cited on page 284

[288] M. Stamp and S. Thaker, Software watermarking via assembly code
transformations, *Proceedings of the 2004 Conference on Computer Science
and its Applications*, June 2004, at
`www.cs.sjsu.edu/faculty/stamp/papers/iccsaSmita.doc`
Cited on page 149

[289] S. Staniford, V. Paxson, and N. Weaver, How to Own the Internet in
your spare time, at
`www.icir.org/vern/papers/cdc-usenix-sec02/`
Cited on page 429

- Excellent article on the future of malware.

[290] M. Stigge, et al, Reversing CRC — Theory and Practice, at
`sar.informatik.hu-berlin.de/research/publications/`
    `SAR-PR-2006-05/SAR-PR-2006-05_.pdf`
Cited on page 132

[291] H. L. Stimson and M. Bundy, *On Active Service in Peace and War*,
Hippocrene Books, 1971.
Cited on page 37

[292] D. Stinson, Doug Stinson's visual cryptography page, at
`www.cacr.math.uwaterloo.ca/~dstinson/visual.html`
Cited on page 145

- An excellent introduction to a fascinating topic.

[293] B. Stone, Breaking Google captchas for some extra cash, *New York
Times*, March 13, 2008, at
`bits.blogs.nytimes.com/2008/03/13/`
    `breaking-google-captchas-for-3-a-day/`
Cited on page 306

[294] A. Stubblefield, J. Ioannidis, and A. D. Rubin, Using the Fluhrer, Mantin and Shamir attack to break WEP, at www.isoc.org/isoc/conferences/ndss/02/papers/stubbl.pdf
Cited on pages 56 and 181

[295] C. Swenson, *Modern Cryptanalysis: Techniques for Advanced Code Breaking*, Wiley, 2008.
Cited on page 168

[296] P. Ször, *The Art of Computer Virus Defense and Research*, Symantec Press, 2005.
Cited on page 427

[297] P. Ször and P. Ferrie, Hunting for metamorphic, Symantec Corporation White Paper, at www.peterszor.com/metamorp.pdf
Cited on page 430

- An excellent discussion of polymorphism and metamorphism, along with various detection techniques.

[298] A. S. Tanenbaum, *Computer Networks*, fourth edition, Prentice Hall, 2003.
Cited on pages 377, 523, and 552

- Probably the best networking book for self-study or casual reading. The book is comprehensive, yet Tanenbaum has plenty of stories to keep the reader interested and awake.

[299] TechnoLogismiki, Hackman, at www.technologismiki.com/en/index-h.html
Cited on page 448

[300] D. Terdiman, Vegas gung-ho on gambling tech, *Wired*, September 19, 2003, at www.wired.com/news/print/0,1294,60499,00.html
Cited on page 243

[301] The Warhol, at www.warhol.org/
Cited on page 430

[302] C. Thomborson and M. Barrett, NGSCB: a new tool for securing applications, at www.cs.auckland.ac.nz/~cthombor/Pubs/barrettNZISF120804.pdf
Cited on pages 503, 504, and 505

[303] K. Thompson, Reflections on trusting trust, *Communication of the ACM*, Vol. 27, No. 8, pp. 761–763, August 1984.
Cited on pages 436 and 446

- A classic paper that probes the limits of security in software.

[304] B. C. Tjaden, *Fundamentals of Secure Computing Systems*, Franklin, Beedle & Associates, 2004.
Cited on page 300

- An introductory information security textbook. The chapter on intrusion detection is well worth the (modest) price of the book.

[305] W. A. Trappe and L. C. Washington, *Introduction to Cryptography with Coding Theory*, Prentice Hall, 2002.
Cited on pages 148 and 176

- An excellent and mathematically sound introduction to many aspects of cryptography.

[306] Trusted Computing Group, at `www.trustedcomputinggroup.org/home`
Cited on page 500

[307] B. W. Tuchman, *The Zimmermann Telegram*, Ballantine Books, 1985.
Cited on page 32

- An entertaining historical account by one of the better writers of popular history.

[308] Ultra, at `en.wikipedia.org/wiki/Ultra`
Cited on page 169

[309] United States Department of Defense, *Trusted Computing System Evaluation Criteria*, 1983, at
`csrc.nist.gov/publications/history/dod85.pdf`
Cited on pages 266, 267, 269, and 302

- The infamous "orange book." Like most government publications, this one is a sure cure for insomnia.

[310] US v. ElcomSoft & Sklyarov FAQ, at
`www.eff.org/IP/DMCA/US_v_Elcomsoft/us_v_elcomsoft_faq.html`
Cited on page 471

[311] R. Vamosi, Windows XP SP2 more secure? Not so fast, at
`reviews.zdnet.co.uk/software/os/0,39024180,39163696,00.htm`
Cited on pages 416 and 438

[312] S. Venkatachalam, Detecting undetectable computer viruses, Master's Thesis, Department of Computer Science, San Jose State University, 2010, at

```
www.cs.sjsu.edu/faculty/stamp/students/
        venkatachalam_sujandharan.pdf
```
Cited on page 430

[313] R. Venkataramu, Analysis and enhancement of Apple's Fairplay digital
rights management, Master's Thesis, Department of Computer Science,
San Jose State University, 2007, at
```
www.cs.sjsu.edu/faculty/stamp/students/
        RamyaVenkataramu_CS298Report.pdf
```
Cited on page 463

[314] R. Venkataramu and M. Stamp, P2PTunes: A peer-to-peer digital
rights management system, *Handbook of Research on Secure Multimedia Distribution*, IGI Global, March 2009, at
```
www.cs.sjsu.edu/faculty/stamp/papers/Ramya_paper.doc
```
Cited on page 464

[315] VENONA, at `www.nsa.gov/public_info/declass/venona/index.shtml`
Cited on page 31

- VENONA is an interesting topic, both for the crypto and for the
  historical material. Many of those who vehemently denied they
  had any role in espionage are implicated by VENONA decrypts.
  Also, of the hundreds of traitors mentioned (by cover name) in the
  decrypts, the true identities of most remain unknown.

[316] VeriSign, Inc., at `www.verisign.com/`
Cited on page 113

- The leading commercial certificate authority (CA).

[317] J. Viega and G. McGraw, *Building Secure Software*, Addison Wesley,
2002.
Cited on pages 404, 406, 455, 457, 472, and 474

- This is a worthwhile book that provides considerable detail on issues related to secure software development. About the only conceivable criticism is that it provides no evidence of the effectiveness
  of its suggestions.

[318] VMware is virtual infrastructure, at `www.vmware.com/`
Cited on page 449

[319] L. von Ahn, M. Blum, and J. Langford, Telling humans and computers apart automatically, *Communications of the ACM*, Vol. 47, No. 2,
pp. 57–60, February 2004, at

www.cs.cmu.edu/~biglou/captcha_cacm.pdf
Cited on pages 13 and 285

- A fascinating, informative and entertaining article. This is the place to start your research into CAPTCHAs.

[320] L. von Ahn et al., The CAPTCHA project, at www.captcha.net/
Cited on page 286

[321] J. R. Walker, Unsafe at any key size; an analysis of the WEP encapsulation, at www.dis.org/wl/pdf/unsafe.pdf
Cited on pages 185 and 398

- A clever title and a good description of the some of the problems created by WEP's use of IVs. However, one of the most serious problems is the devastating cryptanalytic attack discussed in [112], which is not mentioned here.

[322] What is reCAPTCHA?, at
recaptcha.net/learnmore.html
Cited on page 305

[323] D. J. Wheeler and R. M. Needham, TEA, a tiny encryption algorithm, at www.cix.co.uk/~klockstone/tea.pdf
Cited on page 70

- Less than four pages to present TEA in all of its wonderful simplicity.

[324] O. Whitehouse, An Analysis of Address Space Layout Randomization on Windows Vista, at
www.symantec.com/avcenter/reference/
        Address_Space_Layout_Randomization.pdf
Cited on page 418

- A readable analysis of the randomness (or lack thereof) in ASLR as implemented in Windows Vista.

[325] Wi-Fi Protected Access, at
en.wikipedia.org/wiki/Wi-Fi_Protected_Access
Cited on page 380

[326] R. N. Williams, A painless guide to CRC error detection algorithms, at www.ross.net/crc/crcpaper.html
Cited on pages 81 and 131

[327] N. Winkless and I. Browning, *Robots on Your Doorstep*, Robotics Press, 1978.
Cited on page 301

- While it seems dated today, this classic and off-beat book presents the conventional wisdom of its time in an unconventional way.

[328] Wireshark, at `www.wireshark.org/`
Cited on pages 391 and 392

[329] W. Wong, Revealing your secrets through the fourth dimension, *ACM Crossroads*, at
`www.cs.sjsu.edu/faculty/stamp/students/wing.html`
Cited on page 211

- An elementary and highly readable description of the basic ideas behind RSA timing attacks.

[330] W. Wong and M. Stamp, Hunting for metamorphic engines, *Journal in Computer Virology*, Vol. 2, No. 3, December 2006, pp. 211–229.
Cited on pages 430, 442, and 554

- This paper covers some research problems related to metamorphic malware. A number of real-world metamorphic generators are analyzed and a reasonably practical detection technique is given.

[331] T. Ylonen, The Secure Shell (SSH) Authentication Protocol, RFC 4252, at `www.ietf.org/rfc/rfc4252.txt`
Cited on page 391

[332] B. Yee, et al., Native client: a sandbox for portable, untrusted x86 native code, at
`nativeclient.googlecode.com/svn/data/docs_tarball/nacl/`
        `googleclient/native_client/documentation/nacl_paper.pdf`
Cited on page 510

[333] T. Ylonen, The Secure Shell (SSH) Transport Layer Protocol, RFC 4253, at `www.ietf.org/rfc/rfc4253.txt`
Cited on page 391

[334] G. Yuval, How to swindle Rabin, *Cryptologia*, Vol. 3, No. 3, 1979, pp. 187–189.
Cited on page 129

[335] M. Zalewski, Strange attractors and TCP/IP sequence number analysis—one year later, at `lcamtuf.coredump.cx/newtcp/`
Cited on page 334

  - Fascinating scatter plots of the distribution of TCP initial sequence numbers for many different vendor's products. Many are extremely non-random.

[336] L. Zeltser, Reverse engineering malware, at
`www.zeltser.com/sans/gcih-practical/`
Cited on pages 448 and 571

  - An excellent discussion of malware as well as reverse engineering principles. Highly recommended. See also [337].

[337] L. Zeltser, SANS malware FAQ: reverse engineering `srvcp.exe`, at
`www.sans.org/resources/malwarefaq/srvcp.php`
Cited on pages 448 and 571

  - Much overlap with [336], but this one also includes a link to the malware executable that is reverse engineered.

[338] J. Zhang, Improved software activation using multithreading, Master's Thesis, Department of Computer Science, San Jose State University, 2010, at `www.cs.sjsu.edu/faculty/stamp/students/zhang_jianrui.pdf`
Cited on page 456

[339] M. Zorz, Basic security with passwords, at
`www.net-security.org/article.php?id=117`
Cited on page 241

Index

write access rule, 278
Biham, Eli, 186
biometric, 242–251
    attack, 250
    authentication, 242
    enrollment phase, 243
    equal error rate, 244
    error rate, 250
    errors, 244
    fingerprint, 244
    fraud rate, 244
    hand geometry, 246
    ideal, 242
    identification, 242
    insult rate, 244
    iris scan, 246–249
    recognition phase, 243
birthday paradox, *see* birthday problem
birthday problem, 128–129
    and hash functions, 129
block cipher, 40, 57–76
    bit errors, 75
    cut-and-paste attack, 75, 84, 86
    design, 202–203
    modes of operation, 72–76
    round function, 57
Blowfish, 70
    S-box, 70
BLP, 276–279, 303, 304
    simple security condition, 276
    star property, 276
    strong tranquility, 277
    system Z, 277
    weak tranquility, 277
BMA, *see* British Medical Association
Bob, 1
Bob's Cave, 335–336, 348
Bobcat hash, 155
BOBE, 459
    resistance, 467, 486
Boeing 777, 405
Bonaparte, Napoleon, 203

botmaster, 433
botnet, 433, 443
Brain, 422
break once break everywhere resistant, *see* BOBE
British Medical Association, 280
buffer overflow, 9, 407–414, 440
    example, 411–415
    prevention, 415–417
Burleson, Donald Gene, 436

C-list, *see* capabilities
C#, 416
CA, *see* certificate authority
Caesar's cipher, 22, 43
Caesar, Julius, 22
canary, 416, 417
capabilities, 272, 302
    and digital signatures, 303
    delegate, 302
CAPTCHA, 13, 285–287, 305
    Gimpy, 304
Carroll, Lewis, 1, 19, 51, 125, 313, 317
Catch-22, 363
CBC mode, 73–76, 78, 85, 236
    and random access, 84
    cut-and-paste attack, 84
    repeated IV, 84
    residue, 77, 85
cell phone
    cloning, 381, 399
    first generation, 381
    second generation, 381
    third generation, 381
CERT, 424
certificate
    authority, 112
    revocation, 113
certificate revocation list, *see* CRL
challenge-response, 316, 319, 320
change detection, 427–428
Chinese Remainder Theorem, 100, 217
chosen plaintext attack, 212